Tests
and
Assessment

second edition

W. Bruce Walsh
Nancy E. Betz

The Ohio State University

Prentice Hall, Englewood Cliffs, New Jersey 07632

Library of Congress Cataloging-in-Publication Data
Walsh, W. Bruce, (date)
  Tests and assessment/W. Bruce Walsh, Nancy E. Betz.—2nd ed.
    p.   cm.
  Includes bibliographical references.
  ISBN 0-13-904970-3
  1. Psychological tests.   2.   Ability—Testing.   3.   Psychometrics.
I. Betz, Nancy E.   II. Title.
BF176.W335   1990
150′.28′7—dc20

                                                                  89-37813
                                                                  CP

Editorial/production supervision and
  interior design: *bookworks*
Cover design: *Ray Lundgren*
Manufacturing buyer: *Ray Keating/Bob Anderson*

 © 1990, 1985 by Prentice-Hall, Inc.
A Division of Simon & Schuster
Englewood Cliffs, New Jersey 07632

Printed in the United States of America
10   9   8   7   6   5   4   3   2

ISBN 0-13-904970-3

Prentice-Hall International (UK) Limited, *London*
Prentice-Hall of Australia Pty. Limited, *Sydney*
Prentice-Hall Canada Inc., *Toronto*
Prentice-Hall Hispanoamericana, S. A., *Mexico*
Prentice-Hall of India Private Limited, *New Delhi*
Prentice-Hall of Japan, Inc., *Tokyo*
Simon & Schuster Asia Pte. Ltd., *Singapore*
Editora Prentice-Hall do Brasil, Ltda., *Rio de Janeiro*

Contents

PART II
THE ASSESSMENT OF PERSONALITY

PART III
THE ASSESSMENT OF COGNITIVE ABILITY

Preface

This edition of the book, like the preceding one has two basic assumptions. The first assumption is that assessment is apt to be sounder if based upon meaningful—that is, reliable and valid—information. Secondly, assessment skills may be developed by improving one's knowledge of tests used to gather meaningful information about people and environments. Thus, in a practical sense a primary objective of this book is to help students develop some assessment skills and to improve their knowledge about assessment techniques and tests.

The general rationale of the book is that human behavior tends to be influenced by many determinants both in the person and in the environment. Therefore, within this framework it is our belief that any assessment of the person is incomplete without some assessment of the environment. People clearly affect and change environments and situations, but at the same time we cannot ignore the fact that environments, like people, have personalities and influence behavior. Thus, within this context our book focuses on theory and assessment techniques used to assess and understand both the person and the psychological environment.

The past five years have been a period of significant advances in psychological and educational testing. Advances in theory, practice, and professional responsibility reflect rapid growth in the field. The first revision of Tests and Assessment attempts to reflect this growth by contributing to a more intelligent understanding and use of psychological and educational tests and assessment. The revision updates and expands content areas in an effort to make the book more meaningful and useful for teachers, practitioners, and students in the field. The most profound revisions were made in chapters 3, 4, 6, 7, 9, 11, and 14. Chapter 3, focusing on Concepts of Reliability and Validity in Testing and Assessment, was revised to provide a more detailed discussion of the test construction procedures. Chapter 4, on objective personality assessment, was revised to include the 1987 edition of the California Psychological Inventory. In addition, the Sixteen Personality Factor Questionnaire, the Tennessee Self-Concept Scale, and the Millon Clinical Multiaxial Inventory are reviewed and discussed. In Chapter 6 (The Nature and Assessment of Intelligence) and Chapter 7 (The Assessment of Aptitudes) new versions of the Stanford-Binet, the Cognitive Abilities Test, the Employee Aptitude Survey, and the Armed Services Vocational Aptitude Battery are discussed. Also, several tests reviewed in the first edition of the book are now covered in chapters 6 and 7; these include the Kaufman Assessment Battery for Children, culture fair tests, the DAT-Adaptive, and the Multidimensional Aptitude Battery. In chapter 9, The Assessment of Interests, new editions of the Strong-Campbell Interest Inventory, the Kuder Occupational Interest Survey, the Self-Directed Search, and the Career Assessment Inventory are reviewed and discussed. The recent revisions of these inventories reflect active growth in the content area of interests. Chapter 10 now reflects revisions in the ACT Assessment and in SIGI and SIGI Plus. Chapter 11, on Environmental Assessment, was revised to include the College Student Experiences Questionnaire, the School Environment Preference Survey, and the Home Observation for Measurement of the Environment. These are relatively new tests assessing the psychological environment. Finally, in Chapter 14, Professional and Ethical Standards and Social Issues in Assessment, the 1985 American Psychological Association Standards for Tests and Educational and Psychological Testing are reviewed and discussed. Also, since 1985, there have been some additional major works on test usage with minorities and women, and these are discussed here. This chapter was further revised to include some additional general considerations for the purpose of test interpretation.

The book continues to be primarily for courses at the undergraduate or graduate level, in which consideration of tests and assessment is a main objective. Basic principles of tests, measurements, and assessment are reviewed, and some of the most useful and meaningful person and environment assessment techniques are described and evaluated in detail. The book is primarily oriented toward students in undergraduate and graduate psychology courses and programs, including courses in testing and assessment at the undergraduate levels and in graduate programs in counseling psychology, vocational psychology, educational psychology, and industrial psychology. The book would also be useful to students in counselor education, guidance and counseling, educational administration, and other disciplines and areas in which a background in testing and assessment is needed.

The first revision is divided into 6 sections: Foundations of Tests and Assessment; The Assessment of Personality; The Assessment of Cognitive Ability; The Assessment of Interests and Career Development; The Assessment of Environment, Person-Environment Interaction and Human Development; and Ethical Standards of Tests and Assessment. Section 1, Foundations of Tests and Assessment, consists of three chapters focusing on the history and meaning of tests and assessment, basic statistical concepts important to testing and assessment, and the concepts of reliability, validity, and test construction. Methods of test construction and item analysis are also covered. These chapters present some basic principles of tests, measurements, and assessment. The second section, the Assessment of Personality, is made up of two chapters. The first focuses on objective personality assessment; the second deals with projective and behavioral personality assessment. This section of the book attempts to highlight the importance of personality and social intelligence in everyday living. Stated differently, a large part of coping successfully on a daily basis involves getting along with people. Section 3, the Assessment of Cognitive Ability, consists of three chapters focusing, in order of appearance, on the assessment of intelligence, aptitudes, and achievement. These chapters present basic concepts and techniques concerned with the assessment of cognitive ability. Section 4, the Assessment of Interests and

Career Development, includes two chapters. The first focuses on the assessment of interests, the second on the assessment of career development and career maturity. These chapters attempt to show the utility of assessing interests and career development variables in the fields of vocational, counseling, and educational psychology. Section 5 focuses on the assessment of environment, person-environment interaction, and human development. These chapters focus on the convergence of theory and assessment in the fields of person-environment psychology and human development. Selected theories are reviewed that have implications for assessment and other practical applications. The integration within this book of psychological assessment and person-environment psychology is a unique and valuable feature. The final section of the book focuses on ethical standards of tests and assessments. This is a vital chapter providing extensive coverage of the uses and misuses of tests and assessments. In addition, this chapter comprehensively considers standards and ethics pertaining to the use of tests and assessment.

It is hoped that this first revision will continue to assist the consumer of test information and, furthermore, contribute to a more intelligent understanding and use of psychological and educational tests and assessment.

W. Bruce Walsh and Nancy E. Betz
The Ohio State University

1

The History and Meaning of Assessment

INTRODUCTION

The notion of human assessment as a means of knowing and understanding another person, has been with us for a long time. Human behavior has been assessed in a variety of settings and by individuals in many different disciplines. Everyone is to some extent an assessor of human behavior, but each person probably performs the task in his or her own distinct way, drawing on hunches and personal rules of thumb and frequently ending up with results different from anyone else's. Even the experts vary in their approach to assessment psychology and many times arrive at equally reasonable, yet different, conclusions. In time we will develop a body of laws to define and order the assessment process; the history of assessment certainly suggests strides in this direction.

No attempt is made in this book to present a comprehensive history of assessment, but Tables 1.1 and 1.2 provide an overview of historical events in (Table 1.1), and significant tests developed for (Table 1.2), the assessment of people and environments. Some of the topics are discussed here and others are discussed later in the book. For additional information on the history of psychological assessment, see DuBois (1970), Linden and Linden (1968), and McReynolds (1975).

HISTORY OF ASSESSMENT

Individual Differences and Intelligence

The theory and study of individual human differences had origins in the late nineteenth and early twentieth centuries with the work of Francis Galton, Wilhelm Wundt, James Cattell, Emil Kraepelin, Hermann Ebbinghaus, and Karl Pearson. Francis Galton, an English gentleman, studied individual differences by measuring a variety of human characteristics, such as height and head size. He was particularly interested in intelligence and devoted much of his time to the study of inherited genius. In the main, his motto was "Whenever you can, count." Wilhelm Wundt and Hermann Ebbinghaus, two German psychologists, continued the quest by suggesting that psychological events, like physical events, can be interpreted in quantitative terms. Wundt developed the first psychological laboratory, in Leipzig, Germany, and Ebbinghaus explored the learning and retention rates of children through a completion test he developed. James Cattell, an American, carried Galton's methods and concepts to the University of Pennsylvania and developed a testing laboratory. Cattell introduced the term *mental test* and made an effort to relate scores on mental tests to reaction time, but the findings were not very revealing.

It was not until 1905 that a French psychologist, Alfred Binet, working with Theodore Simon, produced the first widely used intelligence scale. To identify children who could not profit significantly from schooling, Binet and Simon developed an individually administered test consisting of 30 problems of increasing difficulty. A profound social issue underlying the Binet and Simon test was the notion that slow children should be excluded from schooling. This way of thinking has haunted the education world ever since. Only recently has the United States formed a policy that all children deserve and have a right to an appropriate education. In any event, the Binet and Simon scale was the beginning of intelligence testing and the main model for subsequent developments. It was brought to this country by H. H. Goddard in 1911, then revised by Lewis M. Terman in 1916 and called the Stanford-Binet Intelligence Scale. About this same time (1917), the first paper-and-pencil group intelligence tests were developed under the leadership of Arthur Otis and Robert M. Yerkes. These

Table 1.1 Some Historical Events in Assessment

Year	Significant Person or Association	Event
1869	Francis Galton	Study of individual differences
1879	Wilhelm Wundt	Developed first psychological laboratory, at Leipzig, Germany
1888	James McKeen Cattell	Developed a testing laboratory at the University of Pennsylvania and the term *mental test*
1896	Emil Kraepelin	Classification of mental disorders
1897	Hermann Ebbinghaus	Explored learning and retention rates
1901	Karl Pearson	Theory of correlation
1904	Charles Spearman	Introduced the two-factor theory of intelligence
1906	Edward L. Thorndike	Published first textbook in educational psychology
1909	Frank Parsons	Founder of the vocational guidance movement and author of *Choosing a Vocation*
1910	Charles Spearman	Psychometric theory
1922	Lewis M. Terman	Studied gifted children
1922	James McKeen Cattell	Founded the Psychological Corporation
1934	J. L. Moreno	Sociometric technique
1935	Louis L. Thurstone	Developed factor analysis technique
1935	Kurt Lewin	Field theory
1938	Oscar K. Buros	First *Mental Measurements Yearbook* for test reviews
1939	L. Frank	Introduced the term *projective technique*
1939	U.S. Department of Labor	*Dictionary of Occupational Titles*
1948	Office of Strategic Services	Situational techniques
1952	American Psychiatric Association	Published the *Diagnostic and Statistical Manual of Mental Disorders* (DSM I)
1954	American Psychological Association, American Education Research Association, and National Council on Measurement in Education	Technical recommendations for tests
1954	Paul Meehl	Published *Clinical vs. Statistical Predictions*
1957	C. E. Osgood	Semantic differential
1963	R. Glaser	Criterion-referenced testing
1966	American Psychological Association	Published *Standards for Educational and Psychological Tests and Manuals*
1966	J. P. Guilford	Model of the structure of intellect (operations, contents, and products)
1968	American Psychiatric Association	DSM II
1969	American Psychological Association	Guidelines for testing the disadvantaged
1973	K. H. Craik	Review of environmental assessment in *Annual Review of Psychology*
1974	American Psychological Association, American Education Research Association, and National Council on Measurement in Education	Revised standards for tests
1974	James F. Buckley	Author of Family Educational Rights and Privacy Act
1978	Oscar K. Buros	*Eighth Mental Measurements Yearbook* for test reviews
1980	American Psychiatric Association	DSM III
1981	Buros Center, University of Nebraska	Founded to continue the work of Oscar K. Buros and the test reviews

Table 1.1 Cont.

Table 1.1 Some Historical Events in Assessment

Year	Significant Person or Association	Event
1984	Test Corporation of America	Test Critiques (Vol. I) for test reviews
1985	American Psychological Association, American Education Research Association, and National Council on Measurement in Education	Established joint technical standards for educational and psychological testing
1987	American Psychiatric Association	DSM III-Revised

two tests (the Army Alpha Test for Literates and the Army Beta Test for Illiterates) were administered to American soldiers during World War I to measure mental ability.

Developments in the area of intelligence testing were slow until 1938, when David Wechsler developed the Wechsler-Bellevue Intelligence Scale. This was followed by the development of the Wechsler Intelligence Scale for Children in 1949; the Wechsler Adult Intelligence Scale in 1955 (a revision of the 1939 Wechsler-Bellevue Intelligence Scale), which was revised in 1981; and the Wechsler Preschool and Primary Scale of Intelligence in 1967. The Wechsler scales were a good contribution to intelligence testing for a number of reasons, one of which was that the long-used Stanford-Binet Intelligence Scale was not very effective with adults. The Wechsler scales were able to improve the assessment process at the adult level. More recently, in 1978, Jane Mercer developed her System of Multicultural Pluralistic Assessment to make testing fairer to people from minority cultures. This assessment system combines the Wechsler Intelligence Scale for Children (Revised) with a one-hour interview with the child's parents and a complete medical examination. All of this information is now used to estimate the child's adjusted IQ and/or learning potential. Advocates of this assessment system view it to be a good nondiscriminatory assessment battery, but more work is needed in order to verify this claim.

Aptitudes and Achievement

The assessment of aptitudes and achievement began some time later than the assessment of intelligence and was aimed primarily at identifying more specific abilities. Intelligence tests (Stanford-Binet and the Wechsler scales) were useful in that they produced valuable assessment information about overall intellectual level (global intelligence), but limited in that they yielded little information about special abilities. The development of aptitude and achievement tests was an attempt to bridge this gap. Aptitude tests were thought to measure people's ability to learn if given the opportunity (future performance), while achievement tests were thought to measure what people had in fact learned (present performance).

An initial attempt at developing an aptitude test was made by Carl Seashore in 1918, with his Measures of Musical Talent. Other pioneers in the development of aptitude and achievement tests were T. L. Kelley, with the Stanford Achievement Test in 1923; Edward F. Lindquist, with the Iowa Every Pupil Test in 1936; Louis L. Thurstone, with the Primary Mental Abilities Test in 1938; and the United States Employment Agency, which

Table 1.2 Some Significant Tests in Assessment

Year	Significant Person or Association	Event
1905	Alfred Binet and Theodore Simon	First Binet-Simon intelligence scale
1905	Carl Jung	Word-Association Test
1916	Lewis M. Terman	Stanford-Binet Intelligence Scale (American Revision)
1917	Arthur Otis and Robert M. Yerkes	Army Alpha and Beta group intelligence tests
1918	Carl Seashore	Seashore Measures of Musical Talent
1919	Louis L. Thurstone	Psychological Examination for College Freshmen
1920	Robert S. Woodworth	Personal Data Sheet, first personality inventory
1921	Hermann Rorschach	Published *Psychodiagnostics*, inkblot projective test
1923	T. L. Kelley	Stanford Achievement Test
1926	Florence Goodenough	Draw-A-Man Test
1927	E. K. Strong, Jr.	First edition of the Strong Vocational Interest Blank for men
1934	G. F. Kuder	First edition of the Kuder Preference Record—Vocational
1936	Edgar Doll	Vineland Social Maturity Scale
1936	Edward F. Lindquist	Iowa Every Pupil Test
1937	Lewis M. Terman and Maud Merrill	Revised Stanford-Binet Intelligence Scale
1938	Lauretta Bender	Bender Visual-Motor Gestalt Test for assessing personality and brain damage
1938	Henry Murray	Thematic Apperception Test
1938	Louis L. Thurstone	Primary Mental Abilities Test
1939	David Wechsler	Wechsler-Bellevue Intelligence Scale
1943	Starke Hathaway and Fred McKinley	Minnesota Multiphasic Personality Inventory
1947	U.S. Employment Agency	General Aptitude Test Battery
1949	David Wechsler	Wechsler Intelligence Scale for Children
1953	William Stephenson	Q-sort
1955	David Wechsler	Wechsler Adult Intelligence Scale
1956	Harrison Gough	California Psychological Inventory
1958	C. R. Pace and G. G. Stern	College Characteristics Index, a measure of perceived environment
1960	Maud Merrill	Revised (2nd edition) Stanford-Binet Intelligence Scale
1967	David Wechsler	Wechsler Preschool and Primary Scale of Intelligence
1968	G. F. Kuder	Kuder Occupational Interest Survey (KOIS)
1971	John L. Holland	Self-Directed Search, a measure of interests and personality
1974	David P. Campbell	Strong Vocational Interest Blank and the Strong-Campbell Interest Inventory (SVIB and SCII)
1974	Rudolf H. Moos	Social climate scales to assess the social environment
1974	David Wechsler	Wechsler Intelligence Scale for Children—Revised
1977	G. F. Kuder	Kuder Occupational Interest Survey—Revised
1977	John L. Holland	Self-Directed Search—Revised
1978	Jane Mercer	System of Multicultural Pluralistic Assessment, a nondiscriminatory assessment battery
1981	David P. Campbell and Jo Ida C. Hansen	SVIB and SCII—Revised
1981	David Wechsler	Wechsler Adult Intelligence Scale—Revised
1985	Jo Ida C. Hansen and David P. Campbell	SVIB and SCII—Revised
1985	G. F. Kuder and Donald Zytowski	Kuder Occupational Interest Survey—Revised
1985	John Holland	Self-Directed Search—Revised
1985	Robert L. Thorndike, Elizabeth Hagen, and Jerome Sattler	Stanford-Binet (4th edition)
1987	Harrison Gough	California Psychological Inventory—Revised

developed the General Aptitude Test Battery in 1947.

Personality Assessment

Another aspect of assessment psychology is concerned with the nonintellectual aspects of behavior, or what is frequently called "personality." As Boring (1950, p. 51) has said, "The most important and greatest puzzle which every man faces is himself, and secondarily, other persons."

The first personality inventory (self-report inventory) to assess persons was the Personal Data Sheet developed by Robert S. Woodworth in 1920. This inventory was a screening technique for indentifying seriously disturbed men who were not socially capable of military service and served as a model for the development of subsequent inventories of emotional adjustment. The Woodsworth Personal Data Sheet was followed by two significant contributions in the area of projective techniques: the Rorschach Inkblot Test, developed by Hermann Rorschach in 1921, and Henry Murray's Thematic Apperception Test, developed in 1938. Both were projective techniques that asked the individual to respond to vague and unstructured tasks or stimuli. The assumption underlying the technique is that individuals will project their personality into the tasks to which they are responding. Both of these projective techniques have survived the test of time and are being used today. Another major contribution in the area of personality assessment was the development of the Minnesota Multiphasic Personality Inventory by Starke Hathaway and Fred McKinley in 1943. To this day, it is the best self-report measure of emotional disturbance in the assessment repertoire.

Interest Assessment

The assessment of interests was introduced in 1927, when E. K. Strong, Jr., developed the Strong Vocational Interest Blank (SVIB) for men. The SVIB was an empirically based inventory that showed how an individual's likes and dislikes were similar to the likes and dislikes of individuals employed in a variety of other occupations. Strong later developed scales for women's occupations in the same way. The 1974 edition of the SVIB was expanded by the work of David P. Campbell and renamed the Strong Vocational Interest Blank and the Strong-Campbell Interest Inventory (SVIB and SCII). The SVIB and SCII was again revised in 1981, and a further revision was published in 1985. On the SVIB and SCII, John L. Holland's (1973) theory of personality types and model environments has been used to structure the profile and interpret the scores. Two other important inventories are used to assess interests. The Kuder Preference Record was introduced by G. F. Kuder in 1934. The most recent revision of this inventory, now called the Kuder Occupational Interest Survey, occurred in 1985. John Holland's Self-Directed Search was introduced in 1971 and revised in 1977 and 1985. In general, all three interest inventories attempt to give people some idea of how their likes and dislikes are similar to the likes and dislikes of individuals actually working in various other occupations.

Environmental Assessment

An important additional feature of the assessment process, which has gained more emphasis in recent years, is the environmental perspective. As will be stated many times throughout this text, any assessment of a person is incomplete without some assessment of the environment in which the person's thought and behavior occurs.

Kurt Lewin introduced his "field theory" in 1936, contending that scientific psychology must take into account the state of both the person and the environment. In 1938, Henry Murray's *Explorations in Person-*

ality developed a "need-press" model based on the assumption that behavior is a function of the relationship between the person (needs) and the environment (presses or perceived pressures). C. R. Pace and G. G. Stern operationalized the press concept in 1958 by developing the College Characteristics Index, a measure of perceived environment. The work of Rudolf Moos (1974) has also focused on the perceived environment. Moos suggests that environments, like people, have personalities and that how we perceive environments influences our behavior. Based on this notion, he has developed a series of social climate scales to assess perceived social environments. In 1973 K. H. Craik published the first review of environmental assessment in the *Annual Review of Psychology*. These and other contributions, to be discussed later in this book, suggest that the environment perspective is an important part of the assessment process.

Historic Professional Publications

Certain professional publications are historic in the development of assessment over the years. Edward Thorndike's *The Principles of Teaching: Based on Psychology* (1906) was the first book published in educational psychology. Emil Kraepelin's classification of mental disorders, published in his book, *Clinical Psychiatry* (1907), helped organize a mass of symptoms associated with mental disorders. The vocational guidance movement, founded by Frank Parsons, was a significant event in the development of assessment. Parson's book, *Choosing a Vocation* (1909), suggested a model for matching people and jobs that is still meaningful and useful today. The basic idea is that if we have self-knowledge (awareness of our aptitudes, interests, and personality) and knowledge of occupational environments through "true reasoning" or matching, we can choose an appropriate occupation.

The next highly significant publication was the first *Mental Measurements Yearbook* (1938), which was the work of Oscar K. Buros. The field of testing had grown rapidly, and the Buros book was the first good publication that described and reviewed tests. Buros produced eight such yearbooks, his last in 1978, shortly before his death. In 1981 the Oscar K. Buros Center was established at the University of Nebraska to continue his work. In 1985 the *Ninth Mental Measurements Yearbook* was published, edited by James V. Mitchell, Jr. More recently, Daniel Keyser and Richard Sweetland of the Test Corporation of America edited the first volume of *Test Critiques*, which was published in 1984. Since that time five additional volumes have been published, and these have been primarily concerned with describing and reviewing tests. In 1939 the Occupational Analysis Section of the United States Employment Service published the *Dictionary of Occupational Titles* (DOT). The DOT was the first sound attempt to present an occupational classification and comprehensive description of job duties. The fourth edition of the DOT appeared in 1977. In 1952 the American Psychiatric Association published the *Diagnostic and Statistical Manual of Mental Disorders* (DMS I), which was the first manual of mental disorders to contain descriptions of the different diagnostic categories. The most recent edition of the manual (DSM III-R, 1987) reflects a renewed commitment to basing an understanding of mental disorders on hard evidence. In the course of all this activity, the need for testing standards, guidelines, and principles had emerged. In 1954 the American Psychological Association published its technical recommendations for tests. The 1966 revised version of this document was called *Standards for Educational and Psychological Tests and Manuals*. It was revised again in 1974 and 1985. These standards have served as reasonable guides for those who wish to use and construct tests.

THEORY AND ASSESSMENT

Personality Theory and Assessment

Personality theory, in its various forms, has had considerable influence on assessment. Psychoanalysis, as developed by Sigmund Freud in the early part of the century, was primarily concerned with making unconscious motives conscious in order to help people develop more socially acceptable ways of dealing with their impulses. Freud believed that the individual is involved in a lifelong struggle between the pleasure-oriented id impulses on the one hand and perceived socially based responsibility on the other. There is no question that psychoanalytic concepts have had a profound impact on the assessment process. For example, most projective techniques (the Rorschach, the Incomplete Sentences Blank, Draw-A-Person) are based on psychoanalytic theory. As previously mentioned, Kurt Lewin introduced field theory in 1936, suggesting that psychology must view behavior in terms of both the person and the environment. The impact of this idea is probably more important in assessment today than ever before. In 1913 John Watson introduced behavioristic psychology, stressing the science of behavior. According to Watson, current behavior is a function of past experiences and antecedent conditions. The best predictor of future behavior is past behavior. From Watson's work developed the modern behavioral modification movement and the behavioral assessment of clients. Behavioral assessment, as we shall see later in this text, is concerned with understanding behavior in relation to the environment. Carl Rogers' "self-theory" (person-centered theory) (1951) stressed the importance of perception and self-assessment. Growing as a person, understanding and liking self and others, called upon the person to be relatively good at self-assessment.

The above theories of personality and others have had and will continue to have significant impact on the assessment process. In addition, in the next two sections we see the continued significance of personality concepts in theories of person-environment psychology and theories of human development.

Person-Environment Psychology and Assessment

A second body of theory relevant to assessment is in the area of person-environment psychology. This theoretical base is nested in Lewin's (1936) idea that the environment is as important as the individual and both must be analyzed to understand behavior. As we have already mentioned, Murray (1938) introduced one of the first theoretical views, a need/press model that was subsequently operationalized by Pace and Stern (1958). From an assessment perspective, this theory suggests that behavior is a function of personality needs and perceived environmental pressures. Holland's (1973) theory of personality types and model environments indicates that congruent person-environment relations lead to predictable behavior. People tend to enter and remain in environments that match their personality. Barker's (1968) theory of behavior settings proposes that environments tend to have a coercive influence on behavior, so that, for example, when in school we behave like school and when in church we behave like church. Some of the Moos (1974) work previously mentioned suggests that environments, like people, have personalities and that how we perceive environments in which we live and work directly influences our behavior. These theories and others dicussed in this text make some reasonable predictions about the individual within a person-environment framework, and for this reason alone have clear implications for the assessment process.

Human Development and Assessment

A third group of theories relevant to assessment focuses on human development. Theories of development are suggestive of how human development occurs over the life span. We know, for example, that the human being develops through a period of growth, a period of stability, and a period of decline. This developmental approach has stimulated two families of developmental theories having clear implications for assessment. One family of theories, the cognitive development theories, examines how we reason, think, or make meaning of our experiences. The main theorists in this group include Piaget, Kohlberg, Perry, and Loevinger. The second family of theories, the psychosocial theories, are concerned with the "what," or content, of human development. These theories combine feelings, thinking, and behavior into a description of the life span. Thus, for example, these theories explore the questions "Who am I?"; "Who am I to love?", and "What am I to believe?" Significant theorists here are Erikson, Chickering, and Levinson. The above developmental theories are discussed in this text primarily in the context of their meaning and implications for assessment.

THE USE OF TESTS

The use of various tests and inventories is a topic on which little information is available. One survey conducted by Watkins, Campbell, and McGregor (1988) sampled 1,000 randomly selected American Members of the American Psychological Association, Division of Counseling Psychology. Of the 1,000 potential participants, 630 returned usable questionnaires. The 630 participants were at the time working in private practice, college and university counseling centers, hospital settings, or community mental health centers. The findings are reported in Table 1.3 in rank order. Nine of the tests listed by Watkins, Campbell, and McGregor assess

Table 1.3 Most Frequently Used Assessment Instruments

Rank	Test
1	Minnesota Multiphasic Personality Inventory
2	Wechsler Adult Intelligence Scale—Revised
3	Strong-Campbell Interest Inventory
4	Sentence Completion Blanks
5	Bender-Gestalt
6	Wechsler Intelligence Scale for Children—Revised
7	House-Tree-Person
8	Draw-A-Person
9	Thematic Apperception Test
10.5	Rorschach
10.5	Sixteen Personality Factor Questionnaire
12	Wide Range Achievement Test
13.5	Edwards Personal Preference Schedule
13.5	Kuder Occupational Interest Survey
15	California Psychological Inventory
16	Wechsler Memory Scale
17	Wechsler Preschool and Primary Scale of Intelligence
18	Differential Aptitude Test

Source: Adapted from Watkins, Campbell, and McGregor (1988).

personality, seven assess intelligence, achievement, and aptitude factors, and two are interest inventories.

Table 1.4 takes a look at assessment instruments most frequently researched, based on the total number of references accumulated over the years. These findings are similar to those in Table 1.3 (Test Usage). Nine of the tests assess personality, seven assess intellectual factors, and two assess interests. Ten of the assessment instruments (Minnesota Multiphasic Personality Inventory, Wechsler Adult Intelligence Scale, Strong-Campbell Interest Inventory, Bender Visual-Motor Gestalt Test, Wechsler Intelligence Scale for Children, Thematic Apperception Test, Rorschach, Sixteen Person-

ality Factor Questionnaire, Edwards Personal Preference Schedule, and the California Psychological Inventory) appear in both Table 1.3 and Table 1.4, indicating that they are used frequently and, in addition, are often evaluated for meaning and validity. Notice, however, that the three highest ranking tests in Table 1.4 are primarily concerned with the assessment of personality.

Table 1.5 looks at the research on assessment instruments by focusing on the work since 1971. Again, we see findings similar to those in Tables 1.3 and 1.4: Ten of the tests assess personality, seven assess intellectual ability, and one is an interest assessment instrument. All ten of the assessment instruments mentioned above are listed in Tables

Table 1.4 Most Frequently Researched Assessment Instruments, Based on Total Number of Cumulative References to Midyear 1984

Rank	Test	References (Cumulative Total)
1	Minnesota Multiphasic Personality Inventory	5,382
2	Rorschach	5,021
3	Thematic Apperception Test	2,058
4	Wechsler Intelligence Scale for Children and Revision	1,883
5	Strong Vocational Interest Blank and the Strong-Campbell Interest Inventory	1,720
6	Edwards Personal Preference Schedule	1,648
7	Stanford-Binet Intelligence Scale—Third Revision	1,625
8	Sixteen Personality Factor Questionnaire	1,584
9	Wechsler Adult Intelligence Scale and Revision	1,580
10	California Psychological Inventory	1,447
11	Bender Visual-Motor Gestalt Test	1,082
12	Study of Values	1,027
13	Kuder Preference Record—Vocational	903
14	College Board Scholastic Aptitude Test	813
15	Eysenck Personality Inventory	809
16	Progressive Matrices	766
17	Illinois Test of Psycholinguistic Abilities	681
18	Maudsley Personality Inventory	671

Source: Adapted from Buros (1978) and Mitchell (1985).

Table 1.5 Most Frequently Researched Assessment Instruments, Based on the Number of References Since 1971 to Midyear 1984

Rank	Test	References since 1971
1	Minnesota Multiphasic Personality Inventory	1,527
2	Wechsler Intelligence Scale for Children	847
3	Sixteen Personality Factor Questionnaire	686
4	Wechsler Adult Intelligence Scale	642
5	California Psychological Inventory	513
6	Eysenck Personality Inventory	495
7	Personal Orientation Inventory	455
8	Tennessee Self-Concept Scale	442
9	Rorschach	439
10	State-Trait Anxiety Inventory	425
11	Close Procedure	399
12	Edwards Personal Preference Schedule	334
13	Bender Visual-Motor Gestalt Test	317
14	Illinois Test of Psycholinguistic Abilities	307
15	Thematic Apperception Test	293
16	Strong Vocational Interest Blank and the Strong-Campbell Interest Inventory	288
17	College Board Scholastic Aptitude Test	246
18	Torrance Tests of Creative Thinking	229

Source: Adapted from Buros (1978) and Mitchell (1985).

1.3, 1.4, and 1.5, suggesting that they are highly used, frequently explored for their meaning and benefit, and of frequent current interest in society.

Table 1.6 takes a contemporary look at the research on assessment instruments by focusing on the work from 1978 to midyear 1984. Again, we see some findings similar to those in Tables 1.3, 1.4, and 1.5: Eleven of the tests assess personality, six assess intellectual ability, and one is a neuropsychological test battery. Seven of the assessment instruments are listed in Tables 1.3, 1.4, 1.5, and 1.6. However, Table 1.6 identifies a number of instruments not previously mentioned in Tables 1.4 and 1.5 and also not mentioned in the most frequently used assessments Table 1.3. Thus, Table 1.6 does suggest that some changes in research emphasis may be taking place.

THE MEANING OF PSYCHOLOGICAL ASSESSMENT

Definition

Psychological assessment has been defined in different ways. McReynolds (1975) views assessment as a process whereby one person attempts to know, understand, or size up another person: One attempts to develop a picture of what the other person is like. Sundberg (1990) suggests that assessment is a process of developing images, making decisions, and checking hypotheses about another person's behavior in interaction with the environment. This definition of the assessment process suggests the need to develop images of the person, images of the environment, and person-environment theories to understand and predict behavior.

Table 1.6 Most Frequently Researched Assessment Instruments, Based on the Number of References from 1978 to Midyear 1984

Rank	Test	References from 1978 to 1984
1	Minnesota Multiphasic Personality Inventory	339
2	Wechsler Intelligence Scale for Children—Revised	299
3	Wechsler Adult Intelligence Scale—Revised	291
4	State-Trait Anxiety Inventory	158
5	Bem-Sex Role Inventory	121
6	Peabody Picture Vocabulary Test—Revised	117
7	Wide Range Achievement Test, 1978 Edition	103
8	Eysenck Personality Inventory	91
9.5	Halstead-Reitam Neuropsychological Test Battery	79
9.5	Rorschach	79
11.5	Present State Examination	71
11.5	Matching Familiar Figures Test	71
13.5	Progressive Matrices	67
13.5	Sixteen Personality Factor Questionnaire	67
15	Bender Visual-Motor Gestalt Test	65
16.5	Symptom Check List-90-R	61
16.5	California Psychological Inventory	61
18	Tennessee Self-Concept Scale	60

Source: Adapted from Mitchell (1985).

Maloney and Ward (1976) propose a less complex definition in suggesting that assessment is a process of solving problems, in which tests are frequently used as a method of collecting important information. To Maloney and Ward the process involves three demands: the problem, data collection, and answering the question.

Our definition of assessment is similar to these, yet different in an important way. To us, psychological assessment is a process of understanding and helping people cope with problems. In this process, tests are frequently used to collect meaningful information about the person and his or her environment. In an applied sense, the assessment process has four parts: the problem, information gathering, understanding the information, and coping with the problem.

The Problem

Part one of the process involves defining the problem or asking the question. Problem clarification, at least initially, is usually carried out in an interview situation. For example, a client may say, "I can't decide what I want to do after high school [or college]"; "I don't know what makes me so nervous all the time"; "Why do I find is so hard to make friends?"; "I'm afraid of not being able to find a job after graduation"; "I'm just not sure of what I can do"; "I just don't know what to believe about God"; "I have sexual conflicts"; "I just don't know who I am." Frequently the reported problem suggests, and may be linked to, a content area (e.g., personality, ability, interests, values, achievement, or the social climate). For example, the problem "I can't decide what I want to do" may be linked to the content area of vocational interests; the problem "I don't know what makes me so nervous all the time" may be linked to the content area of personality; the problem of having no friends may be linked to the personality area; concern about unemployment after graduation may be linked to social climate; and the problem of not being sure about one's abilities may be linked to the cognitive ability area. The important point being made is that making a link between a reported problem and the content of the problem is of significant help in the information-gathering part of psychological assessment. If we are able to link the reported problem of "no vocational goal" to the content area of interests, this link then tends to be suggestive of the kind of information needed to attempt to cope with the problem. However, be careful not to oversimplify the "link" concept, because in some situations a stated problem may certainly suggest more than one problem content area.

Information Gathering

Part two of the assessment process involves gathering meaningful information. A basic assumption we want to keep in mind here is that the person and the environment are in constant transaction, and any assessment of the person is incomplete without some assessment of the environment in which the thought or the behavior occurs. Most certainly the person has an impact on the environment and the behavior, but also the environment most certainly has an impact on the person and his or her behavior. How the individual perceives the situation, context, or the enviroment is a determinant of that person's behavior.

    Most of the time in the information-gathering process a psychological test or inventory of some kind may be used to collect relevant information. Other methods (interview, observation, reports of others, case study information) are certainly appropriate for gathering information and should be used, but psychological tests are a primary tool used to collect information about people and environments, and as such will be the main focus of this text. Once a link between a reported problem and a content area has been suggested, we may begin to consider various psychological tests that may be used to collect useful information about the person and the environment. Consider the identity problem previously mentioned. The link between this problem and the personality content area suggests the use of a personality inventory to collect some meaningful information about the client. In addition, this linkage suggests the use of an environmental inventory to collect some information about the client's perceptions of his or her family climate, family interactions, and values that may have an impact on self-concept. Keep in mind that our task here is to develop an image of the person and some image of the environment or context in which the behavior occurs. As these images emerge, a related task for us becomes one of organizing, interpreting, and understanding the information.

Understanding the Information

Part three of the psychological assessment process involves an attempt to organize, interpret, and understand the person-environment information within some kind of theoretical perspective. In other words, we attempt to use a theory of personality, of human development, and/or of person-environment psychology to help us organize, understand, and predict behavior. Our goal is to develop a set of hypotheses about the person and his or her situation with the help of the various theories of person-environment psychology and development. (These theories are discussed later in the text.) These more formalized theoretical perspectives do not have answers, but they do serve as useful bench marks to help organize and interpret meaningful information about people and environments. Existing theories help us build other theories to understand an individual's behavior in a given context.

Coping with the Problem

The final step in the assessment process is coping with the problem. Actually the coping begins when the client initially reports a problem or asks a question and continues through the data collection and theory-building stages. From our linkage of a reported client problem and a content area emerges an information-gathering plan from which we develop a set of working hypotheses about the person and his or her situation. As we prove or disprove these hypotheses, we make progress toward answering questions and coping with problems. Of course, the testing of hypotheses may suggest other hypotheses. In addition, the psychological assessment process, in its attempts to cope with problems, may suggest a series of alternative solutions or a number of answers to a certain question, or in fact no solution, decision, or answer al all. Thus, psychological assessment does not promise all things to all people. Nor does psychological assessment suggest that given a problem there is one appropriate or right answer or correct way of coping. Psychological assessment is simply an information-based process that is primarily concerned with understanding and helping people effectively cope with their problems and make decisions.

THE JUDGMENTAL AND OBJECTIVE APPROACHES TO ASSESSMENT

The judgmental and objective perspectives represent two main approaches to assessment. In the judgmental approach all available information, whether subjective (interview data, reports of others, observations, descriptive data) or objective (test scores, ratings) in nature, is cognitively processed and used to make some kind of meaningful conclusions. (Cronbach [1984] refers to this approach as "impressionistic.") The judgmental approach, often referred to as the clinical approach, may or may not use test scores and objective data in attempting to understand a client's current behavior or in predicting future behavior. The flexibility of the judgmental approach permits the inclusion of a broad range of information about the person and the environment in the assessment process.

The objective approach is limited to information (test scores, ratings) about the person and the environment that can be quantified or coded for statistical analysis. Meehl (1965) calls this the statistical approach. Cronbach (1984) calls it the psychometric approach, based on Thorndike's (1906) notion that "if a thing exists, it exists in some amount" (p. 56) and "if it exists in some amount, it can be measured" (p. 56). (For example, Thorndike thought that all people possess the trait of intelligence, but in different amounts.) The objective approach maintains that judgments (interview data, reports of others, observations, case study information) may be included in assessments only if they are quantifiable and obtained through the use of a reliable and valid rating instrument. In essence, the objective approach uses quantifiable information to make empirical predictions about current or future behavior, and in some instances it does the job reasonably successfully. The objective approach will use the American College Test scores and high school grade-point average to predict the first-quarter grades of freshmen college students at Ohio State University. In the objective approach the information is processed by a computer; in the judgmental approach the information is cognitively processed by the counselor. However, the objective approach has a major limitation in that it is not feasible to quantify all information about individuals and environments. Thus, the judgmental approach includes a broader range of information about the individual and the environment than the objective approach does. Other data-based comparisons between the two approaches suggest that when the information is quantifiable the objective approach has the edge over the judgmental approach in predicting future behavior.

In any event, the psychological assessment process does not require us to choose one approach over the over. Psychological assessment is essentially an information-based process that is used to help people cope with their problems. This assessment process needs all available meaningful information about the person and the environment, whether generated by the judgmental or by the objective approach. In practice, a solid psychological assessment will be based on information emerging from both the judgmental and the objective approaches.

ASSESSMENT AND SOME BASIC ASSUMPTIONS

The decision of the meaning of psychological assessment and the approaches to assessment suggests a few basic assumptions that need to be kept in mind during the assessment process. These assumptions are in some respects themes that are visible throughout this text. There are other assumptions than the ones cited below, but these seemed most meaningful within the framework and context of this book.

1. People and environments are in constant transaction, and any assessment of the person is incomplete without some assessment of the environment. We can't take the person out of personality (Mischel, 1977a); but,

at the same time, we cannot ignore the fact that environments, like people, have personalities and influence behavior.

2. Cognitive, personality, interest, and value factors are essential determinants of behavior. This person component indicates that an individual's abilities, personality, interests, and values do affect or influence behavior.

3. The psychological meaning of situations for the individual is a determinant of behavior. This situational or environmental component suggests that an individual's perceptions of situations will to some extent determine behavior.

4. Behavior is reasonably predictable, given knowledge of an individual's perception of the situation and of the individual's disposition to respond in that situation. As suggested by Magnusson and Endler (1977a, p. 11), under these conditions "individual behavior across different situations provides a consistent, idiographically predictable pattern."

5. People differ on certain identifiable and measurable dimensions. As suggested by Kluckholn, Murray, and Schneider, (1953, p. 53), "Every person is in certain respects, like all other people, like some other people, like no other person." Psychological tests are an effective means of measuring and describing these differences.

6. The psychological meaning of situations or environments differs on certain identifiable and measurable dimensions. People perceive situations differently, and these differences may be measured and described, using environmental tests and inventories.

7. Person-environment assessment is an information-oriented process used to help people cope with real-life problems. Any information about an individual or his or her environment that contributes to understanding behavior must be considered in the assessment process.

8. The assessment process ideally attempts to link reciprocally the person, the environment, and the behavior in a data-based framework to help people understand and cope with problems. Figure 1.1 describes these reciprocal transactions, which have been suggested by Bandura (1978) and Howard (1979). The essence of the model

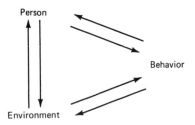

FIGURE 1.1 A model of reciprocal transactions.

is that all variables (person, environment, and behavior) mutually and reciprocally influence one another. The major problem is one of measuring and describing the multidirectional transactions. Currently this is a measurement task that has been very difficult to operationalize and make real. The attempts that have been made to link and relate the person, environment, and behavior variables are reported in the theory chapters.

The above list of assumptions is not exhaustive. However, within the framework of this text they serve as meaningful touchstones for understanding the assessment process.

DIAGNOSIS AND ASSESSMENT

Diagnosis is similar to, yet different from, psychological assessment. The diagnostic process, like the assessment process, involves some statement of the problem, information gathering, and information interpretation, but all for the main purpose of making a diagnosis (a classification on the basis of observed symptoms). According to Rapaport, Gill, and Schafer (1968), *diagnosis*, which is a medical term, is defined as the act or art of identifying a disease from its symptoms. The medical model suggests that there is an underlying cause responsible for specific symptoms. Wolman (1978) defines *diagnosis* as the search for a disease responsible for symptoms. This search is for an invading

germ that exists internally and is the source of behavioral problems. By observing and classifying symptoms, the physician makes a diagnosis regarding the condition. As noted by Maloney and Ward (1976), the most basic feature of the medical model is that diagnosis attempts to suggest the cause and nature of the condition. However, keep in mind that many illnesses and syndromes have unknown causes. Thus, from another perspective, diagnosis may be viewed as a process that tends to reify sets of symptoms or characteristics (making a description into a concrete thing, such as a learning disability or depression) for subsequent treatment. Cause is usually not indicated in the diagnosis of mental disorders, except for specific organic conditions, one of which, for example, may be substance-induced by alcohol or drugs. Thus, when we review the much-used classification system for mental disorders, the *Diagnostic and Statistical Manual of Mental Disorders* (DSM III-R, 1987), published by the American Psychiatric Association, cause is not indicated for most of the functional disorders. The approach is primarily descriptive, in that the definitions consist of descriptions of the clinical features of the disorders.

THE *DIAGNOSTIC AND STATISTICAL MANUAL OF MENTAL DISORDERS* (Third Edition—Revised) (DSM III-R)

The first edition of the American Psychiatric Association's *Diagnostic and Statistical Manual of Mental Disorders* was published in 1952. This was the first manual of mental disorders to contain descriptions of the various diagnostic categories. The 1987 edition of the DSM III-R reflects an increased commitment to rely on data as the basis for understanding mental disorders.

In use, the DSM III-R requires that each individual be evaluated on five axes.

Axis I represents the principal diagnosis; for example:

Axis I: 295.32 Schizophrenia, Paranoid Type, Chronic.

Axis II is generally used to describe personality disorders and specific developmental disorders (e.g., paranoid traits). A code number may be used here to indicate a personality disorder:

Axis II: 301.70 Antisocial Personality Disorder.

On Axis III are noted physical disorders or any other conditions besides mental disorders that are relevant to understanding the individual. For example, it would be important to note that a child has a vision problem associated with an Anxiety Disorder. Axis IV (Severity of Psychosocial Stressors) asks for an evaluation of the stresses judged to have been an important contributor to the development of the identified disorder. Types of psychosocial stressors to be considered are marital and nonmarital, parenting, interpersonal problems, living conditions, occupational problems, financial, legal, developmental, physical illness or injury, and family factors.

On Axis V a global assessment of the individual's psychological, social, and occupational functioning is carried out on a hypothetical continuum of mental health to illness. Two ratings are required on Axis V on what is called the Global Assessment of Functioning (GAF) Scale. A rating is made on the individual's current level of functioning at the time of the evaluation. And a second rating is made on the highest level of functioning for at least a few months during the past year. GAF Scale ratings vary from 1 to 90. A rating of 1 would suggest severe symptoms and a tendency for the individual to be in persistent danger of severely hurting self or others. A rating of 90 would suggest an absence or minimal symptoms and in general good psychological, social, and occupational functioning. A rating of 51 to 60 would suggest moderate symptoms and moderate difficulty in social, occupational, or school functioning.

In general, the DSM III-R is attempting to focus attention on types of disorders, aspects of the environment, and areas of functioning that may be overlooked if only the presenting problem is evaluated.

Why do we discuss the DSM III-R here? For a number of reasons: This is the one official manual that describes and delineates the various psychological disorders, and it is used in a variety of different settings. Therefore counselors and clinicians working in community mental health clinics, hospital settings, and private practice will probably have to become very familiar with the diagnostic classification system of psychological disorders in order to make generally recognizable diagnoses, in order to communicate with other professionals, and in order to follow the relevant literature in the mental health field. In spite of limitations (unclear diagnostic categories, some reliability problems, unclear implications for treatment, category overlap, vague category definitions, and inability to show cause), the DSM III-R is currently at least an attempt to describe psychological disturbances, environmental factors, and other areas of functioning that may be problematic.

MEASUREMENT AND ASSESSMENT

Definition

Psychological measurement and psychological assessment have the idea of process in common, but the function of this process is very different. As we have said, the process of psychological assessment involves the collection of meaningful information to understand and help people cope with problems. Psychological measurement, on the other hand, is the process of assigning numbers according to certain agreed-upon rules. The way of assigning numbers most useful to psychologists was set up by Stevens (1951). Stevens suggests four types of measurement, each having its own rules for the assignment of numbers. In using Stevens's types of measurement and in assigning numbers according to certain rules, we are able to quantify behavior, personality traits, aptitudes, environmental perceptions, and other psychological variables. Once these factors have been quantified, we are able to provide them with additional meaning by relating them to other factors and by making statistical comparisons. The four types of measurement enabling us to quantify personal and environmental factors are Stevens's very important contribution to the psychological assessment task.

The Nominal Scale

Stevens called the most elementary level of measurement the *nominal scale*. Here numbers are used to classify, name, or identify individuals or things by groups to which they belong: The numbers on soccer or basketball jerseys are used to identify the players. Or we may use numerical labels to identify occupational groups: Engineers may be given a code number of 1, chemists a code number of 2, social workers a code number of 3, and so forth. Telephone nubmers are another example of assigning numbers primarily for identification purposes. The only mathematical operation that may be applied to nominal scales is counting. The numerical labels say nothing about order and may not be used to add, subtract, multiply, or divide.

The Ordinal Scale

The second level of measurement is the *ordinal scale*, which involves the assignment of numbers to indicate rank or order from highest to lowest. In a thoroughbred horse race the winner of the race is ranked first, the horse finishing second is assigned the rank of 2, and the horse finishing third is assigned the rank of 3. Notice that this ranking (1, 2, and 3) tells us in which order the horses finished the race but tells us nothing about the differences among the horses. The rank order of finish does not indicate that the winner of the race won by only a nose over the second-place horse and that the second horse finished five lengths in front of the third-place horse. The ranking does not indicate the quantitative differences between the various ranks. As with nominal scales, the mathematical operations of addition, subtraction, multiplication, and division cannot be appropriately used with ordinal scales. However, statistical tools based on rank are appropriate.

The Interval Scale

The third level of quantification in measurement is called the *interval scale*. We like to think that tests and inventories used to quantify psychological variables (personality traits, interests, abilities, values, and environmental perceptions) fall on the interval scale. Interval scales permit the addition and subtraction of scores, but not the division of one score by another. Dividing one score by another assumes an exact zero point, which is not a property of the interval scale. Thus, on an interval scale, distances between each number and the next are equal, but it is not known how far any number is from zero.

For example, the centigrade thermometer is an inteval scale on which the difference between 20 and 30 degrees is the same as the difference between 50 and 60 degrees. The intervals are equal. However, we cannot say that minus 50 degrees is twice $2(50 \div 25)$ as cold as minus 25 degrees, since there is no exact zero point, and division, as we said before, assumes an exact zero point. Let's try a more psychologically oriented example. On the final examination in an introductory psychological assessment course Roy scores 90 and Joan scores 45. Each student received an additional five points for class participation, making Roy's score 95 and Joan's 50. The difference between their scores is the same in either case (45 points), but notice how the quotient of the two scores varies. In the first case (without the class participation points) the quotient is 2(90 ÷ 45), but with the extra five points the quotient is 1.9(95 ÷ 50). Under these circumstances (no exact zero point), it is very difficult to make statements about one person's knowledge being twice that of another. On the other hand, an interval scale does permit us to add and subtract, which means that we are able to describe distributions of test scores by computing an average, the standard deviation, and correlation coefficients. In addition, we are able to translate raw scores on tests into different kinds of derived scores. But keep in mind that these statistical procedures (the mean, standard deviation, correlation coefficient, derived scores) cannot be used with ordinal data.

The Ratio Scale

The fourth level of measurement is the *ratio scale*. This is the highest level of measurement and permits the use of all mathematical operations (addition, subtraction, multiplication, and division). Ratio scales, like interval scales, have equal intervals, plus the additional property of an exact zero point. Height, weight, and volume may be quantified in this way. Thus, we may say that the difference between 10 pounds and 20 pounds is the same as the difference between 20 pounds and 30 pounds. And, in addition, we may say that 50 pounds is twice as heavy as 25 pounds. We may express the two as a ratio.

Few of the measurements made in psychology qualify as ratio scales. The factors that do qualify are generally measured in physical units, galvanic skin response (GSR), electroencephalogram (EEG), and adrenalin excretion. Most of the measurements we make in psychology are assumed to be interval scales and permit the use of inferential statistics. However, as mentioned by Walsh (1989), an important caution to remember is that not all the operations we know how to carry out with numbers may appropriately be used with test scores and other psychological characteristics. Nevertheless, it is important for us to remember that psychological measurement in assigning numbers according to rules permits us the advantage of developing and using psychological tests and inventories to understand human behavior more objectively. Thus, measurement procedures help us estimate the amount or quantity of personal and environmental variables through the use of psychological tests and inventories. The next section of the book focuses on tests and assessment.

TESTS AND ASSESSMENT

The Interview

In the main, tests developed out of the need to find a more objective and efficient method of collecting information about people. The traditional interview method, which is probably as old as the humn race (Matarazzo, 1978), has some distinct advantages, but also some clear disadvantages. An interview, well defined long ago, is simply a conversation with a purpose (Bingham & Moore, 1924). We ask, watch, and share perspectives and information (Sundberg, 1990). However, the strengths of the interview in some respects reflect the weaknesses. The interview is a very individualized procedure that enables us to collect personal and subjective information about a client. This flexibility of the interview is a positive feature of the procedure, but difficult to objectify and/or quantify. Herein lie the weaknesses of the interview. The information is subjective and individual, and the procedure varies from person to person. In other words, it is very difficult to quantify and analyze interview information, and it is difficult to use subjective and unquantified information to compare people. Tests provide us with such objective and quantified information.

The Psychological Test

A test is a method of acquiring a sample of a person's behavior under controlled conditions—"controlled conditions" meaning that all people taking the test do it the same way, to make sure they may be compared. This means that tests are standardized. Procedures for administration, scoring, and interpretation are the same for each person taking the test. Standardized tests produce a sample of a person's behavior that may usually be quantified and reported in an objective and numerical form. By comparison, interview information is qualitative and is difficult to report in numerical form. Actually both kinds of information (interview and test, or qualitative and quantitative) are useful and meaningful in psychological assessment. It's just that the quantitative information (test scores) is more useful in making comparisons among people who have taken the same test under similar conditions.

In summary, the test has certain assets, one of which is objectivity. An objective test that is standardized is administered, scored, and interpreted in a similar way for all people. A second attribute of the test is that it is quantifiable. A test score may be reported in numerical form, which permits more precision and the use of statistical procedures. Finally, under many circumstances tests are thought to be more economical and more efficient than the interview.

Tests and Some Basic Assumptions

As we have indicated, a test is a method of obtaining a sample of behavior under controlled conditions. The conditions are controlled so that we may compare scores for people taking the test. However, for a number of reasons, tests and test scores are at best suggestive. Tests are not "magic" nor do they possess the only "right" answer, but they are useful and meaningful ways of collecting information about people. Below are listed some basic assumptions we must make in using tests and some good reasons why tests are at best suggestive. The first three of these assumptions were suggested by Wiggins (1973) some years ago.

1. It is assumed (at least to some extent) that each item on a test and all the words in that item have some similar meaning for different people. This is a large assumption, and one that is difficult to corroborate. Realistically, test items will vary some in meaning for different people, thus making the scores on a test less comparable. This variance in meaning is a limitation, but not a reason for discarding the use of tests.

2. A second assumption is that people are able to perceive and describe their self-concepts and personalities accurately. This assumption suggests that people need to be sufficiently free from self-distortion and defenses to report accurately about themselves. Of course the other side of this assumption is that these self-distortions may be very much a part of the client's problems.

3. It is assumed that people will report their thoughts and feelings honestly. There are many situations, however—prison, job placement, promotion—where people may think it is not in their best interest to do so. In such situations, individuals may respond in a way they think will make them look good or in a way they think is socially desirable and acceptable.

4. It is assumed that an individual's test behavior (and actual behavior) is rather consistent over time. Fortunately, this assumption may be empirically explored and is called the *reliability* of the test—"reliability"

meaning primarily "consistency." The concept and types of reliability are discussed more comprehensively in Chapter 3.

5. It is assumed that the test measures what it is supposed to measure. For example, a dominance scale is supposed to measure leadership and dominance. An order scale is supposed to measure neatness, orderliness, and organization. Again this assumption may be empirically investigated and is referred to as the *validity* of the test. The meaning and types of validity are discussed in Chapter 3.

6. It is assumed that an individual's observed score (X_i) on a test is equal to his or her true score (true ability) (T_i) plus the error (E_i).

$$X_i = T_i + E_i$$

All test scores have an error factor (a mistake factor) made up of things like testee health, attention span, previous experience, emotional state, fatigue, motor defects, visual defects, sociocultural problems, luck, group attentiveness, test administration, lighting, noise, and so forth. We must remember that tests, like most other things, are not perfect.

SUMMARY

The idea of assessment has been with us for some time. Everybody tends to be some kind of an assessor of human behavior by forming impressions of others and sizing people up. The entire assessment process probably received its biggest push from Francis Galton, who introduced the concept of individual differences. However, it was Binet and Simon who produced the first widely used assessment instrument to collect general intelligence information about people. Aptitude and achievement tests soon after appeared to assess special abilities, a task the more global intelligence tests were not designed to accomplish. In 1920 Woodworth developed the first self-report personality inventory, and the assessment of interests was introduced in 1927, when Strong constructed the Strong Vocational Interest Blank. Lewin presented

an environmental perspective by suggesting that behavior is a function of the transactional relationship between the person and the environment. Thus, over time, the idea developed that assessment of the person is incomplete without some assessment of the environment in which the thought or behavior emerged.

Our definition of psychological assessment suggests a process of understanding and helping people cope with problems. In an applied sense, the assessment process includes defining the problem, gathering information about the person and the environment, understanding and interpreting the information, and problem coping. The assessment process attempts to link person, environment, and behavior in an information-based framework to help people understand and cope with problems. Tests are frequently used as part of this process to collect meaningful information about people and their context.

A psychological test is a method of acquiring a sample of behavior under controlled conditions. Controlled conditions mean that the procedures for administration, scoring, and interpreting the test are the same for each person, so the results may be compared. Such tests usually produce objective numerical scores that may be used for comparison purposes and, in addition, permit the use of statistical procedures. Tests are an important part of the assessment process, but they do not define the process. Psychological tests are less than perfect tools in the assessment process, used to gather meaningful information about people and environments. Other sources of information (including interview behavior, observations, observations of others, physiological responses, nonverbal behavior) are also important and useful in the assessment process. Any information that is thought to be meaningful should be included in an assessment.

2

Basic Statistical Concepts in Testing and Assessment

Chapter 1 defined psychological assessment as a process of understanding and helping people cope with problems. One important stage of this process is that of gathering information about the person and his or her environment, and psychological tests are major tools by which we gather this information. Thus an understanding of the nature of a psychological test and the means by which test scores may be interpreted is essential to the goal of effective and useful psychological measurement. This chapter begins by expanding upon the *definition* of a psychological test introduced in Chapter 1. In subsequent sections, basic *statistical con-* *cepts* necessary to the use and understanding of test scores are described, followed by a discussion of the use of *norms* in test interpretation.

DEFINITION OF A PSYCHOLOGICAL TEST

Of the eight major assumptions concerning assessment, as given in Chapter 1 (p. 15), the most important assumption underlying the concept of a psychological test is that people and environments differ on certain identifiable and measurable dimensions or characteristics. This assumption, known as the concept of "individual differences," is easy to verify by simple observation. For example, you can readily observe differences in the heights and weights of people around you. Similarly, you have undoubtedly known people you considered very intelligent, very good in mathematics, or very capable athletically, and people you felt were less intelligent, less good at math, or less athletic. As you are observing and getting to know the people around you, the fact that they differ from each other in various ways becomes readily apparent.

While our everyday lives involve constant observations of individual differences, these observations are often seemingly automatic and usually relatively unsystematic. Methods of psychological assessment, on the other hand, are designed to provide more *systematic* observations of differences among people or environments. As was stated in Chapter 1, tests in particular are means of observing people's behavior under controlled conditions. As defined by Cronbach (1984, p. 26), a psychological test is a "systematic procedure for observing a person's behavior and describing it with the aid of numerical scales or fixed categories." Similarly, Anastasi (1982, p. 22) describes a psychological test as "essentially an objective and standardized measure of a sample of behavior." Essentially, then, a psychological test is a highly refined and systematized version of the ordinary process of observation of ourselves and the people around us.

While a psychological test, then, bears similarities to the everyday process of observation, its greater refinement and systematization have important implications for the science of psychology in general and the process of assessment in particular. As was described in Chapter 1, one major attribute of tests is that test scores are quantifiable. The process of quantification allows a descriptive precision not possible in the course of everyday observation. For example, you may be quite certain that John is more intelligent than Bill, but the results of an intelligence *test* would provide numerical estimates of the level of intelligence of each and thus add precision and validity to your intuitive comparison of the two. Similarly, a supervisor in a factory may observe that some workers appear to be working faster than others, but by actually counting the number of pieces each worker completes per hour the supervisor would have a precise description of individual differences in work rate or productivity. Thus, the numerical scores yielded by a psychological test differentiate the test from the ordinary process of observation.

In addition to quantification, the terms *standardized* and *objective* were also described in Chapter 1 as referring to essential characteristics of a psychological test. The term *standardized* refers to the controlled conditions under which testing occurs; standardization means that the procedure and materials used and the methods of scoring the test are constant across testings.

By *procedures* we mean the conditions under which the test is administered, including the procedures the test administrator follows, the instructions provided to examinees, the sample questions utilized, and the time limits. For example, if different examinees were given different instructions or different time limits, the testing process would not be standardized, or constant, across individuals, and it would be difficult to interpret and to compare test scores. Consider the degree of unfairness if you were given 30 minutes to complete a mathematics test, while the other students in the class were given one hour in which to complete the test.

Constancy in testing *materials* refers to the fact that the test's *content* should be comparable from one testing to the next. Test content can include paper-and-pencil "items," such as math problems, vocabulary items, or questions about attitudes or personality. Standardization requires that the nature and number of these test items be comparable across examinees and testings. Test content can also be "performance-related," for example, intended to assess the number of pieces produced per hour, motor coordination or perceptual speed when using certain apparatus, or behavior in a social or classroom situation. In this kind of test, standardization requires that the conditions under which the performance is observed be constant across individuals and testings: The working conditions prevailing when productivity is assessed, the apparatus used to measure motor coordination, and the social situation in which behavior is observed must be comparable when different people are tested. Imagine a secretarial applicant taking a test of typing speed on an old manual typewriter when the other applicants were given new electric typewriters. This would clearly be unfair and a case of nonstandardized test materials.

Finally, the methods of scoring the test should be clearly defined and constant across testings. A person responding in the same way another person responds should receive the same score. This means that identical test responses should receive identical scores, while different test responses should receive different scores. On an achievement test, for example, there are correct answers to each question, and the correct answer does not vary depending on who is taking the test. Similarly, if one examinee is penalized for guessing wrong on a multiple-choice test, then any other individuals taking the test should be similarly penalized for guessing wrong.

The idea of constancy in scoring procedures is related to the concept of "objectivity" in testing. Generally, the term *objectivity* refers to the extent to which every observer or judge evaluating the test or performance arrives at the same score or interpretation of the test. Paper-and-pencil tests in which the examinee selects one of several alternative responses provided on the test form are objective tests because any person given the scoring "key" should arrive at the same score for the test. For example, two or more people scoring a "true-false" or multiple-choice answer sheet should arrive at the same number of "trues" or the same number of correct answers. Similarly, a performance test involving number of pieces produced per hour or number of typing errors is objective because two or more people carefully counting the pieces or errors should arrive at the same result. In contrast, paper-and-pencil tests involving open-ended responses—for example, essay tests, tests in which people describe or write about their reactions to a visual cue, such as the inkblots of the Rorschach and the pictures in the Thematic Apperception Tests, and many types of performance tests—are more subjective, in that different evaluators may arrive at different scores. On an essay test, a professor who likes your ideas or the way you write may give you a higher grade than would a different professor who disagreed with your ideas or didn't like your writing style. While tests vary, therefore, in the degree to which scoring is objective or subjective, objectivity is an important consideration in psychological testing.

Finally, two additional points concerning the definition of a psychological test should be noted. First, both Anastasi (1988) and Cronbach (1984) refer to testing as the systematic observation or sampling of behavior. The term *behavior* is used here in its broadest sense, referring to cognitive behaviors, such as abilities and aptitudes, to attitudes and personality, and to overt behaviors. In essence, behavior includes the full range of human responses capable of being observed and recorded. Second, Anastasi's definition refers to tests as measuring a *sample* of behavior. In using this term, Anastasi is making the important point that tests can only sample a portion or segment of the totality of our response capabilities or tendencies. A test measuring knowledge of American history cannot possibly include every possible question that could be asked about the subject. Similarly, a test of social behavior can include our responses in several social situations but cannot possibly cover every possible social situation in which we might find ourselves. A major assumption in testing is that the observations we make from *samples* of behaviors can be *generalized* to the person's behavior over time and across situations. This assumption must be evaluated using the concepts and methods of *reliability*, to be discussed in Chapter 3.

In summary, a psychological test is a systematic and standardized method of observing and quantifying the characteristics of an individual or environment, the individual differences among people, and the ways in which environments differ from each other. Because a test is *quantified* observation, it yields a numerical *score* describing some characteristic of the individual or of an environment. However, since tests are used to gather information about persons and environments for the overall purpose of understanding and solving applied problems, it is essential that the numerical scores yielded are informative, meaningful, and interpretable relative to the purposes for which the information is needed. Test scores become meaningful and interpretable in a variety of ways, but we will discuss one major way in this chapter: the use of *norms*, which are ways of interpreting people's scores in relationship to the scores of some appropriate comparison group of people. In the next chapter we'll discuss how different rationales by which tests are constructed lend different types of meaning and interpretability to test scores. Prior to discussing these

ways of adding meaning to test scores, it is necessary to review the basic *statistical concepts* important to the description and use of numerical test scores.

STATISTICAL METHODS IN TESTING

One of the major purposes of statistics in test use is to allow us to *describe* and *summarize* data—for example, test scores—in efficient and useful ways. Major descriptive methods in statistics are score distributions (including what is called "normal distribution") and measures of central tendency, variability, and relationship.

Nondescriptive statistical concepts include regression analysis, used for predicting behavior or performance, and factor analysis, used to investigate the basic underlying dimensions in a set of variables.

Describing Score Distributions

When we have collected a large amount of data—let's say, test scores for 50 people—it's very difficult to make sense out of the data without descriptive statistics that allow us to summarize *score distributions*. Assume, for example, that we have the following set of 50 scores from our administration of a 100-item test of vocabulary:

```
21 95 73 68 54 87 26  9 17 58
46 72 31 94 33 64 51 58 23 55
62 42 47 74 52 41 35 88 65 15
32 53 25 69 48 76 54 27 13  6
43 39 67 44 37 83 49 78 56 18
```

Arranged this way, the set of scores is not readily interpretable, but when we use a frequency distribution it becomes interpretable.

The first method of summarizing a large set of scores like this is to order the scores from largest to smallest and then tabulate the number of times each score occurs. When there are many possible score values (e.g., 1 to 100), it is helpful to group the possible scores into intervals and tabulate the frequency of scores within each interval. For example, Table 2.1 shows the above set of scores organized into a *tabular frequency distribution*; the table shows the frequency of occurrence of the scores of the 50 people on the hypothetical 100-item test of vocabulary. In constructing a frequency distribution of this type, it is important that *interval size* remain constant and that a manageable number of intervals be used; generally speaking, approximately 8 to 12 intervals are desirable. Note that a frequency distribution of this type also provides information useful in interpreting any given score; it is possible from this table to get a general idea of where a given raw score interval falls relative to the scores of other people. For example, it is clear from Table 2.1 that people scoring in the 80s and 90s have done better than most other people, while people scoring under 20 or so are clearly not performing at the level of most of their peers or classmates.

More immediately informative than a tabular frequency distribution are graphic frequency distributions, as shown in Figure 2.1. The graphs given in Figure 2.1 each have two axes: the horizontal axis, or *abscissa*, along which the test scores or score intervals are arranged, and the vertical axis, or *ordinate*, which represents the frequency of occurrence of each score or score interval. When the graph is drawn as a *bar graph*, or histogram, the frequencies are shown as horizontal bars at the appropriate level on the vertical axis. When the graph is drawn as a *frequency polygon*, a point indicating the number of persons obtaining scores in a given interval is placed at the midpoint of that interval, and the points representing each frequency are connected. Figure 2.1 provides graphic representation of the data shown in Table 2.1 — both a bar graph and a frequency polygon are shown. Note that graphic representation (Figure 2.1) summarizes the scores more easily than tabular representation (Table 2.1) does.

Measures of Central Tendency

A set of scores can also be described in terms of measures of *central tendency*, which summarize the average level, or *magnitude*, of the scores. The most commonly used measure of central tendency is the *mean (M)*, or arithmetic average, found by adding all the scores and dividing the sum by the number of cases (N). Table 2.2 shows the computation of the mean, given the 10 scores of 20, 18, 17, 15, 10, 7, 6, 3, 3, and 1, obtained from a 20-item quiz of knowledge of basic psychological statistics. As shown in Table 2.2 the sum of 100 is divided by the N of 10 to obtain the mean of 10.

The *median* is the score in the exact center of the distribution: An equal number of scores fall below and above the median score. If we had scores of 1, 2, 3, 5, and 9, the score of 3 would be the median, since two scores fall below that value and two scores fall above it. When there are an odd number of scores, the median is simply the $[(N + 1)/2]$th score, when scores are arranged in order of size. When there is an even number

TABLE 2.1 Hypothetical Frequency Distribution of Scores on a Test of Vocabulary

Test Scores In Intervals	Frequency of Occurrence
1–10	2
11–20	4
21–30	5
31–40	6
41–50	8
51–60	9
61–70	6
71–80	5
81–90	3
91–100	2
Number of Cases (N) =	50

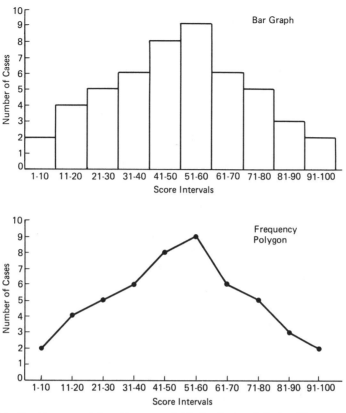

Figure 2.1 Graphic representation of frequency distribution: bar graph (top) and frequency polygon (bottom).

TABLE 2.2 Computation of Hypothetical Mean, Median, and Mode

Scores

20	**Mean** $(M) = \dfrac{\text{Sum of Scores}}{\text{Number of Scores}} = \dfrac{\Sigma \text{Scores}}{N}.$
18	
17	Therefore,
15	
10	
7	$M = \dfrac{100}{10} = 10.$
6	
3	**Median** (with even number of scores) = the value halfway between the $(N/2)$th score
3	and the $[(N + 2)/2]$th score = halfway between the $(10/2 = 5)$ 5th score, score 10,
1	and the $[(10 + 2)/2 = 6]$ 6th score, score 7.
Sum of (Σ) Scores = 100	Therefore,
Number of Scores (N) = 10	$median = 8.5.$
	Mode = the most frequently occurring score.
	Therefore,
	$mode = 3.$

NOTE: The symbol Σ is the upper case form of the Greek letter sigma and means "the sum of."

of scores, as in the example shown in Table 2.2, the median is the numerical value falling halfway between the $(N/2)$th and the $[(N + 2)/2]$th score. As shown, the median of the scores in Table 2.2 is the value halfway between the fifth score $(10/2)$ and the sixth score $[(10 + 2)/2]$.

Finally, the *mode* is the most frequently occurring score in the distribution. For the set shown in Table 2.2, the mode is 3, since that value occurs most often. When scores occur with equal frequency, a distribution may have no mode, and in other cases there may be more than one mode. Thus, while every score distribution has one and only one mean and median, a distribution may have one, several, or no mode(s).

Different measures of central tendency provide different types of information and are appropriate for use with different types of data. The appropriate measure of central tendency for nominal or categorical data is the mode. Both the median and the mode can be used to describe ordinal (i.e., rank order) data. Any of the three measures may be used with interval data.

While interval data may be described using any of the three measures of central tendency, the mean, median, and mode are differentially sensitive to differences in the *shape* of the distribution. When the test scores are distributed symmetrically around a single peak (most frequent score), the mean, median, and mode will have the same value. If, however, the distribution of scores is asymmetrical, or *skewed* (i.e., scores tend to cluster on one side of the distribution, but a few extreme scores are represented at the other end of the distribution), the median or mode may be better measures of central tendency. The mean reflects exactly the position of every score in the distribution and is thus sensitive to the presence of extreme (very high or very low) scores. The median and mode, on the other hand, are generally insensitive to the presence or absence of ex-

treme scores. For example, the *mean* of the scores 5, 5, 7, 8, and 100 would be 25 (125/5), while the *median* and *mode* would be 7 and 5, respectively. Thus, in cases where we have one or more extreme scores, the median or mode may better reflect the *average* magnitude of scores than will the mean.

Measures of Variability

Measures of *variability* describe the degree to which scores vary around the central tendency; they provide single numbers that summarize the degree to which individual scores in the distribution differ from one another. In other terms, variability refers to the *spread* of scores across the distribution. If all scores are equal, then there is *no* variability or spread in scores. In contrast, scores of 100, 200, 300, 400, and 500 differ markedly from each other, so variability is considerable. The most commonly used measures of variability are *range*, *variance*, and *standard deviation*. Table 2.3 illustrates the computation of measures of variability for the set of 10 scores on the 20-item quiz of knowledge of statistics, introduced previously in Table 2.2.

The *range* is simply the distance or difference between the largest and smallest scores. The range of the scores 1, 3, 5, 8, and 10 is equal to 9 (10 − 1). The range of the 10 scores shown in Table 2.3 is equal to 19 (20 − 1).

While the range is useful in describing a score distribution, it is rather unstable because it is based on only two scores. For example, the range of the scores 1, 1, 1, 1, 10 is equal to the range of the scores 1, 3, 5, 8, 10, yet the variability among scores is obviously different. Another example illustrating the instability of the range would be the case where we have 98 people who obtained scores of 50, one who got a score of 100, and one who got a score of 0. The range of scores would be equal to 100, yet except for the two extreme scores there is almost no score variability.

Measures that are more stable because they take into account the variation of every score in the distribution from every other score in that distribution are the *variance* and the *standard deviation*. The variance and standard deviation both indicate the average distance of scores from the mean of scores and are based on calculating the squared deviation of each individual's score from the mean. The variance, defined as the average of the squared deviations from the mean, is calculated using the formula:

$$Variance = \sigma^2 = \frac{\Sigma(X - M)^2}{N}$$

where σ^2 is sigma (a Greek letter) squared, X refers to each individual observation or score, M is the mean of scores, and N is the number of scores. Table 2.3 provides an illustration of the computation of the variance and standard deviation of a hypothetical set of scores. Note that the deviation of each score from the mean is represented by the deviation score x; the sum of the squared values of x becomes the numerator in the formula for computation of the variance. The standard deviation (SD, or σ) is equal to the square root of the variance; its computation is also illustrated in Table 2.3.

While the variance is an extremely useful statistic for inferential purposes, the standard deviation is more useful as a descriptive measure because its value is in numerical units the same as the original scores in the distribution. The standard deviation is especially useful when the distribution of scores approximates a *normal* distribution, to be discussed next.

The Normal Distribution

A very useful property of the distributions of many psychological characteristics is that they are approximately *normally distributed*. A normal distribution, as shown in Figure 2.2, has two easily observable major characteristics: It is *symmetrical* around its mean, and it is *unimodal*. A distribution that is sym-

Figure 2.2 Percentage distribution of cases in a normal distribution of scores.

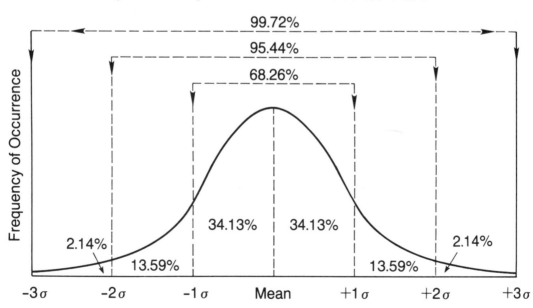

Table 2.3 Computation of Range, Variance, and Standard Deviation for Hypothetical Distribution of Scores

Score (X)	Deviation (x) from the Mean (M) $(x = X - M)$	Deviation Squared (x^2)
20	10	100
18	8	64
17	7	49
15	5	25
10	0	0
7	−3	9
6	−4	16
3	−7	49
3	−7	49
1	−9	81

$\Sigma X = 100$ $\Sigma x^2 = 442$

$N = 10$

$M = 100/10 = 10$

$$\text{Variance} = \sigma^2 = \frac{\Sigma x^2}{N} = \frac{442}{10} = 44.2$$

$$\text{Standard Deviation} = \sqrt{\sigma^2} = \sqrt{\frac{\Sigma x^2}{N}} = \sqrt{44.2} = 6.65$$

$$\text{Range} = \frac{\text{Largest}}{\text{Score}} - \frac{\text{Smallest}}{\text{Score}} = 20 - 1 = 19$$

Note: The symbols Σ and σ are the upper and lower case forms of the Greek letter sigma. Σ means "the sum of," while σ refers to the variance (σ^2) and the standard deviation (σ).

metrical around its mean and unimodal has a single "peak" (the most frequently occurring score or mode) and falls off with about equal frequency in both directions. The frequency polygon shown in the lower portion of Figure 2.1 approximates a normal distribution because it has a single peak (nine scores fall in the range of 51–60) and it drops off with approximately equal frequency on either side of that peak.

The normal distribution is actually a family of distributions described by a mathematical formula using, among other things, the mean and standard deviation of scores to describe each specific normal distribution. Although knowledge of the formula is not really necessary to understand the importance of the distribution (see, for example, Glass & Hopkins, 1984, p. 61, for the formula itself), the fact that the formula uses the mean and the standard deviation of scores is particularly useful to us in the analysis and interpretation of test scores. One way in which a normal distribution of scores is made especially interpretable is that there is a known, invariant relationship between the standard deviation of scores and the proportion of cases falling in any given score interval. This relationship, illustrated in Figure 2.2, means that in any normal distribution approximately—

1. 68 percent of the area under the curve lies within one σ of the mean μ either way (i.e., $\mu \pm 1\sigma$);

2. 95 percent of the area under the curve lies within two σs of the mean;

3. 99.7 percent of the area under the curve lies within three σs of the mean μ.

Note that the majority of cases (68.26 percent) fall within ±1 standard deviation of the mean, while almost all scores (99.7 percent) are within ±3 standard deviations from the mean. The utility of this relationship for practical purposes may be illustrated by an example. Assume that you are told that a normally distributed set of scores has a mean of 100 and a standard deviation of 10. You know automatically that about 68 percent of scores are in the range of 90 to 110 (± 1σ) and that over 99 percent fall between 70 and 130 (±3σ). If your client obtained a score of 65 or 140, you would know without further information that these were highly atypical, improbable scores. The utility of the relationship of the standard deviation in a normal distribution to percentages of cases will be further illustrated in the section on norms.

Measures of Relationship

A final category of descriptive statistics useful in the interpretation of test data is what may be summarized as measures of *relationship*. While the mean, standard deviation, and so forth describe a single distribution of scores, measures of relationship describe the degree of association between two or more sets of scores. These measures are important in describing the relationship of test scores to other variables of interest and are essential to the evaluation of reliability and validity (to be discussed in Chapter 3).

Just as we can summarize a single distribution, we can summarize the relationship between two sets of scores using a bivariate frequency distribution (*scatter plot*, or *scattergram*). As shown in Figure 2.3, a scatter plot contains a horizontal axis labeled with the possible values of one of the sets of scores and a vertical axis labeled with the values of the second set of scores. We have two observations (scores) for each individual, and we plot those scores as a single *point* representing the intersection of the person's score on one variable with his or her score on the second variable. The scatter plot consists of the points representing all individuals in the sample.

The scatter plot shown in Figure 2.3

Figure 2.3 Scatter plot describing possible relationships between scores on two hypothetical tests.

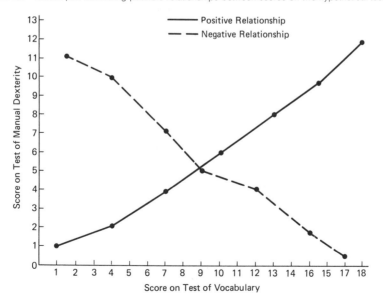

describes two possible relationships between two sets of hypothetical test scores. Each point represents the intersection of an individual's scores on the vocabulary test and the manual dexterity test, and the lines connecting the points summarize the nature of the relationship. When scores are positively associated (shown as the solid line in the figure), high scores on one variable are associated with high scores on the second variable. A negative or inverse relationship (shown by the dotted line) indicates that people with high scores on one variable tend to obtain low scores on the other. Note that, in both cases depicted in Figure 2.3, there is an association between the two sets of scores, and this association is approximately linear.

While a scatter plot provides a graphic representation of relationships between variables, a *correlation coefficient* describes that relationship in numerical form. The most commonly used correlation coefficient, used with two sets of continuous scores, is the "Pearson product-moment correlation coefficient," or r. The basis for the computation of this statistic is the product of the deviations of the two sets of scores from the mean of each distribution. More specifically, r is calculated as shown in the hypothetical example in Table 2.4. The first step in the computation involves the calculation of the means and standard deviations of the two sets of scores. Following this, the deviation of the person's score on the first test from the mean of scores on that test is calculated $(x = X - M_X)$, as is the deviation of the person's score on the second test from the mean of that test $(y = Y - M_Y)$. The product of the two deviation scores (xy) is calculated for each person, and these products are summed across all individuals. Finally, the sum of products is divided by the product

Table 2.4 Calculation of the Pearson Product-Moment Correlation Coefficient (r) for a Hypothetical Distribution of Scores

Person	Score on Test 1 (X)	Score on Test 2 (Y)	x	y	x^2	y^2	xy
1	1	2	−2	−2	4	4	4
2	2	2	−1	−2	1	4	2
3	2	4	−1	0	1	0	0
4	3	2	0	−2	0	4	0
5	3	7	0	3	0	9	0
6	3	3	0	−1	0	1	0
7	4	5	1	1	1	1	1
8	4	6	1	2	1	4	2
9	4	7	1	3	1	9	3
10	4	2	1	−2	1	4	−2
	$\Sigma = 30$	$\Sigma = 40$	$\Sigma = 0$	$\Sigma = 0$	$\Sigma = 10$	$\Sigma = 40$	$\Sigma = 10$
	$M_x = 3$	$M_y = 4$					

$$SD_x = \sqrt{\frac{\Sigma x^2}{N}} = \sqrt{\frac{10}{10}} = 1 \quad SD_y = \sqrt{\frac{\Sigma y^2}{N}} = \sqrt{\frac{40}{10}} = 2$$

$$r_{xy} = \frac{\Sigma xy}{(N)(SD_x)(SD_y)} = \frac{10}{(10)(1)(2)} = \frac{10}{20} = 0.50$$

Note: The symbols X and Y refer to the original obtained test scores; x and y are *deviation scores* obtained by subtracting the mean of scores from the original score, that is, $X - M_x = x$ and $Y - M_y = y$. The symbol Σ, the upper case form of the Greek letter sigma, means "the sum of." SD_x and SD_y refer to the standard deviations of the deviation scores x and the deviation scores y, respectively. r_{xy} is the correlation between sets of scores X and Y. M stands for mean and SD for standard deviation.

of the sample size (*N*) and the standard deviations of the two sets of scores (SD_X and SD_Y) to yield the coefficient *r*.

In interpreting Pearson product-moment correlation coefficients it is important to note that the *sign* indicates the *direction* of the relationship while the *value* indicates the *magnitude* of the relationship. Pearson product-moment correlation coefficients may range from +1 to −1. A positive sign indicates a positive, or direct, relationship, in that high scores on one variable are associated with high scores on the other variable; the relationship shown by the solid line in Figure 2.3 would be described by a positive value of *r*. In contrast, negative values of *r* indicate a negative, or inverse, relationship between the two variables; high scores on one are associated with low scores on the other. A negative value of *r* would describe the relationship shown by the dotted line in Figure 2.3.

In terms of the magnitude or strength of relationship, the larger the absolute value of *r* (up to a maximum of +1), the stronger

the relationship. In other words, values of *r* at or near zero indicate that the two variables are not linearly related to each other. An *r* of ±0.50 would indicate a moderate degree of relationship, while values of ±1.0 indicate a perfect relationship between the two variables.

Several additional points in interpreting the value of *r* should be noted. First, *r* describes only *linear* relationships. A value of *r* near zero indicates that the two variables are not related in a *linear* fashion, but in some cases variables may be curvilinearly related; such relationships will not be reflected in the value of *r*. An example of a possible curvilinear relationship between test anxiety and score on a math test is shown in Figure 2.4. Examining the scatter plot makes it clear that there *is* a systematic relationship between test anxiety and performance on a math test, but that this relationship is *not* linear. Rather, it appears that people reporting moderate levels of test anxiety obtain high math test scores, while those reporting either very low or very high levels of anxiety per-

Figure 2.4   Hypothetical example of a curvilinear relationship between two variables.

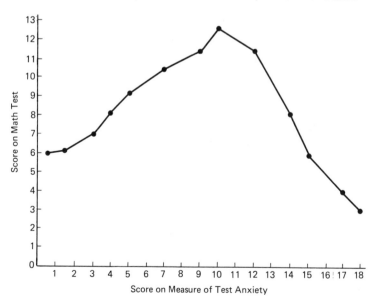

form less well on the test. Perhaps people with very high levels of anxiety are too anxious and upset to perform well and to focus on the test itself, while those low in anxiety don't particularly care how well they do or haven't studied for the test. The appropriate measure of relationship when there is the possibility of curvilinearity is the statistic *eta*. Methods for the calculation and use of the eta statistic are described, for example, in Hays (1981).

A second issue in interpreting the value of *r* is the degree to which the value is statistically significant. Recall that in *inferential* statistics we attempt to determine the extent to which our findings actually represent a real finding, rather than one that could have happened solely by chance. Stated in another way, we attempt to decide whether or not findings obtained in a given sample of subjects represent what is actually true in the population of interest. Although we can never make this decision with complete certainty, we can derive an estimate of the probability that our findings from a sample are in error (do not accurately represent what is true in the population).

One major type of error, Type I error, is the probability of rejecting the "null hypothesis" when the null hypothesis was actually true. Although the reader should consult an elementary statistics text for a more complete review of the concepts of hypothesis testing and statistical significance (see, for example, Glass & Hopkins, 1984; Hays, 1981), recall that the null hypothesis, the hypothesis to be tested, is usually that of "no difference." For example, the null hypothesis might be that there are no differences between males and females on a test of personality or no differences between the "treatment" groups and the control groups on the dependent variable of interest. When we reject the null hypothesis, we derive a value indicating the probability that we have wrongly done so. This probability is called the *level of significance* and is the symbol α (alpha). Usually we decide a priori that the null hypothesis should be accepted unless the probability of error is small enough, usually $\alpha < 0.05$, although often set even lower than that, say, $\alpha < 0.01$.

In testing the statistical significance of a correlation coefficient, the null hypothesis is usually that there is *no* relationship in the population—in other words, p (the value of *r* in the population) $= 0$. Assuming that we wish to generalize our conclusions regarding the existence of a relationship beyond the immediate sample of subjects, we must ask whether the obtained value of *r*, when not zero, could have been obtained solely through sampling fluctuation. For example, a sample from a population in which there actually is *no* relationship between the two variables could yield a correlation larger or smaller than zero simply because of the specific sample we utilized in calculating the value of *r*. Thus, determination of statistical significance allows us to estimate the probability that the obtained value of *r* actually came from a population in which $p = 0$. When we say that *r* is significant at or below the 0.01 level, we are saying that the chances are no greater than 1 out of 100 that the correlation in a population is actually equal to zero.

The statistical significance of a value of *r* varies directly with the sample size used in its calculation. The larger the *N*, the smaller the *r* necessary to attain statistical significance. Conversely, the smaller the sample size, the larger the obtained *r* must be for us to conclude that it is significantly different from zero. The minimum values of *r* for statistical significance at the 0.05 and 0.01 levels for different sample sizes are shown in tables of the significance of correlations in statistics books (e.g., Glass & Hopkins, 1984; Hays, 1981). These tables should be consulted in determining whether an obtained value of *r* actually represents a relationship between the two sets of scores. Significant values of r differ quite markedly, depending on the sample size. For example, with an N of 10 the value of r must be equal to 0.63 to be significant at the 0.05 level. If the N is 100, however, a value of $r = 0.20$ is statistically significant at the 0.05 level.

In interpreting correlations obtained in large samples, it is important to note that while a value of r may be *statistically* significant it may be so small as to lack *practical* significance. For example, a correlation of $r = 0.09$ is statistically significant in a sample of 500 people, but $r = 0.09$ indicates a negligible degree of relationship in practical terms. By squaring the value of r, we calculate what is known as the coefficient of determination; this value indicates the proportion of variance in one set of scores that is accounted for or explained by variance in the other set of scores. If $r = 0.09$, then $r^2 < 0.01$, meaning that less than 1 percent of the variance in one variable is explained by the other. While in rare instances the capability of explaining 1 percent of the variance in scores may be useful to us, generally it has little practical utility or meaning. Thus the *practical*, as well as the *statistical*, significance of a correlation coefficient must be considered in its interpretation and use.

A final point regarding the interpretation of correlation coefficients involves the concept of *restriction in range*. A variable is restricted in range when scores fall at only a few possible values. If all students taking a test obtain 50 correct answers, there is no *variability* in scores; thus, scores on the test will not be found to be related to other individual difference variables. Generally, the less variability there is in one or both of the variables, the lower the maximum value of the correlation coefficient will be.

The problem of restriction in range has serious ramifications for studies of the predictive validity of tests used in selection. Because selection procedures by their very nature "select" only the most qualified applicants, the pool of individuals that can be used to study the relationship of test scores to criterion performance (e.g., grades in college) represents a restricted range of test scores. Although the effects of restriction in range on selection are beyond the scope of this chapter, they will be discussed more extensively in Chapter 3, as part of the section on criterion-related validity, and in Chapter 14, on issues of test bias in selection.

In interpreting *any* correlation coefficient, it is important to avoid assumptions of causality—that is, assumptions that individual differences in one variable cause or lead to differences in another variable. For example, in the example shown in Figure 2.4 it might seem reasonable to assume that levels of anxiety *caused* the observed variations in math test performance. A correlation, however, does not necessarily imply causality, nor does it suggest that a particular variable causes another. It is possible that math performance caused different levels of anxiety or that some third variable caused or led to variations in both test performance and anxiety.

As another example, assume that we have found a positive correlation between teachers' salaries and the percentage of high school graduates who go on to college. It is possible that well-paid teachers do a better job of teaching, and thus their students are better qualified for admission to college. It is also possible that the greater success of students' applications to college causes the school administrators to give their teachers salary increases. And it is possible that a third variable, such as the socioeconomic status of the families whose children are in various schools, influences both the salaries of teachers, in terms of the available tax bases, and the extent to which families encourage and can pay for higher education. Thus a correlation indicates an *association* between two variables, but other strategies of research design and statistical analysis, such as experimental and quasi-experimental studies (e.g., Campbell & Stanley, 1966; Cook & Campbell, 1979) and causal analysis and modeling (Asher, 1976; Bentler, 1980; Long, 1983), are necessary in making inferences about causality.

Before leaving the topic of correlation, several other correlation coefficients should be mentioned. The Pearson r is best suited for use with two sets of continuous scores, data that are assumed to be interval in nature. When the formula for the product-moment correlation is adapted for use with data that consist of one continuous variable and one dichotomous variable (e.g., sex, "right-wrong"), the resulting correlation coefficient is called the *point-biserial*. Along with the biserial correlation coefficient, the point-biserial is used extensively in the process of evaluating the quality of test items (see the section on test construction in Chapter 3). The *phi coefficient*, also a product-moment coefficient, is used in studying the relationship between two dichotomous variables, while the *contingency coefficient* is used with two polychotomous variables (i.e., categorical variables having more than two possible categories, such as marital status). Formulas for these and other correlation coefficients may be found in Nunnally (1978).

Regression Analysis

Nondescriptive types of statistical analysis are also critical to the use of test scores; *regression analysis* is one of these.

Recall that measures of relationship allow us to *describe* the relationship between two or more variables. While such description has many important uses in the field of testing and assessment, applied uses of test scores have often relied heavily on the use of a relationship between two variables to *predict* scores on one test from knowledge of scores on the other. For example, a relationship between scores on a scholastic aptitude test and college grade-point average (GPA) can be used to predict grades in college from knowledge of aptitude test scores. Similarly, scores on a test of clerical aptitude might be used to predict performance levels of clerical personnel. The use of relationships between variables for purposes of prediction is called *regression analysis*.

Another example of a scatter plot should further our understanding of regression analysis. Figure 2.5 shows a scatter plot describing the relationship between scores on a test of scholastic aptitude and college GPA. In regression, the set of scores used as the

Figure 2.5 Examples of a scatter plot and regression line for the prediction of college GPA from Scholastic Aptitude Test Scores.

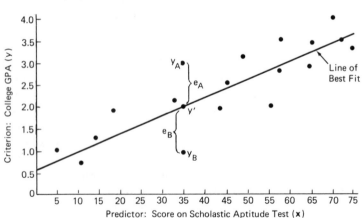

predictor variable is shown on the horizontal axis and is denoted by the variable X, in this case, aptitude test scores are the predictor X. The variable to be predicted is known as the *criterion*; the criterion variable is denoted Y and appears on the vertical axis of the scattergram.

In regression, a "line of best fit" is fitted to the points of the scatter plot. The "line of best fit" is a straight line that best summarizes the relationship between the two variables. Figure 2.5 shows the line of best fit. This line, also known as the "regression line," can be described by the equation $Y' = bX + a$. In this equation, a is what is known as the "Y intercept," the value of Y at the point where the regression line crosses the Y axis or, in other words, the value of Y corresponding to an X of 0. In practical terms, a is a constant number added to the value of bX to obtain a predicted value of Y. The b is the *slope* of the line, the rate at which the value of Y changes in relationship to changes in X. In practical terms, b is a direct function of the value of the correlation r between the two variables. The X refers, of course, to scores on the predictor variable, and the Y' to a *predicted* value of Y, the criterion variable.

Given the formula $Y' = bX + a$, then, we can estimate a person's score on the criterion variable given his or her score on the predictor variable. Assume you are given a regression equation $Y' = 2X + 10$ and are told that John's score on X was 5. You would predict John to obtain a criterion score of $20 [(2 \times 5) + 10]$. And you have a predictor score of 10 for Judy, giving you a predicted Y of 30. A regression equation, therefore, is used to estimate scores on a criterion variable through inserting into the equation a known score (X) on the predictor variable.

A critical aspect of the use of regression analysis is the possibility of error in prediction. Regression equations are calculated within a sample of subjects for whom both the predictor and the criterion scores are available (since the b in the equation is based on the correlation between X and Y and the a on the actual Y intercept, both scores are needed in order to determine the original equation). However, the equations are *used* in samples for whom only the predictor scores are known, so the criterion scores Y are not known and must be predicted or estimated, with the possibility of error in that estimation. Referring back to Figure 2.5 it is possible to observe that most of the points fall above or below the line of best fit. Note, for example, the individuals whose scores are described by points A and B. Both individuals obtained a score of 35 on the predictor variable X, and the regression line (and equation) lead to the prediction of a college GPA of 2.0. Person A in actuality did better than predicted, obtaining an actual GPA of 3.0! Person B, in contrast, did more poorly than predicted, obtaining a college GPA of 1.0. The difference between the actual Y and predicted Y' criterion score is the *error* in prediction; although the regression line is selected to minimize error in prediction, it cannot eliminate error completely (unless $r = 1.0$, an *extremely* rare circumstance). In order to take this potential for error into account when using regression to predict criterion scores, a statistic called the *standard error of estimate* ("see") is computed and used in the prediction process. Similar in concept to a standard deviation, the "see" provides an estimate of the average amount of error in prediction and is dependent on the extent of variability in the criterion scores and the magnitude of the correlation between the predictor and the criterion. The stronger the correlation r between the two variables, the less the extent of error in prediction and vice versa. The importance of the value of r is also indicated by the fact that r^2 is known as the *coefficient of determination*, the proportion of variance in Y explained by X. Extensive descriptions of the computation and use of the standard error of estimate may be found in Glass and Hopkins (1984) and Wiggins (1973).

In addition to the prediction of criterion scores from one predictor variable, *multiple regression* can be used to predict a criterion score from two or more predictor or independent variables. The formula for a multiple regression equation is simply an extension of that used for one predictor variable, taking the form $Y' = b_1 X_1 + b_2 X_2 + \ldots b_n X_n + a$. The quality of prediction is based on the strength of the multiple correlation coefficient R, describing the relationship between a linear composite or summary of the predictor variables and the criterion variable Y. And R^2, like r^2, is referred to as the coefficient of determination. (Although well beyond the scope of this book, a method of analysis called *canonical correlation* is the logical extension of multiple regression to the case where we would like to predict multiple criterion variables from multiple predictor variables.)

In summary, the methods of regression analysis are very useful for applied purposes of predicting future behavior or performance based on test scores. However, the ever-present possibility for error in prediction must be taken into account when using such predictions to make important decisions about people.

Factor Analysis

Factor analysis is used when we wish to investigate the underlying structure or basic dimensions of a set of variables or when we wish to reduce a set of variables to a smaller set. For example, researchers interested in personality may wish to understand whether or not there are key underlying dimensions to 20 or 30 tests of different aspects of personality. Or assume that a business uses 20 different tests to select employees for a certain job: Factor analysis can be used to iden-

tify perhaps 4 or 5 basic dimensions measured by those 20 tests, so that tests of those 4 or 5 basic dimensions can make predictions as accurately and efficiently as the 20 original tests.

Factor analysis begins with a table of the correlations between all the variables of interest, a table known as a *correlation matrix*. The result of a factor analysis is a *factor matrix*, showing the number of important underlying factors and the "loading," or weight, of each original variable on the resulting factors. A factor loading is like a correlation coefficient: The larger it is (in either a positive or a negative direction), the stronger the relationship of the variable to the factor. In factor analytic terms, the loading can also be viewed as related to the proportion of the variable's variance explained by the underlying factor. The square of the factor loading is the proportion of common variance between the test and the factor.

Table 2.5 shows an illustrative factor table, the result of a factor analysis of the Jackson Personality Inventory (JPI, to be described in more detail in Chapter 4's discussion of objective personality assessment). The 16 scales of the JPI appear down the left column, and the four factors extracted appear across the top of the page. The body of the table provides the loadings of each of the variables on each of the factors. Like the correlation coefficient r, the larger the absolute value of the loading is, the stronger its relationship, or *contribution*, to the factor. Values of 0.40 or above are underlined in the table to indicate significant factor loadings—that is, factor loadings indicating that the variable is an important part of the factor.

Thus, it may be noted that Factor I is represented by several variables: Breadth of Interest, Complexity, Innovation, Risk Taking, and Tolerance are positively related to the underlying dimension defined by the factor, whereas Conformity and Value Or-

Table 2.5 A Factor Table from a Factor Analysis of the Jackson Personality Inventory

JPI Scales	Factor Loadings			
	Factor I	Factor II	Factor III	Factor IV
Anxiety	0.05	−0.05	−0.88	−0.06
Breadth of Interest	0.75	0.10	0.03	0.18
Complexity	0.92	−0.09	0.24	0.08
Conformity	−0.67	0.12	0.22	−0.07
Energy Level	0.39	0.18	−0.31	0.24
Innovation	0.51	0.18	−0.13	0.04
Interpersonal Affect	0.33	0.38	0.46	0.44
Organization	−0.33	0.19	−0.11	0.04
Responsibility	0.10	0.03	−0.05	0.96
Risk Taking	0.46	0.15	−0.20	−0.09
Self-Esteem	0.14	0.66	−0.26	0.03
Social Adroitness	−0.14	0.42	0.03	−0.33
Social Participation	−0.16	0.71	0.09	0.08
Tolerance	0.59	0.02	−0.05	0.28
Value Orthodoxy	−0.50	0.01	−0.12	0.33
Infrequency	−0.07	−0.21	−0.10	−0.26

Note: Loadings 0.40 and above are underlined to indicate that those variables loading highly on the factor contribute significantly to its definition.

This was a maximum-likelihood factor analysis with an oblique (Harris-Kaiser) rotation based on a correlation matrix of 115 female subjects (Jackson, 1976b, p. 25).

thodoxy are negatively related to the factor (as indicated by the negative factor loadings). In contrast, Factor II is defined by three variables: Self-Esteem, Social Adroitness, and Social Participation.

In addition to the ability to use and interpret a factor matrix, test users should have some understanding of how factors themselves are named or interpreted. Naming a factor is a process of judgment and summarization by which we examine the tests or variables loading highly on a factor and then attempt to discern what those tests or variables have in common. Table 2.6 shows a possible factor analysis of nine hypothetical tests. The first three tests, (Vocabulary, Verbal Analogies, and Reading Comprehension) load strongly on Factor I; we might call the underlying ability measured by these tests "Verbal Ability." The next three tests (Addition, Multiplication, and Fractions) load highly on Factor II, which we might label "Ability to use Arithmetic." The last three tests (Shotput Distance, Arm Wrestling, and

TABLE 2.6 Hypothetical Factor Matrix from an Analysis of Scores on Nine Different Tests

Test	Factor I	Factor II	Factor III
Vocabulary	0.90	0.40	−0.05
Verbal Analogies	0.80	0.30	0.12
Reading Comprehension	0.75	0.35	−0.08
Addition	0.30	0.80	−0.13
Multiplication	0.35	0.85	0.17
Fractions	0.33	0.70	0.03
Shotput Distance	0.04	0.13	0.75
Arm Wrestling	−0.08	0.05	0.85
Pounds Lifted	0.10	−0.10	0.92

NOTE: The variables loading most strongly on each factor are underlined.

Pounds Lifted) represent Factor III, which we might call "Upper Body Strength." Note that now we can discuss our nine-test battery in more parsimonious terms, as measuring Verbal Ability, Ability to Use Arithmetic, and Upper Body Strength.

While specific mathematical and computational methods in factor analysis are beyond the scope of this book (see, for example, Nunnally, 1979; Rummel, 1970), test users should be aware that a given correlation matrix can be factor analyzed in a number of different ways, and the specific methods used will influence the obtained factor matrix. Among other things, the test developer must make decisions about the type of factor analysis to use, about how many factors to "extract" (or derive from the original variables), and about whether or not, and how to, "rotate" the factors. The rotation of factors is designed to make the resulting factor matrix more interpretable (and therefore more useful). It should always be kept in mind, then, that a factor matrix provided in a manual for a personality inventory or battery represents one, but not the only, way of conceptualizing the underlying structure of the set of tests. Factor analysis has been used extensively in the study and measure-

ment of abilities, personality variables, and other characteristics of persons and environments.

These, then, are the major statistical concepts important in the description of test scores. The next section introduces the concept of norms in the interpretation of test scores.

NORMS IN THE INTERPRETATION OF TEST SCORES

The initial result when we administer a psychological test is what is known as a *raw score*, obtained by counting the number of correct responses (in the case of an ability test) or "keyed" responses (in the case of, for example, an interest or personality inventory) or by adding up numbers that reflect the individual's extent of agreement or disagreement with various self-descriptive statements. By itself a raw score conveys little meaning or information. It is not very useful to know that Jim answered 15 math problems correctly or responded in the keyed direction to 10 items on a measure of anxiety. And even if we know in addition that Jim got 50 percent of the math problems correct or answered 50 percent of the anxiety items in the keyed direction, we are still lacking a basis on which to *compare* these scores or percentages to something meaningful. In other words, test scores themselves are meaningless unless we have a frame of reference from which to interpret them.

Probably the most common frame of reference used in attributing meaning to test scores is the performance of other people. If we know that Jim got 15 math problems correct, while John got only 10 correct, we have somewhat more information than we had knowing only Jim's score. If we are told further that only 10 percent of the students in the class got scores of 15 or better, we have still more information with which to interpret Jim's score. The concept of comparing one person's test score to those of other people is the basis for test *norms*, the characteristics of the test scores of a representative sample of people. Usually test norms are obtained using a standardization sample, a sample collected with the objective of providing a representative sample of the people for whom the test is designed to be used. Based on the responses of this *standardization*, or *normative sample*, raw scores obtained from any subsequent examinee can be converted into a measure of relative standing in comparison to the normative group.

More specifically, the derivation of norms begins when we administer the test to a standardization sample, a very large sample of individuals representative of those for whom the test is designed to be used. If a test is designed for use with college students, then the standardization sample should consist of a representative group of college students. Similarly, if a test is designed to predict the vocational interests of adults in professional-level occupations, then these should constitute the normative sample. Following administration of the test to the standardization sample, the resulting scores are described and summarized using the statistical approaches discussed in the previous section (frequency distributions, measures of central tendency, and measures of variability). These descriptive measures are the basis for the derivation of norms used in the interpretation of scores on the test.

Percentiles

The first method of interpreting scores with reference to norms is to calculate the *percentile equivalent* of each possible score on the test. A percentile refers to the proportion of people in the standardization sample whose scores were *below* a particular test score. Thus, if 15 percent of the people in the original sample obtained scores below 20, then the score of 20 is said to lie at the 15th percentile. Similarly, if 80 percent of persons obtained scores below 50, then people who obtain scores of 50 have achieved at the 80th percentile.

The derivation of percentiles is based on the calculation of a *cumulative frequency distribution*, where for each score point we calculate the percentage of persons whose scores fall at or below that score point. This percentage would become the percentile equivalent of that score. The *median* corresponds to the 50th percentile; scores above the 50th percentile represent above-average performance, while those below the 50th percentile represent below-average performance. Two other convenient points are what are known as the first *quartile* (the 25th percentile) and the third quartile (the 75th percentile). The first and third quartiles cut off the top and bottom quarters of the distribution from the middle half. The median and first and third quartiles are often useful markers in the comparison of two or more score distributions.

Percentiles should not be confused with percentage scores. Percentage scores are simply another way of stating a raw score—for instance, 50 correct responses on a 100-

item test corresponds to 50 percent correct. But 50 percent correct may represent superior, average, or inferior performance, depending on the performance of other people; it is the comparison of any raw score to the scores of other people that distinguishes norms in general and percentiles in particular. Thus 50 percent correct may correspond to any percentile between 0 and 100, depending on the comparison group.

In interpreting percentile scores it should be recalled that the higher the percentile is, the higher the person's score is, relative to other people. Conversely, lower percentiles correspond to lower scores relative to those of other people. Percentiles have the advantage of being easily understood by, and making intuitive sense to, test takers as well as to test users. Their disadvantage, however, is that the distance between percentile scores describes different absolute score differences, depending on the area of the distribution we are describing.

The reason for this is that a normal distribution concentrates individuals around the center or mean of the score distribution—the large majority of people obtain scores near the mean, with only a few obtaining the highest and lowest scores. Because people are "lumped" around the middle, large percentages of people and, thus, a large range of percentile scores characterize a relatively small range of actual test scores. On the other hand, because there are considerably fewer individuals scoring beyond +1 or −1 standard deviations from the mean, more actual score values are needed to encompass a given percentage (or percentile range) of the normative sample.

Figure 2.6 shows the relationship between scores on a normal distribution and their percentile equivalents. The mean of

Figure 2.6 Relationship of a normal distribution of scores to their percentile equivalent scores.

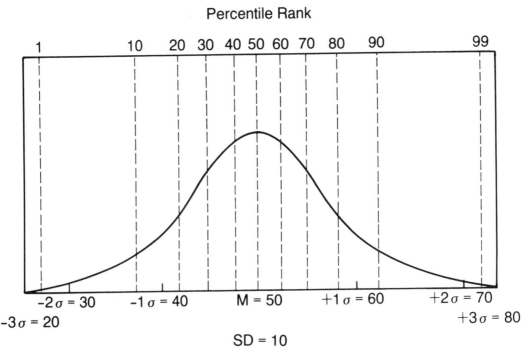

the original distribution was 50, and the standard deviation was 10. Notice that because scores in a normal distribution cluster around the mean and decrease in frequency with increasing distance from the mean, a wide range of percentile ranks describes scores near the mean. Thus score differences near the mean are exaggerated when converted to percentiles, while score differences at the extremes become very small percentile differences.

As an example, notice that people obtaining scores of 60, the 84th percentile, versus those obtaining scores of 50, the 50th percentile, differ by 10 score points, but by 34 percentile points. In contrast, the 10-point difference between scores of 70 (98th percentile) and 80 (essentially the 100th percentile) is reflected as a difference of only 2 percentile points. Thus, if we are comparing the percentile scores of two people, we should remember that the closer scores are to the 50th percentile, the smaller the actual difference in raw score points between the two people is. To summarize, the marked inequality of percentile score points at different locations on the distribution is essential to the interpretation of this type of normative score.

Standard Scores

The most commonly used type of normative score is the *standard score*, which expresses the distance of the individual's score from the mean of the distribution in standard deviation units.

Most standard scores are derived using a *linear transformation* of the original raw scores. A linear transformation is one that follows the general form $Y = AX + B$, where X and Y are variables and A and B are constants. In the computation of standard scores, the Y refers to the original test score, the A to the standard deviation of the score distribution, the B to the mean of the distribution, and the X to the new, or "standard," score. Using algebra with the formula $Y = AX + B$, we subtract B from both sides ($Y - B = AX + B - B = AX$) and divide each side by A ($(Y - B)/A = AX/A = X$) yielding the result $(Y - B)/A = X$ or $X = (Y - B)/A$. If the letters are replaced by their meanings, we have the equation for the standard score known as a Z-score; that is, Z(new score) = (original score $- M$)/SD. For purposes of consistency with statistical convention, the original score in this formula will be denoted as X, yielding the formula $Z = (X - M)/SD$.

The most basic standard score is the Z-score, which assumes a normal distribution having a mean of 0 and a standard deviation of 1. Any score can be converted into a Z-score, simply by subtracting from the score the mean of the scores and dividing by the standard deviation of the scores. As was shown above, the formula for the calculation of Z-scores is $Z = (X - M)/SD$. Table 2.7 illustrates the calculation of Z-scores, based

Table 2.7 Calculation of *Z, T,* and *CEEB* Standard Scores

Raw scores: $M = 40$; $SD = 8$

	Person 1 $X = 56$	Person 2 $X = 40$	Person 3 $X = 28$
$Z = \dfrac{X - M}{SD}$	$Z = \dfrac{56 - 40}{8} = 2.0$	$Z = \dfrac{40 - 40}{8} = 0$	$Z = \dfrac{28 - 40}{8} = -1.5$
$T = 10Z + 50$	$T = 10(20) + 50 = 70$	$T = 10(0) + 50 = 50$	$T = 10(-1.5) + 50 = 35$
$CEEB = 100Z + 500$	$CEEB = 100(Z) + 500 = 700$	$CEEB = 100(0) + 500 = 500$	$CEEB = 100(-1.5) + 500 = 350$

Note: *M* = mean; *SD* = standard deviation; *X* = raw score; and *CEEB* stands for the College Entrance Examination Board score.

on a score distribution having a mean of 40 and a standard deviation of 8.

Z-scores typically range from -3 to $+3$ and are *directly interpretable* in terms of distance from the mean in standard deviation units. A Z-score of $+2$, as obtained by Person 1 in the table, indicates that the score is 2 standard deviations above the mean. A Z-score of -1 is one standard deviation below the mean. While Z-scores have the advantage of providing a direct statement of the number of standard deviations above or below the mean corresponding to a given test score, their disadvantage is that they include both negative numbers and decimal points—for example, $Z = 1.5$ in Table 2.7.

In order to provide standard scores using positive, integer values, several other commonly used standard scores have been developed. For example, T-scores, used in many personality and vocational interest inventories, are standard scores adjusted to a mean of 50 and a standard deviation of 10. The basic procedure involved in calculating other types of standard scores involves computing the Z-scores and then using the formula $SS_{New} = SD_{New} Z + M_{New}$. For T-scores, as shown in Table 2.7, the formula becomes $T = 10Z + 50$. Thus, Z-scores of $+2$ and -1.5 are equivalent to T-scores of 70 and 35, respectively.

Another common standard score is that used by the College Entrance Examination Board (CEEB) in its scholastic aptitude tests (e.g., the Scholastic Aptitude Test [SAT] and the Graduate Record Examination [GRE]). These scores have a mean of 500 and standard deviation of 100. As shown in Table 2.7, Z-scores of $+2$, 0, and -1.5 correspond to CEEB scores of 700, 500, and 350, respectively.

While test users should be familiar with and able to immediately interpret the common types of standard scores, the principles used in their derivation may be used to convert a set of raw scores into standard scores

having any desired mean and standard deviation using the general formula $SS_{New} = SD_{New} Z + M_{New}$. And an understanding of Z-scores allows the immediate interpretation of any test score, given only the mean and the standard deviation of the score distribution. Assume that the manual for the Charismatic Personality Inventory reports that the mean score on the charisma scale is 30, while the standard deviation is 5. Your client's score is 40, which you can easily see is 2 standard deviations above the mean ($+2$ in Z-score units).

One problem in the use of linear-derived standard scores to compare scores on two or more tests is that their meaning differs if the original score distributions are shaped differently. For example, if one distribution is normal while the other is negatively skewed (i.e., scores are concentrated at the upper end of the distribution and tail off at the lower end), a Z-score of $+1$ could exceed 84 percent of the cases in the former distribution, but only 50 percent of the cases in the latter distribution. If we wish to compare scores across distributions that may differ markedly in shape, we can use what are known as *normalized standard scores*, or standard scores that have been transformed to fit a normal distribution. In normalization, a *nonlinear* transformation, the percentage of persons in the standardization sample falling at or above each raw score point is found. This percentage is transformed into a Z-score by reference to a normal distribution frequency table found in most statistics books. Referring back to Figure 2.2, it may be noted that a Z-score of $+1$ ($+1\sigma$ above the mean) corresponds to approximately the 84th percentile (50 percent of cases fall below the mean, and 34.13 percent fall between the mean and $+1\sigma$). Thus, the score value at or below which 84 percent of the standardization sample falls would be assigned a Z-score of $+1$. Note that in the case of normalized standard scores the meaning of a Z-score of, for example, +1 does *not* necessarily describe a score one standard deviation above the mean. Rather, it describes the percentile equivalent of scores in Z-score terms.

Normalized standard Z-scores, like linear-derived Z-scores, can easily be converted into normalized standard scores having any desired mean and standard deviation, using the formula shown previously. One commonly used type of normalized standard score is the *stanine*, developed by the United States Air Force during World War II. Stanines (based on the abbreviation of "standard nine") have a mean of 5, a standard deviation of approximately 2, and can take only the integer values 1 through 9. Raw scores can be readily converted to stanines by reference to the values shown in Table 2.8. Scores are arranged from lowest to highest; the lowest 4 percent of scores receive a stanine of 1, the next 7 percent receive a 2, and so on. Stanines have the advantage of using only single-digit numbers and are being used increasingly, especially with aptitude and achievement tests and in the armed services and industry.

A final commonly used standard score is the deviation IQ score. Generally, the mean of IQ scores has been set at 100, although the standard deviation has been set to 15 (e.g., the Wechsler Adult Intelligence Scale)

or 16 (e.g., the Stanford-Binet Intelligence Scale). Scores on the General Aptitude Test Battery are also normed using a mean of 100, and the standard deviation has been set to 20. In interpreting IQ scores, then, a score of 100 has been taken to indicate the average IQ, but scores above or below 100 are interpreted slightly differently, depending on the standard deviation specified.

One particular advantage of standard scores in general is that because they are based on the concepts of Z-scores and the normal distribution they can be readily understood in terms of percentiles, as well as in terms of distance from the mean in standard deviation units. Figure 2.7 demonstrates the relationship of various commonly used standard scores, including stanines and IQs, to each other and to their percentile equivalents. A test user should be able to recall immediately the approximate percentile scores corresponding to Z-scores. In this way, knowledge that a person's score is, for example, about one standard deviation above the mean allows automatic estimation of his or her percentile standing in comparison to the normative group. Of course, using the frequency tables for the normal distribution allows precise calculation of the percentile equivalent of any standard score value.

Summary

In summary, norms allow us to readily compare obtained test scores to those of other people and provide, therefore, an essential basis for the interpretation of the scores. In using norms, however, it is essential that the standardization group be appropriate for the type of individuals for whom we are using the test. Knowing, for example, that an 11th grade student scores at the 90th percentile on an ability test would not be particularly informative if the standardization sample consisted of 8th graders. Many tests provide

TABLE 2.8 Percentages of Hypothetical Sample Receiving Various Stanine Scores

Stanine	Percentage Receiving Score	Cumulative Percentage
1	4	4
2	7	11
3	12	23
4	17	40
5	20	60
6	17	77
7	12	89
8	7	96
9	4	100

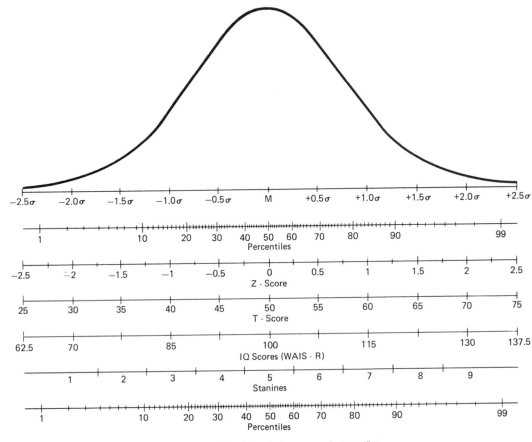

Figure 2.7 Relationships of standard scores and percentiles.

normative data for several different populations, and test users may select the normative population most appropriate for the individuals with whom they work. For example, the American College Test (ACT), used to predict success in college, provides norms based on a national sample of college students, but most colleges have what are known as "local" norms, norms characterizing the students at that university or college. In working with a student at a highly selective college or university, for example, knowledge of national norms may not be very helpful; an ACT score at the 70th percentile in comparison to entering college students in general may be equivalent to the 20th percentile in comparison to students at a highly selective college. If we used national norms, we might conclude that the student should easily be able to achieve good grades in college courses, while the use of local norms would suggest that the student may be less academically able than most of his or her classmates. Thus, consideration of the appropriateness of norm groups and the development of local norms, if appropriate, are important to the usefulness of norms in the interpretation of test scores.

SUMMARY

This chapter has considered the basic principles and statistical concepts underlying the interpretation and use of psychological test scores used to understand and solve applied problems. Methods of describing test scores and score distributions, the use of norms to provide meaningful frames of reference for the interpretation of test scores, and the concept of the rationale for test construction are essential in the provision of the needed information. Distributions of test scores may be described graphically—for example, using a bar graph or frequently polygon—and may be summarized by measures of central tendency and variability. Relationships among test scores may be described using coefficients of correlation and may be further utilized in prediction, through the use of regression analysis, and in exploring the underlying structure of several tests or variables, through factor analysis. As will be seen in Chapter 3, regression analysis is used extensively in the study of criterion-related validity and in the empirical approach to test construction, and factor analysis is very useful in the study of construct validity and in the factor-analytic approach to test construction.

Norms, based directly on the concepts of score distributions and measures of central tendency and variability, are used to compare an individual's test score to the score distribution obtained in some relevant comparison group of people. Different types of norms include percentiles and standard scores—for example, Z-scores, T-scores, stanines, CEEB scores, and IQs. Without norms, most tests would be nearly impossible to interpret meaningfully and therefore useless for most applied needs.

Thus, knowledge of basic statistics and a thorough acquaintance with the types of normative data available for a given test are crucial to the effective and responsible use of tests and assessments.

3

Reliability, Validity, and Test Construction

INTRODUCTION

Chapter 2 provided an overview of the principles and statistical concepts underlying the interpretation and use of tests and assessments. Among other things, understanding the concepts of norms was described as essential to the usefulness and interpretability of test scores. The availability to test users of information concerning the interpretation of test scores is, however, part of a much larger issue, the overall *technical quality* of tests and assessments.

Concern about the technical quality of

psychological tests is based on an awareness on the part of professionals that tests and assessments can be very powerful, useful tools when used correctly, but useless, misleading, or even dangerous tools if they yield inaccurate information. As an analogy, consider the gasoline gauge, which is normally a very useful tool, particularly when one is setting out on a trip. If the gas gauge is providing erroneous information—for example, reading "full" as one begins a trip into the desert, when in actuality the tank is half empty—the consequences are potentially dangerous.

Poor-quality tests, like inaccurate gasoline gauges, can also have damaging consequences or, at a minimum, provide the user with useless or misleading information. It is the responsibility of psychologists and other test professionals to ensure that tests they develop and tests they use are of high quality and thus will provide useful information that will contribute to the solving of applied problems and to the making of important decisions for both individuals and organizations.

In order to define the components of a high-quality, or "good," test and to assist tests developers in constructing tests of high quality, representatives of the professional organizations involved in the development and use of tests cooperated in the development of standards of quality in tests. These standards, developed and endorsed by a joint committee of the American Psychological Association (APA), the American Educational Research Association (AERA), and the National Council on Measurement in Education (NCME), were most recently published in 1985. Although these standards for tests will be described and discussed more extensively in Chapter 14 ("Professional and Ethical Standards and Social Issues in Assessment"), the present chapter will discuss, first, the two most basic components of test quality, *reliability* and *validity*, and, second, methods of test construction that are essen-

tial to the development of high-quality tests. Finally, since it requires an informed test user to *evaluate* carefully the quality of available tests, sources of information about various tests and their quality will be reviewed.

THE CONCEPT OF RELIABILITY

The first requirement for a high-quality, or "good," test is that the test possesses what is called "reliability." Synonyms for the word *reliability* include terms such as *consistency, stability, replicability*, and *repeatability*. Reliability involves the extent to which we are measuring some attribute in a systematic and therefore repeatable way. A ruler or yardstick is an example of a reliable measuring instrument; assuming that the user is careful in using the ruler, repeated measurements of the same object should yield very similar results.

In classical test theory, the concept of reliability is defined using three assumptions. The first assumption is that each person (or environment) to be described by the test has some fixed amount of the attribute of interest; this amount is known as the person's *true score*. For example, a client being tested is assumed to possess some "true" level of intelligence. The second assumption, however, is that every *observation* of an attribute—intelligence, for example—contains some degree of *error*. The third assumption, which follows from the first two, is that any *observed score* reflects both the "true" score and some error. Thus, a score on an intelligence test, for example, reflects some degree of "true" variance and some degree of "error" variance. Because the usefulness of a test depends at least in part on the degree to which it is reflecting "true" rather than "error" variance, the proportion of observed score variance that is true score variance is an index of the test's quality. A reliability coefficient indicates this kind of test quality because it provides an estimate of the proportion of observed score variance that is "true" variance rather than "error" variance.

Sources of Error in Test Scores

Before we proceed to a discussion of different types of reliability and reliability coefficients, the major types of error in test scores should be noted. Although there are many ways of categorizing the types of error in test scores, Lyman (1978) presents one useful system, in which errors in test scores are related to five major factors: time influence, test content, the test examiner or scorer, the situation in which testing occurs, and the examinee.

The first major source of error in test scores, time influence, is due to fluctuations in test performance over time. Errors in scores occur when measurements taken at one point in time do not yield the same result as measurements taken at another point in time. Sometimes this error is due to people remembering the responses they gave on a previous administration of the same test, or it may be due to people having practiced with the specific test items used. In other cases, however, changes in scores over time reflect real changes in the individual being tested; in such cases, changes in scores are reflecting "true" rather than "error" variance.

The second major source of error variance involves the content of the test items. Test items are usually selected to be representative of or reflective of the characteristic of interest, but the items selected represent only a *sample* of those that could measure the characteristic. The items on a test represent a sample from a population, or "domain," of possible test items. Many people have had the experience of studying most but not all of the materials for a test, only to find that most of the test covered the small amount of material not studied. The instructor's selection of test questions was not representative of the course material, and, consequently, students who should have done well on the test did poorly. If another test more representative of the course material were given, these individuals might do very well. The fact that the particular selection of test content could greatly influence an individual's test performance illustrates this type of error variance.

A third kind of error is that which can occur if the test administrator fails to administer the test correctly or if the test is improperly scored. A test administrator may lose track of the passage of time and, through carelessness, give examinees 25 minutes to work instead of the 20 minutes specified in the instructions; or the test administrator may forget to ask the examinees to read the instructions or to complete the practice questions, thus detracting from performance on the test. Errors in scoring can occur through lack of correct scoring information or through carelessness.

A fourth factor, the situation in which testing occurs, can contribute to error if conditions are not constant from one situation to the next or if conditions distract the individual from full attention to the testing process. For example, a noisy, poorly lit, or excessively warm testing room may detract from performance.

Finally, the examinee may also be a source of error. Sickness or fatigue during testing may cause an individual's score to reflect inaccurately one's "true" score and to be poorly related to scores that would be obtained when the person was healthy and rested. Similarly, individuals who aren't motivated to do well on the test and don't care about providing accurate information (or, worse, who purposely make mistakes or provide inaccurate information) can contribute error to their test scores.

The objective of developing reliable tests is to minimize the extent to which these kinds of error influence tests scores. Basic, commonsense approaches to minimizing the effects of error include the development of detailed instructions for both administration and scoring, and making sure that individuals administering and scoring tests are responsible and careful in following instructions. It is also necessary to establish testing conditions that permit the examinee to work without distractions and physical discomfort and to do everything possible to ensure that examinees understand the instructions for taking the test and are motivated to do their best on the test.

Beyond these ways of standardizing and optimizing testing conditions, different types of reliability focus on the examination of different types of error variance in test scores. These different types of reliability should be viewed as guidelines to the construction of high-quality tests and as means by which a test's quality can be evaluated. The types of reliability to be discussed include (1) test-retest reliability, (2) alternate forms reliability, (3) split-half reliability, and (4) internal consistency reliability.

Test-Retest Reliability

Test-retest reliability, also known as "stability," is an assessment of the degree to which test scores are similar or stable over time versus the degree to which scores change or fluctuate upon repeated testings. In other words, stability is the extent to which individuals tend to obtain a similar score, relative to other individuals, upon retaking the *same* test. If test scores are relatively stable across repeated testings separated by a time interval, we have some basis for believing that the test is measuring something in a consistent and generalizable (across time) manner.

The design for a study of test-retest reliability involves two administrations of the same test to the same individuals, with a time interval separating the two administrations. Typically, a test-retest design should involve a time interval of at least one week between test and retest. The reliability (stability) coefficient is the correlation between the two sets of scores (i.e., the correlation of scores obtained at Time 1 with those obtained from the same individuals at Time 2).

Stability coefficients can be obtained using any time interval, but, generally, the longer the time interval, the less stability we are likely to find. In other words, the longer the interval between testings is, the greater the likelihood is that individuals will actually change on the dimension measured. Thus, for purposes of interpreting a stability coefficient, it is important to know the time interval represented; for example, a coefficient of $r = 0.80$ representing a one-year interval would indicate greater stability than would an identical value representing a one-week interval.

Several conceptual considerations are essential to using and interpreting test-retest designs as an index of the reliability of a test.

First, a test-retest design is appropriate only to the extent that the trait or dimension itself is postulated to be somewhat stable over time. For example, characteristics like intelligence and extraversion are postulated to be relatively enduring characteristics of an individual; thus the stability of measures of these variables is an appropriate dimension by which to evaluate them. On the other hand, some characteristics of individuals, such as mood states, are postulated to vary considerably across time. The Minnesota Multiphasic Personality Inventory (MMPI) depression scale, since it reflects mood at the time of testing, is relatively unstable upon repeated testings. Thus stability may not be an appropriate criterion upon which to evaluate this scale or other measures presumed to fluctuate over time.

In contrast to mood states that may simply fluctuate over time, other attributes of an individual may be strongly influenced in the test-retest interval by experience, training, or practice specifically related to the content of the test. Consider, for example, a test of typing speed and accuracy given to two individuals. Following the first testing, one extensively practices his or her typing, while the other doesn't. On retest, we would expect the first individual's scores to improve considerably but would not expect such improvement from the second individual. Practice or experience effects such as this reduce the magnitude of the correlation between scores obtained from the test and scores obtained from the retest. Thus, we must lower our estimate of the test's stability, even though differential experiences, rather than the test per se, caused the instability in scores. Hence, to obtain meaningful indices of the stability of such tests, it is important to control for, or at least assess, the nature of experiences relevant to test performance that occur in the test-retest interval.

We must also consider the extent to which having previously taken the same test influences a person's performance on the retest. For example, memory of one's previous responses may artificially inflate the stability coefficient. Practice with the test materials themselves (for example, verbal analogies or numerical word problems) is likely to improve the performance of some people more than others and may thus reduce the stability of scores. Generally, the longer the interval between testings is, the less influence memory and the effects of practice with the specific test items will have. Unfortunately, longer time intervals increase the odds that the differential experiences and learning discussed here will occur. Thus, the merits of shorter time intervals in test-retest studies must be carefully considered. Gen-

erally, the best approach in test development is to implement test-retest studies using several different time intervals, including both short-term and longer-term designs.

One final problem with test-retest designs, especially with those using longer time intervals, involves loss of subjects between the first and the second testing. For example, if freshmen in college are tested during the fall term and retested in the spring term, a percentage of those initially tested may have left school or changed address before the second test is administered. It is important to attempt to retest as many as possible of the subjects initially tested and to determine whether subjects who do not take the second test differ in important respects from those individuals tested twice. Where significant loss of subjects has occurred, interpretation of stability coefficients should be done with great caution.

In summary, while test-retest reliability studies are relatively easy to design and implement, considerations involving appropriate time intervals, the conceptualization of the characteristic to be measured, the possible effects of memory, practice, and experience, and the possible loss of subjects should accompany the use and interpretation of coefficients of stability.

Alternate Forms Reliability

Alternate forms reliability assesses the degree to which two different *forms* of the same test yield similar results. This type of reliability addresses those sources of variance associated with test content sampling. If an individual's score on one form of a test is similar to the person's score on an "alternate" form of the test, we have increased confidence that the test items reflect some common characteristics, or dimension, and are measuring that dimension in a relatively consistent manner.

A study of alternate forms reliability requires the development of two forms of the test, with the idea that the two forms are equivalent, or "alternate," measures of the same attribute or dimension. For example, if a test constructor developed a pool of 100 items designed to measure numerical ability, those items could be used to construct two 50-item tests of numerical ability, designated Form A and Form B. It is essential that pairs of similar items be assigned to the two forms of the test, one to each form. If there are ten subtraction and ten multiplication items, for example, five of each should be assigned to Form A and five of each to Form B.

Once the two alternate forms have been constructed, the alternate forms design involves administration of the two forms to a single group of examinees. The reliability coefficient is the correlation between the two sets of scores. If the interval between the administration of the first form and the second form is very short (usually the two forms are administered in the same testing session), the resulting reliability coefficient reflects the adequacy of content sampling and the extent to which the items on the two forms are measuring the same thing. In other words, to the extent that scores on one form of the test are related to scores on an alternate form of the test, the test constructor has evidence that the test is measuring some attribute in a relatively systematic and representative manner.

In addition to providing information regarding the degree to which the test items themselves are indicative of true variance or error variance, alternate forms can be used to estimate the test's *stability*, if a longer time interval—for example, two weeks or a month—separates the administration of the two forms. Stability coefficients obtained in this way will generally be lower than coefficients obtained from readministering the same test, because they reflect not only

changes over time, but also differences in the two forms of the test.

Care should be exercised in ensuring the equivalence of alternate forms. The two forms should contain the same number and type of items and, in tests of ability or achievement, should be approximately equal in difficulty. (The notion of item difficulty, to be discussed extensively in this chapter's section on test construction, technically refers to the probability of an individual answering the item correctly. Items for which most people are able to give the correct answer are relatively easy, while those that few people are able to get right are the more difficult items. Thus, alternate forms of a test should contain the same numbers of easier items and more difficult items.) When alternate forms are administered, the order in which the two forms are given should be counterbalanced. In other words, half the subjects should receive Form A first, while the other half should receive Form B first. This counterbalancing controls for the possible occurrence of fatigue, practice, or motivational effects on the test scores.

In summary, while the construction of alternate forms is somewhat time-consuming and requires considerable care, alternate forms reliability provides a good estimate of the degree to which performance fluctuates from one set of test items to a second set of theoretically equivalent items and, in addition, can provide information regarding the degree to which test scores fluctuate or are relatively stable over time.

Split-Half Reliability

From the discussion of alternate forms reliability the reader may have noted that, instead of constructing two forms of a test, it would be possible to divide a test into two halves and examine the relationship between the two half-scores. This approach, known as *split-half reliability*, is conceptually similar to alternate forms reliability in that we are interested in sources of error variance associated with content sampling. If scores obtained from one half of the test are similar to those obtained from the other half, we have reason to believe that the test items are measuring the same dimension or characteristic.

A split-half design, then, involves dividing one test into two comparable halves. The test is administered as a whole, but test scores are computed separately for each half. The correlation between the two half-scores is related to the index of reliability. Temporal stability of test scores does not enter into this type of reliability, since only one test administration is used.

The major consideration in a split-half design is the means by which the test should be divided into halves. Generally, the division should lead to the same kind of equivalence expected of alternate forms. A common approach to split-half test division is to assign the odd-numbered items to one half and the even-numbered items to the other half. In other cases, item assignment may be accomplished using a random numbers table. It is usually unwise to divide a test at its midpoint, since factors such as fatigue or practice may operate to affect the latter portion of the test.

The correlation between the two half-scores gives an estimate of the reliability of each half-test, but not of the reliability of the full test. Other things being equal, the more items in a test, the more reliable it will be (Cureton, 1965). Thus, the correlation between the scores on the two halves is an underestimate of the reliability of the test itself. To estimate the reliability of the full complement of items, the Spearman-Brown formula is used. Although the general form of this formula can be used to estimate the effect on reliability of lengthening or shortening a test by any number of items, a sim-

plified version of use in split-half designs is given below.

$$r_{test} = \frac{2r_{12}}{1 + r_{12}}$$

In this formula, r_{test} is the estimate of the reliability of the whole test, and r_{12} is the observed correlation between scores obtained from the two halves of the test. For a more thorough discussion of the use of the Spearman-Brown formula in split-half designs, see Thorndike (1951).

In summary, split-half reliability provides a relatively simple method of evaluating the degree to which the test items are measuring something in a relatively consistent manner. Care in ensuring the equivalence of the two halves, and in the use of the Spearman-Brown formula, should of course be exercised.

Internal Consistency Reliability

Alternate forms and split-half reliability examine the degree to which equivalent, or alternate, forms of a test are measuring the same thing and, similarly, the degree to which two halves of the same test are measuring the same thing. The logical extension of these questions is the degree to which each item on a test is measuring the same thing as each other item. This inter-item consistency is known as *internal consistency*, or *homogeneity*. A test is internally consistent, or homogeneous, to the extent that an individual's response to, or performance on, one item is related to his/her responses to all of the other items in the test.

Internal consistency is directly related to the "unidimensionality" of the test. The term *unidimensionality* refers to the extent to which the test items reflect one dimension rather than several dimensions (or *multidimensionality*). To illustrate the concept of unidimensionality versus the concept of multidimensionality, consider a test of numerical ability using only multiplication items, in contrast to a test containing addition, subtraction, multiplication, and division items. While adding, subtracting, multiplying, and dividing are all indicative of numerical ability, people may differ in their skill in using the different operations. Mark may be very skilled at addition and subtraction, but poor at multiplication and division. Cindy, on the other hand, knows her multiplication tables but has trouble with subtraction and division. Thus, while the test using all four operations is measuring important and probably *related* skills, it is less clearly measuring only one dimension than would be a test using only multiplication items.

Another example is a test of numerical ability that requires the examinee to perform arithmetic calculations and to solve the types of word problems found in mathematics tests. Some people are better at making calculations, while others are better at solving word problems. Furthermore, performance on the word problems might also be related to reading ability, thus possibly adding another *dimension* of test performance. An internal consistency reliability coefficient is a reflection of the unidimensionality versus multidimensionality of test items; the more internally consistent a test is, the more evidence there is for the unidimensionality of test items. Internal consistency is also often referred to as *homogeneity* (sameness of content) as distinguished from *heterogeneity* (differences in content), of test items.

It should be noted that estimates of internal consistency reliability will not necessarily be similar to estimates of alternate forms or split-half reliability, even though all three types of reliability address the content of the test items. If the reliability of the tests discussed above—that is, those composed of all four types of arithmetic operations or of calculations plus word problems—were studied using an alternate forms or split-form design, we would ensure that the two forms

or the two halves of the test contained equivalent numbers of items representing each operation or type of problem. In these cases, the reliability of the test could be equivalent to that of the test using only multiplication items. Thus, the homogeneity or heterogeneity of test content is best studied using estimates of internal consistency reliability.

The design of an internal consistency reliability study, like that of a split-half study, involves a single administration of one test. Following administration of the test, the internal consistency reliability, also thought of as inter-item consistency, is computed, using one of several formulas designed for this purpose. These formulas—the most commonly used of which are Cronbach's (1951) alpha coefficient and the Kuder and Richardson (1937) coefficient known as Kuder-Richardson-20, or KR-20—estimate the proportion of true score variance, herein defined as inter-item consistency, relative to the amount of observed score variance.

More specifically, a set of items is measuring some attribute only if the average correlation among items is positive. If the average correlation is zero or near zero, the items as a group have no common core, and it makes no sense to think of them as measuring a single attribute. In the same way a correlation coefficient of zero between scores obtained from two alternate forms of a test would cast doubt on the degree to which they are measuring the same thing and on the adequacy of our method of test construction, a correlation of zero between two test items would suggest that they are not measuring the same dimension.

Thus, formulas for estimating internal consistency reliability are based on the values of the inter-item correlations and the number of items in the test. The formula known as KR-20 is appropriate for use with dichotomously scored items (for example, right-wrong, yes-no), while Cronbach's alpha is appropriate for use with nondichotomous items as well (for example, items scored using a five-point response continuum ranging from "strongly agree" to "strongly disagree"). Formulas for these and other internal consistency reliability coefficients may be found in Nunnally (1978), Guilford (1954), and other texts on the theory of psychological measurement.

One important caution in the use of internal consistency reliability coefficients is that they are inappropriate for use with tests having highly restrictive time limits. In such tests, which are often used to assess abilities and skills, individual differences in scores depend entirely on the speed of performance. Generally, the items are relatively easy, and it's assumed that most or all items attempted will be gotten right; consequently, a person's total score depends on how quickly the person moves through the test. The inappropriateness of using an internal reliability coefficient with such tests may be demonstrated by the fact that inter-item correlations are dependent not on the extent to which the items are measuring the same thing, but on the placement of items in the test and on the time allotted to testing. If the time allotted to so easy a test permitted everyone to finish, most or all examinees would obtain perfect scores, and item responses would be perfectly correlated with one another. On the other hand, a restrictive time limit would result in correct responses to items appearing early in the test and in largely incorrect (i.e., unattempted) responses to later items, thus reducing the inter-item correlations and, consequently, the internal consistency reliability. Given the arbitrariness of item placement and time limits, the use of formulas such as Cronbach's alpha and KR-20 would not yield a meaningful result.

The more appropriate ways of estimating the reliability of highly speeded tests are test-retest and alternate forms designs. Split-half designs are not appropriate unless the two halves of the test are administered separately, using identical time limits; an ordinary odd-even design occurring in a single test administration would result in inflated estimates of reliability, because the correlation between the two half-scores would be close to $r = 1.0$.

Interpreting Reliability Coefficients

Although the meaning of a reliability coefficient will vary as a function of the type of characteristic measured and the method of obtaining the estimate(s) of reliability (e.g., test-retest versus split-half), there are several ways of interpreting a reliability coefficient of a given value.

The first method is to interpret a reliability coefficient as the proportion of observed score variance that is "true" rather than "error" variance. In other words, a reliability coefficient of 0.80 indicates that 80 percent of the variance is true score variance, while the remaining 20 percent is error variance.

Related to reliability as the proportion of true variance in observed test scores is the concept of the *standard error of measurement* (SEM). In keeping with the assumption in classical test theory that observed scores consist of a true component plus an error component, SEM allows us to estimate the relative size of the error component for any individual tested. In other words, it allows us to estimate the degree of closeness of the observed test score to the person's true level of the trait, using the same units by which the test itself was scored.

The formula for the standard error of measurement is as follows:

$$SEM = \delta_{test} \sqrt{1 - r_{test}},$$

where δ_{test} is the standard deviation of the test score distribution and r_{test} is the estimated reliability of the test. It should be noted that the higher the reliability is, the smaller the standard error is, relative to the standard deviation of the test. If the reliability were 1.0—which is theoretically possible, although highly unlikely—the standard deviation of test scores would be multiplied by zero, resulting in an SEM equal to zero. This would imply that there was no error in the estimation of true scores; the observed score would be an exact estimate of the true score.

To the extent, however, that the test is less than perfectly reliable, there will be some degree of error of measurement. Assume, for example, that the reliability of a test is 0.89 and that the standard deviation of test scores is 15. Using the formula given above, the SEM is equal to $15[\sqrt{(1 - 0.89)}] = 15 (\sqrt{0.11}) = 15 (0.33) = 5$. Based on the useful properties of the normal distribution discussed in Chapter 2 (see pp. 22, Figure 2.2), knowledge of the SEM allows us to construct a confidence interval around a person's observed score such that we can estimate the probability that the person's true score falls within a certain interval around his or her observed score. If John's observed score is 100, we know from our knowledge of the normal distribution that there is a 95 percent probability that John's true score falls within 1.96 standard errors (like standard deviations) of his observed score. In other words, there is a high probability that, although John's true score is not exactly equal to 100, it does fall somewhere between 109.8 [(5 × 1.96) + 100] and 90.2 [100 − (5 × 1.96)].

Note the effect on the SEM if the test's reliability were only 0.75, rather than 0.89. The SEM in this case would be 7.5, and the 95 percent confidence interval around John's score of 100 would range from 85.3 to 114.7. Our confidence in the accuracy of John's observed score of 100 would be reduced because of the larger range in which his true score could possibly fall.

In summary, as a test is more highly reliable, the confidence we can place in the resulting test scores increases. Using the SEM

we can determine the likelihood that an individual's *true score* falls within any given interval around the person's obtained score on the test.

An additional important aspect of reliability is that the degree of reliability can influence the *validity* of test. Validity, the second major important characteristic influencing a test's quality, will be extensively discussed in the next section but, in brief, may be defined as evidence that the test measures what we say it measures. A test may be reliable, yet not measure what it was designed to measure. However, unreliability in a test restricts its potential validity; thus, a test's reliability establishes an upper limit on its validity. One of the ways of studying validity is based on the correlation of test scores with external or other indices of the attribute. Generally, the maximum possible correlation between the test and some external criterion is equal to the square root of the reliability coefficient (see, for example, Helmstadter, 1964). If the reliability coefficient were 0.90, the largest validity coefficient would be 0.94; if the reliability were only 0.70, the largest correlation of the test with an external criterion would be 0.84. Thus, reliability is not only an important characteristic itself but also serves as a limiting factor in the test's validity.

Finally, examining evidence regarding reliability is the first step in evaluating a test's quality. Although the specific kinds of reliability evidence desired and the approximate minimum levels of the obtained reliability coefficients necessary to establish quality depend on the test and the uses to which it is to be put, some evidence for a test's reliability and estimates of the standard error of measurement in test scores should always be provided. Generally, it may be said that tests used in admissions or selections decisions (and thus where the lives of individuals may be seriously affected by the resulting decisions) should have reliabilities equal to or above 0.90 (see, for example, Nunnally, 1978) and that reliabilities of 0.80 or above are desirable for most other kinds of tests. Stability coefficients are generally expected to be somewhat lower than alternate forms, split-half, or internal consistency reliability coefficients, especially with longer time intervals or with measures of highly modifiable attributes.

It is also important to note that any given test can be described by many different reliability coefficients. The test-retest, alternate forms, and internal consistency reliabilities of a test will usually differ from each other; thus a coefficient cannot be meaningfully interpreted without reference to the type of reliability study utilized. Similarly, reliability coefficients will not necessarily be identical across samples of subjects, and test-retest and alternate forms coefficients will differ as a function of the time interval between testings. Therefore test users must pay attention not only to the value of a reliability coefficient but also to the method and conditions under which it was obtained. Also, in using reliability evidence to evaluate the quality of a test, it is most essential that test users keep in mind the *purposes* for which the test is to be used and then consider the degree to which reliability data describing the test render it adequate and useful for *those purposes*.

Summary

We have discussed the concept of *reliability* as the first of two major ways in which the quality of a psychological test is evaluated. Sources of error in test scores and various methods of studying reliability and obtaining reliability coefficients have been described. While we have emphasized some of the practical aspects of obtaining and interpreting reliability coefficients, it is important to note that the concept of reliability is fundamental to the assumption that we can

measure psychological and environmental characteristics. An unreliable test is not "measuring" anything other than random or error variation; thus, it is essentially useless. Similarly, the dependence of validity on reliability suggests that an unreliable test will not correlate with anything else and thus is useless. In other words, if we lack confidence in the accuracy, consistency, or repeatability of our measurements, there is no point in attempting to relate the instrument to other behaviors, characteristics, or measures. Hence, reliability is a necessary prerequisite for validity and is the essence of the concept of measurement itself. Reliability is of necessity a primary concern of both test constructors and test users.

THE CONCEPT OF VALIDITY

While reliability indicates the degree to which a test is measuring *some attribute* in a consistent manner, it does not provide evidence that we are measuring *what we intend to measure*. The term *validity* refers to the extent to which the test we're using actually measures the characteristic or dimension we intend to measure. If a test designed to measure intelligence measures something else, then it is not a valid measure of intelligence. Validity is the second major requirement for a test of good quality that has some usefulness for applied purposes.

Some examples should serve to clarify the distinction between reliability and validity and the fact that a test can be reliable but not valid. Assume that the yardstick you recently bought is, through an error in manufacturing, only 33 inches long, even though it shows 36 "inch marks." You measure a 33-inch board five times and conclude each time that its length is 36 inches. Your yardstick is highly *reliable* in that it gives the same result (or "score") each time you use it; but it is not *valid*, because it is not accurately representing length, the dimension you are interested in.

As another example, assume that a researcher decides that the height of an adult might be a measure of his or her intelligence. The researcher measures John's height several times and finds that it is a reliable measure—that is, John is six feet tall each time he is measured. However, in trying to relate height to other indices of intelligence (e.g., IQ tests, educational level achieved), the researcher finds that height is unrelated to these variables. Thus, height is a reliable, but not valid, measure of intelligence. In both examples given, an attribute is being measured consistently—*reliably*—but our "test" does not actually reflect what it was intended to measure.

In addition to the question of whether the test measures what it is intended to measure, the concept of validity is concerned with the theoretical and applied usefulness of a test. Tests are the means by which we measure people and environments for purposes of understanding, explaining, and predicting behavior. The usefulness of tests depends on our ability to make inferences about people or environments from the test scores. The kinds of inferences we wish to make of course depend on the purposes of our test, but it is the range and accuracy of possible inferences to other real-world phenomena that constitute evidence for a test's validity.

Thus, validity concerns both the extent to which the test measures what it was intended to measure and the extent to which test scores permit inferences to other variables, as postulated in the definition of the characteristic being measured. The following sections review the kinds of information pertinent to establishing the validity, and thus evaluating the quality, of a test. Although there are many different kinds of such evidence, three major kinds of information relate to content validity, criterion-related validity, and construct validity. Other types of

validity discussed here (e.g., face validity) are appropriate for particular uses of the test.

Content Validity

The term *content validity* refers to how well the particular sampling of behaviors used to measure a characteristic reflects performance in the entire domain of behaviors that constitutes that characteristic. That is, we are interested in the behavior of a person as expressed in a variety of situations or toward a universe of possible "items." Although we are interested in, and wish to generalize to, an entire domain of behaviors, it is rarely feasible to include on a test all possible situations or items that might be relevant to that domain. Content validation, however, allows us to judge whether or not the content of a test is representative of the desired universe of content.

For example, if we were trying to assess an individual's level of achievement in an American history course, it would be impractical to ask the person questions about every event in the history of America. Similarly, if we were interested in assessing a person's behavior in social situations, it would be impossible to observe the person's behavior in every possible social situation that might be encountered. Thus, for practical reasons, we must take a sampling of social situations. Content validity describes the extent to which our sample of items or situations is reflective of the dimension, domain, or characteristic to which we wish to generalize.

It should be evident that to ensure content validity it is first necessary to define carefully the dimension of interest—that is, the dimension the test items are intended to reflect. This definition should be as specific as possible, including delineation of both what *is* included in the dimension and what *is not* included. For example, the dimension "knowledge of American history" would need to include specification of the time period involved and the extent to which "American" referred only to the United States or included the whole of North America and/or South America. Once the domain is defined, the sampling of items from that domain should be sufficiently broad and representative to allow direct inferences to it.

The achievement test situation, where there is a defined body of knowledge to be learned, provides the most obvious application of the principles of content validity. The test items should be taken from *that* body of knowledge and not some other, and the items should be taken systematically from each segment of the subject area so that specific gaps or emphases in the knowledge of any one individual will not have a disproportionate effect on the assessment of the person's knowledge. The more precisely the instructor has clarified and organized the relevant subject matter, the easier it will be to construct a test that adequately samples from that subject matter.

However, these principles are important in the construction of any psychological measuring instrument, for content validity is directly related to our conceptualization and definition of a construct. For example, in defining the construct of anxiety, it is necessary to specify what behaviors may indicate anxiety (e.g., increased heart rate, sweaty palms, or simply the person's report of feeling anxious) and to specify a universe of situations in which anxiety might be felt. Some people may feel anxious in social situations, some in academic or job situations, some while driving a car or grocery shopping, and some in all of these situations. If we are to obtain an estimate of a person's overall tendency toward becoming anxious (our trait or attribute of interest), it is important to sample from the entire range of situations in which the behavior could be exhibited. Thus, as in the achievement test situation, the more precisely we have clarified and organized the set of behaviors we believe to represent the

attribute of interest, the better able we will be to make generalizations to it from a sampling of those behaviors.

Evidence in Support of Content Validity. The most usual kind of evidence presented in support of content validity is the judgment of those who construct the test or of other experts familiar with the subject area or trait definition. Because this kind of evidence is usually somewhat subjective, it should be accompanied by a detailed definition of the behavioral domain or universe of interest and by a clear specification of the methods used to select items from that universe. In a sense, content validity is best ensured by a detailed, thoughtful plan used to guide the initial construction of the test (ways of constructing tests to ensure content validity will be discussed in the section of this chapter devoted to test construction).

Content validity can be indirectly evaluated through the degree to which the test shows high internal consistency reliability, or homogeneity, as was discussed in the previous section. A high internal consistency reliability coefficient indicates that each of the items reflects the behavioral domain each other item does and, consequently, that performance on each item is related to performance on the test as a whole. What is still lacking, however, is the demonstration that the total test score actually reflects the attribute of interest. For example, it would be possible to construct a quite internally consistent test of "mathematics achievement" that was composed only of addition items. All the items could be highly related to total score, but this total score would certainly not have great generalizability to the domain of mathematics achievement or content validity relative to that domain.

Thus, high internal consistency tells us that all the items are measuring the same variable. It provides some evidence that we are sampling a single domain of content. If an attribute is postulated to be unidimensional, then internal consistency reliability is a necessary part of the body of evidence for content validity. The other evidence required, however, is that provided by careful test construction, expert judgment, and methods of construct validation to be discussed in a subsequent section.

In summary, content validation is an essential *first* step in the establishment of a test's validity. To interpret, and to attribute psychological meaning to, test scores requires knowledge of what behavioral domain the test items reflect. It is perhaps most straightforward to evaluate content validity in achievement tests, since the domain consists of stated instructional goals within a defined body of content or knowledge. However, evidence for the content validity of tests of other attributes—for example, personality characteristics—is valuable because it forces careful definition of the behaviors relevant to the attribute of interest. Furthermore, the content validity focus requires a specification of the means by which a sampling of those behaviors will permit generalizations to or conclusions about some broader universe or domain of behavior.

Criterion-Related Validity

The term *criterion-related validity* usually refers to the extent to which a measure of an attribute demonstrates an association with some independent or external indicator of the same attribute. This external indicator, called the *criterion*, often represents the behavior we are actually interested in, and we wish to use test scores or other measurements to predict status or performance on the criterion. For example, scholastic aptitude tests are used to predict success in completing a college curriculum. Success in college is the behavior of interest, and the magnitude of the correlation between test

scores and success is an important index of the applied usefulness of the test.

There are two kinds of criterion-related validity. *Predictive validity* is studied when the criterion is measured some time after scores are obtained on the predictor. We are interested in how *present* status on the test predicts *future* status on the criterion variable. Thus, the correlation between the aptitude test scores of high scool seniors and their grades as college juniors would be a predictive validity coefficient. *Concurrent validity* is studied when both the predictor and the criterion scores are obtained at the same time; we are interested in the relationship between *present* status on the test and *present* status on the criterion. The observed relationship between scores on scales of the MMPI and present psychiatric status would be concurrent validity data. Similarly, correlations between ability test scores and present performance in school or on the job are examples of concurrent validity coefficients.

The basic kind of evidence in support of criterion-related validity is that which shows a relationship between the test (called the *predictor* in this case) and another variable postulated to be related to the test (called the *criterion*). The two major ways of demonstrating a relationship of this kind are through correlational data and data regarding differences between groups.

Correlational Approaches to Criterion-Related Validity. The Pearson product-moment correlation coefficient (r) is appropriate for use with two sets of continuous variables and is frequently used in criterion-related validity studies. For example, if we predict that Scholastic Aptitude Test (SAT) scores in high school should be related to grades in college, the correlation between the SAT score and the college grade-point average (GPA) is an index of predictive validity. Alternatively, assume we've developed a test of speed of reaction time that we postulate to be related to skill as a pilot. We administer the test to pilot trainees and at the end of training obtain instructor evaluations of each trainee. The correlation between test scores and performance in pilot training school is an index of the predictive validity of our test. Or say we've developed a measure of introversion/extraversion; the correlations of our test with such variables as number of friends, others' ratings of the person's popularity, and/or number of social club memberships would be indices of the concurrent validity of our test.

Note that if such correlations are zero or in a direction other than that predicted, the criterion-related validity of our test is cast in doubt. For example, if people scoring in the introverted direction on our test of introversion/extraversion are those people who have the most friends, belong to the most social groups, and are rated most popular by others, the validity of our test must be questioned. In other words, our test does not relate meaningfully to other variables. Thus, the test is not valid and consequently is not useful for applied purposes.

Prediction is probably the main practical use of criterion-related validity coefficients, based on the methods of regression analysis discussed in Chapter 2. Recall that a regression equation is used to predict the score on the criterion variable Y using the score on the predictor variable X. And recall that the b in the regression equation, which is the slope of the regression line, is based on the *correlation* between the predictor and the criterion, that is, the criterion-related validity coefficient. For example, if scores on the SAT are shown to be highly related to performance in college, the correlation coefficient can be used in developing a regression equation for the prediction of performance in college, based on SAT scores obtained in high school. Although some degree of error accompanies any type of prediction, this kind of regression equation might be used

by college admissions officers to predict the degree to which any prospective student will obtain an acceptable GPA at that college. Regression equations of this sort, based on criterion-related validity studies, are used extensively in the selection of people for educational and job-training programs.

Cautions in the use of correlational methods, as discussed in Chapter 2, should be recalled when considering the use of correlation to examine criterion-related validity. First, it should be recalled that the Pearson product-moment correlation is an appropriate index of the relationship between two variables only if that relationship can be assumed to be linear. If the relationship is curvilinear, for example, as observed from the scatterplot, the eta coefficient is the appropriate index of relationship. If it assumed that very high or very low levels of test anxiety will be associated with lower levels of test performance, the relationship of anxiety to performance is not assumed to be linear. Thus the eta coefficient would be appropriate for use in this case.

Also remember that correlation does not imply causation; a correlation indicates an association between two variables, but does not imply that one causes another. Thus, it is important to avoid speaking of correlational relationships in ways that imply causation, especially when one variable is being used to predict another variable.

Finally, it is important to consider both the statistical and the practical significance of obtained correlation coefficients. As was discussed in Chapter 2, with large sample sizes, smaller *absolute* values of r may be statistically significant (i.e., significantly different from zero and thus indicating a nonzero relationship between the two variables). Conversely, the smaller the sample size is, the larger the value of r must be to conclude that there actually is a nonzero relationship between the variables. With small sample sizes, then, it is important to note the statistical significance of the obtained coefficient, because even a moderately sized coefficient may not be significantly different from zero. With very large sample sizes, on the other hand, small correlations can be statistically significant, but relatively useless in practical terms. For example, a correlation of 0.15 or 0.10 will be statistically significant if the sample size is large enough, but correlation coefficients of that size indicate insignificant degrees of actual association between two variables. Thus, in using correlation coefficients as evidence of criterion-related validity, both the statistical and the practical significance must be considered.

A number of issues are important in the use of regression equations to predict criterion performance. Very often regression data are used to *select* individuals predicted to perform best on the criterion. As has been mentioned, scores from scholastic aptitude tests are used to select applicants to colleges and universities because of criterion-related validity data showing relationships between test scores and performance in college. Any time a test is used in ways having the effect of selecting some people while rejecting others, it is essential that any possible unfairness in the selection procedures be considered and then minimized or eliminated. One way that unfairness could occur is if a given test were differently predictive for different groups of people—for example, blacks versus whites, males versus females, persons for whom English is a second language versus persons for whom English is a first language. For example, if scores on a given test were highly related to college grades in one group of people but not in another group, it would be fair to use test scores to select applicants for college in the first group but not in the second. Although the issue of *differential predictability*, or *selection bias*, will be covered in depth in Chapter 14, a major point relevant to the current topic of criterion-related validity is that va-

lidity coefficients and any resulting regression equations should be obtained separately for significant subgroups of examinees until and unless it is demonstrated that validity coefficients can be generalized across groups. (For further discussion of this issue and other critically important considerations concerning the use of tests in selection the reader is referred to Chapter 14.)

Group-Differences Approaches to Criterion-Related Validity. A second approach to the study of criterion-related validity involves the extent to which test scores can differentiate between groups of people. In applied situations, we may wish to use test scores to predict success or failure in a job training program, to separate people who have psychotic tendencies from normal individuals, or to separate people who'll be satisfied in a particular occupation from those who won't be satisfied. In addition, our definition of the characteristic our test is intended to measure generally includes testable hypotheses concerning score differences across different groups of people or different types of environments. For example, on the test of speed of reaction time for pilot trainees, we would expect to find score differences between those trainees who successfully complete the course and those who fail or drop out of the course. We would expect to find higher mathematical ability in a group of mathematicians than in a group of lawyers. We would expect to find that scores on a measure of "interest in working with others" are higher in a group of teachers and social workers than in a group of research scientists. Thus, the nature of the characteristic our test is designed to measure leads us to predictions concerning group differences in test scores.

Generally, this approach to criterion-related validity involves calculation of the mean test scores within the groups and comparison of the differences between the means of the different groups. Figure 3.1 presents three sets of hypothetical data describing mean test score differences between a group of successful clerical employees and a group of unsuccessful clerical employees. Assume that the test they took was a clerical aptitude test. In Figure 3.1, example (a) illustrates a case where the mean test scores of the successful employees were higher than those of the unsuccessful employees, which, given that this was a test of clerical aptitude, illustrates the relationship we would *expect* to find between test scores and success versus failure. Assuming that a *t*-test or analysis of variance allowed us to conclude that the difference between group means was statistically sig-

nificant, the finding that scores were higher in the successful group than in the unsuccessful group would provide evidence for the criterion-related validity of the test scores.

In contrast, examples (b) and (c) in Figure 3.1 show relationships which would *not* be supportive of criterion-related validity. In example (b), both the successful and the unsuccessful group obtained the same mean score on the test of clerical aptitude; the lack of association is reflected by the horizontal line connecting the means of the two groups. In example (c), the unsuccessful employees actually obtained scores on the test *higher* than the scores of successful employees. Findings such as these would cast consid-

Figure 3.1 Hypothetical Data Describing Possible Mean Score Differences Between Groups of Successful ("S") and Unsuccessful ("U") Clerical Employees on a Test of Clerical Aptitude.

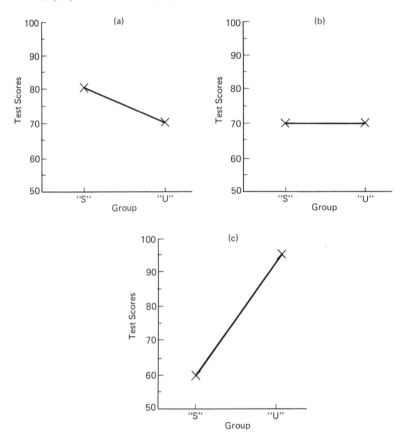

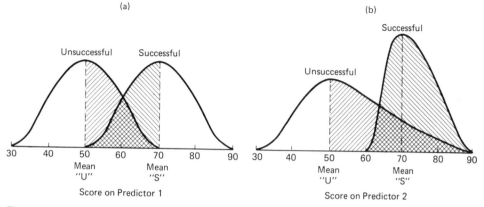

(a)

(b)

Figure 3.2 Two Possible Sets of Score Distributions for Groups of Employees on a Test of Clerical Aptitude.

erable doubt on the extent to which the test was actually measuring an attribute related to success in clerical work and thus on the criterion-related validity of the test.

Group-differences data, like correlational data, can be used in both predictive and concurrent validity studies. The example using successful versus unsuccessful clerical employees would be a study of concurrent validity if the test were administered to people who had already been judged successful or unsuccessful; in other words, we obtain test scores and criterion data (i.e., group membership) at the same approximate time, that is, concurrently. If, on the other hand, we administered our test to a group of prospective clerical employees and then later compared the test scores of those who had been judged successful with the scores of those who had been judged unsuccessful, we would have evidence for the predictive validity of the test.

For predictive purposes, an important aspect of group-differences data is not only the degree of difference between group *means*, but also the amount of overlap between the score distributions of the two groups. Figure 3.2 illustrates two possible cases where the difference between the group *means* is the same, but the amount of overlap

differs. In both cases, the successful group obtained a mean score of 70, while the unsuccessful group obtained a mean score of 50, a difference of 20 points. In example (a) in Figure 3.2, the area of overlap between the two score distributions (shown as the shaded area) is in the score range of 50 to 70. Thus, a person scoring in this range could be a member of either the successful or the unsuccessful group. However, scores above 70 can be uniformly predicted to be successful, while those below 50 can be uniformly predicted to be unsuccessful. Although there is some uncertainty, then, in predictions based on scores in the mid-range, much of the score range allows overall certainty in prediction.

In contrast, example (b) in Figure 3.2 shows a case with an unusually large score range among people judged unsuccessful, a range of 30 to 90. Although a certain prediction of "unsuccessful" can be made for examinees scoring below 50, examinees in the range of 50 to 90 can be successful *or* unsuccessful. Assuming that the maximum score is 90, there is no way in which a reasonably certain prediction of "successful" can be made. It should be apparent from example (b) in Figure 3.2 that a large amount of overlap between two score distributions reduces the utility of test scores in differentiating groups and thus in making accurate predictions.

The amount or percentage of overlap between two score distributions may be described exactly through the calculation of Tilton's (1937) overlap statistic. A high percentage of overlap (e.g., 75 percent) indicates a test with little utility for predictive (e.g., classification) purposes, while overlap percentages below about 50 percent indicate that the test can be useful in prediction of group membership, for example, the "successes" versus the "failures" (Dunnette, 1966).

While correlational and group-differences data are the major approaches to the investigation of criterion-related validity, virtually any statistical index of relationship between variables may also be appropriate. Such approaches include chi-square analyses (Glass & Hopkins, 1984), other types of correlation coefficients, such as the biserial and point-biserial (McNemar, 1969), multivariate techniques (e.g., Weiss, 1974), and experimental designs utilizing analyses of variance (Winer, 1971).

Construct Validity

While content and criterion-related validity are useful in addressing the question "Does the test measure what it is intended to measure?", the type of validity most directly addressing this question is *construct validity*. In understanding the notion of construct validity, it is essential to recall that tests and test scores by themselves are not really of either theoretical or applied interest. Rather, tests are of interest because they are reflections of some real-world phenomenon, characteristic, or behavior that we view as important and that we think is related in meaningful ways to other important phenomena, behaviors, or characteristics. Therefore the test is merely an indirect or operational way of attempting to describe the extent to which

individuals or environments possess some theoretically postulated characteristic, or *construct*. For example, intelligence is a construct assumed to be present to varying degrees in different people. However, one's IQ is stamped neither on one's forehead nor on one's social security card; in other words, we cannot directly *observe* intelligence. Rather, we develop tests that we *think* reflect a person's intelligence in an indirect way. Construct validation is the process of gathering data to support our contention that this test of intelligence is actually a reflection of the construct or attribute it is designed to reflect.

Construct validation occurs within the context of a theory or set of hypotheses concerning the construct in which we are interested. The constructs of the theory are made *observable*, or operationalized, through tests or assessments, and then the hypothesized relationships among variables can be studied through studies of the relationships between the tests/assessments that are thought to indicate them. One way of visualizing a theory and the role of tests in the theory is through what is called a "nomological network" (the word *nomological* means *lawlike*). A hypothetical nomological network illustrating a set of possible relationships between intelligence and other variables is shown in Figure 3.3.

The upper portion of Figure 3.3 represents the theory, which uses constructs or ideas that are not observable by themselves. We can hypothesize that something called "intelligence" exists, but, as was mentioned, we can't observe it directly. Our theory of intelligence suggests that intelligence should be related to both school performance and learning ability, but neither of these latter ideas is directly observable either. In order to study whether or not intelligence is actually related to school performance and learning ability, we must operationalize the constructs—that is, we must make them observable (see the lower portion of Figure 3.3).

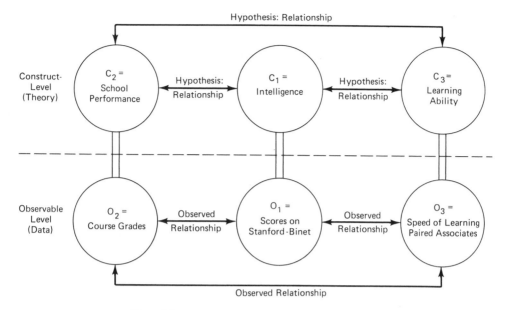

Figure 3.3 Illustration of a Hypothetical Nomological Network.

Tests and assessments are one of the major means of operationalizing constructs; for example, the Stanford-Binet Intelligence Scale is used in the present example to operationalize the abstract notion of intelligence.

Once the constructs can be operationalized, or *measured*, studies of their interrelationships can take place. In the present example, we have postulated that intelligence should be related to school performance and learning ability. We could also postulate that intelligence, as we conceptualize it, should *not* be related to height, eye color, or the state in which one was born. Examination of the relationships of scores on our intelligence test to these other variables is the means by which we would evaluate the construct validity of our intelligence test. Only when the observed pattern of relationships is correspondent with predictions based on our understanding of the construct can it be said that the construct validity of the test is supported.

Thus, the process of construct validation involves the following steps: First, the construct of interest is carefully defined and hypotheses regarding the nature and extent of its relationships to other variables are postulated. Second, an instrument designed to measure that construct is developed. Third, after the degree to which the test is reliable has been examined, studies examining the relationship of the test to other variables (as formulated in the hypotheses about the construct of interest) are undertaken.

Studies pertinent to the establishment of construct validity include those discussed previously in the discussions of criterion-related and content validity. The methods of criterion-related validation—for example, correlational data and data regarding group differences—would be appropriate to examine hypotheses about our construct. We might use correlational methods to examine the hypothesized relationship between intelligence and school performance. We might postulate that school children should perform better on our test of intelligence than should children in an institution for the mentally retarded. Thus, group differences in test scores would be an appropriate focus of study. From approaches to the examination of content validity come analyses of internal consistency, or homogeneity. For example, if our conception of intelligence involves the assumption that it is a unidimensional trait, then studies of the homogeneity of our intelligence test, using internal consistency reliability coefficients, would be appropriate.

Factor analysis is another method that can also provide some evidence supporting the construct validity of a measuring instrument. The results of a factor analysis of the intercorrelations of test items yield information about how many dimensions or traits are needed to summarize or explain test performance. If a test is constructed to measure one trait, and items are sampled only from behaviors reflecting that trait, a factor analysis yielding a single large "general" factor would be evidence of construct validity. On the other hand, if the factor analysis yielded several factors, the conclusion would have to be that the test measures more than one trait. Conversely, factor analysis of the items of a test designed to measure several variables (e.g., anxiety, dependence, sociability) should result in factors identifiable as these variables, if the test is to have demonstrated construct validity. Thus, the results of factor-analytic studies should be in agreement with the assumed dimensionality of the construct, if evidence for construct validity is to be provided.

Generally, the methods of evaluating construct validity include any empirical study and method of statistical analysis capable of examining the hypotheses about the construct. For example, our conceptual definition of assertiveness might include the assumption that assertiveness is a skill that can be taught. An appropriate construct validity study for our measure of assertiveness might be a controlled experimental study where half the subjects are taught assertiveness skills while the other half are not. If treated subjects improve more on our assertiveness test than do untreated subjects, we have evidence for both the construct validity of the test and the effectiveness of the treatment. If treated subjects do not improve, we can hypothesize that (1) our treatment was not effective, (2) assertiveness is not a skill that can be taught, or (3) our test is not a valid measure of assertiveness. While further studies would be necessary to discern which one or more of these explanations explains the lack of a treatment effect, the construct validity of our test has not been supported by our research findings.

It is important to note that evidence supportive of construct validity depends not only on the validity of the test we're interested in, but also on the reliability and validity of the measures of the other variables studied in relationship to our test. For example, if we postulate that intelligence should be related to numerical problem-solving ability, we would expect to find a correlation between our test of intelligence and a test of numerical problem-solving ability. However, unless the latter test is a reliable and valid measure of that problem-solving ability, we cannot expect to find a relationship between the two sets of scores. Essentially, a strong relationship between two tests suggests the validity of *both* as measures of what they are intended to measure, while a weak relationship between two variables assumed in theory to be related casts doubt on the validity of at least one, and possibly both, measures.

In summary, to the extent that our hypotheses about the construct are supported in research studies using our measure of that construct, the construct validity of our test is supported. If, on the other hand, our test scores are not related to other variables, as suggested by our hypotheses about the construct, the construct validity of the test is in doubt. Thus, such studies are essential to the establishment of construct validity, and the more evidence such studies enable us to accumulate about the test's construct validity, the greater the meaning and usefulness of the test will be. When we have information concerning relationships of the construct, as measured by our test, to other real-world phenomena, we are better able to explain and understand the meaning of the construct and to use the test for applied purposes. Hence, construct validity is not only a necessary part of a test's basic quality but is also the characteristic by which the test acquires meaning, interpretability, and usefulness. Construct validity is the major basis on which tests contribute to theoretical understanding and to the solving of applied problems.

Convergent and Discriminant Validity

Pertinent to both criterion-related and construct validity, as well as important themselves, are *convergent validity* and *discriminant validity*. As has been discussed, part of the process of validation involves examining the relationships of our test to other variables hypothesized to measure the same construct or to be related to the construct. For instance, if we develop a new measure of creativity, we would expect it to have some relationship to other valid measures of creativity. Thus, we would examine the relationship of our test to other tests of creativity and/or to others' judgments regarding a person's artistic, literary, musical, or scientific productivity. The relationship of our test to independent measures or indices of the same trait is known as *convergent validity* (Campbell & Fiske, 1959).

In addition to demonstrating relationships between the test and independent measures of the same trait, the validation process should also demonstrate moderate or *negligible* relationships between the test and certain other variables. For example, if

our test of creativity were found to have a very high relationship to intelligence, there would be little need for the test of creativity, since a measure of intelligence would provide the same information about individuals. In other words, our test of creativity would have little predictive utility beyond that offered by an intelligence test. Further, if creativity and intelligence were found to be essentially the same thing (i.e., through a very high correlation between the two), the two constructs would be redundant. The law of parsimony in science, which encourages simplicity in explanation, suggests that two or more constructs are unnecessary if one will explain behavior just as well. Thus, a very high correlation between two theoretically different constructs suggests that one of them is unnecessary.

It is also necessary to demonstrate that our test is unrelated to variables that it is *not* postulated to reflect, which is known as *discriminant validity* (Campbell & Fiske, 1959). If our conception of creativity involves the assumption that it is unrelated to physical size, we would hope to find a zero correlation between creativity scores and height. Similarly, if we postulate that creative people are found equally across sex and racial groups, we would hope to find an *absence* of mean differences between males and females and across racial groups.

Thus, test validation should involve examination of both convergent and discriminant validity as part of, and in addition to, the process of criterion-related and construct validation.

One important consideration with convergent and discriminant validity studies concerns what is known as *method variance* (Campbell & Fiske, 1959). Method variance concerns the extent to which scores on two different tests are correlated not because the constructs they measure are related, but because they used the same format—for example, true-false, multiple-choice, essay—and to whether or not speed in taking the test is required. For example, some people are more comfortable than others in taking highly speeded, multiple-choice tests like the SAT or the Graduate Record Examination (GRE). If three different abilities are all tested this way, the correlations among scores on the three different tests could be artificially inflated due to the common method of measurement. Method variance, because it inflates the correlations between test scores, operates to *increase* estimates of convergent validity—for example, if three tests of intelligence all used the same method of measurement—and to *decrease* estimates of discriminant validity—for example, when three different abilities were all measured using multiple-choice tests.

To control for method variance, Campbell and Fiske (1959) propose the use of what is called a *multitrait-multimethod matrix*. To use such a matrix, a validation study should include measures of two or more traits, each measured by two or more of the same methods. A hypothetical example might include the traits of anxiety, dominance, and introversion/extraversion. Each trait is measured three ways: by a self-report personality inventory, by ratings obtained from others who know the person, and by a situational test (e.g., likelihood of speaking to a stranger as a measure of introversion/extraversion). Table 3.1 shows a hypothetical example of a multitrait-multimethod matrix based on the example above.

The correlation matrix shown in the table includes the correlations of each test with each other test. The correlations of a test with the two other measures of that same trait indicate the convergent validity of the test. In the sample shown, notice that the correlations of the test of introversion/extraversion with other indices of the trait are higher than are the correlations of the anxiety or dominance tests with other measures of those traits, which indicates greater convergent validity for the measure of introversion/extraversion. The correlations indi-

TABLE 3.1   Hypothetical Example of a Multitrait-Multimethod Matrix

	Trait	Method 1 (Self-Report)			Method 2 (Others' Ratings)			Method 3 (Situational Test)		
		A_1	B_1	C_1	A_2	B_2	C_2	A_3	B_3	C_3
Self-Report	Anxiety (A_1)	(0.85)								
	Dominance (B_1)	0.48	(0.88)							
	Introversion-Extraversion (C_1)	0.40	0.38	(0.79)						
Others' Ratings	Anxiety (A_2)	0.50			(0.90)					
	Dominance (B_2)	0.30	0.54		0.40	(0.86)				
	Introversion-Extraversion (C_2)	0.22	0.18	0.68	0.44	0.36	(0.88)			
Situational Test	Anxiety (A_3)	0.50	0.25	0.15	0.55	0.30	0.42	(0.86)		
	Dominance (B_3)	0.28	0.50	0.16	0.40	0.58	0.32	0.56	(0.90)	
	Introversion-Extraversion (C_3)	0.19	0.15	0.60	0.30	0.36	0.66	0.53	0.48	(0.80)

cating convergent validity should be higher than the correlations between tests of different traits; lower values of these correlations suggest greater discriminant validity. Although a complete explication of the idea of method variance and the usefulness of a multitrait-multimethod matrix in the study of test validity is beyond the scope of this book, interested readers are referred to Campbell and Fiske's (1959) article.

Incremental Validity

Tests are widely used for selection and placement in educational institutions and in business and industry. While the users of tests for these purposes have generally found them to be useful, testing programs also require purchasing tests, hiring test administrators, and scoring and interpreting the tests. Thus, the benefits of testing include some costs to the organizations as well. Because of this, Sechrest (1963) suggests that, before using a new test for purposes of selection and placement, one evaluate the extent to which the test *improves* the accuracy of decision making beyond that possible using already available or less expensive methods of assessment. The capacity of a test to lead to improved prediction over already available predictive tools is known as *incremental validity*. For example, a test having a correlation of $r = 0.90$ with the criterion measure (e.g., job performance) would not have incremental validity if some already available method of selection had the same degree of predictive accuracy. On the other hand, a test with low-to-moderate predictive validity, (e.g., $r = 0.30$ or $r = 0.50$) might have considerable incremental validity and, consequently, utility, if there were few or no other bases upon which to make the necessary decision.

Related to the idea of incremental validity is that of *base rates* (Meehl & Rosen, 1955), which are the proportions of people expected a priori to fall into given categories—for example, success versus failure in a training program. If 90 percent of unselected people routinely succeed in a given training program, the base rate for success is 90 percent, and the base rate for failure is 10 percent. If we predicted a successful outcome for every person starting training, we would be correct 90 percent of the time without having to use any kind of test. In this sense, then, incremental validity is the extent to which a test can improve the accuracy of prediction beyond that possible by simply using base-rate data.

Face Validity

The term *face validity* concerns the extent to which the test appears to look like a test of the concept it is intended to measure. For example, if you're told to begin an intelligence test, yet all the items ask about your feelings about your parents, you might be skeptical of the test administrator's real purposes. Face validity is of concern primarily in terms of the acceptability of the test to potential test takers and test users. If a test advertised for use in the prediction of a person's performance as a police officer has no obvious relationship to the job duties and responsibilities of police officers, police departments may be skeptical about its usefulness, and applicants for training as police officers may perceive the test as irrelevant and/or unfair.

Face validity is not necessarily equivalent to content validity. In some cases, appropriate test items may not bear an obvious relationship to the construct of interest. Indirect or subtle ways of getting at certain characteristics may be necessary, especially if people's knowledge of themselves or their honesty in self-description is in doubt. Thus, a test's items may have *content* validity as judged by experts in the field, but may not have *face* validity for test users and test takers.

Although in some cases face validity may be necessary for public relations purposes, it is not necessary to the establishment of a test's validity, nor does it contribute to the establishment of validity. A test is *not* valid just because it *appears* to be valid, and face validity is not among the types of validity information required in the *Standards for Educational and Psychological Testing* (1985) developed by a joint committee of the AERA, APA, and NCME. However, the effective use of tests depends on the establishment and maintenance of trust and "rapport" between test users and the "public" (which includes test takers), and face validity may be very important in this regard.

Interpretive Validity

A final consideration in the establishment of a test's validity concerns the extent to which a test and a test manual facilitate accurate and useful interpretations by a test user, a quality known as *interpretive validity*. A test can be highly reliable and supported by considerable evidence for validity, but if scoring and interpretation procedures, or the design of the test-score reporting sheet or "profile," are unclear and/or overly complicated, test users may have difficulty using the test as it was intended to be used.

Thus, test constructors have a responsibility to clearly define the purposes of a test, including its strengths and weaknesses, to specify the populations for which it is and is not appropriate, and to specify exact procedures for the administration, scoring, and interpretation of the test. The test constructor is therefore responsible not only for the demonstration of the test's reliability and validity but also for providing guidelines to test users that will ensure that the test is used accurately, effectively, and in ways the test constructor intended.

Summary

Several different types of validity are important in the evaluation of a psychological test or measuring instrument. The importance of validation data cannot be underestimated, for they are the means by which a test gains meaning, interpretability, and usefulness. Given this fact, it should not be surprising that it is not possible to say that a test *is* valid or has a certain degree of validity. Rather, validation is a continual process of studying the empirical network of interrelationships of the test and of verifying, modifying, or proposing sets of hypotheses that provide logical meaning and interpretability to obtained test results. A test has some degree of validity when we can say what the scores *mean* in practical terms, when we have supported the relationship of the test items to the construct of interest, when test scores are useful in the prediction of other real-world phenomena, and when the pattern of observed relationships with other variables facilitates our understanding of the construct of interest. Validity data, then, not only constitute an essential psychometric characteristic of a test, but are also the means by which tests gain practical and scientific utility.

TEST CONSTRUCTION

Introduction

Although the reliability and validity of a test are evaluated after the test is constructed, the best way (probably the only way) to ensure a high-quality test is through proper and careful methods of test construction. If a test was well constructed in the first place, chances are good that it will be found to be reliable and valid.

In general, test construction should proceed with the following steps:

1. careful definition of the attribute or construct to be measured
2. development of a large pool of items logically related to the attribute of interest
3. administration of the items to a large sample of subjects, often called the "development sample"
4. refinement of the original item pool through item analyses and expert judgment
5. administration of the revised test to a new sample of subjects
6. based on the new samples, examination of evidence for reliability and validity and computation of normative data

Definition of the Construct. Test construction begins with a careful, detailed definition of the characteristic to be measured. This definition should include both what the attribute is and what it isn't; it should include a specification of both behaviors/tasks included in the definition and those not included.

If we are measuring knowledge of American history, we need to define the term *American* (Does it refer only to the United States, or does it also include Canada, Mexico, Central and South America?) and delineate the time period to be included in our measure. Less obvious than defining the characteristic "knowledge of American history" would be defining the characteristics of dominance, sociability, or anxiety, for example. It is important to include in such definitions the meaning of the construct, its implications for behavior, and the kinds of other characteristics it is postulated to be related to.

For example, the Jackson Personality Inventory (JPI) (Jackson, 1976a) measures the construct of anxiety. Anxiety is defined as characterizing people who tend to worry over inconsequential matters, are more easily upset than the average person, and are apprehensive about the future. Anxiety is associated with such words as *tense*, *nervous*, *worried*, *edgy*, and *fearful*. Persons low in the

trait are, in contrast, able to remain calm in stressful situations, take things as they come without worrying, relax in difficult situations, and are usually composed and collected (Jackson, 1976b, p. 10). Similarly, the construct of risk taking is defined as the willingness to gamble and take chances and to expose oneself to dangerous situations or to situations with uncertain outcomes. Persons who score high on risk taking enjoy adventure and are bold, daring, and enterprising, while those who score low on risk taking are cautious, hesitant, careful, wary, security-minded, and conservative (Jackson, 1976b, p. 10).

In many cases, actually delineating the meaning of the construct is the most difficult step. Although we all have intuitive, commonsense understanding of characteristics such as intelligence, anxiety, dominance, and sociability, it is not easy to carefully specify *exactly* what behaviors and responses should be assumed to indicate the construct. Yet, while probably the most difficult step in test construction, this is a most interesting and challenging step, and probably the most important, since everything that follows depends on the specificity and clarity of the definition of the construct.

Developing Test Items. Once the dimension or construct of interest is defined, the test constructor develops test items that are related to the *content* (i.e., the definition) of that dimension. This kind of item development requires that the test developer carefully examine the definition of the construct and then infer specific behaviors or responses that should reflect components of that definition. For example, anxiety measured by the Jackson Personality Inventory (Jackson, 1976b) is defined as characterizing people who tend to worry over inconsequential matters, are more easily upset than the average person, and are apprehensive about the future. Anxiety is associated with words such as *tense, nervous, worried, edgy,* and *fearful.* The test constructor would examine this definition and then write items that reflect the characteristics indicated by the definition. The initial item pool might include items such as "Occasionally I get so nervous that I begin to get all choked up" (an actual JPI item), "I worry a lot about the future," and "I often get upset about little things." These items bear a logical or rational relationship to the construct as defined by the test constructor. The test constructor should develop (i.e., write or adapt from previously available tests or other materials) a pool of items larger than that needed in the final version of the test. A large pool of items is necessary so that items that do not relate as postulated to the dimension of interest may be eliminated. In other words, while an item may appear to the test constructor to be logically related to the dimension, the item analysis procedures to be discussed next may suggest that it is not highly related to the dimension.

Administration of Test Items to a Development Sample.

The next stage of test construction involves administration of the items to a preliminary sample of subjects (often referred to as the "development sample"). The subjects in this group should be representative of the population of subjects for whom the test itself is intended. In other words, if the test is designed to measure school achievement in grades seven through nine, the subjects should be representative of students in grades seven through nine. Similarly, if the test is designed to measure personality characteristics of adults, then a representative sample of adults should be used. Subjects in the development sample are administered the test under conditions identical to those that will be used in the administration of the completed test, and the responses obtained from this pilot testing are used in the item analyses to be discussed next.

Item Analysis.

Although definition of the construct and development of relevant test items are intended to ensure that the items in the initial item pool are reasonably good representatives of the construct, knowledge of other properties of the test items is used in *refining* the item pool. By "refining an item pool" we mean eliminating items that, when actually administered in the development sample, do not have the properties we had hoped for and, further, selecting items that have particularly desirable properties. Sometimes the process of item refinement requires us to write new items, because in the process of eliminating items we've eliminated so many we don't have enough left to constitute a test of the desired length. Because of the importance of item analysis procedures to both constructing and evaluating tests, they will receive separate, more detailed discussion in the next section.

Administration and Examination of the Completed Test.

Finally, the completed test is administered to groups of examinees for the purposes of studying the reliability and validity of the test and computing normative data. This process usually requires considerable time and should involve studies in various different groups with whom the test is to be used—for example, males and females, minority-race groups and majority-race groups, students in urban and rural areas, schools in higher and lower socioeconomic areas. Types of studies and methods of statistical analysis could include any or all of the methods described for the study of reliability and validity (e.g., test-retest studies, analyses of internal consistency reliability, factor analyses, criterion-related validity). Ideally, the careful, systematic methods by which the test was initially constructed will result in a test that possesses reasonable levels of reliability and validity and that consequently is of both theoretical interest and applied utility.

Item Analysis

Item analysis is an important part of test construction because it allows the test constructor to select only the best test items, in terms of reliability and validity. By selecting the best items from the initial pool of items, the test can be kept relatively short without sacrificing the quality of measurement. The two major criteria used to select test items are item difficulty and item discrimination.

Item Difficulty. The concept of *item difficulty* was originally developed for use with test items where there are right and wrong answers, as in the assessment of ability and achievement. With items of this kind, item difficulty is usually defined statistically as the percentage of persons who respond correctly to an item. The higher the percentage of people who answer an item correctly, the easier the item is considered to be, and vice versa. Item difficulty levels are usually expressed as p values: An item answered correctly by 70 percent of subjects has a p of 0.70, while an item answered correctly by only 20 percent of subjects has a p of 0.20. (Some formulas for the calculation of item difficulty include corrections for guessing; see, for example, Nunnally [1978].)

Methods of selecting test items based on their p values depend considerably on the purposes for which the test is constructed, but it should be apparent to the reader that the difficulty of the test is a direct function of the difficulty of the test items we choose. If we include only very difficult items, the test will be very difficult; likewise, if all the items we include are relatively easy, the test also will be easy.

We want to select test items such that the overall level of difficulty is appropriate for the groups with whom the test is to be used and so that the test yields a relatively wide range of scores, preferably having a normal distribution. If a test does not yield a range of scores, it does not provide us with information about individual differences in the attribute or trait of interest.

To illustrate how item difficulty influences the characteristics of the resulting test scores, consider, first, an item that everyone in our standardization or normative sample answered correctly. The difficulty or p value of the item is 1.0 as 100 percent of the examinees answered it correctly. This item is too easy for the group and does not distinguish between individuals in the group—thus, it provides us with no new information about individuals. A test constructed using too many easy items would result in a skewed score distribution with too little of what has been called "ceiling"; that is, the capacity to discriminate individuals at the upper end of the distribution.

Assume, on the other hand, that we have an item that everyone in our normative sample answers incorrectly; this item has a difficulty or p value of 0.0. This item is too difficult for the group and, like the item that was too easy, provides us with no new information about individual differences. A test constructed with items that are too difficult yields a skewed distribution of scores, which is said to "have too little floor," meaning that it does a very poor job of distinguishing individuals at the lower end of the score distribution.

Generally, a set of test items should include items with a range of difficulties, varying, for example, from $p = 0.10$ to $p = 0.90$, with most values of p clustering around 0.50. This will produce a test of appropriate difficulty yielding a range of scores that are approximately normally distributed. This selection of test items will also ensure that even the least able examinees will be able to answer a few items correctly.

Although the idea of item difficulty is used primarily in connection with aptitude and achievement tests, it can also be applied to measures of traits that do not assume right or wrong answers but rather use Likert scales or other methods of obtaining examinees' responses. Let's say that we used a Likert scale with the following response options: Strongly Agree (5), Agree (4), Not Sure (3), Disagree (2), and Strongly Disagree (1). The average of all responses to that item across individuals in the normative sample would be an item "score," analogous in many respects to item difficulty. An item that everyone strongly agreed with would have an item score near 5 and would provide us with very little information about individual differences in the attitude or trait we were trying to assess. As in the case of ability test items, we would probably want to select items having a range of "difficulties" (that is, mean item scores), so that the resulting score distribution was characterized by sufficient variability among individuals.

Item Discrimination. The property of *item discrimination* is important for almost all types of tests designed to assess some unitary attribute. Item discrimination refers to the extent to which people's responses to a given item measuring a construct are related to their scores on the measure as a whole. If item responses *do not* relate to performance on the scale as a whole, we have reason to suspect that the item is not measuring what it was intended to measure. Assume, for example, that the brightest child in the class scores 99 on an achievement test, and that the one item answered incorrectly was an item that the poorest student (who got only 10 right altogether) answered correctly: We would wonder about the extent to which that item was actually measuring achievement in the subject matter. Or assume that on one of the items we developed to measure anxiety the examinees scoring highest (most anxious) on the anxiety test as a whole responded negatively to that item: Again, we would question the effectiveness of that item as a measure of anxiety. The discriminatory

power of test items is directly related to the resulting internal consistency reliability. Reliable tests result from items that discriminate well.

Items such as these may be *poorly discriminating* because they are not clearly worded, are ambiguous in meaning, are subject to alternate interpretations, or simply are not related to the dimension of interest. Indices of item discrimination allow the test constructor to select the "good" items (i.e., those that actually appear to measure the dimension of interest) and to eliminate from the test the "bad" items.

There are many indices of item discrimination. Two correlation coefficients used extensively in the examination of discriminating power are the biserial and point-biserial coefficients. The point-biserial r_{pb}, which is a Pearson product-moment correlation coefficient, describes the relationship between a dichotomous variable (e.g., true-false, right-wrong, male-female), and a continuous variable, such as total score on a test. The biserial r_{bis}, on the other hand, describes the relationship between a *dichotomized* variable (a dichotomous item response assumed to summarize an underlying normal distribution) and a continuous variable. The computation of both r_{pb} and r_{bis} is based on comparing the mean test scores of those who pass the item and of those who fail it, in relationship to the difficulty of the item itself. Evidence for item discrimination requires that the overall test scores of those who respond correctly to an item be higher than the mean scores of those who respond incorrectly to the item.

Table 3.2 shows the calculation of the biserial correlation coefficient for two items, item 1 and item 2. Note that the formula compares the mean total test scores of examinees who responded correctly to the item (M_1) to those of examinees responding incorrectly (M_0). The larger the difference between these means, the larger the value of

Table 3.2 Illustration of the Calculation of the Biserial Correlation Coefficient for Two Test Items

| | | Item Responses | |
| | | (1 = correct, 0 = incorrect) | |
Examinee	Total Test Score	Item 1	Item 2
Ann	20	0	1
Bill	24	1	1
Carol	29	1	1
Dave	27	1	1
Ellen	31	1	1
Frank	19	0	0
George	23	0	0
Hal	26	0	0
Jane	21	1	1
Kate	30	1	1

$\Sigma x = 250$
$N = 10$
$M = 250/10 = 25$
$S_x = 4.05$

For Item 1: $M_1 = 27$, $M_0 = 22$

For Item 2: $M_1 = 25.5$, $M_0 = 24.25$

$$r_{bis} = \frac{M_1 - M_0}{S_{x \, un2}} \, n_1 n_0$$

$$r_{bis} = \left(\frac{27-22}{4.05}\right)\left(\frac{24}{.386-100}\right)$$
$$= (1.23)(.62)$$
$$= .76$$

$$r_{bis} = \left(\frac{25.5-24.2}{4.04}\right) \times (.62)$$
$$= (.31)(.62)$$
$$= .19$$

Where u = the ordinate of the unit normal distribution at $p = n_{1/n}$. To find u enter p or 1-p (.60 and .40 in this case) in a normal distribution table and read u in adjacent column, .3863 in this case.

Note. Data are for illustrative purposes only. For sample sizes less than 100, r_{bis} is a crude approximation of r and should be used only with caution. Also, it is assumed that the x scores are normally distributed, and to the extent that this assumption is violated, r_{bis} is a poor estimate of the item-total score relationship (Glass & Hopkins, 1984).

the correlation, because larger differences indicate a closer relationship of item responses to test scores. That is, correct responses to the item are obtained by people who did better on the test, while incorrect responses are obtained by people who generally did more poorly. In the table, r_{bis} for item 1 = .76, while for item 2 it is only .19. The poorer discriminating power of item 2 can be traced directly to the responses of examinees Ann and Carol. Since Ann obtained a total score of only 20 (versus a group mean of 25), her "correct" response to item 2 is indicative of poor item discrimination. Conversely, Carol obtained a total score of 29 yet responded incorrectly to item 2. Readers should note that a biserial correlation coefficient differs from members of the

Pearson product-moment correlation family (which includes r, phi, and the point biserial) in that it can exceed the range of ± 1, when sample sizes are small. In such cases, or if the distribution of total test scores deviates substantially from the normal, the biserial is a crude index of the item-test relationship. See Glass and Hopkins (1984) and Guilford and Fruchter (1978) for further information about using the biserial and point-biserial correlations.

Another index of item discrimination is the phi coefficient (ϕ), a Pearson product-moment correlation coefficient. Phi expresses the relationship between two dichotomous variables. As an index of item discrimination it tells us the degree to which the percentage of subjects passing the item (pass-fail) is related to their position in the upper or the lower group of overall scorers (expressed as U-L). An example of a U-L dichotomy would be to divide the score distribution at the median; scores above the median would be in the upper group (U), while those below the median would be in the lower group (L). U-L could also be designated as the top third of scorers versus the bottom third of scorers.

Other indices of item discrimination include a simple comparison of the percentages of subjects answering correctly in extreme groups. This has been referred to as the "U-L index," or simply as "D." For example, assume that an item was answered correctly by 70 percent of subjects scoring above the median, but by only 30 percent of those scoring below the median. The U-L index, or D, would be equal to $70 - 30 = 40$. Assume, in contrast, that an item was answered correctly by 70 percent of the top scorers, but also by 65 percent of the low scorers. The U-L index, or D, would equal only $5 (70 - 65)$. Clearly, the first item would be doing a better job of discriminating groups than would the second item. Test constructors usually select items that do have discriminating power and eliminate those that are poorly discriminating.

Although specific criteria for deciding upon minimum levels of discriminatory power necessary to include an item in a test are beyond the scope of this book (see Brown, 1983; Nunnally, 1978), a few general strategies can be suggested. First, a test constructor should administer more pilot test items (to the development sample) than are needed in the final test. Following examination of obtained values of item difficulty and discrimination, the test constructor would select items such that the objectives of a range of item difficulties and good item discriminating power would be met. One approach to doing this would be to arrange items in groups of similar item difficulty and, within those groups, in order of discriminating power (e.g., the value of r_{bis} or "D"). Within each level of difficulty, the most discriminating item would be selected. Table 3.3 illustrates how this might work. Let's assume that we want an equal distribution of p values across the difficulty continuum ranging from $p = 0.10$ to $p = 0.90$. In order to achieve that goal, we'll select the two most discriminating items within each difficulty range. Note that the two most difficult items and the two least difficult items we'll choose (items 10 and 14 in category 1, and items 12 and 15 in category 4) have lower values of r_{bis} than do items we *won't select* in categories 2 and 3. However, we will meet our *overall* objectives of selecting items with a range of difficulties and the best possible discriminating power given the items available at each level of difficulty.

Item Response Theory

Most of the discussion of test construction to this point is based on the assumptions of classical test theory, as presented in the beginning of this chapter. As was mentioned, classical test theory assumes the existence of a "true score" on a test for each individual and that the observed or obtained test score represents the true score plus a certain amount of error in measurement. We assume a linear relationship between the true score and the observed score, and the reliability coefficient indicates the percentage of observed score variance that can be attributed to true scores.

Although classical test theory is still in wide use today, a more recent development in test theory is what has been called "latent trait theory," item response theory (IRT), or item characteristic curve (ICC) theory. (See Weiss, 1983, for an excellent review.) The theory uses information about item difficulty and item discrimination in mathemat-

Table 3.3 Illustration of Item Selection for an Eight-item Test Designed to Have a Rectangular or Balanced Set of Item Difficulty Values

Item Difficulty Ranges	Item Discrimination ('bis)	Item Selected?
Category 1 p = .10 to p = .30 (Most Difficult)		
Item 4	.30	no
7	.35	no
10	.50	yes
14	.40	yes
Category 2 p = .31 to p = .50 (Moderately Difficult)		
Item 1	.40	no
3	.60	yes
8	.55	yes
13	.51	no
Category 3 p = .51 to p = .70 (Most Difficult)		
Item 2	.58	yes
5	.46	no
11	.38	no
16	.52	yes
Category 4 p = .71 to p = .90 (Easiest)		
Item 6	.28	no
9	.35	no
12	.39	yes
15	.41	yes

ical equations, which then guide test construction.

More specifically, latent trait theory (or IRT or ICC) is based, not surprisingly, on the assumption that test scores reflect the amount of a "latent trait" possessed by the individual. A latent trait, symbolized by the Greek letter theta (θ), is similar to a hypothetical construct, as used in the discussion of construct validity. Items, on the other hand, can be described using one or more of three properties: item difficulty, item discrimination, and the probability of a correct response

as a result of guessing on a multiple-choice test. The theory provides mathematical models or equations expressing the relationship between responses to a given test item and amount of the latent trait the person is estimated to have. The equations use information about item difficulty, discrimination, and probability of guessing correctly to estimate the amount of the trait possessed by individuals making a given response.

These mathematical models are illustrated graphically by what are known as *item characteristic curves*, examples of which are

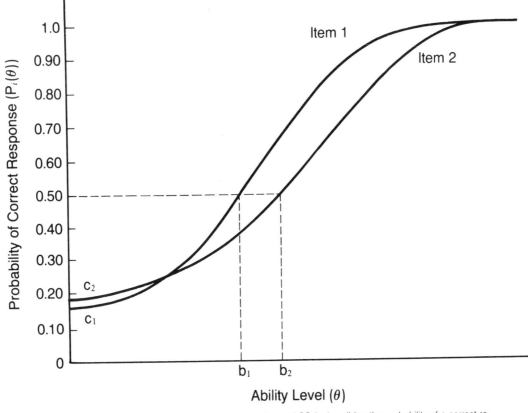

Figure 3.4. Examples of Item Characteristic Curves (ICCs), describing the probability of a correct response to a test item as a function of ability level (θ). The item difficulty is represented as b_1 or b_2 (for item 1 or item 2), probability of guessing correctly as C_1 or C_2, and item discrimination is related to the steepness of the curve.

shown in Figure 3.4. An ICC portrays the cumulative probability of a correct response to an ability test item as a function of ability level. The shape of this curve approximates what is called a "normal ogive" curve, which is a cumulative normal distribution. Item discrimination is shown graphically as the slope or steepness of the curve, and the difficulty level of the item corresponds to that level of ability where 50 percent of the examinees obtained a correct response. In Figure 3.4, item 1 is somewhat easier than item 2, as shown by a lower ability level (b_1) where 50 percent of the examinees pass the item. Item 1 is also more highly discriminating, as

shown by the steeper curve of the ICC. Since both are multiple-choice items, there is a c parameter indicating the probability of a correct response through guessing. Assuming five response choices, even the least capable examinee has a 50 percent chance of responding correctly to the item (shown as values c_1 and c_2 in the graph).

Many advantages accrue to the use of latent trait theory in test construction. For example, each test item can provide an estimate of ability for any individual, and the use of more test items provides more precise estimates. What this means in practical terms is that individuals may be tested with different items and even different numbers of items, yet the same "latent trait" can be measured, and the scores will be on the same numerical scale and thus comparable to one another.

This concept has been used in what is called "adaptive" testing of ability (Weiss, 1974, 1982; Weiss & Betz, 1973), where examinees receive a set of items "tailored" or customized to their ability levels. For example, in the two-stage test (Betz & Weiss, 1973), a preliminary "routing test" is computer-administered and scored, and then the scores are used to assign examinees to a more or less difficult second-stage test. Thus, examinees doing poorly on the routing test would receive an easier set of second-stage items than would examinees doing well on the routing test. Adaptive testing procedures can maximize the reliability of measurement while minimizing the number of items that need to be administered to any given examinee.

Another advantage of latent trait theory is that the formulas also yield what are known as *information functions*. A given test item discriminates better at some ability levels than others, and an information function tells us which ability levels will be most accurately assessed by each of our test items. Using such information, we can assemble a group of items that provide acceptable levels of reliability across a desired range of ability levels. We also know at what levels of ability our test measures less accurately than it does at other ability levels. The practical implications of this type of information might include using other measures with people who we know are not as accurately measured by our test, or placing less confidence in the results for examinees at some levels of ability than we can in the results for examinees at other levels of ability.

In summary, although latent trait theories and adaptive testing are relatively new in test construction, they hold great promise

for the future. Some of the major tests, like the Armed Services Aptitude Battery (see Chapter 7), are already available in computer-administered adaptive form (Moreno, Wetzel, McBride, & Weiss, 1984). Thus, readers should be alert to further developments in this area.

Other Approaches to Test and Scale Construction

The previous section focused on test construction methods used primarily with ability and achievement tests, where there are right and wrong answers. However, there are many variables we wish to measure for which there are no right or wrong answers, including personality traits and vocational interests, and attitudes, opinions, values, and self-perceptions. Although a complete discussion of methods of developing measures of such variables is beyond the scope of this book, they will be briefly mentioned here so that the reader will be somewhat familiar with the general terms when they appear later in the text, in the chapters on the assessment of interests, personality, values, etc. First, several alternative approaches to the measurement of personality and interests will be briefly discussed and, finally, approaches to attitude measurement will be mentioned.

Rational Scale Construction. The *rational approach* to test construction is based on the assumption that the content of the test items directly reflects the characteristic or dimension we are interested in measuring. If we are measuring one's interest in becoming a florist, we would assume that "agree/disagree" responses to the statement "I enjoy looking at flowers" would reflect interest. Similarly, as was mentioned earlier in the discussion of test construction, the Jackson Personality Inventory Anxiety Scale might include the items "I worry a lot about the future" and "Occasionally I get so nervous that I get all choked up."

These items bear logical or rational relationships to the construct as defined by the test constructors, while an item such as "I enjoy taking care of small children" does not have a logical relationship to either anxiety or risk taking and so would not be used to measure these traits. For a scale assessing interest in being a veterinarian, the item "I like animals" would bear an obvious relationship to that interest, while the item "I enjoy listening to music" would not. Generally, the test constructor develops (i.e., writes or adapts from previously available tests or other materials) a pool of items larger than that needed in the final version of the test. These items are administered to the development sample and are then subject to item analysis, as was discussed in the previous section.

Finally, based on item analysis findings, the test constructor selects from the initial pool the number of good items desired in the final version of the test. These, then, are items *logically related* to the construct of interest. In interpreting scores on a rationally constructed test we not only know the person's score on the dimension of interest, but also are able to make inferences about the specific ways in which the person described himself or herself. In other words, we know that a high score on the risk-taking scale indicates a willingness to take chances and a relative lack of concern with safety and security. On the Strong-Campbell Interest Inventory, the "Basic Interest" scales represent rational test construction; a high score on the "Mechanical Activities" scale may be interpreted directly as expressing a liking for mechanical activities, and a high score on the "Music/Dramatics" scale is directly interpretable in terms of a liking for musical and dramatic activities. Thus, the name of the scale itself dictates the content of test items and is used directly in the interpretation of test scores.

Empirical Scale Construction. In contrast to the rational approach to scale construction, empirical scale construction is based on the differences in the responses of people postulated or found to vary on the dimension of interest, rather than on item content itself. In other words, test construction begins with a search for items that will *predict* a criterion measure or status. For example, the Minnesota Multiphasic Personality Inventory (MMPI) was originally designed to permit clinicians to detect persons suffering from serious forms of psychological disorder (e.g., schizophrenia); the responses of diagnosed schizophrenics to a large number of items were compared to the responses of "normal" individuals, in this case visitors to the same hospital in which the schizophrenic individuals were patients. Items on which the responses of the patient group were significantly different from those of normal individuals were used in constructing the schizophrenia scale of the MMPI. Other examples of empirical test construction are the occupational scales of the Strong-Campbell Interest Inventory (SCII). In this case, the criterion groups were people satisfied in various occupations (e.g., physicians). Items on which the responses of people in a given occupation differed from the responses of people in general were used in constructing the occupational scale.

Item *content* per se was not considered in the construction of the MMPI and SCII scales. These scales, then, could contain items bearing no obvious relationship to the dimension being measured. If physicians were more likely than people in general to endorse the item "I would enjoy composing music," then that item would be included on the physician scale. In other cases, keyed item responses might be inconsistent with what would be expected from a logical standpoint. If florists were more likely than people in general to disagree with the item "I enjoy looking at flowers," then responses of "disagree" to that item would contribute positively to scores on the "florist" scale.

Several points concerning empirical test construction should be noted. First, the practical purposes of psychological testing have emphasized the capabilities of test scores to *predict* important real-world phenomena (e.g., mental illness, success or failure in a training program, satisfaction in an occupation). Since empirical test construction is based on the capacity of a test item to predict a criterion, rather than on consideration of item content, this approach has had considerable utility for applied purposes. Second, empirical test construction is based on a theoretical rationale which postulates that criterion groups differ from each other in ways that will be reflected in test scores. However, the ways in which groups will differ is not known or postulated a priori; it is discovered empirically, post hoc. Thus, the underlying rationale for test construction differs from that of the rational approach.

Finally, interpretation of empirically based test scores is in terms of the *similarity* of the individual's responses to those of various criterion groups, rather than in terms of item content. Unless we have familiarity with the specific items used in constructing the scale, we cannot make inferences about the person's *item* responses simply from knowledge of the test score. As an example, if an individual obtained a high score on a *rationally* constructed "florist" scale, we could say that the person had indicated a liking for activities associated with the occupation of florist (e.g., growing flowers). If, on the other hand, the high score was on an *empirically* constructed "florist" scale, we could say that the individual's pattern of likes and dislikes was similar to that of florists as a group, but

we could not necessarily make inferences about the kinds of things the individual reported liking and disliking, *unless* we knew the specific response patterns of florists.

Factor-Analytic Scale Construction. In factor-analytic scale construction a large pool of items, perhaps taken from many different tests, is factor-analyzed to determine the basic dimensions underlying the test items. These basic dimensions become the scales (i.e., the dimensions to be measured), and the items loading highly on each factor are those used in constructing the test. One of the first test batteries constructed in this way was the General Aptitude Test Battery (GATB), developed by the United States Employment Service (U.S. Department of Labor, 1970). Beginning in the 1930s, the Employment Service began the process of developing tests that would predict success in specific occupations. It soon became clear, however, that developing a test for each of the thousands of possible occupations would be an inefficient and never-ending effort. Accordingly, the items of the tests already developed were factor-analyzed. The results of the analysis indicated that there were nine basic dimensions of aptitudes, including numerical aptitude, spatial aptitude, manual dexterity, and finger dexterity. Tests of these nine factors were developed and constitute the GATB as it is today.

Factor analysis has also been used in the construction of personality inventories. For example, the Guilford-Zimmerman Temperament Survey (Guilford & Zimmerman, 1956) was based on factor analyses of the items from many personality tests. From these analyses, 10 basic dimensions of personality and 30 items measuring each dimension were specified and combined to constitute the personality inventory. Similarly, the Sixteen Personality Factor Questionnaire (16PF; Cattell, Eber, & Tatsuoka,

1970) was based on factor-analytic research directed at identifying primary or basic personality traits.

In interpreting factor-analytically derived test scores, one should keep in mind that the primary objective of this approach to test construction is the derivation of scales that are homogeneous (internally consistent) and relatively independent of each other. The primary criterion for item selection is that the item loads highly on that factor. Thus, factor-analytic approaches may provide a blend of the content-relevance of items found in the rational approach to test construction and the high correlation with a criterion (in this case the factor itself) found in the empirical approach to test construction.

Attitude Scale Construction. An *attitude* can be defined as one's view of or reactions toward a given class of stimuli. The stimuli can vary widely and could include such things as attitudes toward political candidates, racial/ethnic groups, women's roles in society, religion, gay lifestyles, abortion, etc. Other attitude measures would include those of job satisfaction, work values (e.g., money versus security, as discussed in Chapter 10), and commitment to one's career or company.

Although techniques of attitude scale construction are beyond the scope of this book, interested readers may wish to consult Dawis (1987), Fitzgerald and Hubert (1987), and Maranell (1974). Four well-known techniques are the Thurstone, Likert, and Guttman scales and the method of paired-comparisons. The first three techniques begin with statements about the stimulus object, to which respondents indicate the extent of their agreement. Let's say we wanted to assess "favorability of attitudes toward working mothers." To the statement "Mothers of young children should stay at home with their children," the respondent might choose from

Likert scale categories of Strongly Disagree, Disagree, Not Sure, Agree, and Strongly Agree. Each response would be assigned a numerical score, from 1 to 5 in this case, and the examinee's total score would indicate the extent to which he or she had favorable or unfavorable attitudes toward mothers working outside the home.

With Thurstone scales, items are scored or scaled in advance by using expert judges to rate each item on the dimension of favorableness toward the object of measurement. Then, an examinee's total score on the measure is the sum of the scale values of the items to which he or she responded "yes" or "agree." Again, let's say that expert judges rated the item "Mothers of young children should stay at home . . ." as a 1.5 on a 5-point scale of favorableness (where 5 is most favorable toward mothers working). An examinee responding "agree" to that item would receive a value of 1.5, to be cumulated along with the scale values of the other items with which the respondent agreed.

Guttman scales also assure a prior scoring ("scaling") of items. In constructing a Guttman scale, the test constructor's goal is to assemble a set of items so high in discriminating power that higher total scores are perfectly associated with responses to a given item.

Finally, in paired comparisons or "forced choice" scaling, a person selects from one of a pair of stimuli. Usually each stimulus is paired with every other stimulus, and the result is a ranking of the stimuli in order of preference. Paired comparisons (or its more primitive form, simple rank ordering of stimuli by the examinee) is used extensively in the assessment of work values and other types of preferences. The Minnesota Importance Questionnaire (described in detail in Chapter 10) uses paired comparisons to assess the examinee's preferences for 20 work values, such as security, advancement, and compensation.

Summary

In summary, knowledge of methods of test construction is extremely important to the test user for purposes of both evaluating and interpreting tests. For those also interested in constructing tests and/or scales, the previous discussion should provide a beginning point, to be followed by additional reading and study so that the tests constructed will be of good psychometric quality and yield meaningful and interpretable test scores.

SOURCES OF INFORMATION ABOUT TESTS

Chapters 2 and 3 have focused heavily on the various kinds of information needed for the effective use and evaluation of tests. Information regarding methods of test construction, reliability and validity, and norms is all necessary to informed and responsible test use. For example, if a test one is considering does not appear to be sufficiently reliable and/or if evidence for validity is lacking, the test should probably not be used for applied purposes (e.g., selection, placement, or counseling) or for research purposes other than studies further investigating the characteristics of the test itself.

To find out about the characteristics of a test, a variety of sources of information helpful to the potential test user is available. These sources of information are helpful in determining what tests are available, in evaluating their psychometric characteristics and potential utility for the user's needs, and in providing information regarding scoring, interpretation, and recommended uses of the test.

The major sources of information concerning available tests are Buros's *Tests in Print* and *Mental Measurements Yearbook* series. *Tests in Print* (1961) and *Tests in Print II* (1974) are comprehensive bibliographies covering all types of published tests available in English-speaking countries.

The *Mental Measurements Yearbook* series, probably the most important source of information about tests, was first published in 1938 and now comprises nine volumes, the ninth volume having been published in 1985. The yearbooks provide descriptive information, critical reviews by test experts, and a complete list of published references pertaining to each test. Information regarding publishers, price, forms, and the ages of subjects for whom the test is appropriate are also provided. In using the yearbooks it is important to note that each volume covers tests published during the period following publication of the previous volume; thus, the yearbooks are designed to supplement rather than supplant previous yearbooks.

An additional helpful source in the Buros series is volumes that reprint the information contained in all the yearbooks for a particular category of test. For example, monographs entitled *Vocational Tests and Reviews* (Buros, 1975c) and *Personality Tests and Reviews* (Buros, 1970) may be particularly useful for users interested in those types of tests.

The most direct source of information about tests is provided by the catalogues of test publishers and the manuals describing each test. A comprehensive list of test publishers and their addresses is provided in the *Mental Measurements Yearbook*. The test manual should provide the information necessary both to evaluate the psychometric properties and potential utility of the test and to effectively administer and interpret the test. Requirements concerning the kinds of information to be provided by test publishers are described more fully in the *Standards for Educational and Psychological Testing* (AERA, APA, & NCME, 1985).

Another excellent source of information is test reviews, which provide information to test users in terms of selection, use, and interpretation of test data. Test reviews are found in the *Mental Measurements Yearbook* series and in journals in the fields of psychology and education. For example, the journal *Measurement and Evaluation in Counseling and Development* contains test reviews in each issue; reviews of educational and vocational tests, like the Self-Directed Search and the Strong-Campbell Interest Inventory are most frequent. The *Journal of Educational Measurement* contains a section in which new, unpublished tests are described and reviewed.

Numerous other journals publish articles of interest to test users. *Educational and Psychological Measurement* includes a "Validity Studies" section in most of its issues; in a typical issue, studies of the validity of 10 to 15 tests may be reported. Most of the articles contained in *Applied Psychological Measurement* concern the development and evaluation of psychological measuring instruments; a recent article examining the reliability and validity of the Ghiselli Self-Description Inventory (see Raben, Snyder, Hoffman, & Farr, 1978) is illustrative. The *Journal of Consulting and Clinical Psychology* and the *Journal of Clinical Psychology* contain numerous articles examining measures of personality and psychopathology. Finally, other journals publishing articles of interest to test users include the *American Educational Research Journal, Journal of Counseling Psychology*, and the *Journal of Vocational Behavior*.

In addition to the previously described sources of test information, major tests like the Minnesota Multiphasic Personality Inventory (MMPI) and the Strong-Campbell Interest Inventory (SCII) have been the subject of entire books. For example, the books of Dahlstrom, Welsh, and Dahlstrom (1972, 1975) on the MMPI are recognized resources in the field.

Finally, ethical considerations in the use of tests are outlined in the *Standards for Educational and Psychological Testing* (1985) and in the ethical standards of relevant professional organizations (e.g., American Psychological Association, 1981). These issues are discussed more completely in Chapter 14, and should be part of the basis of knowledge of all test users.

SUMMARY

This chapter has described the concepts of reliability and validity and various methods of evaluating the reliability and validity of a psychological test or measure. Tests are only useful to the extent that they measure something in a consistent way and that what they measure is what we think they measure. The construction of a reliable and valid test or measure is not easy; it requires careful thought and considerable time and effort. Test construction is, however, a central basis for both theoretical and applied advances in the field of psychology, for until we can measure our constructs we cannot make effective use of them. Thus, for both the test developer and the test user, the evaluation of a test's reliability and validity should be viewed as a challenge that, although time-consuming, contributes to scientific progress and to the effective application of psychology to applied problems.

4

Objective Personality Assessment

The term *personality* has many meanings. (See Allport, 1937; Hall & Lindzey, 1970.) The "person" in personality suggests an individual identity having a certain uniqueness. Some view personality as a cluster of characteristics (abilities, interests, attitudes, and values) indicative of a pattern of behavior. Personality has also been defined as an individual's actual behavior in social situations. While there are many definitions of personality, we want to talk about personality in terms of assessment. Thus, for our purposes there are five different definitions of, or ways of thinking about, personality—stated differently, five different ways of collecting information about an individual's personality.

MODELS AND DEFINITIONS IN PERSONALITY PSYCHOLOGY

As in the assessment of intelligence and abilities, various conceptual models in personality psychology have stimulated considerable research and test development. The major models that have generated this work are the trait, the phenomenological, the psychodynamic, the situational, and the interactional models.

The *trait model* has clearly been the dominant force in personality research over the years (Endler & Magnusson, 1976a,b). This model assumes that human behavior may be ordered and measured along dimensions of defined traits (dominance, achievement, affiliation, and responsibility) and that individuals may be reasonably well characterized in terms of these defined traits. Thus, traits are viewed as the prime determinants of behavior in that they represent a person's tendencies to behave in certain ways regardless of environmental conditions. The trait model recognizes the impact of environmental or contextual conditions, but it suggests that traits are inner dispositions that tend to be associated with relatively consistent behavior across a variety of situations. In order to describe personality dimensions and explain individual differences, a variety of self-report tests, inventories, and questionnaires based on the trait model have been developed. Notice that the assumption made here is that self-reported behavior is a reliable and valid way of collecting information about actual behavior. Some examples of the self-report inventories based on the trait model are the Minnesota Multiphasic Personality Inventory, the California Psychological Inventory, the Omnibus Personality Inventory, and the Comrey Personality Scales. With its focus on person variables, the trait model has been our most productive means of understanding and exploring social behavior.

The *phenomenological model*, which focuses on the individual's subjective perceptions of the world, is also concerned with person factors (e.g., self-concept and subjective experiences). The individual's self-concept (picture of self) is thought to be the main determinant of behavior, and behavior is viewed as being reasonably consistent across different situations. Within this model and definition of personality, some hold that subjective experiences, for example, cannot be measured or quantified. However, others (Kelly, 1955; Rogers, 1951, 1961) have made efforts to operationalize the model by developing self-report inventories such as the Tennessee Self Concept Scale (Fitts, 1965). Again, notice the assumption that self-reported perceptions represent the individual's self concept (picture of self). In the main, this model and definition of personality has produced few tests and inventories.

The *psychodynamic model*, like the trait model and the phenomenological model, emphasizes person variables, but in a different sense. This basically Freudian model assumes a personality core made up of the id, the ego, and the superego. These personality elements and associated motives and instincts represent a person's tendencies to behave in certain ways. It is assumed that sources of behavior are within the individual and that behavior is relatively stable across a variety of situations. The basic assumption for assessment is that the individual's responses to vague or ambiguous stimuli (such as inkblots) tend to portray a personality style. In general, the projective techniques associated with the psychodynamic model are difficult to administer and interpret. Often the scores are not quantifiable, and thus reliability and validity are difficult to examine. In spite of limitations, projective methods are one way of collecting meaningful information about people. Some examples of projective methods are the Rorschach Test, the Thematic Apperception Test, the Rotter Incomplete Sentence Test, and the Draw-A-Person Test.

The *situational model* (or performance model) defines personality in terms of the individual's actual overt behavior. Behavior is assumed to be primarily a function of antecedent conditions or prior experiences. The individual's personality is defined in terms of what he or she does (behavior), and therefore personality is considered to be composed of a pattern of behavioral responses that the individual makes with some consistency. Here clients are not asked to report about themselves, but instead they are asked to perform (behaviorally) some task in a given situation. Behavior may then be discussed in terms of excesses, deficits, and appropriateness. The situational model is receiving considerable attention these days and producing a great number and variety of behavioral questionnaires. Other behavioral methods include self-observation and naturalistic observation.

A related behavioral approach involves the reports of others or assessment through the opinions of others: The individual's personality is in some respects defined through the observations and perceptions of other people. Examples of such methods are ratings of behavioral statements, ranking from highest to lowest, noting frequency of occurrence, and various nominating techniques on dimensions of friendship or cooperativeness. Although this kind of information is frequently used in a variety of settings, there is some concern about the adequacy of such information. For example, raters frequently disagree in their judgments or perceptions of the same person. The limitations do influence the stability and accuracy of the information collected using these methods; however, these methods continue to be a way of collecting information about people.

The final model, the *interactional model*, is mentioned here but dealt with comprehensively in Chapter 12's discussion of person-environment psychology. This model assumes that human behavior tends to be influenced by many determinants both in the person and in the situation (Mischel, 1977a). Thus, this model emphasizes person-situation interactions in personality and suggests that behavior involves a continuous interaction between individuals and situations (Endler & Magnusson, 1976a). To collect data, interactionists have developed tests,

questionnaires, and observational methods. However, a host of measurement problems are introduced when we attempt to develop inventories that simultaneously take into account individuals, responses, and situations. Suffice it to say that this model has been difficult to apply, but it does hold considerable hope for the future. Mounting evidence (Endler & Magnusson, 1976a; Magnusson & Endler, 1977a) indicates that behavior is much more a function of person-situation interactions than a function of person variables or situation variables.

The remainder of this chapter looks primarily at objective personality tests. Chapter 5 deals with projective and behavioral techniques. Although all inventories discussed here have reliability and validity limitations, they still represent useful ways of collecting meaningful information to help people cope with problems. As mentioned in Walsh (1989), we don't throw away a dull tool until we find a sharper one.

RESPONSE SETS

One other subject needs to be discussed before we consider tests of personality. An individual's observed score on a personality test may be determined to some extent by *response sets*, conscious or unconscious tendencies to answer test questions in a certain way. One such response set is *social desirability*, a tendency to respond in terms of what is believed to be right or appropriate as judged by society. Another response set that may influence personality test scores is *acquiescence*, tendency to agree, regardless of the question being asked or the content of the item. A third response set, *deviance*, is the tendency to make unusual answers to questions about personality.

The data over the years have not strongly supported the response set concept. However, in certain individual cases a response set may be a meaningful perspective from which to view test scores. An opposing opinion suggests that response tendencies comprise and/or reflect the individual's personality: If answers to questions about self are consistent with the individual's behavior, they are creditable and valid components of personality, not response sets. From this perspective the notion of response sets tends to have diminished meaning.

OBJECTIVE PERSONALITY TESTS

Most of the objective personality tests existing today are associated with the trait model. The trait model has been easier to use and implement than the other models of personality: It is simply more practical and applicable. Also, a number of personality researchers take the trait-model position that people may be reasonably well characterized in terms of 9 or 10 well-selected traits (Allport, 1937). Without question, this rather straightforward trait assumption has proved worthwhile in advancing our knowledge and understanding of social behavior, but, like most things, the trait approach has limitations. There are concerns that the approach is too mechanistic, static, and point-in-time oriented to adequately describe human behavior and development. In spite of limitations, the trait approach has produced a large number of useful person-centered inventories that afford us meaningful information about people.

As mentioned in earlier chapters, objective tests are so named because they produce an objective quantifiable score. The fact that an objective test produces a quantitative score means that the test results may be compared with the scores of others who have taken the same test under similar conditions.

In terms of format, the objective test asks a client to respond to questions (items) about self and in so doing uses self-reported behavior to estimate actual behavior. For example, on a scale of dominance a client might be asked to answer 20 questions about being aggressive, confident, persuasive, self-reliant, independent, and so on. The client simply reports whether the content of an item is present or absent in his or her behavior. The person's self-report is assumed to be an honest self-description. In addition, the assumption is made that the client who says yes to 16 of the items is more dominant than the person who says yes to 9 of the items. This example is oversimplified in some respects but in general represents the primary strategy of the objective test.

There are problems with the rather straightforward style of the objective test, some of which we commented on in Chapter 1 and some of which deserve to be mentioned again here. One is that the client may not report honestly. The client may deliberately distort or fake the test or inventory in order to get the desired job or promotion. This problem has led (as we shall see) to the construction of a number of scales that attempt to evaluate faking and distortion. Another problem may be that, because of a psychological disturbance or defensive reaction, the client may not be able to adequately describe self or behavior. Work by Silverman (1976) has shown that unconscious motives do in fact influence our behavior, as suggested by Freud some time ago. A third problem is that a client's self-perceptions (self-reports) may to some extent reflect situation variables and show variance from one context to another. Test questions (items) by and large do not take situational variables, or, for that matter, developmental variables, into account. All the above is simply repeating what we said before, namely, that tests certainly are not perfect. Like most things they have their limitations. Still they continue to be useful ways of collecting meaningful information about people.

A number of personality inventories use

self-reports to estimate actual behavior. The first major inventory of this type was the Personal Data Sheet developed by Robert Woodworth in 1920 to screen American army recruits for maladjustment. A second historical landmark was the development in 1943 of the Minnesota Multiphasic Personality Inventory by Starke Hathaway and Fred McKinley. This inventory has clearly withstood the test of time and is currently the most useful psychological test available for assessing emotional upset and/or psychological disturbance. It and a number of other objective personality inventories are discussed below. Remember that these inventories are not infallible, nor do they make decisions; but they are useful ways of collecting some meaningful information about people.

The California Psychological Inventory (CPI)

The California Psychological Inventory (CPI), developed by Harrison G. Gough (1968, 1975) and recently revised by Gough (1987), is intended primarily for use with reasonably well-adjusted individuals. The scales focus on the assessment of personality characteristics important for social living and social interaction. The total of 1,447 published studies using the CPI (Buros, 1978; Mitchell, 1985) is ample evidence of the wide use of the CPI in different research and practical settings. The CPI has been found to provide useful information related to social, educational, vocational, and family issues. For example, the CPI could be used to collect meaningful social interaction information for a college student with personal adjustment problems, to gather personality information for a very social college student who is interested in being a research chemist. In addition, the CPI has been effectively used with problems of asocial behavior and delinquency.

In its present 1987 form the CPI Test Booklet consists of 462 items (194 of which were taken from the Minnesota Multiphasic Personality Inventory) and produces 20 standard scores. In the revision of the CPI, 18 items were dropped, 29 items were changed in wording so as to make them easier to understand, and two new scales (Independence and Empathy) were added to the profile sheet. In addition, the new version of the CPI includes three new scales for use in assessing the underlying theoretical dimensions of the CPI. The inventory may be given under normal conditions beginning in the seventh grade, or at about age 13. The normative samples of 1,000 males and 1,000 females, on which the profile sheets are based, were assembled from the CPI archives so as to approach the general population in regard to age, education, and status. The mean standard score for each scale on the profile sheet is 50, with a standard deviation of 10.

The basic purpose of each scale is to identify individuals who behave in a certain way. Thus, the names of the scales were selected to describe as much as possible the kinds of behavior they are designed to reflect. For example, a person scoring high on the Sociability scale would probably be perceived by others as outgoing, enterprising, competitive, and forward; an individual scoring low on the Sociability scale would be perceived as conventional, quiet, and unassuming.

The scales are clustered together into four different classes on the profile sheet in order to facilitate interpretation. The scales are presented in a sequence moving from the more interactional socially observable qualities (e.g., Dominance), through a group of scales assessing internal values and control mechanisms (e.g., Responsibility), and ending with measures of stylish variables related to different functional modes (e.g., Flexibility). Cluster I (Measures of Poise, Ascendency, Self-Assurance, and Interpersonal Adequacy) consists of seven scales: Dominance, Capacity for Status, Sociability, Social Presence, Self-Acceptance, Independence, and Empathy. Cluster II (Measures of Socialization, Maturity, Responsibility, and Intrapersonal Structuring of Values) is made up of seven scales: Responsibility, Socialization, Self-Control, Good Impression, Communality, Sense of Well-Being, and Tolerance. Cluster III (Measures of Achievement Potential and Intellectual Efficiency) consists of three scales: Achievement via Conformance, Achievement via Independence, and Intellectual Efficiency. Cluster IV focuses on Measures of Intellectual and Interest Modes and is made up of three scales: Psychological-Mindedness, Flexibility, and Femininity/Masculinity. The CPI scale descriptions for high scorers and low scorers are reported in Figure 4.1.

In addition, as noted above, the 1987 version of the CPI includes three new scales for use in assessing the underlying theoretical dimensions of the CPI and in combination give rise to a model of personality. The first two scales assess Interpersonal orientation (externality to internality) and a Normative perspective (norm favoring to norm questioning). The combination of the Interpersonal and Normative orientations yields four ways of living or four kinds of people. These four lifestyles have been labelled Alpha, Beta, Gamma, and Delta types. The degree to which the potentials associated with these four lifestyles have been realized is indicated by the score on the Realization scale. Persons scoring high on the Realization scale tend to be reflective, capable, and optimistic concerning their present and future status. Low scorers perceive themselves to be vulnerable to life's traumas and not very fulfilled or actualized.

As noted above, the combination of the Interpersonal and Normative scales yields four ways of living or lifestyles. The manual (Gough, 1987) reports psychological expec-

tations attached to membership in each of the four categories. Alphas tend to be enterprising, dependable, and outgoing. Betas tend to be reserved, responsible, and moderate. Gammas tend to be adventurous, restless, and pleasure seeking. Deltas tend to be withdrawn, private, and to some extent disaffected.

Three scales may be used to detect faking or misrepresentation on the CPI: Good Impression, Sense of Well-Being, and Communality. The Good Impression scale is primarily concerned with identifying persons who are concerned about how others respond to them. However, very high scores on this scale suggest the possibility of either overconcern about making a good impression or test faking. The Sense of Well-Being scale primarily attempts to identify persons relatively free from self-doubt and worry. Below-average scores suggest some personal concerns, but very low scores may be suggestive of persons attempting to exaggerate their personal distress. This scale needs to be carefully interpreted, since a very low scale may reflect an honest report of personal distress or low sense of well-being. Average scores on the Communality scale tend to indicate that the individual has responded to the inventory in a conscientious manner. Very low scores introduce the possibility that the responses to the inventory have been given in some random or unmeaningful way. For additional information on these scales and their interpretation see the CPI Manual (Gough, 1987).

In terms of development, most of the scales were constructed using the empirical approach with an external criterion strategy. Four scales (Social Presence, Self-Acceptance, Self-Control, and Flexibility) were developed using the empirical approach, but with an internal consistency analysis. These and other methods of test construction were discussed in Chapter 3 and will not be reviewed here. For additional information on

Figure 4.1. The 20 Folk Concept Scales of the CPI and Their Intended Meanings

Scale Name	Intended Implications of Higher and Lower Scores	
Do (Dominance)	Higher:	confident, assertive, dominant, task-oriented
	Lower:	unassuming, not forceful
Cs (Capacity for Status)	Higher:	ambitious, wants to be a success, independent
	Lower:	unsure of self, dislikes direct competition
Sy (Sociability)	Higher:	sociable, likes to be with people, friendly
	Lower:	shy, feels uneasy in social situations, prefers to keep in the background
Sp (Social Presence)	Higher:	self-assured, spontaneous; a good talker; not easily embarrassed
	Lower:	cautious, hesitant to assert own views or opinions; not sarcastic or sharp-tongued
Sa (Self-acceptance)	Higher:	has good opinion of self; sees self as talented, and as personally attractive
	Lower:	self-doubting; readily assumes blame when things go wrong; often thinks others are better
In (Independence)	Higher:	self-sufficient, resourceful, detached
	Lower:	lacks self-confidence, seeks support from others
Em (Empathy)	Higher:	comfortable with self and well-accepted by others; understands the feelings of others
	Lower:	ill at ease in many situations; unempathic
Re (Responsibility)	Higher:	responsible, reasonable, takes duties seriously
	Lower:	not overly concerned about duties and obligations; may be careless or lazy
So (Socialization)	Higher:	comfortably accepts ordinary rules and regulations; finds it easy to conform
	Lower:	resists rules and regulations; finds it hard to conform; not conventional
Sc (Self-control)	Higher:	tries to control emotions and temper; takes pride in being self-disciplined
	Lower:	has strong feelings and emotions, and makes little attempt to hide them; speaks out when angry or annoyed
Gi (Good Impression)	Higher:	wants to make a good impression; tries to do what will please others
	Lower:	insists on being himself or herself, even if this causes friction or problems
Cm (Communality)	Higher:	fits in easily; sees self as a quite average person
	Lower:	sees self as different from others; does not have the same ideas, preferences, etc., as others
Wb (Well-being)	Higher:	feels in good physical and emotional health; optimistic about the future
	Lower:	concerned about health and personal problems; worried about the future
To (Tolerance)	Higher:	is tolerant of others' beliefs and values, even when different from or counter to own beliefs
	Lower:	not tolerant of others; skeptical about what they say
Ac (Achievement via Conformance)	Higher:	has strong drive to do well; likes to work in settings where tasks and expectations are clearly defined
	Lower:	has difficulty in doing best work in situations with strict rules and expectations

Figure 4.1. The 20 Folk Concept Scales of the CPI and Their Intended Meanings (continued)

Scale Name		Intended Implications of Higher and Lower Scores
Ai (Achievement via Independence)	Higher:	has strong drive to do well; likes to work in settings that encourage freedom and individual initiative
	Lower:	has difficulty in doing best work in situations that are vague, poorly defined, and lacking in clear-cut methods and standards
Ie (Intellectual Efficiency)	Higher:	efficient in use of intellectual abilities; can keep on at a task where others might get bored or discouraged
	Lower:	has a hard time getting started on things, and seeing them through to completion
Py (Psychological-mindedness)	Higher:	more interested in why people do what they do than in what they do; good judge of how people feel and what they think about things
	Lower:	more interested in the practical and concrete than the abstract; looks more at what people do than what they feel or think
Fx (Flexibility)	Higher:	flexible; likes change and variety; easily bored by routine life and everyday experience; may be impatient, and even erratic
	Lower:	not changeable; likes a steady pace and well-organized life; may be stubborn and even rigid
F/M (Femininity/Masculinity)	Higher:	sympathetic, helpful; sensitive to criticism; tends to interpret events from a personal point of view; often feels vulnerable
	Lower:	decisive, action-oriented; takes the initiative; not easily subdued; rather unsentimental

Reproduced with permission from the *Manual for the California Psychological Inventory* by Harrison G. Gough, pp. 6–7. Copyright 1987 by Consulting Psychologists Press, Inc., Palo Alto, Calif. 94306.

test construction see Megargee's (1972) *The California Psychological Inventory Handbook* and the manual (Gough, 1987).

Reliability coefficients for the scales of the CPI were computed on samples of 200 college males and 200 college females randomly drawn from the archival samples of college students. Alpha coefficients were also computed on the combined sample of 400 students (Gough, 1987). The Alpha coefficients for the male college students ranged from a low of 0.45 to a high of 0.85, with a median of 0.72. For females, the range was from 0.39 to 0.83, with a median of 0.73. The range for the total sample was 0.52 to 0.85.

Scale reliability was also explored via the test-retest method for a sample of high school students tested first in the eleventh grade and then a year later in the twelfth grade (Gough, 1987). The high school student samples consisted of 102 males and 128 females. Test-retest coefficients for males ranged from a low of 0.43 to a high of 0.76, with a median of 0.68. For females, the values ranged from a low of 0.58 to a high of 0.79, with a median of 0.71. Scale consistency, although lower than desirable, does not detract from the usefulness of the scales.

Most of the 1,447 studies investigating the validity of the CPI have explored the concurrent or predictive validity of the CPI scales. In general, validity coefficients for individual scales tend to be low, but the use of multiple scales to predict certain criteria has been more successful. For example, through the use of multiple regression techniques the CPI scales have been used to predict delinquency, leadership, parole outcome, college attendance among bright students, high school graduation, high school grades, college grades, performance in student teaching, and achievement in dental school, medical school, optometry, accounting, business, health care, computer programming, mathematics, and nursing. Additional information on validity and interpretation may be found in "An Interpretive Syllabus for the California Psychological Inventory" by Gough (1968), *The California Psychological Inventory Handbook* by Megargee (1972), and *A Practical Guide to CPI Interpretation* (McAllister, 1986).

In terms of interpretation, the name of the CPI scale serves as a guide as to the scale's meaning. A sample CPI profile (Case 4) interpretation is given in Figure 4.2. The basic purpose of each scale is to identify individuals who tend to behave in certain ways. Individuals scoring above average on a given scale tend to evidence more behavior consistent with the high scorers' description.

Individuals scoring below average on a given scale demonstrate more behavior consistent with the low scorers' description. Scale overlap contributes to some overlap in the high and low scorers' descriptions, which ultimately led to clustering the scales in order to facilitate interpretation. In general, the characteristics of high and low scorers tend to be more descriptive than behavioral in nature.

The Omnibus Personality Inventory (OPI)

The Omnibus Personality Inventory (OPI) was developed by Heist and Yonge (1968) for use in research on college students. The personality dimensions assessed (see Figure 4.3) are primarily concerned with effective functioning in college settings. These OPI dimensions were selected for their relevance to academic activity and for their importance in understanding the college student. Thus, in constructing the inventory, emphasis was placed on the assessment of intellectual versus nonintellectual values and interests, liberal versus conservative attitudes, and social emotional adjustment (Heist & Yonge, 1968). An additional feature of the OPI is its focus on the intrinsic characteristics of learning.

The OPI test booklet is composed of 385 true/false items, 88 percent of which were taken from 13 other tests, including the Minnesota Multiphasic Personality Inventory and the California Psychological Inventory. The inventory is used with college students to assess academic activity and social adjustment. Norms are based on standard scores for 3,540 male and 3,743 female college freshmen at 37 diverse institutions. The mean standard score for each scale is 50, with a standard deviation of 10. Raw scores are transformed to standard scores using a table in the manual.

The purposes of the OPI scales were to provide a meaningful description of college students and a means of assessing change on dimensions of academic activity and social adjustment. The evidence indicates that individuals scoring above average on a given scale tend to reflect certain values, attitudes, and behaviors. For example, people scoring above average on the Thinking Introversion scale are characterized by a liking for reflective thought, academic activities, and ideas. Low scorers would tend to be more practical and action oriented.

On the OPI profile sheet used to record a subject's scores, the scales make up three different groupings that tend to assist the interpretive process (shadings on the profile sheet indicate these groupings). The

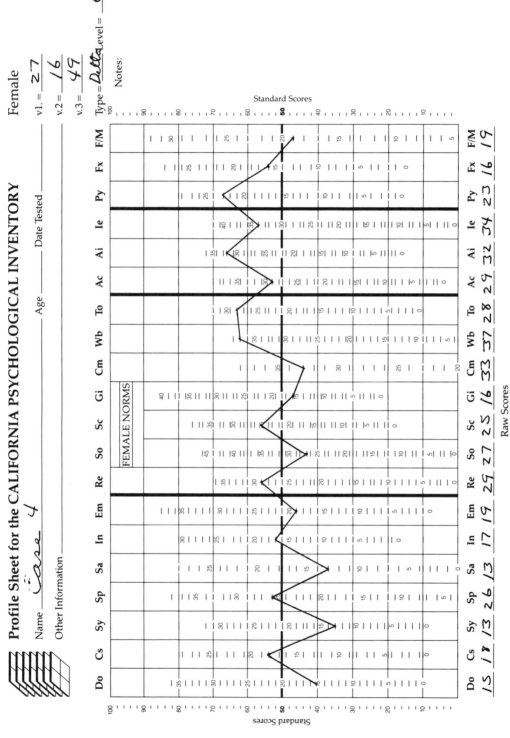

Figure 4.2. CPI Profile of a Successful Woman in Early Middle Age (Case 4). (Reproduced with permission from the California Psychological Inventory Administrator's Guide, by Harrison G. Gough, pp. 81–82. Copyright © 1987 by Consulting Psychologists Press, Inc., Palo Alto, Calif. 94306).

FEMALE NORMS

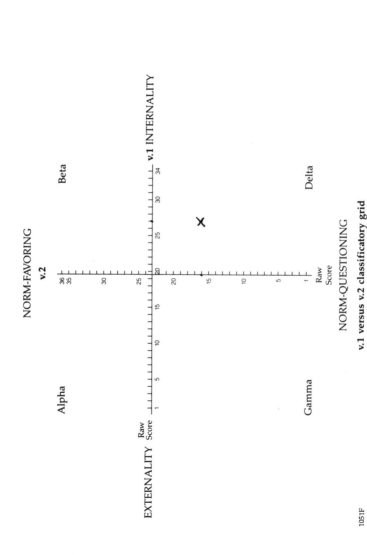

EXTERNALITY

NORM-FAVORING
v.2

Alpha

Beta

v.1 INTERNALITY

Raw Score

Gamma

NORM-QUESTIONING

Delta

Raw Score

v.1 versus v.2 classificatory grid

1051F

v.3

Level

Raw Score
REALIZATION

CASE 4

This is a woman in early middle-age, with two children, married to an eminent scholar. She herself is a very successful person in the same field as her husband, with a national if not an international reputation for her work. Her CPI Type/Level classification is Delta-6, indicating an excellent resolution of the problems and potentialities of the Delta way of life. She is an internally-oriented individual, private and highly articulated in her thoughts and fancies. Her values and preferences are her own, not merely the internalization of the norm or status quo. from the personological side, she is capable of creative innovation at her best, but of inner conflict and warring polarities at her worst.

97

1. *Thinking Introversion* (TI): Persons scoring high on this measure are characterized by a liking for reflective thought and academic activities. They express interests in a broad range of ideas found in a variety of areas, such as literature, art, and philosophy.

2. *Theoretical Orientation* (TO): High scorers indicate a preference for dealing with theoretical concerns and problems and for using the scientific method in thinking. High scorers are generally logical, analytical, and critical in their approach to problems and situations.

3. *Estheticism* (Es): High scorers endorse statements indicating diverse interests in artistic matters and activities and a high level of sensitivity and response to esthetic stimulation.

4. *Complexity* (Co): High scorers are tolerant of ambiguities and uncertainties; they are fond of novel situations and ideas. Very high scorers are disposed to seek out and to enjoy diversity and ambiguity.

5. *Autonomy* (Au): High scorers show a tendency to be independent of authority as traditionally imposed through social institutions. They oppose infringements on the rights of individuals and are tolerant of viewpoints other than their own; they tend to be realistic, intellectually and politically liberal, and much less judgmental than low scorers.

6. *Religious Orientation* (RO): High scorers are skeptical of conventional religious beliefs and practices. Persons scoring around the mean are manifesting a moderate view of religious beliefs and practices; low scorers are manifesting a strong commitment to Judaic-Christian beliefs.

7. *Social Extroversion* (SE): High scorers display a strong interest in being with people, and they seek social activities and gain satisfaction from them.

8. *Impulse Expression* (IE): High scorers have an active imagination, value sensual reactions and feelings; very high scorers have frequent feelings of rebellion and aggression.

9. *Personal Integration* (PI): The high scorer admits to few attitudes and behaviors that characterize socially alienated or emotionally disturbed persons. Low scorers often intentionally avoid others and experience feelings of hostility and aggression along with feelings of isolation, loneliness, and rejection.

10. *Anxiety Level* (AL): High scorers deny that they have feelings or symptoms of anxiety, and do not admit to being nervous or worried. Low scorers describe themselves as tense and high-strung.

11. *Altruism* (Am): The high scorer is an affiliative person and trusting and ethical in his relations with others. He has a strong concern for the feelings and welfare of people he meets. Low scorers tend not to consider the feelings and welfare of others and often view people from an impersonal, distant perspective.

12. *Practical Outlook* (PO): The high scorer on this measure is interested in practical, applied activities and tends to value material possessions and concrete accomplishments.

13. *Masculinity-Femininity* (MF): High scorers deny interests in esthetic matters, and they admit to few adjustment problems, (feelings of anxiety, or personal inadequacies). Low scorers, besides having stronger esthetic and social inclinations, also admit to greater sensitivity and emotionality.

14. *Response Bias* (RB): High scorers are responding in a manner similar to a group of students who were explicitly asked to make a good impression by their responses to these items. Low scorers, on the contrary, may be trying to make a bad impression or are indicating a low state of well-being or feelings of depression.

Figure 4.3 OPI Scale Descriptions. (Reproduced by permission from the Omnibus Personality Inventory. Copyright © 1968 by The Psychological Corporation. All Rights Reserved.)

first four scales (Thinking Introversion, Theoretical Orientation, Estheticism, and Complexity) are called the Intellectual scales and focus on a person's interests in working with ideas and abstractions. The next two scales (Autonomy and Religious Orientation) are the Liberalism, or Nonauthoritarian, scales and are concerned with an individual's freedom to learn. The third group (Social Extroversion, Impulse Expression, Personal Integration, and Anxiety Level) focus on Social-Emotional Adjustment. The remaining scales (Altruism, Practical Outlook, and Masculinity-Femininity) are not members of a group. One additional score may be obtained from a weighted combination of six scales (Thinking Introversion, Theoretical Orientation, Estheticism, Complexity, Autonomy, and Religious Orientation). These six scales follow in consecutive order on the profile sheet and make up a continuum of Intellectual Disposition ranging from not intellectual to broadly intellectual interests—or, stated differently, the Intellectual Disposition score represents a continuum from vocational orientation to intrinsic learning for its own sake. This emphasis on intellectual variables is probably the unique feature of the OPI. Very few other personality inventories reflect this kind of intellectual orientation.

One scale, Response Bias, has been developed to detect faking on the OPI. This scale attempts to evaluate the student's test-taking attitude by assessing the individual's motivation to make a good impression. High scorers tend to be responding in a style similar to a group of students asked to make a good impression by their answers to the items. It may also be that low scorers are attempting to make a bad impression. However, a low score needs to be interpreted carefully because such a score may represent an honest report of depression or low state of well-being (Heist & Yonge, 1968).

The OPI manual (Heist & Yonge, 1968) has little to say about scale development. What information is available suggests the use of a content, or rational, approach to scale construction. This approach follows a rather logical procedure that assumes a firm relationship between a person's self-report and the person's internal state and/or behavior.

In order to estimate the reliability of the OPI, a test-retest procedure was used for two different samples. The time between the two administrations for both samples was between three and four weeks. The stability coefficients on a sample of 67 women attending three different colleges ranged from 0.79 to 0.94. Stability coefficients for 71 upperclassmen at one college ranged from 0.84 to 0.93. Most of the coefficients fell above 0.85, suggesting overall reasonable scale reliability for the OPI. For additional information on estimates of reliability see the manual (Heist & Yonge, 1968).

Concurrent validity has been explored by looking at the correlations with a variety of other inventories, including the California Psychological Inventory; the Myers-Briggs Type Indicator; the Edwards Personal Preference Schedule; the Strong Vocational Interest Blank; the Minnesota Multiphasic Personality Inventory; the Allport, Vernon, and Lindzey Study of Values; and the Kuder Preference Record (Vocational). In general, these obtained correlation coefficients are consistent with expectations and suggest that the OPI scales are related to similar scales on other tests. For example, the correlations between the Altruism scale and scores on the Economic ($r = -0.48$) and Social ($r = 0.46$) scales of the Study of Values are consistent with the interpretation that the altruistic person is not materially oriented, but more concerned for the welfare of others. Additional types of validity data are needed, and some attempts have been made to explore various scale scores and actual behavior.

Although the OPI was primarily developed for research purposes, it does seem to have some meaningful applications in counseling and assessment. For example, counselors have found the OPI valuable in obtaining information on academic motivation and intellectual orientation. Such information may be helpful in understanding why a student's performance is inconsistent with his or her ability. Scores on the Autonomy and Religious Orientation scales may be suggestive of authority problems or a student's readiness for new experiences. The four Social-Emotional Adjustment scales may suggest personal concerns or a disturbing level of anxiety.

In interpreting OPI scores, it is helpful to interpret the Intellectual scales together, then the Liberalism scales, and then the Social-Emotional Adjustment scales. In addition, these scale clusters tend to take into account scale relationships and overlap in scale descriptions. On most scales, persons with standard scores of 60 or above may to some extent be appropriately characterized by the definition of attitudes, interests, and values illustrated in the sample profile interpretation in Figure 4.4.

Student C: Interpretation of Scores. The OPI scores for Student C, in Figure 4.4, result from administration of the OPI at the time of the student's enrollment in a large state university in the Midwest. The interesting pattern of scores represents the responses of a young woman who is considerably above average in her interest in the world of ideas and in scholastic activities, as indicated by the first four scales, Thinking Introversion (TI) through Complexity (Co). Noteworthy in these scores is the level of the Theoretical Orientation (TO) score falling significantly above the Estheticism (Es) score, especially with the high elevation on the Co scale. This pattern implies a readiness to pursue work in areas involving analytical thinking, mathematics, and scientific concerns.

The high Co score, together with the Autonomy (Au) and Religious Orientation (RO) elevations, indicates an openness to new thoughts and ideas, if not a need to seek out the new and the different. This generally strong orientation to learn and to experience may be amplified by the motivational concomitants implied in the Impulse Expression (IE) score being above a standard score of 60. However, in view of the low Personal Integration (PI) and Anxiety Level (AL) scores, it may well be that Student C flits from one immediate experience to another without integrating or learning much of anything from these experiences. The Au and RO pattern, with the second score being exceedingly high for a student from a Protestant background, probably indicates a freedom and emancipation of behavior somewhat beyond the social-emotional development of the individual.

The general consistency in the pattern for the scores in the first six scales is not found for the scales encompassed by the third factor, Social Extroversion (SE) through Anxiety Level (AL). Here we find the extremes of the relatively high IE score and the low pattern on the other three. The Altruism (Am) and Response Bias (RB) scores, also below the mean, serve to indicate further a definite degree of difficulty in Student C's relationships with others and acceptance of self. The IE score probably denotes some feelings of strong aggression and hostility, along with a basic impulsiveness. However, with Student C's tendencies toward rational thinking (TI and TO scores) and her mild introversion-alienation (SE, PI, and Am), her aggression will be directed more toward herself than toward others. In brief, the social-emotional problems manifested through Student C's scores must be seen as factors complicating her early achievement and ease of relationships in the large, public university.

The Comrey Personality Scales (CPS)

The Comrey Personality Scales (CPS) developed by Andrew L. Comrey (1970) are intended primarily for use with "normal," socially functioning individuals. Based on existing research, the eight scales were constructed to represent the major factors determining and describing personality (see Figure 4.5). It is predicted that the CPS will find its greatest use in school, college, and business environments.

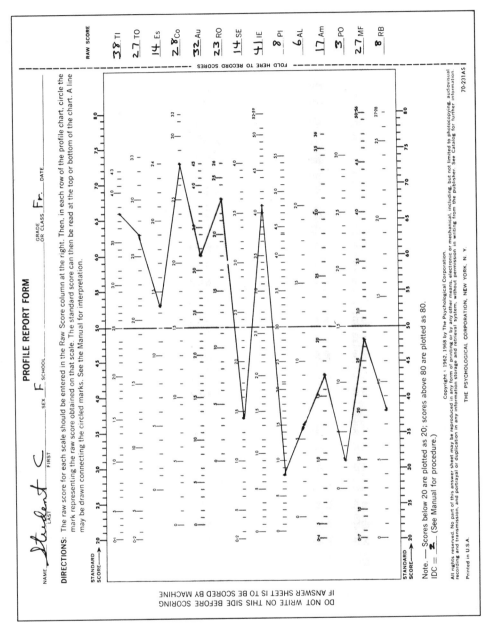

Figure 4.4 OPI Profile of Student C, a Female College Freshman Enrolled at a Large State University. (Reproduced with permission from the Omnibus Personality Inventory. Copyright © 1968 by the Psychological Corporation. All Rights Reserved.)

101

Interpretation of scores

V **Validity Check.** A score of 8 is the expected raw score. Any score on the V scale which gives a T-score equivalent below 70 is still within the normal range, however. Higher scores are suggestive of an invalid record.

R **Response Bias.** High scores indicate a tendency to answer questions in a socially desirable way, making the respondent look like a "nice" person.

T **Trust vs Defensiveness.** High scores indicate a belief in the basic honesty, trustworthiness and good intentions of other people.

O **Orderliness vs Lack of Compulsion.** High scores are characteristic of careful, meticulous, orderly, and highly organized individuals.

C **Social Conformity vs Rebelliousness.** Individuals with high scores accept the society as it is, resent non-conformity in others, seek the approval of society, and respect the law.

A **Activity vs Lack of Energy.** High-scoring individuals have a great deal of energy and endurance, work hard, and strive to excel.

S **Emotional Stability vs Neuroticism.** High-scoring persons are free of depression, optimistic, relaxed, stable in mood, and confident.

E **Extraversion vs Introversion.** High-scoring individuals meet people easily, seek new friends, feel comfortable with strangers, and do not suffer from stage fright.

M **Masculinity vs Femininity.** High-scoring individuals tend to be rather tough-minded people who are not bothered by blood, crawling creatures, vulgarity, and who do not cry easily or show much interest in love stories.

P **Empathy vs Egocentrism.** High-scoring individuals describe themselves as helpful, generous, sympathetic people who are interested in devoting their lives to the service of others.

Figure 4.5 CPS Scale Descriptions. (Reproduced with permission from the *Profile and Interpretation Sheet* for the Comrey Personality Scales by Andrew M. Comrey. Copyright 1970 by the Educational and Industrial Testing Service, San Diego, Calif. 92107.)

The CPS test booklet is reasonable in length: 160 items comprising ten scales, two of which attempt to identify faked profiles. The response format is somewhat different from other personality tests, in that clients respond to the items using two 7-point Likert scales, one ranging from "always" to "never" and the other from "definitely" to "definitely not." The inventory has been used extensively with college students, but past experience indicates that it may be used in the 16–60 age range. Norms are based on standard scores (*T*-scores) for 365 male and 362 female university students, their friends, family members, and other university-affiliated people. As mentioned in the manual (Comrey, 1970), these norm groups are small, and additional norm groups may be needed, depending upon the situation in which the inventory is being used. The mean standard score for each scale is 50, and the standard deviation is 10.

The CPS inventory was developed to assess the major personality dimensions descriptive of the "normal" personality. Scores on the scales indicate what you say about yourself, in comparison with what other people say about themselves. More specifically, a high score on a given trait suggests that the client tends to be very much like the CPS description of that trait. For example, a high score on the Trust vs. Defensiveness scale suggests a person who tends to believe in the basic honesty, trustworthiness, and good intentions of people. Low scorers, who tend to be just the opposite of the CPS trait description, would be somewhat more cynical and suspicious about the intentions of others.

Two scales have been developed to detect faking on the CPS: Validity Check and

Response Bias. The Response Bias scale attempts to identify individuals responding in a socially desirable way. In other words, a high score may suggest that the individual is trying to look good or like a "nice person" compared to others, while a low score may suggest that a person is trying to look unrealistically bad compared to others. However, keep in mind that such scores may be viewed from different perspectives and that a high score may accurately reflect an individual who is honest, considerate, and unselfish when compared to others. At the same time it is possible that an individual lacks self-knowledge or, because of existing concerns, honestly reports a poor impression of self. The Validity Check scale consists of items that, theoretically, should be answered with extreme responses (i.e., "always"/"never" or "definitely"/"definitely not"). Examples of such items are "If I were asked to lift a ten-ton weight, I could do it" and "When I wake up in the morning, my heart is beating." The manual suggests that any score on the Validity Check scale that gives a T-score of 70 or below is within the normal range. Higher scores tend to suggest an invalid profile.

A factor-based construct approach was used in developing the CPS. Early studies using the Minnesota Multiphasic Personality Inventory and additional research were undertaken in order to identify important dimensions of personality. Ideas and data from these early studies provided the basis for developing a factor-analytic taxonomy of personality traits. As we pointed out previously, the factor-analytic approach stresses the importance of couching the test development process in an empirical data base.

To obtain reliability estimates of the factor scales, a split-half procedure was used by dividing each personality factor scale into two equivalent halves. Split-half reliability coefficients for the scales, based on 746 volunteer subjects (362 males and 384 females), ranged from 0.87 to 0.96, with a median of 0.93. Coefficients for the Validity Check scale ($r = 0.45$) and the Response Bias scale ($r = 0.62$) were lower. In general, these data suggest that the personality factor scales tend to be internally consistent. Additional reliability information such as test-retest data would be desirable.

The concurrent validity of the CPS has been explored by looking at the relationships between the CPS and other investigators' scales of personality factors: the Guilford-Zimmerman Temperament Survey, the Cattell Sixteen Personality Factor Questionnaire, and the Eysenck Personality Inventory. Some of the relationships between the CPS and the Guilford-Zimmerman survey and the Eysenck inventory are reasonable and consistent with expectations. Many of the factors have been confirmed with different types of samples, but evidence is only beginning to accumulate concerning the relationships between the CPS and behavioral criteria (Comrey, 1970). One such study (Knecht, Cundick, Edwards, & Gunderson, 1972) found in a sample of 135 undergraduate students at Appalachian State University (North Carolina) that those scoring high on Social Conformity and Orderliness reported less use of marijuana. In a review of the CPS, Howarth (1978) suggests that it is one of the better-constructed inventories using the factor-based construct approach. Additional information on validity may be located in the CPS manual (Comrey, 1970).

The manual indicates that the CPS may be used in research, in schools and colleges, in counseling, in clinics, and in business and industry (Comrey, 1970). The inventory has been used most extensively with college students, and colleges probably continue to be the most meaningful context for using the CPS. Although the CPS was developed to assess normal personality rather than psychological pathology, initial evidence suggests that, for clinical purposes, extremely high or low scores on the scales may be associated with lifestyle problems and difficulties in life adjustment. For example, Comrey suggests in the manual that very low scores on the Emotional Stability vs. Neuroticism scale may be indicative of serious personality difficulties. In sum, more research findings are needed to document the value, and the clinical and other uses of the CPS.

For interpretive purposes the traits of the CPS are primarily concerned with describing normal personality and represent what an individual reports about self, in comparison with what other people report about themselves. It is assumed that all persons to some extent ·possess the traits represented by the Comrey scales. The scales are interpreted individually, although some scale overlap does exist (e.g., the relationship between Orderliness vs. Lack of Compulsion and Social Conformity vs. Rebelliousness is 0.47). Scores between 40 and 60 are reported to be in the average range. A high score suggests that the individual is very similar to the scale trait description. A low score suggests that the person is just the opposite of the scale trait description. A score in the average range indicates that the individual tends to be neither like nor unlike the scale trait description. For example, a high score on the Orderliness vs. Lack of Compulsion scale suggests that the individual is careful, orderly, and organized. A low score suggests that a person tends to be careless and untidy.

Figure 4.6 presents a sample CPS profile, representing a 30-year-old first-year female graduate student in counseling psychology. The above-average (T-scores of 60 or above) scores on this profile suggest a person who is concerned about the social impression she makes and who wants to be perceived as a nice person. The high scores on the Activity vs. Lack of Energy and Emotional Stability vs. Neuroticism scales indicate that this individual has a great deal of energy, works hard, strives for excellence,

and is optimistic and confident. The high score on the Extraversion vs. Introversion scale further suggests a sociable person who meets people easily, seeks new friends, and feels comfortable with strangers.

The Jackson Personality Inventory (JPI)

The Jackson Personality Inventory (JPI; Jackson, 1976a) was developed primarily for use with reasonably well-adjusted people of average or above-average intelligence. The scales (see Figure 4.7) assess personality on a variety of interpersonal, cognitive, and value orientations believed to be relevant to the functioning of a person in a variety of interpersonal and performance oriented settings.

The JPI consists of 320 true/false items comprising 16 scales, 15 substantive scales and 1 validity scale to assess faked profiles. The inventory may be used with grades 10 through 16 and with adults. The wording is such that the average high school student should have no trouble responding. The JPI may be hand-scored in about 10 minutes. The norms are based on standard scores for 2,000 males and 2,000 females drawn from 43 North American colleges and universities. Sampling procedures were designed to ensure that the college students participating represented the various college ranks (freshmen, sophomore, junior, and senior). The mean standard score for each scale is 50, and the standard deviation is 10. In addition, separate high school norms are available, based on 400 male and 554 female eleventh and twelfth grade students.

The JPI was developed on the assumption that all individuals to some extent possess the traits assessed by the personality scales. It was further assumed that the higher a person's score on a given scale is, the greater the probability is that the person will evi-

COMREY PERSONALITY SCALES

PROFILE SHEET

PUBLISHED BY
EDUCATIONAL AND INDUSTRIAL TESTING SERVICE
SAN DIEGO, CALIFORNIA 92107

Name *Graduate Student* Occupation *Psychology*

Address ______

City ______ Schooling Completed ______

State ______ Zip ______ Age *30* Date ______

SCORES:

- V Validity
- R Response Bias
- T Trust vs Defensiveness
- O Orderliness vs Lack of Compulsion
- C Social Conformity vs Rebelliousness
- A Activity vs Lack of Energy
- S Emotional Stability vs Neuroticism
- E Extraversion vs Introversion
- M Masculinity vs Femininity
- P Empathy vs Egocentrism

FEMALE NORMS

T	V	R	T	O	C	A	S	E	M	P
79	29	74	124	133	122	133	134	138	114	134
77	27	73	122	126	119	127	130	133	104	132
75	26	72	120	123	117	125	128	130	101	130
73	25	71	118	121	115	123	126	128	99	129
71	23	70	116	119	112	121	124	126	97	128
69	22	65	114	116	109	117	122	124	95	127
67	21	64	112	115	107	115	120	121	93	126
65	19	61	108	111	104	112	116	118	89	123
63	18	59	106	108	102	109	114	113	86	121
61	17	57	103	104	100	107	112	110	84	118
59	16	56	101	101	98	104	110	107	81	115
57	15	54	99	98	95	101	108	103	77	111
55	14	52	97	95	90	98	105	99	74	109
53	13	50	94	92	86	96	102	95	71	106
51	12	49	91	89	82	93	98	92	68	102
49	11	48	88	86	78	90	94	88	65	99
47	10	46	85	83	74	87	90	84	63	96
45	9	44	82	80	69	84	86	81	59	93
43	9	42	80	77	65	81	82	76	56	89
41	9	41	77	74	61	78	78	72	53	85
39	9	40	75	71	58	76	75	70	51	82
37	8	38	73	68	54	73	71	65	49	79
35		37	71	65	50	69	66	61	46	76
33		35	68	62	45	64	61	53	43	74
31		34	66	59	42	61	58	50	41	72
29		33	64	56	40	58	54	48	39	70
27		32	59	53	39	57	52	45	38	68
25		31	54	50	37	56	50	42	37	66
23		30	50	45	35	54	43	38	35	57
21		29	47	38	33	50	37	32	30	49
T	V	R	T	O	C	A	S	E	M	P
	14	*73*	*100*	*80*	*98*	*120*	*111*	*117*	*74*	*104*

MALE NORMS

V	R	T	O	C	A	S	E	M	P	T
29	68	119	131	125	131	129	136	120	132	79
28	66	114	124	118	127	127	134	118	126	77
27	64	113	117	114	125	125	131	116	125	75
	62	112	114	111	123	124	128	114	124	73
26	60	111	112	109	122	122	125	112	123	71
25	59	108	110	105	121	121	122	111	121	69
24	58	105	108	102	120	120	117	109	119	67
22	56	101	106	99	116	118	112	106	117	65
21	54	99	102	96	112	115	108	103	113	63
19	52	97	99	93	109	113	103	101	110	61
18	51	95	96	91	107	111	99	99	107	59
17	50	93	93	87	105	109	96	97	104	57
16	48	91	90	83	101	106	93	95	101	55
15	46	89	87	79	98	103	90	92	98	53
14	45	87	83	74	96	100	87	89	95	51
13	43	84	80	70	93	96	84	87	92	49
12	41	81	77	66	90	93	80	85	89	47
11	40	78	74	62	87	89	76	83	86	45
10	39	76	72	58	84	84	74	80	83	43
9	37	73	69	55	81	80	71	78	80	41
	36	70	67	52	78	77	68	75	77	39
8	35	67	65	49	75	73	64	73	74	37
	33	62	61	46	71	68	60	71	71	35
	31	60	56	42	67	64	56	68	67	33
	30	58	53	40	64	61	53	65	65	31
	29	55	50	38	62	59	50	61	63	29
	28	52	48	36	60	56	47	58	60	27
	27	49	46	35	54	52	43	53	57	25
	25	45	44	34	45	49	39	47	52	23
	23	38	39	28	30	43	30	36	39	21
V	R	T	O	C	A	S	E	M	P	T

Figure 4.6 CPS Profile of a Graduate Student in Psychology. (Reproduced with permission from the *Profile and Interpretation Sheet* for the Comrey Personality Scales by Comrey, 1970).

Figure 4.7 JPI Scale Descriptions for High Scorers and Low Scorers

TRAIT DESCRIPTIONS FOR THE JACKSON PERSONALITY INVENTORY

Scale	Description of High scorer	Defining trait Adjectives of High scorer	Description of Low scorer	Defining trait Adjectives of Low scorer
Anxiety	Tends to worry over inconsequential matters; more easily upset than the average person; apprehensive about the future.	Worried, tense, nervous, preoccupied, anxious, edgy, distressed, agitated, fearful.	Remains calm in stressful situations; takes things as they come without worrying; can relax in difficult situations; usually composed and collected.	Easy-going, patient, calm, serene, tranquil, relaxed, contented, placid, imperturbable.
Breadth of Interest	Is attentive and involved; motivated to participate in a wide variety of activities; interested in learning about a diversity of things.	Curious, interested, inquiring, involved, inquisitive, seeking, exploring.	Has narrow range of interests, remains uninterested when exposed to new activities; has few hobbies; confined tastes.	Inflexible, unobservant, narrow, insular, uninvestigative.
Complexity	Seeks intricate solutions to problems; is impatient with oversimplification; is interested in pursuing topics in depth regardless of their difficulty; enjoys abstract thought; enjqys intricacy.	Complex, contemplative, clever, discerning, intellectual, thoughtful, analytical.	Prefers concrete to abstract interpretations; avoids contemplative thought, uninterested in probing for new insight.	Uncomplicated, unreflective, straightforward, predictable, matter-of-fact.
Conformity	Is susceptible to social influence and group pressures; tends to modify behavior to be consistent with standards set by others; follows suit; fits in.	Compliant, agreeing, acquiescent, adapting, accomodating, cooperative, concurring, emulating.	Refuses to go along with the crowd; unaffected and unswayed by others' opinions; independent in thought and action.	Individualistic, self-directed, self reliant, unyielding, nonconforming, unrestricted, contradicting, disagreeing.
Energy Level	Is active and spirited; possesses reserves of strength; does not tire easily; capable of intense work or recreational activity for long periods of time.	Lively, vigorous, active, persevering, industrious, tireless, dynamic, enthusiastic, eager.	Tires quickly and easily; avoids strenuous activities; lacks stamina; requires a great deal of rest; slow to respond.	Passive, listless, drowsy, lazy, languid.
Innovation	A creative and inventive individual, capable of originality of thought; motivated to develop novel solutions to problems; values new ideas; likes to improvise.	Ingenious, original, innovative, productive, imaginative.	Has little creative motivation; seldom seeks originality; conservative thinker; prefers routine activities.	Unimaginative, deliberate, practical, sober, prosaic, literal, uninventive, routine.

Interpersonal Affect	Tends to identify closely with other people and their problems; values close emotional ties with others; concerned about others.	Emotional, tender, kind, affectionate, demonstrative, warmhearted, sympathetic, compassionate.	Emotionally aloof; prefers impersonal to personal relationships; displays little compassion for other people's problems; has trouble relating to people; is emotionally unresponsive to those around him.	Unresponsive, distant, hard-hearted, taciturn, unsentimental, indifferent, cold.
Organization	Makes effective use of time; completes work on schedule; is not easily distracted.	Orderly, disciplined, planful, tidy, consistent, methodical, precise, neat, meticulous, systematic.	Frequently procrastinates; easily distracted; falls behind in assignments or duties; often loses things; personal effects frequently in disarray; handles situations in an unsystematic, unpredictable way; rarely plans before doing things.	Disorganized, inefficient, orderless, absentminded, forgetful.
Responsibility	Feels a strong obligation to be honest and upright; experiences a sense of duty to other people; has a strong and inflexible conscience.	Responsible, honest, ethical, incorruptible, scrupulous, dependable, conscientious, reliable, stable, straightforward.	Apathetic about helping others; frequently breaks a promise; takes little interest in community projects; can't be relied on to meet obligations; refuses to be held to answer for his actions.	Unreliable, indifferent, unfair, remiss, neglectful, thoughtless, negligent, inconsiderate, self-centered, careless.
Risk Taking	Enjoys gambling and taking a change; willingly exposes self to situations with uncertain outcomes; enjoys adventures having an element of peril; takes chances; unconcerned with danger.	Reckless, bold, impetuous, intrepid, enterprising, incautious, venturesome, daring, rash.	Cautious about unpredictable situations; unlikely to bet; avoids situations of personal risk, even those with great rewards; doesn't take chances regardless of whether the risks are physical, social, monetary or ethical.	Cautious, hesitant, careful, wary, prudent, discrete, heedful, unadventurous, precautionary, security-minded, conservative.
Self Esteem	Confident in dealing with others; not easily embarrassed or influenced by others; shows presence in interpersonal situations; possesses aplomb.	Self-assured, composed, egotistical, self-possessed, poised, self-sufficient.	Feels awkward among people, especially strangers; ill at ease socially; prefers to remain unnoticed at social events; has low opinion of himself as a group member; lacks self-confidence; easily embarrassed.	Self-depreciating, timid, unassuming, modest, shy, humble, self-conscious.

Social Adroitness	Is skillful at persuading others to achieve a particular goal, sometimes by indirect means; occasionally may be seen as manipulative of others, but is ordinarily diplomatic; socially intelligent.	Shrewd, sophisticated, tactful, crafty, influential, subtle, persuasive, discreet, worldly.	Tactless when dealing with others; socially naive and maladroit; speaks in a direct straightforward manner; insensitive of the effects of his behavior on others.	Direct, frank, tactless, candid, unpolished; undesigning, outspoken, impolite, blunt, naive.
Social Participation	Will eagerly join a variety of social groups; seeks both formal and informal association with others; values positive interpersonal relationships, actively social.	Sociable, friendly, gregarious, outgoing, "joiner," convivial, companionable, funloving extrovert, congenial, cordial, good natured.	Keeps to himself; has few friends; avoids social activities.	Nonparticipant, solitary, "loner," unsociable, retiring, uncommunicative, withdrawn.
Tolerance	Accepts people even though their beliefs and customs may differ from his own; open to new ideas; free from prejudice, welcomes dissent.	Broadminded, openminded unprejudiced, receptive, judicious, impartial, dispassionate, lenient, indulgent.	Entertains only opinions consistent with his own; makes quick value judgments about others; feels threatened by those with different opinions; rejects people from different ethnic, religious, cultural or social backgrounds; identifies closely with those sharing his beliefs.	Intolerant, cocksure, dogmatic, opinionated, narrow-minded, prejudiced, uncompromising.
Value Orthodoxy	Values traditional customs and beliefs; his values may be seen by others as "old fashioned"; takes a rather conservative view regarding contemporary standards of behavior; opposed to change in social customs.	Moralistic, conventional, strict, prim, devout, prudish, puritanical, righteous, rigid.	Critical of tradition; liberal or radical attitudes regarding behavior; questions laws and precedents; acts in an unconventional manner; believes that few things should be censored.	Modern, radical, liberal, unorthodox, contemporary, permissive.
Infrequency	Responds in implausible or apparently random manner, possibly due to carelessness, poor comprehension, passive non-compliance, confusion or gross deviation.			

dence behavior consistent with that trait. Therefore the JPI tends to place greatest importance upon the definitions of the scales on which the individual has high and low scores. For example, an individual with an above-average score on the Anxiety scale tends to worry more, to be more easily upset, and to be apprehensive about the future. Some adjectives describing the persons obtaining high scores are worried, tense, nervous, anxious, agitated, and fearful. Persons obtaining below-average scores tend to remain calm, composed, and collected and to take things as they come. Adjectives associated with low scores are easygoing, calm, relaxed, and contented.

Of the 16 JPI scales, one scale, Infrequency, was developed to identify faked profiles. This scale is composed of items suggestive of very improbable happenings. For example, "Everyone in my family has the same birthday" and "All jokes seem pointless to me." High scores on the Infrequency scale tend to suggest implausible responses or a random response style, possibly due to deficiencies in reading or thinking, carelessness, or lack of motivation.

A construct approach was used in developing the JPI scales. Scales were developed from large item-pools based upon explicit definitions of each scale. The main goal of the construct approach is the development of a content-coherent homogeneous scale for each trait of interest. This is followed by an attempt to demonstrate that performance on the inventory scales is related to other variables or traits in the expected direction.

The scale reliability of the JPI has been explored using an internal consistency procedure and two samples of college students (Jackson, 1977a,b). In the California sample ($N = 82$), coefficients ranged from 0.84 to 0.95, with a median of 0.93. The Pennsylvania sample ($N = 307$) produced a range of 0.75 to 0.93, with a median of 0.90. These coefficients suggest that the scales tend to be internally consistent. However, test-retest data are needed to investigate the reliability issue more thoroughly.

Some concurrent validity data are presented in the manual (Jackson, 1976b). The JPI scales have been correlated with a number of other inventory scales (e.g., the Minnesota Multiphasic Personality Inventory, the Jackson Vocational Interest Survey, the Bentler Interactive Psychological Inventory, and the Personality Research Form). In general, these correlations between JPI scales and other inventories are consistent with expectations. Two studies have explored the relationships among JPI scales, adjective checklist ratings, self-ratings, and peer ratings. In the first of these studies the median correlation of JPI scales for the adjective checklist was 0.70; for self-rating, 0.56; and for peer rating, 0.38. Correlations in the second study tended to be lower. In sum, these data suggest some meaningful relationship among the JPI scales, what people say about themselves, and what others say about them.

The JPI manual (Jackson, 1976b) and the Interpreter's Guide to the JPI (Jackson, 1978) suggest that the JPI is appropriate for use in personality research, in business and industry, and in schools, colleges, and universities as an aid to counseling. Probably the most reasonable use of the JPI at the present time is for personality research. Little evidence is available to evaluate the use of the JPI in applied settings. However, the limited evidence (college norm groups and the reliability and validity studies with college students) suggests that the JPI could probably be used to assess the functioning of persons primarily in educational environments.

In interpreting the JPI scales, the assumption is made that all people possess to some extent each trait being assessed by the inventory. The higher or lower an individual's score is, the greater the tendency is for the individual to exhibit behavior consistent with the trait being assessed. Thus, high and low scores on the JPI tend to have more behavioral meaning than average scores do. Individuals scoring high on a given scale tend to evidence more behavior consistent with the description of high scorers, and low-scoring individuals tend to behave like the description of low scorers. The scales are interpreted individually. The manual makes no attempt to cluster the scales for interpretive purposes, although results of the factor analysis could be used for scale clustering and to facilitate interpretation.

The factor analysis carried out by Jackson and Skinner (1975) used 215 college students and produced five factors of interest to us here. Factor 1 (a general factor) included 8 of the 16 scales: Breadth of Interest, Complexity, Conformity, Energy Level, Innovation, Risk Taking, Self-Esteem, and Tolerance. A high score on this factor suggests broad interests, a liking for complex solutions to problems, high energy, motivation to be creative, willingness to take risks, good self-confidence, acceptance of a variety of people and ideas, and a tendency to be independent in thought and action. Factor 2, which consists of Interpersonal Affect, Social Participation, and the Anxiety scale, suggests a preference for warm interpersonal relationships. A person scoring high on Factor 3 (Self-Esteem and Social Adroitness) tends to be at ease with other people and to influence them. High scorers on Factor 4 (Organization, Responsibility, and Value Orthodoxy) tend to be orderly, honest, law-abiding planners who are conservative in terms of social values. Factor 5 loads only on the Infrequency scale, and high scores tend to reflect carelessness in completing the inventory. Clearly the above factors and scale groupings need to be explored in terms of their interpretive validity. However, at the present time the scale groupings at least offer a different perspective or tentative way

of organizing and thinking about the JPI information.

Figure 4.8 provides a sample profile taken from the JPI manual (Jackson, 1976b).

The Guilford-Zimmerman Temperament Survey (GZTS)

The Guilford-Zimmerman Temperament Survey (GZTS; 1978) is a revision and condensation of Guilford's Inventory of Factors (two forms) and the Guilford-Martin Personnel Inventory. The GZTS was developed to reduce the redundancies in the above inventories and to assess the traits that are proved to be most unique and useful. The ten traits assessed by the GZTS are described in Figure 4.9. The inventory is designed primarily for use with normally functioning individuals. Evidence indicates that the GZTS has been used in a variety of settings: educational, vocational, marital, counseling, evaluation, selection, and placement. The total of 575 published studies using the GZTS (Mitchell, 1985) is evidence of the use of the GZTS in different research and applied settings.

The GZTS test booklet consists of 300 items or ten scales. The response format is yes, no, or ?. A ? response means that the client is unable to decide. The manual (Guilford, Guilford, & Zimmerman, 1978) reports that the inventory may be used with high school and college students and with adults. Norms are based on three reference scales (standard scores, centile ranks, and C-scores) on the profile sheet for high school, college, and adult ages. Each person's raw scores are located on the various trait scales on the GZTS profile charts. The manual indicates that the profile chart was based on rather large samples of individuals, mostly at the college level, but does not report the Ns.

The instruments on which the GZTS was based were initially developed to assess

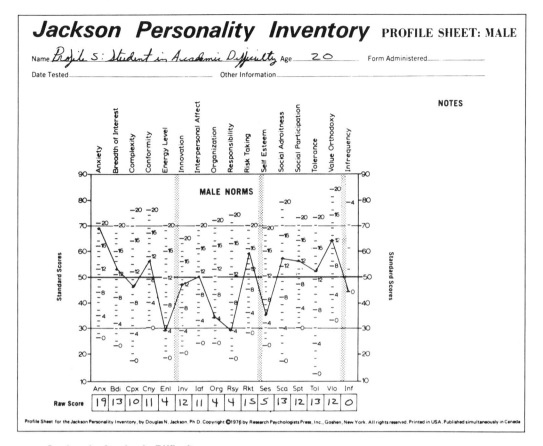

Jackson Personality Inventory PROFILE SHEET: MALE

Name *Profile 5: Student in Academic Difficulty* Age 20 Form Administered _____

Date Tested _____ Other Information _____

MALE NORMS

NOTES

Standard Scores

Standard Scores

	Anx	Bdi	Cpx	Cny	Enl	Inv	Iaf	Org	Rsy	Rkt	Ses	Sca	Spt	Tol	Vlo	Inf
Raw Score	19	13	10	11	4	12	11	4	4	15	5	13	12	13	12	0

Student in Academic Difficulty

This 20 year old male was administered the JPI in connection with his receiving counseling. He reported that he was failing three courses in computer science and mathematics, that he experienced feelings of loneliness and unhappiness, that he enjoyed working with computers—in fact talked about them incessantly—but had not been successful in his advanced work. An examination of his JPI profile reveals low scores in Energy Level, Organization, Responsibility and Self Esteem, and a notably high score in Anxiety. Other testing revealed that he had the requisite ability to succeed in his major, but the low scores in Energy Level and Organization were not consistent with a potential for success in a highly specialized and demanding field. After vocational interest testing results were discussed with him, he decided to transfer into a business administration program, which he successfully completed.

Figure 4.8 JPI Profile of a Student in Academic Difficulty. (Reproduced with permission from the Manual for the Jackson Personality Inventory by Douglas Jackson, p. 20. Copyright 1976 by the Research Psychologists Press, Inc., Port Huron, Mich. 48060.)

Jung's constructs of introversion and extraversion. Three inventories were subsequently developed to assess a number of traits. The GZTS was constructed to assess the most useful of these traits, and the items were selected mainly from the earlier inventories.

The inventory was designed for use with reasonably well-adjusted individuals. A high score on a given scale suggests that the individual is fairly similar to the trait description being assessed. For example, a high score on the Personal Relations scale suggests a

G— General Activity: a tendency toward quick and vigorous activity.

R— Restraint: serious-mindedness and self-control as contrasted with an impulsive, carefree disposition.

A— Ascendance: tendency to take the initiative in social situations as contrasted with the tendency to remain in the background.

S— Sociability: interest in and enjoyment of social contacts and activities in contrast to shyness or seclusiveness; a need for other people as opposed to an indifference toward them.

E— Emotional Stability: a combination of qualities opposite to those characteristic of D (depression) and C (cycloid) dispositions; a tendency to remain optimistic, cheerful, and even-tempered independent of external influences.

O— Objectivity: lack of hypersensitivity and self-centeredness; tendency to view situations realistically and dispassionately.

F— Friendliness: tendency to be friendly and compliant with desires of others as opposed to a tendency to be defensive, hostile or belligerent.

T— Thoughtfulness: tendency to be introspective, reflective, observant and analytical as opposed to the tendency to avoid such contemplation.

P— Personal Relations: cooperativeness, tolerance, and acceptance of things and people as they are as opposed to critical faultfinding and demanding that others live up to personal standards.

M— Masculinity: masculinity of interests and emotional reactions as contrasted with feminine interests and reactions.

Figure 4.9 GZTS Scale Description. (Reproduced, with permission, from the Manual for the Guilford-Zimmerman Temperament Survey by J.P. Guilford, J.S. Guilford, and W.S. Zimmerman, pp 15–18. Copyright 1978 by Sheridan Psychological Services, Inc., Orange, Calif. 92667.)

person who tends to be cooperative, tolerant, and accepting of things and people. A low score suggests a person who tends to be more fault finding, demanding that others live up to his/her personal standards.

No scales on the GZTS were developed to detect faking, but two indices of response tendencies are thought to be indicative of faking or response bias. One such index is the number of question-mark answers given by a person. A large number of question marks may be suggestive of poor self-knowledge, poor self-concept, or low confidence, or, alternatively, of a tendency to be secretive or evasive. In any event, the manual suggests that it is unwise to score an answer sheet for any trait with a large number of question mark responses (defined as three or more for any one trait), because they always contribute to an unfavorable score. A second index of possible response bias is suggested by an overall high profile pattern. For example, a profile pattern with all or most scores above the median (C-score of 5) may be indicative of a "faked good" or "look good"

response style. The scales are sufficiently independent statistically that it would be difficult for a person to obtain ten, nine, or eight scores above the median. More extensive information on what are called the "GZTS Falsification Scales" is included in the *Guilford-Zimmerman Temperament Survey Handbook* (Guilford, Zimmerman, & Guilford, 1976).

A factor-based construct approach was used in developing the GZTS scales. Prior to the development of the GZTS, considerable research explored Jung's constructs of introversion and extraversion by means of factor analysis of self-report items. Three inventories were developed representing 13 factor traits. Upon a reanalysis of the above findings, the GZTS was constructed, representing 10 of the 13 factors (traits) that were found to be the most unique and useful. These 10 traits provide the basis for Guilford's factor-analytic taxonomy of personality traits.

Estimates of scale reliabilities were made using samples of 523 male and 389 female college students. Split-half procedures yielded reliability coefficients ranging from 0.75 to 0.87. Test-retest reliability was examined with the help of teachers in training who were retested after one year ($N = 322$), two years ($N = 104$), and three years ($N = 104$). The mean stability coefficient for the one-year period was 0.67; for the two-year period, 0.54; and for the three-year period, 0.51. In sum, these data indicate that the scales of the GZTS are moderately reliable.

Concurrent validity data are available from correlations of the GZTS scores with scores from other instruments (e.g., the Thurstone Temperament Schedule, the Comrey Personality Scales, the Sixteen Personality Factor Questionnaire, the Minnesota Multiphasic Personality Inventory, the California Psychological Inventory, and the Taylor Manifest Anxiety Scale). The findings of these studies indicate that the GZTS scales are meaningful variables. Additional evidence of this kind is presented in the handbook (Guilford, Zimmerman, & Guilford, 1976). In addition, concurrent validity of the GZTS has been explored by describing and comparing a variety of special groups (e.g., drinking drivers, military personnel, dental students, engineering students, business school students, managers, executives, teachers, social workers, secretaries, musicians, salespeople, police officers, skilled business owners, student nurses, and numerous other samples). In general, these studies' findings provide evidence that the GZTS describes groups in ways consistent with existing knowledge. Again, additional information pertaining to these studies and groups may be found in the handbook, which provides patterns of scores for more than 100 groups including some 15,000 cases.

The GZTS has been used with some effectiveness to predict leadership and academic achievement. For example, the General Activity scale often bears a positive relationship to academic success. Many studies have explored differences among occupational groups in terms of the GZTS trait scores. The handbook contains data on a variety of different sample groups. The GZTS has also been used in counseling. Low scores on the Emotional Stability, Objectivity, Friendliness, or Personal Relations scales may be suggestive of emotional problems. Social problems may be indicated by low scores on the Ascendance and Sociability scales, and academic problems may be indicated by low scores on the Restraint and Thoughtfulness scales. Although the GZTS was not designed for use with the emotionally disturbed, it has been used with individuals assigned to a variety of diagnostic categories (schizophrenics, anxiety reaction clients, hysterical personalities, delinquents, and alcoholics). In general, findings from this work suggest that individuals evidencing symptoms of behavior disorder tend to have lower scores on the Emotional Stability, Objectivity, and Sociability scales. The manual (Guilford, Guilford, & Zimmerman, 1978) points out that the most frequent counseling and clinical use of the GZTS is in educational and vocational counseling in college and university counseling centers.

In interpreting the GZTS scales the usual trait assumption is made, namely, that all people possess to some extent each characteristic being assessed by the inventory. The higher or lower an individual's score is, the greater the tendency is for the person to display behavior consistent with the trait being assessed. On the profile chart raw scores are transformed using three reference scales: the C-scale, the centile scale, and the T-scale. The *Interpretation System for the Guilford-Zimmerman Temperament Survey* (Guilford, Guilford, & Zimmerman, 1976) provides a program for interpretation based on C-scores derived from the profile chart. In general, a C-score of 7 or above tends to be above average and a C-score of 3 or below tends to be below average. On the profile chart the most closely related traits are placed near one another to aid in the interpretation process. In addition, the second-order factors identified as Social Activity (SA), Introversion-Extraversion (RT), Emotional Stability (EO), and (freedom from) Paranoid Disposition (FP) may be scored and used in interpretation. The Social Activity factor loads on the Sociability and Ascendance scales; the Introversion-Extraversion factor on the Restraint and Thoughtfulness scales; the Emotional Stability factor on the Emotional Stability and Objectivity scales; and the Paranoid Disposition factor loads on the Friendliness and Personal Relations scales. More evidence is currently needed to document the use of these experimental factors. In any event, the second-order factors offer a different way of looking at the GZTS scores.

Figure 4.10 provides a sample profile of a college freshman having academic problems. This 19-year-old student came to the counseling center reporting poor academic performance.

The low score on the Restraint scale (R) suggests a person who is spontaneous and flexible, but who can change his or her mind on a whim. This person tends to have

Figure 4.10 Guilford-Zimmerman Temperament Survey of a Freshman College Student with Academic Problems. (Reproduced with permission. Copyright 1975 by Sheridan Psychological Services, Inc., Orange, Calif. 92667.)

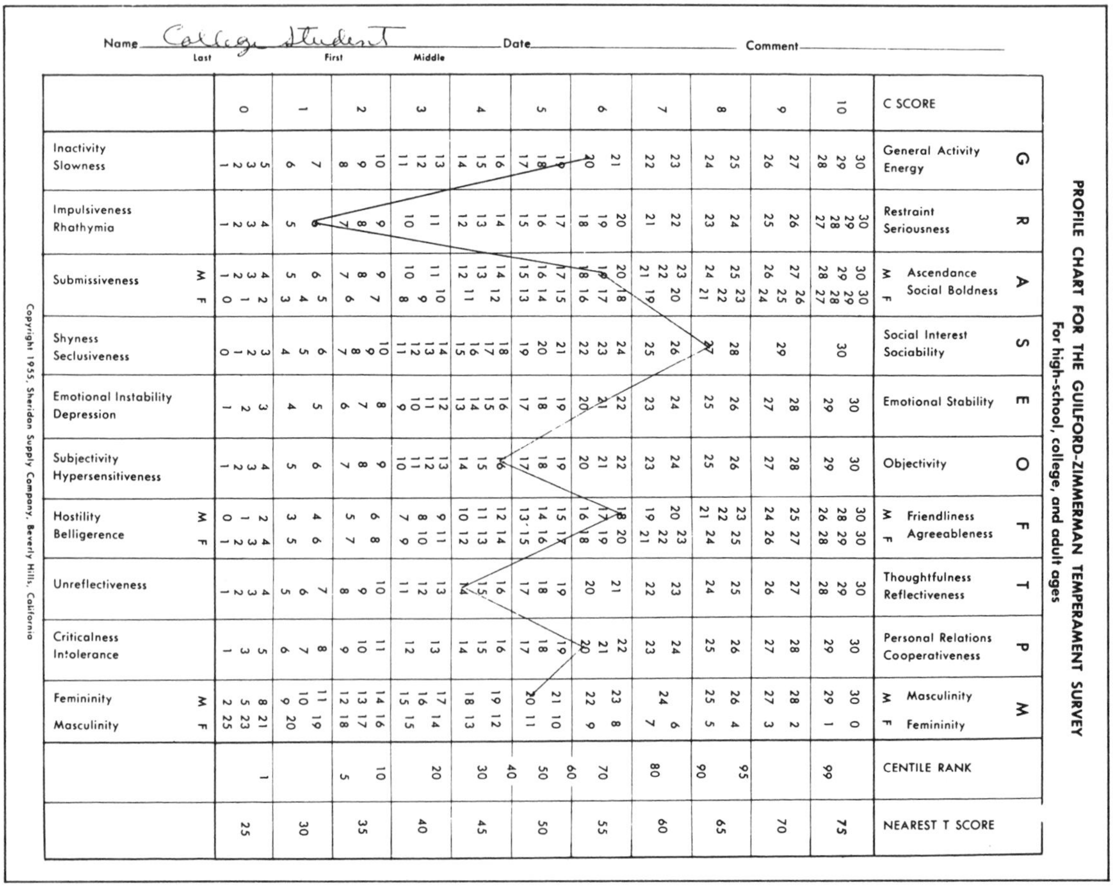

problems where sustained effort, self-denial, and discipline in pursuing long-range goals are required. People who score high on the Social Interest scale (S), as this subject does, have a need for other people and enjoy social contacts to the point where they may have difficulty doing things alone, such as in this case, studying. In general, the GZTS profile suggests that this student's academic problems may be to some extent related to the person's carefree disposition and very sociable personal style. The profile further suggests that the student may tend to be more productive in a person-oriented college major.

The Myers-Briggs Type Indicator (MBTI)

The Myers-Briggs Type Indicator (MBTI) was specifically developed to describe Carl Jung's personality types. The types (see Figure 4.11) tend to suggest different kinds of people who are interested in different things. It is assumed that an understanding of personality type may help in making a career choice and in dealing with problems and people in one's life (Myers & McCaulley, 1985; Myers, 1987).

The revised MBTI (Form G) consists of 126 two-choice items and may be scored for four pairs of scales: Extroversion (E) vs. Introversion (I), Sensing (S) vs. Intuition (N), Thinking (T) vs. Feeling (F), and Judgment (J) vs. Perception (P). All possible combinations of these four paired scales result in 16 possible personality types (see Figure 4.11). Comparative evidence indicates that the original Form F (166 items) and the revised Form G (126 items) produce identical distribution of types (Myers & McCaulley, 1985). Form G is the standard form of the MBTI.

There is also now an abbreviated version (Form AV, earlier referred to as Form H), which includes the first 50 items from Form G in a self-scoring format (Myers &

McCaulley, 1985). Form AV is designed for group situations and workshops where pretesting and scoring by template are not very feasible. Myers and McCaulley (1985) indicate that persons will tend to come out the same on Form G and Form AV about 75 percent of the time.

Norms for samples of high school students, and college students, in a variety of different occupations are reported in the manual (Myers & McCaulley, 1985). The original normative sample consisted mainly of college preparatory students of above-average social economic status. The MBTI data bank now consists of more than 250,000 MBTI records. The data bank is generated from the MBTI Scoring Program at the Center for Applications of Psychological Type (CAPT) in Gainesville, Florida. The more recent data indicate that the MBTI may be used as early as the fifth grade to explore type differences. However, the manual warns that when the MBTI is used with poor readers the scores need to be interpreted with caution.

An individual's personality type on the MBTI may be summarized in four letters which indicate the direction and strength of the individual's preference for Extraversion (E) or Introversion (I), Sensing (S) or Intuition (N), Thinking (T) or Feeling (F), and Judgment (J) or Perception (P). Thus, for example, ESTJ means an extrovert who enjoys sensing and thinking and who has mainly a judging attitude toward the outer world. INTP means an introvert with a preference for intuition and thinking and who has mainly a perceptive attitude toward the outer world. ENFP means an extrovert inclined toward intuition and feeling and who has mainly a perceptive attitude toward the outer world. Each of the 16 types tends to produce a different set of characteristics, interests, values, needs, and traits. (More elaborate descriptions for each type are reported in Figure 4.11.) A potential limitation of the scheme

CHARACTERISTICS FREQUENTLY ASSOCIATED WITH EACH TYPE AMONG YOUNG PEOPLE

SENSING TYPES		INTUITIVE TYPES	
ISTJ Serious, quiet, earn success by concentration and thoroughness. Practical, orderly, matter-of-fact, logical, realistic and dependable. See to it that everything is well organized. Take responsibility. Make up their own minds as to what should be accomplished and work toward it steadily, regardless of protests or distractions.	**ISFJ** Quiet, friendly, responsible and conscientious. Work devotedly to meet their obligations and serve their friends and school. Thorough, painstaking, accurate. May need time to master technical subjects, as their interests are usually not technical. Patient with detail and routine. Loyal, considerate, concerned with how other people feel.	**INFJ** Succeed by perseverance, originality and desire to do whatever is needed or wanted. Put their best efforts into their work. Quietly forceful, conscientious, concerned for others. Respected for their firm principles. Likely to be honored and followed for their clear convictions as to how best to serve the common good.	**INTJ** Usually have original minds and great drive for their own ideas and purposes. In fields that appeal to them, they have a fine power to organize a job and carry it through with or without help. Skeptical, critical, independent, determined, often stubborn. Must learn to yield less important points in order to win the most important.
ISTP Cool onlookers—quiet, reserved, observing and analyzing life with detached curiosity and unexpected flashes of original humor. Usually interested in impersonal principles, cause and effect, how and why mechanical things work. Exert themselves no more than they think necessary, because any waste of energy would be inefficient.	**ISFP** Retiring, quietly friendly, sensitive, kind, modest about their abilities. Shun disagreements, do not force their opinions or values on others. Usually do not care to lead but are often loyal followers. Often relaxed about getting things done, because they enjoy the present moment and do not want to spoil it by undue haste or exertion.	**INFP** Full of enthusiasms and loyalties, but seldom talk of these until they know you well. Care about learning, ideas, language, and independent projects of their own. Tend to undertake too much, then somehow get it done. Friendly, but often too absorbed in what they are doing to be sociable. Little concerned with possessions or physical surroundings.	**INTP** Quiet, reserved, brilliant in exams, especially in theoretical or scientific subjects. Logical to the point of hair-splitting. Usually interested mainly in ideas, with little liking for parties or small talk. Tend to have sharply defined interests. Need to choose careers where some strong interest can be used and useful.
ESTP Matter-of-fact, do not worry or hurry, enjoy whatever comes along. Tend to like mechanical things and sports, with friends on the side. May be a bit blunt or insensitive. Can do math or science when they see the need. Dislike long explanations. Are best with real things that can be worked, handled, taken apart or put together.	**ESFP** Outgoing, easygoing, accepting, friendly, enjoy everything and make things more fun for others by their enjoyment. Like sports and making things. Know what's going on and join in eagerly. Find remembering facts easier than mastering theories. Are best in situations that need sound common sense and practical ability with people as well as with things.	**ENFP** Warmly enthusiastic, high-spirited, ingenious, imaginative. Able to do almost anything that interests them. Quick with a solution for any difficulty and ready to help anyone with a problem. Often rely on their ability to improvise instead of preparing in advance. Can usually find compelling reasons for whatever they want.	**ENTP** Quick, ingenious, good at many things. Stimulating company, alert and outspoken. May argue for fun on either side of a question. Resourceful in solving new and challenging problems, but may neglect routine assignments. Apt to turn to one new interest after another. Skillful in finding logical reasons for what they want.
ESTJ Practical, realistic, matter-of-fact, with a natural head for business or mechanics. Not interested in subjects they see no use for, but can apply themselves when necessary. Like to organize and run activities. May make good administrators, especially if they remember to consider others' feelings and points of view.	**ESFJ** Warm-hearted, talkative, popular, conscientious, born cooperators, active committee members. Need harmony and may be good at creating it. Always doing something nice for someone. Work best with encouragement and praise. Little interest in abstract thinking or technical subjects. Main interest is in things that directly and visibly affect people's lives.	**ENFJ** Responsive and responsible. Generally feel real concern for what others think or want, and try to handle things with due regard for other people's feelings. Can present a proposal or lead a group discussion with ease and tact. Sociable, popular, active in school affairs, but put time enough on their studies to do good work.	**ENTJ** Hearty, frank, able in studies, leaders in activities. Usually good in anything that requires reasoning and intelligent talk, such as public speaking. Are usually well-informed and enjoy adding to their fund of knowledge. May sometimes be more positive and confident than their experience in an area warrants.

(Left margin: INTROVERTS / EXTRAVERTS; Right margin: INTROVERTS / EXTRAVERTS)

Figure 4.11 Characteristics Frequently Associated with Each Myers-Briggs Type Among Young People. (Reproduced with permission from the *Manual: A Guide to the Development and Use of the Myers-Briggs Type Indicator*, by Isabel Briggs Myers and Mary McCaulley, pp. 20–21. Copyright 1985 by Consulting Psychologists Press, Inc., Palo Alto, Calif. 94306.)

is that each pair of scales assumes that people must go one way or the other. The empirical support for this dichotomy assumption is tenuous (Coan, 1978; Devito, 1985).

As a psychometric instrument the MBTI operationalizes Jung's theoretical concepts or types. Thus, a personality theory construct approach was used in test development. Scale construction was a function of theoretical concerns. Content-coherent scales were developed for each theoretical variable of interest. As mentioned previously the scales rest on a dichotomous, "either-or" assumption that people clearly have one preference or another, but the evidence supporting this notion of a dichotomy is not substantial. Reliability of the four scores has been explored using the split-half procedure; resulting coefficients range in the 0.70s and 0.80s.

The manual (Myers & McCaulley, 1985)

also includes a number of test-retest reliability studies. Test-retest reliability coefficients range from 0.48 (14 months) to 0.87 (7 weeks). The test-retest reliability of males on the TF scale seems to be the least stable of the four scales.

Concurrent validity studies have related MBTI scores in a variety of occupational and academic groups to creativity, academic achievement, vocational preferences, aesthetic preferences, values, needs, abilities, and work behavior. The MBTI has been used in some 320 published studies (Buros, 1978; Mitchell, 1985). In general, these data tend to be supportive of the concurrent validity of the scales (Coan, 1978; Devito, 1985). The MBTI scores tend to be associated with a variety of variables in ways consistent with expectations: The MBTI does operationalize and assess the Jungian types to at least some extent.

The MBTI is an interesting and somewhat unusual personality inventory, and the manual suggests that it may be used to assist in career choice and to help deal with interpersonal problems. In general, the concurrent validity studies are supportive and consistent with expectations; however, additional research would be useful in helping to clarify and elaborate the applied value of the inventory.

For interpretive purposes each combination of the 16 preferences tends to be characterized by its own interests, values, and traits. These are reported on the back of the profile sheet. Clients are asked to match their four-letter type and see if the description fits their personal style. Included is a sample MBTI profile (see Figure 4.12.) This 21-year-old second-year nursing student has the four-letter code ESFJ, suggesting that she tends to be warm-hearted, talkative, conscientious, and cooperative. She tends to like doing nice things for other people and works best with some encouragement and praise. Her main interest is in things that directly affect people's lives and in the here-and-now. She enjoys variety but adapts well to routine. In general, she prefers to base plans and decisions upon known facts.

The Minnesota Multiphasic Personality Inventory (MMPI)

There is little question that the Minnesota Multiphasic Personality Inventory (MMPI), developed by Hathaway and McKinley in 1943, is the most useful psychological test available in clinical and counseling settings for assessing the degree and nature of emotional upset. As the MMPI manual (Hathaway & McKinley, 1967) indicates, it was designed to assess some major personality characteristics that affect personal and social adjustments. The total of 5,382 published studies using the MMPI (Buros, 1978; Mitchell, 1985) is clear evidence of the wide use of the MMPI in a variety of different research and applied settings. Approximately 1,527 of these publications have appeared since 1971. The MMPI has more references than any other instrument in print today.

The MMPI is a lengthy inventory containing 566 statements covering a range of subject matter including physical condition, moral attitude, and social attitudes. The subject is asked to respond to each item as "true," "false," or "cannot say." Originally, the inventory was composed of nine clinical scales named for the psychiatric-psychological condition assessed: Hypochondriasis (Hs), Depression (D), Conversion Hysteria (Hy), Psychopathic Deviate (Pd), Masculinity-Feminity (MF), Paranoia (Pa), Psychoasthenia (Pt), Schizophrenia (Sc), and Hypomania (Ma). In addition, a Social Introversion (Si) scale and four validating scales—Cannot Say (symbolized by a question mark), Lie (L), Frequency or Confusion (F), and Correction (K)—are now routinely scored. The validity scales are concerned with faking

Report Form for the Myers-Briggs Type Indicator™

Name: _Nurse_   Sex: ☐ Male ☒ Female   Date: _____

The MBTI® reports your preferences on four scales. There are two opposite preferences on each scale. The four scales deal with where you like to focus your attention (E or I), the way you like to look at things (S or N), the way you like to go about deciding things (T or F), and how you deal with the outer world (J or P). Short descriptions of each scale are shown below.

E	You prefer to focus on the outer world of people and things	or	**I** You prefer to focus on the inner world of ideas and impressions
S	You tend to focus on the present and on concrete information gained from your senses	or	**N** You tend to focus on the future, with a view toward patterns and possibilities
T	You tend to base your decisions on logic and on objective analysis of cause and effect	or	**F** You tend to base your decisions primarily on values and on subjective evaluation of person-centered concerns
J	You like a planned and organized approach to life and prefer to have things settled	or	**P** You like a flexible and spontaneous approach to life and prefer to keep your options open

The four letters show your Reported Type, which is the combination of the four preferences you chose. There are sixteen possible types.

REPORTED TYPE: | E | S | F | J |

PREFERENCE SCORES: | 60 | 40 | 50 | 50 |

Preference scores show how consistently you chose one preference over the other; high scores usually mean a clear preference. Preference scores do *not* measure abilities or development.

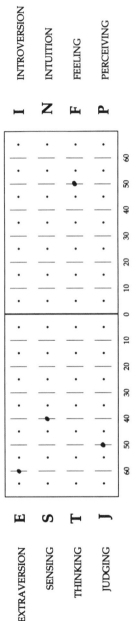

EXTRAVERSION	**E**			**I**	INTROVERSION
SENSING	**S**			**N**	INTUITION
THINKING	**T**			**F**	FEELING
JUDGING	**J**			**P**	PERCEIVING

Each type tends to have different interests and different values. On the back of this page are very brief descriptions of each of the sixteen types. Find the one that matches the four letters of your Reported Type and see whether it fits you. If it doesn't, try to find one that does. For a more complete description of the types and the implications for career choice, relationships, and work behavior, see *Introduction to Type* by Isabel Briggs Myers. Remember that everyone uses each of the preferences at different times; your Reported Type shows which you are likely to prefer the most and probably use most often.

Consulting Psychologists Press, Inc.
577 College Avenue, Palo Alto, California 94306

Figure 4.12 MBTI of a Second-year Student in a Nursing Program. (Copyright © 1976 by Isabel Myers. Copyright © 1988 by Consulting Psychologists Press and reproduced with permission of

and attempt to pick up distorted responses, a "fake sick" response set, and a defensiveness response style. The validity scales attempt to determine the client's mood or mental state at the time of test administration. The test-taking attitude of the person needs to be taken into account in interpreting the clinical scales. The above clinical, validity, and Social Introversion scales are described in Figure 4.13.

Some 500 experimental scales have been constructed; 11 of these are frequently scored as part of the regular profile by various computer services: Conscious Anxiety (A), Conscious Repression (R), Ego-Strength (Es), Low Back Pain (Lb), Caudality (Ca), Dependency (Dy), Dominance (Do), Social Responsibility (Re), Prejudice (Pr), Social Status (St), and Control (Cn). These new scales are helpful in interpreting the MMPI, but to date little information about them has appeared in the research literature.

In general, a high score on a scale is defined as one that is two standard devia-tions above the normal population mean (a T-score above 70). Subjects 16 years of age or older with at least 6 years of successful schooling can be expected to complete the MMPI without difficulty.

The original clinical scales of the MMPI were empirically derived. They consist of items that distinguished between a certain psychiatric group of carefully studied clinical cases and a control group of approximately 700 normal people who visited the hospitals at the University of Minnesota. The sampling was reasonably adequate for ages 16 to 55 and for both sexes. About 800 clinical cases were available from the neuropsychiatric division of the university hospitals when the inventory was developed and published. An important point to keep in mind here is that the chief criterion of interest was valid prediction of clinical cases, as confirmed by the neuropsychiatric staff diagnosis. For some years the major function of the MMPI was to place persons into various diagnostic categories. The idea was that

Figure 4.13 MMPI Scale Descriptions.

Cannot Say Scale (?). The number of items the client has left unanswered.

Lie Scale (L). This scale is measuring the degree to which a person is trying to look good in an obvious way.

Frequency or Confusion Scale (F). This scale is measuring the degree to which a person's thoughts are different from those of the general population.

Correction Scale (K). This scale measures defensiveness and guardedness.

Hypochondriasis (Hs) (Scale 1). This scale measures the number of bodily complaints claimed by a person.

Depression (D) (Scale 2). This is a mood scale that measures the degree of pessimism and sadness the person feels at the time of testing. This scale is rarely elevated by itself.

Conversion Hysteria (HY) (Scale 3). This measures the degree of denial being used by people to avoid facing personal difficulty and conflict.

Psychopathic Deviate (Pd) (Scale 4). This scale is measuring the degree to which an individual is fighting something (parents, friends, spouse, society, school).

Masculinity-Femininity (MF) (Scale 5). This scale is attempting to measure whether a person is more or less masculine or feminine. A problem here is that these definitions have changed significantly over the past years.

Paranoia (Pa) (Scale 6). This scale is measuring a person's suspiciousness, sensitivity, and self righteousness.

Psychasthenia (Pt) (Scale 7). This scale measures anxiety and a tendency to worry a great deal.

Schizophrenia (SC) (Scale 8). This scale measures mental confusion.

Hypomania (Ma) (Scale 9). This scale measures a person's level of psychic energy in terms of thought and behavior.

Social Introversion (Si) (Scale 0). This scale measures a person's preference for being alone (high score) or being with others.

a person taking the test would have an elevation on one scale that would indicate his/her diagnosis. At the time this was a meaningful, though somewhat limited, approach to, and interpretation of, the MMPI.

Recent developments, as noted by Duckworth and Anderson (1986), have expanded the interpretation of the MMPI. One such development is that now an effort is made to describe the behavior associated with the various elevations, rather than just place people into diagnostic categories. This provides useful information for treatment. A second development involves using the scale elevations to describe the intensity of behavior and thinking. For example, the Depression scale (Scale 2) may be used to distinguish people who are simply feeling "down" (lower elevations on the D scale) from those who are severely depressed (higher elevations on the D scale). A third interpretative development is the use of the whole MMPI profile, instead of one or two high-point scales, for analysis. This permits a review of a client's problem areas, strengths, and coping behaviors, and in general adds to the richness of the interpretation.

Test-retest reliability studies for the MMPI scales are reported in the manual (Hathaway & McKinley, 1967). These studies were carried out in the 1940s and early 1950s with groups of normal individuals and, in one case, a group of psychiatric patients. Hathaway and McKinley (1943) reported test-retest coefficients for six of the clinical scales, with intervals of three days to more than one year between testings. Their coefficients ranged from a low of 0.57 to a high of 0.83. Cottle (1950) reported test-retest coefficients for a group of "normals" tested and retested within a one-week interval. The test-retest coefficients for the validity scales and the clinical scales ranged from a low of 0.46 to a high of 0.91. Holzberg and Alessi (1949) reported test-retest coefficients for psychi-

atric patients where both testings occurred within three days. These test-retest coefficients ranged from a low of 0.52 to a high of 0.93. In general, the samples for these studies were small, but the evidence does suggest that the MMPI scales tend to be reasonably reliable.

As far as validity is concerned, the findings of some 5,382 studies conducted using the MMPI show that a high score on a scale will predict positively the associated clinical diagnosis in more than 60 percent of new psychiatric admissions. A high score on an MMPI scale is suggestive of the presence of the trait and the related symptoms. The MMPI remains matchless as the best objective instrument for the assessment of psychopathology. There is no question that the MMPI is the most reliable and valid instrument for assessing psychological and/or emotional disturbance. In addition, the MMPI has become a valuable assessment tool for investigating emotional components of physical disease.

Machine scoring and computer interpretation are often used with the MMPI. A profile sheet for a manually scored MMPI is shown in Figure 4.14. The "F Minus K" raw score index $(9 - 7 = +2)$ of less than 12 indicates that this is a valid profile (see raw score in Figure 4.14). (An "F Minus K" index of $+12$ or more may suggest that a client is "faking bad" on the MMPI. An "F Minus K" index of -12 or more may suggest that a client is attempting to "fake good.") This profile (Figure 4.14) suggests a person with a combination of severe depression and long-standing somatic complaints, which is typical of persons with this profile pattern. Such people see themselves as physically sick and frequently exhibit symptoms of depression, tension, nervousness, anxiety, and multiple somatic complaints. In general, people with such profiles have learned to tolerate great unhappiness and a high level of discomfort

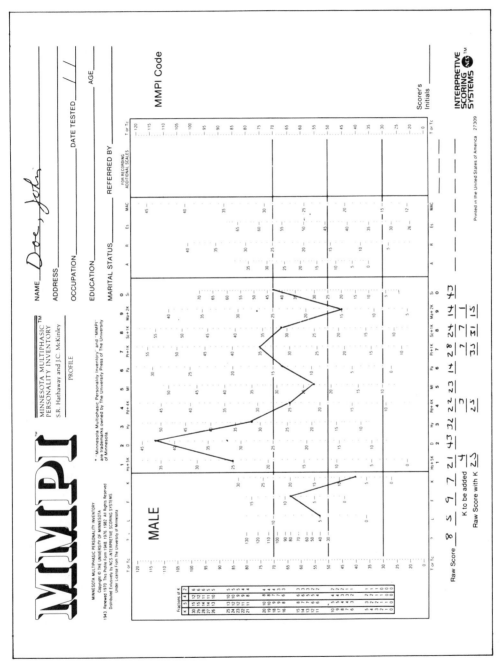

Figure 4.14 Profile Sheet for a Manually-scored MMPI. (Reproduced with permission from the *Minnesota Multiphasic Personality Inventory*. Copyright © The University of Minnesota 1943, renewed 1970. This form 1948, 1976, 1982.)

and consequently tend to display little motivation to receive help and poor response to treatment.

There are a number of sources of interpretative information about the MMPI. Two that we have found helpful are Lachar's (1974) *MMPI: Clinical Assessment and Automated Interpretation* and the *MMPI Interpretation Manual for Counselors and Clinicians* by Duckworth and Anderson (1986). All MMPI materials may be obtained from National Computer Systems, 4401 West 76th Street, Minneapolis, Minnesota.

The MMPI is currently being revised in order to make it more appropriate for the assessment of personal-adjustment problems. People have changed significantly in the last half century, making some of the MMPI items outdated or old-fashioned in their wording. Thus, about 14 percent of the test items are being revised because their wording is antiquated or sexist. In addition, the new test will focus more on contemporary issues such as eating disorders and drug abuse, which were not thought of as problems in the 1940s. For example, for adolescents, there will be more items that deal with sex, drugs, and parent and teacher problems. The new version of the MMPI will contain 704 true-false items in the version for the adults and 654 in the version for adolescents. It will probably take about two hours to complete. About 20,000 people throughout the country have already taken the new MMPI as part of its validation and standardization. In addition, many special groups have been tested: college students, military personnel, adolescents, the elderly, the residents of Indian reservations, those living in Hispanic communities, drug and alcohol abusers, patients in psychiatric hospitals, and patients with medical problems like chronic pain. The data are currently being analyzed and the revised form of the MMPI is expected to be available in about 1990.

Other Personality Inventories

As we pointed out at the beginning of this chapter, many different personality inventories are available. For example, another personality inventory that has stood the test of time is the Sixteen Personality Factor Questionnaire (16 PF) (Cattell, Eber, & Tatsuoka, 1980; Krug, 1981). The Sixteen Personality Factor Questionnaire was originally developed in 1949 by Raymond Cattell through factor analysis of items that were constructed to measure personality source traits. The 16 PF is primarily concerned with measuring personality attributes of more normal rather than pathological populations. The inventory assesses 16 personality attributes: Warmth, Intelligence, Emotional Stability, Dominance, Impulsivity, Conformity, Boldness, Sensitivity, Suspiciousness, Imagination, Shrewdness, Insecurity, Radicalism, Self-Sufficiency, Self-Discipline, and Tension. Additional factor scores are also computable based on combinations of the 16 primary scales. A total of five forms now exist: Forms A, B, C, D, and E. Form A is recommended as the standard form of the 16 PF. Forms A and B each have 187 items and require approximately 45 to 60 minutes of testing time. Forms A and B have reading grade levels of approximately 7.5. Forms C and D are shorter (105 questions) and have a reading grade level of approximately 6.5. Form E is a special low literate personality inventory with a reading level of approximately the 3.3 grade level. Form E in 1985 was renormed for highly diverse populations, including prison inmates, culturally disadvantaged, and physical rehabilitation clients. Test-retest reliability coefficients for short intervals (a few days) between administrations demonstrate relatively acceptable stability. Coefficients of equivalence (intercorrelations between factor scales generated from different test forms) are generally lower.

When Forms A and B are compared, few equivalence coefficients are greater than 0.50. In general, most of the reliability and validity data for all forms except Form E are based on data collected about 15 to 20 years ago. However, as noted above, the 16 PF is a research instrument that has stood the test of time and has been translated or structurally adapted into over 50 languages in Europe, South America, Africa, and Asia.

An assessment of self-concept was developed by William H. Fitts in 1965. The Tennessee Self-Concept Scale (TSCS) (Fitts, 1965 & 1972) consists of 100 self-descriptive items by means of which an individual reports what he or she is, does, likes, and feels. The scale is intended to assess an individual's feelings of self-worth and the degree to which the self-image is realistic. The TSCS provides an overall assessment of Self-Esteem, measures five external aspects of self-concept (Moral-Ethical, Social, Personal, Physical, and Family), and three internal variables (Identity, Behavior, and Self-Satisfaction). Test-retest reliability coefficients based on a sample of 60 college students over a two-week period range from 0.60 to 0.90. In the manual, Fitts reports correlations between the TSCS and scales of the MMPI, the Edwards Personal Preference Schedule, and a number of other well-known measures. Many of these correlations are significant. In addition, the TSCS has proven its usefulness as an instrument that is able to distinguish between different groups, particularly clinical and nonclinical groups.

The Millon Clinical Multiaxial Inventory (MCMI) was developed by Theodore Millon to provide a personality inventory useful for assessing and making a clinical diagnosis. The Minnesota Multiphasic Personality Inventory (MMPI) has long been the established inventory for assessing mental disturbance. The MCMI was designed to compete with the MMPI on this clinical dimension. The MCMI is a 175-item personality inventory with a true-false response format that produces scores on 20 scales: Schizoid, Avoidant, Dependent, Histrionic, Narcissistic, Antisocial, Compulsive, Passive Aggressive, Schizotypal, Borderline, Paranoid, Anxiety, Somatoform, Dysthymic, Alcohol Abuse, Drug Abuse, Psychotic Thinking, Psychotic Depression, Psychotic Delusion, and Validity. The scales are organized into three broad categories to assess differences among persistent personality features, current symptom states, and level of pathological severity. One form of the inventory is appropriate for individuals over 17 years of age with reading skills at or above the eighth-grade level. The MCMI was developed to identify clinical patterns in a manner easily related to the Diagnostic and Statistical Manual of Mental Disorders (Third Edition—Revised) (1987). Presently, the data base is not sufficient to make a judgment regarding how well the MCMI is competing with the more established MMPI. However, the evidence so far suggests that the inventory shows good promise to become a major clinical screening inventory of the future.

SUMMARY

Various conceptual models in personality psychology have stimulated research and test development over the years. The trait, psychodynamic, and behavioral models in particular have accounted for a very large percentage of the existing 220 personality inventories. For a number of reasons, most of the objective personality inventories we discussed and noted in this chapter are associated with the trait model. The trait model has been easier to use and implement compared to the other models of personality; it is more practical and applied in nature. However, there are some concerns that the trait approach may be too mechanistic and point-in-time oriented to adequately describe human behavior and development. In spite of limitations, the trait approach has produced a large number of person-centered inventories that are useful and afford meaningful information about people. Thus, in this chapter we have discussed seven objective personality inventories based on the trait model. These inventories and many others are called "objective" personality inventories because they produce an objective, quantifiable score. The fact that an objective test produces a quantitative score means that the test results may be compared with the scores of others who have taken the same test under similar conditions. With regard to the inventories, we included the Minnesota Multiphasic Personality Inventory and the California Psychological Inventory be-

cause they have demonstrated ample evidence of use in different research and practical settings. The Guilford-Zimmerman Temperament Survey and the Myers-Briggs Type Indicator are also solid objective personality inventories that show evidence of empirical investigation and support. The Omnibus Personality Inventory was included because of its rather unique emphasis on intellectual variables. It was developed primarily for research purposes, but clearly does have some practical applications. The Jackson Personality Inventory and the Comrey Personality Scales are more recently developed objective personality inventories that show promise for the future. There are many other personality inventories available, a few of which we discussed, but at the present time these seem to be representative of the population.

5

Projective and Behavioral Personality Assessment

INTRODUCTION TO PROJECTIVE AND BEHAVIORAL MEASURES OF PERSONALITY

This chapter focuses on two other models of personality that have stimulated considerable test development: the *psychodynamic model* and *situational*, or *behavioral, model.*

    The *psychodynamic model* is the interpretive basis for projective techniques that were developed to assess an individual's motives, drives, and defenses. The basic assumption of the projective techniques is that client responses to vague or ambiguous stimuli will tend to portray personality style. Inkblots and pictures of human situations are the most common projective techniques. Since an inkblot is not really a picture of anything, the interpretation a person gives must come from the way that individual perceives and organizes the world. In essence, one is said to project into the picture one's own emotional attitudes and ideas about life. In general, projective techniques tend to be more difficult to administer and interpret than objective measures are, and there are problems with reliability and validity. However, in spite of limitations, projective techniques are very clearly a meaningful and useful way of collecting information about people. A number of projective techniques are discussed in this chapter.

The *situational,* or *behavioral, model* defines personality in terms of the individual's actual overt behavior. Behavior is assumed to be primarily a function of past experiences. Past behavior is thought to be the best predictor of future behavior. Thus, within this context the individual's personality is defined in terms of actual behavioral performance, or what he or she does. Clients are asked to perform some activity or task in a specific situation. Behavior in that situation may then be observed and commented upon in terms of frequency, duration, intensity, and appropriateness. Recently a number of behavioral questionnaires have been developed, primarily because of the inconvenience and cost of observing clients' behavior in different situations. Therefore we have included a section in this chapter on behavioral questionnaires and their reliability and validity.

PROJECTIVE TECHNIQUES AND TESTS

As we mentioned previously, psychoanalytic concepts and psychoanalysis itself have had a rather profound impact on the assessment process. Psychoanalysis, as developed by Sigmund Freud in the early part of the twentieth century, is primarily concerned with making unconscious motives conscious in order to help people develop more socially acceptable ways of dealing with their impulses. At first, interview and case history methods were used to collect information about an individual's psychodynamics (motives, drives, intentions, defenses, and instincts). These methods were quite consistent with the traditional psychoanalytic framework. Eventually, however, projective methods appeared, in which psychoanalytic theory was used to understand the results of projective techniques. The basic assumption of the projective approach is that the individual's re-

sponses to vague or ambiguous stimuli or tasks will tend to reflect his or her basic personality. Psychologists who use projective techniques attempt to obtain a general impression of an individual's personality by focusing on the outstanding or significant features in a pattern of responses; an attempt is made to identify consistencies across a series of responses. The administration and scoring of a typical projective technique requires considerably more training than does the use of an objective self-report personality inventory. Even with more training, we frequently find differences among various people's interpretations of projective responses.

Projective techniques are different in various ways from the more objective tests discussed in Chapter 4. Projective techniques tend to be less obvious in their intent, and thus clients tend to be less aware of the type of interpretation that will be made of their responses. The tasks required by projective techniques are more unstructured than those required by objective tests, permitting clients to impose or project their personality onto the test material. However, the comparative structurelessness of projective techniques means that they are less likely than objective tests to produce quantitative scores. Qualitative interpretations are certainly meaningful when based on the counselor's or the clinician's experience and expertise, but such interpretations have difficulty meeting basic standards of reliability and validity. In the main, projective techniques have complex scoring procedures and therefore scoring problems, thus making reliability and validity complex issues. Since it is difficult to produce a quantifiable and objective score for a projective technique, norms and norm groups for comparative purposes tend to be rather limited.

In a more favorable light, projective techniques do make an attempt to assess the whole person in terms of personality, conflicts, needs, emotions, and intellectual processes. In addition, projective techniques attempt to tap unconscious processes by exploring the client's world of fantasy and make-believe. The idea is that vague and unstructured tasks will help the client verbalize material, thoughts, and needs previously not verbalized—or, stated somewhat more psychoanalytically, that the unstructured tasks will help the client make the unconscious conscious. Thus, like all other tests and inventories, projective techniques have problems and limitations, but nevertheless continue to be meaningful ways of collecting important information about people.

In the basic procedure common to most projective techniques, a client is presented with a series of unstructured tasks and asked to describe what something looks like or to tell a story or draw a picture. The client is expected to "project" his or her private view onto the subject of attention (Sundberg, 1990). The instructions for a projective technique emphasize freedom of response, and the intent of ambiguous tasks is not very obvious. Ideally, these two factors create a less anxiety-producing situation for the client. The client's responses to the ambiguous situations are subsequently analyzed to give insight into basic personality dynamics. Impressions of personality dynamics are obtained by focusing on the consistencies across patterns of responses to the ambiguous tasks. As previously mentioned, most test responses are interpreted on a qualitative or impressionistic basis. However, most projective techniques also provide procedures by which numerical scores may be obtained. Thus, it is usually possible (although not always practical) to provide normative data for projective test scores and to evaluate the reliability and validity of obtained scores.

There are a number of different types of projective techniques. Lindzey (1959, 1961) has categorized these into five groups based on the type of response required of the clients.

Association techniques ask the client to respond to a stimulus with the first word or image that comes to mind. The Rorschach Inkblot Test is a good example of this technique. Clients are presented inkblots and asked to report what they see. Another association technique is the Word Association Test, which is based on the notion of free association and asks clients to respond to words by indicating the first word that comes to their mind.

Construction techniques ask clients to tell a story about a given situation or picture. A good example of this technique is the Thematic Apperception Test (TAT). The instructions to the TAT ask clients to tell a story about a picture: what is currently happening in the picture, what led up to what is happening in the picture, and how the story ends.

In *completion techniques* clients are requested to complete some task or situation. For example, in various sentence-completion tests clients are presented with sentence stems and asked to complete the sentence, usually in writing and in a way that is true for them as individuals.

Ordering techniques instruct clients to choose from a number of alternatives presented or to order the stimuli or pictures presented to them. The Id, Ego, Superego Test (IES) (Dombrose & Slobin, 1958) is in many respects an example of this technique. The IES assesses the comparative strength of an individual's id, ego, and superego.

Expressive techniques, as the name suggests, are primarily concerned with having the client perform some activity or task. For example, on the Draw-a-Person Test clients are asked to draw a picture of a person. Thus, these techniques ask clients to express themselves through drawing, painting, or some kind of psychodrama. We will talk more specifically about a number of these techniques as we move through this chapter.

One of the first projective techniques

(the Word Association Test) was developed by Carl Jung in about 1905. The word association method was initially developed by F. Galton in 1879, but Jung (1923) was the first to apply the method for diagnostic reasons in order to identify unconscious conflicts. In 1921 Hermann Rorschach published his *Psychodiagnostiks*, a book linking inkblot responses to personality. Equally important was a publication by Henry Murray, entitled *Explorations in Personality* (1938), which introduced the Thematic Apperception Test (TAT). These two projective techniques (the Rorschach and the TAT) have had a profound impact on the process of assessment and tend to represent the core of the projective techniques. They continue to be among the most frequently used and researched assessment instruments. Thus, these and other projective techniques continue to be widely used in spite of considerable criticism. In any event, projective techniques do make a valuable contribution to the assessment process and permit a global assessment of personality. The Rorschach, TAT, and a number of other projective techniques are discussed below.

The Rorschach Inkblot Test

The Rorschach Inkblot Test was developed by Hermann Rorschach in 1921 for purposes of analyzing and understanding personality. As a youngster Rorschach had a favorite pastime of analyzing paintings and pictures in an attempt to understand what artists were trying to say with their images. His favorite game involved putting ink on a piece of paper and folding the paper various ways to form inkblots. It was then the responsibility of the author of the inkblot to explain and interpret the meaning of the blot. Rorschach was known far and wide for his inkblot game and eventually developed the Rorschach Inkblot Test to help in understanding hospital patients. Although Ror-

schach died at a very young age, his inkblot test was brought to the United States by Beck (1944) and Klopfer (Klopfer & Kelley, 1942) and the Rorschach Test has continued to be useful ever since. The Watkins, Campbell and McGregor (1988) data suggest that the Rorschach is the tenth most frequently used assessment instrument, and the Buros (1978) and Mitchell (1985) data suggest that it is the second most frequently researched assessment instrument, accounting for some 5,021 cumulative total references over the years. Without question, Rorschach's test is easily the most complex of the assessment instruments in use by psychologists today.

The Rorschach Inkblot Test itself consists of ten $6\frac{5}{8}$-by-$9\frac{1}{2}$-inch cards. Each card contains one inkblot. Five of the cards are black or gray, and five are colored. Figure 5.1 displays the Rorschach inkblots. The cards are presented one at a time, and the client (who must be age 3 or older) is asked to report what he or she sees or is reminded of by the inkblot image or what might be represented by the inkblot itself. After recording the client's responses, the examiner repeats the procedure, asking the client to report where he or she saw the things reported and to indicate the characteristics of the blot that led to the perceptions and responses. The answers to these questions are frequently needed for scoring procedures.

To illustrate, a young male graduate student in psychology gave the following response to the inkblot (card 10) in Figure 5.1 five seconds after it was shown:

> My first impression is that of two people walking in a garden. The two people holding hands are in the center of the picture and they are surrounded by a variety of different kinds of flowers. The flowers are represented by a variety of different kinds of colors and forms. They are in full bloom and represent the fullness of springtime. The area at the top and center of the picture represents a bench area for relaxation and enjoyment.

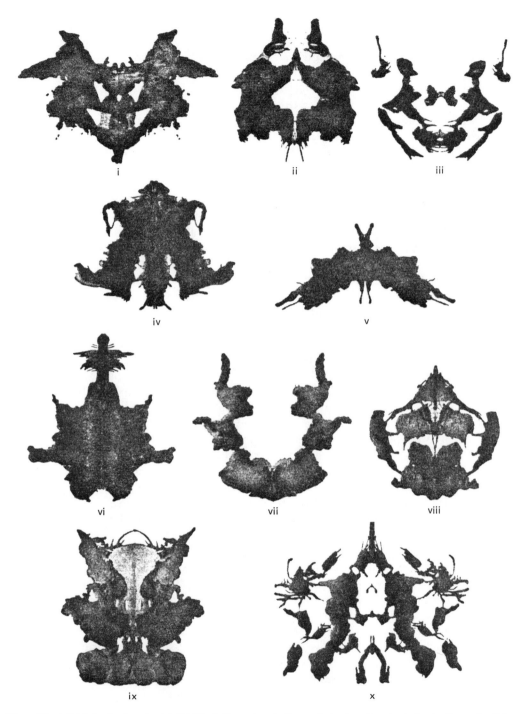

Figure 5.1 Inkblots for the Rorschach Inkblot Test. (Reproduced with permission from Rorschach: Psychodiagnostics Schemablock [Recording Blanks]. © 1947 by Verlag Hans Huber, Bern. Printed in Switzerland.)

For purposes of scoring the Rorschach, the examiner generally focuses on the location of responses, the "determinants" of responses, the content of responses, and the originality of the responses. The *location* of the response indicates where on the card the concept or image was seen and whether or not the whole blot or part of the blot was used. Location is primarily concerned with personality integration. The *determinants* of the response are concerned with the qualities of the blot used in the response and therefore focus on the form, color, texture, and apparent movement in the response. Response determinants are primarily interpreted as emotions or emotional drives. The *content* category simply refers to the content of the response in terms of human, animal, clothing, building, and so forth. Content is interpreted as reflecting the client's interests. Popular responses reveal information about the subject's similarities to people in general. More *original* responses are interpreted as reflecting creativity and productivity. Thus, from responses to a series of inkblots we can tell four things: the part of the blot used; the properties of the blot in terms of form, color, or shading; the content, be it human, animal, or thing; and the popularity of the response. In a sense, as noted by McArthur (1972) the Rorschach is a slice of total behavior, a sample of behavior.

The scoring of this slice of behavior, the responses to the Rorschach inkblots, varies a great deal. In general, the Rorschach is difficult to score, and all scoring systems require considerable training and practice with the technique. Exner's (1974, 1978) books are probably the most definitive textbooks on the Rorschach, providing a comprehensive review of contemporary Rorschach usage. There are a variety of other scoring systems, including those by Beck (1937), Klopfer and Kelley (1942), Munroe (1942), and Exner and Exner (1972). The

Beck system seems to be the most frequently used, although the Exner system is increasing in popularity. Exner's recent Comprehensive System (Viglione & Exner, 1983; Wiener-Levy & Exner, 1981) heavily emphasizes research in order to validate interpretive thinking. In general, the scoring systems seem to be derived from the projective hypothesis that every response, everything a person does, tends to reflect in some way some aspect of personality.

Over the years the Rorschach has been the focus of considerable research, but unfortunately the data continue to support only weakly the reliability and validity of the inkblot test. Reliability of scores (split-half reliability and test-retest reliability) varies widely. Also, as noted by Sundberg (1990), reliability of interpretation is a problem. A number of validity studies have been carried out on the Rorschach, but again the results are very mixed. The majority of studies that have explored suicide using the Rorschach have not faired well. The lack of predictive validity for the Rorschach raises some serious questions about its use in applied settings. In general, the recent reviews in the Buros *Mental Measurements Yearbooks* (1972, 1978) and *Test Critiques* (1985) indicate that the evidence for the reliability and validity of the Rorschach are weak at best. However, in spite of these data, the Rorschach's popularity seems to continue in practice and use. The obvious question is, What is the special attraction of the test?

In terms of current status, the Rorschach ranks tenth in the list of most frequently used assessment instruments and second in the list of most frequently researched assessment instruments. As noted by McArthur (1972) and Lerner and Lerner (1985), it continues to be one of the few assessment techniques that permit us to observe a broad band of the person's behavior; the perceptual, cognitive, emotional, and social aspects of a Rorschach behavioral sample permit us to get to know a client with a richness provided by very few other assessment techniques.

A number of variations of the Rorschach, designed primarily to overcome its psychometric limitations, have developed over the years. A very sound variation demonstrating good potential is the Holtzman Inkblot Technique (HIT) (Holtzman, 1975, 1981). The HIT was initially developed in an attempt to improve the reliability of the Rorschach Test and to increase the total number of responses a given client would make. For example, on the Rorschach a client may give 40 responses to the 10 cards and another client may give only 15. The client making 40 responses to the 10 cards will have a much richer profile. Holtzman solved this problem by using 45 cards, rather than 10 cards, and by asking the client to make only one response per card. Thus, the HIT consists of two parallel forms (A and B), each of which contains 45 inkblots constituting the test series and two practice blots (X and Y) that are identical on the two forms. This means that standardized responses may be obtained from a total of 92 different inkblots rather than just 10. In addition, the HIT has been demonstrated to have good alternate-forms reliability.

For scoring purposes the HIT system includes 22 variables. The Location and Space variables deal with the particular parts of the inkblot used by individuals in organizing their responses. Form Definiteness, Form Appropriateness, Color, Shading, and Movement are related to the stimulus qualities often referred to as the determinants of the response. Content variables are labeled Human, Animal, Anatomy, Sex, and Abstract. The quality of the response content is assessed by the variables of Anxiety, Hostility, Barrier, Penetration, and Pathognomonic Verbalization. Integration, Balance, Popular, Reaction Time, and Rejection complete the set of 22 variables for which standard-

ization data have been compiled and are available. For more specific definitions of these 22 variables see Holtzman (1981).

A clear advantage of the HIT over the Rorschach is that norms are available for individuals of different ages, psychiatric conditions and backgrounds, and some cross-cultural data are also available. Holtzman (1981) reports substantial correlations between similar scores on the Rorschach and the HIT, but to date few significant relationships have been found between the HIT and personality inventories. In general, the studies that have investigated the relationships among the HIT variables and various paper-and-pencil approaches to the study of personality have met with little success. Correlations between HIT scores and standard measures of intelligence, scholastic achievement, and convergent thinking are low, but statistically significant (Holtzman, 1981). Studies exploring the specific behavioral measures of personality as they relate to HIT variables are not common, although a number of investigations have demonstrated the effectiveness of the HIT in the classification of groups and in differential diagnosis (Holtzman, 1981).

In summary, the HIT differs from the Rorschach in a number of respects. First, the HIT contains more inkblots than the Rorschach, thus contributing to the richness of the stimuli and of the profile produced. Second, the client is encouraged to give only one response per card, rather than as many as he or she wishes; this adds to the consistency of the number of responses made by each client. Third, a brief inquiry follows immediately after each response made by a client. Fourth, parallel forms of the HIT permit the use of test-retest designs and the study of change or growth within the individual. Fifth, standardized percentile norms are provided for the 22 inkblot scores on a variety of samples and populations; these normative data clearly add to the interpretive validity of the HIT. Finally, group methods of administration and computer scoring add to the practical utility of the HIT. In general, the HIT seems to be one of the most promising variations of the Rorschach available.

The Thematic Apperception Test

The Thematic Apperception Test (TAT) was developed by Henry Murray and Christina Morgan in 1938 and was subsequently published in 1943 (Murray, 1938, 1943). The TAT is a procedure in which the subject makes up stories in response to a series of pictures. It is a construction technique based on the idea that subjects' responses to the pictures will reveal something about their dominant drives, emotions, sentiments, and conflicts of personality. The TAT is administered in an interview situation with one examiner and one client. It is more structured than the Rorschach and more obvious in intent. The procedure is simply that of presenting a series of pictures to a subject and encouraging that person to tell stories about them. Murray (1943) has aptly described the test as an aid to the exploration of personality, and evidence suggests that as such it has been successful. For example, the Watkins, Campbell, and McGregor (1988) data suggest that the TAT is the ninth most frequently used assessment instrument, and the Buros (1978) and Mitchell (1985) data suggest that it is the third most frequently researched assessment instrument, accounting for some 2,000-plus cumulative total references over the years. In research, the TAT ranks immediately behind the Rorschach Inkblot Test.

The TAT consists of a pool of 30 black-and-white picture cards, plus 1 blank card, and may be used with individuals age four and over. Each card pictures a person or persons in various ambiguous situations. Figure 5.2 displays one of the TAT pictures.

Figure 5.2 Pictures from the Thematic Apperception Test. (Reproduced by permission of the publisher from Henry A. Murray, *Thematic Apperception Test*, Cambridge, Mass.: Harvard University Press. Copyright 1943 by the President and Fellows of Harvard University. Copyright 1971 by Henry A. Murray.

When administered, a full TAT consists of 19 of the 30 picture cards, selected as appropriate for age and sex, and the single blank card. The pictures are presented one at a time, and the subject is asked to make up a story in response to each picture. More specifically, in telling a story about a picture, a subject is asked to indicate what is currently happening in the picture, what led up to what is happening in the picture, and how the story ends. From such stories the examiner gains information about the subject's needs, emotions, and personality conflicts. If the full series of 20 cards is used (generally a complete assessment consists of about ten cards), they are usually broken down into two sessions, ten cards per session on two different days. The manual (Murray, 1943) suggests that the average length of stories for adult subjects is about 300 words and the average length of stories for ten-year-old children is about 150 words. In summary, as indicated by Murray (1943), the TAT is no more than 20 small samples of the subject's thought. It is a good method of exploring personality and developing some hypotheses about the individual and his or her environment.

Murray's scheme for analyzing and interpreting the stories told in response to the various TAT pictures is primarily based on his "need-press" approach to personality (Murray, 1938). Murray believed that the stories people tell about the various pictures will tend to be in terms of their past experiences and present wants or needs. Thus, to Murray the basic assumption underlying the interpretation of the TAT is that the stories reflect the individual's internal needs (achievement, aggression, dominance, and abasement) and perceptions of the environment (presses). These personality needs and environmental pressures are usually evident in the hero, or the person that the subject identifies with, in each picture. According to Murray, the personality needs and environmental forces tend to combine to produce an outcome of the story that Murray calls a "thema." These themas may reflect the individual's coping style, success, failure, unresolved problems, contents, and/or problem areas. Thus, from these stories about the pictures the examiner can develop some hypotheses about the subject's personality needs and how the subject tends to cope with different kinds of perceived situations.

Murray's need-press system for interpreting the TAT is not commonly used today. Other scoring systems have been proposed (Bellak, Parsquarelli, & Branerman, 1949; Tomkins, 1947; Rotter, 1946), but these systems by and large are not very popular. In fact, to this very day there is considerable variation in the administration, scoring, and interpretation of the TAT. In the main, interpretation is a subjective process focusing on the personality needs of the main character (the hero or the heroine) and the environmental forces that are perceived to be affecting the hero.

Over the years the TAT has been the focus of considerable research, but unfortunately, as with the Rorschach, the reliability and validity of the TAT construction technique are only weakly supported by the data. Eron, in a review of the TAT (1972), concluded that reasonable reliability is obtained for the TAT when the measure is agreement between two judges in their ratings of responses to TAT pictures. Concurrent validity has been explored by looking at the relationships among TAT-scored personality needs and the assessment of needs using other procedures. The relationships among the TAT-scored needs and the needs as assessed by the Adjective Check List and the Edwards Personal Preference Schedule were low, and thus the tests cannot be viewed as equivalent. Other validity studies have explored the relationship between story content and overt behavior. These studies have been concerned with the relationship between fantasy thought, as reflected in TAT stories, and overt behavior in real life. The findings tend to be ambiguous and difficult to interpret, regardless of age or sex. A variety of other validity studies have successfully differentiated paranoid from nonparanoid psychiatric populations, brain-damaged patients from controls, patients with heart complaints from normals, and foster home children from children living with their natural parents. In addition, the TAT is being used in a variety of cross-cultural studies in Brazil, the Yucatan, Tibet, and West Africa. In general, based on a long history with the TAT, Eron (1972) and Ryan (1985) have suggested that the TAT is a useful indicator of general interest, motives, and areas of emotional disturbance, but is not a very specific measurement device for personality traits of individuals.

In terms of current status, the TAT ranks sixth in the list of most frequently researched assessment instruments. It continues to be one of the more popular projective techniques. As suggested by Murray (1943), the conclusions reached by analysis of TAT stories are good leads for working hypotheses to be verified by other methods. As we noted earlier, the TAT draws forth no more than 20 small samples of the subject's thought. However, to say the least, these samples of thought tell us something about the subject's personality needs and perceptions of environment—about the subject's problems of achievement, rivalry, love, deprivation, cohesion, restraint, conflicts and social interactions.

The Sentence-Completion Technique

The sentence-completion technique for studying personality asks the subject to complete a task, usually a sentence for which the first word or words are supplied. Thus, subjects are presented with sentence stems and asked to complete the sentence in a way that is true for themselves. In a projective sense, the idea is that a subject's self-report in the sentence generated will tend to reflect wishes, fears, and attitudes. How and why it works is not yet clear (Goldberg, 1965). The Watkins, Campbell, and McGregor (1988) data suggest that the sentence completion method is the fourth most frequently used assessment instrument. It is without question a useful and simple procedure for collecting meaningful information about people.

The Rotter Incomplete Sentence Blank (Rotter ISB; Rotter & Rafferty, 1950) is probably the best known of the sentence-completion techniques. The Rotter ISB consists of 40 stems (see Figure 5.3 for example systems) to be completed by the subject. The ISB manual (Rotter & Rafferty, 1950) gives examples for scoring the responses to the items as conflict, neutral, or positive reactions. For example, to the stem "I like," re-

Figure 5.3 Incomplete Sentences Blank, Adult Form. (Reproduced by permission from the Rotter Incomplete Sentence Blank. Copyright © 1950 by The Psychological Corporation. All Rights Reserved.)

INCOMPLETE SENTENCES BLANK — ADULT FORM

Name_____ Sex_____ Age_____ Marital Status_____

Place _____ Date_____

Complete these sentences to express your real feelings. Try to do every one.
Be sure to make a complete sentence.

1. I like _____

2. The happiest time _____

3. I want to know _____

sponses such as "to know if I'm going crazy" and "to be alone" would receive a high score on conflict, and responses such as "a great many things," "most everything," and "cold beer" would receive a high positive rating. As suggested by Rotter and Rafferty, the scoring plan makes the technique useful as a gross screening instrument. Individuals scoring above a predetermined cutting score may have some adjustment problems. Thus, a positive feature of the Rotter ISB is that it does produce a single overall adjustment score.

In terms of research, the Buros (1978) and Mitchell (1985) data suggest that the Rotter ISB is the 73rd most frequently researched assessment instrument, accounting for some 155 cumulative total references over the years. Reliability estimates are reasonable. The items on the Rotter ISB were divided into halves deemed as nearly equivalent as possible. The split-half reliability procedure produced a coefficient of 0.84 when based on the records of 124 male college students, and a coefficient of 0.83 when based on the records of 71 female students. Inner scorer reliability for two scorers was 0.91 when based on 50 male records, and 0.96 when based on 50 female records. There is also some evidence for the validity of the instrument. For example, Getter and Weiss (1968) found that the adjustment scores of the Rotter ISB differentiated between university students who made many visits to the college health center and those who made few visits. In general, the validity studies suggest that the Rotter ISB has been most consistently successful at assessing the psychological adjustment of adults and the severity of psychiatric disturbance. Those studies that have used the Rotter ISB to predict academic success have not been very productive. Normative data on the Rotter ISB are available for 85 female and 214 male college freshmen. These norms are dated, and more recent normative data are needed.

In terms of current status, the sentence-completion technique ranks fourth in the list of most frequently used assessment instruments, and the Rotter ISB ranks 73rd in the list of most frequently researched assessment instruments. Thus, this technique, of which the Rotter ISB is the most well-known example, continues to be a popular and efficient method of collecting meaningful information about people. It is assumed that in completing the sentences, subjects reflect their own wishes, desires, fears, and attitudes about self and life.

Draw-a-Person Expressive Technique

Expressive techniques include a variety of procedures such as painting, psychodrama, and drawing. By far the most popular and commonly used expressive technique is the Draw-a-Person Test. Florence Goodenough's Draw-a-Man test was originally published in 1926 and was revised in 1963 by Dale Harris. The revision by Harris (1963) included a much more extensive scoring system. In 1949 the Machover Draw-A-Person Test was published. The House-Tree-Person Test by Buck (1948) is a similar kind of expressive technique.

A fundamental assumption for the use of this device is that the drawing of a person represents the unconscious projection of the client's self-image. The drawing of a person is also used as a rough estimate of intelligence; some evidence suggests that it is a more reliable and valid estimate of intelligence than of personality. In addition, the Draw-a-Person expressive technique is used to estimate how a client is feeling at the time of testing. In any event, the drawing of a human figure is one of the most widely used projective tests in psychological clinics. The Watkins, Campbell and McGregor (1988) data suggest that the House-Tree-Person Test and Draw-a-Person Test rank seventh and eighth, respectively, as most frequently used assessment instruments.

The procedure simply involves giving subjects a blank sheet of paper with instructions to draw a person. Subjects may be instructed to draw any person they wish, or to draw themselves, or to draw a man, a woman, a friend, a house, or a tree. Generally, each person or object is drawn separately on a different sheet of paper. Drawings are then interpreted in terms of size, quality, positions, clothing, physical features, and so forth. For example, large nostrils are thought to be a sign of hostility, a mouth turned downward is seen as a sign of depression, Little Orphan Annie eyes indicate a feeling of emptiness, absence of feet indicates insecurity, and the drawing of pockets may indicate concern about saving or keeping things. Ogdon's (1978) handbook provides a good interpretive aid for the Draw-a-Person and House-Tree-Person tests. Ogdon notes that no single sign is conclusive evidence of anything and that broader interpretive hypotheses are more likely to hold up than those with high degrees of specificity. In essence, Ogdon indicates that the configuration of signs must be considered more important than any single sign. In general, Ogdon does seem to think that the human figure drawings tend to represent the drawer's perception of self and body image. Other scoring systems have been developed by Jolles (1964), Buck (1948), and Harris (1963).

In spite of the fact that the human-figure drawing technique has been around for more than 50 years, the reliability and validity data are still not very supportive. In comprehensive reviews of the human-figure drawing technique, Swensen (1968) and Kahill (1984) concluded that global ratings are more reliable on the Draw-a-Person Test than ratings of specific components such as the mouth, eyes, nose, or feet. Therefore, ratings of the overall quality of the drawing tend to be more reliable and useful than rat-

ings of specific components or physical features. However, Swensen and Kahill further note that a number of studies suggest that when an overall approach to drawings is used rather than a sign approach, the artistic ability of the subject or the skill of the drawing seems to become a factor. In general, Kahill (1984), Ogdon (1978), Swensen (1968), and Harris (1972) indicate that the empirical justification for the clinical use of the Draw-a-Person technique has increased over the years, but that global judgments seem most data-based. Finally, Goodenough (1926) and Harris (1963) report data supporting the relationship between intellectual ability and the Draw-a-Person technique. Goodenough and Harris suggest that the correlations are positive with higher mental age among children and, to a lesser extent, with intelligence of adults (see Ogdon, 1978, for additional information).

In terms of current status, the Draw-a-Person technique ranks high on the list of most frequently used assessment instruments. It ranks lower on the list of most frequently researched assessment instruments, but more research seems to be exactly what is needed. Harris indicates (1972) that his years of work with the Draw-a-Person technique suggest to him the persisting belief that drawings must tell something about the person's interests, preoccupations, and perhaps unconscious dynamics. However, Harris also asserts that if this belief is to be documented, research must be initiated along psychological dimensions different from those used to date.

Thus, although the Draw-a-Person expressive technique has been and continues to be quite popular in use, additional reliability and validity data clearly are needed.

The Bender Visual Motor Gestalt Test

The *Bender Visual Motor Gestalt Test* (usually referred to as the Bender Gestalt Test) is a different kind of expressive technique, developed by Loretta Bender (1938) for purposes of detecting brain damage. The test, a drawing technique, is based on the assumption that damage to the brain causes some measurable visual motor coordination problems and/or other behavioral deficits. In developing the test, Bender simply asked children to copy certain designs rather than to verbally describe them. Hutt and Briskin (1960), in a revision of the Bender Gestalt Test, attempted to extend the test's use to understanding personality; however, the evidence gives little support to the use of the Bender Gestalt Test in this area.

The Bender Gestalt Test continues to be a popular method for detecting brain damage and for assessing problems in visual motor coordination due to brain damage. The Watkins, Campbell and McGregor (1988) data suggest that the Bender Gestalt Test is the fifth most frequently used assessment instrument, and the Buros (1978) and Mitchell (1985) data suggest that it is the eleventh most frequently researched assessment instrument, accounting for some 1,082 cumulative total references over the years.

The Bender Gestalt Test is short: nine cards showing simple figures consisting of dots, curves, or lines (see Figure 5.4). It may be used with individuals age four and over. Subjects taking the test are simply asked to copy the nine geometric figures that are visually presented. No memory is involved, since the figures remain present during the administration. The subject must see the stimulus, develop a perception of the stimulus, and reproduce the perception of the stimulus. If visual acuity and motor control problems may be ruled out, the assumption is that faulty reproductions are probably the result of brain damage. For example, errors on the test involving the rotation of figures, gross integration, or perseveration tend to support brain damage.

The total time to complete the Bender

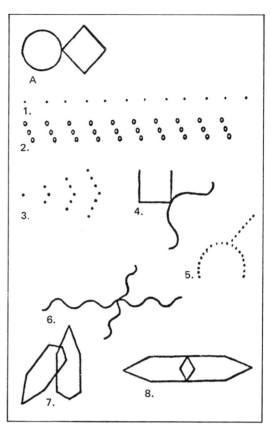

Figure 5.4 Copies of nine Bender ® Gestalt Figures. (Reproduced with permission from *A Visual Motor Gestalt Test and Its Clinical Use*, Research Monographs No. 3 by Lauretta Bender, p. 4. Copyright 1938 by the American Orthopsychiatric Association, New York, N.Y.)

Gestalt Test is also of consequence and interest. Individuals with organic problems will tend to spend excessive time, and obsessive-compulsive individuals have been known to spend more than three or four minutes on each design. On the other hand, hasty drawings tend to suggest impulsiveness and impatience. Formal scoring systems have been developed (Pascal & Suttell, 1951; Hutt, 1951, 1977; Koppitz, 1975), but many experienced clinicians prefer to interpret and analyze the results by visual inspection. Handbooks with some good interpretive notions and hypotheses have been written by Lacks (1984) and Ogdon (1978). They present a good review of existing research evidence in an applied and useful framework.

In studying the reliability of the Bender Gestalt Test, Tolor and Schulberg (1963) found test-retest coefficients to be about 0.70 for a sample of normal adults over a 24-hour period. Scorer reliabilities of about 0.90 were reported for trained scorers. More recently, Koppitz (1975) carried out a rather elaborate standardization of the Bender Gestalt Test with children. Test-retest reliability coefficients over a four-month period within grade groups varied from a low of 0.55 to 0.66. These coefficients do tend to be rather low.

Most of the validity data on the Bender Gestalt Test tend to be concurrent in nature, and additional work is clearly needed on different samples and with a variety of criteria. Some validity work of interest by Tolor and Schulberg (1963) suggests that performance on the Bender Gestalt Test is significantly related to amount of education. In his standardization study with children, Koppitz (1975) found that performance on the Bender Gestalt Test is related to school readiness and subsequent educational achievement of first-grade children. In addition, Koppitz found Bender Gestalt Test performance differences between brain injured and normal children between the ages of five and ten. The work of Koppitz and his developmental scoring system seem to provide very productive aids for the study of the use of the Bender in exploring children's problems.

In summary, Kitay (1972) and Whitworth (1984) support the use of the Bender Gestalt Test in diagnostic examination of adults and children because of its unique contributions to the evaluation of perceptual motor functioning, neurological impairment, expressive styles, and maladjustment. Kitay and Whitworth further suggest that the Bender Gestalt is a brief and useful test that deserves its popularity among clinicians. However, it goes without saying that additional reliability and validity data are needed. (Other tests that may be used to assess the behavioral affects of central nervous system impairment are the Memory for Design Test, the Halstead Neurological Test Battery, the Tactile Performance Test, the Wechsler Scale Block Design Subtest, the Wechsler Memory Scale, and the Benton Test of Visual Retention.)

BEHAVIORAL TECHNIQUES AND TESTS

The behavioral, or performance, model of personality psychology defines personality in terms of the individual's performance, or actual overt behavior, in a given situation. Behavior is assumed to be primarily a function of antecedent conditions or prior experiences. Thus, the best predictor of future behavior is thought to be past behavior or behavior that has been reinforced in the past. The behavioral approach permits us to say something about how an individual will behave in a specific situation. When this approach is operationalized, clients are asked to perform some task in a specific given situation. Behavior in that situation may then be observed by the client and others and commented upon in terms of behavioral excesses, deficits, inappropriateness, and assets. This kind of information is generally organized through a functional analysis of relevant behavior, which is discussed below. However, over the years a variety of behavioral questionnaires and self-monitoring techniques have developed, primarily because it is not very feasible to send observers into clients' work, social, or family environments. Thus, in many cases behavioral questionnaires may be a primary source of behavioral kinds of data. These questionnaires have proven to be a valuable source of behavioral information, but the reliability and validity data pertaining to these techniques is very limited.

Functional Analysis

In behavioral assessment a *functional analysis* is frequently used to organize behavior and to identify problem behaviors. The functional analysis (Bijou & Peterson, 1971; Kanfer & Saslow, 1969; Osipow & Walsh, 1970) makes the basic assumption that problematic behavior is behavior learned in relation to an environment and, in addition, that behavior is maintained and reinforced by conditions that exist in the current environment. In this framework the task of the functional analysis is to collect behavioral data on antecedent conditions, the relation of behavior to the environment and reinforcements in the environment, and the meaning of the behavior. An attempt is made to compare the individual's response repertoire to the behavioral potential of the environment. This is operationalized by focusing on behavioral excesses, behavioral deficits, and behavioral inappropriateness. These general classes serve as behavioral problem categories in behavioral assessment.

A *behavioral excess* suggests that a given overt response occurs too frequently and from that standpoint is a behavioral problem. Examples of behavioral excesses would be overeating, compulsive hand washing, alcohol or drug problems, and a smoking problem. Behavioral excesses suggest a treatment that would involve a nonreward of the behavior. On the other hand, a *behavioral deficit* suggests that the individual has not learned a specific adaptive response that is acceptable and rewarded by a given environment. Examples include inadequate study skills and poor social skills. A response deficit in terms of treatment suggests some kind of training that would eventually lead to environmental reward. *Behavioral inappropriateness* suggests

that certain responses are situationally inappropriate, such as talking to imaginary people in public and stealing. Here in terms of treatment an attempt is made to identify and define more appropriate situations in which the behavior may be emitted.

Another important part of the functional analysis is to identify *behavioral assets* of the client. In essence, these are abilities, skills, behaviors, and achievements that have helped the client function with some degree of effectiveness and that may be used in replacing more undesirable kinds of behaviors. Some focus on the behavioral assets helps the client realize that in spite of problematic behavior he or she possesses some productive and positive behaviors. Thus, the functional analysis focuses on the client's complaints by analyzing behavioral excesses, deficits, and inappropriateness, as well as assets, in the individual's family environment, work environment, and interpersonal environment. It is important to determine how the behavioral excesses and deficits are maintained and reinforced in the client's current environment.

Behavioral Questionnaires

A variety of different methods for the collection of behavioral data have been used over the years. The most traditional of these approaches has been the interview method focusing on the client's self-report. More contemporary procedures are direct observations of the client's behavior by the counselor, observations of others such as family members or friends, role-playing, the use of a diary or daily log, rating scales, and various nominating techniques. As noted by Sundberg (1990), the traditional psychological tests tend to be rarely used in the functional analysis of relevant behavior.

Ideally, as discussed above, behavioral data for a functional analysis is collected using some kind of observation of behavior in the current environment. However, since observations of behavior in natural settings are frequently difficult to obtain, from the standpoint of practicality and economics, samples of behavior must be obtained in other ways. This necessity has led to the development of a number of behavioral questionnaires. Recent increased interest in cognitive therapy, with its assumption that beliefs and values influence a significant amount of behavior, has also encouraged the development and use of questionnaires to assess a variety of behaviors. Questionnaires have been developed to assess behavior in the areas of assertiveness, social interactions, marital interactions, ingestive behaviors, and sex roles. The questionnaires have been chiefly concerned with identifying behavioral problems, client fears, and client reinforcements or preferences. Some of these questionnaires are discussed below. In general, the questionnaires have been designed to provide self-report data from clients or ratings of clients by others. It is vitally important that questionnaires provide quantitative data on specific behaviors in specific situations. Many of these questionnaires lack reliability and validity data, however.

As noted by Haynes and Wilson (1979) and Nelson and Hayes (1982), a number of questionnaires have been developed to assess *assertiveness* in a wide variety of adults, including drug abusers, psychiatric patients, and college students. Generally the scales employed have been of the self-report type and have focused on behaviors such as interpersonal skills, social skills, social expectations, and responsiveness to assertion skill training. For example, the Generalized Expectations of Others Questionnaire (Eisler, Frederiksen, & Peterson, 1978) is designed to assess differences between individuals high and low in assertiveness with respect to expectations of others in everyday situations. On the Assertion Inventory (Gambrill & Richey, 1975) individuals indicate the de-

gree of discomfort to a range of situations calling for an assertive response. The Action Situation Inventory (Friedman, 1971) measures the individual's degree of assertiveness in a range of different situations. In general, the validity of these and other such inventories has received limited attention. However, the limited data do suggest that many of the scales tend to be sensitive to changes in behavior (Haynes & Wilson, 1979; Nelson & Hayes, 1982; Haynes, 1983).

In assessing *social interactions*, behavioral questionnaires have been used with infants, preschool and school-age children, and adults. Generally, the format of these behavioral questionnaires involves teacher and caretaker ratings for child behaviors and self-report responses for adults. Behavior questionnaires used with children have focused on the assessment of social interactions, isolation, and nonconformity. Questionnaires used with adults have focused on heterosexual social anxiety and dating patterns and trends (Haynes & Wilson, 1979; Nelson & Hayes, 1982; Haynes, 1983). Some questionnaires with potential for behavioral assessment in this area include the Social Competence Scale (Kohn, 1977), which is primarily concerned with the assessment of overt classroom behavior with respect to interpersonal relationships; the Survey of Heterosexual Interactions (Twentyman & McFall, 1975), which is concerned with past dating history and males' assertiveness with females in social situations; the Social Competence Scale (Lanyon, 1967), which collects data on dating and confidence in heterosexual situations; and the Peer Contact Form (Becker, 1977), which is a parental questionnaire asking about children's social interactions. Again, as with most behavioral questionnaires, the validity of these questionnaires has been lightly explored (Haynes & Wilson, 1979; Nelson & Hayes, 1982; Haynes; 1983).

The behavioral questionnaires assessing *marital interaction* and satisfaction have primarily focused on marital discord and marital stress. These behavioral questionnaires have used a self-report format and the assessment's function is usually to identify problem behaviors. Questionnaires measuring marital interaction include the Dyadic Adjustment Scale (Spanier, 1976), used in a self-report format to measure marital adjustments, cohesion, and affection expressed; the Knox Marital Adjustment Scale (Knox, 1971), used to assess overall marital happiness; and the Marital Conflict Form (Weiss & Margolin, 1977), which is a self-report questionnaire designed to identify marital problem areas. Some limited data suggest that these behavioral questionnaires are sensitive to behavior change, but again there is little evidence investigating the validity of these questionnaires (Haynes & Wilson, 1979; Nelson & Hayes, 1982; Haynes, 1983).

Questionnaires assessing *ingestive behaviors* have been used with overweight adults, alcoholic adults, and adult smokers. These questionnaires using a self-report format tend to focus on demographic variables, eating characteristics, lifestyle characteristics, dietary issues, antecedents of drinking patterns and smoking behaviors, and consequences of drinking patterns. Some questionnaires measuring ingestive behaviors include the Eating Patterns Questionnaire (Wollersheim, 1970), which is a self-report questionnaire measuring patterns of eating; and the Scale of Internal versus External Control of Weight (Tobias & MacDonald, 1977), which explores whether weight is hereditary, due to childhood problems, or due to the need for reinforcement. In general, these behavioral questionnaires have been found to be sensitive to behavioral changes, but few studies have explored scale validities (Haynes & Wilson, 1979; Nelson & Hayes, 1982; Haynes, 1983).

Behavioral questionnaires have been used in the assessment of *sex role attitudes and behaviors* of children and adults. Behaviors targeted for assessment have included masculine and feminine patterns of behavior, feminine role inadaptability, feminine self-concept, sexual performance and satisfaction, sexual behaviors, and reinforcing imagery. The questionnaires have used a self-report format and have been primarily concerned with the outcome of intervention programs. Some examples of questionnaires used to assess sexual attitudes and behaviors are the Sexual Activities Checklist (Bentler, 1968), on which clients report heterosexual behaviors, and the Sexual Orientation Questionnaire (Feldman & MacCulloch, 1971), which is used primarily to assess heterosexual and homosexual interests.

Problem behaviors assessed by questionnaires have focused on conduct problems, noncompliance, hyperactivity, drug usage, disturbed behaviors within families, suicidal intent, depression, obsessive-compulsive complaints, anger, stuttering, and pain. These behavioral questionnaires have been used with children, children and their parents, adolescents, and adults. Questionnaire formats vary and have included ratings by others, self-reports, and self-ratings. In the main, these questionnaires are used for problem identification, but they have not been very effective in providing information about the situational conditions of problem behaviors.

One of the oldest of these questionnaires used in problem identification is the Mooney Problem Checklist (Mooney & Gordon, 1950), which is a self-administered checklist of problems. The college form of the checklist contains 330 items, with 30 items in each of 11 areas. The problem areas assessed include health, social-psychological relations, personal relations, sexual needs, home and family, morals and religion, adjustment, and the future. The checklist has been used frequently in college counseling centers to identify student areas of concern. There are a number of other questionnaires used to assess and identify problem behaviors. A few of these are the Affect Adjective Checklist (Zuckerman, 1977), used to describe one's current emotional states; the Beck Depression Inventory (Beck, 1967); the Anger Inventory (Novaco, 1977); the Irrational Beliefs Test (Jones, 1968), which consists of statements believed to reflect irrational thinking; the Obsessive-Compulsive Questionnaire (Hodgson & Rachman, 1977); the Suicidal Intent Scale (Kovacs & Beck, 1977), and the Teacher Problem Listing (Azrin, Azrin, & Armstrong, 1977). Most of the questionnaires seem fairly responsive to behavior change, but in general, as noted by Haynes and Wilson (1979), other kinds of validity have not been explored; the most usual application of behavioral questionnaires has been in the assessment of problem behavior and traits.

Another area in which behavioral questionnaires are frequently being applied is in the assessment of *fear responses*. Most of these questionnaires use a self-report format (although there are some checklist formats) and have been directed at male and female adult populations. Target behaviors include spider phobias, rat phobias, snake phobias, fears of height, dental fears, fears of public transportation, fears of bodily injury, social and heterosexual fears, public-speaking and speech fears, achievement anxiety, test anxiety, and generalized anxiety. A number of different questionnaires have been constructed, and their names are very indicative of the fear being assessed. For example, the Acrophobia Questionnaire (Cohen, 1977) is a 40-item self-report questionnaire for fears of heights. Other questionnaires include the Fear of Snakes (Lang, Melamed, & Hart, 1970), the Mathematics Anxiety Scale (Richardson & Suinn, 1973), the Personal Report of Confidence as a Speaker (Paul, 1966), the Spider Anxiety Questionnaire (Denny & Sullivan, 1976), and the Suinn Test Anxiety Behavior Scale (Suinn, 1969a,b). Probably

the major function of these questionnaires has been to assess the outcome of a given intervention, but at times, and with increased frequency, questionnaires are being used for purposes of problem identification. In general, evidence indicates that the fear questionnaires tend to be sensitive to changes in behavior, but other validity data are lacking (Haynes & Wilson, 1979; Nelson & Hayes, 1982; Haynes, 1983).

Some questionnaires have been constructed to assess sources of *client reinforcement* and perceptions of reinforcers. The formats of these questionnaires have been based on self-reports, ratings by self and others, and checklists. The questionnaires have functioned to assess client preferences for various reinforcements prior to treatment and to assess treatment outcome. As with most behavioral questionnaires, reliability and validity data are limited, to say the least. Some examples of behavioral questionnaires in this area include the Reinforcement Survey Schedule (Cautela & Kastenbaum, 1967), developed to identify reinforcers to be used in behavior therapy. The Rotter I.E. Locus of Control Scale (Rotter, 1966) is primarily concerned with the client's perceived control over reinforcers and assesses the client's perceptions of reinforcements being internally or externally controlled. People viewing their rewards as being externally controlled may attribute their successes to good luck and accident.

The above behavioral questionnaires are but a few of those available. The total number of available behavioral questionnaires runs into the hundreds. For a more elaborate list and discussion of these questionnaires see Haynes (1978), Haynes and Wilson (1979) and Nelson and Hayes (1982). In the main, these questionnaires cover the ground we have indicated: behavioral problems, client fears, and client reinforcements. Formats of the questionnaires include self-reports, ratings by self and others, and checklists by self and others. In many cases the questionnaires are used to identify client problems and to assess treatment outcome. In general, reliability and validity data are weak for the questionnaires, but evidence suggests that many of the questionnaires are sensitive to behavioral changes. In any event, caution should be employed in the application and interpretation of questionnaires that lack reliability and validity data.

Self-Monitoring

Another behavioral procedure receiving increased attention is that of *self-monitoring*, which is the observation and recording of one's own behavior. It is a procedure of interest for a number of reasons, one of which is that it permits data collection on certain behaviors (headaches) that are difficult for someone else to observe. Self-monitoring may also be applied to a variety of overt behaviors (smoking and drinking) in order to reduce the time commitment of external observers, the cost, and/or the inefficiency. In addition, as noted by Haynes and Wilson (1979) and Goldfried (1982), self-monitoring may have a therapeutic impact by increasing a client's awareness of his or her behavior and its impact on others. Furthermore, self-monitoring seems likely to increase a client's awareness of the impact of environment on behavior.

As an assessment instrument, self-monitoring has been applied in a variety of settings with a variety of behaviors, such as ingestive behaviors, addictive behaviors, sexual behaviors, work behaviors, academic behaviors, and emotional responses. Smoking behavior has been a frequent target of self-monitoring procedures. Self-monitoring procedures have also been applied to a variety of different populations, including children, adolescents, college students, teachers, adult outpatients, families, and institutionalized individuals. The recording

methods used in the self-monitoring procedures have included talley sheets, data sheets, daily weighings, self-report postcards, recording on charts, daily record cards, recording before or after smoking, logbooks, daily headache forms, diaries, wrist counters, and video taping of the behavior.

A question important to us concerns the validity of self-monitoring procedures. We need information supporting the correspondence between self-monitoring data and other measures of the targeted behavior. For example, self-recorded frequencies of cigarette smoking should accurately reflect the actual number of cigarettes smoked. However, there are problems here because data suggest that self-monitoring procedures have associated reaction effects. For example, as noted by Haynes and Wilson (1979) and Hartman and Wood (1982), self-monitoring may function to modify the rates of targeted behaviors, thus influencing the reliability and validity of the assessment. In addition, data obtained through self-monitoring may accurately reflect a current behavior rate, but inaccurately reflect behavior rates before and after the self-monitoring procedure. Furthermore, data obtained through self-monitoring may not accurately reflect behavior rates when self-monitoring is not occurring. Any factors that tend to increase or decrease the behavior-change qualities of self-monitoring may also influence the validity of self-monitoring. These issues and problems need to be kept in mind when using and interpreting self-monitoring behavioral procedures.

Observation in Natural Environments

Naturalistic observation procedures have been used for assessment in a wide variety of environments, in the home and in a number of community settings, including restaurants, schools, and other institutions. The procedure has received increased attention primarily because of the commonsense basis of the technique. One simply observes and codes the behavior of an individual in a given situation or environment. Thus, the procedure seems to have greater content validity and to require less inference (Haynes & Wilson, 1979; Hartman & Wood, 1982). Target behaviors assessed include parent-child interactions, ingestive behaviors, eliminative behaviors, stereotypic responses, aggressive behaviors, noncomplaint behaviors, social skills, and academic behaviors. These target behaviors have been assessed in a variety of populations, using external observers in some assessment formats and participant observers in others.

In general, the evidence suggests that the employed observation instruments tend to be sensitive to intervention effects in home and community settings (Haynes & Wilson, 1979; Hartman & Wood, 1982). However, a number of factors seem to affect the reliability and validity of naturalistic observation. Observer accuracy is an issue, for example. How reliable and valid is the performance of observers? Related to the performance of observers is the problem of "observer drift," which is defined as the deterioration of the accuracy of observers over some period of time. It goes without saying that changes in recording performance influence the reliability and validity of the observations reported. In addition, the motivation and/or expectations and/or naiveté of observers may be variables that could influence the observations reported. Likewise, the activity of observation measures may be a problem. For example, the naturalness of behavior may be influenced when a subject is aware of being observed. Furthermore, as we increase the number of behaviors to be recorded we may in fact have a detrimental impact on the reliability and validity of the data obtained, actually decreasing the reliability and validity of these observations. Still, the evidence suggests that in spite of potential problems affecting reliability and validity, observation in natural environments is to some extent an effective measure of treatment outcome. However, there is little evidence that naturalistic observation is being applied as a preintervention assessment, that is, for problem identification purposes (Haynes & Wilson, 1979).

SUMMARY

This chapter has focused on the psychodynamic and the situational, or behavioral, approaches to personality test development. The psychodynamic approach is the interpretive basis for the projective techniques discussed. The basic assumption of projective techniques is that the individual's responses to vague or ambiguous stimuli will tend to reflect his/her basic personality. In general, the projective techniques tend to be less obvious in their intent, and thus clients tend to be less aware of the type of interpretation that will be made of their responses. In this chapter we discussed five different projective techniques and tests associated with them: the association technique (e.g., the Rorschach Inkblot Test), the construction technique (e.g., the Thematic Apperception Test), the completion technique (e.g., the Incomplete Sentence Blank), the ordering, or choice, technique (e.g., the Id, Ego, Superego Test), and the expressive technique (e.g., the Draw-a-Person Test). Each projective test discussed seemed to represent appropriately one of five different approaches to projective assessment.

The behavioral, or performance, approach defines personality in terms of the individual's actual overt behavior in a given situation. It assumes that behavior is primarily a function of antecedent conditions or prior experiences. To operationalize this approach, clients are asked to perform some task in a specific situation. Behavior in that situation may then be observed by self and others and analyzed in terms of behavior excesses, deficits, inappropriateness, and assets. This chapter has discussed a variety of behavioral techniques, including behavioral questionnaires that have developed primarily because of the inconvenience and the cost of observing people or clients in different situations.

6

The Nature and Assessment of Intelligence

Chapter 1 provided an overview of the history of the measurement of intelligence, mentioning such important figures as Francis Galton, James McKeen Cattell, Alfred Binet, and David Wechsler and their attempts to measure overall intellectual level, or global intelligence. The measurement of intelligence was indeed one of psychology's earliest and most useful contributions to applied practice. This chapter dealing with the nature and assessment of intelligence will begin with an overview of how intelligence has been conceptualized since Galton's work in the 1800s. It will then proceed to a discussion of various types of intelligence tests.

Throughout the chapter, issues in the use and interpretation of intelligence test scores will be highlighted.

THE NATURE OF INTELLIGENCE

As was discussed in Chapter 3, psychological test contruction ordinarily begins with a theory about the construct to be measured. The way in which we conceptualize the construct determines our approach to measuring it. A psychological test is an operational definition, or *observable translation*, of an abstract, unobservable entity or construct. Theories of the *nature* of intelligence have influenced approaches to its assessment. Conversely, results obtained from using various measures of intelligence have contributed to further clarification of the meaning of the construct. Because of the close and necessary relationship between theory and measurement, our discussion of intelligence will begin with theories of the construct.

The concept of intelligence and the idea that individuals possess different levels, or amounts, of intelligence had their origins in ancient philosophy; discussions of these ideas are found in numerous writings predating the birth of Christ, for example, those of the Greek philosophers Plato and Aristotle. The philosopher Thomas Acquinas (1225–1274) defined intelligence as the "power to combine and separate," the capacity to see similarity among dissimilar things and dissimilarity among similar things (cf. Jensen, 1980). Until the nineteenth century, however, the concept of intelligence remained a philosophical and intuitive one. People undoubtedly observed differences in the "quickness" or "brightness" of others, but these differences were not understood or studied scientifically.

Beginning in the late nineteenth century, scientists in the infant field of psychology began to investigate and attempt to measure intelligence, and from that time to the present day this concept and its measurement have intrigued and engaged the attention of many brilliant and creative psychologists. Different scientists have had different ideas concerning the nature of intelligence and how to measure it, but all these ideas have contributed to our current understanding of the nature, meaning, and measurement of mental ability.

The Galton-Cattell Approach to Intelligence

The first scientific attention to the concept of human intelligence is attributed to the Englishman Sir Francis Galton (1822–1911). Galton, a first cousin of Charles Darwin (who was instrumental in developing the theory of evolution), postulated the existence of a "general mental ability" in humans. Galton's theory of this general mental ability, or intelligence, was based on the idea that since all information reaches us through our senses (e.g., sight, hearing, and touch), intellect was the sum of all of the simple, component parts of sensory functioning. Galton (1883, p. 27) wrote, "The only information that reaches us concerning outward events appears to pass through the avenue of our senses; and the more perceptive the senses are of difference, the larger is the field upon which our judgment and intelligence can act." Thus, Galton postulated that intelligence derives from the speed and refinement of our sensory responses to environmental stimuli.

At the same time Galton was formulating his ideas about human mental ability, the now well-known American psychologist James McKeen Cattell (1860–1944) was completing his doctoral work in experimental psychology under Wilhelm Wundt in Leipzig, Germany. An avid student of individual differences, Cattell was attracted to Galton's work and, after finishing his doctorate under Wundt, went to work with Galton in England. Galton and Cattell developed numerous laboratory devices for measuring the sensory capacities they thought were the component parts of human intellect. Tests were developed to measure the capacity to discriminate sizes, colors, weights, and pitch and to measure visual and hearing acuity, reaction time, strength of handgrip, memory span, and numerous other sensory and motor capabilities. These original *mental tests* (a term first coined by Cattell in 1890) were widely used in Galton's anthropometric laboratory in London and in the psychological laboratory Cattell established at Cornell University in New York.

Extensive use and study of these mental tests prior to and around the turn of the century began to cast doubt on the degree to which measures of sensory discrimination, perceptual speed, and motor coordination were measuring what was intuitively thought to be intelligence. First, scores on the various mental tests were not found to be highly correlated with each other (see Sharp, 1898–1899; Wissler, 1901) and thus did not seem to be reflecting some "general mental ability." Second, scores on the mental tests were not highly related to common-sense, intuitively reasonable indices of intelligence, such as teacher's ratings (Bolton, 1891–1892) or school grades (Wissler, 1901).

In 1904 Charles Spearman pointed out numerous methodological and statistical problems with earlier studies and presented data indicating that the mental tests were related to school performance in children, but his work was not widely considered. Furthermore, the need for special laboratory equipment, the necessity for repeated measurements to ensure a reliable score, and the large number of separate mental tests used made the Galton-Cattell approach somewhat impractical. Thus, this approach to the measurement of human intelligence was abandoned shortly after the turn of the twentieth century.

Binet's Conception of Intelligence

At the same time that the Galton-Cattell approach was declining in popularity, two Frenchmen, Alfred Binet (1857–1911) and Théophile Simon (1873–1961), were developing a markedly different approach to the conceptualization and measurement of intelligence. In 1904, Binet and Simon were commissioned by the French Ministry of Education to develop a means by which mentally retarded children could be distinguished from normal children. Means of easily and readily identifying retarded children were necessary so that special programs of education could be provided for them. In approaching this applied problem, Binet and Simon conceived of intelligence as involving the "higher mental processes" of *judgment* and *reasoning*, rather than the sensory-motor capabilities of the Galton-Cattell approach. Thus, while the first Binet-Simon intelligence test, available in 1905, retained Galton's tests of weight discrimination and short-term memory, it *emphasized* the capacity to make good judgments, to reason well, and to use common sense.

In addition to their emphasis on judgment and reasoning, Binet and Simon contributed the essential notion that the capacity to demonstrate the "higher mental processes" should increase as a child aged; they wisely used this notion in constructing their intelligence test. Test items were grouped according to the age at which the majority of children responded correctly to an item, and items that did not differentiate among age levels were not used. For example, items grouped at age three included "repeats two digits" and "enumerates common objects in a picture." Items to which most eight-year-olds responded correctly included "counts backward from 20 to zero" and "notes omissions from pictures of familiar objects." Items grouped at age 12 included "defines three abstract words" and "discovers the sense of a disarranged sentence." Scores on the intelligence test were expressed in terms of the age of children whose performance the examinee equaled; the term *mental level*, or *mental age*, was therefore used to describe the examinee's intellectual level. For example, a six-year-old child who scored at the level of normal three-year-olds would be considered somewhat retarded, while a six-year-old who scored at the level of the average nine-year-old would be assessed as highly intelligent.

The Binet-Simon tests, the first practically useful tests of intelligence, attracted wide attention and were soon translated and adapted for use in many countries throughout the world. In 1916 Lewis M. Terman, a psychologist at Stanford University, revised, expanded, and standardized the Binet-Simon test for use in the United States. Terman also made use of the idea (first suggested by William Stern) of dividing the tested mental age (*MA*) by the child's chronological age (*CA*) and multiplying by 100 to obtain an "intelligence quotient" or "IQ." In the example presented previously, the six-year-old scoring at the three-year-old level would have an IQ of 50 ($MA/CA \times 100 = 3/6 \times 100 = 50$), while the six-year-old scoring at the nine-year-old level would have an IQ of 150 ($MA/CA \times 100 = 9/6 \times 100 = 150$). Terman's revision of the Binet tests, now known as the Stanford-Binet Intelligence Scale, is the most widely used intelligence test in the world. The Stanford-Binet will be described in detail later in the chapter, but its origins with Binet and Simon in France should be given due credit, for their test was the progenitor of all subsequent individual tests of intelligence.

Spearman's Two-Factor Theory

As was mentioned previously, Charles Spearman's (1904) studies of the Galton-Cattell mental tests indicated that various mental tests were positively correlated. These findings, along with other studies using the technique of factor analysis (which Spearman himself originated), led Spearman to the conclusion that a "general mental ability" postulated by Galton did exist and could be measured. In his "two-factor theory" of intelligence, Spearman (1923) postulated that every mental test or test item measured a general factor *g* that was common to all items and a specific factor *s* that was unique to that particular item and not shared by any other item. When scores on a large number of mental test items are summed, the unrelated specific variance should cancel out, and the remaining variability should therefore reflect individual differences in *g*.

Figure 6.1 depicts Spearman's two-factor theory of intelligence. Assume that we have four mental tests, using verbal analogies, vocabulary, numerical reasoning, and number series items, respectively. According to Spearman, what is measured by each of these tests includes *g* (shown as the overlap between the circle and the small oval representing the test) and a specific factor *s* that is unique to that test. The lack of overlap of any specific factor with any other specific factor (e.g., s_1 with s_2, or s_2 with s_3) illustrates Spearman's notion of the uniqueness and independence of the specific factors. To measure intelligence, then, one would search for those mental tests most highly saturated with *g* (in Figure 6.1, those tests showing more overlap with *g* and lesser amounts of specific variance).

Spearman's conception of *g* involved several ideas that endured in terms of how we conceive of and measure intelligence. First, Spearman (1923) formulated the idea of the *indifference of the indicator*, meaning that the specific *content* of the items used to measure intelligence is unessential. Content is merely a vehicle for representing the essential elements of measuring intelligence. These es-

Figure 6.1 Representation of general ("g") and specific ("s") factors postulated in Spearman's two-factor theory.

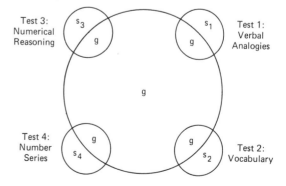

sential elements were summarized by Spearman as the *eduction of relations and correlates.* *Eduction* (meaning "to draw forth or bring out") is essentially the ability to reason and to discover relationships. *Eduction of relations* (or inductive reasoning) is the ability to infer the general rule given instances of the rule. *Eduction of correlates* (deductive reasoning) is the ability to recognize an instance given the general rule. Intelligence tests, therefore, should assess our ability to think, to reason, and to see relationships, and the test *content* can be anything that provides a vehicle for that assessment. For example, the content or, in Spearman's terms, the "fundaments" (as in "fundamental elements") of an analogies test could be verbal, numerical, figural, or pictorial. Intelligence is the ability to see the analogy, not the simple comprehension of, for example, the words used to present the problem. Spearman's principle of the eduction of relations and correlates as the essential indicator of intelligence is still the basis for the measurement of intelligence. His principle of the indifference of the indicator has contributed to the wide variety of content in test items utilized—for example, verbal and nonverbal content, numerical reasoning, pictorial tests, figural problems, and matrices.

While the existence of Spearman's *g* is now generally accepted (and measured by such g-saturated tests as Raven's (1938) Progressive Matrices), researchers, including Spearman himself, soon began to conclude that there were factors of mental ability somewhere in between the global generality of *g* and the absolute uniqueness of specific factors. These factors of intermediate generality, often called "group" factors, were the focus of multiple factor theories of intelligence.

Multiple Factor Theories

Multiple factor theories developed as a result of factor-analytic results showing that the correlations among some groups of tests were higher than would be expected from the loadings of the tests on *g*. In other words, while some common or shared variance could be attributed to the tests' overlap with *g*, there was additional shared variance that seemed to reflect other common factors in mental tests. Figure 6.2 illustrates how multiple factor theory differed from Spearman's two-factor theory (depicted in Figure 6.1). Recall that in Figure 6.1 each of the four tests shown shared some variance with *g* and that the

Figure 6.2 Representation of the concepts of multiple factor theory. The figure shows two group factors. The overlap of Test 1 (Verbal Analogies) and Test 2 (Vocabulary) is the group factor known as verbal ability. The overlap of Test 3 (Numerical Reasoning) and Test 4 (Number Series) is the group factor known as numerical ability.

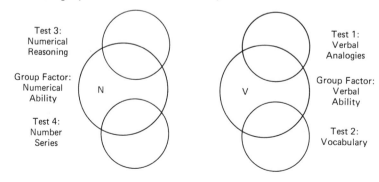

remaining variance was specific or unique variance shared with no other tests. These same four tests are shown in Figure 6.2. Two of the tests, verbal analogies and vocabulary, have variance in common, but this shared variance is not *g*, but a group factor of verbal ability, depicted on the right side of Figure 6.2. Similarly, the tests of numerical reasoning and the number series have in common the group factor of numerical ability, depicted on the left side of Figure 6.2. (It should be noted that the group factors depicted in Figure 6.2 would be only two of several or many possible group factors postulated to describe the dimensions of human mental ability.) Finally, although different multiple factor theorists disagreed about the extent of the existence and importance of Spearman's *g* and *s*, all believed in the existence and importance of group factors. Leon L. Thurstone and J. P. Guilford postulated two of the major multiple factor theories.

Thurstone factor-analyzed the scores from some 60 mental tests and found seven group factors that occurred consistently. These seven factors, which he called the *primary mental abilities* (Thurstone, 1938; Thurstone & Thurstone, 1941), were as follows: *verbal comprehension* (V), measured by, for example, vocabulary tests, reading comprehension, and verbal analogies; *word fluency* (W), measured by anagrams and/or rhyming tests; *Number* (N), the speed and accuracy of arithmetic computation; *space* (S), spatial relations and visualization; *associative memory* (M), including tests for memory of paired associates; *perceptual speed* (P), the ability to quickly grasp details, similarities, and differences in visual material; and *reasoning* (R), for example, number series, arithmetic reasoning, and inductive and deductive reasoning. Working in collaboration with his wife Thelma G. Thurstone, Thurstone developed a battery of tests, called the Primary Mental Abilities Test (PMA), to measure these seven major group factors of ability. These tests were among the first intelligence tests designed to measure multiple factors of ability rather than to focus on the measurement of *g* per se. The PMA continues to be used, although it is now known as the Schaie-Thurstone Adult Mental Abilities Test, published by Consulting Psychologists Press.

Guilford was another major contributor to multiple factor theories of intelligence. After ten years of factor-analytic research, he postulated what he called the *structure of intellect*, or SI model (Guilford, 1967). The SI model proposes that intellectual abilities can be described and classified along three basic dimensions: operations, contents, and products. There are five types of operations, four types of contents, and six types of products. When these are organized into a three-dimensional classification system, they result in 120 (5 × 4 × 6) separate mental abilities, each representing the intersection of one operation, one content, and one product. Figure 6.3 shows the way in which Guilford depicts his model graphically. Note the cross-classification of operations, contents, and products.

The *operation* is what the individual does—that is, the basic kind of intellectual process involved. The five operations are as follows: *cognition*, including recognition, comprehension, and understanding; *memory*, referring to how well a person can remember something very recently learned; *convergent production*, in which the subject must use given information to arrive at a simple correct answer, for example, a logical reasoning test involving syllogisms; *divergent production*, the ability to think in different directions given a simple cue (assessed by questions such as "How many uses can you think of for water?"); and *evaluation*, involving decisions as to whether given information satisfies criteria such as correctness, identity, or consistency.

There are four types of *content*, which is the kind of information or material on

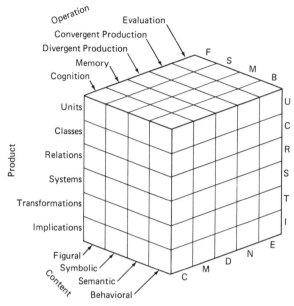

Figure 6.3 Guilford's Three-Dimensional Structure of Intellect Model. [From J. P. Guilford, *The Nature of Human Intelligence* (New York: McGraw-Hill, 1967), p. 63. Copyright © 1967 by McGraw-Hill. Reproduced by permission.]

which the intellectual operation is performed. *Figural content* is concrete material that doesn't represent anything but itself, for example, pictures, geometric forms, and sounds. *Symbolic content* involves letters, numbers, and other conventional signs that have no meaning in and of themselves. *Semantic content* refers to words, often expressing abstract concepts. *Behavioral content* is information about human feelings and interactions between people; the meaning of the expressions or words of another person would be an example of behavioral content.

The *product*, of which there are six types, is the form in which the information must be conceptualized by the examinee. The simplest product is the *unit*, which is a single chunk or item of information such as a word or a number. *Classes* are sets of items having some property or properties in common; we may ask persons to select the item that does not belong in the class represented by the other items. *Relations* are meaningful con-

nections between items of information and are frequently tested by analogies items. *Systems* are organized or structured patterns of information and may be tested with general reasoning or number and letter series tests. *Transformations* are changes in information and may involve redefinitions, shifts in meaning, modifications in structure, and changes in interpretation or use; a similarities test, such as that used in the Wechsler Adult Intelligence Scale, requires the subject to redefine each word several times before finding some common definitional ground between them. *Implications* involve information suggested by other information; a syllogisms test requires the person to generate the conclusion suggested by the premises.

Examples of tests representing the intersection of one operation, one content, and one product include a vocabulary test (*cognition* of *semantic content* represented as a *unit* of information), figural analogies (*cognition* of *figural content* representing a *relation*) and number series, where the subject must fill in the next number in the series (*convergent production* of *symbolic content* involving *relations*).

Guilford's model, because it postulates 120 separate mental abilities, not all of which have even been measured, may be unwieldy for general purposes of measuring intelligence. In addition, the extent to which each of the 120 cells represents a different and important ability has not been satisfactorily demonstrated. The model does, however, have several useful aspects. First, the three-dimensional model with its 120 cells led to the postulation and measurement of many new abilities. Second, while the large number of separate abilities and tests are unwieldy for general mental measurement, there may be applied purposes for which the measurement of very specific abilities is useful. For example, the postulation of figural content has contributed to the conceptualization of artistic abilities, while the postulation of behavioral content was an important contribution to the idea that there may be a "social intelligence" separate from the kind of intelligence associated with academic performance. Finally, Guilford's operation of divergent production stimulated considerable research on creativity, since the ability to think beyond available information and existing knowledge is an essential component of creativity.

In summary, multiple factor theories expanded our view of intelligence to include major group factors as well as *g* itself. Persons possessing equal amounts of *g* may differ in the specific pattern of their abilities: One person may be especially strong verbally but somewhat weaker in mathematics, while another person may show the reverse patterns of abilities. Such differential patterns of strengths and weaknesses may have important implications for applied problems, such as the selection of educational and/or occupational goals and emphases. A va-

riety of multiple aptitude batteries are now available and have contributed greatly to the applied utility of the concept of human abilities.

Hierarchical Theories

One important aspect of multiple factor theories was their postulate that the separate factors were equal in importance and generality; none was superior to, or of higher order in generality than, any of the others. Other researchers, however, were emphasizing the finding that when factors themselves were factor-analyzed (as opposed to factor-analyzing individual tests or test items), it was possible to extract higher-order factors that summarized shared variance or overlap among the factors themselves. This approach to the analysis of mental test scores resulted in hierarchical models of the nature of mental abilities. In these models, for example, that of Vernon (1960), ability factors may be arranged or "layered" in terms of generality versus specificity.

The British theorists Burt (1949) and Vernon (1960) and the Americans Humphreys (1962) and R. B. Cattell (1963b, 1971) proposed hierarchical theories of intelligence. Vernon's (1960) model, shown diagrammatically in Figure 6.4, proposed Spearman's *g* as the most general component of intelligence. Next in generality, according to Vernon, were two broad "major" group factors, verbal-educational (*v:ed*) and spatial-mechanical (*k:m*). These two broad group factors were further subdivided into "minor" group factors at the same level of generality as those postulated in multiple factor theory, for example, verbal and number as components of *v:ed* and spatial and mechanical as components of *k:m*. Last in generality were specific factors or components of the minor group factors.

The two major group factors postu-

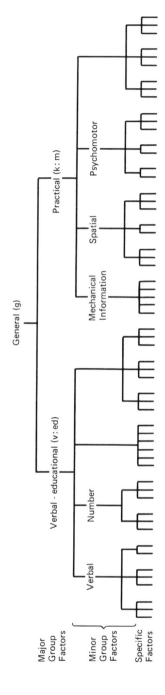

Figure 6.4 Illustration of Vernon's (1960) hierarchical model of intelligence. [Adapted from P. E. Vernon, *Intelligence and Cultural Environment* (London, England: Metheuen & Company, LTD., 1960), p. 22. Copyright © 1960, Metheuen & Company, LTD. Reproduced by permission.]

lated by Vernon—that is, *v:ed* and *k:m*—bear much in common with Cattell's (1963b, 1971) second order factors of *g*, known as "crystallized" and "fluid" intelligence, respectively. *Crystallized intelligence (g_c)* was measured by tests that used informational content drawing on already acquired knowledge and skills, for example, vocabulary, arithmetic, mechanical information, and verbal analogies using relatively difficult words. *Fluid intelligence (g_f)* was measured by tests using little informational content but requiring the ability to see relationships, for example, number and letter series, block designs, spatial visualization, and verbal analogies using very easy words. Thus, g_c was related to acquired knowledge, while g_f was intended as a "purer" (content-free) reflection of reasoning ability. It should be noted that Cattell's distinction is not a verbal-nonverbal distinction. For example, complicated verbal analogies using words familiar to most people in a culture would measure g_f, since the size of one's vocabulary should not influence ability to see the analogy. On the other hand, less complicated verbal analogies using less generally familiar words, perhaps learned as a result of higher education, would be a measure of g_c.

Although Cattell postulated g_f and g_c as separate components of overall *g*, they are in fact highly correlated with each other. It seems that persons high in g_f are able to learn more quickly and to retain information more effectively, thus leading to higher g_c as well. Thus, g_f and g_c are often difficult to distinguish practically, especially in populations homogeneous in terms of educational and cultural background. Even though practical distinctions may be difficult, the conceptual distinction between ability as acquired knowledge gained through the educational system and ability as a purer form of reasoning and capacity to see relationships and think abstractly, independent of test content, is an important one having major implications for the use and interpretation of test scores.

Summary of Psychometric Theories

Each of the theories described thus far has its basis in the *differential*, sometimes known as the psychometric or correlational, school of psychology. The major focus of this approach to psychology is the study and measurement of individual differences in psychological characteristics, most notably, latent or inferred traits such as intelligence. The primary methods of statistical analysis—that is, correlational and, in particular, factor-analytic methods—are designed to discover the underlying sources of variation among individuals. Research is directed primarily toward determining or postulating the *structure* of mental abilities. Because the interest is on latent (unobservable) traits, the nature of such traits is *inferred* from theory and from research findings, such as the results of factor-analytic studies and validity studies.

While these major psychometric theories are diverse in emphasis, each has contributed to the kinds of inferences we make about the nature of the latent variables of intelligence and thus to our understanding of what is measured by intelligence tests. Binet's emphasis on judgment and reasoning and, similarly, Spearman's principle of education of relations and correlates formed the foundation of most current conceptions of intelligence. Intelligence (*g*) is not what we know at a given time, but how well we can reason, solve problems, think abstractly, and manipulate information flexibly and efficiently, particularly when the stimulus materials present some degree of novelty. Novelty is common to *g* tests because the subject cannot fall back on already acquired knowledge or skill.

The multiple factor theorists contributed the now-accepted concepts and measures of group factors of ability, for example, verbal, numerical, and spatial abilities. Thus, they contributed the suggestion that intelligence is not a single unitary ability, but rather a composite of several or many components of ability, each of which may be important for different kinds of human endeavors.

Vernon's hierarchical model is particularly useful in summarizing those aspects of intelligence related to academic performance. While present-day IQ tests measure g, they are often also heavily loaded with that cluster of abilities summarized by Vernon as $v:ed$, especially verbal abilities, and to a lesser extent numerical and spatial abilities. Because one of the major uses of intelligence tests has been to predict level of performance in schools, including colleges and universities, an emphasis on testing the verbal and symbolic (primarily numerical and spatial) abilities has developed. Tests emphasizing Vernon's $v:ed$ are often referred to as "school ability" or "scholastic aptitude" tests. The important point about such tests is that although they are considered "intelligence" tests, they tend to assess those aspects of intelligence that are highly related to academic performance but *may not assess* other important aspects of ability.

Cattell's concepts of "fluid" and "crystallized" intelligence have been useful in clarifying the differences between intelligence and achievement and in suggesting the addition of "learning ability" to our definition of intelligence. Essentially, Cattell's crystallized intelligence might be termed "achievement," since it pertains to and measures acquired knowledge. Cattell's fluid intelligence is more similar in conception to Spearman's g—that is, the ability to see relationships in any content, familiar or novel. However, the causal analysis of the high correlations between g_f and g_c suggest that persons high in g_f learn more readily and thus are more likely to score high on g_c as well. An important aspect of intelligence, then, may be learning ability.

To summarize these concepts: intelligence may be considered a combination of (1) a general, or g, component reflecting overall reasoning and problem-solving abilities, judgment, and learning ability; and (2) subcomponents reflecting school ability and more specific group factors of ability representing various content areas or types of mental operations. The existence of g is inferred from the positive correlations among tests of mental ability *varying* in content and type of intellectual process involved, as long as those processes involve some form of mental manipulation rather than simple demonstration of acquired knowledge. The existence of separate components of g is inferred from factor-analytic studies. Different tests of intelligence differentially emphasize these components of mental ability, so an understanding of these components and their importance in different tests is important to the careful and effective use of tests of human mental ability.

Other Approaches to Intelligence

Although psychometric theories of intelligence are the basis of the testing movement, other theoretical approaches to the study of intelligence have as their objective the *description* of the processes underlying intelligent behavior. Rather than emphasizing individual differences in performance, these approaches attempt to discover the *common elements* in intelligent performance.

Developmental Theories. Developmental theories of intelligence can be said to go back to Binet's concept of intelligence as something that should increase with age, at least until adulthood. Although Binet used the idea of mental age, or mental level, in developing and scoring his intelligence tests, use of this idea to investigate the *nature* of intelligence awaited the developmental psychologists, in particular Jean Piaget. (The broader field of theories of human development and their utility in assessment is covered in Chapter 13.)

Piaget began his work in Binet's lab, assisting in the development of the Binet scale. Most intriguing to Piaget were his own observations relating the age of children to the nature of their *incorrect answers*. In other words, although all average children below the age of nine might respond incorrectly to a particular item, children of a given age under nine tended to give the *same kinds* of wrong answers. Furthermore, the wrong answers given by, say, six-year-olds were different from the kinds of wrong answers given by children of a different age. Piaget began to wonder if age led not only to quantitative differences in mental functioning but also to qualitative differences in how we think and process information. Based on intensive laboratory observation of, and experimentation with, children of different ages, Piaget formulated his "stage" theory of intellectual development.

Piaget's (1952) theory postulated the existence of three major *stages of intellectual development*. These stages, or periods, were postulated to occur sequentially and universally and thus were intended to describe the general processes in, or nature of, intellectual functioning and growth: sensorimotor, concrete operations, and formal operations.

Piaget's first stage of intellectual development is the *sensorimotor*, which lasts from birth to about two. At the beginning of this period, intelligent behavior is action oriented, in that it is primarily reflexive or instinctual; sucking and grasping are such primitive intelligent actions. With growth and experience, overt actions become better coordinated with perceptions, leading to more complex behaviors, such as reaching out to grasp something. The sensorimotor stage can be essentially characterized as "knowing" through the process of sensory and motor interaction with the environment.

The second stage, that of *concrete operations*, occurs during the age range of two to eleven and is that period of development concerned with the acquisition of language, the ability to use symbols, and the ability to think logically and representationally about the world. In essence, "knowing" becomes more than what can actually be seen, touched, tasted, and so forth, because the child learns to represent material concepts internally through the use of language and thought. Concepts of past, present, and future emerge, as well as the ability to fantasize in play. This stage is divided into two substages, the *preoperational* (ages two to seven) and the *concrete operational* (ages seven to eleven). These substages are differentiated by virtue of the dominance of perception in thinking in the former and the movement to logical thinking in the latter. The conservation experiments in which children judged the relative amounts of water by the shape of the bottles containing the water, even when they observed the water in one bottle being poured into the next, illustrate the dependence of thought upon perceptions at the preoperational substage, rather than upon the logic characterizing the concrete operational substage.

Finally, the stage of *formal operations*, which occurs from age eleven on, involves the development of abstract thought, including the ability to hypothesize and to conceptualize all possible solutions to a problem without trying any of them. Abstract thinking represents the final, adult stage of intellectual development.

Although Piaget's theory provides ages during which the three stages occur, these are not assumed to perfectly describe the development of every child; there may be some individual variation in the ages during which stages occur. What *is* thought to be invariant, however, is the order of the stages and the dependence of more complex thought on the mastery of earlier stages. In other words, progression to the formal operations stage depends on the acquisition of the thought processes characteristic of the concrete operational stage. Piaget's description of the nature of thought processes at various stages of development contributes to our understanding of the nature of intelligence.

Cognitive Psychological Theories.

Based on human experimental psychology, including the studies of learning, memory, perception, problem solving, and reasoning, cognitive psychological theories, like developmental theories, have focused on the *description*, rather than the measurement, of intelligence. Cognitive psychologists investigate the phenomenon of human intelligence through their work on human information processing. The study of human information processes follows the assumptions and methods of experimental psychology. In experimental psychology the emphasis of research is on performance variations as a function of variation in stimulus attributes, rather than on individual differences. For example, experimenters might vary the characteristics of a given type of test item and observe the effects on subjects' response time or the number of wrong answers given.

While in the past there was little interaction between researchers pursuing the differential, or psychometric, approach to intelligence and researchers in the area of cognitive psychology, research attempting to integrate the two approaches is currently increasing in popularity (Sternberg, 1981). Several areas of cognitive research may have implications for the understanding of the nature of intelligence; these areas include research on cognitive correlates, cognitive components, cognitive training, and cognitive contents (Sternberg, 1981).

Research in the area of *cognitive correlates* involves investigating the relationship of performance on tasks believed to represent basic information-processing ability—for example, letter matching or memory scanning—to scores on standardized intelligence or ability tests (Hunt, 1978; Hunt, Lunneborg, & Lewis, 1975; Jensen, 1979; Keating & Bobbitt, 1978). The objective of such research is to learn more about the mental tasks/behaviors constituting intelligent performance as measured on tests. Correlations of information-processing task scores with intelligence test scores are generally relatively low in magnitude, around 0.30 (see Sternberg, 1981), thus suggesting that the information-processing tasks utilized do not sufficiently reflect the complexity of intelligent functioning.

In the *cognitive components* approach, the types of problems actually used in intelligence tests are studied in an effort to discover the basic or essential components of successful problem solution (e.g., Mulholland, Pellegrino, & Glaser, 1980; Sternberg, 1977a, 1977b, 1978, 1979, 1980). For example, Sternberg's research has examined the basic processes underlying the solution of such common intelligence test items as analogies, series completions (i.e., letter series), and inductive and deductive reasoning (see Sternberg, 1977a, 1977b). Sternberg postulates that understanding the roles of such information-processing tasks as inference, encoding, and mapping in the solution of intelligence test items will contribute further to our understanding of intelligence as measured by intelligence tests.

Researchers in the area of *cognitive training* (e.g., Feuerstein, 1979a, 1979b; Holzman, Glaser, & Pellegrino, 1976) attempt to differentiate those aspects of mental functioning that can be improved significantly through reasonable amounts of training from those that are not amenable to improvement through training. This type of research has numerous implications for education and training. Finally, research on cognitive contents investigates differences between experts and novices in their strategies for approaching and solving complex problems—for example, in physics (Chi, Feltovich, & Glaser, 1981), and chess (Chase & Simon, 1973)—and in their methods of acquiring information (Chiesi, Spilich, & Voss, 1979).

In summary, research in cognitive psychology can contribute knowledge of the component tasks, processes, and strategies involved in intelligent functioning. Such knowledge not only adds to our understanding of intelligence but has potential for the diagnosis and treatment of some kinds of problems in mental functioning.

Neurological-Biological Theories. Developmental and cognitive approaches to the study of intelligence focus on describing its content—that is, the thought processes and information-processing tasks and strategies that underlie correct solution of intelligence test problems. At an even more basic level, however, are theories that attempt to understand intelligence in terms of the functioning of the brain itself. Based on research on neurophysiology and neuroanatomy, such theories generally postulate some relationship between measured intelligence and physiological characteristics of the brain and/or postulate that different areas of the brain are differentially specialized for different mental functions. Halstead's (1961) concept of "biological intelligence" and Hebb's (1972) theory of "Intelligence A" (innate and biologically based) and "Intelligence B" (the result of the environment and experience) are examples of neurological-biological theories of intelligence. Although these theories are currently of relatively minor importance, advances in the sciences of neuroanatomy and neurophysiology will probably lead to increases in the utility of research in these areas for the understanding of intelligence.

In summary, there are several different theoretical and methodological approaches to the study of intelligence. Although the psychometric theories have been the primary basis for the construction of intelligence tests, all the theories contribute to the understanding of the concept of intelligence and to the extent to which the assessment of intelligence has utility in the solution of applied problems. The next section describes the major intelligence tests in use today.

MAJOR INTELLIGENCE TESTS

While many theorists have focused on the *nature* of intelligence and abilities, the demonstrated *practical utility* of the original Binet-Simon intelligence test stimulated the development of numerous different tests of intelligence designed for a variety of applied purposes. Before we present some of the major intelligence tests used today, it may be helpful to provide several dimensions along which intelligence tests can be classified. These dimensions—including individually administered versus group administered intelligence tests, tests emphasizing verbal, nonverbal, and performance tasks, and the cultural-specificity of item content—have general implications for the use of intelligence tests across different applied problems and settings. Thus, they should be considered along with other criteria in the selection of specific intelligence tests for use in various applied situations.

Individually administered tests are administered to one individual at a time by an examiner well-trained in both the procedures of test administration and the methods of test scoring. Individual administration is required because such tests may involve the manipulation of materials such as blocks, the timing of speed of performance with a stopwatch, or the oral presentation of words, sentences, or numbers, and because in many cases the examiner must observe the performance in order to score it. Individual tests are particularly appropriate for testing children because instructions and examples are presented orally (thus requiring no reading ability on the part of the examinee) and because the interaction between examiner and subject can facilitate the maintenance of a child's attention and level of motivation.

Generally, individual test administration also permits the examiner to note the occurrence of conditions that may detract from performance (e.g., low motivation, distracting environmental conditions, and sickness). The examiner may take such conditions into account when interpreting the resulting test scores or, alternatively, may suggest postponing testing until conditions are more conducive to an accurate assessment of the individual. Finaly, individual testing allows the examiner informally to assess other attributes of the individual, including motivation, cooperativeness, ability to follow instructions, and emotional state. Thus, individual test administration can result in a richer description of the individual than would be provided by a numerical intelligence test score alone. Major individual tests include the Stanford-Binet and the Wechsler scales.

While individually administered intelligence tests have several advantages for the assessment process, they have obvious disadvantages in that they are expensive and time-consuming both to administer and to score. For the practical needs of classifying thousands of World War I recruits, the first group intelligence tests, the Army Alpha Test (for literates) and the Army Beta Test (for illiterates), were developed. *Group-administered tests* can be administered to large numbers of individuals simultaneously.

In contrast to individual tests, materials used with group tests are suitable for mass administration, utilizing paper-and-pencil formats and machine-scorable answer sheets.

Printed instructions are provided and are usually read to the group prior to the start of the test. Most group intelligence tests are timed and utilize the verbal skills of reading and writing. Because group tests are efficient to administer, normative data can generally be obtained from much larger samples of subjects than is possible with individual tests. Group tests are also less prone to slight differences in examiner procedures and scoring than are individual tests. However, group test administration does not take into account many of the conditions that can adversely affect test scores; a person who is ill or upset on the day of the administration of a college entrance examination has little choice but to take the exam and do one's best under the circumstances. Major group tests include the Cognitive Abilities Test and the California Test of Mental Maturity. Probably the best-known tests of this type are scholastic aptitude tests such as the Scholastic Aptitude Test (SAT), the American College Test (ACT), and the Graduate Record Examination (GRE); these tests will be covered in Chapter 7's discussion of the assessment of aptitudes.

While the individual-versus-group distinction pertains primarily to differences in the method of test administration and scoring, the *verbal, nonverbal, and performance distinction* describes different types of test content. *Verbal test* items involve language, either spoken or written, and are appropriate measures of intelligence only for people who can speak and write the language. Individually administered tests usually use spoken language, while group tests usually use written language. *Nonverbal tests* are often designed to measure the same kinds of reasoning abilities measured by verbal tests, but they use figural materials, symbols, pictures, or geometric patterns instead of language. Such tests are appropriate for individuals who cannot read and for those who speak a foreign language; the Army Beta, a nonverbal test, was used during World War I to measure the abilities of thousands of illiterate and foreign-born recruits. *Performance tests* require the examinee to manipulate materials in some way; mazes, puzzles, and block designs like those used on the Wechsler scales are examples. Performance tests usually need to be individually administered and scored and consequently are found primarily in individual intelligence tests.

The final dimension useful in describing intelligence tests is that of the *cultural specificity of test content*. "Culture-loaded" tests (e.g., Jensen, 1980) are those that emphasize types of knowledge and skill acquired in the culture's educational system (e.g., reading and arithmetic) or that use objects and concepts peculiar to a particular culture or time period (e.g., vehicles, household appliances, and furniture). "Culture-reduced" items are nonverbal and performance items that are not specific to a particular culture or taught in school. Culture-reduced content includes colors, simple geometric figures, and mazes. The degree of cultural specificity of test content is a particularly important consideration when evaluating the intelligence of any person whose educational and/or cultural background is different from, or less advantaged than, that of, for example, the typical middle-class and white American citizen. The use of intelligence tests with such groups will receive extensive further consideration in Chapter 14's discussion of ethical and social issues in testing.

In the remaining sections of this chapter, the major individual and group tests of intelligence will be described. Individually administered tests, the Stanford-Binet and the Wechsler Intelligence Scales, will be presented first, followed by several of the major group tests used to assess the intelligence, and more specifically the school ability, of children and adolescents. Tests used for the assessment of scholastic aptitude in the post-high-school years will be covered in Chapter 7.

Individually Administered Intelligence Tests

The Stanford-Binet Intelligence Scale. The Stanford-Binet Intelligence Scale, probably the best-known intelligence test in the world, is a direct descendent of the original Binet-Simon scales, first developed in 1905. As was mentioned earlier in this chapter, Lewis Terman of Stanford University was the dominant figure in the initial revision of the Binet-Simon scales for use in this country; the first Stanford revision of the Binet-Simon scales, known as the Stanford-Binet, was available in 1916. Subsequent revisions of the Stanford-Binet were the work of Terman and his colleague Maude A. Merrill. In 1937 Terman and Merrill produced a revised Stanford-Binet that had two alternate forms, known as Forms L and M. The third revision of the test occurred in 1960 and resulted in a single form (known as L-M) using the best items from the previous Forms L and M (Terman & Merrill, 1960). In 1972 Form L-M was restandardized (Terman & Merrill, 1973).

Finally, in 1985 the Stanford-Binet was revised extensively (Thorndike, Hagen, & Sattler, 1985), resulting in the Stanford-Binet: Fourth Edition in use today. In the discussion to follow, an overview of the Stanford-Binet administration and scoring will be provided. For more detailed information about use of the test, the reader is referred to the *Guide for Administering and Scoring the Fourth Edition* (Thorndike, Hagen, & Sattler, 1986a), the *Technical Manual* (Thorndike, Hagen, & Sattler, 1986b), and the *Examiner's Handbook* (Delaney & Hopkins, 1987).

The Stanford-Binet: Fourth Edition consists of 15 subtests, of which 6 are "core tests" administered to all examinees, and the remaining 9 are administered to different age groups of examinees. The youngest examinees (age 2 and above) are administered a total of 8 tests, while the oldest (age 16 through adult) receive 13 tests. The 15 subtests are described below. The items within each subtest are arranged in levels of difficulty from easiest to most difficult, with two items at each level of difficulty.

Vocabulary. The first 14 items are picture vocabulary items, where the examinee is asked to name the stimulus in the picture (e.g., car, flag). The remaining items (15 through 46) are oral vocabulary, where the examinee is asked to define a stimulus word ("dollar," "envelope").

Bead Memory. For the first 10 items, the examinee is asked to identify beads in a picture after being briefly shown the actual bead(s). For the more difficult items, the examinee is to construct a model of the bead layout shown in a picture.

Quantitative. Examinees use numbered blocks to match, add, count, and order (easier items) and to respond to numerical word problems.

Memory for Sentences. Examinees are read oral stimuli and asked to repeat them exactly. At the easiest level, the phrase "tall girl" is to be repeated, while at a more difficult level the sentence "Ruth fell in a puddle and got her clothes all muddy" would be administered.

Pattern Analysis. The examinee is asked to replace pieces in a three-hole form board or use pattern cubes to replicate picture stimuli or the examiner's models.

Comprehension. The examinee is asked to identify body parts using a picture of a child or to answer questions requiring a logical or commonsense answer.

Absurdities. The examinee is shown pictures and asked to say what is wrong or silly in them (e.g., square bicycle wheels).

Memory for Digits. The examiner reads a series of digits and the examinee is asked to repeat them. Parts 1 and 2 are forward and reversed repetition, respectively.

Copying. The examinee duplicates the examiner's block models or copies designs in the record booklet from picture stimuli.

Memory for Objects. Examinees are shown a series of pictures and then asked to point to the pictures in the sequence they were shown when presented in a larger array of pictures.

Matrices. Examinees are shown figural stimuli with a portion missing and are asked to complete the stimuli.

Number Series. The examinee is shown a series of numbers and asked to provide the next two numbers that would occur in the sequence (e.g., the sequence 2, 4, 6 would be continued by 8, 10).

Paper Folding and Cutting. The examinee is shown paper being cut and folded and asked to identify the correct picture of the paper if it were unfolded.

Verbal Relations. Given four words, the examinee is to tell the examiner how three words are similar to each other and different from the fourth.

Equation Building. The examinee is to rearrange a set of numerals and mathematical signs to yield a true equation (e.g., 2 3 5 + = would be arranged to make the true equation $2 + 3 = 5$).

Administration of the revised Stanford-Binet, like earlier versions of the test, is *adaptive*, that is, geared to the examinee's estimated ability level (see the discussion of adaptive testing in Chapter 3). The vocabulary test (Test 1) is used to obtain a rough estimate of ability level, which, along with chronological age, is then used in turn to determine the entry point for the other 14 subtests. The point of beginning the vocabulary test is determined based on the examinee's chronological age.

For example, a 4-year-old child would begin the vocabulary test at item 7, while a 10-year-old would begin at item 19. Based on an entry-level chart combining the numbers of the most difficult pair of vocabulary items administered with chronological age, an entry level designated by a letter A through Q is specified. To show the joint use of vocabulary test performance and age, a 16-year-old reaching the 17th vocabulary item, a 10-year-old reaching the 21st item, and a 6-year-old reaching the 29th item would all begin the subtests at level I.

The entry level also determines *which* subtests are given, as well as the specific entry point for each subtest. As an example, an examinee at the lowest level, A (corresponding to chronological ages 2.0 to 3.11 depending on vocabulary score), would receive seven subtests in addition to the vocabulary test used to determine entry level. Each of the seven subtests (Bead Memory, Quantitative, Memory for Sentences, Pattern Analysis, Comprehension, Absurdities, and Copying) would be entered at the 1st item. In contrast, an examinee at level T (corresponding to chronological ages 6.0 to 15.11 depending on vocabulary test performance) would receive the following subtests, with entry item number in parentheses: Bead Memory (15), Quantitative (15), Memory for Sentences (19), Pattern Analysis (19), Comprehension (19), Absurdities (19), Memory for Digits (Forward 1, and Backward 1), Copying (19), Memory for Objects (1), Matrices (3), and Number Series (3).

Following determination of the entry level for a subtest, the examiner administers items until both a "basal level" and "ceiling level" have been established. The basal level is established when all four items at two consecutive levels are passed; when this occurs, it is assumed that the examinee would pass all the items easier than those at the basal level, so it is not necessary to administer them. After the basal level is determined, the examiner proceeds with progressively more difficult items until a ceiling level is reached. The ceiling level is attained when the examinee fails three out of four or all four items at two consecutive levels; the examiner assumes that all items above this level would be failed, and thus there is no need to administer them.

Once both the basal and ceiling levels have been determined, the subtest can be scored. For each test, the raw score is equal to the number of items failed, subtracted from the highest item number administered. The raw score is converted to a standard age score (SAS) based on the norm tables corresponding to the individual's chronological age. Figure 6.5 shows an example of the record booklet used to compute total scores. Note that the 15 subtests are organized in terms of four cognitive areas, viewed as group factors of ability. The four postulated group factors are Verbal Reasoning, Abstract/Visual Reasoning, Quantitative Reasoning, and Short-Term Memory. The report form provides columns for a raw score and standard age score for each test administered.

Within each ability area, the SAS values for all tests administered are added; this value is then taken to the appropriate norm table to obtain an SAS for each area, beginning with Verbal Reasoning. Finally, the four area scores are added; the result is again taken to the appropriate table to obtain a composite score.

The composite score on the Stanford-Binet: Fourth Edition is an overall index of intellectual performance. It is an estimate of Spearman's *g*, general mental ability, the capacity to deduce relationships and correlates (Delaney & Hopkins, 1987, p. 80). Like the

![Stanford-Binet Intelligence Scale logo]

STANFORD-BINET INTELLIGENCE SCALE

RECORD BOOKLET

Stanford-Binet Intelligence Scale: Fourth Edition

Name **John C.**

Sex **M**

Ethnicity   NA   H   B (W/NH) O/AA   PI   Other _____

	YEAR	MONTH	DAY
Date of Testing **B**	86	6	29
Birth Date	72	1	18
Age	14	5	11

School **Hillview High School**

Grade **9th**   **A**

Examiner **Robinson**

Father's Occupation: **Civil engineer**

Mother's Occupation: **Social worker**

FACTORS AFFECTING TEST PERFORMANCE
Overall Rating of Conditions   **C**

Optimal	Good	(Average)	Detrimental	Seriously detrimental

	1	2	3	4	5	
Attention						
a) Absorbed by task				✓		Easily distracted
Reactions During Test Performance						
a) Normal activity level				✓		Abnormal activity level
b) Initiates activity			✓			Waits to be told
c) Quick to respond		✓				Urging needed
Emotional Independence						
a) Socially confident			✓			Insecure
b) Realistically self-confident				✓		Distrusts own ability
c) Comfortable in adult company			✓			Ill-at-ease
d) Assured				✓		Anxious
Problem-Solving Behavior						
a) Persistent				✓		Gives up easily
b) Reacts to failure realistically			✓			Reacts to failure unrealistically
c) Eager to continue				✓		Seeks to terminate
d) Challenged by hard tasks			✓			Prefers only easy tasks
Independence of Examiner Support						
a) Needs minimum of commendation				✓		Needs constant praise and encouragement
Expressive Language						
a) Excellent articulation				✓		Very poor articulation
Receptive Language						
a) Excellent sound discrimination			✓			Very poor sound discrimination

Was it difficult to establish rapport with this person?
Easy ✓ Difficult

D

	RAW SCORE	STANDARD AGE SCORE ✱
Verbal Reasoning		
1 Vocabulary	27	47
6 Comprehension	39	61
7 Absurdities *(Est. ceiling)*	31	57 (Est.)
14 Verbal Relations		
Sum of Subtest SAS's ③		165
Verbal Reasoning SAS		(171)
Abstract/Visual Reasoning		
5 Pattern Analysis	40	56
9 Copying		
11 Matrices	14	48
13 Paper Folding & Cutting		
Sum of Subtest SAS's ②		104
Abstract/Visual Reasoning SAS		(105)
Quantitative Reasoning		
3 Quantitative	19	39
12 Number Series	6	37
15 Equation Building		
Sum of Subtest SAS's ②		76
Quantitative Reasoning SAS		(73)
Short-Term Memory		
2 Bead Memory	28	51
4 Memory For Sentences	32	60
8 Memory For Digits *(Est. basal)*	12	47 (Est.)
10 Memory For Objects	9	55
Sum of Subtest SAS's ④		213
Short-Term Memory SAS		(108)
Sum of Area SAS's		397

		COMPOSITE SCORE ✱
Test Composite		(97)
Partial Composite		109
Partial Composite based on **VR, A/VR, STM**		

✱ Be sure that all Standard Age Scores (SAS's) are based on the tables in the *Guide* with the number 9-74502 on the cover.

The Riverside Publishing Company

Robert L. Thorndike
Elizabeth P. Hagen
Jerome M. Sattler

Figure 6.5 Front cover of the record booklet of the Stanford-Binet Intelligence Scale: Fourth Edition. Reprinted with permission of The Riverside Publishing Company from p. 7 of *Stanford-Binet Intelligence Scale Examiner's Handbook: An Expanded Guide for Fourth Edition Users* by E. A. Delaney and T. F. Hopkins. Copyright 1987. © The Riverside Publishing Company, 8420 W. Bryn Mawr Avenue, Chicago, Ill. 60631.

IQ score yielded by previous editions of the Stanford-Binet, the composite SAS has a mean of 100 and a standard deviation (SD) of 16.

Examiners should report the composite SAS along with its corresponding confidence bands, which are based on the magnitude of the standard error of measurement (SEM). The composite SAS plus or minus one SEM gives the 68 percent band of confidence (i.e., the chances that the examinee's "true score" lies within this range of scores is 68 percent). The 95 percent confidence band would be the composite SAS plus or minus 1.96 SEMs, while the 99 percent confidence interval would be the SAS plus or minus 2.56 SEMs. For example, the 95 percent confidence band for a 6-year-old obtaining a composite score of 120 would be from 114 to 126, while the 99 percent confidence interval would be 112 to 128.

Although any labels should be used carefully and tentatively, especially given the ever-present possibility of measurement error, the composite SAS scores are associated with ability classifications as follows: Very Superior, 132 and above; Superior, 121 to 131; High Average, 111 to 120; Average, 89 to 110; Low Average, 79 to 88; Slow Learner, 68 to 78; and Mentally Retarded, 67 and below.

The standardization sample for the revised Stanford-Binet consisted of about 5,000 individuals aged 2 to 23, selected to be representative of the U.S. population in 1980. Although designed to be representative, the final sample somewhat overrepresented middle- and upper-class children and underrepresented lower-class children. This problem was dealt with by differential weighting of individual scores in the calculation of normative data. The standard scores for each subtest are normalized standard scores with a mean of 50 and a standard deviation of 8 within each age group. As has been mentioned, the composite SAS is standardized to a mean of 100 and a standard deviation of 16.

The Stanford-Binet:Fourth Edition is highly reliable. The internal consistency reliability of the composite score ranges from 0.95 to 0.99 across age levels. Those for the cognitive areas range from 0.80 to 0.97, and those for the individual subtests are generally in the high 0.80s and low 0.90s except for reliabilities ranging from 0.66 to 0.78 depending on age group. Reliabilities tend to be somewhat higher at older than younger levels and, consequently, error bands are smaller for the scores of older versus younger examinees. For instance, in the example given earlier, the 95 percent confidence band around a composite SAS of 120 is 114 to 126 for a 6-year-old examinee, 116 to 124 for a 14-year-old, and 117 to 123 for a 17-year-old.

Test-retest reliability coefficients of 0.91 and 0.90 obtained on samples of 57 five-year-olds and 55 eight-year-olds indicate that the composite score is stable. However, the stability coefficients for the area scores and subtests were generally lower.

Results from factor analysis indicate that the Stanford-Binet: Fourth Edition does assess a general factor of intelligence. However, the extent to which the test distinguishes the four group factors is less clear. The *Technical Manual* reports support for the Verbal Reasoning, Quantitative, and Short-Term Memory group factors, although not the Abstract/Visual Reasoning Area. In contrast, Reynolds, Kamphaus, and Rosenthal (1988) report factor analytic findings that strongly supported the ability of the intelligence (with Vocabulary, Quantitative, and Comprehension loading most strongly on g) but which did not show consistent group factors across age groups.

Validity data available to date include a high correlation ($r = 0.81$) with the IQ scores obtained from the earlier version of the Stanford-Binet, moderately high correlations with scores on other intelligence tests, and excellent differentiation among gifted, learning-disabled, and mentally retarded examinees.

Like all previous versions of the Stanford-Binet, the individual administration of the test allows not only for *adaptive* administration but also for the administrator to observe the examinee's in-test behavior, adding to the informative value of the test. On the record booklet for John C., shown in Figure 6.5, a section guiding the observation and recording of other behaviors is provided. Note the sections describing the examinee's attention during testing, reactions during test performance, problem-solving behavior, independence of examiner support, and expressive and receptive language skills. The last question concerns the relative ease versus difficulty of establishing rapport with the examinee. This kind of additional information can prove very helpful to those using test results.

In summary, the Stanford-Binet is a highly reliable intelligence test useful particularly in the testing of children, for the diagnosis of mental retardation, and for the prediction and explanation of academic achievement.

The Wechsler Adult Intelligence Scale. As its name implies, the Wechsler Adult Intelligence Scale was developed specifically for intelligence testing in adult populations. The first form of the test, known as the Wechsler-Bellevue Intelligence Scale, was published in 1939. The first version of the revised test, the Wechsler Adult Intelligence Scale (WAIS), was published in 1955. The revised version of the WAIS, known as the WAIS-R, was published in 1981 (Wechsler, 1981).

The WAIS-R is similar to the Stanford-Binet: Fourth Edition in many respects. Both are individually administered and are adaptive in that the administration of too-difficult

and too-easy items is minimized. The WAIS-R has been organized according to subtests since it was first developed, while only the most recent version of the Stanford-Binet uses subtest organizational structure.

The subtests of the WAUS-R are grouped into a Verbal Scale and a Performance Scale. The Verbal Scale, consisting of six subtests, and the Performance Scale, consisting of five subtests, constitute the Full Scale of 11 subtests. Thus, the WAIS-R yields a Verbal IQ, a Performance IQ, and a Full Scale IQ. The subtests of the Verbal Scale and the Performance Scale are described below.

WAIS-R Verbal Scale

INFORMATION: includes 29 questions presented in ascending order of difficulty. The range of item content is broad and includes general information (e.g., naming presidents of the United States), cultural information (e.g., "What is the Vatican?"), and basic scientific and numerical information. While the content assumes normal exposure to United States culture and society, it is not designed to assess academic or highly specialized knowledge.

DIGIT SPAN: involves the repetition of from three to nine digits as enunciated by the examiner. The first part of the test involves repetition in the same order as presented, while in the second part the examinee must repeat the digits backwards—that is, in reverse order. Scoring is based on the number of digits the examinee can successfully repeat forwards and the number he/she can repeat backwards.

VOCABULARY: involves defining 35 words presented both orally and visually and in increasing order of difficulty.

ARITHMETIC: includes 14 problems based on simple arithmetic, including addition, subtraction, fractions, and percentages. The problems are orally presented, are timed, and are to be solved without the use of pencil and paper.

COMPREHENSION: involves 16 items designed to assess practical judgment and commonsense. Item content includes problem solving, the meaning of proverbs, and factual questions assessing commonsense understanding of the sociocultural environment.

SIMILARITIES: uses 14 questions requiring the examinee to state ways in which two things are alike. High scores require the examinee to provide abstract concepts that summarize essential characteristics of the objects or concepts presented, for example, being able to see that a fly and a tree are similar because both are living things.

WAIS-R Performance Scale

PICTURE COMPLETION: presents 20 cards depicting objects or scenes from which something is missing. The examinee must indicate what is missing from each picture. Examples include a girl with her nose missing and an American flag with too few stars.

PICTURE ARRANGEMENT: presents 10 sets of cards. Each set of cards contains a series of pictures that when arranged in the correct order, tell a coherent story. The pictures resemble those of comic strips. The single frames are presented in disarranged order, and the examinee must arrange them in the order that tells the story.

BLOCK DESIGN: presents 9 cards representing colored designs that the examinee must reproduce using colored cubes. The cards are presented one at a time, and the examinee is asked to reproduce that particular design.

OBJECT ASSEMBLY: consists of 4 puzzles, each containing six or seven pieces. The examinee is asked to put the pieces together to form a picture of a familiar object but is not told a priori what objects the puzzles represent. The objects are to be assembled within specified time limits.

DIGIT SYMBOL: involves showing the examinee a key containing 9 symbols, each of which is paired with a digit. With the key in front of him/her, the examinee must fill in the symbol corresponding to each of the digits presented in several rows. The examinee is given 90 seconds to fill in as many symbols as he/she can within that time limit. This test involves motor coordination, speed, visual acuity, and rote memory.

The WAIS-R subtests are administered by alternating one Verbal and one Performance subtest as follows:

1. Information
2. Picture Completion
3. Digit Span
4. Picture Arrangement
5. Vocabulary
6. Block Design
7. Arithmetic
8. Object Assembly
9. Comprehension
10. Digit Symbol
11. Similarities

Each subtest score is computed and then converted to a standard score in which the mean is 10 and the standard deviation is 3. The subtest standard scores are added and, using tables provided in the manual, this total is converted into standard IQ scores having a mean of 100 and a standard deviation of 15. The 6 verbal subtest scores are added to derive a Verbal IQ, the 5 performance test scores are added to obtain a Performance IQ, and the sum over the 11 subtests is converted to a Full Scale IQ. (Note that while the means of both the Stanford-Binet and the WAIS-R IQs are equal to 100, the standard deviations are 16 and 15, respectively). The normative group used in the most recent standardization of the WAIS-R (done for the 1981 revision) included 1,880 individuals, half of them male and half of them female, distributed over nine age levels ranging from 16–17 to 70–74. The sample is representative of the population of the United States in terms of race, geographical and rural/urban background, and occupational and educational levels.

The WAIS-R is a highly reliable test. The split-half reliabilities of the Verbal, Performance, and Full Scale IQs range from 0.95 to 0.97, 0.88 to 0.94, and 0.96 to 0.98, respectively (Wechsler, 1981). The reliabilities of the subtests for which split-half coefficients are appropriate (all except Digit Span and Digit Symbol) range from 0.52 to 0.71 for Object Assembly to 0.94 to 0.96 for Vocabulary. Test-retest coefficients for Digit Span ranged from 0.70 to 0.89, while those for Digit Symbol ranged from 0.73 to 0.86 (Wechsler, 1981). For more information about the psychometric characteristics of the WAIS-R, refer to the manual (Wechsler, 1981) and to reviews by Kaufman (1985) and Matarazzo (1985).

Scores on the WAIS-R (and previously on the WAIS) were highly related to scores on earlier versions on the Stanford-Binet; correlations between the WAIS Full Scale IQ and the Stanford-Binet IQ have typically been around 0.80. Relationships of WAIS-R scores to scores on the Stanford-Binet: Fourth edition are currently under investigation and are expected to be comparable in magnitude to those found with earlier versions of the Stanford-Binet.

Although factor analysis of the WAIS (Cohen, 1957a, 1957b) indicated a large general factor and three group factors (Verbal Comprehension, Perceptual Organization, and Memory), more research investigating the factor structure of the WAIS-R is needed (Kaufman, 1985). Kaufman (1985) also sug- gests that more validity data are needed, particularly for uses of the test with individuals under age 20.

In addition to its usefulness in the assessment of intellectual level, the WAIS-R is used extensively in certain kinds of clinical assessment and diagnosis. More specifically, experienced users of the WAIS-R have developed numerous hypotheses pertaining to the relationships between certain types of atypical subtest performance and such forms of psychological disorder as brain damage, schizophrenia, and depression. Furthermore, large discrepancies between the Verbal IQ and the Performance IQ may have clinical significance. While the majority of individuals tested obtain Verbal and Performance IQs within 10 points of each other, some people have differences greater than 15 points. Such discrepancies indicating either Verbal or Performance deficits may be used as hypotheses in the assessment of brain damage (see Matarazzo, 1972; Zimmerman & Woo-Sam, 1973). Thus, in the hands of an experienced clinician, the WAIS-R can provide tentative diagnostic hypotheses in addition to, or instead of, its provision of an intelligence test score. For further information on these and other clinical uses of the WAIS, see, for example, Maloney and Ward (1976), Matarazzo (1972), and Zimmerman and Woo-Sam (1973).

Comparison of the WAIS-R with the Stanford-Binet. Since the WAIS-R and the Stanford-Binet are by far the best known and most widely used intelligence tests in the world, a brief comparison may be helpful to readers. Although both are highly reliable instruments measuring a general component of intelligence, there may be some situations where they are differentially useful. First, the Stanford-Binet was designed primarily for use with children and young adults, and earlier versions of the test did not have enough "ceiling" (difficult items) for use with superior adolescents and young adults. However, it would be better for the assessment of retarded adults, because the WAIS-R has too little "floor" (not enough easy items) for use with such individuals. The WAIS-R, on the other hand, is useful with adults of all ages—the standardization sample ranged from ages 16 to 74. And the WAIS-R would probably be preferable for use with superior adolescents and adults. It should be noted that these generalizations are based on earlier versions of the Stanford-Binet—more complete understanding of the usefulness of the Stanford-Binet: Fourth Edition relative to the WAIS-R will require further research and clinical experience.

The Wechsler Intelligence Scale for Children. The Wechsler Intelligence Scale for Children (WISC) was originally adapted directly from the Wechsler-Bellevue Intelligence Scale (Seashore, Wesman, & Doppelt, 1950). In 1974 a revised version known as the WISC-R was published. The WISC-R is appropriate for use with children age 6 to about age 17 and, together with the Wechsler Preschool and Primary Scale of Intelligence (appropriate for ages 4 to 6½), it constitutes a major well-known individually administered alternative to the Stanford-Binet for the assessment of the intelligence of children.

The WISC-R contains ten basic subtests and two subtests that can be used as alternates or as supplementary tests, if desired. Like the WAIS-R, the WISC-R is organized into a Verbal Scale and a Performance Scale. The Verbal Scale contains five tests similar to their WAIS counterparts: Information, Similarities, Arithmetic, Vocabulary, and Comprehension. The alternate verbal test is Digit Span. The Performance Scale also contains five subtests, and these are also similar to the same-named tests in the WAIS-R. The tests are Picture Completion, Picture Arrangement, Block Design,

Object Assembly, and Coding (like the WAIS-R Digit Symbol, except that an easier part was added to the WISC-R). A new test, Mazes, is the alternate for the Performance Scale; Mazes utilizes nine paper-and-pencil mazes presented in order of increasing difficulty. Essentially, the WISC-R is quite similar to the WAIS-R, but the content is easier and more interesting to children.

As in the scoring of the WAIS-R, raw scores on each subtest of the WISC-R are converted into standard scores having a mean of 10 and a standard deviation of 3. These standard scores are provided separately for age groups ranging from 6 years to 16 years, 11 months, so conversion to standard scores uses the table provided for the age of the child tested. Subtest standard scores are summed to yield a Verbal IQ, a Performance IQ, and a Full Scale IQ. The WISC-R standardization sample was relatively large, consisting of 100 boys and 100 girls at each of 11 age levels ranging from 6½ to 16½, and was representative of the United States population.

The WISC-R is highly reliable; split-half reliability coefficients ranged from 0.90 for the Performance IQ to 0.96 for the Full Scale IQ, and test-retest reliability coefficients ranged from 0.90 (Performance IQ) to 0.95 (Full Scale IQ). The Verbal and Performance IQs are relatively highly correlated ($r = 0.67$), and the WISC-R appears to have a factor structure similar to that of the WAIS-R—that is, a large common factor and group factors representing verbal, perceptual, and memory capacities. Thus, in terms of format, content, and psychometric properties, the WISC-R is very similar to the WAIS-R.

The Wechsler Preschool and Primary Scale of Intelligence. The Wechsler Preschool and Primary Scale of Intelligence (WPPSI) is appropriate for use with children ages 4 to 6½. It consists of six verbal tests, one of which is supplementary, and five performance tests. Most of the tests are analogous to the same-named tests on the WAIS-R and the WISC-R, although there are three new tests. One of the new tests, Animal House, is analogous to the WAIS-R Digit Symbol and WISC-R Coding tests. The key for Animal House has a dog, cat, fish, and chicken, each paired with a different-colored "house" (a cylinder-shaped form). The test board gives animals, and the child's task is to match the appropriately colored house to each animal. The new test Sentences requires the child to repeat a series of sentences after oral presentation of each sentence by the examiner; this test is a substitute for the WISC-R Digit Span and is a supplementary test on the Verbal Scale. Finally, Geometric Design involves the copying of ten simple geometric designs using a pencil. Incorporating these new tests, the Verbal Scale consists of Information, Vocabulary, Arithmetic, Similarities, and Comprehension; Sentences is the alternate or supplementary test. The Performance Scale includes Animal House, Picture Completion, Mazes, Geometric Design, and Block Design.

Like its counterparts the WAIS-R and the WISC-R, the WPPSI yields Verbal, Performance, and Full Scale IQs based on the same types of standard score conversions. The normative sample was a relatively large and representative group of children ages 4 to 6½. The test has been shown to be highly reliable in terms of both internal consistency and test-retest reliability. Factor-analytic findings suggest the presence of a general factor and two group factors, Verbal (including the six verbal tests) and Performance (including the five performance tests).

To summarize, the WAIS-R, WISC-R, and WPPSI are a "family" of intelligence tests that together cover the full range of age levels. Because they are similar in format, administration procedures, and types of scores provided, an examiner experienced in the administration of one of them is able to quickly gain competence in administering and scoring the others. They are well standardized and highly reliable tests that appear to measure major aspects of intellectual functioning.

Kaufman Assessment Battery for Children. The Kaufman Assessment Battery for Children (K-ABC; Kaufman & Kaufman, 1983a, 1983b) is an individually administered intelligence test developed to accomplish the same general purposes as the Stanford-Binet. In addition, it is designed to be especially appropriate for use with handicapped individuals, cultural and linguistic minorities, and in the diagnosis of learning disabilities.

The rationale for test development was based on information processing theory and research, grounded in cognitive psychology. Two basic types of information processing, that is, simultaneous and sequential, served as the basis for test construction. The K-ABC yields four scores based on 16 subtests for use with children ages 2½ to 12½. The four scores are Simultaneous Processing, Sequential Processing, General Mental Processes (a combination of the first two), and Achievement. Test content was selected to deemphasize the verbal and language material traditionally used in intelligence tests and to be independent of knowledge taught in school so that the scores would be a purer measure of "intelligence" versus "achievement." The content of the processing subtests includes spatial, visual-perceptual, memory, numerical, and some verbal content. The Achievement tests assess ability in reading, arithmetic, word knowledge, and general information, but the subtests avoid use of content taught in schools.

The K-ABC was standardized using 8,000 children ranging in age from 2½ to 12½. The scores provided are normalized standard scores (mean of 100, SD of 15) and as percentile ranks within each 6-month age interval (i.e., ages 2½, 3, 3½, 4, etc.). Handicapped, retarded, gifted, and ethnic minority children were oversampled, and norms within race and socioeconomic status (parental education) groups are also provided.

Even though the K-ABC is reliable, there is a lack of evidence for its construct validity. Although the processing subtests were designed as a "culture-fair" (see the last section of this chapter) measure of g, they don't appear to measure g since they don't load highly on the large general factor now accepted as indicative of g and they don't correlate highly with the g indices of the WAIS-R and Stanford-Binet (Anastasi, 1985; Page, 1985). The Achievement subtests of the K-ABC actually seem to do a better job of measuring g than do the information-processing subtests (Anastasi, 1985; Page, 1985).

Overall, the K-ABC has promise as a measuring instrument as long as its questionable degree of utility as a general measure of intelligence is kept in mind. The accompanying interpretive materials in the *Interpretive Manual* (Kaufman & Kaufman, 1983b) are excellent and eloquently demonstrate the careful use of test scores for diagnostic purposes. And although use of the information-processing scores reduces the size of race differences in test scores, it also reduces the extent to which the test measures intelligence. Although the word "intelligence" is not used in the title of the test, the authors do claim to measure it. This claim needs further support before it should be accepted.

Group-Administered Tests of Intelligence

The development of group tests of intelligence, like the first Binet-Simon intelligence test, was stimulated by an urgent practical need, the classification of recruits for the American armed services during World War I. A group of psychologists headed by Robert M. Yerkes (1921) developed the first group tests of intelligence, the Army Alpha Test and the Army Beta Test, to use for the purpose of rapid and efficient screening of new recruits. The Army Alpha was a verbally oriented test, while the Army Beta was a nonlanguage test used with illiterate or foreign-born recruits (Yerkes, 1921). The Army Alpha and the Army Beta served as models for subsequent group-administered intelligence tests.

As has been noted, group intelligence tests can be administered to large numbers of individuals at one time. This capability allows the utilization of very large standardization samples and has facilitated the development of large-scale testing programs used particularly in the armed services, business and industry, and education. In other words, the efficiency and relatively low costs associated with group testing have made it an almost routine occurrence in the lives of most Americans.

The following sections describe the major group tests of intelligence used at different age levels. It should be noted that the titles of the tests to be described use terms such as *scholastic ability, mental ability, school ability, cognitive ability,* and *mental maturity* rather than the term *intelligence*. Because the criteria used to validate intelligence tests have usually been measures of academic achievement and success, terms like *school ability* represent appropriate alternatives to the term *intelligence* in describing these tests. In addition, terms like *school ability* and *mental ability* are less likely than the term *intelligence* to be misunderstood and misinterpreted. Since the tests to be described are used primarily in educational settings and for the prediction and understanding of educational achievement, the use of terms that will be correctly understood and interpreted by the consumers of test results—usually parents, children, and teachers—is particularly important. Essentially, terms like *scholastic ability* more directly convey the *practical* implications of varying levels of intellectual ability and are thus more readily understood and more appropriately utilized.

The tests described in the remaining portion of this chapter are various measures of cognitive, mental, or school ability used primarily with children in kindergarten through grade 12. Ability tests used at the elementary and secondary school level are often referred to as "multilevel" batteries (e.g., Anastasi, 1982) because they consist of a series of analogous tests of varying yet overlapping difficulty levels that, taken together, are suitable for the measurement of intelligence across grade levels. In other words, the same test battery can be used in a school system including grades kindergarten through 12 because the particular *segment* of the battery administered depends on the grade level of the students being tested at a particular time. For example, grade-5 students might be administered the tests for grade levels 3 through 7; the use of the grade levels below those of the students being tested would help to ensure that even the poorest grade-5 students were able to respond correctly to some items. The use of higher grade-levels would provide a "ceiling" with which to adequately assess the intelligence of the brightest students. While this is a somewhat simplified and over-generalized description of multilevel batteries, it should convey the desired purposes or utility of one battery across age levels and the provision of sufficient "floor" and "ceiling" to adequately assess individual differences.

Multilevel test batteries are designed for use in the schools; thus the levels are usually referred to in terms of school grades. The youngest grade/age for which group tests are appropriate is generally considered to be the kindergarten or first-grade level. With children younger than about five, individual administration is necessary to establish and maintain the child's attention and to administer the orally presented and performance items.

The Cognitive Abilities Test. The Cognitive Abilities Test (CogAT), a revision of the Lorge-Thorndike Intelligence Tests (Lorge, Thorndike, & Hagen, 1964) was developed by Robert L. Thorndike and Elizabeth Hagen (1978). In its most recent revision, the 1986 CogAT Multilevel Edition, Form 4, the test is organized into two primary batteries (Primary 1 for kindergarten and first grade and Primary 2 for second and third graders) and one multilevel battery designed for use in grades 3 through 12.

The three sections of the test—the Verbal, Quantitative, and Nonverbal Batteries—are intended to assess reasoning abilities with the three major types of symbols used in cognitive reasoning—verbal, quantitative, and spatial or geometrical. Accordingly, the Verbal Battery includes sentence completion, verbal classifications, and verbal analogies subtests. The Quantitative Battery has sections for quantitative relations, number series, and equation building. Figure 6.6 shows examples of the types of items used in the Verbal and Quantitative Batteries of the CogAT. The Nonverbal Battery does not use numbers or language, but rather geometric forms and other figures; subtests include figure analogies, figure classification, and figure analysis. Examples of the types of items in the Nonverbal Battery are shown in Figures 6.7 and 6.8. The Nonverbal Battery of the CogAT is designed to minimize the influence of formal schooling on test scores and is thus especially appropriate for the appraisal of poorly educated individuals, those for whom English is a second language, and poor readers.

Based on normative groups of approximately 18,000 students from each school

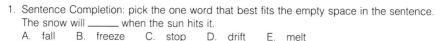

Verbal Battery

1. Sentence Completion: pick the one word that best fits the empty space in the sentence.
   The snow will _____ when the sun hits it.
   A. fall   B. freeze   C. stop   D. drift   E. melt

2. Verbal Classification: think in what way the words in dark type go together. Then find the word in the line below that goes with them.
   winter   summer   autumn
   A. season   B. spring   C. temperature   D. weather   E. year

3. Verbal Analogies: figure out how the first two words arae related to each other. Then from the five words on the line below find the word that is related to the third word in the same way.
   west → east: up →
   A. down   B. hill   C. shot   D. tight   E. town

Quantitative Battery

1. Quantitative Relations: If the amount or quantity in Column A is more than in Column B, mark A; if it is less, mark B; if they are equal, mark C.
   Column A   Column B
    7 dimes   10 nickels

2. Number Series: the numbers at the left are in a certain order. Find the number at the right that should come next.
   5 7 9 11 13   A. 11   B. 13   C. 14   D. 15   E. 16

3. Equation Building: Arrange the numbers and signs below to make true equations and then choose the number at the right that gives you a correct answer.
   12   18—   A. 6   B. 8   C. 16   D. 26   E. 30

Figure 6.6 Sample items from the verbal and quantitative batteries of the Cognitive Abilities Test (Cog AT). [From R. L. Thorndike & E. Hagen, *Examiner's Manual for the Cognitive Abilities Test* (Boston: Houghton Mifflin Company, 1979, The Cognitive Abilities Test is copyrighted by The Riverside Publishing Company. Reproduced by permission of The Riverside Publishing Company, 8420 Bryn Mawr Avenue, Chicago, Ill. 60631.]

grade and representative of the school population of the United States, raw scores on each battery of the multilevel CogAT are converted into scores called *universal scale scores*. Using tables supplied in the manual, the universal scale scores for each battery can be converted into percentile and stanine normative scores across both age and grade levels for each battery separately. In addition, the universal scale scores can be converted into *standard age scores* having a mean of 100 and a standard deviation of 16, that is, identical to deviation IQ scores. Figure 6.9 shows several sample score profiles derived from the multilevel CogAT; it should be noted that five different normative scores (percentile and stanine by grade, and standard, percentile, and stanine scores by age)

are provided for each battery (Verbal, Quantitative, and Nonverbal), thus allowing comparisons of the battery scores for a given individual, as well as comparisons to normative groups of examinees.

The CogAT is a highly reliable test and an excellent predictor of academic achievement. Internal consistency reliability coefficients (Kuder-Richardson-20) are very high, averaging 0.94 (Verbal), 0.92 (Quantitative), and 0.93 (Nonverbal) across grade levels. Test scores are also relatively stable over time; retests using alternate forms after a six-month interval yielded correlations ranging from 0.85 to 0.93 for the Verbal Battery, 0.78 to 0.88 for the Quantitative Battery, and 0.81 to 0.89 for the Nonverbal Battery.

Scores on the CogAT are highly cor-

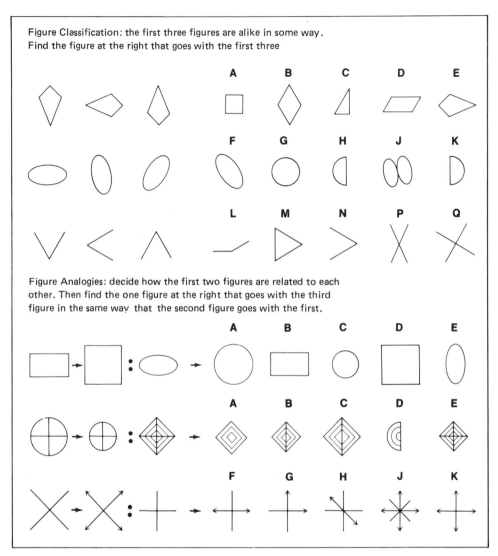

Figure 6.7 Sample test items from the nonverbal battery of the cognitive battery of the Cognitive Abilities Test, Form 3, Levels A-H. [Reproduced by permission of the Publisher, The Riverside Publishing Company, 8420 Bryn Mawr Avenue, Chicago, Ill. 60631.]

related with indices of academic achievement, particularly achievement test scores. Correlations with the composite score of the Iowa Tests of Basic Skills (used in grades 3 through 8) or the Tests of Achievement and Proficiency (used in grades 9 through 12) range from 0.86 to 0.89 (Verbal), 0.78 to 0.83 (Quantitative), and 0.71 to 0.75 (Non-verbal). Correlations of CogAT scores with other indices of academic achievement (e.g., course grades and overall grade-point averages) are in the neighborhood of $r = 0.50$ to $r = 0.60$, values typical of those found for well-constructed and standardized scholastic aptitude tests. Of the CogAT batteries, the Verbal scores are the best predictors of

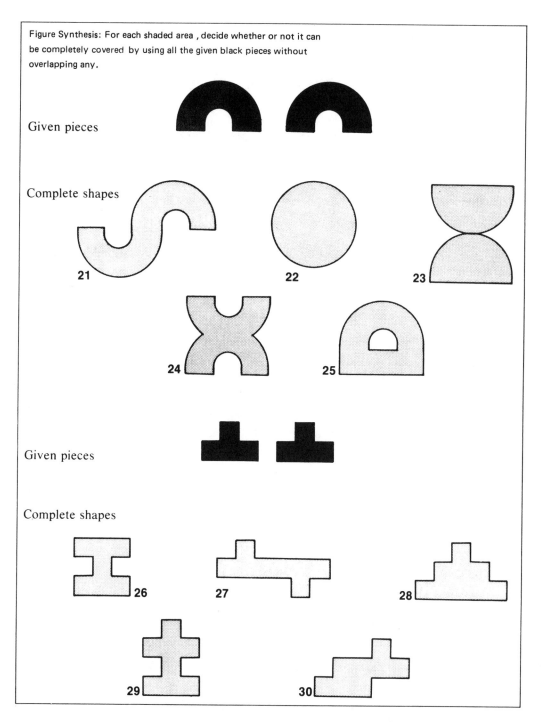

Figure Synthesis: For each shaded area , decide whether or not it can be completely covered by using all the given black pieces without overlapping any.

Given pieces

Complete shapes

21

22

23

24

25

Given pieces

Complete shapes

26

27

28

29

30

Figure 6.8 Sample test items from the nonverbal battery of the cognitive battery of the Cognitive Abilities Test, Form 3, Levels A-H. [Reproduced by permission of the Publisher, The Riverside Publishing Company, 8420 Bryn Mawrn Avenue, Chicago, Ill. 60631.]

Case 2: D.B., Male Chronological Age 13 Years 3 Mos. Grade 7

	Number of Answers Marked	Number of Answers Correct	Norms by Grade		Norms by Age		
			Percentile Rank	Stanine	Standard Age Score	Percentile Rank	Stanine
V	100	40	22	3	87	21	3
Q	60	25	16	3	83	14	3
NV	80	36	15	3	82	13	3

Case 3: K.L., Male Chronological Age 10 Years 6 Mos. Grade 5

	Number of Answers Marked	Number of Answers Correct	Norms by Grade		Norms by Age		
			Percentile Rank	Stanine	Standard Age Score	Percentile Rank	Stanine
V	100	48	34	4	94	35	4
Q	60	38	49	5	100	50	5
NV	79	54	48	5	98	45	5

Case 4: T.T., Female Chronological Age 14 Years 5 Mos. Grade 9

	Number of Answers Marked	Number of Answers Correct	Norms by Grade		Norms by Age		
			Percentile Rank	Stanine	Standard Age Score	Percentile Rank	Stanine
V	100	92	99	9	144	99	9
Q	60	56	97	9	132	98	9
NV	80	75	98	9	133	98	9

Case 6: R.M., Male Chronological Age 12 Years 3 Mos. Grade 7

	Number of Answers Marked	Number of Answers Correct	Norms by Grade		Norms by Age		
			Percentile Rank	Stanine	Standard Age Score	Percentile Rank	Stanine
V	100	45	30	4	95	38	4
Q	60	48	82	7	118	87	7
NV	80	66	83	7	117	86	7

Case 7: M.B., Female Chronological Age 15 Years 2 Mos. Grade 9

	Number of Answers Marked	Number of Answers Correct	Norms by Grade		Norms by Age		
			Percentile Rank	Stanine	Standard Age Score	Percentile Rank	Stanine
V	100	77	90	8	117	86	7
Q	60	51	85	7	115	83	7
NV	80	50	33	4	92	31	4

Figure 6.9 Sample score profiles from the Cognitive Abilities Test (CogAT). [From R. L. Thorndike & E. Hagen, *Examiner's Manual for the Cognitive Abilities Test* (Boston: Houghton Mifflin Company, 1979). The Cognitive Abilities Test is copyrighted by the Publisher, The Riverside Publishing Company. Reproduced by permission of The Riverside Publishing Company, 8420 Bryn Mawr Avenue, Chicago, Ill. 60631.]

overall achievement test scores and of achievement in a variety of academic subjects. This finding is consistent across academic aptitude tests designed for use in the elementary and secondary grades. Only in the prediction of grades or achievement in mathematics is the Quantitative score a better predictor of academic achievement; CogAT Quantitative scores are better predictors of math achievement than are CogAT Verbal scores.

In terms of the relationships of CogAT scores to other measures of mental aptitude, correlations with the Stanford-Binet range from $r = 0.65$ (Nonverbal) to $r = 0.77$ (Verbal). The separate battery scores are themselves highly correlated, ranging from $r = 0.66$ (Verbal scores with Nonverbal scores) to $r = 0.75$ (Verbal scores with Quantitative scores). Consistent with the high intercorrelations among Verbal, Quantitative, and Nonverbal scores is the finding of a large general factor resulting from factor analyses of the ten subtests (i.e., four verbal, three quantitative, and three nonverbal). This general factor, accounting for over 50 percent of the variance in scores, appears to reflect relational thinking and reasoning abilities. Since separate Verbal, Nonverbal, and Quantitative factors resulting from the analysis accounted for only about 8 percent, 5 percent, and 2 percent of the variance, respectively, the CogAT may be described as primarily a measure of general intelligence or scholastic aptitude (Spearman's g) rather than as a measure of different academic abilities.

Reference to the score profiles shown in Figure 6.9 provides several examples of the practical utility of CogAT scores. The first three cases shown (numbered 2, 3, and 4) illustrate a typical pattern of scoring on the CogAT in that the individual's performance is roughly equivalent across the three batteries. In Case 2, D.B. is somewhat slower in cognitive development than the average child of his grade or age and uses each type of symbol with equivalent skill (e.g., grade percentiles of 22, 16, and 15 for the Verbal, Quantitative, and Nonverbal subtests, respectively). While below average, D.B. can probably perform satisfactorily in seventh grade if his learning experiences are highly structured and include frequent step-by-step presentations. Case 3, K.L., shows a student with average scores relative to other children of his age and grade, and Case 4 depicts T.T., a gifted ninth-grader. The primary educational concern for students like T.T. is the provision of adequate opportunities for use of their exceptional abilities.

Cases 6 and 7 demonstrate instances of uneven patterns of cognitive development in that scores on two of the batteries are very high relative to the score on the third battery. Case 6, R.M., shows a relatively low Verbal score but relatively high Quantitative and Nonverbal scores. Case 7, M.B., shows an opposite pattern, a low Nonverbal score but high Verbal and Quantitative scores. In terms of his educational progress, R.M. is likely to do well in math and science but poorly in language-oriented courses. M.B., on the other hand, will need help in developing her spatial-visual reasoning abilities for successful pursuit of higher-level mathematics such as geometry.

One aspect of multilevel school ability batteries particularly useful in educational settings is that many of these tests were standardized concurrently with (i.e., using the same normative samples and testing concurrently) major academic achievement tests (to be described in Chapter 8 in discussion of the assessment of achievement). The major advantage of concurrent standardization is that for each grade and age level, the average levels of academic achievement associated with various ability or intelligence test scores are determined precisely. This knowledge can be translated into expectancies for subsequent educational achievements (at least as measured by the achievement tests) and can be used to assess the extent to which a student at a given level of scholastic aptitude is achieving at a level similar to other students with comparable levels of ability. The CogAT levels corresponding to grades 3 through 8 were standardized concurrently with the Iowa Tests of Basic Skills (ITBS), and grades 9 through 12 were standardized with the Tests of Achievement and Proficiency (TAP). Further information about these achievement tests and their uses may be found in Chapter 8.

For further information about the psychometric characteristics and interpretive aspects of the CogAT, see the CogAT manual (Thorndike & Hagen, 1979) and reviews by Kenneth D. Hopkins and Robert C. Nichols in the *Eighth Mental Measurements Yearbook* (Buros, 1978) and Ansorge (1985) in the *Ninth Mental Measurements Yearbook.*

The School and College Ability Tests. The School and Ability Tests (SCAT,

Series III) were developed and refined under the auspices of the Educational Testing Service. The tests, designed to assess academic aptitude for students in grades 3 through 12, are organized in three difficulty levels and are available in alternate forms X and Y for all grade levels. The SCAT includes a 20-minute Verbal test, composed of 50 verbal analogies, and a 20-minute Quantitative test containing 50 quantitative comparison items. Figure 6.10 shows the types of items used. Three scores are provided (i.e., Verbal, Quantitative, and Total); raw scores may be converted into standard scores, percentiles, and/or stanines for each grade level.

The SCAT and its companion achievement test, the Sequential Tests of Educational Progress (STEP III), were standardized in samples of approximately 5,000 to 7,000 students at each grade level; the standardization sample represented a cross section of the United States school population in grades 3 through 12. Internal consistency reliability is high; Kuder-Richardson-20

Figure 6.10 Sample items from the verbal and quantitative test of the School and College Ability Tests (SCAT III, Intermediate level). Used by permission of the publisher, CTB/McGraw-Hill, 2500 Garden Road, Monterey, Calif. 93940. Copyright © by Educational Testing Service. All Rights Reserved. Printed in the U.S.A.

Part I— Verbal: each question begins with two words. These two words go together in a certain way. Find the lettered pair of words that go together in the same way as the first pair of words.

hammer: carpenter

A. beret: artist
B. gavel: judge
C. nurse: doctor
D. curtsy: ballerina

Part II— Quantitative: Each of the following questions has two parts, one part in Column A and the other part in Column B. You must find out if one part is greater than the other, or if the parts are equal, or if not enough information is given for you to decide. Mark A if the part in Column A is greater, B if the part in Column B is greater, C if the two parts are equal and D if not enough information is given for you to decide.

Column A	**Column B**
1. The average of 3, 5, and 7	The average of 4, 5, and 6.
2. 0.001	0.01
3. $11 + x$	14

coefficients range from 0.86 to 0.92 for the Verbal section, 0.87 to 0.93 for the Quantitative section, and 0.92 to 0.95 for the Total scores. Alternate forms reliability coefficients (the correlation of scores on Form X with those on Form Y) range from 0.69 to 0.92, but are generally in the high 0.80s. Test-retest reliability coefficients range from $r = 0.78$ to $r = 0.85$ for the Verbal score, from $r = 0.70$ to $r = 0.84$ for the Quantitative score, and from $r = 0.83$ to $r = 0.88$ for the Total score (Educational Testing Service, 1980).

Like CogAT scores, SCAT scores are strongly related to indices of academic achievement. Correlations with STEP scores range from $r = 0.60$ to $r = 0.80$. The total score shows the highest correlations with achievement test scores, followed by the Verbal test score for all but mathematics achievement, where, like the CogAT, the Quantitative score is the better predictor of the two. Correlations with course grades and grade-point average are somewhat lower than those with achievement test scores but are well within the range typical of high-quality tests of this type. Also similar to the CogAT are the high correlations between the Verbal and Quantitative scores, ranging from 0.61 to 0.75 across grade levels.

A particularly useful feature of the SCAT is that its scores are highly correlated with scores on the Scholastic Aptitude Test (SAT), used extensively in selecting applicants to colleges and universities. The SCAT manual provides expectancy tables by which the probabilities of various levels of performance on SAT-Verbal given SCAT-Verbal scores and on SAT-Quantitative given SCAT-Quantitative scores are shown. These tables can be used in the counseling of high school students when they are making decisions concerning the colleges and universities to which they will apply for admission. Since colleges and universities have differentially selective admissions criteria, esti-

mates of expected levels of SAT performance can be helpful in selecting colleges where admission is likely and in evaluating the likelihood of admission to preferred colleges and universities.

For example, Figure 6.11 shows the SCAT test report of a hypothetical student. The score report shows the raw, standard, percentile, and stanine scores for the Verbal, Quantitative, and Total sections of the SCAT. It may be noted that this student's level of both verbal and quantitative ability is well above average (e.g., scores at the mid-90th percentiles nationally and at the eighth or ninth stanines). Not surprisingly, the student is predicted to perform reasonably well on the SAT. Gerry has a 60 percent chance of receiving at least a 550 on SAT-Verbal and a 62 percent chance of receiving a 550 on SAT-Quantitative. Thus, Gerry's chances of admission to a college requiring minimum scores of 550 on both SAT-Verbal and SAT-Quantitative would appear reasonably good. If, however, Gerry indicates that he's interested only in highly selective colleges—for example, those in which SAT scores of 650 or 700 on the Verbal and Quantitative portions are typical—we may wish to urge him to apply to somewhat less selective schools, because his chances of scores that high are quite low.

It may also be noted that Gerry's superior standing as a high school student fades somewhat in terms of projected SAT performance; SCAT norms are in comparison to all high school students, while SAT norms are based only on *college-bound* high school students. Thus, SAT norms are based on a more selective comparison group than are SCAT norms. This difference in comparison groups should be kept in mind. Students like the hypothetical Gerry may be disturbed and upset when they find themselves performing at less than the 80th or 90th percentile levels they became accustomed to in elementary and secondary school.

STUDENT REPORT:
SCHOOL AND COLLEGE ABILITY TEST   STEP   TEST DATE: 04/79

NAME: BOGATZ, GERRY A.
SPECIAL CODES: 187453494   GRADE: 9   NATIONAL NORMS: 9 SPRING   FORM USED: X

REPORT FOR: ANNA WILLIS   SCHOOL: SIR FRANCIS DRAKE

SCHOOL AND COLLEGE ABILITY TEST	RAW SCORE/ MAXIMUM POSSIBLE/ LEVEL TAKEN	STANDARD SCORE	NATIONAL PERCENTILE/ STANINE	LOCAL PERCENTILE/ STANINE
Verbal	38/50/AD	481	94/8	91/8
Quantitative	38/50/AD	498	95/8	97/9
TOTAL	76/100/AD	488	96/9	95/8

CHANCES IN 100 THAT SAT SCORE WILL EQUAL OR EXCEED	VERBAL				QUANTITATIVE			
	95	93	60	10	97	95	62	12
	350	450	550	650	350	450	550	650

Figure 6.11 Sample test report from the School and College Ability Test; also shows prediction of future Scholastic Aptitude Test (SAT) scores as estimated from SCAT scores. [Used by permission of the Publisher, CTB/McGraw-Hill, 2500 Garden Road, Monterey, Calif. 93940. Copyright © by Educational Testing Service. All Rights Reserved. Printed in the U.S.A.]

Because the SCAT was normed concurrently with the STEP, aptitude-achievement discrepancies are another useful aspect of score interpretation and application. Since SCAT and STEP scores are highly correlated, students who score significantly higher on one than on the other may be dealing with issues of attitude, motivation, interest, and so on. For example, if Sue's performance on the STEP Reading or Vocabulary test is significantly lower than the level expected from students with her level of SCAT Verbal ability, we might question the degree to which she is satisfactorily adjusting to school in terms of her attitudes and motivation. On the other hand, a student whose STEP achievement test scores were significantly higher than those of other students with his or her level of SCAT ability would likely be postulated to be a highly motivated and hard-working student who was achieving at his or her maximal level of potential. In general, large aptitude-achievement discrepancies indicate that the stu-

dent's performance may be influenced by factors beyond the scope of either the SCAT or the STEP and thus suggest special caution in using these test scores.

One final noteworthy feature of the SCAT manual (Educational Testing Service, 1980a) is its explicit description of the test as a measure of academic aptitude and of the importance of the quality and amount of education in determining test performance. While these ideas are generally accepted among test constructors and publishers, the developers of the SCAT can be credited for making the purpose of their test explicit.

Further information about the SCAT-III can be found in the manual. Reviews of the SCAT-III may be found in the ninth edition of the *Mental Measurements Yearbooks;* see Ahmann (1985) and Passow (1985).

The Otis-Lennon School Ability Test. The Otis-Lennon School Ability Test (OLSAT) is the continuation of an ability test series that dates back to 1918. Its predecessors include the Otis Group Intelligence Scale, the Otis Quick-Scoring Mental Ability Tests, and Otis-Lennon Mental Ability Test. The OLSAT was developed by Otis and Lennon in 1980, and the second edition of the test became available in 1988. The OLSAT is designed to measure abstract thinking and reasoning ability. As the title implies, the test is most appropriately used to assess examinees' ability to cope with school learning tasks and to evaluate school ability-school achievement discrepancies.

The OLSAT, second edition, is organized into levels designated A through G, corresponding to kindergarten (Level A) up to grades 9–12 (Level G), respectively. Item content is classified as Verbal or Nonverbal depending on whether knowledge of language is necessary to answer the items. Verbal sections include Verbal Comprehension and Verbal Reasoning. Nonverbal sections include Pictorial Reasoning, Figural Reasoning, and Quantitative Reasoning. Separate scores for Verbal and Nonverbal sections and a Total Score are provided.

The OLSAT and the Metropolitan Achievement Tests were standardized concurrently in a sample of 130,000 students representative of the United States school population in grades 1 through 12. Raw scores are converted into what is called the "School Ability Index," essentially a deviation IQ score ($M = 100$, $SD = 16$). The School Ability Index may also be converted into percentiles and/or stanines for each age and grade level.

The test manual (Otis & Lennon, 1980) provides excellent coverage of data concerning reliability and validity. Kuder-Richardson-20 reliability coefficients equal or exceed 0.90 for all age and grade levels, as do alternate forms correlations for grades 5 and above and ages ten and above. Alternate forms reliability coefficients for grades 4 and below and below age ten range from $r = 0.81$ to $r = 0.90$. Test-retest correlations for a six-month

interval range from $r = 0.84$ to $r = 0.92$. Scores on the OLSAT are related to several indices of academic achievement, including achievement test scores and course grades.

While the OLSAT is clearly a highly reliable test and an excellent predictor of academic achievement, factor-analytic studies are necessary to support the theoretical basis for the test (i.e., Vernon's *v:ed*). The OLSAT manual and a review by John E. Milholland (1978) in the *Mental Measurements Yearbook* provide more information about the test.

The Henmon-Nelson Tests of Mental Ability. The Henmon-Nelson Tests of Mental Ability were first published in 1931 and were revised in 1973 (Lamke, Nelson & French, 1973a). The tests include a Primary Battery for kindergarten through second grade and three additional levels, covering grades 3 through 6, 6 through 9, and 9 through 12. (A college-level battery, published in 1961, was not included in the most recent revision of the test.) The Henmon-Nelson Tests are designed to measure general mental ability of the type important to scholastic success. The Primary Battery includes three separate subtests. The Listening test samples general information, reasoning, and the ability to understand abstract relationships, the Picture Vocabulary test assesses vocabulary and verbal comprehension, and the Size and Number test assesses numerical and spatial comprehension and reasoning. Scores on the three Primary subtests are summed to give a single raw score that can be converted into a deviation IQ ($M = 100$, $SD = 16$) and percentiles and stanines by age and grade.

The test battery used for grades 3 through 12 contains 90 items of different types, including vocabulary, sentence completion, verbal analogies, number series, and figure analogies. Items are arranged in a spiral omnibus format—that is, different item

Easiest Section of the Test

1. **When we sleep we:**
   (1) run (2) march (3) play (4) rest (5) eat.................................. ☐1 ☐2 ☐3 ☐4 ☐5

2. **The weather is warm in summer and ... in winter.** A word for the blank is:
   (1) cold (2) heat (3) long (4) plenty (5) very .... ☐1 ☐2 ☐3 ☐4 ☐5

3. **A sheet of music always has:**
   (1) rhythm (2) words (3) covers (4) notes (5) players......................... ☐1 ☐2 ☐3 ☐4 ☐5

4. To **allow** means the same as to:
   (1) take (2) pursue (3) store (4) cease (5) permit.......................... ☐1 ☐2 ☐3 ☐4 ☐5

5. **A shore is:**
   (1) land (2) sunny (3) certain (4) a stream (5) hot........................... ☐1 ☐2 ☐3 ☐4 ☐5

6. ◯ is to ◡ as ｜ is to: (1) ◯ (2) ｜ (3) ☐ (4) ⸱⸱ (5) ___ .... ☐1 ☐2 ☐3 ☐4 ☐5

7. △ is to ▷ as ◣ is to: (1) ◁ (2) Z (3) M (4) P (5) ◿ .... ☐1 ☐2 ☐3 ☐4 ☐5

8. **A suburb is near a:**
   (1) hospital (2) paragraph (3) city (4) creamery (5) drama..................... ☐1 ☐2 ☐3 ☐4 ☐5

9. **Man** is to **boy** as **cat** is to:
   (1) kitten (2) snake (3) dog (4) mouse (5) rat .... ☐1 ☐2 ☐3 ☐4 ☐5

More Difficult Section of the Test

71. **Mock** means about the same as:
    (1) copy (2) respect (3) chicken (4) imitate (5) sober .... ☐1 ☐2 ☐3 ☐4 ☐5

72. A **hoax** is a:
    (1) truck (2) deception (3) tool (4) persuasion (5) hotel .... ☐1 ☐2 ☐3 ☐4 ☐5

73. **Two pints equal one liter. Three liters equal one rabeck. What is the cost of 5 rabecks of milk at 6¢ a pint?**
    (1) 90¢ (2) 30¢ (3) $1.80 (4) 60¢ (5) $3.60 .... ☐1 ☐2 ☐3 ☐4 ☐5

74. **The big oak tree near the cottage had lost its.....** A word for the blank is:
    (1) growl (2) cones (3) blossoms (4) foliage (5) needles .... ☐1 ☐2 ☐3 ☐4 ☐5

75. **8, 4, 2, 1, $\frac{1}{2}$,...,....** What two numbers should come next?
    (1) $\frac{1}{4}$ and $\frac{1}{6}$ (2) $\frac{1}{3}$ and $\frac{1}{4}$ (3) 1 and $\frac{1}{2}$ (4) $\frac{2}{3}$ and $\frac{2}{4}$ (5) $\frac{1}{4}$ and $\frac{1}{8}$ .... ☐1 ☐2 ☐3 ☐4 ☐5

76. To **insinuate** is to:
    (1) devise (2) err (3) hint (4) convict (5) officiate .... ☐1 ☐2 ☐3 ☐4 ☐5

77. **27, 9, 3, 1, $\frac{1}{3}$,...,....** What two numbers should come next?
    (1) $\frac{1}{9}$ and $\frac{1}{27}$ (2) $\frac{2}{3}$ and $\frac{1}{9}$ (3) $\frac{2}{3}$ and $\frac{1}{3}$ (4) $\frac{1}{9}$ and $\frac{1}{18}$ (5) $\frac{1}{6}$ and $\frac{1}{9}$ .... ☐1 ☐2 ☐3 ☐4 ☐5

78. To be **frank** is to be:
    (1) enraged (2) argumentative (3) candid (4) sealed (5) joyful .... ☐1 ☐2 ☐3 ☐4 ☐5

79. **The director of a museum is most often known as its:**
    (1) chief (2) conductor (3) curator (4) president (5) logician .... ☐1 ☐2 ☐3 ☐4 ☐5

Figure 6.12 Sample sections illustrating the spiral omnibus format of the Hermon-Nelson Tests of Mental Ability. [Reproduced by permission of the Publisher, The Riverside Publishing Company, 8420 Bryn Mawr Avenue, Chicago, Ill. 60631.]

types of the same difficulty level occur together and the different types of items recur regularly but at increasing levels of difficulty. Figure 6.12 shows a sample section from the form of the test used in grades 6 through 9. The battery used for grades 3 through 12 was normed in a national sample of 40,000 students in grades 3 through 12. Raw scores on the 90-item test may be converted into deviation IQs and age and grade percentile and stanine normative scores.

Split-half (odd-even) reliability coefficients for the Henmon-Nelson suggest that it is a highly reliable test; values (corrected by the Spearman-Brown formula) range from 0.94 to 0.96. Most validity data reported in the test manual (Lamke, Nelson & French, 1973b) describe the previous version of the test, but those data do suggest strong relationships of Henmon-Nelson test scores to achievement test scores and, to a lesser extent, school grades. Further data regarding the psychometric characteristics of the test may be found in the manual (Lamke, Nelson, & French, 1973b).

Summary. To summarize, the group-administered tests described for use at the elementary and secondary school levels have much in common. Generally, they are well constructed and well standardized, highly reliable, and show strong relationships with academic achievement criteria. Although none contains the word *intelligence* in its title, all provide a standard score using the same mean and standard deviation as the deviation IQ scores provided by either the Stanford-Binet or the Wechsler scales. Although the CogAT and the SCAT provide factor scores (e.g., verbal, quantitative) instead of, or in addition to, total scores, the large general factors, the high subtest intercorrelations of the CogAT and the SCAT, and the high internal consistency reliabilities of all these tests suggest the common presence of a general mental ability important to

achievement in the American educational system. Thus, even though the theoretical bases used in the construction of these tests differ, they all appear to be successfully measuring a common ability important to scholastic success.

"Culture-Fair" Intelligence Tests

As will be more fully discussed in Chapter 14, there has been growing concern in recent decades about using intelligence tests with individuals from subcultural, minority, and disadvantaged backgrounds. A related concern is the adaptation of tests for use in other countries, particularly non-Western countries with values and belief systems different from those represented by most Western societies. In response to these concerns, much attention has been directed toward the possibility of developing "culture-fair" tests of intelligence. Developers of culture-fair tests have attempted to minimize the importance of language, culture-specific content, and speed in test performance to maximize fairness across cultures. In the following section, tests developed to minimize the importance of culturally specific knowledge are briefly described.

Raven's Progressive Matrices. This test was developed to measure Spearman's g. It includes 60 matrices that are each missing a section; examinees are required to choose the missing section from six alternatives provided. The test can be used with the deaf and non-English-speaking examinees and is available in several forms, including one for gifted individuals aged 11 and over and one for use with children ages 5 to 11, retarded adults, and mental patients.

Culture-Fair Intelligence Test (CFIT). The CFIT was developed by Raymond Cattell and is published by the Institute for Personality and Ability Testing (IPAT). The CFIT is a nonverbal intelligence test designed to overcome, as much as possible, the influences of verbal fluency, cultural background, and educational level. The test was designed to measure Cattell's postulated "fluid ability," involving basic reasoning skills that are less influenced by training and experience than are measures of "crystallized ability," which include the vocabulary, knowledge, and numerical skills resulting from education and experience. The test is available in three levels spanning ages 4 through superior adulthood. The item content includes figural, graphic, and pictorial material that must be organized or classified in some manner by the examinee.

The Leiter International Performance Scale. This test was developed and first used in Hawaii and is distinguished by the almost complete lack of instructions, either spoken or pantomime. The materials consist of a response frame and a series of cards used to indicate the examinee's response; in one sense, comprehension of *how* to do the task becomes part of the test. Some of the tasks required include matching colors, picture completion, similarities, and memory for a series. Scores are reported in terms of Mental Ages, like earlier versions of the Stanford-Binet, which can be converted into IQs. A shorter version of the test, called the Arthur Adaptation, appropriate for use with children aged 2 through 12, is also available.

Goodenough-Harris Drawing Test (G-HDT). The G-HDT requires examinees to draw three pictures—a man, a woman, and themselves. Scoring is based on the degree to which the drawing demonstrates observational accuracy and conceptual thought regarding the human body. Norms are available for children aged 3 through 15. The correlations of G-HDT scores with those on other intelligence tests average about 0.50, and there is evidence that the test does not completely overcome differences in cultural and socioeconomic backgrounds.

More generally, attempts to develop culture-fair tests have not been completely successful. Questions about whether it is actually possible to remove the effects of culture from a test and, if it *is* possible, the question of what is measured by the remaining culture-free test content are still being addressed. As with the K-ABC, there remains the difficulty of removing race and socioeconomic class differences from a test without also reducing the extent to which the test measures the desired attribute of *g*, or general intelligence. Clearly, *g* is not an attribute specific to *any one* culture or subculture, but the best ways to measure it validly across and within cultures are still under study by researchers. An expanded discussion of these and related issues will be found in Chapter 14.

SUMMARY

This chapter has reviewed theories of the nature of intelligence and has described the major individually administered and group administered tests of intelligence. We have reviewed the contributions of Galton, Cattell, Binet, Spearman, multiple factor theorists such as Guilford, and hierarchical theorists such as Vernon to both the understanding and the assessment of intelligence. We have also described the potential contributions of developmental, cognitive, psychological, and neurological/biological theories to the conceptualization of intellectual functioning. The chapter discussed the major individually administered intelligence tests, that is, the Stanford-Binet, the Wechsler Adult Intelligence Scale, the Wechsler Intelligence Scale for Children, and the Wechsler Preschool and Primary Scale of Intelligence. Finally, group administered tests of school or mental ability used in the assessment of elementary and secondary school children were described.

7

The Assessment of Aptitudes

INTRODUCTION

In Chapter 6 we described the concept of intelligence and the major individually administered and group-administered tests of intelligence. Although the concept of intelligence has had tremendous value for the field of psychology, another related concept having great practical as well as theoretical utility is that of *aptitude*, which may be defined as "a condition or set of characteristics regarded as symptomatic of an individual's ability to acquire with training some (usually specified) knowledge, skill, or set of re-

sponses, such as the ability to speak a language [or] to produce music" (Bennett, Seashore, & Wesman, 1982a, p. 2). Essentially, an aptitude is the *capacity* to learn: Clerical aptitude is the capacity to acquire clerical skills; scholastic aptitude (described in Chapter 6 as an alternative label for what is measured by many tests of intelligence) is the capacity to learn what is taught in a given educational curriculum.

In the field of psychological assessment the concept of aptitude has two *major* uses, that is, in the assessment of scholastic aptitude and in the assessment of the aptitudes necessary for successful performance in different occupations. Because scholastic aptitude is significantly related to one's *performance* in an educational program, measures of scholastic aptitude are used extensively in the *selection* of applicants to post-high-school educational prorams, most notably in the selection of students for colleges, graduate schools, and professional schools. Selection is probably the most common use of such tests, although they can also be very helpful in assisting people to plan the amount and kind of education they wish to pursue and in assisting schools to place people in the most appropriate levels of coursework given their aptitudes. The first section of this chapter will describe the major measures of scholastic aptitude used in the selection of students to post-high-school education programs.

Although the concept of scholastic aptitude is an important and useful one, the overall ability to do well in school is clearly not the only ability having relevance for individual and institutional decisions. In particular, the tradition begun by multiple-factor theorists such as Louis L. Thurstone and J. P. Guilford specifies that overall "intelligence" includes several of many *group* factors of ability, each of which may have importance in the prediction of specific aspects of performance. The multiple-factor theory led to the development of a large number of aptitude tests for use in personnel selection and placement in business, industry, and government. Single aptitude tests such as the Minnesota Paper Form Board, the Minnesota Clerical Test, and the Bennett Mechanical Comprehension Test have been widely used in the selection of candidates for specific job-training programs.

Although single aptitude tests have often been useful in the selection of employees for a specific kind of job—for example, clerical work—the process of educational and vocational decision making

ideally requires a more complete picture of the individual's pattern of aptitudes, that is, the individual's particular pattern of strengths and weaknesses. Thus, the counseling needs of individuals were a major impetus for the development of the multiple-aptitude test batteries also described in this chapter.

Prior to discussing specific aptitude tests, we should emphasize a few additional points concerning the concept of aptitude. First, the importance of the idea of aptitude to educational and career planning should be noted. In order to select a given course of study or occupation it is not necessary to have *already* acquired the necessary knowledge or skill of the curriculum or job, but rather to possess the capacity to *learn* the necessary knowledge base and/or to *acquire* the necessary skills. Applicants to medical schools, for example, are not assumed to already be knowledgeable concerning medical practice, but rather are evaluated in terms of their potential or *capacity to learn* medicine once admitted to a medical school. Because aptitude test scores are thus designed to predict the areas of knowledge and/or skill a person *could* develop with the appropriate training, they are very helpful to individuals wishing to make decisions about their educational and career directions.

Second, although aptitude tests help us assess learning capacity, the capacity must be accompanied by the appropriate learning experiences in order to become a *developed* skill or competency or ability (e.g., Anastasi, 1982). In other words, musical aptitude must be accompanied by training in music in order for a person to become a musician and thereby demonstrate achievement in music. Similarly, mathematics aptitude must be accompanied by coursework in mathematics in order for the individual to become competent in, that is, demonstrate "achievement" in, mathematics. Further, individuals possessing sufficient aptitude to learn and to perform well in an educational or training program or job may fail to perform well for a variety of reasons *not assessed* by aptitude tests—for example, low motivation, poor study skills, personal problems, and illness. Thus, aptitudes are related to subsequent achievements, but other factors, such as opportunities and personal and environmental characteristics, will influence the extent to which individuals fully develop their capacities.

With these points in mind we may move to a discussion of the major scholastic aptitude tests and multiple aptitude batteries in use today.

MEASURES OF SCHOLASTIC APTITUDE

As was mentioned previously, tests of scholastic aptitude are used extensively in the selection of students for entrance to programs of higher education and for decisions regarding the award of financial aid, scholarships, and fellowships. Tests used for selection and financial aid at the undergraduate level are the American College Test (ACT), the Scholastic Aptitude Test, and the Preliminary Scholastic Aptitude Test/National Merit Scholarship Qualifying Test. Tests used for selection to graduate schools are the Graduate Record Examination and the Miller Analogies Test. Tests used in the selection of professional school applicants include the New Medical College Admissions Test and the Law School Admissions Test.

Selection for College and Graduate School

The ACT Assessment. The ACT Assessment, developed by E. F. Lindquist and his associates with the University of Iowa Testing Programs, was first administered in 1959. The assessment was designed to assist college and university personnel to screen out students who would not likely profit from a college education and to describe their educational needs and abilities in meaningful differential terms (Lindquist, 1970). Like other national testing programs used extensively in the selection of students for undergraduate and graduate educational programs, administration of the ACT is strictly controlled by the test program; the ACT is administered to high school juniors and seniors five times yearly (in February, April, June, October, and either November or December). Test development is a continuous process—new forms are developed frequently. A limited number of forms are available for release nationally; students are informed regarding the test dates after which the test form will be released for view by students and their parents and teachers. Three new forms of the ACT are published annually. The ACT was originally used primarily for selection to large state universities but is now used by about 3,000 colleges, universities, and agencies. The ACT Assessment is the predominant college admission testing program in 28 states.

The ACT contains four tests of educational development. The English Usage Test (E) is a test of the individual's understanding of the conventions of standard written English and the use of the basic elements of effective writing. Many of the 75 items are concerned with aspects of diction, style, sentence structure, punctuation, and organization. The test is not intended to measure rote memory for details of grammar, but rather to assess one's ability to differentiate effective from ineffective written communication.

The ACT Mathematics Usage Test (M) assesses general mathematical reasoning ability; the 40 items include the solution of practical quantitative reasoning problems and problem exercises taken from geometry and first-year algebra.

The 52-item Social Studies Reading Test (SS) measures the student's ability to interpret and evaluate reading selections in the area of social studies and to do the types of reasoning and problem-solving characteristic of the social studies. The 52-item Natural Science Reading Test (NS) assesses the student's ability to interpret and evaluate reading materials in the natural sciences and to utilize the critical, analytical, and problem-solving skills required in the natural sciences.

Raw scores on the four tests of the ACT are converted into standard scores, and a composite score representing the average level of performance across the four subtests is also computed. The standard scores provided utilize a different scale than the common types of standard scores described previously. Essentially, the mean and standard deviation of the standard scores differs for each subtest and for the overall composite score. The minimum possible standard score is always 1, while the maximum varies across subtests as follows: E,33; M,36; SS,34; NS,35; and composite (35). The means of the standard scores for the national sample of high school students taking the ACT range from 17.7 (Mathematics) to 21.7 (Natural Sciences). The standard deviations range from 5.2 (English) to 7.9 (Mathematics), as reported in *College Student Profiles* (ACT, 1987). Also reported therein are extensive tables of norms for specific groups of students, for example, in particular types of colleges, particular geographic regions, and for students of different ages, family incomes, and college major intentions. Norms are provided for men and women separately and for the total group within each subgroup for which norms are provided.

In addition, expectancy tables providing the probabilities of achieving various grade-point averages (GPAs) at a given college based on the student's ACT Composite score and high school GPA are particularly useful for counseling purposes.

The content of the ACT subtests is somewhat more dependent on previous schooling than is that of other tests used for the selection of college students. In particular, there is a heavy emphasis on reading ability, especially in the Natural Sciences and Social Sciences subtests.

The ACT Assessment is highly reliable; the average value of the KR-20 coefficient for the 15 different forms used between 1983 and 1986 ranged from 0.84 (Natural Sciences Reading) to 0.91 (English Usage) for the Subtests, with a value of 0.96 for the Composite Score. Alternate forms test-retest reliability coefficients (that is, two forms of the test administered between two and six weeks apart) ranged from 0.69 to 0.89 and from 0.73 to 0.90 when uncorrected and corrected for restriction in range, respectively. Again, Natural Sciences Reading was the least reliable subtest, although Mathematics Usage rather than English Usage was the most reliable subtest. Not surprisingly, the Composite Score was most reliable.

In addition to providing extensive reliability data, the *ACT Assessment Program Technical Manual* (American College Testing Program, 1988) provides a wide variety of criterion-related validity data. For example, the correlations between ACT subtest scores and college GPA range from 0.37 (Mathematics Usage) to 0.56 (English Usage), with a correlation of 0.51 between ACT Composite score and college grades. Subtest scores are also related to grades in analogous college courses as follows: English (0.51), Math (0.38), Social Studies Reading with Psychology (0.48), and Natural Sciences Reading with Biology (0.36). Finally, multiple regression equations using all subtest scores yield high multiple correlations with both individual course grades and overall college GPA (0.55), but predictive accuracy is increased still further when self-reported high school grades are added to the equation (0.62 for overall GPA).

The ACT is administered in combination with a vocational interest inventory (the ACT Interest Inventory, which provides a profile of student interests in science, the creative arts, social service, business contact, business detail, and technical areas) and a "Student Profile" that collects a variety of demographic information. The score profile received by the student contains, then, not only ability test scores but information regarding vocational interest patterns and major and career plans. Figure 7.1 shows a sample student profile resulting from the ACT test administration. The upper left portion of the profile provides the ability test scores themselves; standard scores and both national and local percentile norms for the four subtests and the composite score are shown. These scores can then be used in deriving predicted grade point averages (shown in percentile equivalents in comparison to comparable groups of freshmen) and the probability of obtaining at least a C average; these predictions for general areas of study and for specific courses are shown to the right of the ACT test scores.

Note that the student shown in Figure 7.1 demonstrates higher ability in the verbal than in the quantitative area. Not surprisingly, expectancies for a C-average or better are higher in colleges of education (89 percent probability), business administration (92 percent), and liberal arts (81 percent), than they are in engineering (32 percent). Although such data should not necessarily be used to dissuade a student like this one from pursuing a major in engineering, they do suggest that greater effort and persistence would be required for success in that major because of its heavy emphasis on mathematics.

In addition to test scores and predictions of level of performance in collegiate curricula, the ACT student profile shows information regarding educational and vocational plans and needs (left middle), vocational interest patterns (left bottom), and high school performance (right middle). Thus the test user or counselor has immediate access to a rich variety of information regarding a student's abilities, achievements, interests, background, and future plans. This information can be particularly useful in assisting students in making educational and career decisions and in understanding and solving problems related to students' decisions and plans.

The ACT has recently been extensively revised, and the new version of the test will begin to be used in 1989. The contents of the four ACT tests are being changed to reflect changes in the high school curriculum. The four tests will be English, Mathematics, Reading, and Science Reasoning. Also, for more detailed score information, the ACT Assessment will yield 12 scores, the four overall test scores, the Composite Score, two English Subscores, two Reading Subscores, and three Mathematics Subscores. Further information about the ACT test battery may be found in materials supplied by the publisher and in a review by John R. Hills in *The Eighth Mental Measurements Yearbook* (Buros, 1978).

The Scholastic Aptitude Test. The Scholastic Aptitude Test (SAT) is part of a large-scale testing program administered for the College Entrance Examination Board (CEEB) by the Educational Testing Service (ETS) of Princeton, New Jersey. The SAT and the ACT are the most widely used tests for the prediction of achievement in higher education. The SAT is administered to high school juniors and seniors seven times annually (in January, March, May, June, October, November, and December) at testing centers established by the test publishers. The SAT, a direct descendent of the Army Alpha Test, is a 2½-hour multiple-choice test measuring the verbal and mathematical reasoning abilities important to success in college.

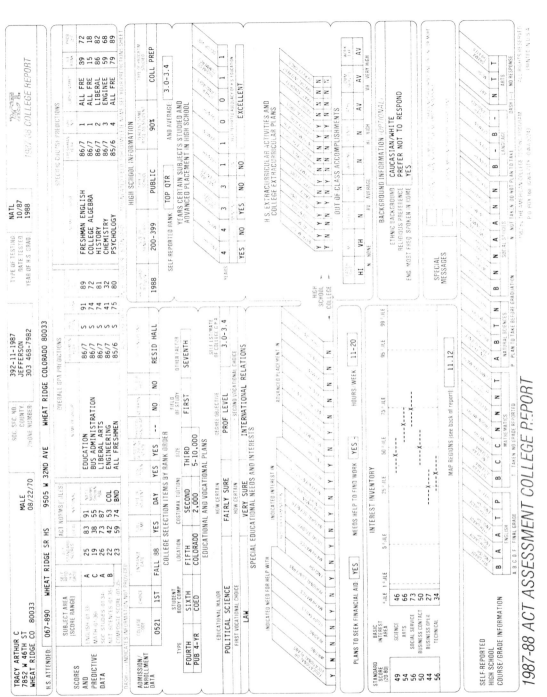

Figure 7.1 A sample student profile report for the ACT Assessment. (Reproduced with permission of the ACT Assessment Program. Copyright © 1987 by The American College Testing Program.)

1987-88 ACT ASSESSMENT COLLEGE REPORT

The verbal portion of the test (SAT-V) contains 85 questions similar to those used on the other tests of verbal abilities, including verbal analogies, antonyms, sentence completions, and reading comprehension. Items used in the verbal portion of the SAT are drawn from a variety of subject matter, including social, political, scientific, artistic,

Verbal Items (Analogies)

Directions: Each question below consists of a related pair of words or phrases, followed by five lettered pairs of words or phrases. Select the lettered pair that best expresses a relationship similar to that expressed in the original pair.

1. YAWN : BOREDOM :: (A) dream : sleep (B) anger : madness (C) smile : amusement (D) face : expression (E) impatience : rebellion

2. Verbal Items (Antonyms)
   GOOD: (A) sour (B) bad (C) red (D) hot (E) ugly
   Mathematics Items

3. If $x + y = 8$ and $xy = 15$, then $x - y$ could equal
   (A) 2
   (B) 4
   (C) 6
   (D) 7
   (E) 9

4. Of 100 freshmen, 30 are taking history but not calculus and 50 are taking calculus but not history.
   A. The number of freshmen taking both history and calculus
   B. 19
      Compare quantities A and B and respond as follows:
   A) If A is greater
   B) If B is greater
   C) If A and B are equal
   D) If the relationship cannot be determined from the information given.

philosophical, and literary content. The quantitative portion of the test (SAT-M) contains 60 items organized into two parts; the items emphasize logical reasoning and the perception of mathematical relationships but require as math background only the math taught in grades one through nine. Figure 7.2 shows examples of items from the SAT.

Raw scores on SAT-V and SAT-M are converted into standard scores based on the performance of the original norm groups, for which a scale based on a mean of 500 and a standard deviation of 100 was used. Mean scores for current groups of examinees have had means lower than 500 but usually standard deviations above 100. Means, standard deviations, and percentile equivalents for each group of examinees are reported by ETS. For example, means of 439 and 483, with standard deviations of 105 and 121, were reported for the verbal and mathematical sections for students taking the November 1986 SAT (Table 2 in the 1988/89 ATP Guide). For the 1,080,000 students in the class of 1987 who took the SAT, a Verbal score of 430 is at the 50th percentile, while a score of 500 is at the 72nd percentile. On the Mathematical Section, a score of 480 is at the 51st percentile, and a score of 500 is at the 58th percentile. Knowledge of these current data is important if students associate scores of 500 with "average" and then become upset when they get scores below that value. The SAT score report is also very helpful in this regard because it reports score ranges based on the SEM as well as the obtained standard scores themselves. The SEMs vary across score levels but average about 30 for Verbal and 35 for Mathematical. They tend to be smaller at the higher score ranges (about 20 points for scores above 700). Thus, the profile for a student with a Verbal standard score of 480 would show a score range of 450 to 510 (plus and minus one SEM). The SAT score report and ATP (Admissions Testing Program) Guide for School and College Personnel convey the idea of error in testing so that neither students nor their parents view a single number as "true aptitude."

In addition to the two aptitude tests, the examinee may elect to take between one and three achievement tests as specified by college or scholarship program requirements. The achievement tests include such fields as American history and social studies, biology, chemistry, mathematics, English composition, literature, Latin, Hebrew, and German.

The SAT represents high standards of test construction and evaluation. Like the ACT, new forms are developed each year, since previously used forms become part of the public domain. A different form is used in each administration. Thus the psychometric characteristics of the test are those referring to or summarizing the numerous forms of the test developed and utilized each year. The SAT possesses high internal consistency reliability (in the low 0.90s). Parallel-forms reliability coefficients are in the high 0.80s.

Careful attention has been paid by the test constructors at ETS to ensure that item content remains up-to-date. Also, analyses of items to remove cultural bias and sexist language have been performed at both psychometric and psychological levels. And panels of experts representing various cultural/ethnic and other subgroups have been consulted to find and remove any language that may be offensive to some subgroups.

Scores on the SAT are strongly predictive of college achievement, especially when used in combination with high school rank data. As with other tests of this type, the verbal and quantitative scores are highly correlated; recent SAT-V/SAT-M correlations were in the 0.60s.

Studies of the effects of large amounts of coaching show that this leads to increases of only about 15 standard score points, equal to about one-half of one SEM or only one-

fourth the size of the score range band shown on the student's score report. This score increase is about the same as that resulting from retaking the test. In order to ensure that all students have the opportunity for this degree of practice, the pamphlet "Taking the SAT" offers detailed descriptions of each item type and a complete form of the SAT for practice. In addition, 10 "retired" forms of the exam are available to the public, so a highly motivated student has ample opportunity to become familiar with test format and types of content.

One advantage of the SAT for applied purposes is the provision by ETS of a service analyzing the predictive validity of SAT scores, high school grades, and other relevant variables for purposes of predicting achievement at a particular college or university. In other words, a given college may have ETS develop a specific regression equation by which the nature and strength of the predictors of achievement *at that college* may be used in the selection and/or placement of students.

While the SAT and the ACT are generally quite similar in terms of the purposes for which they are used and their ability to predict academic achievement at the college level, some differences should be noted. First, while the ACT battery supplies an interest inventory as well as the aptitude tests, the SAT program supplies tests of achievement or knowledge in 15 different academic areas. Thus, the ACT battery may be more useful in career counseling because it contains both aptitude and vocational interest test information. The SAT, on the other hand, is more widely used in the selection of scholarship recipients, and especially for scholarships awarded to individuals pursuing specific academic fields (e.g., chemistry, engineering, history), because it contains the advanced achievement tests. Probably the major difference between the SAT and the ACT is in the nature and content of the tests' scales;

the more achievement-related content of the ACT's English and mathematics usage and social science and natural science reading subtests is in contrast to the more typically used scholastic aptitude dimensions of verbal and quantitative aptitude found in the SAT. Recent *Mental Measurements Yearbook* reviews of the SAT were done by Cohn (1985a) and Cronbach (1985).

The Preliminary Scholastic Aptitude Test/ National Merit Scholarship Qualifying Test. Although the SAT and the ACT are by far the most commonly used measures of scholastic aptitude for the prediction of achievement in college, the Preliminary Scholastic Aptitude Test (PSAT)/National Merit Scholarship Qualifying Test (NMSQT) also has several important uses. The PSAT/ NMSQT is appropriate for administration to students in grades 10 through 12 but is most usually administered to eleventh graders competing for scholarships or as a trial run for the SAT. The test, administered each October at participating secondary schools, provides three scores: verbal, mathematics, and what is known as the "Selection Index" for scholarship consideration. The verbal section contains 65 items similar to those used in most verbal sections of intelligence tests— sentence completion, analogies, antonyms, and reading comprehension. The 50 items in the math section utilize math reasoning and problem-solving items, but the content does not go beyond elementary algebra and informal geometry. Correlations between the verbal and mathematics scores are high and comparable to those found with the SAT— that is, in the middle 0.60s. The PSAT/ NMSQT is highly reliable and valid in terms of the academic achievement criteria for which the test may be used.

While the SAT or the ACT are the predominant tests used in the selection of students for colleges and universities, the PSAT/ NMSQT has two particular and somewhat unique uses. First, the PSAT is constructed such that it scores are roughly comparable to those that would be obtained on the SAT, which, for most students, would be administered the following year. Thus, PSAT scores can be used to provide rough estimates of the levels of SAT scores that can be expected the following year; these estimates in turn can be used in planning strategies for applications to colleges. Assume, for example, that John's PSAT-Verbal score led to a prediction of a SAT-V score in the approximate range of 500 to 600. Based on this predicted SAT-V score, John may wish to reconsider his chances of being admitted to a highly selective college and make sure that he applies to some less selective colleges where his probable level of SAT performance would be acceptable.

Second, the NMSQT "Selection Index" is used to select semifinalists for the National Merit Scholarship competition. The selection of National Merit semifinalists is the first step in a process of further evaluation of the scholarship candidates that culminates in the award of numerous scholarships and other forms of financial aid. For further information about the PSAT/NMSQT see reviews by Jerome E. Doppelt and J. Thomas Hastings in *The Eighth Mental Measurements Yearbook* (Buros, 1978).

An important point that should be reiterated at this point is that high school grades predict achievement in college as well as do scholastic aptitude test scores. Thus, in the prediction of future academic performance, test scores are *not* a substitute for knowledge of the student's *past* academic performance. However, the combination of high school record *and* scholastic aptitude test scores is a better predictor of subsequent academic performance than is either one alone. Thus selection for programs of higher education almost invariably utilizes both aptitude and achievement data.

The Graduate Record Examination. The Graduate Record Examination (GRE) is the scholarship aptitude test most often used in the selection of candidates for graduate programs. It is also used in making decisions concerning the awarding of scholarships, fellowships, and departmental financial aid such as teaching and research assistantships. Like the SAT and the ACT, the GRE is administered several times annually (usually in February, April, June, October, and December) at centers established by the test publisher.

The GRE contains verbal, quantitative, and analytical aptitude sections and advanced achievement tests in a variety of academic fields. The verbal section (GRE-V) includes verbal analogies, antonyms, sentence completion, and reading comprehension. The quantitative section (GRE-Q) involves algebra, geometry, quantitative comparisons and reasoning problems, and the interpretation of graphs, diagrams, and data. The analytical section (GRE-A, added in 1977) includes analytical and logical reasoning items.

Figure 7.3 shows examples of the types of items contained in the analytical subtest and explanations of how the correct answers are derived. Essentially these items assess such functions as recognizing logical relations, drawing conclusions from statements, and determining complex relationships.

Raw scores on the GRE aptitude tests are converted to standard scores based on a norm group with a mean of 500 and a standard deviation of 100. Percentile equivalent scores are also provided. In addition to the aptitude tests, the GRE test battery contains a variety of optional academic achievement tests in various fields, including psychology, biology, economics, mathematics, philosophy, physics, engineering, French, and geology. These tests will be covered in Chapter 8's discussion of the assessment of achievement.

Analytical Reasoning

1. A farmer plants only five different kinds of vegetables—beans, corn, kale, peas, and squash. Every year the farmer plants exactly three kinds of vegetables according to the following restrictions:

   If the farmer plants corn, he also plants beans that year. If the farmer plants kale one year, he does not plant it the next year. In any year, the farmer plants no more than one of the vegetables he planted in the previous year.

   Which of the following is a possible sequence of combinations for the farmer to plant in two successive years?
   (A) Beans, corn, kale; corn, peas, squash
   (B) Beans, corn, peas; beans, corn, squash
   (C) Beans, peas, squash; beans, corn, kale
   (D) Corn, peas, squash; beans, kale, peas
   (E) Kale, peas, squash; beans, corn, kale

   Explanation for Answer:
   Options (A) and (D) are not possible because corn appears as a vegetable without beans in a given year. Option (E) is not possible because kale appears in two successive years. Option (B) is not possible because two vegetables are repeated in two successive years. Option (C) contains a possible sequence of combinations.

Logical Reasoning

2. If Ramon was born in New York State, then he is a citizen of the United States

   The statement above can be deduced logically from which of the following statements?
   (A) Everyone born in New York State is a citizen of the United States.
   (B) Every citizen of the United States is a resident either of one of the states or of one of the territories.
   (C) Some people born in New York State are citizens of the United States.
   (D) Ramon was born either in New York or in Florida.

Figure 7.3 Sample items from the Analytical and Logical Reasoning Sections of the Graduate Record Examination. Answers are as follows: 1 (c), 2 (a). (Reproduced with the permission of Educational Testing Service from the 1987–88 GRE Student Information Bulletin, pp. 39–40. Copyright © 1987 by the Educational Testing Service.)

(E) Ramon is a citizen either of the United States or of the Dominican Republic.

Explanation for Answer

The question here is which of (A) through (E), if true, would guarantee that Ramon cannot have his birthplace in New York State without being a United States citizen. Since, crucially, the relationship between birthplace and citizenship is at stake, any statement that concerns itself with birthplace alone, like (D), or citizenship alone, like (E), or with the relationship between residence and citizenship, like (B), will be unsuitable for providing any such guarantee. This leaves (A) and (C), both of which deal with the relationship at issue here. Of these, (C) makes the weaker claim: It leaves open the possibility that there might be people born in New York State who are not United States citizens, and it leaves open whether or not Ramon is one of those people. (A), on the other hand, rules out any possibility of anyone being born in New York State and yet not being a United States citizen. Therefore, (A) rules out that possibility for Ramon also, and (A) is thus the correct answer.

Figure 7.3 Continued

The GRE aptitude tests are highly reliable; Kuder-Richardson internal consistency reliability coefficients are consistently around or above 0.90 for the verbal, quantitative, and analytical tests. In terms of criterion-related validity, typical studies would involve determining the relationship of GRE scores (and/or other aspects of the undergraduate record) to various criteria of success in graduate school, such as faculty ratings, grades, performance on Ph.D. exams, amount of time needed to complete the Ph.D., and probability of completing the Ph.D.

Although there are a variety of possible types of studies of validity, these studies are often complicated by the problem of restriction in range. It may be recalled from Chapter 2 that the maximum size of a correlation coefficient is dependent on the extent of individual differences in the characteristics being studied. Homogeneity (lack of significant variation) in one or both variables limits the size of the correlations that can be obtained. For several reasons, studies of the predictors of success in graduate school usually involve restriction in the range of both predictors and criteria. Predictors such as GREs and undergraduate GPAs are usually of major importance in *selecting* students for graduate programs, thus automatically eliminating low scores from the distribution available. For example, if a graduate program only selects applicants with minimums of 650 on both GRE-V and GRE-Q, the relationships of GRE scores to outcome criteria such as graduate school grades, performance on comprehensive examinations, and time required to receive a particular advanced degree will be much weaker (or even nonexistent) than if applicants with significantly lower GRE scores had also been admitted. Similarly, one of the major criterion variables, graduate school grades, typically shows little significant variation among those highly select students admitted; most students obtain reasonably good GPAs.

In spite of this serious limitation of the potential magnitude of criterion-related validity coefficients, GRE scores do show the ability to predict various indices of success in graduate school. Figure 7.4 provides a graphic illustration of the relative efficacy of GRE aptitude scores (denoted as V and Q), undergraduate grades (U-GPA), and GRE Advanced Test (S) scores in predicting grades in graduate school. The numbers at the left (0.2 and 0.4) represent the correlations of the various predictor variables with the criterion of graduate school grades. Across fields of academic study the best *single* predictor of grades was the GRE advanced test in the appropriate subject area, such as the advanced psychology test for graduate students in psychology or the advanced chemistry test for graduate students in chemistry. The best overall predictor, however, was the combination of GRE verbal and quantitative

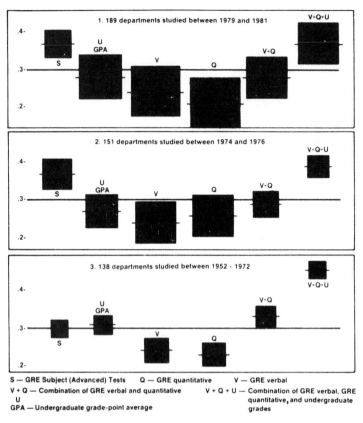

Figure 7.4 Correlations between predictors of success in Graduate School and Graduate School grades. (Reproduced with the permission of the Educational Testing Service from the *GRE 1982–83 Information Bulletin*, p. 56. Copyright © 1982 by the Educational Testing Service.)

scores and undergraduate grades, and recent studies suggest that adding the advanced test score to this combination increases predictive accuracy still further. Although the data depicted in Figure 7.4 describe the prediction of graduate school grades, the strength of the GRE advanced test or, even better, the GRE-GPA composite, as a predictor applies as well to most other criteria of graduate school success, for example, faculty ratings, chances of completing the Ph.D., and time needed to complete the Ph.D. Reviews of the GRE were provided by Cohn (1985a) and Jaeger (1985) in the *Ninth Mental Measurements Yearbook*.

To summarize, the utility of GRE scores for the prediction of success in graduate school is moderate in magnitude. Graduate programs in general appear to use aptitude and achievement test scores and previous academic grades to select students possessing a sufficient level of scholastic aptitude to succeed academically. Given a student group with generally sufficient levels of academic ability, other personality and attitudinal factors may begin to be more important in influencing academic performance. Assume, for example, that Sue and Sandy are enrolled in the same graduate program and that both received scores of 700 on GRE-V and GRE-Q and scores of 650 on the GRE Analytical test. Sue is highly motivated to learn about the field, has excellent study habits, and regularly attends classes. Sandy, on the other hand, is more concerned with impressing her friends and family by getting a Ph.D. than she is interested in her field of study and is constantly having personal problems that distract her from her studies. Even though both women are extremely able academically, Sue will probably be the better graduate student. Thus, aptitude assessment is very useful, but it is always important to also consider the possible influence of attitudinal, motivational, and situational factors in understanding people's performance.

The Miller Analogies Test.

The Miller Analogies Test (MAT) is another major test used in the selection of candidates for graduate school and, in addition, is used in the evaluation of personnel for high-level jobs in industry. The test consists of complex analogy items whose content is drawn from many academic fields. Test items are in many cases extremely difficult, so the MAT is capable of differentiating among people of superior intellect. Raw scores are converted to percentile norms based on several different academic fields and different groups of industrial employees and applicants. Performance on the MAT varies *widely* as a function of the academic or business fields used as the comparison groups. For example, a raw score of 60 might correspond to the 90th percentile among applicants for one type of graduate program, but to the 10th percentile among applicants to a different graduate program. Thus, while the comparison group is always important in the interpretation of normative data, the wide intergroup differences on the MAT make use of the relevant comparison group *essential* to the resulting utility of test scores.

The MAT is highly reliable; split-half reliability coefficients range from $r = 0.92$ to $r = 0.95$ in different samples, while parallel-forms coefficients range from $r = 0.85$ to $r = 0.90$. Scores on the MAT are highly correlated with other tests of intelligence and scholastic aptitude, but since the test is used as a predictor in a variety of industrial as well as educational settings, the test's validity must be evaluated and discussed relative to the specific purpose for which, and in the specific setting in which, the test is to be used.

Selection for Professional School

Even though high-quality scholastic aptitude tests are available for use in the selection of applicants for both undergraduate and graduate education, several professions have developed their own programs of aptitude testing for use in selecting applicants to professional schools. The New Medical College Admission Test, the Law School Admission Test, the Graduate Management Admission Test, and the Dental Admission Testing Program are examples of scholastic aptitude tests used in selecting applicants to schools of medicine, law, business, and dentistry, respectively.

Generally speaking, these tests assess the same types of verbal (V) and quantitative (Q) aptitudes assessed by the major scholastic aptitude tests (e.g., the SAT and the GRE), although the emphasis on verbal versus quantitative abilities differs, and some tests may contain sections pertinent to the specialty area. For example, the Medical College Admission Test assesses achievement in science as well as verbal and quantitative ability, the Law School Admission Test emphasizes the writing ability so important in law, and the Dental Admission Testing Program includes subtests for the perceptual and motor ability required in dentistry. Overall, though, the measurement of verbal and quantitative aptitudes is the most important objective, so these tests represent not so much new types of tests but, rather, specially administered testing programs. The aptitudes universally important for academic success appear to be the verbal and quantitative aptitudes found in all measures of scholastic aptitudes, and this is true for professional as well as undergraduate and graduate programs.

Thus, tests in this category usually include a general test of scholastic aptitude and one or more achievement tests relevant to preprofessional training (e.g., the premedicine or predentistry curriculum). The objectives of the scholastic aptitude portions of these tests are similar to those of other such tests, but their content may be slanted somewhat toward the particular professional field for which the test is used.

An important point regarding the use of tests of this type is that *such tests are by no means the only criterion* used in selecting applicants to professional schools. Undergraduate grades, letters of recommendation, autobiographies and personal statements, and, often, personal interviews are used in the selection process. The following section describes two of the major tests of this type—the New Medical College Admission Test and the Law School Admission Test.

The New Medical College Admission Test.

The New Medical College Admission Test (MCAT), developed by the American Institutes for Research in cooperation with the Association of American Medical Colleges, is required for admission to virtually every medical school in the United States. The test is administered twice yearly (spring and fall) by American College Testing (ACT) at designated testing centers across the country. The MCAT is taken by approximately 50,000 students each year.

The MCAT is administered in four sections: Science Knowledge, which covers knowledge of biology, chemistry, and physics; Science Problems, which applies knowledge in the above areas to the solving of problems; Skills Analysis: Reading, which

assesses analytical and reasoning abilities with verbal material; and Skills Analysis: Quantitative, which assesses analytical and reasoning abilities with quantitative material. These four tests of the MCAT yield six scores per person: Biology, Chemistry, Physics, Science Problems, Skills Analysis: Reading, and Skills Analysis: Quantitative. Examples of items from the Science Knowledge practice test are shown in Figure 7.5 and examples of items from the Science Problems practice test are shown in Figure 7.6. The manual provided to potential examinees (Association of American Medical Colleges, 1977) contains detailed descriptions of the types of test items to be expected, along with a practice test and an illustrative (sample) test.

The New MCAT was standardized in a sample of about 31,000 examinees tested in the spring of 1977. Each of the six scores is reported on a 1 to 15 scale; score means are around 8.0, with standard deviations of about 2.5. No composite or total scores are provided. The score report to examinees contains the scaled (1 to 15) scores and the means, standard deviations, and percentile equivalents for the group of examinees tested at the same time. Test users (i.e., medical admissions officers) each year receive interpretive information providing percentile equivalent scores separately as a function of sex, year in college, racial/ethnic group, and undergraduate major. Thus, the performance of, for example, students who were *not* science majors in college can be compared to that of other nonscience majors.

Reliability coefficients available for the MCAT scores include both Kuder-Richardson-20 (KR-20) and split-half coefficients. Values of both types of coefficients range from 0.76 (Skills Analysis: Reading) to 0.86 (Chemistry) and cluster in the low 0.80s. Thus, the MCAT is not as reliable as other tests in this category, although this may be due in part to the somewhat restricted range of ability and achievement levels of individuals tak-

1

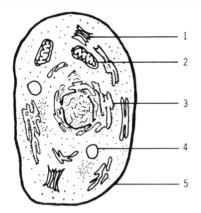

The figure above represents a generalized animal cell as seen with an electron microscope. (The structures are not drawn to scale.) Interference with the function of structure 3 would first affect

A mitosis.

B RNA synthesis.

C protein synthesis.

D oxidative phosphorylation.

---

2 A mouse species is divided into two populations. Population A breeds true for long tails and Population B breeds true for short tails. When a member from Population A is bred with a member from Population B, all of the off-spring, or F_1 generation, have long tails.

The hypothesis that long tail is dominant is

A *supported* by the data.

B *contradicted* by the data.

C *neither supported nor contradicted* by the data.

---

3 Which of the following substances is NOT generally absorbed into the blood capillaries of the intestinal villi?

A Water

B Glucose

C Amino acids

D Sodium chloride

E Fats (triglycerides)

---

4 A simple hypothetical ecosystem contains five animal species whose relative numbers have remained stable for a long time. To study the interactions of these species, one species was removed from the system and the resultant change in the number of individuals of all four remaining species was recorded. This species was then replaced, and, after the system had restabilized, a different species was removed, and so on. The results are compiled in the table below.

Species Removed	Change in numbers of individuals in				
	Species 1	Species 2	Species 3	Species 4	Species 5
1	▨	NC	NC	NC	
2	NC	▨	NC	NC	NC
3	NC	NC	▨		NC
4	NC	NC	+	▨	NC
5	NC	NC	NC	NC	▨

+ = increase in numbers of individuals
− = decrease in numbers of individuals
NC = no change in numbers of individuals

Species 5 is most likely a

A prey species.

B predator species.

C parasitic species.

D symbiotic species.

E cohabitant species.

Figure 7.5 Sample items from the Science Knowledge practice test. (Reproduced by permission from the Science Knowledge practice test, in the *New Medical College Admission Test Student Manual*, p. 23. Copyright © 1977 by the Association of American Medical Colleges.)

Sickle cell anemia is a genetic disease. It is manifested by a change in shape of the erythrocyte in conditions of low oxygen tension. The disease is transmitted as an autosomal recessive trait. The gene shows incomplete dominance (i.e., heterozygous individuals are affected) in its expression.

15 If a man and a woman, both heterozygous for sickle cell anemia, had two children, both of whom had only normal hemoglobin, what would be the probability that the third child would also have *only* normal hemoglobin?

  A 0%

  B 25%

  C 50%

  D 75%

  E 100%

16 If two heterozygous parents had children, what would be the probability that any one child would show some aspect of the disease?

  A 25%

  B 50%

  C 75%

  D 100%

  E None of the above

17 If, contrary to the condition that actually exists, the gene were transmitted as an X-linked recessive, what would be the probability of a male child being born with the disease if his mother were heterozygous for the disease and his father were homozygous normal?

  A 0%

  B 25%

  C 50%

  D 75%

  E 100%

Barbiturates have the general formula shown below.

Sedative activity is found for most alkyl and aryl substituents in the R and R′ positions.

18 The barbiturates are insoluble in water. They are quite soluble in aqueous base in spite of the lack of $O-H$ groups. This is best explained by

  A the polarization of N H bonds.

  B the ease with which amides are hydrolyzed.

  C resonance stabilization of the anion formed by removal of the proton bound to nitrogen.

  D resonance stabilization of the cation formed by addition of a proton to nitrogen.

19 The fastest-acting barbiturates display the highest lipid solubility. Which of the following R and R′ groups would cause the resulting barbiturate to act *most rapidly*?

	R	R′
A	H	CH_3
B	C_2H_5	C_2H_5
C	$(CH_2)_2CH_3$	$(CH_2)_3CH_3$
D	CH_2OCH_3	CH_2OCH_3
E	$(CH_2)_2COOH$	CH_3

Figure 7.6 Sample items from the Science Problems practice test. (Reproduced by permission from the Science Problems practice test, in the *New Medical College Admission Test Student Manual*, pp. 25–26. Copyright © 1977 by the Association of American Medical Colleges.)

ing the test. As with other aptitude and achievement batteries, subtests are moderately to strongly correlated; correlations range from $r = 0.50$ (the Reading test with the Physics test) to $r = 0.73$ (the Quantitative test with the Science Problems test; the Physics test with the Chemistry test). The various science achievement scores are, as would be expected, related to each other, but each also seems to be measuring a somewhat independent dimension of science achievement.

A small amount of concurrent validity evidence based on several 1976 studies using a research form of the New MCAT with students already in medical school is provided in the interpretive manual for test users (Association of American Medical Colleges 1977). Although the sample sizes used in these studies are quite small, they generally suggest a relationship between MCAT scores and performance in the first year of medical school. A larger number of concurrent validity studies are reported in brief form in a recent annotated bibliography of research (Jones & Adams, 1982). Over all, these studies appear to support the concurrent and predictive validity of the New MCAT.

To summarize, the New MCAT is a test of scholastic aptitude and science achievement and in this country is required for all medical school applicants. Because the test results, along with other criteria such as college grades and letters of recommendation, determine who will be given the opportunity to pursue medical training, care in the construction and use of the test has been essential. In order to help students prepare for the test, a comprehensive and detailed student manual is available (Littlemeyer & Mauney, 1977); this manual contains detailed descriptions of the subtests and provides several practice tests. Thus, students taking the MCAT may familiarize themselves with the item content and test format.

The Revised Law School Admissions Test.

The Revised Law School Admissions Test (Revised LSAT) is the 1982 version of a test originally developed in 1947 and widely used to select students for admission to law school. The test is administered five times annually at designated testing centers.

The Revised LSAT consists of seven sections, including six 35-minute multiple-choice sections and one 30-minute essay section. Two of the six multiple-choice sections consist of experimental items and are not used in calculating the LSAT score. The remaining four sections are those on which the

LSAT score is based and contain four different types of questions designed to measure abilities in reasoning, reading comprehension, problem identification, and logic. More specifically, the item types are as follows: (1) passages of about 450 words forming the basis for six or more questions directed at assessing the ability to comprehend the various meanings and implications of the passage; (2) sets of three to seven related conditions describing a relationship structure, followed by questions pertaining to the implications of that structure; (3) principles and rules applied to cases; and (4) understanding and analysis of arguments.

Within the first six sections, the placement of the two experimental sections is varied across test forms; thus, examinees are not informed as to which sections do or do not affect their scores. The 30-minute essay section presents candidates with a topic about which they must write a logical and reasonable essay. The topic presents a factual context and designates an audience to whom the essay is to be addressed.

Performance on the multiple-choice sections of the LSAT is summarized by one LSAT score; the LSAT standard scores have a range of 10 to 50, with a mean of 30 and a standard deviation of approximately 8. The extreme scores of 10 and 50 are, respectively, only 2.5 standard deviations below and above the mean; thus, the LSAT standard scores truncate the extremes of the raw score distribution. The writing sample taken from the essay test is not scored, but a copy is sent to each law school to which the examinee has applied.

The LSAT is, in general, heavily oriented toward the verbal skills so important to both the study and the practice of law. In particular, the use of a writing sample assesses the degree to which the law school applicant possesses the effective writing skills essential in law, and the presence of the writing sample on the LSAT undoubtedly serves to encourage prospective law school applicants to develop good writing skills.

The LSAT is highly reliable, with average KR-20 reliabilities of 0.92. In terms of validity, the heavily verbal nature of the LSAT and the fact that scholars in the legal profession assist in its construction support the validity of the test's content to the study and practice of law. Studies suggest that LSAT scores, like other types of general scholastic aptitude test scores, predict grades in the first year of law school with about the same degree of effectiveness as does undergraduate GPA. The combination of LSAT scores and undergraduate grades, however, yields better prediction than does either one alone (e.g., Schrader, 1977). Also, the LSAT is a better predictor of first year law school grades than is undergraduate GPA, but the latter increases in predictive efficacy with years in law school (Powers, 1982). Such findings support the importance of past behavior in the prediction of future behavior, that is, the necessity of such qualities as persistence and motivation, in addition to intellect, in academic performance. The LSAT is not designed to predict success in the practice of law, but LSAT scores are as good a predictor of scores on the law bar exam as are law school grades (see Melton, 1985). Although the LSAT does predict law school grades and bar exam performance, there is no real evidence that the LSAT is anything more than a long test of verbal aptitude, similar to GRE-V. In fact, other verbal aptitude tests may be better predictors of performance in law school, a hypothesis worth empirical examination (see Melton, 1985).

The materials accompanying the LSAT suggest several cautions in the use of LSAT scores by law school faculty and administrators. These cautions include the recommendation that test users avoid using LSAT scores as the sole criterion for admitting people to law school, avoid using cutoff scores below which all applicants are rejected, and postpone using scores for *decisions* until local validity data have been collected and evaluated. To facilitate the collection and evaluation of local validity data, the publishers of the LSAT offer a Validity Study Service providing expert advice and consultation on the validation process. Thus, used carefully, the LSAT may provide helpful information for use in evaluation of applicants to law schools.

Summary

This section has described several measures of scholastic aptitude used heavily in the selection of students for undergraduate, graduate, and professional degree programs. Although the administrators and faculty of educational institutions have found such tests very useful in the selection of students for admission, there are also many groups and individuals who contend that such tests may not be fair for use with various racial minority and/or economically disadvantaged groups. We discuss some evidence about this issue in Chapter 14's consideration of ethical and social issues in assessment, but two general issues should be noted at this point.

First, even though these tests are described as measures of aptitude or "capacity" to learn, they cannot avoid assessing the *quality of past learning experiences* as part of the assessment of future learning potential. At the same time that such tests have their greatest utility in predicting future academic achievements, performance on such tests is not independent, of *past* educational experiences and achievements. Thus, the quality of an individual's educational background must also be considered in interpreting aptitude test scores. Second, the assessment of aptitudes cannot be separated completely from the *cultural context* in which it is imbedded, which suggests that special caution should be used in assessing and using scores obtained from individuals who are not of the dominant culture or subculture.

MULTIPLE-APTITUDE BATTERIES

In contrast to scholastic aptitude tests, multiple-aptitude barriers generally assess a wide variety of aptitudes important to success in both educational and occupational areas. They are used extensively to help individuals make educational and career decisions and are also used in the selection of people for vocational training programs and for specific jobs and occupations.

The following section describes four of the *major* multiple aptitude batteries: the Differential Aptitude Tests, the General Aptitude Test Battery, the Armed Services Vocational Aptitude Battery, the Employee Aptitude Survey and the Multi-dimensional Aptitude Battery.

The Differential Aptitude Tests

The Differential Aptitude Tests (DAT) were first published in 1947 and have been subject to three major revisions since first constructed. The tests were originally developed to provide a well-standardized procedure for measuring the multiple aptitudes of students in grades 8 through 12. The resulting ability profile was designed to be helpful to students making educational and vocational decisions and to counselors helping students. The DAT were revised and restandardized in 1962 (Forms L and M), in 1972 (Forms S and T), and again in 1980 (Forms V and W).

The DAT measures the following eight aptitudes:

1. Verbal Reasoning (VR): the ability to reason with words and to understand and use concepts expressed in words. VR is measured by verbal analogies items.
2. Numerical Ability (NA): the understanding of numerical relationships and the ability to handle numerical concepts. NA is assessed using standard types of arithmetic computation items. (Numerical Ability and Verbal Reasoning are, in combination, an estimate of general learning ability or "scholastic" aptitude as measured by tests such as the SAT.)
3. Abstract Reasoning (AR): nonverbal, nonnumerical reasoning abilities. In these test items, four figures are arranged in a series and the examinee must select one of five figures provided as the one that represents the next logical step in the series. Figure 7.7 shows items from the Abstract Reasoning test. It may be noted that the test provides a third measure of general *reasoning* ability, complementing the verbal and numerical reasoning abilities assessed by VR and NA.
4. Clerical Speed and Accuracy (CSA): perceptual and response speed in simple clerical tasks. Each test item gives the examinee five pairs of numbers and/or letters (e.g., AB, 7B, 17, Aa, b3) one pair of which is underlined. The same five pairs appear on the answer sheet, but in a different order. The task of the examinee is to locate on the answer sheet the combination that was underlined in the test booklet and to fill in the space beneath it. Figure 7.7 illustrates the types of items found on the DAT Clerical Speed and Accuracy Test. Since the items themselves are easy, score differences are the result of the extent of speed and accuracy of response.
5. Mechanical Reasoning (MR): comprehension of mechanical principles and devices and of the laws of everyday physics. Test items, examples of which are shown in Figure 7.8, pictorially present a mechanical problem or situation, together with a simply worded question.
6. Space Relations (SR): spatial visualization abilities. Test items ask the examinee to indicate which of four figures would result if the pattern given were folded. Figure 7.9 shows examples of the items used on this test. The ability measured by this test is, according to the DAT manual and interpretive materials, important in such areas as drafting, carpentry, art and design, architecture, and sewing/clothing design.
7. Spelling (SP): spelling ability. The test presents 100 words, for each of which the ex-

Remember—you are to select, from among the Answer Figures, the one figure that belongs next in the series.

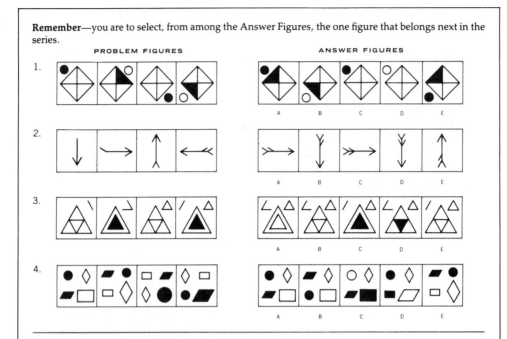

This is a test to see how quickly and accurately you can compare letter and number combinations. Each test item contains five groups of these combinations. These same combinations appear after the number for each test item on the Practice Answer Sheet, but they are in a different order. You will notice that in each test one of the five is **underlined**. You are to look at the **one** combination that is underlined, find the same one after that item number on the Practice Answer Sheet, and fill in the circle under it.

Examples

V. <u>AB</u> AC AD AE AF

W. aA aB BA Ba <u>Bb</u>

X. A7 7A B7 <u>7B</u> AB

Y. Aa Ba <u>bA</u> BA bB

Z. 3A 3B <u>33</u> B3 BB

Figure 7.7 Sample items from the practice sections for the Abstract Reasoning test (top) and the Clerical Speed and Accuracy test (bottom) as shown in the orientation booklet for the Differential Aptitude Tests, Forms V and W. (Reproduced by permission. Copyright © 1982, 1980, 1975, 1973, 1972 by The Psychological Corporation. All Rights Reserved.)

aminee must indicate whether it is spelled correctly or incorrectly. For example, an examinee should indicate that the word *inferier* is incorrectly spelled, while the word *astronaut* is correctly spelled. The words used occur frequently in everyday vocabulary. The spelling test is basically an achievement

test assessing the individual's ability to correctly spell common English words.

8. Language Usage (LU): ability to detect errors in grammar, punctuation, and capitalization. The test items present a sentence and ask the examinee to indicate whether or not the sentence contains an error and,

Find the space for Mechanical Reasoning on the Practice Answer Sheet.

This test consists of a number of pictures and questions about those pictures. Look at the two examples below, to see just what to do.

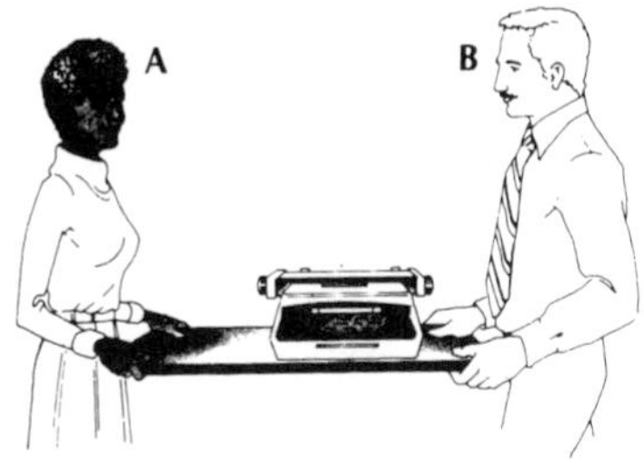

Example X.

Which person has the heavier load?
(If equal, mark C.)

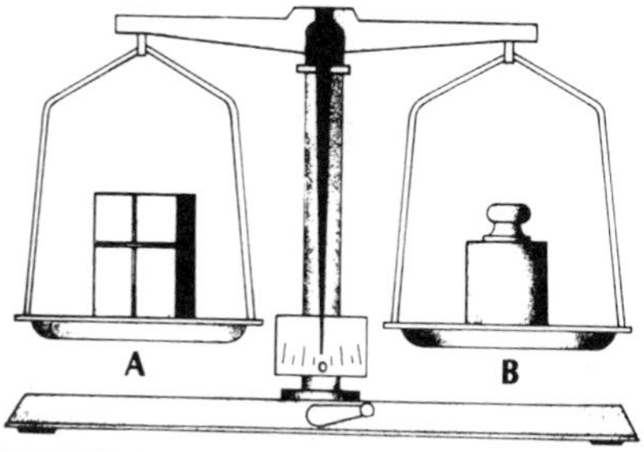

Example Y.

Which weighs more?
(If equal, mark C.)

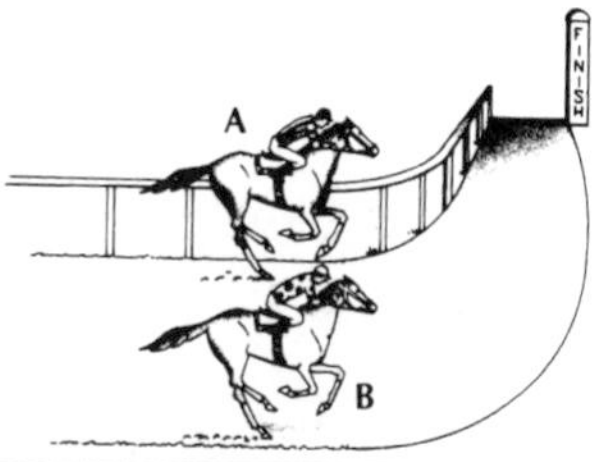

1.

Which horse has to run faster to win the race?
(If neither, mark C.)

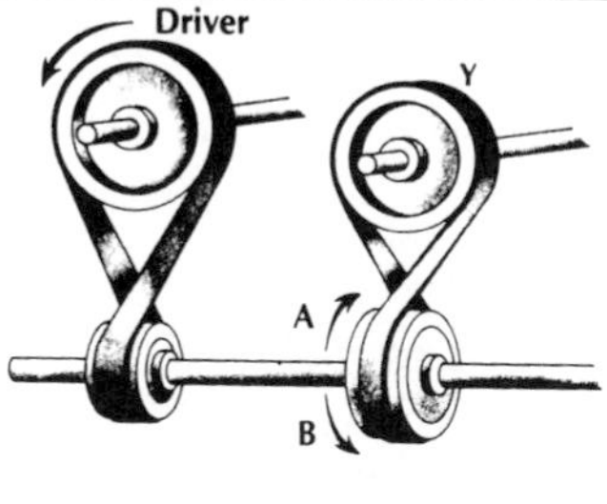

2.

If the driver turns in the direction shown, which way will pulley "Y" turn?
(If either, mark C.)

Figure 7.8 Sample items from the practice sections for the Mechanical Reasoning test as shown in the orientation booklet for the Differential Aptitude Tests, Forms V and W. (Reproduced by permission. Copyright © 1982, 1980, 1975, 1973, 1972 by The Psychological Corporation. All Rights Reserved.)

Study the pattern carefully and decide which figure can be made from it.

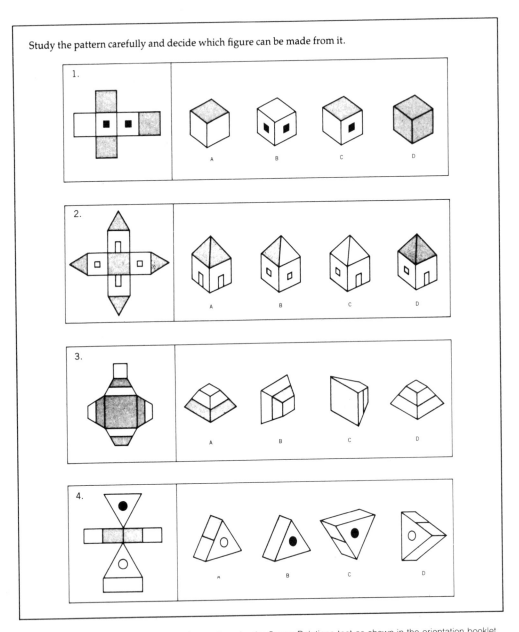

if so, where the error occurs. For example, in the sentence "I just left my friends house" the examinee should indicate that an error occurred because "my friend's house" (with the apostrophe) was the correct usage. (Like the Spelling test, Language Usage is primarily an achievement test. These two tests, even though achievement rather than aptitude tests, are included in the DAT because of the importance of language skills to so many academic and vocational pursuits.)

The normative sample for Forms V and W of the DAT consisted of approximately 62,000 students in grades 8 through 12, selected from 64 public and parochial school systems designed to be representative of the national population of high school students. A stratified sample of public school districts representative of American school districts in both size and socioeconomic status and a sample of parochial schools were used. Sample sizes ranged from 11,200 in grade 12 to 13,400 in grade 9. Although the major standardization sample was as described, normative data were also obtained from Catholic school students, students in grades 10 through 12 of vocational schools, and students enrolled in postsecondary educational institutions.

The score reports for the DAT provide raw scores (number of correct answers) and percentiles based on the 1980 standardization for each of the eight separate tests and for the combination of VR and NA, used as an index of scholastic aptitude. Percentiles are reported separately by sex and for students tested in the spring and the fall semester of grades 8 through 11 and the fall semester of grade 12. The percentile equivalents reported have been rounded off to 23 percentile values, in groups of five between the 5th and 95th percentiles, plus the 97th and 99th percentiles at the top and the 1st and 3rd percentiles at the bottom.

Each student receives an "Individual Report Form" that shows the student's raw scores, percentiles, and resulting profile of aptitude scores. Figure 7.10 shows a sample profile as provided in the test manual. Note that the percentile scores shown at the top of the profile are represented graphically on the profile itself; such graphic representation highlights the individual's strengths and weaknesses across aptitudes. For example, the student depicted in Figure 7.10 appears to be especially strong in numerical aptitude, abstract reasoning, and spelling, and relatively weak in clerical speed and accuracy.

For interpreting differences between aptitude test scores it is especially important to note that the score profile shows percentiles as a range rather than as a single score. This use of a range of percentiles takes into account the error of measurement and also facilitates accurate interpretation of differences in the scores obtained on different tests. The instructions provided on the report suggest that if the bars overlap, caution in assuming significant differences between levels of two or more aptitudes should be used. In the example shown in Figure 7.10, the percentile bars for NA, AR, and Sp (this student's highest scores) overlap to some extent with VR + NA, MR, SR, and LU, thus suggesting that these aptitude scores may not be significantly different from each other even though they appear different on the profile. In contrast, the NA and AR percentile bars show no overlap with the VR or the CSA. Thus, it is reasonable to conclude that this student's aptitude for numerical and abstract reasoning tasks *is* significantly greater than is his aptitude for verbal reasoning tasks.

In interpreting DAT profiles it should also be noted, however, that while an individual's strengths and weaknesses as shown in the profile are important in educational and vocational planning, the general level of scores must also be considered when making decisions. For example, two individuals may both achieve their highest scores on the Mechanical Reasoning test, yet for one individ-

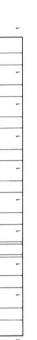

Figure 7.10 Sample score profile from the manual for the Differential Aptitude Tests, Forms V and W. (Reproduced by permission. Copyright © 1982, 1980, 1975, 1973, 1972 by The Psychological Corporation. All Rights Reserved.)

ual that score may be at the 95th percentile, while for the other the score may be at the 40th percentile. The first individual clearly possesses superior mechanical aptitude. If we were selecting among applicants for training as auto mechanics and other factors were equal, we would probably prefer to select the individual with the superior aptitude.

The tests of the DAT are highly reliable. Split-half reliability coefficients for all but CSA are generally in the low to mid 0.90s across sexes, grade levels, and test forms. Test-retest reliability coefficients for CSA (appropriate because CSA is a speeded test) range from 0.93 to 0.97.

As might be expected, the major type of validity evidence pertinent to the use of the DAT is criterion-related validity, that is, predictive and concurrent validity. When discussing the predictive validity of multiple- or differential-aptitude batteries, it is important to consider what is known as "differential" predictive validity. The original development of multiple-aptitude batteries was based on the assumption that different aptitudes would be differentially predictive of different applied criteria; this is the issue of differential validity. Assume, for example, that our test of clerical aptitude is designed to predict capacity to acquire clerical skills and that our test of mechanical aptitude is designed to predict capacity to acquire mechanical skills. For multiple aptitudes to be a useful concept, we should find that grades in typing courses are more highly related to scores on the clerical aptitude test than to scores on the mechanical aptitude test and, conversely, that grades in an auto mechanics training course are more highly related to mechanical than to clerical aptitude. In other words, a special aptitude is a useful concept only to the extent that it predicts certain practical criteria better than does any other special or more general aptitude.

In the case of the DAT, criterion-related validity data reported in the manual include the correlations of DAT scores with course grades in a variety of high school and vocational school courses, with some college courses, and with scores on other aptitude and achievement tests. Generally the DAT is useful in prediction, but it is not really *differentially* useful. The manual for the DAT (Bennett, Seashore, & Wesman, 1974) reports several thousand validity coefficients describing the correlations of DAT scores with a variety of external or other test criteria in many different samples. Median correlations of the VA + NA (scholastic aptitude) score, the best overall predictor of high school grades, are in boys and girls, respectively, 0.51 and 0.56 with grades in English and literature courses, 0.48 and 0.51 with grades in mathematics courses, 0.54 and 0.53 with grades in science courses, 0.56 and 0.58 with grades in social studies and history, and 0.42 and 0.56 with grades in business and business skills. The lack of differential validity is illustrated, for example, by the failure of CSA to be related to grades in business and business skills courses; for both boys and girls the CSA score shows the *lowest* correlation of all eight aptitudes to business grades. As another example, the best single predictor of boys' grades in English and literature is not VA but rather NA, and among girls VR and NA are equally strongly related to English grades.

Finally, the correlations of DAT scores with grades in vocational school courses are in some cases nonsignificant for all nine scores and in other cases significant, but not for the DAT aptitudes that should be logically related to course grades. For example, grades in auto mechanics courses were *unrelated* to MR scores, but show some relationships to NA, AR, and SR. The most consistent predictors of grades in machine shop courses are VR + NA, VR, NA, and AR, while NA, VR + NA, VR, and Sp are significantly related to course grades in electronics. In addition to VR + NA, the best predictors of all high school grades are VR, NA, and LU, possibly because of their assessment of the "verbal intelligence" expected to play an important role in scholastic achievement. In general, these data suggest that the effectiveness of the DAT in predicting school grades is largely due to the subtests or scores oriented toward the assessment of scholastic aptitude: VR + NA, VR, NA, and to some extent AR, LU, and Sp. The DAT has not yet been demonstrated, however, to be a consistent predictor of vocational/occupational criteria.

In addition to their correlations with course grades, scores on the DAT are highly correlated with scores on other scholastic aptitude and achievement tests. The VR + NA score is moderately to strongly related to scores on other aptitude tests; correlations range from 0.48 to 0.89, with the majority above 0.70. Correlations with the SAT verbal (0.48 boys, 0.62 girls) and quantitative (0.63 boys, 0.72 girls) scores, and with the ACT English (0.84 boys, 0.80 girls), math (0.82 boys, 0.72 girls), and composite (0.86 boys, 0.82 girls) scores, indicate that the DAT VR + NA score is essentially comparable to scores provided by the major tests of scholastic aptitude, in particular the ACT. With the exception of CSA, the other DAT scores are also strongly related to other aptitude measures' scores. For example, the correlations of MR with ACT composite scores are 0.71 (boys) and 0.56 (girls), and those of SR with ACT composite scores are 0.73 (boys) and 0.55 (girls).

The DAT may be used at any level from the eighth through the twelfth grade. Testing in the eighth or ninth grade may be used as a supplement to other criteria used to decide upon the specific educational curriculum to be followed in high school—commercial, college preparatory, or technical—to make decisions concerning the election of coursework in, for example, mathematics and languages, and/or for placement of students from several junior highs into senior high school courses. Testing in the tenth through twelfth grades may be used to assist a student in deciding about vocational training programs, post-secondary educational or vocational directions, or changes in previous plans. For example, a student who decides that he or she needs to investigate alternatives to obtaining a college education could be helped to identify occupational alternatives requiring technical or vocational training.

Use of the DAT is facilitated by the excellence and variety of interpretive materials supplied not only to counselors but to parents, teachers, and students. Test users are informed that scores on VR and NA and VR + NA are to be interpreted primarily as indicators of scholastic aptitude, more particularly as indicators of ability to succeed in college, and that, along with other aptitudes, they are also linked to success in specific programs of education and training and in specific occupations. The test materials also contain frequent suggestions concerning the utility of different aptitudes for different types of training programs or occupations. The materials provided to students and their parents suggest specific educational and occupational areas related to each of the aptitude scores. For example, CSA aptitude is described as important in many kinds of office jobs where speed and precision in handling and recording information and data are necessary. The MR score is suggested to be related to mechanical and engineering and traces occupations, while space relations are described as helpful for occupations such as drafting, architecture, carpentry, dentistry, construction, and the machine trades. It must be noted that although these suggested interpretations possess a certain amount of face validity and appear reasonable, there is insufficient predictive validity evidence to actually support the interpretations.

Also available to assist in the process of career planning is a special program titled the DAT Career Planning Program, introduced in 1973. Using a special answer sheet, students who take the DAT respond to a questionnaire covering interests, occupational preferences, and educational plans. This information is summarized and related to the DAT score profile in order to facilitate the process of educational and career planning.

An especially useful feature of the DAT for college-bound students is the provision of regression equations with which DAT scores can be used to predict subsequent performance on the SAT. The DAT VR and grammar (from the Language Usage test) scores are included in the regression equation to predict SAT-Verbal, and the DAT VR and NA scores are used in the equation to predict SAT-Math. Once predicted SAT-Verbal and SAT-Math scores are obtained using these regression equations, an expectancy table showing the probabilities of obtaining various actual SAT scores given the predicted SAT scores can be used. Figure 7.12 provides an example of such an expectancy table, as taken from the DAT manual.

Assume that a male student taking the DAT in the ninth grade obtained VR and NA scores resulting in a predicted SAT-Math score of 530. The expectancy table shown in Figure 7.11 indicates that the odds are 35 out of 100 that he will *actually* obtain an SAT-Math score in the range of 500 to 549, 26 out of 100 that his score will be in the range of 550 to 599, and only 13 out of 100 (9 + 4) that his score will equal or exceed 600. If this student had plans to major in engineering at a somewhat selective college, these plans might have to be reconsidered in light of the relatively low probability that he could obtain a high enough score on the SAT-Math test to be admitted to such colleges.

In summary, the Differential Aptitude Tests are the major differential aptitude battery used for educational and career counseling in the schools. They are well-constructed, carefully standardized, and highly reliable. There are a wealth of purposes for which DAT test scores may be used, and the test developers and publishers have made available an excellent variety of interpretive aids to counselors, parents, and students. For counselors the DAT manual is excellent, as are the casebook (Psychological Corporation, 1977) and the manual for the DAT Career Planning Program (Super, 1973a). For parents and students the Individual Report Form, the Career Planning Report, and a folder entitled "Your Aptitudes" are helpful in facilitating understanding of the concept of aptitudes and the uses of aptitude test scores.

The DAT-Adaptive. The DAT is also available in a computer-administered adaptive form. As may be recalled from Chapter 3, an adaptive test is one in which the test items administered are geared to the examinee's ability level. The Stanford-Binet and the Wechsler scales, because they are individually administered, are adaptive, but computer-controlled test administration makes adaptive testing possible without requiring extensive time from a trained examiner.

Using item response theory (IRT), the computer selects the test items that are most appropriate for the individual examinee. Because of its adaptive nature, the DAT Adaptive requires only half the time required in the paper-and-pencil version of the test. The DAT-Adaptive is equated to the DAT Forms V and W; percentile ranks for males and females in grades 8 through 12 are provided. The DAT-Adaptive and associated Technical Manual, Examiner's Manual, and Counselor's Manual are available through the Psychological Corporation.

BOYS (N = 192)

SAT Score Predicted from DAT Composite	Below 400	400–449	450–499	500–549	550–599	600–649	650 & above	N[b]
Verbal								
600 & above						33	67	3
550–599			11	18	43	25	4	28
500–549	8	8	18	26	21	16	3	38
450–499	15	18	25	32	7	3		60
400–449	44	29	15	3	3	6		34
Below 400	59	28	10	3				29
Math								
600 & above		2	2	2	18	30	45	40
550–599		7	14	19	29	19	12	42
500–549		13	13	35	26	9	4	46
450–499	7	27	41	15	10			41
400–449	35	25	25	10		5		20
Below 400	100							3

GIRLS (N = 194)

SAT Score Predicted from DAT Composite	Below 400	400–449	450–499	500–549	550–599	600–649	650 & above	N[b]
Verbal								
600 & above			10	10		30	50	10
550–599		3	23	23		35	16	31
500–549	6	12	25	38	12	3	3	32
450–499	21	14	42	21	2			43
400–449	24	24	37	11	4			46
Below 400	69	28		3				32
Math								
600 & above				6	17	22	56	18
550–599		5	14	23	27	23	9	22
500–549		15	28	15	28	13		39
450–499	12	26	36	14	8	2	2	50
400–449	31	31	24	9	4			45
Below 400	65	25	10					20

Note.—These expectancy tables are based on the same samples for which equations for predicting SAT scores are given in Table 31. Predicted SAT scores reported here were derived from those equations. Discrimination is likely to be less sharp when the prediction formulas are applied to other samples.

[a]Percentages are based on the total number of cases predicted to fall within a given SAT score interval. Thus, each row of percentages sums to 100 percent, within the limits of rounding error.

[b]Each entry shows the number of cases predicted to fall within the SAT score interval for that row.

Figure 7.11 Sample score expectancy table from the manual for the Differential Aptitude Tests, Forms S and T. (Reproduced by permission. Copyright © 1973, 1974 by The Psychological Corporation. All Rights Reserved.)

General Aptitude Test Battery

Other than the DAT, probably the most widely used multiple-aptitude battery is the General Aptitude Test Battery (GATB). The GATB, developed and distributed by the United States Employment Service, has been used primarily for employment counseling in government employment offices and for vocational rehabilitation counseling in government agencies such as state and Veterans Administration hospitals. Because access to the GATB is controlled by the federal government, special permission must be obtained before it is made available to potential users.

The GATB uses 12 tests to measure nine aptitudes. The nine aptitudes and the tests used to measure them are as follows:

1. Intelligence (G) or General Learning Ability: the ability to reason and make judgments; essentially a measure of overall scholastic aptitude. This aptitude is measured by the combined score across three tests: Three-Dimensional Space, a measure of spatial ability; Vocabulary, a measure of verbal ability; and Arithmetic Reasoning, a measure of numerical ability.

2. Verbal Aptitude (V): the ability to understand the meaning of words and to use them effectively, to comprehend language and to understand relationships between words, and to understand the meanings of whole sentences and paragraphs. V is measured by the vocabulary test.

3. Numerical Aptitude (N): the ability to perform arithmetic operations quickly and accurately. It is measured by two tests, one of arithmetic reasoning (word problems) and one of simple arithmetic computation.

4. Spatial Aptitude (S): the ability to think visually about geometric forms and to comprehend the two-dimensional representation of three-dimensional objects. It is measured by the test called Three Dimensional Space, in which the examinee is asked to look at a drawing of a pattern and indicate which of four pictures would result if the pattern were folded.

5. Clerical Perception (Q): the ability to perceive pertinent details in verbal or tabular material, to observe differences in copy, and to proofread words and numbers. Q is measured by the test known as Name Comparison, wherein the examinee must determine whether or not two names given are identical or different.

6. Form Perception (P): the ability to perceive pertinent details in objects or in pictorial or graphic material and to make visual comparisons and discriminations among shapes, figures, and objects. Form perception is measured by two tests, Form Matching and Tool Matching. The Form Matching Test presents the examinee with an array of numbered stimulus shapes encosed in an outline of a page. The same stimulus shapes are arranged, but in a different manner, at the bottom of the page and are identified by letter. The examinee must find the letter-identified shape identical to each number-identified shape as quickly as possible. In the tool matching test, a stimulus tool is shown and the examinee must indicate which of four answer stimulus tools is shaded identically to the original stimulus tool.

7. Motor Coordination (K): the ability to coordinate the eyes and hands or fingers rapidly and accurately in making precise, speedy movements and to make movement responses accurately and swiftly. K is measured by a test called Mark Making, in which the examinee is asked to make marks in a series of squares as quickly as possible.

8. Manual Dexterity (M): the ability to move the hands easily and skillfully and to work with the hands in placing and turning motions. It is measured by two tests, known as Place and Turn. In Place, the examinee must transfer 48 pegs from their holes in one board to holes in a second board and is allowed to use both hands in doing so. In Turn, the examinee transfers the 48 pegs back to the first board but inverts each peg in making the transfer. Note the requirement of special apparatus for the Place and Turn tests; because the GATB measures physical performance aptitudes as well as cognitive job-related aptitudes, special testing apparatus beyond paper-and-pencil testing materials are used.

9. Finger Dexterity (F): the ability to move the fingers and manipulate small objects with

the fingers rapidly and accurately. F is measured by two tests, one called Assemble and the second called Disassemble. In Assemble the examinee must place 50 rivets and 50 washers in 50 holes on a board. In Disassemble the examinee must remove the rivets and replace them in a bin and remove the washers and place them onto a rod. Note that this test also requires special equipment.

Like the DAT, the GATB was designed to reflect differential levels of aptitude across a number of potentially important job-related aptitudes. In the case of the GATB, these aptitudes were determined through extensive factor-analytic research using a large number of tests that had been developed to predict success in specific occupations. The GATB was standardized in 1952 in a sample that consisted of 4,000 people representative of the working population of the United States in 1940 in terms of sex, age, education, occupation, and geographical distribution. The normative sample ranged in age from 18 to 54 (mean of 30.4 years) and had attained a mean of 11.0 years of education. It may be noted that although the GATB was actually normed in a population of *working* people rather than in a *school* population, these norms are quite old and are based on a world-of-work much more oriented toward blue-collar jobs. The aptitudes required for the kinds of jobs now increasing in frequency—white-collar, service, and professional jobs and particularly the "high-tech" jobs of the 1980s and 1990s—are probably not adequately represented in the GATB (e.g., Weiss, 1972).

The GATB yields standard scores ($M = 100$, $SD = 20$), percentiles, and stanines for each of the nine aptitudes measured. A GATB profile provides raw and standard scores for each aptitude. In addition to providing the aptitude scores, however, the GATB profile takes into account the error of measurement by including a section whereby the value of one standard error of

measurement (SEM) is added to the obtained standard score for each aptitude. For example, the SEM of 6 is added to the G, V, and N standard scores, and a value of 12, the largest SEM, is added to the standard score on Finger Dexterity. The addition of one SEM to each score is based on the assumption that since obtained test scores are used both to select and to eliminate some occupational alternatives, potential error in test scores should be used in such a way as to give the examinee the benefit of the doubt.

One of the major ways of interpreting GATB scores is in relationship to the minimum aptitude test scores necessary for success in various occupations. More specifically, one of the major uses to which GATB scores have been applied involved the establishment of special aptitude test batteries (SATBs). A SATB specifies two or four aptitides that are particularly important for success in a given job and defines the minimum standard scores necessary for successful performance in that occupation. The delineation of each SATB included job analysis to determine the critical aptitudes for the job, and selection criteria included the possession of high means and low standard deviations by people employed in the occupation and significant criterion correlations. For example, the SATB for psychologist is V (120), G (125), and N (95). That for dental hygienist is G (110), S (95), and P (110).

In order to facilitate use of the SATBs in counseling, occupations having similar aptitude requirements were grouped into job families, and minimum, or cutoff, scores for the three most significant aptitudes were determined. Critical aptitudes and the necessary minimum scores on those aptitudes for groups of occupations are called "occupational aptitude patterns" (OAPs). For example, OAP-1 includes the occupations of physician, engineer, and computer programmer; the critical aptitudes for these jobs are G, N, and S. The occupations of secretary, typist, and typesetter require G, Q, and K (OAP-36), while welders and small parts assemblers require S, F, and M (OAP-27). A GATB profile provides the numbers of those OAPs and, thus, those job families for which the examinee possesses the necessary minimum aptitudes.

Another useful aspect of OAP data is that the GATB manual provides cross references to the United States Department of Labor's *Dictionary of Occupational Titles* (DOT; 1977). Thus, if an individual learns from the GATB results that he or she possesses the aptitudes to become a successful welder or dressmaker or upholsterer, that person can refer to the appropriate pages in the DOT to obtain more information about those occupations. The GATB is indeed part of a coordinated career counseling system that includes, in addition to the DOT, an *Interest Inventory* (U.S. Department of Labor, 1981b) and the *Guide for Occupational Exploration* (U.S. Department of Labor, 1981a).

Thus, the GATB and the resulting OAP data are used extensively in counseling, selection, and placement. In employment counseling, particularly in government, hospital, and/or rehabilitation settings, the information provided by the GATB is used to assist people in selecting occupations for which they possess the necessary aptitudes. This information would also have utility in helping people select appropriate vocational or technical training programs. However, some government agencies select candidates for training programs only when their aptitudes exceed those of the relevant OAP selected for a training program.

GATB scores may also be used to determine whether a person is likely to succeed at various educational levels. Minimum levels of G for success in junior college, college, and graduate or professional training have been established at 100, 110, and 120, respectively.

The United States Department of Labor has conducted numerous studies of the psychometric characteristics of the GATB. Reliability coefficients determined primarily by the alternate-forms method range from the 0.80s to the 0.90s. The motor tests are somewhat less reliable than are the paper-and-pencil tests. The GATB manual summarizes numerous studies of the validity of the GATB tests, mostly in terms of the correlations of SATB and OAP aptitudes with the relevant occupational criterion measures (U.S. Department of Labor, 1970, 1980a, 1980b).

Although the GATB is used extensively in employment and rehabilitation counseling, several major limitations of the test should be noted. Probably its major limitation is that all tests are highly speeded; the tests favor examinees who are able to work very quickly. Thus, the GATB tests may not accurately reflect the capabilities of people who, for whatever reasons (e.g., age, inexperience), work less quickly. A highly speeded test is really justifiable only if the criteria in terms of *job performance* are also highly speeded, and the importance of speed has not been demonstrated for most job-related criteria. While speed may occasionally be important in such jobs as dentistry, surgery, or accounting, in most cases accuracy and thoroughness are more important than speed to successful job performance.

Other limitations of the GATB include the out-of-date norms and the GATB's assessment of nine aptitudes based on factor-analytic studies describing the important occupational aptitudes for the world of work as it was in the 1940s and 1950s (Weiss, 1972). Finally, the use of OAPs, or of multiple-cut-off methods in general, is often criticized (e.g., Anastasi, 1982; Weiss, 1972).

To summarize, the GATB is a widely known and widely used multiple-aptitude battery. Like the DAT, the GATB measures verbal ability, numerical ability, spatial ability, and clerical speed and accuracy as well as providing a score reflective of general intelligence or scholastic aptitude. However, the DAT provides a measure of mechanical reasoning ability, while the GATB provides measures of figure dexterity, manual dexterity, and eye/hand coordination. The GATB therefore provides the advantage of measures of physical performance aptitudes, but it has the disadvantages of requiring special apparatus and a specially trained examiner.

The Armed Services Vocational Aptitude Battery (ASVAB)

This is a multiple-aptitude battery used by the military to classify and place recruits to the armed services. It is also offered free of charge by the Department of Defense for use with students in secondary and postsecondary schools. The ASVAB is used in 14,000 schools, testing 1.3 million students annually. The combination of military and civilian uses of the test make it the most widely used multiple-aptitude battery in the United States (ASVAB *Counselor's Manual;* U.S. Department of Defense, 1984).

The latest forms of the ASVAB, Forms 11, 12, 13, and 14, are parallel to Forms 8, 9, and 10, which were used from 1980 to 1984. Current forms are calibrated (or equated) to Form 8a, which was standardized in a nationally representative sample of almost 12,000 youths between the ages of 16 to 23.

The ASVAB-14 consists of 10 subtests as follows: (1) General Science, (2) Arithmetic Reasoning, (3) Word Knowledge, (4) Paragraph Comprehension, (5) Numerical Operations, (6) Coding Speed, (7) Auto and Shop Information, (8) Mathematics Knowledge, (9) Mechanical Comprehension, and (10) Electronics Information.

Results from the ASVAB are provided as composite scores, which are combinations of subtest scores shown to have predictive utility for educational and occupational decisions. The Academic Composites are measures of scholastic aptitude, like the SAT and GRE. Composite scores for Verbal, Math, and Academic Ability are provided. Occupational composites are Mechanical and Crafts, Business and Clerical, Electronics and Electrical, and Health, Social, and Technology. Figure 7.12 shows the subtests included in each occupational composite, along with sample corresponding occupations.

The ASVAB scores are available as both standard scores and as percentiles referenced to appropriate subsamples of the 1980 normative sample of 12,000 young adults. Within the large sample, norms for eleventh graders, twelfth graders, 2-year college, and the youth population aged 18 to 23 are provided separately. The standard scores are based on a mean of 50 and a standard deviation of 10 for both the subtests and the composite scores. Figure 7.13 shows a score report for a high school junior. Note that percentiles are provided within grade, for same sex, for opposite sex, and for the total grade group, as well as for the youth population as a whole. The percentiles for the student's grade and sex are expanded at the bottom of the score report, and score ranges reflecting the standard error of measurement are shown. Note that the student's strengths include math ability in the academic area and Mechanical and Crafts in the occupational area. She is especially weak in the Business and Clerical rating. The use of within-sex percentiles highlights scores in areas outside the range of traditional sex role socialization. For example, this female student's Mechanical and Crafts score is below average if she is compared to eleventh grade rates (40th percentile) or to the youth population as a whole (39th percentile) but is above average when she is compared to eleventh grade females (68th percentile). Thus, her interests in an area less emphasized in

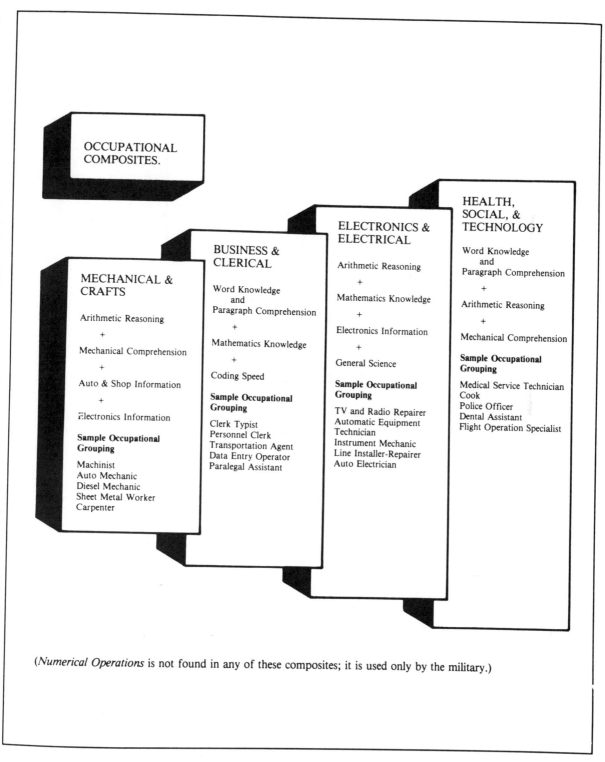

Figure 7.12 Occupational Composites from the Armed Services Vocational Aptitude Battery. Taken from the *Counselor's Manual* for the Armed Services Vocational Aptitude Battery, Form 14 (p. 5). (Copyright © 1984 by the United States Department of Defense. Reproduced by permission).

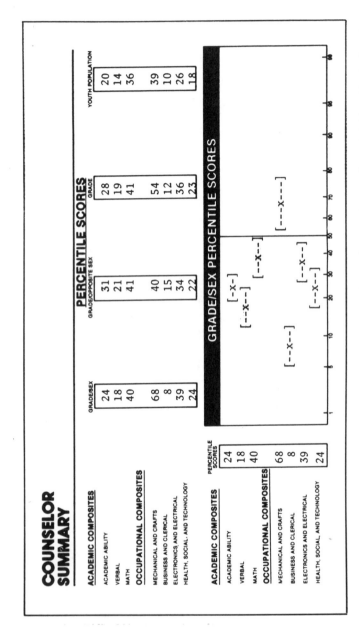

Figure 7.13. Summary profile from the Armed Services Vocational Aptitude Battery. Reprinted from the *Counselor's Manual* for the Armed Services Vocational Aptitude Battery, Form 14. (Copyright © 1984 by the United States Department of Defense. Reproduced by permission).

traditional female socialization are highlighted.

The ASVAB scores are reliable. Alternate forms reliability coefficients for the composite scores range from 0.84 to 0.93 for women and between 0.88 to 0.95 for men. Internal consistency reliability coefficients are almost all in the 0.90 to 0.96 range, with only the Mechanical and Crafts composite showing values in the high 0.80s among women.

Extensive validity data are reported in the *Technical Supplement to the Counselor's Manual* (U.S. Department of Defense, 1985). Validity data include evidence that scores on the composites used in military selection and placement predict performance in the training programs for military occupations. For over 50 military technical training courses, the median correlations of ASVAB composite scores with measures of training performance were over 0.60 (U.S. Department of Defense, 1984).

Validity data regarding use in civilian samples has been extrapolated from the ASVAB Form 5, the academic composite of which is related to that of the ASVAB-14 at above 0.90. The *Counselor's Manual* also suggests that because the verbal and math tests of the GATB are psychometrically equivalent to those of the ASVAB, the validity data for the ASVAB can be extrapolated from that available for the GATB. More directly, however, are correlations of the Academic Ability composite of the ASVAB-14 with grades in high school and college (about 0.40), with the California Achievement Test (0.90), and with the DAT (0.85). Thus, the Academic Ability Composite appears to be comparable to other measures of general cognitive ability. Jensen (1985) argues that the ASVAB *is* primarily useful because of its ability to measure g, particularly as jobs become more complex. He suggests that tests of perceptual-motor factors, *along* with general cognitive ability, add to the prediction of success in the skilled trades but that other

evidence for differential validity is weak. In a factor analysis of the ASVAB-14 subtests, Jensen (1985) reports that a large general factor accounted for 63 percent of the total variance, and the only other interpretable factor included the two highly speeded subtests, Numerical Operations and Coding Speed. The loadings of the subtests on the g factor were uniformly high, ranging from 0.59 for Coding Speed to 0.87 for General Science and 0.86 for Word Knowledge and Arithmetic Reasoning. Loadings of this magnitude do suggest that the test measures primarily g. The composite scores are also highly intercorrelated, ranging from 0.78 to 0.97 for men, with a mean of 0.93, and from 0.76 to 0.97 for women, with a mean of 0.89. These values approach the size of the parallel forms reliability coefficients, suggesting that a given composite score is measured as well by a different composite score as by an alternate form of the test for that composite. Given the lack of evidence for differential validity, overemphasis on score differences among composite scores is probably unwise.

The interpretive materials provided for counselors using the ASVAB are excellent. The *ASVAB Counselor's Manual* (U.S. Department of Defense, 1984) contains detailed information on the meaning and interpretation of scores and extensive suggestions concerning how that information should be communicated to students. A number of case reports are provided, complete with counselor-client dialogue. Most of the case reports provide both ASVAB and interest inventory profiles (e.g., the Self-Directed Search or the Strong-Campbell Interest Inventory, as discussed in Chapter 9). Thus, illustrations of how both ability and interest test results can be integrated into career counseling are provided. The manual also contains extensive occupational information, also very helpful for use with clients.

In sum, the ASVAB is a psychometrically sound instrument accompanied by excellent interpretive materials. It is thus very useful for educational and career counseling in schools, colleges, and the military.

Other Multiple Aptitude Batteries

The Employee Aptitude Survey. Widely used in employment selection, the Employee Aptitude Survey (EAS; Ruch & Ruch, 1980) measures 10 aptitudes predictive of performance in a range of occupational areas. The EAS is published by the Educational and Industrial Testing Service (EDITS). The 10 tests of the EAS are as follows:

1. Verbal Comprehension: the ability to use words in oral and written communication and in planning, measured by a vocabulary test.
2. Numerical Ability: skill in the four fundamental operations of addition, subtraction, multiplication, and division and in the use of decimals and fractions.
3. Visual Pursuit: requires the examinee to follow the paths of lines such as those used in electrical wiring diagrams or electronics schematics.
4. Visual Speed and Accuracy: the ability to quickly see difference (rather than similarity) between two numbers; the test is designed to assess clerical aptitude.
5. Space Visualization: spatial ability; the test requires the examinee to visualize the number of neighboring blocks touched by a given block in a pile of blocks.
6. Numerical Reasoning: numerical aptitude; assessed by use of number series items.
7. Verbal Reasoning: logical reasoning ability; assessed by use of items that provide the examinee with a set of facts, following which he/she must decide which of several conclusions are justified based on the facts given. This ability is thought by the authors of the EAS to be important in decision making in business and other practical settings.
8. Word Fluency: the aptitude originally postulated as one of Thurstone and Thurstone's (1941) primary mental abilities; the test provides the examinee with a letter of the alphabet and requires the person to write down as many words as possible that begin with that letter within five minutes.
9. Manual Speed and Accuracy: examinees must place a pencil dot in as many holes as possible within the five-minute time limit given.
10. Symbolic Reasoning: requires the examinee to evaluate symbolic relations in the form of $<$, $>$, $=$, and $\neq$. For example, the examinee must decide whether the following relation is true, false, or uncertain:

$$X = Y > Z, \text{ therefore } X = Z.$$

(The relation is false, since $X > Z$.)

The scores for the EAS are computed as raw scores that may be compared to tables of percentile scores describing the performance of members of various occupational groups. Norms are provided for, among others, clerical, technical, sales, executive, and supervisory occupations, as well as for skilled, semiskilled, and unskilled trades and jobs. Another helpful feature of the EAS technical manual (Ruch & Ruch, 1980) is its provision, for some occupations, of information regarding the aptitudes most closely related to performance in a given occupation and percentile norms describing the performance levels of people employed in that occupation. Norms are also provided for male and female college students and for students in engineering, electronics, and architectural drafting.

Like the GATB, the tests of the EAS are highly speeded; each test is limited to five minutes or less of testing time. Although this speededness probably increases the usefulness of the tests in employee selection, since testing time can be minimized, the problems of highly speeded testing conditions for some examinees must be kept in mind. Another feature facilitating the ease of using the EAS in employee selection is the availability of simple methods of hand-scoring and of alternate forms for all of the tests. Because of the availability of alternate forms, examinees may be easily retested if there are questions or concerns about the results of the initial testing.

The EAS, then, has utility in the selection of employees for jobs in a number of occupations. This test battery is probably most useful for use in those occupational areas for which norms have been published, but the relative ease of both administering and scoring the battery should facilitate the collection and use of local normative data, that is, within a given organization. Although care in the use of scores obtained under such highly speeded conditions should be exercised, the ease of obtaining, administering, and scoring the battery have made it very useful in personnel selection.

Multidimensional Aptitude Battery. The Multidimensional Aptitude Battery (MAB), developed by Douglas N. Jackson and published by Research Psychologists Press, is designed to accomplish the same purposes as the WAIS-R, except that it provides the efficiency of group administration. Like the WAIS-R, the MAB is designed for use with individuals aged 16 to 74. Also like the WAIS-R, the MAB yields Verbal, Performance, and Full Scale IQs, and these are calibrated to those of the Wechsler scales. There are five verbal and five performance subtests, most of which are analogues to the WAIS-R subtests except that the items have different formats and have been written to be appropriate for group (paper-and-pencil) administration.

The MAB is highly reliable, with both internal consistency and test-retest coefficients of 0.94 to 0.98 for the Verbal, Performance, and Full Scale scores. The correlation between the WAIS-R and MAB Full Scale IQs is 0.91.

Although still relatively new, the MAB appears to be a very promising measure of intellectual abilities for use in both counseling and research. Further information about the test is available in the manual (Jackson, 1984) and in a review by Vernon (1985).

Summary

To summarize, the primary individual uses for multiple-aptitude batteries such as the DAT, GATB, and ASVAB are to help individuals use differential aptitude data in the process of selecting specific educational curricula, occupational training programs, and/or jobs and occupations. *General* measures of intelligence and scholastic aptitude (such as the DAT's VR + NA and the GATB's G) are probably most important in determining the *level* of educational and occupational aspirations (e.g., Crites, 1969; Tyler, 1965). For example, it generally appears that an IQ about one standard deviation above the mean is the usual average for the pursuit of professional occupations; Stanford-Binet mean IQs as a function of attained level of education have been reported as follows: college entrants, $M = 118$; B.A. recipients, $M = 123$; M.A. recipients, $M = 126$; and Ph.D. recipients, $M = 141$ (Tyler, 1965). Thus, to the extent that pursuit of a given occupation requires the attainment of a certain level of formal education, knowledge of IQ or scholastic aptitude test scores will provide information concerning the degree of *realism* of an individual's preferences. For example, a person whose measured IQ was equal to 90 would probably find pursuing a career in medicine or law difficult or impossible because of the extensive amount of education required.

Thus, the importance of G or IQ for occupational selection appears to be in placing limits on people's options. An individual possessing high scholastic aptitude could choose an occupation requiring extensive education—medicine, law, college teaching—or one requiring less extensive education—auto mechanics, carpentry. In contrast, an individual possessing lower scholastic aptitude might have numerous options in terms of technical training to become an auto mechanic or carpenter, but lack the occupational options requiring extensive formal education.

Within a general *level* of aspirations, however, information about one's strengths and weaknesses in ability can be useful in determining specific educational and occupational *directions*. For example, both Bob and Barb may obtain a superior DAT (VR + NA) score—say at the 95th percentile—but Bob's score on VR is significantly higher than his score on NA, while Barb's scores show the opposite pattern. Because of their very high scholastic aptitudes, both Bob and Barb will probably pursue college degrees and possibly graduate or professional degrees, but because of their *differential* aptitudes Bob may be more successful in a highly verbal occupation or profession such as law or writing, while Barb may be highly successful in an occupation or profession requiring quantitative skills such as engineering or stock brokering. Of course, information regarding abilities is only one basis upon which such decisions are made, but abilities *do* to some extent limit the realistic options available to people.

SUMMARY

This chapter and Chapter 6, on the assessment of intelligence, have described the major approaches to the understanding and assessment of human mental abilities and aptitudes. Beginning with Galton's measures of sensory and motor capacities and Binet's charge to develop a means to identify the mentally retarded, the mental testing movement in psychology has developed to its present status as one of the major and most important applications of psychology to practical decision-making and problem-solving situations. Ability testing in the elementary and secondary schools is used in the understanding, prediction, and evaluation of educational achievement and in the design of interventions capable of facilitating the educational development of students. At the postsecondary level, aptitude tests are particularly important in institutional decisions regarding selection, placement, and financial aid and in the educational and career decisions made by individual students. Ability and aptitude tests are an integral part of our educational system and have had widespread use in personnel selection, business, industry, government, and the armed services.

Although the tests described in Chapters 6 and 7 have extensive utility and represent the highest standards in test construction, standardization, and guidelines for use, necessary cautions in their use must be recalled. As has been mentioned, possibilities for bias and unfairness in the tests and/or their use must be carefully evaluated. (Chapter 14 describes the issues and necessary considerations in the fair use of tests.) In addition, aptitudes and abilities are generally related to, but are no guarantee of, successful performance in a given domain. Chapter 8 will describe the assessment of actual achievement in the educational setting.

The Assessment
of Achievement

INTRODUCTION

Achievement is the third major type of cognitive assessment. While the concepts of intelligence and aptitude refer to one's learning *potential* or learning *capacity*, the concept of achievement describes what has already been learned, or *developed capacity*.

Although the concepts of capacity (aptitude) and developed capacity (achievement) are fairly easy to differentiate in theory, they are more difficult to differentiate at the practical level of measurement. Intelligence, aptitude, *and* achievement tests *all* reflect one's capabilities at the time of assessment. The main differences between aptitude (and intelligence) tests on the one hand and achievement tests on the other hand are in terms of (1) the *types* of past experiences they are assumed to reflect, and (2) the *uses* of test scores. According to Anastasi (1982), aptitude tests and achievement tests differ in that they assume different degrees of *uniformity* in the relevant antecedent experiences. In other words, an achievement test is generally designed to measure the effects of relatively standardized sets of experiences, such as a specific educational curriculum. Aptitude tests, on the other hand, do not assume specific prior learning experiences, but instead reflect the person as the product of whatever learning experiences he/she has had up to that point.

Perhaps the most important difference between aptitude tests and achievement tests involves their applied uses. Because aptitude tests are designed to assess capacity to *learn*, they are used primarily in the prediction of *future* performance. Scholastic aptitude tests are used to predict success in future educational work, and clerical aptitude tests may be used to predict success in a typing course. Because of this major purpose of aptitude tests, predictive validity is a particularly important consideration in their evaluation.

Achievement tests, on the other hand, tend to be past and present oriented rather than future oriented. They provide an evaluation of the knowledge or competencies possessed by the individual at the time of testing, and they reflect the effects on the person of a specified prior set of educational or training experiences. Although achievement tests may be used to make decisions concerning areas in which a person needs further education or training, they are more often used to indicate a student's current *level* of attainment in a given subject matter area, such as social studies, or a basic educational skill area, such as reading. Another frequent use of achievement tests is to evaluate the overall quality of educational programs and schools, rather than the individuals within those programs or schools. A third frequent use of achievement testing is within various trades and professions for the purpose of assessing competency to *practice* the trade or profession.

This chapter will describe the major methods of assessing educational achievement and also address the use of achievement testing to establish professional competency. Before we proceed with a discussion of specific tests, a discussion of the concept of *criterion referencing* as used in the assessment of achievement is appropriate.

Criterion-Referenced Testing

The reader should recall from Chapter 3 that a major method for the interpretation of test scores is the use of normative data, that is, data comparing an individual's performance to that of a large group of individuals. Normative data allows us to describe a score as a percentile equivalent, standard score, or stanine *in reference to* a large group of people.

Although the concept of norms has had tremendous utility for the interpretation and use of test scores, there are many applied situations where norms are *not* very helpful in the actual use of test scores. As an example, knowing that the driver in the next car scored at the 80th percentile on the driver's test is not as important as knowing whether or not the driver has mastered the skill of driving and knows the "rules of the road." A score at the 80th percentile on a math achievement test in a school district characterized by very low levels of achievement may not mean that the student is actually able to do the math appropriate for the student's age or grade level. In many cases we care not so much how the person stands relative to other people, but whether or not that person has mastered a given subject or area of knowledge. Thus, the ideas of "criterion referencing" and "criterion-referenced testing," terms first proposed by Glaser (1963), use as their frame of reference a specified domain of *content* rather than a comparative group of individuals.

A good definition of a criterion-referenced test is a test "used to ascertain an individual's status with respect to a well-defined behavior domain" (Hambleton, Swaminathan, Algina, & Coulson, 1978, p. 2; see also Popham, 1978). In most cases the concept of a "well-defined behavior domain" applies to some area of knowledge, skills, or competency, and criterion-referenced tests are used to assess the individual's degree of knowledge, skill, or competency with respect to that domain. For example, criterion-referenced tests are used extensively in educational settings to assess students' levels of competency in reading, mathematics, and foreign languages. Such tests are also the basis for granting a driver's license, a pilot's license, and licenses to practice medicine, psychology, and/or law.

Assessing levels of competency may be done in order to design further instructional sequences—that is, if a person demonstrates sufficient competency in one aspect of a domain, such as arithmetic, he or she progresses to the next instructional module; individuals demonstrating less than sufficient competency receive further instruction in that area. Achievement of competency or "mastery" may also lead to the cessation of instruction in that subject matter or to the granting of a license or certificate to practice the behavior, for example, driving, flying, or medicine. When the interpretation and use of tests is tied to a content area as in these examples, it is what has been called the content, or "performance referral," approach to criterion-referenced testing (e.g., Ebel, 1962).

In constructing a test designed to be content or performance referenced, the first step involves detailed specification of the behaviors/competencies to be assessed and the objectives to be attained. Usually categories of behavior are specified and arranged in a logical order, and items representative of each category are written. For example, competency in arithmetic would include several categories of behavior, such as addition, subtraction, multiplication, division, and fractions. Each subarea and the domain as a whole are measured only as well as the relevance and representativeness of the items written to assess the domain. As in rational test construction (which bears many similarities to criterion-referenced test construction), item analysis data may be used to evaluate the quality of individual test items. Such data, however, must not be used in a way that distorts the representativeness of content sampling.

Following construction of the test, decisions based on its intended uses must be made. For instructional purposes, the learning exercises appropriate to each competency area are designed, and decisions concerning the performance level that will indicate achievement of competency are made. In most cases, a relatively high proportion of correct responses to test items is necessary for a person to demonstrate competency. For purposes of licensure, a minimum cutoff score is often specified; people who score at or above the minimum are licensed, while those scoring below it are not licensed.

The necessity of specifying minimum performance levels for the determination of competency is one of the problems encountered in criterion-referenced testing. In most instances, such levels could be viewed as essentially arbitrary and, because of this, professional standards and judgment and specific formulation of the *objectives* of testing are necessary. Some persons or group of people must determine the criteria for a safe driver or a competent psychologist, and therefore the expertise of professionals in these fields is essential to the specification of minimum levels of performance. The problem of setting minimum performance standards also illustrates an area where the distinction between criterion-referenced and norm-referenced testing blurs. Oftentimes, normative data are used in determining minimal performance levels (Popham, 1978); while decisions based on normative data are still arbitrary, they are less likely to result in the setting of unrealistically high or low standards for acceptable performance.

Note that for many applied purposes, criterion referencing may be more useful and sensible than norm-based interpretations of test scores. The use of tests for designing further instructional modules is probably the primary example of this utility. For example, knowledge that John's competency in mathematics includes algebra but not geometry and trigonometry would probably be of more use in planning his subsequent coursework in mathematics than would knowledge that his score on a mathematics achievement test was at the 50th percentile. Similarly, when we allow people to drive automobiles, fly large commercial airlines, or practice medicine we are probably more interested in the questions of whether or not they can drive, fly, or practice medicine competently than we are in their standing in a normative group.

In summary, the content-based approach to criterion referencing offers an important framework from which to interpret and use achievement test scores. The next sections will describe the assessment of achievement at the elementary, junior high, and high school levels and special-purpose achievement tests used at the college level and beyond.

EDUCATIONAL ACHIEVEMENT TESTS: ELEMENTARY AND JUNIOR HIGH LEVELS

The type of test most frequently and widely used within educational institutions is the achievement test. In addition to the exams used to determine course grades, standardized achievement tests have a number of other important purposes related to the evaluation of both individual students and of educational and instructional programs.

More specifically, a first major use of standardized achievement tests is for the evaluation of *individual* students. Because standardized achievement tests provide norm-referenced scores, teachers can use them to obtain information about students' levels of educational development in comparison to other students in the school system and nationwide. In addition, most major achievement test batteries also provide criterion-referenced interpretations; in other words, they suggest specific content areas in which a student is strong and specific areas in which the student is weak. Practical uses of these norm-referenced interpretations for individual students include the following:

1. to assess the achievement level of a student in relationship to other students
2. to identify a student whose achievement is exceptionally high or low
3. to compare a student's achievement with performance in class
4. to give parents an informative estimate of their son's or daughter's achievement
5. to suggest a level of instruction that is appropriate for an individual student
6. to identify a particular area of a student's strengths or weaknesses to provide a guide for further instruction
7. to group students of similar levels of achievement for some instructional purposes (e.g., grouping students into special classrooms)
8. to evaluate the level of the student's functioning in grade level terms ("functional level testing")

Functional level testing is particularly useful for students in schools, such as "open schools," where traditional grade levels are not used. For students at schools of this type, the average level of functioning of students and of classes of students can be evaluated, as can specific educational strengths and weaknesses.

In addition to their usefulness in providing information about individual students, standardized achievement tests can be used to compare the average levels of performance across different schools of a school system or to compare one particular school or classroom with the performance of a national normative sample of schools and students. A recent example of the use of educational achievement test results for this purpose was described in the January 10, 1983, issue of *Time* magazine, in an article describing the resistance of administrators of two private schools in Michigan to state supervision of their curriculum and teachers (McGrath & Dolan, 1983). Part of the documentation for the administrators' argument that high-quality education was being provided to students even though the curriculum and the qualifications of teachers did not follow state educational requirements was the finding that the standardized test performance of the students in the private schools was above what would be expected for their grade level. In this case, achievement test data were used to document the quality of the education that was being received in these private schools.

Other system-wide uses of achievement test data include the appraisal of average levels and ranges of achievement so that the effectiveness of past educational programs can be evaluated and so that further educational needs can be evaluated and addressed. Criterion-referenced information can be particularly helpful in instructional planning—for example, to obtain an indication of the extent to which specific goals of an educational program are being achieved, to compare the performance of a local group in specific content and skill areas with students nationally, and to identify topics in which the group is exceptionally high or low in relation either to local groups or to the performance of students nationally. This kind of information can also be used to identify topics that are troublesome for a class or for individuals and to determine the kinds of errors that students are making.

Thus, there are a number and variety of purposes for which standardized achievement test data are used. The following section describes several of the most widely used achievement test batteries. The batteries to be described have several characteristics in common.

First, they are multilevel batteries designed for use across a number of grade levels, often as large a range as kindergarten through grade 12. Test booklets are designed with overlapping sections, and students at various grade levels are instructed to begin and to stop at specified places in the test booklet.

Second, the tests tend to be constructed similarly and to measure the same set of basic educational skills. Educators and achievement test constructors tend to agree that the capabilities to understand, to read, and to write the English language and to understand mathematical concepts and perform mathematical operations are the essential goals of the American educational system; the importance of the "three Rs" has apparently not diminished. Considered next in educational importance are knowledge of resource materials and their use (e.g., libraries, dictionaries, maps) and of the social and natural sciences. Knowledge in the humanities area is sometimes included in achievement batteries but is not as consistently included as are the other areas.

Third, these batteries are well-constructed, following the procedures of rational test construction and item analysis described in Chapter 3. Several basic steps are used to ensure the relevance and representativeness of test content:

1. The *purposes* of the test are carefully defined and delineated through consultation with test specialists, educators, and test consumers, such as school administrators and school board members.

2. Once the purposes of the tests are established, specifications for its content are developed, including subtests, item types, and content coverage. Content specifications should be at least partially based on extensive analyses of current curricular materials, such as leading textbook series, syllabi, and state guidelines.

3. The item specifications are given to item writers (e.g., educational consultants, teachers), and the items written are submitted to other expert reviewers.

4. Items that survive expert review are included in a preliminary pool of items that are administered to students representative of those for whom the test is designed.

5. The results of analyses of item difficulty and discrimination are included as criteria in the final selection of test items. Other criteria for item selection include item content, item bias (e.g., difficulty for male versus female or black versus white students), and the quality of the distractors, that is, the incorrect answers in a multiple-choice test.

A final characteristic shared by many of the major achievement test batteries is their concurrent norming with an intelligence or scholastic aptitude test, such as the Iowa Tests of Basic Skills with the Cognitive Abilities Test, the Metropolitan Achievement Tests with the Otis-Lennon School Ability Test. The major advantage of concurrent standardization is that it allows teachers, counselors, and parents to compare a student's actual school achievement as measured by the achievement test battery to the student's *potential* level of achievement as estimated from aptitude test scores. Counseling and teaching might be quite different for a student who is achieving considerably *below* his or her ability than for one whose level of achievement is as good as, or better than, would be expected given his or her aptitude test scores. Thus, knowledge of a student's scholastic aptitude can assist in the interpretation and add to the usefulness of scores on educational achievement tests. Table 8.1 gives examples of the coordinated achievement/aptitude batteries that will be discussed in the remaining parts of this chapter. Aptitude tests were discussed in Chapter 6.

Although many of the test batteries discussed in this section assess achievement in kindergarten through grade 12, they are among the major batteries used mainly in the elementary and junior high grades. Other batteries focusing specifically upon the assessment of educational achievement in the high school years will be discussed in the next section.

Table 8.1 Examples of Coordinated Ability and Achievement Test Batteries

| Publisher | School Ability | Type of Test School Achievement | |
		Grades K–8	Grades 9–12
Riverside Publishing Co.	Cognitive Abilities Test	Iowa Tests of Basic Skills	Tests of Achievement and Proficiency
Psychological Corporation	Otis-Lennon School Ability Test	Metropolitan Achievement Tests	Stanford Achievement Test
CTB/McGraw-Hill	School and College Ability Test (SCAT-III)	Sequential Tests of Educational Progress (STEP-III)	

The Iowa Tests of Basic Skills

The Iowa Tests of Basic Skills (ITBS), published by the Riverside Publishing Company, are a multilevel battery of achievement tests covering grades K–8. (A companion test battery, the Tests of Achievement and Proficiency, measures achievement in grades 9 to 12. This battery is discussed later in this section.) Both batteries were normed concurrently with the Cognitive Abilities Test, facilitating normative comparisons of aptitude and achievement test scores.

The ITBS are designed to measure the basic educational skills important for effective functioning in society, including reading, language, mathematics, and work-study skills (e.g., the use of reference materials). The ITBS underwent a major revision and restandardization in 1985. The revised version of the ITBS is available in Early Primary (K–2), Primary (grades 1–3), and Multilevel (grades 3–9) batteries. The available subtests have been expanded from previous editions of the test and include Listening (primary batteries only), Word Analysis (primary batteries only), Vocabulary, Reading, Language Skills, Work-Study Skills (not in Early Primary battery) and Mathematics Skills. Supplements to the Multilevel battery include Social Studies and Science Achievement Subtests.

As mentioned, the ITBS were recently restandardized, along with the Tests of Achievement and Proficiency (TAP, described in the next section) and the Cognitive Abilities Test (CogAT, discussed in Chapter 6). Extensive pre-norming studies were done to provide information regarding item fairness across gender and ethnic minority groups. Data from 48,000 students in 35 states, with blacks and Hispanics intentionally oversampled so that sample sizes of those groups would be large enough, were used to eliminate items that might be biased against minorities or against one gender. The final standardization, done in the fall of 1984 and the spring of 1985, consisted of about 14,000 students per school grade, selected to be representative of the nation's school students in terms of public/private/parochial schools, larger versus smaller cities and towns, geographic regions, and socioeconomic classes.

The scores available for the ITBS include standard scores, national grade percentiles and stanines, grade equivalents, normal curve equivalents, and age equivalents. The profiles provided for the ITBS emphasize the grade equivalent scores and the national percentiles and stanines.

The tests are highly reliable, with values of the KR-20 reliability coefficient ranging from the high 0.80s to the high 0.90s. The content validity of the tests is based on their careful construction to reflect the content of the educational curricula represented by the tests. In the ITBS *Teacher's Guide*, the content of each subtest is described in detail. The test manual strongly suggests that all users of the test carefully review these content descriptions to determine whether or not the tests' content is appropriate to measure the educational objectives of their particular curricula.

Evidence regarding the construct validity of the ITBS includes information about the intercorrelations of the subtests, the stability of test scores over time, and the extent to which the batteries relate to other measures of achievement and ability. Test intercorrelations are quite high; correlations between different test scores are concentrated in the 0.50s to the 0.80s, depending on the tests and grade levels concerned. The tests are highly stable; test-retest correlations for the ITBS subtest scores range from 0.83 (Vocabulary) to 0.93 (Language) over a one-year interval. The stability of the composite score (V, R, LT, WT, and MT) ranged from 0.82 (four years) to 0.96 (one year), thus indicating an almost disturbing degree of score stability. Achievement test scores that stable suggest that while education may be improving students' skills, the relative quality of performance of different students is remaining almost identical.

Although the present version (Forms G and H) of the ITBS is still relatively new, it was equated to the earlier version of the battery, Forms 7 and 8. Thus, users wishing to compare students' performance levels across years—for example, in a particular school district—can easily do so. And until a large body of predictive validity data becomes available for Forms G and H, validity data from the earlier forms may be somewhat useful. These data suggested moderate relationships of ITBS scores with high school grades (r's of 0.60 were typical) and freshman (college) GPA ($r = 0.41$ to 0.49) and high correlations with scholastic ability test scores (r's in the 0.70s and 0.80s between analogous ITBS and CogAT scores and 0.70 with the ACT Composite score).

Although additional validity data would be helpful in the interpretation of ITBS scores, the interpretive materials accompanying test scores do provide a considerable amount and variety of helpful information. For example, based on the ITBS's concurrent standardization with the CogAT, the ITBS manual contains what are called "norms for ability levels." These norms provide estimates of the ITBS achievement levels expected from students possessing varying degrees of CogAT-measured scholastic aptitude. Thus, the norms can indicate underachievement or maximum use of ability, in comparison with students of similar ability.

Particularly useful features of the ITBS interpretive materials include a "criterion-referenced skills analysis" and suggestions for helping students improve their basic educational skills. A skills analysis allows an assessment of the individual student's strengths and weaknesses across educational skill areas and shows whether these areas of strength and weakness are unique to the student or common to the class as a whole.

To show the value of this type of criterion-referenced analysis, assume that a student named Steve was well below the national average on the "Fractions" skill component of the Math Concepts subtest. In one case assume that Steve's classroom as a whole was also below average on "Fractions," while in the other case the class as a whole was considerably above average. In the first instance we would focus interventions (extra time spent on fractions) on the entire class, whereas in the second case we would attempt to give Steve, but not the entire class, special help with fractions. As can be seen through this example, criterion-referenced skills analyses of this type have definite instructional implications, both for individual students and for classes or schools.

Metropolitan Achievement Tests

The Metropolitan Achievement Tests (MAT) were first developed in 1930 to test the achievement levels of students in the New York City schools. By 1932 a form for use nationally was released, and the tests have been revised in 1947, 1958, 1970, 1978, and 1985, the Sixth Edition. The tests are published by the Psychological Corporation and were standardized concurrently with the Otis-Lennon School Ability Test (OLSAT), discussed in Chapter 6.

The MATs measure achievement across grades K–12 and are available in two related but different test batteries: the Survey Battery, designed for norm-referenced use, and the diagnostic tests, designed for criterion-referenced use. The traditional achievement tests are the Survey Tests, which measure educational achievement in the following basic skill areas: (1) reading, which includes vocabulary, word recognition, and reading comprehension; (2) mathematics, which includes concepts, problem solving, and computation; (3) Language, with spelling and grammar and punctuation sections; (4) Science, both knowledge and skills of inquiry and analysis; and (5) Social Studies, including knowledge and skills in geography, history, economics, political science, and human behavior. A Research Skills score is provided using relevant test items from all 10 subtests.

Both the survey tests and the diagnostic tests, along with the OLSAT, were standardized in the fall of 1984 and the spring of 1985 in a representative sample of American school systems. The scores provided for the Survey Battery include raw scores, stanines, percentile ranks, grade equivalents, and normal curve equivalents for each subtest. In addition, basic scores (reading + mathematics + language) and composite scores (reading + mathematics + language + social studies + science) are provided. An instructional reading level score, defined as the grade level of reading material at which the student is able to answer 70 percent of the questions successfully, is also provided. Also very helpful is a predicted score range based on OLSAT performance, which can be used to suggest underachievement (or overachievement) and a predicted achievement level for schools, based on the socioeconomic status of the students' parents', as reflected by parental levels of education.

The Metropolitan Achievement Tests are highly reliable. The reliabilities (KR–20) of the five content areas range from 0.90 to 0.96, while the total score for the complete battery yielded a KR–20 of 0.98. Alternate forms reliability coefficients are in the 0.80s. The reliability coefficients and associated standard errors of measurement are used to provide error bands for use in score reports. Content validity was ensured by using school curriculum as the basis for item development, followed by extensive item analysis to eliminate gender and race bias prior to the final standardization.

The Sequential Tests of Educational Progress

The Sequential Tests of Educational Progress (STEP-III), published by CTB/McGraw-Hill in cooperation with the Educational Testing Service, are the achievement test battery that serves as companion to the School and College Ability Tests (SCAT-III) discussed previously. The STEP-III is organized into two batteries, one designed for grades K–3, and one designed for use in grades 3–12. The STEP-III assesses the following basic educational skills: reading, writing skills, vocabulary, mathematics computation, and mathematics concepts. In addition to the basic battery, the STEP provides measures of knowledge and understanding in social studies, science, study skills, and listening (oral comprehension).

The STEP-III were standardized in the fall of 1977 and spring of 1978 in a representative sample of 200,000 students from 200 school districts across the country. Scores provided on the STEP profile include percentile bands, both in numerical and graphic terms, the raw score and maximum number correct, standard scores, grade level indicators, national and local percentiles and stanines, and percentiles as a function of high or low socioeconomic status groups.

Figure 8.1 provides the score report for a hypothetical student named Ann Andrews. Percentile bands for the basic skills areas indicate that Ann is, overall, a superior student. Her excellence is supported by the fact that although she is only in the sixth grade, she is performing at the eighth or ninth grade level educationally.

Reliability data for the STEP-III include Kuder-Richardson-20 and alternate-forms reliability. The STEP-III basic tests

SCORING AND REPORTING FORMS Levels C-J

The Basic Service is an alphabetical roster of pupil scores. The service provides raw scores with the test level and maximum raw score indicated; national percentile ranks and stanines; grade level indicators for the basic tests; local percentile ranks and local stanines. Special percentile ranks (i.e., high SES, low SES, and large city) are available as options. When SCAT is administered with STEP, significant score differences will be indicated by an asterisk to the left of the STEP raw score. Data is summarized for the class with the number of students scoring in each stanine reported.

STEP

Educational Testing Service

SCORE ROSTER

REPORT FOR: Andrews Ann D, Brandywine — GRADE: 6 — NATIONAL NORMS: 6 Spring — NUMBER TESTED: 25 — FORM USED: SCAT X, STEP X — TEST DATE: 04 78 — PAGE: 1 — PROCESSING CODES: 02234A, 02233B

NAME CURTIS RUSS P — SPECIAL CODES 155313360

Test	RAW SCORE/ MAXIMUM POSSIBLE/ LEVEL TAKEN	STANDARD SCORE	GRADE LEVEL INDICATOR	NATIONAL -ILE/ STANINE	LOCAL -ILE/ STANINE	OPT
Reading	42 50 H	468	7 5	68 6	64 6	60
Vocabulary	22 28 H	459	8 1	78 7	85 7	70
Writing Skills	44 58 H	463	8 1	78 7	88 7	72
Math Computation	45 55 H	477	7 9	75 6	80 7	60
Basic Concepts	40 50 H	452	7 5	66 6	78 7	50
Study Skills	23 30 H	458	- -	76 6	73 6	- -
Listening	15 20 H	476	- -	79 7	84 7	- -
Social Studies	40 50 H	452	- -	62 6	65 6	- -
Science / Biological Science / Earth Science / Physical Science	35 50 FH	452	- -	66 6	68 6	- -
SCAT Verbal	35 50 IN	475	- -	85 7	80 7	- -
SCAT Quantitative	30 50 IN	484	- -	72 6	75 6	- -
SCAT TOTAL	65 100 IN	478	- -	81 7	76 6	- -

NAME KELL JOH O — SPECIAL CODES 156535219

Test	RAW SCORE/ MAXIMUM POSSIBLE/ LEVEL TAKEN	STANDARD SCORE	GRADE LEVEL INDICATOR	NATIONAL -ILE/ STANINE	LOCAL -ILE/ STANINE	OPT
Reading	39 50 H	464	6 9	58 5	49 5	45
Vocabulary	17 28 H	452	7 1	60 6	65 6	50
Writing Skills	** 52 58 H	470	8 5	92 8	96 9	90
Math Computation	* 30 55 G	454	5 1	32 4	46 5	20
Basic Concepts	35 50 G	447	6 1	42 5	56 5	24
Study Skills	20 30 H	455	- -	68 6	60 6	- -
Listening	13 20 H	467	- -	59 5	56 5	- -
Social Studies	38 50 H	450	- -	56 5	61 6	- -
Science / Biological Science / Earth Science / Physical Science	30 50 FH	448	- -	57 5	58 5	- -
SCAT Verbal	28 50 IN	467	- -	68 6	54 5	- -
SCAT Quantitative	24 50 IN	476	- -	56 5	54 5	- -
SCAT TOTAL	52 100 IN	470	- -	63 6	57 5	- -

NAME LEVINS ANN D — SPECIAL CODES 187453494

Test	RAW SCORE/ MAXIMUM POSSIBLE/ LEVEL TAKEN	STANDARD SCORE	GRADE LEVEL INDICATOR	NATIONAL -ILE/ STANINE	LOCAL -ILE/ STANINE	OPT
Reading	40 50 I	488	9 5	99 9	99 9	99
Vocabulary	25 28 I	471	9 9	99 9	98 9	97
Writing Skills	52 58 I	474	9 1	95 8	97 9	92
Math Computation	53 55 H	482	8 5	86 7	97 9	80
Basic Concepts	46 50 H	461	8 5	83 7	91 8	75
Study Skills	28 30 H	467	- -	93 8	96 9	- -
Listening	18 20 H	485	- -	99 9	97 9	- -
Social Studies	48 50 H	466	- -	92 8	96 9	- -
Science / Biological Science / Earth Science / Physical Science	49 50 FH	466	- -	96 9	99 9	- -
SCAT Verbal	38 50 IN	481	- -	94 8	91 8	- -
SCAT Quantitative	38 50 IN	498	- -	95 8	97 9	- -
SCAT TOTAL	76 100 IN	488	- -	96 9	95 8	- -

SUMMARY DATA

Test	N	MEAN SS	SD	MEDIAN SS	GLI OF MEAN SS	NPR OF MEAN SS	OPT -ILE OF MEAN SS	STANDARD ERROR OF MEASUREMENT
Reading	25	461 9	13 6	461 0	6 5	52	40	4 7
Vocabulary	25	447 8	11 5	447 3	6 5	47	30	4 2
Writing Skills	25	446 3	13 5	444 3	6 1	40	20	4 8
Math Computation	25	458 2	15 6	460 0	6 1	45	22	4 4
Basic Concepts	,25	442 1	11 8	446 8	6 1	38	18	4 8
Study Skills	25	448 4	12 0	451 0	- -	50	- -	4 3
Listening	25	462 4	14 2	464 0	- -	51	- -	3 9
Social Studies	25	442 6	12 6	441 8	- -	37	- -	4 8
Science / Biological Science / Earth Science / Physical Science	25	443 3	10 9	440 8	- -	44	- -	4 5
SCAT Verbal	25	461 0	13 3	461 4	- -	53	- -	5 2
SCAT Quantitative	25	469 5	15 8	470 0	- -	44	- -	6 0
SCAT TOTAL	25	464 1	12 6	465 0	- -	49	- -	3 5

NUMBER OF YOUR STUDENTS IN EACH NATIONAL STANINE

Test	1	2	3	4	5	6	7	8	9
Reading	0	1	4	4	7	4	0	2	3
Vocabulary	0	0	5	5	6	4	3	1	1
Writing Skills	0	2	5	6	4	3	4	1	0
Math Computation	1	1	9	6	2	2	4	0	0
Basic Concepts	1	4	3	4	7	4	1	0	1
Study Skills	1	1	4	2	5	8	3	1	0
Listening	1	1	2	7	3	5	4	2	0
Social Studies	0	2	6	7	4	2	1	3	0
Science / Biological Science / Earth Science / Physical Science	0	2	3	9	3	5	2	0	1
SCAT Verbal	0	2	2	3	7	6	2	2	1
SCAT Quantitative	1	0	5	5	7	3	2	1	1
SCAT TOTAL	0	1	5	3	6	E	2	1	1

Figure 8.1 Example of an individual student report from the Sequential Tests of Educational Progress. (Reproduced by permission from the *Sequential Tests of Educational Progress*, p. 11. Copyright © by the Educational Testing Service. Used by permission of CTB/McGraw-Hill, 2500 Garden Road, Monterey, Calif.

(reading, vocabulary, writing skills, mathematics computation and mathematics basic concepts) are highly internally consistent; values of KR-20 are generally in the 0.90s, although a few values are in the 0.80s. The reliabilities of the additional tests are in the 0.90s for the study skills test, in the high 0.80s and low 0.90s for the social studies and science tests, and in the 0.70s and 0.80s for the listening test. Most alternate-forms reliability coefficients for Forms X and Y are in the 0.80s, although a few are in the high 0.70s or in the low 0.90s. Test-retest stability coefficients are generally in the 0.60s to the 0.80s, with the majority falling in the 0.70s.

As with other well-constructed achievement tests, care and thoroughness in test construction procedures are intended to ensure content validity. Also similar to other major achievement batteries, evidence for other types of validity is somewhat weak. As evidence of construct validity, the correspondence of test intercorrelations to the pattern of correlations that would be expected given our understanding of the constructs is provided. In general, the different skills measured are quite highly correlated with each other. Thus, although there is evidence for the reliability and content validity of the STEP-III, more evidence regarding criterion-related and construct validity is needed.

The Stanford Achievement Series

The Stanford Achievement Series, published by the Psychological Corporation along with the Otis-Lennon School Ability Tests and the Metropolitan Achievement Tests, was revised and restandardized in 1981 in preparation for initial use in the 1982/1983 school year. New norms were collected in 1986, so although the test series revision carries a 1982 publication date, both 1982 and 1986 norms are available to test users.

The Stanford Achievement Series consists of three related test batteries covering grades K–12. The Stanford Early School Achievement Tests: Second Edition (SESAT) are used to assess achievement in kindergarten and first grades. The Stanford Achievement Test: Seventh Edition (Gardner, Rudman, Karlsen, & Merwin, 1982) is designed for use in grades 1–9. The Stanford Test of Academic Skills: Second Edition (TASK) is designed for use with students in grades 8–13 (13 being the first year of college).

The best-known of these tests, the Stanford Achievement Test, is used to assess achievement in the following basic educational areas: word-study skills (similar to the listening or oral vocabulary tests included in other batteries), reading comprehension, vocabulary, listening comprehension, spelling, language, concepts of number, mathematics computation, mathematics applications, social science, and science. Total scores for reading, listening, language, and mathematics are also provided.

Figure 8.2 shows a score report for the Stanford Achievement Test and the Otis-Lennon School Ability Tests. The report includes raw and scaled scores, national percentiles and stanines (PR-S), grade equivalent scores, and achievement-ability comparisons. Percentile bands are profiled on the right side of the report. The lower portion of the report shows the criterion-referenced analysis; raw score (number correct) as a proportion of number of items and an indication of whether this proportion is below average, average, or above average are provided.

Like other major achievement batteries, the Stanford Achievement is highly reliable and has been carefully constructed to reflect important emphases of the school curriculum. And like other batteries, more evidence for criterion-related and construct validity is needed.

Stanford ACHIEVEMENT TEST WITH OTIS-LENNON SCHOOL ABILITY TEST

SKILLS ANALYSIS FOR CHARLES A BALLARD

TEACHER MS WELLENS
SCHOOL LAKESIDE ELEMENTARY
SYSTEM NEWTOWN PUBLIC SCHOOLS

GRADE 4   TEST DATE 10/12/82   COPY 1
STANFORD NORMS GR 4.1   LEVEL PRIM 3   FORM E
OLSAT NORMS   GR 4 FALL   LEVEL ELEM   FORM S

TESTS / NUMBER OF ITEMS	RAW SCORE	SCALE SCORE	NAT'L PR-S	GRADE EQUIV	ACHIEVMNT ABILITY COMPARISN
WORD STUDY SKILLS 54	35	142	50- 5	4.1	LOW
READING COMPREHENSION 60	49	143	50- 5	4.0	LOW
VOCABULARY 38	29	148	52- 5	4.3	LOW
LISTENING COMPREHENSION 40	31	139	44- 5	3.9	LOW
SPELLING 36	18	143	40- 5	3.8	LOW
LANGUAGE 46	37	148	60- 6	4.6	MIDDLE
CONCEPTS OF NUMBER 34	14	137	32- 4	3.5	LOW
MATH COMPUTATION 42	20	145	50- 5	3.9	MIDDLE
MATH APPLICATIONS 38	19	145	50- 5	4.0	LOW
SOCIAL SCIENCE 44	37	161	82- 7	5.5	MIDDLE
SCIENCE 44	19	130	34- 4	3.3	LOW
TOTAL READING 114	84	143	50- 5	4.0	LOW
TOTAL LISTENING 78	60	144	48- 5	4.1	LOW
TOTAL LANGUAGE 82	55	146	52- 5	4.2	LOW
TOTAL MATHEMATICS 114	53	143	44- 5	3.8	LOW

NATIONAL PERCENTILE BANDS
1 5 10 20 30 40 50 60 70 80 90 95 99

OTIS-LENNON SCHOOL ABILITY TEST				
	AGE	PR-S	84-7	RS = 51 SAI = 116
	GRADE	PR-S	82-7	

AGE 9 YRS. 1 MO.

READING SKILLS GROUP—DEVELOPMENTAL

CONTENT CLUSTERS / RAW SCORE/NUMBER OF ITEMS		BELOW AVERAGE	AVERAGE	ABOVE AVERAGE
WORD STUDY SKILLS	35/54		\	
Phonetic Analysis, Consonants	16/18			\
Phonetic Analysis, Vowels	12/18		\	
Word Division	7/18	\		
READING COMPREHENSION	49/60		\	
Textual	15/20		\	
Functional	17/20			\
Recreational	17/20		\	
Literal Comprehension	28/30			\
Inferential Comprehension	21/30		\	
VOCABULARY	29/38		\	
LISTENING COMPREHENSION	31/40		\	
Retention	17/20		\	
Organization	14/20		\	
SPELLING	18/36		\	
Sight Words	6/ 8		\	
Phonetic Principles	4/16	\		
Structural Principles	8/12		\	
LANGUAGE	37/46			\
Punctuation	8/ 9			\
Capitalization	5/ 5			\
Applied Grammar	9/12		\	
Language Sensitivity	7/10		\	
Reference Skills	8/10			\
CONCEPTS OF NUMBER	14/34	\		
Whole Numbers & Dec. Place Value	8/18		\	
Rational Numbers	1/ 5			
Operations & Properties	5/11		\	

CONTENT CLUSTERS / RAW SCORE/NUMBER OF ITEMS		BELOW AVERAGE	AVERAGE	ABOVE AVERAGE
MATHEMATICS COMPUTATION	20/42		\	
Addition with Whole Numbers	9/12		\	
Subtraction with Whole Numbers	8/ 9			\
Multiplication with Whole Numbers	2/12	\		
Division with Whole Numbers	1/ 9	\		
MATHEMATICS APPLICATIONS	19/38		\	
Problem Solving	9/18		\	
Graphs	5/ 6			\
Geometry	1/ 5	\		
Measurement	4/ 9		\	
SOCIAL SCIENCE	37/44			\
Geography	6/ 6			\
History	2/ 4			\
Anthropology	5/ 7			\
Sociology	5/ 6			\
Political Science	3/ 4			\
Economics	8/ 8			\
Inquiry Skills	8/ 9			\
SCIENCE	19/44		\	
Physical Science	4/11	\		
Biological Science	9/20			\
Inquiry Skills	6/13		\	

See back for aids for interpretation.

DATA SERVICES DIVISION   THE PSYCHOLOGICAL CORPORATION
HARCOURT BRACE JOVANOVICH, PUBLISHERS

Figure 8.2 Example of a score report for the Stanford Achievement Test. (Reproduced by permission from the *Score Report for the Stanford Achievement Test, 7th Edition.* Copyright © 1982 by the Psychological Corporation. Reproduced by permission of the publisher, Harcourt Brace Jovanovich, Inc. All Rights Reserved.)

EDUCATIONAL ACHIEVEMENT TESTS: HIGH SCHOOL LEVEL

Although most of the test batteries discussed in the previous section included levels appropriate for use in grades 9 through 12, the high school years, there are several additional achievement batteries designed specifically for use in the high schools. Generally these batteries are accompanied by interpretive information designed to help the ninth through twelfth grade student in immediate educational planning and also in post-high-school educational/vocational planning. Thus, the focus of such testing is more likely to emphasize educational/vocational planning than is true at the lower grade levels.

The Iowa Tests of Educational Development

Of the tests designed for use at the high school level, probably the most academically oriented are the Iowa Tests of Educational Development (ITED). The ITED were developed by E. F. Lindquist and L. S. Feldt at the University of Iowa and were first published in 1942. The current versions of the test, Forms X-8 and Y-8, are published by The Riverside Publishing Company.

The ITED is designed to measure "skills that are important in adolescent and adult life, abilities that constitute a major part of the foundation for continued learning. These skills include understanding the meaning of a wide variety of words, recognizing the essentials of correct and effective writing, solving quantitative problems, critically analyzing discussions of social issues, understanding nontechnical scientific reports and recognizing sound methods of scientific inquiry, perceiving the moods and nonliteral meanings of literary materials, and using a variety of sources of information." (Feldt, Forsyth, & Alnot, 1988, p. 02).

Social Studies

Advertisement
Four out of five doctors surveyed favored

BALM SOAP

Tests show that Balm Soap clears up complexion problems faster than any other product!

On the basis of this advertisement, which of the following conclusions, if any, is valid?

A It has been scientifically demonstrated that the quickest way to get rid of any complexion problem is to use Balm Soap.

B Of the five leading brands of complexion soaps, only one is better than Balm Soap from a medical point of view.

C Of all the doctors who recommended skin care products, four out of five recommended Balm Soap.

D None of theses conclusions is valid.

Natural Sciences

Soon after being bitten by a mosquito, a person became ill with yellow fever. Which conclusion, if any, is justified solely from these observations?

A There is insufficient evidence to draw any of the conclusions that follow.

B Mosquitoes are the direct cause of yellow fever.

C The mosquito introduced a microorganism into the person's bloodstream.

D The mosquito carried an organism that caused yellow fever.

Figure 8.3. Sample items from the Social Studies and Natural Sciences Subtests of the Iowa Tests of Educational Development (ITED). Taken from the *Teacher, Administrator, and Counselor Manual: Iowa Tests of Educational Development*, Forms X-8 and Y-8. Copyright © 1988 by the University of Iowa. Reproduced by permission of the publisher, Riverside Publishing Co., 8420 Bryn Mawr Avenue, Chicago, Ill.

In order to assess the abilities, the battery contains seven subtests: (1) Correctness and Appropriateness of Expression, which contains items related to grammar, punctuation and capitalization, sentence structure, organization of writing, and diction (Part I) and spelling (Part II); (2) Quanti-

Test L: Literary Materials

1 Loveliest of trees, the cherry now
2 Is hung with bloom along the bough,
3 And stands about the woodland ride
4 Wearing white for Eastertide.

5 Now, of my threescore years and ten,
6 Twenty will not come again,
7 And take from seventy springs a score,
8 It only leaves me fifty more

9 And since to look at things in bloom
10 Fifty springs are little room,
11 About the woodlands I will go
12 To see the cherry hung with snow.

What feeling does the poet express in this passage?
A   Delight in beauty
B   Religious faith
C   Fear of death
D   Enjoyment of old age

Which of these words is used as a descriptive figure of speech rather than in its usual meaning?
A   "bloom" (line 2)
B   "twenty" (line 6)
C   "woodlands" (line 11)
D   "snow" (line 12)

The poet apparently feels that
A   he will die while still a young man.
B   his life may last many years but still seem short.
C   his life has passed too quickly.
D   his life will end soon.

Test SI: Use of Sources of Information

For a paper on safety measures in the home, you need some recent statistics on accidental deaths. The best source for such data would be
A   *The World Almanac.*
B   *Encyclopedia Americana.*
C   *U.S. News & World Report.*
D   publications of the Bureau of the Census.

Where could you expect to find a brief summary of the achievements of a famous scientist who lives in your hometown?
A   *Who's Who in America*
B   *Scientific American*
C   *Science Digest*
D   *Information Please Almanac*

If you wanted to find a word to describe an attractive individual while avoiding overworked words, it would be best to consult
A   a thesaurus.
B   a grammar handbook.
C   an abridged dictionary.
D   a dictionary of slang.

Figure 8.4. Sample items from the Literary Materials and Use of Sources of Information Subtests of the ITED. Reprinted from the *Teacher, Administrator, and Counselor Manual for the Iowa Tests of Educational Development, Forms X-8 and Y-8.* Copyright © 1988 by the University of Iowa. Reproduced by permission of the publisher, Riverside Publishing Co., 8420 Bryn Mawr Avenue, Chicago, Ill.

tative Thinking; (3) Social Studies: Concepts and Background (Part I) and Social Studies Reading (Part II); (4) Natural Sciences: Concepts and Background (Part I) and Natural Sciences Reading (Part II); (5) Literary Materials; (6) Vocabulary; and (7) Use of Sources of Information. Examples of items from the Social Studies and Natural Sciences subtests are shown in Figure 8.3, and examples from the Literary Materials and Use of Sources of Information subtests are shown in Figure 8.4.

The ITED were restandardized in 1984 in samples of approximately 3,750 students each in grades 9–12. The scores provided include standard scores for each of the seven tests, a composite score over all seven tests, and a reading total score. The standard scores have a mean of 15, a standard deviation of 5, and a range of 0 to 30. In addition to the standard scores, percentile ranks are also reported. The composite score is derived by converting the total raw score across the seven tests to a standard score having the same mean and standard deviation as the subtest scores. The reading score is the summary of the student's performance on all exercises that require analysis of reading material (i.e., Social Studies Reading, Natural Sciences Reading, and Literary Materials). The report to the student describes each of the tests and provides a profile sheet by which scores on the various subtests may be plotted.

Figure 8.5 shows a sample score report for Student A on the ITED. This profile form is very convenient in that it provides both a global view of performance with standard scores, percentiles, and profile plotting for the seven subtests (E through SI) and the Composite (C) and Reading Total (RT), and also a breakdown of performance scores in the skill areas *within* each subtest area. Thus, the test can be used to differentiate skill areas needing additional work from those in which the student is relatively competent. Notice that Student A is generally weak in Quantitative Thinking (Test Q) but particularly weak in the Exponents skill area, in comparison to the relevant norm group.

The ITED are highly reliable. The KR-20 coefficients are 0.97 for the Composite Score, 0.95 to 0.96 for the Reading Total, and 0.86 to 0.93 for the subtest. Correlations with earlier versions of the test (the Seventh Edition) range from 0.76 (Literary Materials) to 0.92 (Composite). Validity data provided come from studies of both the Seventh and the Eighth editions of the ITED. For example, correlations of the ITED composite score (Seventh Edition) with high school GPA range from 0.66 to 0.74 and with freshman (college GPA) from 0.42 to 0.46. The ITED scores are highly correlated with other measures of scholastic aptitude (0.70 to 0.85 with SAT scores and 0.82 to 0.84 with ACT Composite) and achievement (e.g., 0.92 with the ITBS Composite score taken in the eighth grade). The ITED subtests are highly intercorrelated (0.60s to 0.80s), which Kifer (1985) attributed to the heavy emphasis on reading throughout the test. More evidence for the construct and criterion-related validity and test-retest stability of the Eighth Edition of the ITED is needed.

Because the ITED are so academically oriented, they are generally most useful in educational planning—for example, in making decisions about high school curricula and college entrance—rather than in vocational planning. In addition to the information provided by national high school norms and by the student's profile of educational strengths and weaknesses, ITED composite score norms for special subgroups, such as college-bound students, and tables relating ITED scores to probable grades in college can be provided. A table providing predictions of ACT Composite Scores from ITED Composite Scores is also provided in the *Teacher, Administrator, and Counselor Manual* for Forms X-8 and Y-8 (Feldt, Forsyth, & Alnot, 1988). Thus, the ITED may be used in ways similar to the uses of traditional scholastic aptitude tests, as described in Chapter 7.

The Tests of Achievement and Proficiency

The Tests of Achievement and Proficiency (TAP), like the companion battery, the Iowa Tests of Basic Skills for grades K–8, are designed to measure the basic educational skills important for effective functioning in society. The TAP, designed for use in grades 9–12, cover the relatively advanced levels of educational development associated with high school. The tests assess achievement in reading comprehension, written expression, mathematics, using sources of information, social studies, and science.

The TAP, Form G, were restandardized along with the ITBS and CogAT in the fall of 1984 and the spring of 1985 in a sample consisting of about 14,000 students per grade. Scores provided for the TAP include standard scores, national grade percentiles and stanines, grade equivalents, and normal curve equivalents. As with ITBS, CAT

Figure 4.10*

IOWA TESTS OF EDUCATIONAL DEVELOPMENT

INDIVIDUAL PROFILE—Student A

SERVICE 7

Order No.:

Building: HILLSDALE
Test Date: 9/29/87
Test Level: 01
Test Form: X8
Grade: 9
Norm Group: NATIONAL
Norms: FALL

	E		Q		SS		NS		L		V		SI		C		RT	
	SS	PR	SS	PR	SS	PR	SS	PR	SS	PR	SS	PR	SS	PR	SS	PR	SS	PR
	22	97	8	14	13	55	16	65	12	44	18	75	9	17	14	53	10	29

SKILL AREAS	Number of Items	Number Attempted	Percent Correct	Norm Average % Correct
Correctness & Appropriateness of Expression (TEST E)	69	69	83	58
Capitalization/Punctuation	10	10	80	60
Grammar	12	12	75	58
Sentence Structure	13	13	78	62
Organization	7	7	86	71
Diction/Clarity/Word Choice	12	12	83	50
Spelling	15	15	93	53
Literary Materials (TEST L)	46	46	52	54
Literal Comprehension	6	6	67	50
Interpretation of Nonliteral Forms	7	7	43	58
Inferences and Relationships	16	16	50	56
Generalizations	5	5	40	41
Literary Techniques/Tone	12	12	58	57
Sources of Information (TEST SI)	46	46	46	63
Books	6	6	50	67
Dictionaries	5	5	40	60
Organization of Library Materials	5	5	60	59
Encyclopedias/Almanacs	5	5	40	61
Common References	7	7	29	58
Readers' Guide	7	7	29	71
Maps/Atlases	6	6	67	67
Govt. & Private Agencies	5	5	60	61
Vocabulary (TEST V)	40	40	62	48

SKILL AREAS	Number of Items	Number Attempted	Percent Correct	Norm Average % Correct
Quantitative Thinking (TEST Q)	40	40	30	52
Whole Numbers/Fractions/Decimals	10	10	30	50
Percent	7	7	14	57
Geometry/Measurement	5	5	40	60
Estimation/Rounding	4	4	50	60
Probability/Statistics	4	4	25	50
Exponents	3	3	0	33
Graphs/Tables/Formulas	7	7	43	57
Science (TEST NS)	60	60	55	51
Principles of Inquiry/Measurement	3	3	67	67
Interpretation of Information	11	11	45	55
Inferences and Predictions	9	9	56	44
Classification of Ideas	7	7	43	57
Analysis of Experimental Procedures	20	20	60	50
Evaluation of Evidence	5	5	60	40
Generalization and Extension of Ideas	5	5	60	40
Social Studies (TEST SS)	60	60	50	48
Literal Comprehension	9	9	44	45
Interpretation of Information	13	13	46	54
Inferences and Relationships	7	7	57	56
Classification of Ideas	5	5	40	59
Evaluation of Sources, Evidence, and Conclusions	18	18	56	45
Author's Position and Techniques	8	8	50	38

* The normative data used in this illustration are for illustrative purposes only.

Figure 8.5. Individual score profile from the Iowa Tests of Educational Development, Forms X-8 and Y-8. Taken from the *Teacher, Administrator, and Counselor Manual for the ITED*, Forms X-8 and Y-8. Copyright © 1988 by the University of Iowa. Reproduced by permission of the publisher, Riverside Publishing Company.

ability level norms are available, as are percentile equivalent scores and stanines.

In addition to these already familiar types of scores, the TAP provides two special types of scores designed to indicate the degree to which a high school student has attained sufficient competency to function in the adult world. The first score, known as the Minimum Competency score, indicates whether or not the student has attained at least an eighth grade education, defined as achievement at the median level for eighth grade students. The TAP score reports can indicate "yes," "no," or "may" in reference to competency in reading and mathematics skills. A minimum competency score of "yes" indicates that the student's score exceeds that of the median eighth grader, and a "no" indicates that it does not. A "may" indicates that this level may be reached if the student makes average progress from his or her current grade through grade 12. A second type of competency is the Applied Proficiency Skills score. This score reflects performance on a subset of TAP items particularly relevant to everyday tasks and situations rather than to academically relevant skills. Scores on this scale are indicative of the student's ability to function adequately in everyday adult life.

Like the ITBS, the TAP results can include a Profile Narrative Report and/or a Criterion-Referenced Skills Analysis Report. Also like the ITED, the TAP are highly reliable. The 1986 *Preliminary Technical Summary* of the ITBS, TAP, and CogAT indicated subtest reliabilities of 0.87 to 0.94 for the subtests among tenth to twelfth grades, although values were somewhat lower among ninth graders. The reliability of the Battery Composite was 0.98. Subtest scores are relatively highly intercorrelated, with most values in the 0.60s and 0.70s. Most available validity data are from previous versions of the TAP. These data indicated high correlations of the TAP with ITBS scores (0.70s

and 0.80s), the CogAT (0.60s and 0.70s), high school grades (0.34 to 0.55), and college grades (0.31 to 0.45). More validity data are needed for the TAP Form G, especially for uses of the Minimum Competency and Applied Proficiency scores (Keene, 1985; Wardrop, 1985).

Overall, the TAP are an excellent battery for measuring achievement in high school, although users should be sure that their focus on basic educational skills is appropriate for the intended uses of the tests.

The Tests of General Educational Development

The remaining achievement battery to be discussed in this section, although designed to assess achievement at the high school level, is quite different in *purpose* from the multilevel achievement batteries discussed previously. Although they assess achievement at the high school level, the Tests of General Educational Development (GED) are generally used with *adults* who wish to demonstrate high school equivalency. In other words, the objective of the GED is to allow adults who did not graduate from high school to attempt to demonstrate that they have in other ways obtained the level of knowledge signified by a high school diploma. Many individuals who did not graduate from high school wish later on in their lives to demonstrate that their experiences since leaving high school have enhanced their educational attainments to the level of high school equivalency. Successful performance on the GED allows such individuals to qualify for jobs and/or promotions requiring the possession of a high school diploma and to enter institutions of higher education and work toward college degrees. For others, eventual completion of their high school diploma represents an important personal goal. Thus, the GED provides individuals with the opportunity to demonstrate their level of achievement in, and mastery of, the educational curriculum through the high school level in order to further their educational, occupational, and personal objectives. To illustrate the large numbers of people served by this program, in 1982, a typical year, 800,000 people were administered the GED and more than a half million scored well enough to earn high school equivalency diplomas.

The GED are multiple-choice examinations in each of five educational areas: writing skills, social studies, science, reading skills, and mathematics. The tests, which emphasize broad concepts and generalizations rather than specific facts and details, are intended to assess the important areas of educational competency and knowledge that result from high school education in the United States. The Writing Skills test assesses competency in spelling, punctuation and capitalization, grammar, and sentence organization and logic. The Social Studies test contains materials in the areas of United States history, economics, political science, geography, and behavioral science. Included in the Science test are materials from biology, chemistry, physics, and earth science. The Reading Skills test includes passages from literature, poetry, and drama, as well as popular books, newspapers, and magazines. The Mathematics test assesses achievement in arithmetic, algebra, and geometry.

The GED were first developed in 1942 and were most recently revised in 1978 and restandardized in 1980. The new version was standardized using 3,600 twelfth grade students about to graduate from high school and, to ensure the appropriateness of the tests for individuals of all ages, an additional 300 adult GED candidates. The 1980 norming also included students in grades 9 through 11, because the compulsory age for school attendance has been lowered in some states. The performance of the twelfth grade standardization sample is used in the estab-lishment of minimum scores considered acceptable for the award of a certificate of high school equivalency. Minimum required scores differ somewhat in different states: The test manual contains the minimum acceptable GED scores for the award of high school equivalency in each of the 50 states, the United States territories, and the Canadian provinces. The most commonly used minimum cutoff scores are a minimum of 35 on each of the five tests and a minimum mean score of 45 across the five tests. Requiring both minimums requires that poor performance on one test—for example, the minimum score of 35—would need to be compensated for by strong performance on another in order to obtain an overall mean of 45.

The tests are highly reliable; reliabilities of all but one of the five tests are above 0.90. A useful part of the materials provided to potential GED candidates is two practice tests (Forms A and B) designed to help candidates evaluate their readiness for the official testing. Each practice test contains one-half the number of items contained in the full-length test and is similar to it in both form and content. The practice tests are self-scoring, and tables are provided that allow the individual to estimate one's full test score from the practice test score.

In summary, the GED assesses the extent to which the individual has mastered the competencies and the knowledge base of the secondary school curriculum. Because states, many employers, and most colleges and universities accept a GED certificate in lieu of formal high school graduation, the GED provide an excellent opportunity for individuals who wish to enhance their educational and vocational opportunites and meet personal and career goals.

Other Tests of Basic Skills

In addition to the GED, there are other tests that assess functional literacy, numeracy, and other skills thought to characterize the minimum competence levels attained through United States secondary education.

The Basic Skills Assessment, published by ETS and designed for use in grades 7 through 12, assesses basic skills in reading, writing, and mathematics. The Adult Basic Learning Examination (ABLE) is published by the Psychological Corporation and assesses skills in vocabulary, reading, comprehension, spelling, language, number operations, and problem solving.

The ABLE is designed for use with adults and has three different levels: Level 1 for adults who have had from one to four years of formal education, Level 2 (five to eight years), and Level 3 (eight or more years). The items are oriented toward practical coping skills, those necessary in everyday life.

SPECIAL-PURPOSE ACHIEVEMENT TESTS USED AT THE COLLEGE LEVEL AND BEYOND

A number of achievement tests are used for important applied purposes at the college level and after. These special tests will, for purposes of convenience here, be discussed in terms of two general categories of test: advanced academic achievement tests and tests used to evaluate professional competency.

Advanced achievement tests are those evaluating knowledge of advanced subject matter, generally knowledge at a more advanced and more specific level than was true of the tests of basic educational skills used at the elementary and secondary school level. Of course examinations in college and post college coursework assess specialized achievement, but the tests described here are carefully standardized and used nationally for specific purposes. The test batteries to be discussed under this category include the College-Level Examination Program, one of

two programs by which students can demonstrate college-level achievement worthy of college credit or exemption from college courses, and the GRE Subject (Advanced) Tests, used in admissions, financial aids, and fellowship decisions for students applying to graduate programs.

The second category of tests described here includes tests used for evaluating professional competency—for example, in teaching, law, and psychology. The National Teacher Examination will be discussed as an example of tests in this category.

The College-Level Examination Program

The College-Level Examination Program (CLEP) is one of the two major programs by which individuals can earn college credit by examination rather than by actually enrolling in the courses. (The other major program is the ACT Proficiency Examination Program, administered by the American College Testing Program.) Established by the College Entrance Examination Board (CEEB) with financial support from the Carnegie Corporation of New York, the CLEP program was formed to provide recognition for learning experiences occurring outside the college classroom. Originally aimed toward the nontraditional student, that is, the veteran or older student, CLEP now serves both traditional and nontraditional students who wish to obtain college credit for knowledge gained in other ways.

The CLEP program consists of two major types of achievement tests, the General Examinations and the Subject Examinations. The five General Examinations measure college-level achievement in five basic areas of the liberal arts: English composition, humanities, social science, natural science, and mathematics. Each exam is 90 minutes long and is intended to cover material that would be taught during the first two years of college. Students taking the General Examinations are generally attempting to obtain credit for courses that would meet the school's "basic," "general," or "liberal arts" requirements, for example, those in the humanities or sciences.

The Subject Examinations assess achievement in specific college courses and are used to grant either credit for, or exemption from taking these specific courses. Each of the subject exams is 90 minutes in length, and most of the exams include an optional 90-minute essay section. Although subject exams could theoretically cover any college courses, the CLEP subject exams cover those that are relatively widely taught. Sample courses for which CLEP subject exams are available include introduction to business management, introductory accounting, English literature, statistics, general psychology, college Spanish, and introductory sociology.

The CLEP examinations, both General and Subject, are developed by faculty committees working with test specialists at the Educational Testing Service. In other words, both the specification of content to be covered and the writing of items to cover that content are done by college and university faculty members who teach courses relevant to the content area of the specific examination. Preliminary versions of the tests constructed are tried out in samples of college students and, based on these results, the final versions of the tests are compiled. Finally, the tests are administered to "reference" groups of college and university students.

Although used for the same purpose as the more generally used "normative" or "standardization" groups, the CLEP "reference" groups are somewhat different in that they are composed of different groups of college students for each examination. They are not necessarily representative of the American college population because they are obtained from the voluntary participation of colleges and universities. For the General Examinations, the most recent reference data were collected in 1978; reference group sizes ranged from 2,290 for the English composition General Examination to 757 for the humanities General Examination. Reference group data for the General Examinations are collected by testing students who were completing college courses that would fulfill distribution requirements in the curriculum areas in which they were tested. For example, the humanities test was administered to students completing courses in literature, art, or music.

Reference groups for the Subject Examinations are composed of students who are completing a college course in the area of the examination. For example, the reference group for the examination in introductory accounting was constituted by students completing college courses in that area. The year in which reference group data were collected and the size and nature of the sample differ for every Subject Examination; sample sizes do vary widely in size, including representative Ns of 321 for second year German, 793 for Afro-American history, and 3,106 for general chemistry.

Scores on the CLEP examinations are reported as standard scores with a mean of 500, a standard deviation of 100, and a range of 200 to 800. (Although CLEP General Examination scores use the same standard score scale as do GRE and SAT scores, they are *not* comparable scores and should not be interpreted as such.) Scores on the CLEP Subject Examinations are standard scores ranging from 20 to 80, with a mean of 50 and a standard deviation of 10. Percentile data based on the performance of each relevant reference group are provided along with the standard scores (College Entrance Examination Board, 1981a).

In addition to providing standard scores and percentile equivalent scores, the CLEP user's guide (College Entrance Examination Board, 1981b) provides a variety of information and suggestions concerning ways in which CLEP tests may be used in the granting of college credit. For example, the manual summarizes the policies of universities regarding the minimum levels of CLEP exam performance required for the award of college credit and also provides the recommendations of the American Council on Education's Commission on Educational Credit and Credentials. Recommendations for the use of specific exams are often provided by the relevant professional organizations, such as the American Dental Association for the exams in dental hygiene and the Mathematical Association of America for the exams in mathematics. It should be noted, however, that although the CLEP exams are constructed, administered, and *scored* under the auspices of the College Entrance Examination Board, specific policies concerning the use of the tests and the establishment of minimum scores for the award of credit are determined separately by each college or university using the CLEP program. Also, although anyone can take CLEP exams, not all colleges and universities honor CLEP scores or agree with the general notion of college credit by examination. Materials provided by the publisher list those colleges and universities using the resources of the CLEP program (College Entrance Examination Board, 1981a).

The CLEP tests are, in general, highly reliable. The Kuder-Richardson-20 coefficients for the General Examinations range from 0.91 (mathematics) to 0.96 (humanities). The reliabilities of the Subject Examinations vary somewhat more, with values of KR-20 in the mid-80s to mid-90s for most exams but as low as 0.74 or 0.75 for exams in the dental hygiene and nursing areas. The careful construction of the CLEP tests by faculty members who actually teach the relevant college courses provides good evidence for content validity of the CLEP tests. The publishers strongly urge potential users to carefully *examine* the content of a test to ensure its appropriateness to the course emphases on their particular college campus; in other words, users are asked to make their own judgments concerning the content validity of the tests for *their* unique needs.

Some evidence for the concurrent validity of the Subject Examinations is provided by correlations of CLEP scores with final grades in the appropriate courses; these values range from 0.34 (medical-surgical Nursing) to 0.67 (introductory business law). Most values of r are in the 0.40s and 0.50s. No concurrent validity data are provided, however, for the General Examination. Further evidence of the criterion-related validity of CLEP scores would be helpful but, as is true with most achievement tests, the emphasis has been on ensuring the content validity of CLEP through careful test construction procedures.

In addition to the use of the CLEP exams to grant exemption from, or credit for, college courses, there are two other major ways in which CLEP scores are used. One of these uses has been to allow individuals to establish the equivalent of a college education for qualification for positions in business, industry, and government or in meeting the licensing requirements for certain professions, such as teaching. Four states have "external" college degree programs that enable people to actually *earn* college degrees by passing examinations such as those provided by the CLEP program. Note that the CLEP tests, when used to support "college equivalency," are similar in purpose to the GED for establishing high school equivalency. Tests like the CLEP and the GED, then, are based on the philosophy that the educational objectives of formal schooling may be met in ways other than formal attendance at classes. Standardized educational achievement tests allow individuals to demonstrate that they have in fact met the desired educational objectives. Thus, such tests make the professional and personal gains associated with higher education available to large numbers of people who would not otherwise be able to obtain a college education.

Finally, while providing opportunities for nontraditional students to earn college credit or even college degrees by examination is a noteworthy objective of programs like CLEP, some would contend that this opportunity has been misused by traditional college-age students to essentially avoid some of the basic liberal arts requirements of most institutions of higher education (see Derrick, 1978). For example, a student may be able to pass the humanities general exam on the basis of knowledge of literature and thereby avoid exposing oneself to the riches of art, music, or drama. The CLEP program should be used carefully and in ways designed to encourage and facilitate learning rather than provide ways to avoid it.

The Graduate Record Examination Subject (Advanced) Tests

Although tests such as the Scholastic Aptitude Test (SAT) and the Graduate Record Examination (GRE) are used primarily in the assessment of scholastic aptitude, optional subject matter achievement tests are also included in these testing programs. Advanced tests used with the SAT may be used in admissions decisions or in awarding some types of financial aid to entering college students, and the GRE advanced tests are used in making admissions and financial aids decisions for students applying to graduate programs.

The Graduate Record Examination (GRE) Subject (Advanced) Tests are available in 20 different academic fields, including psychology, music, physics, education, engineering, French, and philosophy. Examinations are used both in selecting students for graduate work and in awarding fellowships and assistantships.

The GRE advanced tests are developed by committees of faculty members in the relevant academic fields, assisted by Educational Testing Service staff members. These committee members are appointed by the Graduate Record Examination Board, with the advice of the appropriate professional organization in the subject area—for example, the American Psychological Association, the American Society for Engineering Education, and the American Association of Teachers of German. The tests are each 2 hours and 50 minutes in length. The number of questions in the tests varies from 66 in the Advanced Mathematics test to 230 in the Advanced Literature in English test. (Questions in the tests in quantitative areas generally require more time to answer, since preliminary figuring/calculation is required.)

The results of the GRE advanced tests are reported on a scaled-score system in which the mean and standard deviation of the scaled scores is tied to the performance of a normative sample of students tested in 1952. The major important aspect of this system is that, although the theoretical range of scores is from 200 to 990, the actual score range and the mean and standard deviation of scores is *different for each of the advanced tests.* In other words, unlike many test batteries, the GRE advanced tests *do not* use the same standard score scale, and thus a score of 500 on one advanced test doesn't necessarily mean the same thing as does a score of 500 on another advanced test. Although the reasons for different standard score scales are beyond the scope of this book, interpretation of scores on a given advanced test must be based on information provided specifically for that test.

So that test users may most effectively use and interpret the scores, data describing the most recent group of GRE examinees are provided for each test. As of this writing, data describing the performance of all students taking the tests between October 1978 and September 1981 are provided. For the 49,973 students taking the advanced test in psychology, the mean score was 532, with a standard deviation of 98 and a range of 320 to 760. Percentile equivalents corresponding to the standard scores are provided. Thus, a student taking the advanced test in psychology in 1983 could be compared on a relative percentile basis to the reference group of almost 50,000 students tested between 1978 and 1981. Another important source of interpretive information is the cumulative experience of admissions and fellowship officers. In other words, because a score of 500 on the advanced test in psychology has the same meaning from year to year, the meaning of given levels of test performance in terms of graduate school criteria can be better understood with successive years of use of the advanced test scores.

In addition to the advanced test total scores, nine advanced tests also provide two or three subscores; for example, the psychology test has subscores in experimental psychology and social psychology, and the history test has European and American history subscores. Scores are reported on a scale ranging from 200 to 990 and, again, means, standard deviations, and percentile equivalents are provided based on examinees tested between October 1978 and September 1981.

The careful test construction procedures for the GRE advanced tests were accompanied by a requirement for minimum acceptable levels of reliability of 0.90 for total test scores and 0.80 for subtests (subscores). The Kuder-Richardson-20 reliabilities of the advanced tests range from 0.92 to 0.97, and those for subtests range from 0.84 to 0.94. Thus, the GRE advanced tests are highly reliable.

The GRE advanced tests are constructed on the assumption, borne out by

evidence from validity studies, that graduate school performance is related to achievement at the undergraduate level. Thus, the tests focus on the measurement of learning in undergraduate curricula. Tests are designed to cover material that would be encountered by the average college senior majoring in a field. As with other well-constructed achievement tests, the objective of content validity in the GRE advanced tests is met by using first-rate scholars in a particular academic field both to specify the overall objectives and content of the test and to write test items. Continual feedback from subject matter experts and test users helps to ensure the relevance and comprehensiveness of test content.

In terms of criterion-related validity the GRE technical manual (Conrad, Trismen, & Miller, 1977) describes the studies of the validity of each of the 20 advanced tests. Both the number and the results of these studies differ somewhat across academic disciplines, but it is generally the case that a GRE advanced test score is the best single predictor of various criteria of graduate school success, for example, graduate school grades and faculty ratings. (It should be noted that although GRE advanced test scores tend to be effective predictors of success in graduate school, a *combination* of both test scores and college grades provides better prediction than does either predictor alone. Course performance and test performance provide somewhat different information about further educational performance, and both types of information are useful to the process of decision making in applied situations.)

To summarize, the GRE advanced tests are highly reliable and valid measures of college-level achievement in 20 academic disciplines representing common fields of graduate study. Because they assess achievement at, or near the end of, undergraduate education, the GRE advanced tests are the most advanced and specialized of the commonly used achievement test batteries. Beyond this level, the comprehensive examinations of graduate programs and for licensing in the professions (e.g., the bar exam for the practice of law, medical boards, or psychology licensure exams) probably represent the remaining levels in the assessment of educational achievement.

National Teacher Examination Programs

The National Teacher Examination (NTE) Programs are an example of the use of standardized achievement testing to evaluate competence to practice a trade or profession. Competency testing is used to grant certificates or licenses in a range of occupations—for example, law, real estate, psychology, medicine, nursing, and accounting.

The NTE Programs, a widely used example of this type of assessment, are designed to provide objective measures of educational achievement for college seniors completing teacher education programs and for advanced candidates who have received additional training in specific fields. Prior to the 1982/1983 academic year, the NTE consisted of a Common Examination (3 hours, 15 minutes) and 25 Area Examinations (2 hours each). As of 1982/1983, however, the NTE Programs have been revised to consist of two types of test batteries: the core battery (previously called the common examinations), assessing general educational achievement; and 25 subject matter exams called the specialty area tests. The NTE test batteries are administered twice a year at testing centers established by Educational Testing Service.

The core battery of the NTE consists of three two-hour tests, including the test of communication skills, the test of general knowledge, and the test of professional knowledge. The test of communications skills assesses the examinee's ability to comprehend and use the English language and includes separate sections for listening comprehension, reading comprehension, and writing ability; the writing ability subtest includes an essay section. The test of general knowledge includes items in the area of literature and fine arts, mathematics, science, and social studies. The test of professional knowledge assesses achievement in the general field of education, such as principles of teaching and learning, and philosophy of education.

The specialty area tests are tests of achievement in specific educational specialties such as art education, mathematics, music education, reading specialty fields, guidance counseling, and languages such as French, German, and Spanish. Each specialty area test is two hours in length; brochures for the specific tests describe the rationale for, and scope and content of, the test and provide sample test items.

Development of the NTE tests has included the efforts of educators, administrators, and test specialists. The preliminary outline for the test in the current core battery was based on the contributions of 75 teacher-educators and classroom teachers. The elaboration and refinement of the preliminary outline was based on the reactions of 3,000 teachers, principals, representatives of boards of education and parent-teacher associations, and teacher-educators to the initial proposals. A large pool of items generated on the basis of the refined test specifications was pretested in a sample of 42,600 students in 149 institutions of higher education in 47 states. The specialty area tests were standardized on groups varying in size from 121 (German) to about 30,000 (the elementary education specialty exam) (Educational Testing Service, 1981). The scores provided are standard scores representing the weighted combination of subtest scores for the core battery and standard scores for each specialty area test. The score range is about 250 to 990, and percentile equivalent data are provided separately for each exam or subtest.

Both core and specialty sections of the NTE are highly reliable. The content validity of the NTE has received careful attention in that the tests are constructed with the help of a large and varied group of subject matter experts and test consumers. Evidence for the test's predictive validity, however, has been lacking throughout the history of the exam. Since the NTE tests are often used as at least *one* criterion in the selection and/or certification of teachers, evidence of a relationship of test scores to teaching effectiveness should be demonstrated. The small amount of data available regarding this relationship show only small correlations; in seven studies relating the NTE composite scores to first-year teaching evaluations, the median correlations were only $r = 0.11$. The NTE materials offer test users instructions for a do-it-yourself validity study to collect local validity data; but although they are excellent supplements to publisher's evidence regarding the overall validity of the tests, local validity data do not compensate for the failure of the test publisher to provide adequate validity data. Test publishers, not test users, must bear the responsibility for the psychometric adequacy of their tests.

Because of the lack of predictive validity evidence, the Educational Testing Service has made it clear that the NTE tests are measures of academic achievement *only* and should not be used to predict effectiveness in classroom teaching. In other words, the tests of the core battery are designed to assess achievement in general academic areas common to most teacher education programs, and the specialty area tests are designed to assess the candidate's academic preparation in certain specific subject fields such as music, German, mathematics, and elementary education. But because NTE scores have not been shown to predict teaching effectiveness, they should not be used as the sole criterion in decisions regarding the selection or certification of teachers, nor should they be used in decisions concerning the retention, tenure, or salary of teachers already in a school system.

Although there are several inappropriate uses of NTE scores, the NTE tests may be (and are) used as *one* criterion in selection and certification decisions. More recently, the core battery is being used to select candidates for entrance into teacher education programs (usually at the end of the second year of college). In this sense, the NTE tests are being used in the same way scholastic aptitude tests like the MCAT, LSAT, ACT, and SAT are used. Other appropriate uses of the NTE include assisting colleges and universities in reviewing their programs for the education of teachers, counseling prospective teachers, and providing state boards of education information regarding teacher preparation programs within their states. Thus, assuming considerable caution in their use, the NTE tests have found a variety of applied uses.

SUMMARY

This chapter has presented a large number and variety of tests used to assess educational achievement at the elementary, junior high school, high school, and college levels. We ended with coverage of advanced achievement tests and of tests used to evaluate competency to practice a trade or profession.

The present chapter also introduced the concept of criterion referencing as an alternative to norm referencing in interpreting test scores and included several examples of tests that provide both kinds of interpretive information. Depending on the purposes for which assessment data are needed, criterion referencing may provide an alternative or a supplementary approach to test use and interpretation.

More generally, in selecting and using methods of assessing cognitive abilities and achievements, then, it is always important to begin with a clear understanding of the purposes and problems for which the scores are needed. Once these purposes are clearly understood, selection of appropriate and useful methods of assessment from among the large number available should be relatively straightforward. It should be noted, of course, that the tests discussed herein are provided as representative examples of available instruments; additional examples may be found in *Tests in Print: III* as well as in the *Mental Measurements Yearbooks* series.

9

The Assessment of Interests

INTRODUCTION

The assessment of interests was introduced in 1927 when E. K. Strong, Jr., developed the Strong Vocational Interest Blank for Men (SVIB). The SVIB was an empirically based inventory that showed how an individual's likes and dislikes were similar to the likes and dislikes of people employed in a variety of different occupations. More than 60 years later, evidence (see Table 1.4) indicates that the Strong inventory is the fifth most frequently researched assessment instrument, accounting for some 1,720 papers and empirical studies. Brown and McGuire (1976), in their survey of assessment instruments, found the Strong inventory to be the eighteenth most frequently used assessment in-

ventory. There is no question that E. K. Strong's work has had a profound impact on interest measurement since the year 1927. The most recent fourth edition of the SVIB was published in 1985 and is called the Strong Vocational Interest Blank/Strong-Campbell Interest Inventory.

In the early years of assessment Strong (1927) thought that interests were tied to abilities. Strong theorized that people participated in activities because of their abilities; if in fact their performance was successful, they grew to like the activity. The liking of the successful performance Strong viewed as an interest. Thus, Strong thought that interests were on a liking-to-disliking dimension. This liking-disliking continuum in time became the basic format for the initial Strong Vocational Interest Blank. However, to this very day the evidence tends not to support the relationship between abilities and interests. Therefore the links among ability, activity, success, liking, and interest have not been validated. Or, stated differently, it is possible that an individual may have likes and dislikes very similar to those of medical doctors, but not have the ability to complete medical school to become a member of the medical profession.

A second milestone in the area of interest measurement was the work of G. F. Kuder. In 1934 Kuder introduced the Kuder Preference Record, made up of a series of content scales assessing one's preferences for outdoor activities, mechanical activities, and so forth. Kuder's early work was not empirically based, but in 1966 he introduced the Kuder Occupational Interest Scale (KOIS), which used empirically defined occupational scales. The most recent revision (second edition) of the Kuder Occupational Interest Survey occurred in 1979 (Kuder & Diamond, 1979). In 1985 a new report form was designed for the KOIS.

During the next two decades a number of theoretical notions were discussed, but none were translated into measurement and application. In 1940, H. D. Carter introduced the concept of the dynamic character of interests and took into account the social forces that influence adolescents in the process of developing interests and an acceptable self-concept and in choosing a career. Carter also thought that one's value system influenced one's range of possible occupations. In 1941 John Darley suggested that differential interests reflect the process of personality development. He, like Carter, believed that interests are dynamic factors and should be viewed as a phase of personality measurement. Consistent with this dynamic theme, E. S. Bordin suggested in 1943 that in answering an interest inventory a person is guided by self-concept and occupational stereotypes. Thus, people who see themselves as lawyers respond as they believe a lawyer would respond. In 1940 Donald Super had suggested that interests were the products of interaction between inherited aptitudes and glandular factors, on the one hand, and opportunity and social evaluation, on the other. Not unlike E. K. Strong, Super seemed to be suggesting that abilities and opportunities were related to the development of interests patterns. A second definition of interests by Super (1949) reflected even greater precision. Super identified four ways of defining interests: expressed interest (verbal statement), manifest interest (evidenced), tested interest (information), and inventoried interest (likes and dislikes). Super further pointed out that the concept of interest has been used to mean degree of interest, strength of motivation, drive, and need.

In 1959, John Holland theorized that behavior is a function of interests, personality, and social environments. In this context, Holland suggested that the choice of an occupation is an expression of personality and that interest inventories are therefore personality inventories. Thus, Holland thought that the choice of an oocupation represented the individual's motivation, knowledge of the occupation, insight and understanding of self, and abilities. In fact, Holland was convinced that people entered vocational environments because of their interests and personalities. In any event, over the years Holland's theory has led to considerable research on a number of new assessment techniques. To measure the interest and personality types, Holland himself developed the Vocational Preference Inventory and more recently the Self-Directed Search. Other inventories that have drawn upon his theoretical concepts include the Strong-Campbell Interest Inventory, the

Unisex Addition of the ACT Interest Inventory, the Career Assessment Inventory, the Harrington and O'Shea System for Career Decision Making, and the United States Employment Service Interest Inventory. It is clear that Holland's theory and subsequent assessment techniques have had considerable impact on the field of interest measurement over the past two decades.

About the same time (1956) Anne Roe introduced a theory of vocational choice based on a series of studies exploring the personalities of research scientists in different fields. The results of these investigations demonstrated differences in the personality needs and childhood experiences of people doing research in different scientific areas. Based on these findings Roe concluded that a major distinction among the scientists was on a dimension of interest toward persons or not toward persons (that is, toward things). Or, stated differently, the evidence was suggesting that early rewarded social activities seem to be related to later person orientation. The person-to-thing dimension has been viewed as a basic interest dimension since its inception by Roe some years ago. To measure Roe's concepts and classification system a number of inventories have been developed over the years: The Remak (meaning in Hebrew a list of occupations), the Career Occupational Preference System Interest Inventory, and the Hall Occupational Orientation Inventory.

A theme running through all of the above interest perspectives is the "Trait Factor Approach," with its long history of extensive use focused on personal characteristics that tend to link the individual to different environments. The Trait Factor Approach, in the main, is based on the idea that human behavior may be ordered and measured along dimensions of defined traits, or factors, and that individuals may be reasonably well characterized and described in terms of these defined traits. There is no question that the evidence to some extent tends to support the validity of the Trait Factor Approach, but at the same time we need to keep in mind the concepts of human development and environment and their subsequent impact and interaction with the concept of interests.

A second theme running through the above interest perspectives is the overall positive direction of interest inventories. As noted by Sundberg (1990), interest inventories look for directions of positive effort, while personality inventories, in contrast, measure maladjustments. That is, interest inventories attempt to measure motivations that determine life decisions (Walsh, 1989).

A final comment worth repeating from above is the fact that, surprisingly, interests and abilities are not highly correlated. For example, a person may have interests very similar to those of artists, but achieve in only a mediocre way in the artistic profession. A person may have a high degree of accounting ability, but not have interests similar to those of individuals in the profession of accounting. The person simply may not like accounting. So, although interests and abilities tend not to be highly related, keep in mind that they do interact. An individual's interests and abilities may be influenced by environmental variables such as education, experience, and learning. Interest patterns do seem to be reasonably stable within broad interest categories for young adults and on into life for many people, but there certainly are exceptions (Campbell, 1971). Evidence (Hansen & Campbell, 1985) indicates that by the time a person is 21 his or her interests have become rather established, and by the time the person is 25, his or her interest patterns are reasonably stable. In any event, remember that interests, like abilities, may be susceptible to environmental influence and human development.

THE MEASUREMENT OF INTERESTS

Information about a person's interests, likes, or preferences for different kinds of activities, events, or people may be obtained in a variety of different ways, as suggested by Super (1949). An individual's interests, likes, or preferences suggestive of directions of positive effort generally link the individual to the world of work. Mitchell (1985) indicates that there are more than 200 vocational interest tests or ways of collecting information about an individual's likes and preferences.

Probably the most direct and simplest method of collecting such information is to ask individuals what they are interested in or what they want to do when they grow up. This is called an *expressed interest*, and the individual is simply asked to make a verbal statement of liking or disliking for various activities, tasks, or occupations. Recent evidence suggests that this is a reasonably valid way of collecting information about an individual's likes and dislikes. The method, to say the least, is consistent with the idea that if you want to know something about someone, simply ask them.

A second method of assessing interests involves observing a person's behavior in different situations. This is called *manifest*, or *evidenced*, *interest* and involves participation in an activity, situation, or occupation. The reasoning behind this method is that individuals tend to participate in the activities or situations they like and find somewhat satisfying.

Tested interests, a third method of assessment, infers interests from an individual's knowledge of special terminology or relevant information about a given topic. Such an assessment is generally made through the use of various objective information-oriented tests. It is assumed that interest in a vocation should result in an accumulation of relevant information about that vocation.

Thus the reasoning is that the more specific knowledge an individual has about a given occupation the more the individual is interested in pursuing that occupation.

Inventoried interest is the fourth way of collecting information about, or assessing, an individual's interests. This method of assessment asks individuals to report their likes, dislikes, and preferences among items in a list of activities, occupations, or people. The method of inventoried interest is the most popular and widely used and permits a broader sampling of behaviors, likes, and preferences. In addition, the inventoried interest method provides objective scores that permit individual and occupational group comparisons. Thus, for example, interest inventories give us some idea how an individual's likes and dislikes are similar to the likes and dislikes of individuals in specific occupations.

The remainder of this chapter will discuss a few of the more than 200 interest inventories that have been found to be reasonably reliable and valid for vocational counseling purposes. Interest inventories discussed below include the Strong-Campbell Interest Inventory; the Kuder Occupational Interest Inventory, Form DD; the Self-Directed Search; the Career Assessment Inventory; and the Career Occupational Preference System Interest Inventory.

The Strong Interest Inventories

The Strong Vocational Interest Blank for Men (SVIB) was first published in 1927 by E. K. Strong, Jr. Since that time the SVIB has clearly set the pace for interest assessment down through the years. Hansen and Campbell (1985) note that the SVIB has the longest history of any psychological test in widespread use today. And, as we noted above, the SVIB has been one of the most widely used and researched assessment instruments.

In the beginning the development of the SVIB was based on the rather interesting observation by E. K. Strong, Jr., and some other psychologists that different groups of professional people showed consistent differences in what they said they liked and disliked. Some of these differences made sense, but other differences turned up on items having no apparent connection with jobs—such as amusements, hobbies, people, books, activities, and other nonvocational aspects of life. These results suggested at least implicitly that a profession may represent a way of life or a kind of life style as well as a way of earning a living. Until his death in 1963, Strong systematically researched men in one occupational group after another, comparing the responses they gave to the test questions with the responses given by men in general. Thus, Strong used an empirical process to construct scoring keys for the various occupational scales on the SVIB. For example, in constructing a scoring key for his accounting scale, he asked several hundred practicing male accountants to take the test. Item by item, he conscientiously tabulated their responses to find out which ones they answered "like," which "indifferent," and which "dislike." Any answer for which the difference between the accountants and men in general was statistically significant was included in the accounting scoring key; that is, those items on the SVIB that differentiated among the professional accountants and the men-in-general group made up the accounting scoring key. Thus, the higher a person's score on the accounting scale, the more similar that individual's likes and dislikes (interests) were to those of professional accountants. Using this empirical procedure, Strong developed norms for all the occupational groups he studied and was able to explore the relationships of interest scores to age, special abilities, and a variety of other human characteristics. In 1933 Strong devised a form of the SVIB for women and

constructed scales for what he viewed as "women's occupations" in the same way.

The Strong Vocational Interest Blank/Strong-Campbell Interest Inventory (SVIB-SCII), the most recent edition of the Strong Vocational Interest Blank, was published in 1974, revised in 1981 and 1985 (Campbell, 1977; Campbell & Hansen, 1981; Hansen & Campbell, 1985). The publication of the SCII in 1974 was marked by at least two major changes: The men's and women's test booklets were merged into a single form, and a theoretical framework was introduced to structure the profile and the interpretation of the scores. The combining of the men's and women's forms into one booklet, answer sheet, and profile was intended to provide equal treatment for both women and men. Items that appeared to have a sexual bias were removed, and references to gender (e.g., "policemen") were revised. In sum, the SCII 1974 edition of the SVIB permitted men and women to be scored on all existing scales of the inventory.

A theoretical framework for organizing and interpreting the 1974 SCII developed from John Holland's theory of personality types and social environments. Holland (1985a) suggests that interests are an expression of personality and that people tend to resemble one or more personality types (Realistic, Investigative, Artistic, Social, Enterprising, and Conventional). The linking of Holland's theory and Strong's empirical work was supported by the fact that Holland's six personality types were found to resemble the dimensions frequently appearing in research with the SVIB scales. In other words, the evidence suggested that Holland's personality types might be useful for organizing, understanding, and interpreting the scales of the SVIB. David Campbell's ingenuity and persistence and follow-up research showed that the Holland types could in fact be used with SVIB items and archival data in a meaningful way for men and women. These findings led to the use of Holland's theory and personality types for organizing the profile of the SCII.

The success of the 1974 SCII from the perspective of sex bias was met with mixed reviews. Johnson (1976) viewed the merger of the male and female forms of the SVIB as a success, but other reviewers were clearly less supportive. Lunneborg (1978) commented that the 1974 SCII did not present gender-free career options. She further commented that the manuals did not present sufficient data to support the decision to continue with occupational scales separately normed by gender and, in addition, that the 1974 SCII continued to have more options for men than for women. The SCII contained 20 unique female-normed scales, compared to 30 unique male-normed scales.

In order to reduce the sex bias of the SCII and to bring the inventory up to date with more contemporary samples, Campbell and Hansen (1981) embarked on an expansive renorming program. The outcome of this program resulted in the SVIB-SCII 1981 Revision (Campbell & Hansen, 1981). There were no theoretical or conceptual changes in the SCII and no change in the instrument itself, but the expansion of coverage of the occupational samples has been extensive. More specifically, a major goal of the 1981 revision was to match all still existing male-normed occupational scales with the corresponding female-normed scales, and vice versa. A second goal was to update the 1974 SCII scales that had been developed with criterion samples collected prior to 1966. A third goal was to add new occupational groups. Thus, the data collection for this 1981 SCII revision turned out to be the largest testing program of employed adults in history. The revised 1981 SCII Profile carried 162 occupational scales representing 85 occupations. All but 8 of the 162 scales were in matched pairs. For each of 77 occupations there was a scale based on a male-normed

criterion sample and a scale based on a female-normed sample. As noted by Campbell and Hansen (1981), this more than doubled the analogous number of matched pairs (37 occupations) on the 1974 SCII. The 162 new occupational samples represent 40,197 individuals who were in fact drawn from a total of 107,807 people actually tested in the course of research. In general, each occupational sample consisted of people who were between the ages of 25 and 60, had been in their occupation for at least three years, reported that they enjoyed their work, met at least some minimal standard of occupational performance, and pursued their occupation with the typical tasks and duties. Of the 162 new occupational samples, half contained men and half contained women; the average sample contained 248 people. The overall mean age (the mean of the sample means) was 39.2 years, the average level of education over all samples was 16.6 years, and the average length of experience over all samples was 12.2 years.

The major goal of the latest revision of the SVIB-SCII (Hansen & Campbell, 1985) was to increase the breadth of occupations represented on the profile to include nonprofessional or vocational technical occupations. To do this nonprofessional occupational scales were added to the profile. About 32 percent of the occupational scales were developed from criterion samples whose mean educational level was less than 16 years or whose requirements for entry into an occupation did not include a college degree. In addition, all of the vocational technical jobs added were judged to have at least an average or an above-average outlook for the future. The vocational technical occupations added to the profile were further selected to represent each of the six areas of interest proposed in Holland's Theory of Careers. Thus, the profile now includes 34 occupations (65 occupational scales) that are categorized as nonprofessional or vocational technical according to educational level. The new focus makes the inventory useful with clients who have a wide range of occupational and educational goals.

Currently, the 1985 SVIB-SCII Profile carries 207 occupational scales representing 106 occupations. All but 5 of the 207 scales are in matched in pairs. For each of the 101 occupations there is a scale based on a male-normed criterion sample and a scale based on a female-normed sample. The occupational samples represent 48,238 individuals who were in fact drawn from a total of 142,610 people actually tested in the course of research. In general, each occupational sample consisted of people who were between the ages of 25 and 60, had been in their occupation for at least three years, reported that they enjoyed their work, met at least some minimal standard of occupational performance, and pursued their occupation with the typical tasks and duties. Of the 202 occupational samples, half contained men and half contained women. The overall mean age (the mean of the sample means) was 38.1 years, the average level of education over all samples was 16.8 years, and the average length of experience over all samples was 11.8 years.

A second goal of the 1985 revision of the SVIB-SCII was the development of a new general reference sample composed of 300 women in general and 300 men in general. These samples are used to standardize the general occupational themes and the basic interest scales and to contrast samples in the empirical construction of the occupational scales. The 1985 general reference sample was drawn from a pool of employed adults (794 females and 794 males) between the ages of 25 and 60 who liked their occupations.

Another goal of the 1985 SCII revision was to reevaluate the single-sex scale perspective of the Strong inventories. The Hansen and Campbell (1985) manual presents new data on this issue and concludes that empirical scales constructed on the basis of same-sex criterion and reference samples work better (are more valid) than scales based on opposite-sex samples. Men and women, on the average, do respond differently to almost half of the inventory items. Hansen and Campbell are careful to point out that these differences should in no way be used to discriminate against, repress, or embarrass any individual of either sex. However, the data demonstrate that the route to equal treatment is not necessarily through identical treatment. Thus, based on their data, Hansen and Campbell (1985) indicate that separate scales and separate norms are necessary—or, stated differently, Hansen and Campbell suggest that combined-sex test construction is not the most reliable and valid approach for most occupations. Therefore single-sex test construction continues to be the strategy used to develop the SCII occupational scales. Other research (Tittle, 1981) is consistent with this perspective, suggesting that the structures of career interests are different for men and women. (For further discussion of issues regarding the use of interest inventories with men and women clients, see Chapter 14.)

In its present form, the SVIB-SCII 1985 Revision consists of 325 items drawn from several areas of life: occupations, school subjects, activities, amusements, types of people, activity preferences, and personal characteristics. It takes the average adult about 30 minutes to respond "like," "indifferent," or "dislike" to each of the items. Over the years, the major use of the Strong inventories has been with 17- and 18-year-olds, or with older college students. However, about 90 percent of the average eighth grade class (students aged 13 to 15) can read and complete the inventory (Hansen & Campbell, 1985).

The answers to the 1985 SVIB-SCII are analyzed by computer (the SCII cannot be scored by hand), and the results are reported on a profile sheet that presents scores in an organized format and offers interpretative information. Hansen and Campbell (1985) suggest that the profile is largely self-explanatory, but it is essential that a counselor assist the client in understanding the scales and in interpreting the scores. Scoring agencies routinely report scores for six general occupational themes reflecting Holland's personality types (Realistic, Investigative, Artistic, Social, Enterprising, and Conventional), for 23 basic interest scales, 207 occupational scales, 2 special scales, and 26 administrative indexes. The six general theme scores reported suggest an individual's overall occupational outlook, the general kinds of activities enjoyed, the type of occupational environment liked, general coping style, and the kind of people a person tends to get along with. The six themes are briefly described below:

> *Realistic:* Outdoor and technical interests
>
> *Investigative:* Scientific and inquiring interests
>
> *Artistic:* Dramatic and self-expressive interests
>
> *Social:* Helping and people-oriented interests
>
> *Enterprising:* Persuasive, political, and power-oriented interests
>
> *Conventional:* Organizational and clerical interests

The 23 basic interest scales measure interests in particular kinds of activities such as science, mechanical activities, and athletics. High scores (standard score of 60 or above) mean strong interest and liking for activities in the area. The 207 occupational scales couple the individual's pattern of interests with the working world by telling the person how one's interests (likes and dislikes) resemble those of experienced workers happily employed in a variety of different occupations. The two special scales (the Academic Comfort Scale and the Introver-

sion-Extroversion Scale) were previously called the "nonoccupational scales." High scorers on the Academic Comfort Scale will be found among people who are well educated or who intend to become well educated. Low scorers on the Academic Comfort Scale will be found among those who are uncomfortable in academic settings and who find intellectual exercises boring. The Introversion-Extroversion Scale suggests the person's interest in being alone as opposed to working with other people. High scores on this scale are earned by people who would rather work with things or ideas. Low scores are earned by people who enjoy working with others. Scores on the six general themes, the basic interest scales, the occupational scales and the special scales are reported on the profile as standard scores with a mean of 50 and a standard deviation of 10.

The 26 administrative indexes of the SCII are routine clerical checks performed by computer on each answer sheet to make sure that errors have not occurred in the administration, completion, or processing of the answer sheet. As noted in the manual (Hansen & Campbell, 1985), the indexes examine three statistics: total responses; infrequent responses; and the percentages of like, indifferent, and dislike responses. The meaning of the scores is explained on the back of the profile sheet the testee receives and more completely in the manuals. Two manuals are available to assist users in learning about the SVIB-SCII profile: the manual for the SVIB-SCII (Hansen & Campbell, 1985) and the users Guide to the SVIB-SCII (Hansen, 1984b). Both have information on interpretation that includes an outline of a counseling procedure and a number of detailed case studies. Figure 9.1 shows what a profile sheet looks like, and Figure 9.2 gives an example of a score summary.

Very recent test-retest reliability data (Hansen & Campbell, 1985) were collected for three different samples (a two-week sam-

STRONG VOCATIONAL INTEREST BLANK

PAGE 1 PROFILE REPORT FOR:

DATE TESTED: January 12, 1986

ID:
AGE: 32 SEX: Male

DATE SCORED: February 17, 1986

SPECIAL SCALES: ACADEMIC COMFORT 48
INTROVERSION-EXTROVERSION 59

STANDARD SCORES

TOTAL RESPONSES: 321 INFREQUENT RESPONSES: 8

OCCUPATIONAL SCALES

REALISTIC

GENERAL OCCUPATIONAL THEME – R   30 40 50 60 70
Very Low (35)

BASIC INTEREST SCALES (STANDARD SCORE)
AGRICULTURE — Low (37)
NATURE — Very Low (25)
ADVENTURE — Low (40)
MILITARY ACTIVITIES — Very Low (40)
MECHANICAL ACTIVITIES — Moderately Low (42)

INVESTIGATIVE

GENERAL OCCUPATIONAL THEME – I   30 40 50 60 70
Average (49)

BASIC INTEREST SCALES (STANDARD SCORE)
SCIENCE — Average (57)
MATHEMATICS — Average (52)
MEDICAL SCIENCE — Moderately Low (41)
MEDICAL SERVICE — Moderately Low (41)

ARTISTIC

GENERAL OCCUPATIONAL THEME – A   30 40 50 60 70
Very Low (31)

BASIC INTEREST SCALES (STANDARD SCORE)
MUSIC/DRAMATICS — Low (33)
ART — Very Low (28)
WRITING — Average (42)

Code F	Code M	Occupation	F	M
(CRS)	RC	Marine Corps enlisted personnel	(CRS)	18
RC	RC	Navy enlisted personnel	30	28
RC	RC	Army officer	26	27
RI	RIC	Navy officer	29	21
R	R	Air Force officer	27	27
(C)	R	Air Force enlisted personnel	(C)	30
R	R	Police officer	24	24
R	R	Bus driver	33	39
R	R	Horticultural worker	35	26
RC	R	Farmer	34	37
R	RCS	Vocational agriculture teacher	30	25
RI	R	Forester	27	28
(IR)		Veterinarian	(IR)	37
RIS	(SR)	Athletic trainer	16	(SR)
RS	R	Emergency medical technician	31	31
RI	RI	Radiologic technologist	46	35
RI	R	Carpenter	27	17
RI	R	Electrician	25	22
RIA	(ARI)	Architect	29	(ARI)
RI	RI	Engineer	36	34
IRC	IRC	Computer programmer	49	45
IRC	IRC	Systems analyst	45	35
IRC	IRC	Medical technologist	41	34
IR	IR	R & D manager	38	33
IR	IR	Geologist	37	45
IR	I	Biologist	44	(I)
IR	IR	Chemist	42	36
IR	IR	Physicist	42	38
IR	(RI)	Veterinarian	38	(RI)
IRS	IRS	Science teacher	33	37
IRS	IRS	Physical therapist	33	23
IRS	IRS	Respiratory therapist	43	34
IC	IR	Medical technician	48	37
IC	IE	Pharmacist	48	38
(ISR)	(CSE)	Dietitian	39	(CSE)
(SI)	ISR	Nurse, RN	(SI)	22
IR	I	Chiropractor	22	34
IR	IR	Optometrist	43	39
IR	IR	Dentist	32	21
I	IA	Physician	46	45
(IR)	I	Biologist	(IR)	46
I	I	Mathematician	51	48
IR	I	Geographer	46	51
I	I	College professor	57	61
IA	IA	Psychologist	54	57
IA	IA	Sociologist	51	47
AI	AI	Medical illustrator	11	6
A	A	Art teacher	-9	16
A	A	Artist, fine	35	33
A	A	Artist, commercial	13	27
AE	A	Interior decorator	0	25
(RIA)	ARI	Architect	(RIA)	28
A	A	Photographer	28	23
A	A	Musician	38	37
AR	(EA)	Chef	10	(EA)
(E)	AE	Beautician	(E)	16
AE	A	Flight attendant	12	21
A	A	Advertising executive	23	35
A	A	Broadcaster	22	41
A	A	Public relations director	15	18
A	A	Lawyer	35	30
A	AS	Public administrator	40	29
A	A	Reporter	23	42
A	A	Librarian	33	40
AS	AS	English teacher	18	30
(SA)	AS	Foreign language teacher	(SA)	39

CONSULTING PSYCHOLOGISTS PRESS
577 COLLEGE AVENUE   209 0223 001226
PALO ALTO, CA 94306

SVIB-SCII profile form, upper half.

Figure 9.1 Profile for the Strong Vocational Interest Blank/Strong-Campbell Interest Inventory. (Reproduced with special permission of the Publisher, Consulting Psychologists Press, Inc., Palo Alto, Calif. 94306, from Strong-Campbell Interest Inventory by Edward K. Strong, Jr., David P. Campbell, and Jo-Ida Hansen. Copyright © 1933, 1938, 1945, 1946, 1966, 1968, 1974, 1981, 1983, 1985. Further reproduction is prohibited without the publisher's consent.)

Figure 9.1B SVIB-SCII profile form, lower half.

Your answers to the test booklet were used to determine your scores; your results are based on what you said you liked or disliked. The results can give you some useful systematic information about yourself, but you should not expect miracles.

Please note that this test does not measure your abilities; it can tell you something about the patterns in your interests, and how these compare with those of successful people in many occupations, but the results are based on your *interests,* not your abilities. The results may tell you, for example, that you like the way engineers spend their day; they do *not* tell you whether you have an aptitude for the mathematics involved.

Although most of us know something of our own interests, we're not sure how we compare with people actively engaged in various occupations. We don't know "what it would be like" to be a writer, or receptionist, or scientist, for example. People using these results are frequently guided to considering occupations to which they had never given a thought before. In particular, this inventory may suggest occupations that you might find interesting but have not considered simply because you have not been exposed to them. Or the inventory may suggest occupations that you ignored because you thought they were open only to members of the opposite sex. Sexual barriers are now falling, and virtually all occupations are open to qualified people of either sex — so don't let imagined barriers rule out your consideration of any occupation.

Men and women, even those in the same occupation, tend to answer some items on the test differently. Research has shown that these differences should not be ignored — that separate scales for men and women provide more meaningful results. Generally, the scales for your sex — those marked in the "Standard Scores" column corresponding to your sex — are more likely to be better predictors for you than scales for the other sex would be.

Your answers have been analyzed in three main ways: first, under "General Occupational Themes," for similarity to six important overall patterns; second, under "Basic Interest Scales," for similarity to clusters of specific activities; third, under "Occupational Scales," for similarity to the interests of men and women in 106 occupations. The other two groups of data on the profile — labeled "Administrative Indexes" and "Special Scales" — are of interest mainly to your counselor. The first are checks to make certain that you made your marks on the sheet clearly and that your answers were processed correctly. The second are scales that have been developed for use in particular settings and require special interpretation; your counselor will discuss them with you.

■■■■■■ **The Six General Occupational Themes**

Psychological research has shown that vocational interests can be described in a general way by six overall occupational-interest Themes. Your scores for these six Themes were calculated from the answers you gave to the test questions. The range of these scores is roughly from 30 to 70, with the average person scoring 50.

Men and women score somewhat differently on some of these Themes, and this is taken into account by the printed statement for each score; this statement, which might be, for example, "Very High," is based on a comparison between your score and the average score for your sex. Thus, you can compare your score either with the scores of a combined male-female sample, by noting your numerical score, or with the scores of only members of your own sex, by noting the phrasing of the printed comment.

The differences between the sexes on these Themes also are shown on the profile; the open bars indicate the middle 50 percent of female scores, the shaded bars show the middle 50 percent of male scores. The extending, thinner lines cover the middle 80 percent of the scores, and the mark in the middle is the average.

Following are descriptions of the "pure," or extreme, types for the six General Occupational Themes. These descriptions are only generalizations; none will fit any one person exactly. In fact, most people's interests combine several Themes to some degree or other.

R-Theme: People scoring high here usually are rugged, robust, practical, physically strong; they usually have good physical skills, but sometimes have trouble expressing themselves or in communicating their feelings to others. They like to work outdoors and to work with tools, especially large, powerful machines. They prefer to deal with things rather than with ideas or people. They enjoy creating things with their hands and prefer occupations such as mechanic, construction work, fish and wildlife management, radiologic technologist, some engineering specialties, some military jobs, agriculture, or the skilled trades. Although no single word can capture the broad meaning of the entire Theme, the word REALISTIC has been used here, thus the term R-Theme.

I-Theme: This Theme centers around science and scientific activities. Extremes of this type are task-oriented; they are not particularly interested in working around other people. They enjoy solving abstract problems, and they have a great need to understand the physical world. They prefer to think through problems rather than act them out. Such people enjoy ambiguous challenges and do not like highly structured situations with many rules. They frequently are original and creative, especially in scientific areas. They prefer occupations such as design engineer, biologist, social scientist, research laboratory worker, physicist, technical writer, or meteorologist. The word INVESTIGATIVE characterizes this Theme, thus I-Theme.

A-Theme: The extreme type here is artistically oriented, and likes to work in artistic settings that offer many opportunities for self-expression. Such people have little interest in problems that are highly structured or require gross physical strength, preferring those that can be solved through self-expression in artistic media. They resemble I-Theme types in preferring to work alone, but have a greater need for individualistic expression, and usually are less assertive about their own opinions and capabilities. They describe themselves as independent, original, unconventional, expressive, and intense. Vocational choices include artist, author, cartoonist, composer, singer, dramatic coach, poet, actor or actress, and symphony conductor. This is the ARTISTIC Theme, or A-Theme.

S-Theme: The pure type here is sociable, responsible, humanistic, and concerned with the welfare of others. These people usually express themselves well and get along well with others; they like attention and seek situations that allow them to be near the center of the group. They prefer to solve problems by discussions with others, or by arranging or rearranging relationships between others; they have little interest in situations requiring physical exertion or working with machinery. Such people describe themselves as cheerful, popular, and achieving, and as good leaders. They prefer occupations such as school superintendent, social worker, high school teacher, marriage counselor, playground director, speech therapist, or vocational counselor. This is the SOCIAL Theme, or S-Theme.

E-Theme: The extreme type of this Theme has a great facility with words, especially in selling, dominating, and leading; frequently these people are in sales work. They see themselves as energetic, enthusiastic, adventurous, self-confident, and dominant, and they prefer social tasks where they can assume leadership. They enjoy persuading others to their viewpoints. They are impatient with precise work or work involving long periods of intellectual effort. They like power, status, and material wealth, and enjoy working in expensive settings. Vocational preferences include business executive, buyer, hotel manager, industrial relations consultant, political campaigner, realtor, sales work, and sports promoter. The word ENTERPRISING summarizes this pattern, thus E-Theme.

(Continued on page 2 back)

Figure 9.1C SVIB-SCII profile form, reverse side, upper half.

ple, a 30-day sample, and a three-year sample) to determine the stability of the SVIB-SCII 1985 scales. The median test-retest correlations for the two-week, 30-day, and three-year periods were 0.92, 0.89, and 0.87, respectively—almost identical to the comparable statistics for the 1981 occupational scales. These data suggest that the SVIB-SCII scales are reasonably stable over short and longer periods of time.

Long-term research has revealed a great deal about what Strong inventory scores do and do not predict. With a few exceptions, such scores do not tell us just how successful a person is likely to be in an occupation or in the training program leading to it. What

(Continued from back of page 1)

C-Theme: Extremes of this type prefer the highly ordered activities, both verbal and numerical, that characterize office work. People scoring high fit well into large organizations but do not seek leadership; they respond to power and are comfortable working in a well-established chain of command. They dislike ambiguous situations, preferring to know precisely what is expected of them. Such people describe themselves as conventional, stable, well-controlled, and dependable. They have little interest in problems requiring physical skills or intense relationships with others, and are most effective at well-defined tasks. Like the E-Theme type, they value material possessions and status. Vocational preferences are mostly within the business world, and include bank examiner, bank teller, bookkeeper, some accounting jobs, mathematics teacher, computer operator, inventory controller, tax expert, credit manager, and traffic manager. The word CONVENTIONAL more or less summarizes the pattern, hence C-Theme.

These six Themes can be arranged in a hexagon with the types most similar to each other falling *next* to each other, and those most dissimilar falling directly *across* the hexagon from each other.

Few people are "pure" types, scoring high on one and only one Theme. Most score high on two, three, or even four, which means they share some characteristics with each of these; for their career planning, such people should look for an occupational setting that combines these patterns.

A few people score low on all six Themes; this probably means they have no consistent occupational orientation and would probably be equally comfortable in any of several working environments. Some young people score this way because they haven't had the opportunity to become familiar with a variety of occupational activities.

The Basic Interest Scales

These scales are intermediate between the General Occupational Themes and the Occupational Scales. Each is concerned with one specific area of activity. The 23 scales are arranged in groups corresponding to the strength of their relationship to the six General Themes.

On these scales, the average adult scores about 50, with most people scoring between 30 and 70. If your score is substantially higher than 50, then you have shown more consistent preferences for these activities than the average adult does, and you should look upon that area of activity as an important focus of your

interests. The opposite is true for low scores. Your scores are given both numerically and graphically, and an interpretive comment, based on a comparison between your scores and the average score for your sex, also is provided.

Your scores on some of the Basic Interest Scales might appear to be inconsistent with scores on the corresponding Occupational Scales. You might, for example, score high on the Mathematics scale and low on the Mathematician scale. These scores are not errors; they are in fact a useful finding. What they usually mean is that although you have an interest in the subject matter of an occupation (mathematics), you share with people in that occupation (mathematicians) very few of their other likes or dislikes, and you probably would not enjoy the day-to-day life of their working world.

The Occupational Scales

Your score on an Occupational Scale shows how similar your interests are to the interests of people in that occupation. If you reported the same likes and dislikes as they do, your score will be high and you would probably enjoy working in that occupation or a closely related one. If your likes and dislikes are different from those of the people in the occupation, your score will be low and you might not be happy in that kind of work. Remember that the scales of your sex — marked in the "Standard Scores" column with the sex corresponding to yours — are more likely to be good predictors for you than scales for the other sex.

Your score for each scale is printed in numerals — for those scales normed for your sex — and also plotted graphically. Members of an occupation score about 50 on their own scale — that is, female dentists score about 50 on the Dentist F scale, male fine artists score about 50 on the Fine Artist M scale, and so forth. If your score high on a particular scale — say 45 or 50 — you have many interests in common with the workers in that occupation. The higher your score, the more interests you have. But note that on these scales *your scores are being compared with those of people working in those occupations;* in the scoring of the General Themes and the Basic Interest Scales you were being compared with "people-in-general."

The Occupational Scales differ from the other scales also in considering your dislikes as well as your likes. If you share in the same *dislikes* with the workers in an occupation, you may score moderately high on their scale, even if you don't agree with their *likes.* But a higher score — 50 — reflects an agreement on likes *and* dislikes.

To the left of each Occupational Scale name are one to three letters indicating the Theme characteristic of that occupation. These will help you to understand the interest patterns found among the workers in that occupation, and to focus on occupations that might be interesting to you. If you score high on two Themes, for example, you should scan the list of Occupational Scales and find any that have the same two Theme letters, in any order. If your scores there are also high — as they are likely to be — you should find out more about those occupations, and about related occupations not given on the profile. Your counselor can help you.

There are two Special Scales derived from your Strong responses that may give you additional insight into your interests and expectations.

The Academic Comfort Scale differentiates between people who enjoy being in an academic setting and those who do not. Remember, however, that the Academic Comfort Scale *does not measure ability.* About 2/3rds of all people who take the Strong score in the range of 32 to 60. People with low scores (below 40) often are inclined to view education as a necessary hurdle for entry into a career. People with high scores (above 50) typically seek out courses that allow them to explore theory and research in their chosen field.

The Introversion-Extroversion Scale is associated with a preference for working with things or ideas (high scores, say, above 55) or with people (low scores, say, below 45). Scores between 45 and 55 indicate a combination of interests that include working with people and ideas or things in the same occupation.

Using Your Scores

Your scores can be used in two main ways: first, to help you understand how your likes and dislikes fit into the world of work, and second, to help you identify possible problems by pointing out areas where your interests differ substantially from those of people working in occupations that you might be considering. Suppose, for example, that you have selected some field of science, but the results show that you have only a moderate interest in the daily pursuit of the mathematical skills necessary to that setting. Although this is discouraging to learn, you at least are prepared for the choice among (1) abandoning that field of science as a career objective, (2) trying to increase your enthusiasm for mathematics, or (3) finding some branch of the field that requires less mathematics.

In the world of work there are many hundreds of specialties and professions. Using these results and your scores on other tests as guides, you should search out as much information as you can about those occupational areas where your interests and aptitudes are focused. Ask your librarian for information on these jobs and talk to people working in these fields. Talk with your counselor, who is trained to help you, about your results on this test and other tests, and about your future plans. Keep in mind that choosing an occupation is not a single decision, but a series of decisions that will go on for many years. Your scores on this inventory should help.

Figure 9.1D SVIB-SCII profile form, reverse side, lower half.

---

the scores do predict is how likely individuals are to enter and remain in particular occupations or shift to others. For example, some of the most significant predictive validity work by Dolliver, Irvin, and Bigley (1972) suggests that the chances are about one to one that a person would end up in an occupation for which one received an A score (high score) on a Strong occupational scale. In addition, Dolliver, Irvin, and Bigley suggest that the chances are about eight to one that a person will not end up in an occupation for which

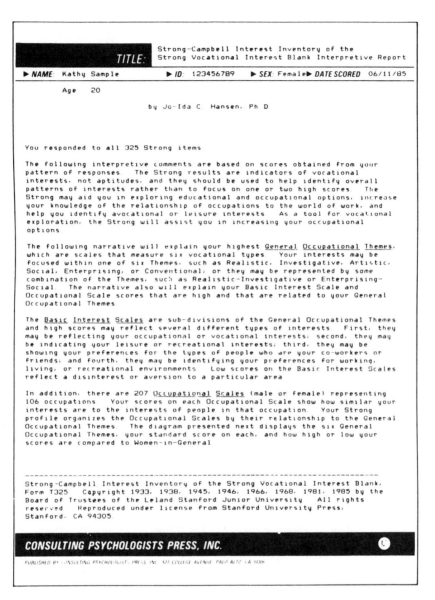

Figure 9.2 SVIB-SCII interpretive report, portion of a sample report generated by computer. (Reproduced with special permission of the publisher, Consulting Psychologists Press, Inc., Palo Alto, Calif. 94306 from the Manual for the SVIB-SCII, 4th edition, by Jo-Ida Hansen and David P. Campbell. Copyright © 1985. Further reproduction is prohibited without the publisher's consent.)

he or she received a C score (low score). A study by Spokane (1979) examined the predictive validity of the SCII for college women and men over a 3½-year span. Good predictive validity was found for 42.5 percent of the females and 59.3 percent of the males. Thus, Hansen and Campbell (1985) note that the SCII's predictive validity hit rates compare favorably with the older SVIB hit rates, which averaged about 50 percent. An im-

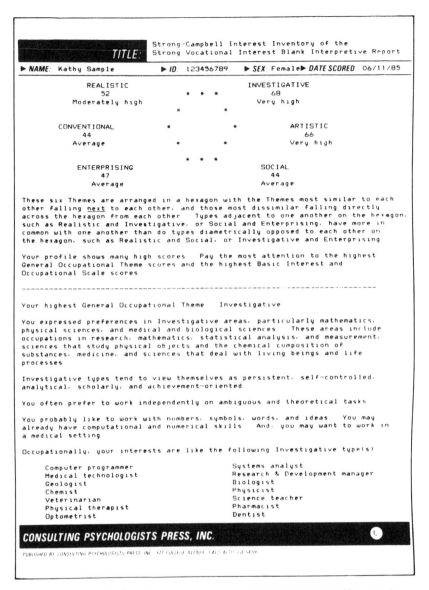

Figure 9.2B SVIB-SCII interpretive report, portion of a sample report generated by computer.

portant study of predictive accuracy for black adults tested with the earlier SVIB occupational scales was reported by Borgen and Harper (1973). They compared predictive accuracy for white and black students who had been winners of the National Achievement and National Merit Scholarships. Their findings indicate that membership in career groups was predicted at least as well for the blacks as it was for the whites. In general, the evidence suggests that those who are in occupations on which they obtained high Strong inventory scores are on the whole better satisfied with their positions than are others whose interest scores did not point in the particular direction they took.

It goes without saying that the SVIB-SCII 1985 revision is a useful assessment technique and one of the best existing today. For example, the SVIB-SCII may be used in counseling students or employees, as an aid in making educational and occupational choices, as a vehicle in discussions between student and counselor, as a selection device in employment decisions, and as a tool in helping people understand their job dissatisfaction. These are only a few of the more common applications. However, keep in mind that interest inventories, like other tests and inventories, are at best suggestive. Interest inventories do not make decisions, nor do they tell you what to do, but they are helpful ways of collecting meaningful information about people.

In summary, the earliest versions of the Strong inventory were primarily designed to measure how similar a person's interests were compared to those people in specific occupations (Hansen, 1986). However, with the addition of the Basic Interest Scales and the General Occupational Themes the uses for the inventory were expanded. Now the inventory may be used to identify an individual's occupational interest, interest in being around different types of people, interest in various leisure activities, and interest in working or living in a variety of environments. But the most frequent use of the inventory continues to be the career counseling of students and employees (Hansen, 1986).

The Kuder Occupational Interest Survey

The first Kuder interest inventory, the Kuder Preference Record—Vocational, was introduced by G. F. Kuder in 1934. Kuder's early inventories contained fairly homogeneous content scales, but in 1966 he introduced the first form of the Kuder Occupational Interest Survey (KOIS), Form D, which represented a departure from his previous work. The KOIS, like Strong's inventories, used empirically defined occupational scales and was based on the idea that people in a given occupation usually have characteristic preferences that distinguish them from people in other occupations (Kuder & Diamond, 1979). However, Kuder's work was different from Strong's in that he eliminated the general reference group and compared the responses of a client to the typical or representative responses of an occupational group or a college major group. A unique feature of the second form of the KOIS, Form DD, is the college-major scales; no other interest inventory has such scales. Thus, in its present form (second edition, a new report form for the KOIS was published in 1985), the KOIS, Form DD, is a 100-triad inventory asking the respondent to choose in each group of three activities the one activity preferred most and the activity preferred least. The individual's preferences are then compared with the responses of many occupational and college-major groups. Each comparison group is represented by about 200 men or women. The assumption is that an individual who has an interest pattern similar to the interest pattern of people in a particular occupation or college-major group is likely to find satisfaction in that occupation or college-major group. Or, stated differently, scores on the KOIS reflect the similarity of the person's responses to the typical responses of each group. Zytowski (1981, 1985) suggests that the KOIS may be given to anyone interested in making plans for the future who is in the tenth or eleventh grade or beyond. It takes about 30 minutes on the average to complete the KOIS, but the inventory cannot be scored by hand. However, Zytowski (1981, 1985) points out that results are mailed from the publisher, Science Research Associates, within three days of receipt of answer sheets.

Over the years more than 60,000 people have cooperated in the development of scales for the KOIS, Form DD. Currently the inventory is scored for 174 scales. Forty-seven of the occupational scales and 19 of the college-major scales were normed on female criterion groups. Seventy-nine occupations and 29 college majors were normed on male criterion groups. Twenty-seven of the occupations and 12 college majors have both male and female criterion groups, and these twin scales are noted by an arrowhead on the profile sheet. Each group is represented by 200 or more men or women.

The back of the profile sheet lists the complete titles of the scales in alphabetical order and may be used when a counselor asks a client to name the occupations and college majors that the client expects to prefer the most. In addition, the profile sheet reports several experimental scale scores in its lower right-hand corner. The men (M) and women (W) scores represent a comparison with the responses of unselected groups of men and of women in general, without regard to their occupations (Zytowski, 1981, 1985). The MBI and WBI ("Men, Best Impression" and "Women, Best Impression") scores represent a comparison with the same group's responses when they are instructed to mark their answers to make the best impression possible. Zytowski (1981, 1985) points out that the M or W scores are generally at least 10 to 30 points higher than their "Best Impression" counterparts. The evidence suggests that persons whose high-ranking occupational scales are essentially nonprofessional tend to have lower "Best Impression" scores. The four scales labeled S, F, D, and MO were developed, respectively, on groups of sons and their fathers and of daughters and their mothers. Zytowski (1981, 1985) suggests that at times it may be informative to note how close the S and F or D and MO scores are. Kuder and Diamond (1979) and Zytowski (1981, 1985) note that differences between the appropriate pair

for a test taker's gender may be a rough index of the maturity of that person's interests.

On the profile sheet testees are scored on all scales regardless of the sex-grouped norms, and the main headings at the top of the report form indicate whether the scale was developed from the responses of males or females. Kuder has retained separate male and female norms despite the increasing number of people in nontraditional fields, primarily because men and women, even when they are in the same occupation, tend to respond differently to certain items in interest inventories (Kuder & Diamond, 1979). Thus, the current thinking of Kuder and Diamond (1979) is that norms for the two sexes cannot be combined without discriminating seriously against one sex or the other and probably the sex for whom the occupation is less traditional. However, Kuder and Diamond (1979) and Zytowski (1981) do indicate that persons should be encouraged to examine the data from scales normed on the gender other than their own.

The KOIS, Form DD, profile indicates some error messages that are worth noting. For example, if 15 or more responses are unscorable, the validity of the profile is sufficiently questionable that no scale scores are printed. In addition, each profile sheet reports a Verification (V) score. The Verification score consists of a number of items marked often by sincere respondents, but marked with significantly less frequency by persons trying to make a good impression (Zytowski, 1981). A person who earns a V score well under 45 may not have been sincere in his or her responses. An individual who scores a few points under 45 may be sincere but may be a poor reader or may have some genuinely unusual interests (Zytowski, 1981).

For interpretation purposes, the similarity of a person's responses to those of each norm (criterion) is represented by means of the Lambda score. The Lambda score indicates the sum of the similarities between a person's KOIS, Form DD, responses and those of the persons who formed the norm or criterion group. Thus, according to Zytowski (1981), a score represents the degree to which the person shares the occupational interests of the group as measured by the KOIS. Virtually all of the individuals who have been included in a norm group have (with a few exceptions) worked in their occupation for at least three years and have been satisfied. About 80 percent of people actually in the occupations or college majors listed scored 0.45 or higher on the scale for their job or field of study. On the other hand, clients' profiles that show no Lambda scores over 0.30 are generally viewed as being uninterpretable, especially if the verification score is less than 45. However, profiles on which the highest scores are in the 0.40s are perfectly valid. In general, Lambda scores rarely go higher than 0.70. For interpretation purposes, the important point to keep in mind is that the Lambda score should be used to assign the rank (1, 2, 3) to the scales. The rank order of the scales based on the Lambda scores is what needs to be paid attention to.

Testees are scored on all scales regardless of the gender-grouped norms, and the main headings at the top of the report form indicate whether the scale was developed from the responses of males or of females. The individual's scores are listed in order of similarity (see Figure 9.3) in order to aid the interpretation of the results. In Sections 3 and 4 of the Profile Sheet the most similar occupational groups represent the individual's highest scores. These should be given primary consideration. All scores within 0.06 of the individual's highest score may be considered nearly equivalent. The next most similar section identifies the next 0.06 range (see Figure 9.3). The greater the difference between two scores, the greater the difference in the testee's preferences and those of people actually in occupations or college majors. The manual (Kuder & Diamond, 1979) and the Interpretive Booklets by Zytowski (1981, 1985) contain additional information on background, development, and interpretation.

In 1985 a new report form for the KOIS (Zytowski & Kruder, 1986; Zytoswki, 1985) was designed, clearly identifying the four different types of scales reported and providing explanatory comments for each type. In Section 1 as shown in Figure 9.3 a statement is made about the dependability and the trustworthiness (Dependability Scale) of the inventory results. Section 2 gives the results of scoring 10 Vocational Interest Estimates (VIE) scales. This section shows the relative rank of the individual's preferences for 10 different kinds of vocational activities. Each vocational activity is explained on the back of the report form. Sections 3 and 4 report occupational and college major similarities. The KOIS has been given to groups of persons who are experienced and satisfied in many different occupations. Their patterns of interests are compared to the reported interests of the individual taking the inventory and placed in order of their similarity. Finally, new information to guide in the interpretation of the results are printed on the back of each copy of the report form. In sum, the intent of the new KOIS report form was to enhance self-knowledge, the exploration of more alternatives, and the exploration of nontraditional alternatives.

In terms of reliability the manual (Kuder & Diamond, 1979) reports a study by W. Scott Gehman that involved 93 Duke University engineering students. The students—33 majoring in electrical engineering, 37 majoring in mechanical engineering, and 23 majoring in civil engineering—had taken the KOIS as freshmen and again as seniors. Median reliabilities for the three groups were, respectively, 0.92, 0.88, and

Kuder Occupational Interest Survey Report Form

Name: EVANS RICCARDO

Sex: MALE Date: 07/16/85

Numeric Grid No. SRA No. 004C0

7-3881

1 Dependability

How much confidence can you place in your results? In scoring your responses several checks were made on your answer patterns to be sure that you understood the directions and that your results were complete and dependable. According to these:

YOUR RESULTS APPEAR TO BE DEPENDABLE.

2 Vocational/Interest Estimates

Vocational interests can be divided into different types and the level of your attraction to each type can be measured. You may feel that you know what interests you have already — what you may not know is how strong they are compared with other people's interests. This section shows the relative rank of your preferences for ten different kinds of vocational activities. Each is explained on the back of this report form. Your preferences in these activities, are as compared with other people's interests, are as follows:

Compared with men		Compared with women	
HIGH		HIGH	
OUTDOOR	92	OUTDOOR	95
SOCIAL SERVICE	86	MECHANICAL	87
CLERICAL	77	MUSICAL	80
AVERAGE		AVERAGE	
MUSICAL	75	CLERICAL	65
MECHANICAL	45	SOCIAL SERVICE	61
COMPUTATIONAL	29	COMPUTATIONAL	39
LOW		LOW	
ARTISTIC	23	SCIENTIFIC	12
LITERARY	12	ARTISTIC	11
PERSUASIVE	08	PERSUASIVE	11
SCIENTIFIC	08	LITERARY	05

3 Occupations

The KOIS has been given to groups of persons who are experienced and satisfied in many different occupations. Their patterns of interests have been compared with yours and placed in order of their similarity with you. The following occupational groups have interest patterns most similar to yours.

Compared with men

WELDER	.67
PAINTER, HOUSE	.66
PLUMBER	.66
CARPENTER	.66
MACHINIST	.65
AUTO MECHANIC	.65
POSTAL CLERK	.64
BRICKLAYER	.64
TRUCK DRIVER	.62
ELECTRICIAN	.62
SUPERVSR, INDUST	.61

THESE ARE NEXT MOST SIMILAR:

BLDG CONTRACTOR	.41
FARMER	.40
PLUMBING CONTRAC	.40

THE REST ARE LISTED IN ORDER OF SIMILARITY:

BOOKKEEPER
POLICE OFFICER
X-RAY TECHNICIAN
TV REPAIRER
FORESTER
EXTENSION AGENT
PRINTER
BUYER
BANKER
NURSE
VETERINARIAN
DENTIST
ELEM SCH TEACHER
PLANT NURSRY WKR
MATH TCHR, HS
FLORIST
PHARMACIST
PHYS THERAPIST
BOOKSTORE MGR
ENGINEER
REAL ESTATE AGT
METEOROLOGIST
INSURANCE AGENT
SCIENCE TCHR, HS
SCHOOL SUPT
PHYSICIAN
MATHEMATICIAN
AUTO SALESPERSON
MINISTER
PHOTOGRAPHER
CLOTHIER, RETAIL
ARCHITECT
TRAVEL AGENT
OPTOMETRIST
COMPUTER PRGRMR
CHEMIST

COUNSELOR, HS	.48
LIBRARIAN	.46
RADIO STATION MGR	.45
JOURNALIST	.45
PHARMACEUT SALES	.45
STATISTICIAN	.43
PERSONNEL MGR	.43
SOCIAL WORKER	
PODIATRIST	
AUDIOL/SP PATHOL	
LAWYER	
ACCT, CERT PUB	.41

Compared with women

BEAUTICIAN	.67
DEPT STORE-SALES	.46
NURSE	.46
OFFICE CLERK	.46
X-RAY TECHNICIAN	.45
PHYS THERAPIST	.45
BOOKKEEPER	.44

THESE ARE NEXT MOST SIMILAR:

BANK CLERK	.41

Compared with women MOST SIMILAR, CONT.

FLORIST	.57
ELEM SCH TEACHER	.55
SECRETARY	.55
MATH TEACHER, HS	
DENTAL ASSISTANT	
EXTENSION AGENT	
OCCUPA THERAPIST	
SCIENCE TCHR, HS	

THE REST ARE LISTED IN ORDER OF SIMILARITY:

BOOKKEEPER	.54
POLICE OFFICER	.54
X-RAY TECHNICIAN	.54
TV REPAIRER	.53
VETERINARIAN	.51
BOOKSTORE MGR	.50
DIETITIAN	.48
PHYSICIAN	.48
DENTIST	.47
BANKER	.47
COMPUTER PRGRMR	.47
RELIGIOUS ED DIR	.47
NUTRITIONIST	.47
ENGINEER	.46
LIBRARIAN	.46
SOCIAL WORKER	.45
COUNSELOR, HS	.45
COL STU PERS MKR	.45
LAWYER	.43
AUDIOL/SP PATHOL	.43
ACCT, CERT PUB	.43
INSURANCE AGENT	.42
ARCHITECT	.42
PSYCHOLOGIST	.42
INTERIOR DECOR	.41
JOURNALIST	.41
FILM/TV PROD/DIR	.39

REST, CONT.

	Compared with men	Compared with women
INTERIOR DECOR	.41	.25
PSYCHOLOGIST	.40	.23
FILM/TV PROD/DIR	.40	.20

4 College Majors

Just as for occupations, the KOIS has been given to many persons in different college majors. The following college major groups have interest patterns most similar to yours.

Compared with men

FORESTRY	.47
AGRICULTURE	.46
ANIMAL SCIENCE	.45

THESE ARE NEXT MOST SIMILAR:

ELEMENTARY EDUC	.38
PHYSICAL EDUC	.37

THE REST ARE LISTED IN ORDER OF SIMILARITY:

ENGINEERING	.34
MATHEMATICS	.32
MUSIC & MUSIC ED	.31
PHYSICAL SCIENCE	.31
FOREIGN LANGUAGE	.28
ARCHITECTURE	.28
BIOLOGICAL SCI	.28
PREMED/PHAR/DENT	.28
SOCIOLOGY	.27
SERV ACAD CADET	.26
HISTORY	.24
BUSINESS ADMIN	.24
ECONOMICS	.23
ART & ART EDUC	.21
POLITICAL SCI	.18
PSYCHOLOGY	.18
ENGLISH	.13

Compared with women

NURSING	.36
PHYSICAL EDUC	.36
HEALTH PROFESS	.33
MATHEMATICS	.33
BIOLOGICAL SCI	.30
MUSIC & MUSIC ED	.30

THESE ARE NEXT MOST SIMILAR:

ELEMENTARY EDUC	.28
HOME ECON EDUC	.28
HISTORY	.26
FOREIGN LANGUAGE	.25

THE REST ARE LISTED IN ORDER OF SIMILARITY:

BUSINESS EDUC	.24
ART & ART EDUC	.24
SOCIOLOGY	.20
PSYCHOLOGY	.19
POLITICAL SCI	.16
ENGLISH	.15
DRAMA	.08

Experimental Scales.

V-SCORE	58				
M .53	MBI -.02	F .55		W .41	MBI -.01
S .36				D .26	MQ .42

Figure 9.3 Sample copy of the 1985 KOIS Report Forms Reprinted from the Kuder Occupational Interest Survey Report Form, Form DD, Revised. Copyright © Frederic Kuder, 1985. By permission of the publisher, Science Research Associates, Inc. All rights reserved.

0.82. Ranges of the reliabilities were, respectively, 0.66 to 0.97; 0.35 to 0.98; and 0.57 to 0.95. These data demonstrate reasonable stability of individual profiles over a period of approximately three years.

The reliability of the Vocational Interest Estimates was also explored using a sample of 192 college students. Test-retest reliabilities for a two-week period for the 10 scales ranged from a low of 0.73 to a high of 0.84. The median profile stability for the Vocational Interest Estimates was found to be 0.80 (Zytowski, 1985). Some follow-up research by Zytowski (1976) has revealed considerable information about what the KOIS scores do predict. Zytowski contacted 882 men and women 12 to 19 years after they had taken an early form of the Kuder Occupational Interest Survey in either high school or college. The follow-up data show that 50 percent of the total group were employed in an occupation that would have been suggested to them had the inventory been interpreted 12 to 19 years previously. Zytowski found the predictive validity of the college-major scales to be slightly superior to that of occupational scales. The College-major scales from a high school testing session correctly predicted the third-year college major of 55 percent of the students. The average span of prediction represents five years, with a range from three to eight — that is, the majors of more than half the students who had decided on a college major were correctly predicted by a scale in the top 0.06 range on the KOIS administered during high school. If the top 0.12 range of scores on the KOIS is used, 80 percent of the students are correctly predicted. However, individuals in occupations consistent with their early interest profiles did not report greater job satisfaction or success, though they did demonstrate more persistence in their occupations. In general, evidence suggests that better prediction is achieved when the individual has attended or graduated from college or entered a high-level occupation.

A second predictive study by Zytowski and Laing (1978) drew from the same population as the 1976 Zytowski study. The authors followed up 206 persons who had taken an early Kuder inventory, the Kuder Preference Record—Occupational, from 12 to 19 years earlier and who were in occupations predictable by one of the 27 KOIS twin scales (27 same named male and female scales). The study explored the predictive validity of own-gender and other-gender normed scales, as well as the rank order correlations between male and female norm scales. The evidence suggests that the predictive validity of the two sets of norms was about equivalent, regardless of the gender of the person taking the inventory. More specifically, slightly over 43 percent of the sample were in occupations corresponding to their five highest ranked scales on own-gender norms, and more than 50 percent were in occupations corresponding to their five highest ranked scales on other-gender norms. These data are consistent with the stated encouragement by Kuder and Diamond and Zytowski for individuals to examine the data from scales normed on the gender other than their own.

Another study of interest by Zytowski (1977) explored the effects of receiving the results of the KOIS on several aspects of vocational behavior among 157 eleventh and twelfth grade high school students. He found that receiving results increased self-knowledge, when compared to a control group that received no KOIS results. However, KOIS results did not seem to influence confidence in, or satisfaction with, vocational plans, unless the person had reported high interest in the inventory results beforehand. In general, the above validity data and effects information suggest that the KOIS may be used with more confidence than previously believed. An additional interpretive aid by Zytowski (1981), *Counseling with the Kuder Occupational Interest Survey*, is of solid practical value in using the KOIS. The manual supplement (Zytowski, 1985) and a recent chapter by Zytowski and Kuder (1986) report advances in the KOIS and describe the new report form.

As noted by Zytowski (1981, 1985), the KOIS is probably best used to enhance self-understanding, to reduce too many choices to a manageable few, or to suggest new possibilities to consider. In particular the KOIS may be useful in identifying a number of alternatives that a person may want to investigate in a variety of other ways. In addition, it is important to keep in mind that the KOIS is not an ability test. Interest inventories do not measure abilities, they attempt to assess how an individual's likes and dislikes are similar to the likes and dislikes or preferences of individuals in a variety of different occupations.

Holland's Self-Directed Search

A more recent important figure to dominate the interest assessment scene is John L. Holland. Holland's Vocational Preference Inventory initially defined his theoretical personality types and model environments (Realistic, Investigative, Artistic, Social, Enterprising, and Conventional) and led to the development of the very practical and useful Self-Directed Search (SDS). The SDS was first published in 1971 to fill the need in the field of counseling for a reasonably short, self-administered, self-scored, and self-interpreted inventory that would reflect a person's interests and relate them to appropriate occupational groups. The SDS was thus a vocational counseling experience for people who did not have access to professional counselors or could not afford their services.

The SDS underwent a number of minor revisions from 1971 to 1978, including several format and word changes. The ma-

jor changes in the most recent 1985 revision include new items to increase the validity of the SDS scales, reducing overlap among scales, omitting items that are too easy or difficult, and increasing the Occupations Finder from 500 to more than 1,100 occupations. Minor changes include rewriting the directions to increase understanding, providing a more useful list of resource materials, and redesigning the booklets so that they are easier to complete (Holland, 1985). Holland (1985) notes that because of these changes the new SDS Booklet is more easily self-administered and takes less time to complete.

Most people can complete the SDS in 40 to 50 minutes, and the manual (Holland, 1985b) indicates that the SDS is suitable for persons aged 15 and older. In its present form the 1985 SDS is composed of two parts. The first part is an assessment booklet (228 items) that asks the individual to report daydreams about occupations, preferences for various activities and occupations, competencies in performing various tasks, and self-estimates of abilities. From these self-reported activities, competencies, occupations, and self-ratings one obtains a summary code representing an individual's resemblance to each of the six personality types, (Realistic, Investigative, Artistic, Social, Enterprising, and Conventional). In the second part of the inventory, the individual is directed to use the Occupational Classification Booklet containing 1,156 occupational titles (99 percent of the labor market in the United States) to identify occupational groups corresponding to the summary code (highest three scores, also called the three-letter code). The user is encouraged to use all combinations of the three-letter code (IAS) in the search for occupations.

Holland's hexagonal structuring of people in occupations (see Figure 9.4), based on his six personality types, is the core of both the Vocational Preference Inventory and the

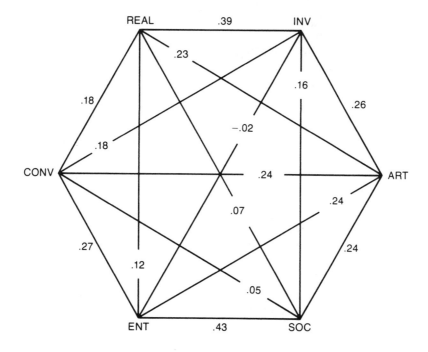

Note: Correlations are between the SDS scales (1985 Revision) for 175 women age 26-65.

Figure 9.4 A hexagonal model for interpreting inter and intra-class relationships. Source: J. L. Holland (1985). Professional Manual for the Self Directed Search. Odessa, FL: Psychological Assessment Resources. Copyright 1985 by Psychological Assessment Resources and reproduced with permission.

Self-Directed Search. The six types are arranged in a hexagon as shown in Figure 9.4 in such a way that types falling next to each other (Realistic and Investigative, for example) are the most similar to each other. Types directly across the hexagon from each other (Conventional and Artistic, for example) are the most dissimilar.

Few people score high on one type and low on all the others. Stated differently, few people are pure types. Most people score high on two or three types which indicates that they share some traits with each of these. For purposes of vocational planning, these people should seek an occupational environment that cuts across these patterns. (It has been also incorporated into the Strong Vocational Interest Blank/Strong-Campbell Interest Inventory as a means of organizing

the large amount of occupational data the SVIB-SCII generates.)

The various assessment methods of the SDS are included for different reasons. The occupational daydreams section encourages the individual to engage in some occupational exploration and may be used to predict a person's future occupation. The six activities scales of 11 items each are measures of personal involvement in each of the six types of activities. The six competency scales of 11 items each are self-reported estimates of a person's proficiencies and aptitudes. The six occupation scales of 14 items each are measures of occupational preferences. Finally, the two sets of self-estimates consist of self-ratings (talents and traits) found to be most identified with one type.

Test-retest reliability data are available

on the old SDS for 118 high school boys, 57 high school girls, and 65 college freshmen. The test-retest time interval for the high school students was three to four weeks and for the college freshmen sample, seven to ten months. The median correlations for the six summary scales for the high school boys and girls and college freshmen were, respectively, 0.61, 0.64, and 0.75. The median rank order of summary codes for the high school boys and girls and college freshmen were, respectively, 0.81, 0.83, and 0.92. In general, the summary code coefficients tend to be higher than the summary scale coefficients, and, as expected, college students' codes and scales are more stable than those of high school students (Holland, 1979). Test-retest data on the 1977 SDS for a small sample of adults, ages 22 to 59, are also reported in the manual (Holland, 1979). The test-retest period was from one to four weeks. Coefficients are reported for all subscales and for the summary scales. The stability coefficients for the summary scales ranged from a low of 0.70 to a high of 0.89. Holland (1979) notes that the test-retest estimates have a larger error component because of the small sample size, but nevertheless range from moderate to high.

The 1985 manual (Holland, 1985b) reports the internal consistency coefficients of the 24 SDS scales for the 1977 and 1985 editions. In general, the 1985 revision alpha coefficients are higher, suggesting that the 1985 SDS is slightly more reliable than is the 1977 revision. For example, when the summary scales for the 1977 and 1985 editions are compared, 69 percent of the scales are more reliable, 17 percent show no difference, and 14 percent are less reliable.

One very positive feature of the SDS is the fact that it is one of the few inventories that has been studied to determine the effects of its use with people. These effects studies have shown that the SDS has positive influences on both men and women and that these positive effects are similar to those of counselors. The positive and productive effects on people take the form of expanding vocational alternatives, reinforcing a current vocational alternative, stimulating vocational exploration, reducing indecision, increasing self-understanding, and stimulating more satisfaction with choice. The data and the effects studies tend to indicate that the SDS has positive beneficial influences for users.

On the basis of extensive research, we now know a number of things about the SDS. In the main, the evidence suggests that college students tend to enter college-major environments consistent with their dominant personality types. Other work, again using college students, suggests that students in college-major environments consistent with their personality types tend to report being more stable (personally and vocationally) and satisfied. Students reporting educational programs inconsistent with their personality types do not seem to be as well off in terms of their academic and personal adjustment. The research on employed men and women (with and without college degrees) is not as abundant as the work with college students, but it continues to increase. In general, these data suggest that men and women tend to enter and remain in occupational environments consistent with their personality types, and these findings tend to obtain for white and black men and women. Thus, the mounting evidence continues to suggest that the SDS may be successfully applied in work environments.

Holland (1985b) and Holland and Rayman (1986) note that in terms of use the SDS serves a large proportion of students and adults whose need for vocational assistance is minimal. A simple straightforward confirmation or reassurance they receive from taking the SDS, or the alternatives generated by the experience of taking the SDS, provide the help or information needed. Thus, the SDS is used in high schools, colleges, adult centers, correctional institutions, women centers, and employment offices for career education, vocational guidance, and placements. However, Holland (1985b) points out that the SDS is not helpful for people who are grossly disturbed, uneducated, or illiterate. Nor will it replace counselors in many instances, because clients often have vocational difficulties and decision-making problems that require personal counseling and other forms of assistance (Holland, 1985b). There is no question that a clear advantage of the SDS is the fact that it is self-directed. The SDS may be used in private at a time a person wishes to use it. It is a self-directed form of assessment that has made a valuable contribution in the area of interest measurement. An example summary of SDS scores is presented in Figure 9.5.

The SDS has an "Easy" form (E) developed for adolescents and adults with limited reading skills (Holland, 1985b). The directions include only fourth grade words. The scoring is simplified and only two, rather than three, letter codes are used throughout. In addition, each occupational title in the occupation section is followed by a simple sentence of explanation. Form E, which consists of 203 items, is also shorter than the regular form of the SDS.

The Career Assessment Inventory: The Vocational Version

Developed by C. B. Johansson, the Career Assessment Inventory (CAI) is suitable for individuals interested in beginning work immediately or in careers requiring some postsecondary education in technical school, business school, or community college. The completion time of the CAI (Johansson, 1982) is about 30 minutes, and the inventory is suitable for sixth grade students through adults. Individuals respond to the 305 items—composed of activities, school subjects, and occupations—by marking each item "Like very much," "Like somewhat," "Indifferent," "Dislike somewhat," or "Dislike it very much." Responses to the CAI are then computer scored, producing four main sets of scores: theme scales, basic interest area scales, occupational scales, and administrative indices. Actually the development and format of the CAI is very similar to that of the SCII (see Figure 9.6 for a sample CAI profile sheet). Holland's theoretical scheme is used to organize the format for the general themes, the basic interest areas, and the occupational scales. Thus, the six general occupational theme scales (Realistic, Investigative, Artistic, Social, Enterprising, and Conventional) describe an individual's overall orientation to the world of work. Standard scores with a mean of 50 and a standard deviation of 10 are used and plotted on the profile format sheet. The 22 basic interest scales provide measures of the strength of specific interests in areas such as electronics, sales, social service, and so forth. Again, standard scores are reported and plotted on the profile sheets. Ninety-one occupational scales relate interests to specific careers and indicate areas of career satisfaction. These scales indicate the degree of similarity of likes and dislikes to those of employed people in specific occupations.

For the 1982 CAI, combined gender occupational scales were developed. This was done by utilizing the core interests of an occupation that effectively differentiates females and males from the general reference samples. Stated differently, only those items that significantly differentiated for both genders were used to construct the occupational scale. The combined scales are somewhat shorter than the earlier separate female and male scales, but they still maintain high stability (Johansson, 1982). For example, Johansson (1982) reports high stability (correlations in the 90s) for intervals of 30 days and correlations in the 80s for intervals as long as five to seven years.

Profile A-1 Age 21

Activities (pp. 4-5):
9 2 3 2 1 1
R I A S E C

Competencies (pp. 6-7):
8 0 0 3 1 0
R I A S E C

Occupations (p. 8):
1 0 0 0 0 0
R I A S E C

Self Estimates (p. 9) (What number did you circle?):
5 2 5 4 3 3
R I A S E C

5 4 4 4 4 4
R I A S E C

Total Scores (Add the five R scores, the five I scores, the five A scores, etc.):
28 8 12 13 9 8
R I A S E C

SUMMARY CODE
Diff = 40% ile
| R | S | A | C = 1 |
Highest | 2nd | 3rd |

Person A. Person A completed the SDS at 14, 19 and 21. The profiles for the 1977 edition, taken when he was 21, are shown in profile A-1. Profiles A-2 and A-3 show his SDS profiles at 19 and 14. The 1970 edition has been converted to the 1977 format and scoring to make the profiles in all three tables comparable. Note the stability of his high-point R-code for this seven year period as well as the fluctuations in the other codes and scales.

He did not do well in high school, considered joining the army, and worked at a series of unskilled and semi-skilled jobs. At 20 he attended an electronics trade school (RIE), but dropped out. He entered truck-driving school (RIE) at 21, which he enjoyed. Note that his SDS codes resemble the codes implied in his work and training history and that the code for the second training school is closer to his last SDS assessment than the first school was. His history also illustrates the floundering and trial that many young people undergo.

Profile A-2 Age 19

Activities (pp. 4-5):
8 1 0 1 1 7
R I A S E C

Competencies (pp. 6-7):
4 0 0 2 1 1
R I A S E C

Occupations (p. 8):
1 1 0 1 1 1
R I A S E C

Self Estimates (p. 9) (What number did you circle?):
4 2 3 3 4 3
R I A S E C

4 5 3 4 5 4
R I A S E C

Total Scores (Add the five R scores, the five I scores, the five A scores, etc.):
21 9 6 11 12 16
R I A S E C

SUMMARY CODE
Diff = 17% ile
| R | C | E | C = 2 |
Highest | 2nd | 3rd |

Profile A-3 Age 14

Activities (pp. 4-5):
8 7 5 5 7 3
R I A S E C

Competencies (pp. 6-7):
5 1 1 1 0 0
R I A S E C

Occupations (p. 8):
0 1 1 0 0 0
R I A S E C

Self Estimates (p. 9) (What number did you circle?):
7 4 5 3 6 2
R I A S E C

6 5 4 7 3 2
R I A S E C

Total Scores (Add the five R scores, the five I scores, the five A scores, etc.):
26 18 16 16 16 7
R I A S E C

SUMMARY CODE
Diff = 35% ile
| R | I | A /S/E |
Highest | 2nd | 3rd C = 3 |

Figure 9.5 Summary of scores for person A. *Source:* J. L. Holland (1985). Professional Manual for the Self-Directed Search, Odessa, Fla.: Psychological Assessment Resources. Copyright © 1985 by Psychological Assessment Resources and reproduced with permission.

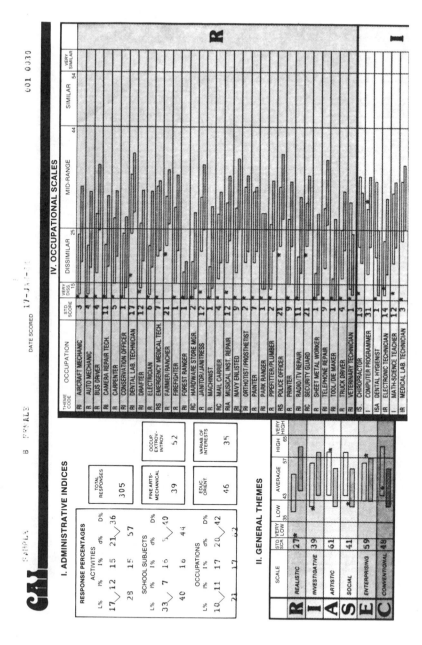

Figure 9.6 Career Assessment Inventory Profile Sheet. (Reproduced with permission from the *Career Assessment Inventory Profile* by C. B. Johansson. Copyright 1982 by the NCS Interpretive Scoring Systems, Minneapolis, Minnesota.)

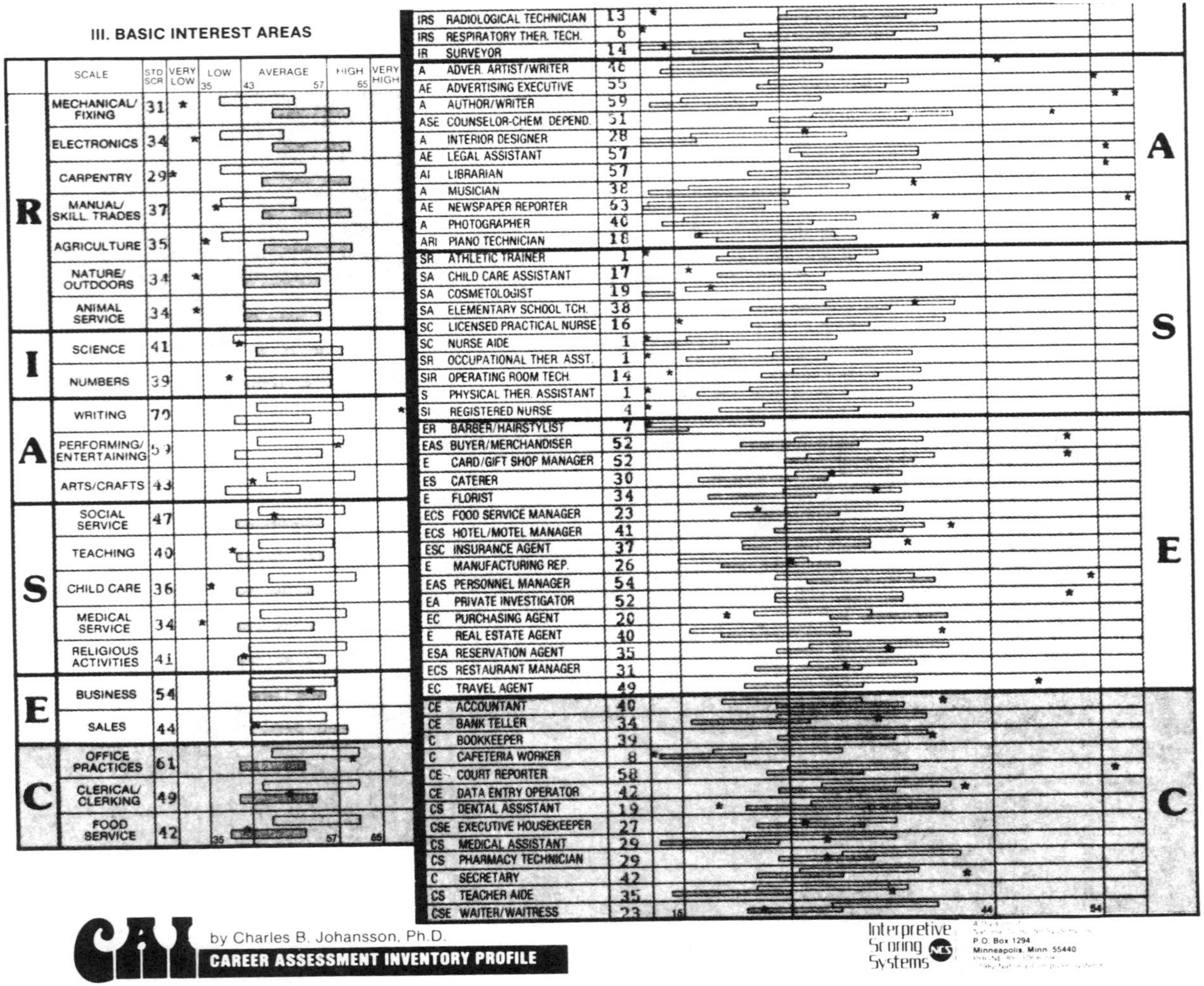

III. BASIC INTEREST AREAS

Figure 9.6 (cont.)

CAI by Charles B. Johansson, Ph.D
CAREER ASSESSMENT INVENTORY PROFILE

Interpretive
Scoring
Systems

P.O. Box 1294
Minneapolis, Minn. 55440

UNDERSTANDING YOUR RESULTS

Your results, which are shown on the other side of this sheet, are from the responses you provided when you answered the *Career Assessment Inventory*. These results are based on your like and dislike answers to the Inventory, and they can be important in helping you to understand better how your interests fit into the world of work.

These results can give you some helpful information about yourself, but do not expect miracles. You may feel that the scores tell you nothing more than you already know; however, they will help you determine how high or low your interests are in comparison to the interests of others. They also will point out interest areas which you may not have considered before.

Most importantly, remember that these results are measures of your interests and *not* your abilities. For example, your scores may show that you like art or sales, but they will not show if you have the talent or training for art or sales work.

Four main sets of scores are given for you on the reverse of this sheet. First are your results on the Administrative Indices — they give some overall indication on how you responded to the inventory. Second are your results on six General Themes — they give an overall view of your interests as compared to adults in a general population. Third are your scores on twenty-two Basic Interest Area scales — they tell about the strength of your interests in specific areas such as sales, writing, carpentry, and so forth in comparison to adults in a general population. Fourth are your scores on the Occupational scales — they tell how similar or dissimilar your interests are to those of people in various occupations, such as accountants, mechanics, computer programmers, librarians, and so forth.

ADMINISTRATIVE INDICES

In the top left-hand corner on the reverse of this sheet are the Administrative Indices. On the *Career Assessment Inventory* you answered whether you liked or disliked certain ACTIVITIES, SCHOOL SUBJECTS, and OCCUPATIONS. Numbers in the Administrative Indices box show your response percentages to these three sections. For example, if 10 appears under L%, then you answered "Like very much" to 10 percent of the items; the number under l% shows the percentage for "Like somewhat"; the number under I% is your "Indifferent" percentage; the number under d% is your "Dislike somewhat" percentage and the number under D% is your "Dislike very much" percentage. Also, notice that the two "Like" percentages and two "Dislike" percentages are added together for each section (some rounding error may occur). This is done to give you an overall view of your "Like-Indifferent-Dislike" response percentages for each of the three sections of the inventory.

Total Responses merely indicates that number of items answered on the inventory. There are 305 items on the inventory. If your Total Responses are 291 or more, then your results will be an accurate reflection of your preferences. If your Total Responses are 290 or fewer, then you should interpret the results cautiously.

The Fine Arts—Mechanical Index gives an overall view of how you responded to aesthetic and mechanical items on the inventory. Scores of 42 and lower indicate a strong preference for creative and social service occupations. Scores of 58 and higher indicate a stronger preference for mechanical activities and for skilled trades and technical occupations. Scores between 43 and 57 indicate an overall preference for both fine arts and mechanical activities or an indifference to these activities.

The Occupational Extroversion—Introversion index gives an overall view of whether you prefer to work alone or with people. Scores of 42 and lower indicate a preference for working with people more than with just things; people in sales occupations and social service professions tend to have low scores. Scores of 58 and higher indicate a preference for working with things more than with people; people in skilled trades occupations and technicians tend to have high scores. Scores between 43 and 57 fall in the average range.

The Educational Orientation Index indicates how your interest preferences compare to the overall interest preferences of individuals who attend a liberal arts college. Scores of 40 and higher indicate a liking for studying and for creative, mathematic, fine arts, and scientific activities generally offered by a community college or liberal arts college. Scores between 31 and 39 usually are obtained by adults who have pursued vocational, technical, business, or some community college course work and by students in high school and young adults. Scores of 30 and lower generally reflect an indifference or a disliking for school course work; adults who do not continue their education beyond high school and young adolescents typically have scores in this range.

The Variability of Interest Index indicates the diversity of your interest preferences. Scores of 60 and higher indicate a preference for a wide range of activities, while scores of 40 and below indicate that a more narrow range of activities is found rewarding. Scores between 41 and 59 are in the average range and are typical of most people.

These administrative indices can be explained in greater detail by a counselor and are useful when people are seeking further career guidance.

THEME SCALES

Research has shown that interests can be grouped into six very broad categories and that each category can be described by a General Theme. Your score on each of these six Theme scales tells how high or low your interest is when compared with that of people in the general population. Most people have scores ranging between 43 and 57 on these scales and so this range, 43-57, is called the *average range of scores*. Scores below 43 generally are considered low and scores above 57 generally are considered high. Your score is printed in the *Std. Score* column and it is plotted on the graph. You also will notice that there are two printed bars for each Theme; the open bar shows the average range of scores for females, and the shaded bar shows the average range of scores for males. Males *tend* to have higher scores on some of these Themes, such as Realistic, while females *tend* to have higher scores on other Theme scales, such as Artistic.

To help you better understand these Themes, descriptions are given below for each Theme. These descriptions describe a group of people, and therefore, all the characteristics may not fit any one person. A few people will have no really high scores; this indicates that these Theme scales do not adequately measure the person's preferences or that the person is uncertain about what he/she finds rewarding. Some people will have a high score on just one Theme scale and low scores on all others; this indicates that only this one area is of primary importance to the individual. Most people will have high scores on two or even three Theme scales; thus, they share some of the characteristics of several Theme areas. Finally, a few people will have high scores on all six Theme scales; this indicates that they have a wide range of interests and find many different activities rewarding. Generally, the higher your score, the more likely the following descriptions will be true for you.

Realistic — People who have high Realistic scores like to work with their hands and tools to build things such as a radio or cabinets, and to fix things such as broken toys or furniture. These people like to work outside rather than inside and prefer working alone or with one or two people rather than with a large group. They describe themselves as having good physical skills, as being practical and rugged, and as generally preferring to work with things, such as machines, rather than with people. They prefer occupations such as mechanic, skilled tradesperson, farmer, military officer, forester, and park ranger. The word *Realistic* has been used to describe this area.

Investigative — These people like activities and occupations that are related to science and mathematics. They are similar to Realistic people in that they prefer to work by themselves. They like to solve problems that require thinking to find the correct answer, and they do not like to work where there are a lot of rules. They enjoy working with ideas and words to find their own answers and solutions, especially in the scientific areas, and they frequently describe themselves as achieving, confident, curious, inventive, and scientific. They prefer occupations such as laboratory research worker, medical technician, computer programmer, dental hygienist, drafter, and other scientific occupations. The word used to describe this theme is *Investigative*.

Artistic — People of this type have an artistic bent to their nature and like to work in a job with many possibilities for expressing themselves by making and creating works of art. They usually like to work alone and wrap themselves up in what they are doing. Generally, they like to do such things as writing poetry or drawing and sketching. They are similar to Investigative people in not liking to work where there are a lot of rules and regulations, but they are more interested in creating artistic things that mean something to them personally. They frequently describe themselves as imaginative, original, expressive, and artistic. Occupational choices include those of artist, author, cartoonist, singer, poet, actor/actress, newspaper reporter, photographer, librarian, and interior designer. *Artistic* is the word used to describe this Theme area.

Social — People who have high scores on this scale tend to have a very strong concern for other people and like to help them solve personal problems. They see themselves as cheerful, popular, and good leaders. They prefer to solve problems by talking things out, and they get along well with many types of people. They usually have little interest in working with machines and prefer being in groups and activities that let them be helpful. They frequently describe themselves as thoughtful, considerate, patient, giving, and generous. Some occupations preferred by these people are social worker, recreation leader, camp counselor, teacher, child care assistant, and nurse. *Social* is used to describe the Theme area.

Enterprising — People who have high scores on this scale are good at talking and using words to persuade other people. Often they are in sales work and they are clever at thinking of new ways to do things that lead and convince people. They see themselves as full of energy, enthusiastic, adventurous, ambitious, competitive, outspoken, and confident. They like power, status, and wealth, and they frequently work in business. Many times they are in occupations such as real estate sales, buyer/merchandiser, hotel manager, advertising manager, insurance sales, and other kinds of sales work. The word *Enterprising* describes these interests.

Conventional — These people prefer activities and jobs where they know exactly what is expected of them and what they are supposed to do. They work well in large offices, but they usually do not seek leadership jobs. Such people describe themselves as conventional, stable, well-controlled, moderate, conforming, cautious, and dependable. Generally, they have little interest in problems that need a lot of creative thinking. They like to do activities such as bookkeeping, typing, filing, and general business types of work. They prefer jobs in the business world such as bank teller, bookkeeper, accountant, computer operator, keypunch operator, administrative assistant, and secretary. The word *Conventional* has been used to describe these activities and jobs.

BASIC INTEREST AREA SCALES

Your scores on the twenty-two Basic Interest Area scales show the strength of your interest in a variety of pure types of areas such as Electronics, Science, Sales and so forth. Each of these twenty-two scales is related to one of the six Theme areas; for example, the first seven Basic Interest Area scales (Mechanical/Fixing through Animal Service) all are related to the R-Realistic area; therefore, these first seven scales are color-coded the same as R-Realistic. The next two scales (Science and Numbers) are related to I-Investigative, and so forth. These Basic Interest Area scales give you a finer breakdown of your interests in more specific areas than the Theme scales.

The average adult score is between 43 and 57 on each scale and so this range, 43-57, is considered the *average range of scores*. Scores 58 and higher are considered as indicating high interest and they show areas where you probably will find enjoyable types of activities. Scores 42 and lower are considered as indicating low interest and show areas that may be less satisfying to you. Your scores are printed in the *Std. Score* column and are plotted on a graph. You also will notice that for each scale there are two printed bars; the open bar shows the average range of scores for females, and the shaded bar shows the average range of scores for males.

To help you better understand your scores, brief descriptions of each of these twenty-two scales and some examples of occupations that score high on each scale follow. Remember, the higher your score in an area, the more you liked related activities in that area; the lower your score, the more you tended to dislike activities in that area.

MECHANICAL/FIXING — Using tools to repair or adjust things such as repairing damage to a car, adjusting a carburetor, and fixing a sink are measured by this scale. Mechanics, skilled trades workers, and service repair people have high scores in this area.

ELECTRONICS — Working with electrical things such as building or fixing a radio, studying electronics, and doing electrical wiring are interests of an electronics technician, electrician, radio/tv repairperson, and mechanic.

CARPENTRY — Working with wood, such as fixing antiques or broken furniture, or making things, such as cabinets, are interests that carpenters and other building tradespeople have.

MANUAL/SKILLED TRADES — Operating machinery, equipment, or vehicles and skilled trades occupations are interests measured by this area. Some occupational examples are truck

Figure 9.6B

Formation of the CAI occupational criterion samples involved the selection of employed individuals who fulfilled five criteria. The individual had to be in an appropriate job, had to have at least two years' experience, had to like the work, had to be under 60, and had to have the proper accreditation or degree required for the occupation. The median combined sample size for the occupational criterion groups was about 150 CAI forms that met all five criteria. Average age for most samples was in the 30s or 40s. Average number of years of experience was usually between 10 and 15 years. Average education usually was two or three years of postsecondary education and this occurred most frequently at a community college or a vocational technical or business school (Johansson, 1982).

As noted above, the CAI occupational scales represented interests shared by both females and males in an occupation and excluded those interests that were not significant for either gender or were only signifi-

driver, bus driver, sheet metal worker, firefighter, machinist, plumber, and construction worker.

AGRICULTURE — Agricultural or forestry occupations that are worked at outdoors are in this area. Some examples of occupations that have high scores on this scale are farmer, forest ranger, park ranger, horseshoer, veterinarian assistant, and conservation officer.

NATURE/OUTDOORS — Being outdoors, going canoeing or camping, growing flowers, or raising a garden, or just walking through the woods are similar types of activities related to this area.

ANIMAL SERVICE — Working with animals and taking care of them are interests related to such occupations as being a dog trainer, working at a zoo, managing a pet shop, or being a veterinarian's assistant.

SCIENCE — Studying biology, astronomy, geology, and physics, reading books on science, and doing scientific activities are interests of people who have high scores on this scale, such as scientists and laboratory technicians.

NUMBERS — Working with numbers to keep a budget, drawing graphs and charts, and studying arithmetic, algebra, and general math are things liked by accountants, computer programmers, technicians, and bookkeepers.

WRITING — Covering news stories, writing poetry, doing creative writing, and writing stories are things liked by reporters, writers, advertisers, librarians, and journalists.

PERFORMING/ENTERTAINING — Being in front of people and acting in a play, directing a play, being in a band, playing a musical instrument, being an actor/actress, and so forth are part of this general interest area.

ARTS/CRAFTS — Doing fine arts activities such as going to concerts or art galleries as well as hobby pastimes such as making pottery, leather goods, or rugs are activities liked by interior designers, fashion designers, and other creative types of people.

SOCIAL SERVICE — Being with people and helping them, making new friends, working on a group project, and doing volunteer work for your town or city are activities related to being a high school counselor, social worker, scout troup leader, camp counselor, or marriage counselor.

TEACHING — Helping individuals to learn, especially in school, is an important part of this area. Teachers, instructors, child care assistants, teacher aides, and physical therapy assistants are some examples of people who have high scores on this scale.

CHILD CARE — Being with children, such as caring for them or assisting in a school, and helping children to read, spell, or play are interests related to being a nursery school teacher, elementary teacher, teacher aide, or child development specialist.

MEDICAL SERVICE — Giving medical aid to people, working in a hospital, studying first-aid, and helping at an accident are interests of medical occupations such as nurse, nurse aide, respiratory therapy assistant, radiological technician, operating room technician, and other hospital occupations.

RELIGIOUS ACTIVITIES — Singing in a choir, being a religious leader, working at a religious camp, and being a religious ambassador are activities liked by people who have a high score on this scale.

BUSINESS — Interviewing people, working in an office, being a manager, and working on a sales campaign are activities enjoyed by salespeople, advertisers, hotel managers, personnel directors, insurance agents, realtors, restaurant owners, and travel bureau agents.

SALES — Doing things that involve selling something to people are included in this area. People who like to be with the public in this way enjoy selling life insurance, real estate, clothes in a department store, or being a buyer/merchandiser. In general, there are many types of sales occupations that fit this area.

OFFICE PRACTICES — Typing letters, operating office machines such as typewriters, copying machines or adding machines, and working at a desk are activities measured by this scale. Occupations such as secretary, stenographer, administrative assistant, and receptionist are related to this area.

CLERICAL/CLERKING — Working with files of some sort, often to give information to the public, is related to occupations such as bank clerk, dental assistant, post office clerk, library clerk, and telephone operator.

FOOD SERVICE — Preparing or serving food, planning a dinner for guests, and working in a kitchen, at home or in a restaurant are activities related to being a short order cook, cafeteria worker, food service manager, and waiter/waitress.

OCCUPATIONAL SCALES

The next group of scales is the Occupational scales. These scales indicate the degree of similarity of your likes and dislikes to

those of employed people in specific occupations. These scales are more complex than the other scales and measure the significant preferences of people employed in each occupation.

In front of each Occupational scale name are one, two, or three capital letters which show how the scale relates to the Theme scales. For example, the Aircraft Mechanic scale has a capital RI in front of it; this shows that the scale has R-Realistic interests and I-Investigative interests related to it. However, for this scale, R-Realistic is more important than I-Investigative and therefore it is coded as RI and not IR. The Auto Mechanic scale just has the letter R in front of it; this indicates that the R-Realistic interest is a very important part of it, and none of the other Theme interests plays a significant role, and so only the R is listed.

Your score on each of the Occupational scales is printed in the Std. Score column. Generally, scores 45 and higher show a strong similarity of interests with employed people in the occupation. Scores 25 and lower generally are considered as showing strong dissimilarity of interests with people in an occupation. Most people in a general population have scores ranging between 26 and 44 and this range, 26-44, is considered the mid-range of scores. For each scale there is an open bar that indicates the middle 33 percent range of scores for females not in the occupation and a shaded bar that indicates the middle 33 percent range of scores for males not in the occupation.

You will have the best chance of finding satisfaction if you decide on occupations — or related occupations and careers not on the profile — where your scores are among the highest for you and less chance where your scores are among your lowest. If your answers to the inventory were different from people employed in a particular occupation, your score will be low and you probably would not like the every-day routine of that occupation. If your answers to the inventory were similar to those of people employed in a particular occupation, your score will be high and you probably would find that kind of work rewarding.

However, you should not conclude that because you have a high score on a scale, that you will be good in that occupation. Other factors, such as ability, past life experiences, personality, and educational training are other important considerations. For example, you may have interests similar to musicians, but you also need the talent to be successful in this career. Also, since some careers today are predominantly either females or males, some CAI occupational scales are based on predominantly females or males in some occupations (see CAI Manual for a complete description). Therefore, you are strongly encouraged to consider an occupation or related career where your score is considerably higher than the average for your gender (open or shaded bar) even if your score is not in the similar to very similar range. All careers are available for all individuals and you should be open-minded about considering occupations that may have been associated with just one gender in the past.

To find out additional information about these occupations and other related careers, your local professionally-trained guidance counselor and local library have a variety of informational sources to help you. In particular, you may wish to look through the following books — the Occupational Outlook Handbook and the Dictionary of Occupational Titles. These books can provide you with information about various careers, training requirements, and the employment outlook for specific occupations.

SUMMARY

Your like and dislike responses have been scored on a broad range of general interests and specific Occupational scales. You should not be totally set on any one particular occupation where your score is high, especially not at an early age. In the world of work there are hundreds of specialties and professions, and you should use this information as a guide for further thinking.

Remember, each person is unique and no test can predict with perfect accuracy the many differences among individuals. You should consider the information on this profile form together with other relevant information — skills, accomplishments, experiences, other test scores, and so forth — in making any career decision. These results should be used as guidelines to help you to better understand your interests and career possibilities.

Figure 9.6C

cant for one gender. According to Johansson (1982) this focus resulted in somewhat shorter but still valid and reliable scales. On the occupational scales standard, scores are reported for each scale and plotted on the profile sheet in a range from very similar to very dissimilar. Each occupational scale is normed so that criterion samples have a mean of 50 and a standard deviation of 10. Generally, scores of 45 and higher represent considerable similarity between an individual's preferences on the CAI and employed workers in an occupation. Scores of 44 and lower indicate less similarity with the average preferences of people in the occupation (Johansson, 1982).

There are a number of administrative indices on the CAI. The total responses index and the infrequent responses index are checks on each answer sheet to make sure that errors have not occurred in the administration, completion, or processing of the answer sheets. Other administrative indices tally the response percentages to activities, school subjects, and occupations on a continuum from "very similar" through "average" to "very dissimilar." The Fine Arts–Mechanical Index reports an overall view of how an individual responded to the items on the inventory. Scores of 58 and higher indicate a strong preference for mechanical activities and for skilled trades and technical occupations. Scores of 42 and lower indicate a strong preference for creative and social service occupations. The occupational Extroversion-Introversion Index gives an overall view of whether an individual prefers to work alone or with people. Scores of 58 and higher indicate a preference for working with things more than with people, and scores of 42 and lower indicate a preference for working with people more than with things. The Educational Orientation Index indicates how an individual's interest preferences compare to the overall interest preference of individuals who attend a liberal arts college. Scores of 40 and higher indicate a liking for studying and for creative, mathematic, fine arts, and scientific activities usually offered by a community college or liberal arts college. Scores of 30 and lower generally reflect an indifference to, or a dislike of school course work. The Variability of Interest Index indicates the diversity of individuals' interest preferences. Scores of 60 and higher indicate preference for a wide range of activities, while scores of 40 and below indicate interest in a more narrow range of activities.

The interpretive information on the back of the profile sheet (see Figure 9.6) indicates that people who enter occupations or choose careers where they have scores in the "similar" to "very similar" range tend to remain in those occupations. In addition, it is suggested that people tend to be more satisfied if they enter occupations where their interests are similar to those of the workers in that particular occupation. A person will probably tend not to be happy in an occupation in which his or her interests are dissimilar to those of the workers actively involved in the occupation. Finally, the interpretive information suggests that individuals with interests similar to those of workers in a given occupation probably find that kind of work to be personally rewarding. However, it does seem that more empirical data are needed in order to validate these rather specific interpretations of the findings of the CAI. Nevertheless, the CAI developed by Johansson is making a good effort at helping students and adults with career decisions related to beginning work immediately.

To broaden the applicability of the Career Assessment Inventory, Johansson (1986) developed the new enhanced version, which is written at the eighth-grade reading level and focuses on careers requiring up to four years of college. (The vocational version discussed above is written at the sixth-grade reading level and concentrates on careers requiring little or no postsecondary education.) Completion time is about 40 minutes. Individuals respond to the 370 items composed of activities, school subjects, and occupations by marking each item "Like very much," "Like somewhat," "Indifferent," "Dislike somewhat," or "Dislike it very much." Responses to the CAI-enhanced version are then computer scored, producing 6 general occupational theme scores, 25 basic interest scale scores, 111 occupational scale scores, and 6 administrative index scores. New features of the 1986 enhanced version include the addition of a validity check index, an increase in the number of basic interest area scales to 25, and an increase in the number of occupational scales to 111. As with the vocational version (Johansson, 1982), all scales on the 1986 edition of the enhanced version were constructed to be applicable to both genders. According to Johansson (1982, 1986) the combined gender scales help eliminate sex-restricted or sex-biased results. This cross-gender scale construction constitutes a major difference between the Career Assessment Inventory and the Kuder and Strong-Campbell inventories (Johannson, 1986). Similar to the vocational version, the scales on the enhanced version compare the individual's responses to those of workers successfully engaged in specific occupations. The primary difference is that the new enhanced version focuses on careers requiring up to four years of college and the vocational version concentrates on careers requiring little or no postsecondary education.

The Career Occupational Preference System Interest Inventory

The Career Occupational Preference System Interest Inventory Form R (COPS-R) (Knapp & Knapp, 1980a) is designed to help individuals in the career decision-making process. Like the COPS Interest Inventory, the COPS-R was developed to meet the need for a brief inventory of interests providing systematic measurement of job activity preferences. Thus, the COPS-R is appropriate for both college-oriented individuals and those vocationally oriented. (Other existing COPS Interest Inventories are the COPS Professional Level Interest Inventory for the professional world of work and the COPS II Intermediate Inventory for younger students elementary through high school.) The COPS-R is a self-contained unit that is essentially self-administering, with items written at the sixth-grade level. Approximately 20 to 30 minutes is required to respond to the items and an additional 15 to 20 minutes is required to score and plot the profile. The inventory booklet consists of 168 job activity descriptions reflecting work performed in a wide variety of occupations. Testees respond to these items by indicating "Like very much," "Like moderately," "Dislike moderately," or "Dislike very much." Based on Roe's (1956) classification of occupations into groups and

levels within each group, the COPS-R is scored on five major groups (arts, service, science, technology, and business) at two levels (professional and skilled), plus three other groups of scales (communication, clerical, consumer economics and outdoor). These groups and levels hypothesized by Roe (1956) have been validated and replicated in a number of primarily factor-analytic studies. In general, the factor-analytic studies have been based on items written to reflect the focus of activity performed in a wide range of occupations (Knapp & Knapp, 1980b).

For purposes of interpretation, the COPS-R profile compares the testees' interests with those of others at a comparable educational level in the major occupational groupings. After plotting their profile, testees are instructed to look at the peaks of highest interest on their profile sheets. In essence, these are the occupational groups in which the individuals' interests are strongest as compared with others at that educational level (Knapp & Knapp, 1980b). Scores are reported in percentile form, so if a score falls, for example, at a point represented by the percentile score of 75, the interest indicated in that occupational group would be greater than about 75 percent of the others. Knapp and Knapp (1980b) note that the greater the score, the greater the interest is in that occupational group, as compared to others who have taken the COPS-R. The normative group is made up of some 8,000-plus boys and girls from grades seven through twelve, and these data were collected in the spring of 1979. For a sample COPS-R profile see Figure 9.7.

In an effort to look at the sex fairness of the inventory, Knapp and Knapp (1980b) explored differences among 200 male and 200 female high school students. Students in the samples were drawn from all five regions represented in the national sample. Obtained F ratios across the COPS-R scales were not found to be significant.

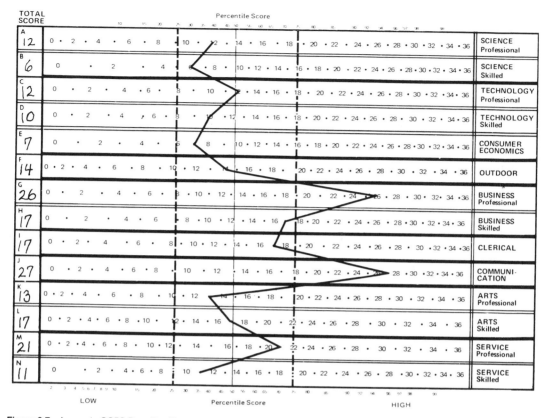

Figure 9.7 A sample COPS-R profile. (Reproduced with permission from the *Manual for the California Occupational Preference System—Form R* by L. Knapp and R. R. Knapp, pp. 12–13. Copyright 1980 by Educational and Industrial Testing Service, San Diego, Calif.)

In terms of reliability, split-half reliability coefficients are reasonably high, ranging from 0.80 to 0.90. The sample group was composed of 200 students. In another study the COPS-R inventory was administered twice within one week to 49 students. Test-retest stability coefficients ranged between 0.78 and 0.87. These data suggest some stability in the COPS-R scores for a one-week interval. The above data are reported in the manual (Knapp & Knapp, 1980b).

Some validity data are reported in the manual, but clearly additional work needs to be done. Correlations of the COPS-R scales with the corresponding scales from the original COPS Interest Inventory range from a low of 0.61 to a high of 0.78 for a group of 284 students. These concurrent validity coefficients suggest that the two forms of the COPS are assessing similar variables. Another validity study reported in the manual explored the relationship between declared major of entering college freshmen ($N = 366$) and measured interests using the COPS. The findings showed that when the three highest interest groups were examined, 71 percent of the students would have had a correct prediction of the cluster containing their declared major. Ninety-two percent had interest scores greater than those of 50 percent of the norm population in the cluster determined by their declared major. Another study explored the validity of the COPS using 404 community college students who

NOTE:: If you have taken the CAPS and COPES, get the Summary Guide from your instructor before completing this page.

⑤ To relate your high interest areas to sample occupations, complete the table below.

Identify the areas (for example, Business, Science) and the level (either skilled or professional) in which you have high or low interest. Relate your highest interest areas to sample occupations listed under each area-level cluster on pages 7, 8 and 9. Sample occupations are further classified into subgroups within each area-level cluster. Interests and, in many cases, the skills required for successful performance of individual jobs within the cluster are highly transferrable to other jobs in the cluster. Note how certain skills are required in many different jobs as you review different occupations.

Check the clusters you are considering

— 1. SCIENCE, Professional	— 4. TECHNOLOGY, Skilled	✓ 7. BUSINESS, Professional	✓ 10. COMMUNICATION	✓ 13. SERVICE, Professional
— 2. SCIENCE, Skilled	— 5. CONSUMER ECONOMICS	✓ 8. BUSINESS, Skilled	— 11. ARTS, Professional	— 14. SERVICE, Skilled
— 3. TECHNOLOGY, Professional	— 6. OUTDOOR	— 9. CLERICAL	— 12. ARTS, Skilled	

A. List your high interest areas.	B. Choose five occupations from each interest area in column A.	C. Look up occupations listed in B in sources of information (see page 11)			D. Choose three occupations from your list in column B.	E. List required skills and tasks for job performance in these three occupations.	F. List courses and training available to you for these three occupations.
		OOH	DOT	Other			
Communication	Lawyer	✓	✓	✓	Lawyer	University 3yr and Lawschool, Pass bar	Am Government Student Government
	Lawyer, Criminal	✓	✓			argue convincingly	Speech Media
	District Attorney	✓	✓			work with people	English
	Lecturer	✓	✓			think logically	Business Law
	Reporter	✓	✓	✓			
Business	Corporation Lawyer	✓	✓		Manager Hotel & Restaurant	Univ. or College→Useful but not necessary	American Hotel & Motel Association
	Lobbyist	✓	✓			work with all	JR. COLLEGE
	Political Scientist	✓	✓			kinds of people	accounting
	Manager Hotel & Restaurant	✓	✓	✓		On the Job training	economics
	Labor Relations Specialist	✓	✓				sales
Service	Social Psychologist	✓	✓		Social Psychologist	Phd required	Minority, Literature
	Case Worker	✓	✓			Be emotionally stable	Psychology
	Counselor	✓	✓			interest in people	Social Studies
	Police Chief	✓	✓			work independently	Sociology
	Physician	✓	✓			interpret research	Humanities

Figure 9.7 (cont.)

were in a variety of vocational classes: air conditioning, auto mechanics, drafters, retail sales, legal secretaries, bookkeepers, nursing, operating room technicans, and licensed vocational nurses. In general, the findings showed evidence of the relationship between vocational major and COPS Interest Inventory scores. In other words, the results lend some support to the use of COPS scores for helping students identify vocational classes.

Other Interest Inventories

There are a number of different interest inventories, as we pointed out at the beginning of this chapter. For example, the Picture Interest Inventory (PII), published by the California Test Bureau (Weingarten, 1958), asks testees to mark the activity they would most like to perform and the one that they would least like to perform in each of 53 triads of pictures. On a second part of the inventory, testees are asked to report whether they like or dislike each of the activities illustrated in 30 pictures. The PII was developed for grade seven through adulthood and takes about 30 to 40 minutes to complete. It is scored in six fields of interest (Personal-Social, Natural, Mechanical, Business, Arts, and the Sciences) and for three supplemental scales (Verbal Computational, and Time Perspective). The test-retest reliabilities for the PII range from a low of 0.76 to a high of 0.92; validity data are clearly limited, however.

Another way to assess interests is through the use of a card sort. This assessment procedure was originally developed by Tyler (1969) and extended by a number of other authors (Dolliver, 1969; Dewey, 1974; Cooper, 1976; and Jones, 1979). Initially, Tyler simply asked individuals to cluster the occupations into categories based on similarities and differences. She then inquired as to the basis or underlying constructs of the clusters that could subsequently be used

for considering additional occupations. In sum, the Tyler card sort does seem to be a sensitive, ideographic assessment technique that may be used to aid client self-understanding. Other card-sort procedures have been developed. For example, one other procedure simply asks the person to sort into categories of most and least liked or preferred some 60 to 100 cards, each indicating an occupational title. The most and least liked areas are then reviewed for futher inquiry.

An additional ideographically oriented interest assessment technique is Hall's (1976) Occupational Orientation Inventory. This inventory samples needs, job characteristics, and worker traits. The items are empirically assigned to three kinds of scales: 13 directional scales reflecting values and needs; the data, people, things orientations of the *Dictionary of Occupational Titles*; 8 degree scales that assess the testee's concerns about job factors such as co-workers and location; and a verification scale that assesses a defensive response. Counselors are subsequently encouraged to investigate with clients the personal meanings assigned to different items and to discuss scores on the various need scales. In addition, scores on the data, people, things scales are explored.

The Jackson Vocational Interest Survey (JVIS) is a new inventory consisting of 34 basic interest scales that assess either a testee's preferences for specific work roles (e.g., creative arts, skill trades, and social work) or preferences for work environments requiring specific behaviors (e.g., planfulness, independence, and interpersonal confidence). The latter preferences Jackson calls "work styles." The JVIS consists of 289 items and may be hand or machine scored. The availability of hand scoring is a distinct advantage. It takes about one hour to complete, and items are at the seventh-grade reading level. A very distinctive feature of the JVIS is the emphasis on work styles rather than interests. Jackson (1977a,b) notes that work styles are not personality dimensions, but preferences in working in environments placing a premium on certain required behaviors. The work-style scales include dominant leadership, job security, stamina, accountability, academic achievement, independence, planfulness, and interpersonal confidence (Jackson, 1977).

The Vocational Interest Inventory (VII) (Lunneborg, 1979a, 1981) is the outcome of a research program started by Lunneborg in 1968. The VII is a 112-item inventory with eight scales designed to measure the occupational types structured by Anne Roe in her Theory of Careers. The eight types are Service, Business Contact, Organizational, Technical, Outdoor, Science, General Cultural, and Arts and Entertainment. As noted by Borgen (1986) the VII has several distinctive features. From the outset, it has been organized by Roe's Occupational Classification System. Secondly, the VII has attempted to minimize sex differences at the item level and it was the first to attempt such an effort. Finally, the VII permits high school students to compare themselves with students of like age who later went on to specific career fields in college. All of these assessment techniques are used to assist clients in self-understanding that may be used in vocational development and planning.

SUMMARY

Information about a person's interests, likes, or preferences for different kinds of activities may be obtained in a variety of different ways.

Probably the most direct method of collecting information is to ask individuals what they are interested in or what they want to do when they grow up. This is called an *expressed interest*, and the individual is simply asked to make a verbal statement of liking or disliking various activities or occupations.

A second method of assessing interests involves observing a person's behavior in different situations. This is called *manifest*, or *evidenced*, *interest* and involves participation in an activity or a situation. The reasoning here is that individuals tend to participate in activities they like and find somewhat satisfying.

Tested interests, a third method of assessment, infers interests from an individual's knowledge of special terminology or relevant information about a given topic. It is assumed that interest in a vocation should result in an accumulation of relevant information about that vocation.

Inventoried interest is the fourth way of collecting information about or assessing an individual's interests. This method of assessment asks individuals to report their likes, dislikes, and preferences of items in a list of activities, occupations, or people. The method of inventoried interests is the most popular and widely used and permits a broader sampling of behaviors, likes, and preferences. This chapter discussed a few of the interest inventories that have been found to be reasonably reliable and valid for vocational counseling purposes. Inventories discussed included the Strong-Campbell Interest Inventory; the Kuder Occupational Interest Inventory, Form DD; the Self-Directed Search; the Career Assessment Inventory; and the Career Occupational Preference System.

The Assessment of Work Values, Career Development and Maturity, and Career Indecision

We will begin this chapter by discussing the assessment of work needs and values. Work needs and values, along with vocationally relevant aptitudes (as discussed in Chapter 7) and vocational interests (as discussed in Chapter 9), are the major individual varia- bles thought to be important in implement- ing the trait-factor, or "matching" approach to career choice. In this approach, individual characteristics such as abilities, interests, and needs are measured with the intent of find- ing their correspondent occupational alternatives. Thus, the assessment of work needs and values is often an important part of helping individuals make career decisions.

Measures of aptitudes, interests, needs, and values are important when considering the *content* of career choices (e.g., Crites, 1974), in that the focus when using them is on specific occupational titles or interest areas, such as law, medicine, and mechanical activities. The emphasis in interpretation and use is on "what to choose."

In contrast to the trait-factor approaches that measure aptitudes, interests, needs, and values are the theories and measures of *career development*. Generally, the emphasis of developmental approaches to career counseling is on the process, rather than the *content* of career choice—the "how to choose," rather than the "what to choose." The emphasis on "how to choose" involves consideration of the kinds of skills needed in effective career decision making, of the individual's maturation as an effective career decision maker, and of the problems and processes of career decision making.

This chapter will describe several different types of assessment methods that have been contributed by the developmental approach to career decision making. First we will describe the theories and measures of career development and career maturity. Then we will describe the concepts and measures of career indecision. The final section of the chapter will briefly describe some of the current approaches to combining individual assessment with systems, some of which are computer-based, that also teach career decision-making principles and skills. An emphasis on the process of career decision making—that is, the "how and when to choose" issues—lends itself readily to the current emphasis on career education, which is the process of *teaching* individuals how to be effective career decision makers. The measures of career indecision described here thus have received considerable use and emphasis not only in career counseling but in the design and evaluation of career education programs.

MEASURES OF WORK VALUES

Consideration of work needs and values, in addition to vocational aptitudes and interests, is important in career decision making. *Work needs* may be defined as preferences for the kinds of rewards to be gained from work. For example, some people don't particularly care what they do as long as the salary and benefits are good. Other people primarily value the work activity itself or the chance to use their abilities to the fullest and are not much concerned with how well the job pays. And, although ideally most people would probably like an exciting, enjoyable job that paid well and still left time for leisure activities, different work needs must be *prioritized* in making choices about work. Although Barbara may want a job that pays well, she may be willing to accept less pay in return for more opportunity to use her special abilities and talents. Thus, the focus of assessment usually includes a ranking or prioritizing of different work needs relative to each other *within* one individual.

The next section describes two measures of work needs or values. These measures, the Minnesota Importance Questionnaire and Super's Work Values Inventory, include probably the most important and commonly discussed work needs. In addition, both provide means by which the importance of a given work need may be compared in strength to a person's other work needs.

The Minnesota Importance Questionnaire

The Minnesota Importance Questionnaire (MIQ; Weiss, Dawis, Lofquist, Gay, & Hendel, 1975), published by Vocational Psychology Research at the University of Minnesota, assesses 20 intrapersonal vocational needs of an individual for specified job-related reinforcers. The MIQ was one of the instruments developed to operationalize the concepts of the "theory of work adjustment" developed by Dawis, Lofquist, Weiss, and their colleagues at the University of Minnesota (see Lofquist & Dawis, 1984). The theory of work adjustment, in brief, postulates that workers whose work-related *abilities* are congruent with the ability requirements of the job will perform satisfactorily on the job, and that workers whose work-related *needs* are congruent with the reinforcers provided in the occupational environment will be *satisfied* workers. The importance of the two variables of *satisfactoriness* and *satisfaction* is that they are postulated to be related to *tenure* in the occupation: The more satisfactory and satisfied the worker is, the greater the likelihood that he/she will remain in the occupation, rather than be fired or quit. To test the theory of work adjustment, the General Aptitude Test Battery (GATB, discussed in Chapter 7) has been used to assess work-related abilities, and the MIQ has been used to assess work-related needs. Both the GATB and the MIQ have also had great utility in individual counseling and personnel selection.

The MIQ requires the examinee to rate the importance of 20 work-related needs, each of which is described by a representative statement. The 20 needs and the statements used to assess them are as follows:

1. *Ability Utilization:* I could do something that makes use of my abilities.
2. *Achievement:* The job could give me a feeling of accomplishment.
3. *Activity:* I could be busy all the time.
4. *Advancement:* The job would provide an opportunity for advancement.
5. *Authority:* I could tell people what to do.
6. *Company Policies and Practices:* The company would administer its policies fairly.

7. *Compensation:* My pay would compare well with that of other workers.
8. *Co-workers:* My co-workers would be easy to make friends with.
9. *Creativity:* I could try out some of my own ideas.
10. *Independence:* I could work alone on the job.
11. *Moral Values:* I could do the work without feeling that it is morally wrong.
12. *Recognition:* I could get recognition for the work I do.
13. *Responsibility:* I could make decisions on my own.
14. *Security:* The job would provide for steady employment.
15. *Social Service:* I could do things for other people.
16. *Social Status:* I could be "somebody" in the community.
17. *Supervision-Human Relations:* My boss would back up the workers (with top management).
18. *Supervision-Technical:* My boss would train the workers well.
19. *Variety:* I could do something different every day.
20. *Working Conditions:* The job would have good working conditions.

The MIQ was revised in 1975, and two forms are available. One form uses a paired-comparison response format, which presents each of the 20 statements in pairs with each of the other 19 statements. A person is asked to indicate which statement in each pair is *more important* in his or her job. For example, examinees are asked to decide which of the following is more important to them in an ideal job: "I could do things for other people" or "I could do something that makes use of my abilities." (The first statement assesses need for Social Service, while the second assesses need for Ability Utilization.)

Because the resulting total of 190 paired comparisons is very time-consuming to administer, a ranked form is also available. In this form, the statements are presented in blocks of five, and the individual ranks the statements within each set in terms of their importance to one's ideal job. Both forms of the MIQ contain a section asking the respondent to indicate whether each statement is or isn't important in one's ideal job. These absolute judgments are used to establish an anchor, or "zero point," to use in interpreting the comparative judgments made in the main section of the test.

The MIQ is usually computer-scored through the services provided at the University of Minnesota. The scores provided include a validity score based on the number of inconsistent comparisons (called the Logically Consistent Triad or LCT score) and a profile of need scores. An example of an MIQ profile is shown in Figure 10.1.

The profile shows the LCT score, at the top left, and the scores for each need. Positive scores indicate needs that *are* important, while negative values indicate needs the examinee said are *not* important. The scores are graphed in relationship to the zero point shown in Figure 10.1. Thus, the profile provides numerical scores and a score profile showing patterns of more-versus-less important needs.

For Client A, shown in Figure 10.1, the most important work needs are Ability Utilization, Advancement, and Creativity, all having scores of 2.1, and the least important need is Social Status (-1.4). Need scores are also provided for the need *Clusters*, into which the 20 needs have been divided. Client A values the Achievement and Autonomy clusters most highly and places little importance on the Comfort and Status clusters.

To further aid in interpretation, occupations have been characterized according to which needs they are more and less likely to satisfy. These descriptions are called Occupational Reinforcer Patterns, or ORPs. In the second part of the MIQ profile, shown in Figure 10.2, the correspondence between the needs of Client A and the reinforcer patterns of a large variety of occupations is used to yield a prediction about whether or not

the client would be satisfied in the occupation. A prediction of Satisfied (S), Likely Satisfied (L), or Not Satisfied (N) is made for each occupation.

Evidence for the reliability of the MIQ is adequate. Internal consistency reliability coefficients for the individual scales have medians ranging from 0.77 to 0.81. Test-retest stability coefficients have averaged 0.47 (six-month interval) and 0.89 (immediate retesting) for the individual scale scores, and 0.70 to 0.95 for the profile scores (four-month interval to an immediate retest). Concurrent validity evidence suggests that people in occupations have needs similar to the appropriate ORPs, but more evidence regarding predictive validity is needed.

In summary, the MIQ is a useful measure of work-related needs. The manual for the MIQ (Rounds, Henly, Dawis, Lofquist, & Weiss, 1981) and a pamphlet entitled the *Counseling Use of the Minnesota Importance Questionnaire* (Lofquist & Dawis, 1975) are helpful in equipping test users to assist clients to understand their vocationally relevant needs and to use that information in selecting potentially satisfying careers.

The Work Values Inventory

The Work Values Inventory (WVI) was developed by Donald E. Super (1970) to measure 15 values important in determining an individual's satisfaction and success in a vocation. The WVI is designed for use with people from seventh grade through adulthood.

The values assessed by the WVI may be divided logically into three categories of work values. The first category includes *intrinsic* work values, meaning aspects of work that are valued for their own sake. Intrinsic values assessed by the WVI include altruism, independence, creativity, intellectual stimulation, esthetics, achievement, and management. The second category, *extrinsic* work values, includes characteristics of the work

```
                    MINNESOTA IMPORTANCE QUESTIONNAIRE
                          Paired Form, 1980
Date--July 20, 1981
LCT Score = 91%                                    Name--Client A

                                        Unimp              Important
                                     -1.0      0.0     +1.0     +2.0      +3.0
                               Score  |.........|.........|.........|.........|
                ACHIEVEMENT    1.7*                  |                  V
Ability Utilization: could make
   use of my abilities..........      2.1           |              --->X-----
Achievement: could give me a
   feeling of accomplishment.....      1.2           |        ->X----

                    COMFORT     .2*                  | V
Activity: could be busy all the
   time........................      -.2          X |
Independence: could work alone
   on the job..................       .2           --->X----
Variety: could do something dif-
   ferent every day.............       .4           |  X-
Compensation: pay would compare
   well with other workers.......     -.4        --->X
Security: would provide for
   steady employment...........       .2           ->X--
Working Conditions: would have
   good working conditions.......      .7           |  -->X-

                    STATUS      .3*                  | V
Advancement: would provide an
   opportunity for advancement...     2.1           |            --->X-----
Recognition: could get recogni-
   tion for the work I do........     1.0           |       ->X--
Authority: could tell people
   what to do...................      -.4        --->X-
Social Status: could be "some-
   body" in the community........    -1.4      X-X

                    ALTRUISM    .7*                  |      V
Co-workers: would be easy to
   make friends with............       .2          |->X--
Social Service: could do things
   for other people............       .8           | -->X--
Moral Values: could work without
   feeling it is morally wrong...     1.0           |  ----->X-----

                    SAFETY      .5*                  |     V
Company Policies: would adminis-
   ter its policies fairly.......     1.0           |      --->X-
Supervision--Human Relations: my
   boss would back up the workers     1.2           |       ->X----
Supervision--Technical: my boss
   would train the workers well..     -.6         ---->X

                    AUTONOMY    1.7*                 |                V
Creativity: could try out some
   of my own ideas..............       2.1          |            --->X-----
Responsibility: could make deci-
   sions on my own..............       1.2          |        ->X----
                               Score  |.........|.........|.........|.........|
                                     -1.0      0.0     +1.0     +2.0      +3.0
                                      Unimp              Important
```

1234/1222334

Figure 10.1   MIQ Report for Client A, including correspondence report, as shown in the MIQ Manual. Copyright © 1981 by Vocational Psychology Research, Department of Psychology, University of Minnesota. Reproduced by permission of the copyright holder.

Correspondence Report for Client A   Date: July 20, 1981
MIQ profile is compared with Occupational Reinforcer Patterns (ORP'S)
for 90 representative occupations. Correspondence is indicated by
the C-Index. A prediction of Satisfied (S) results from C values
greater than .50, Likely Satisfied (L) for C values between .10 and
.49, and Not Satisfied (N) for C values less than .10. Occupations
are clustered by similarity of Occupational Reinforcer Pattern.

	C Index	Pred. Sat.		C Index	Pred. Sat.
Cluster A (ACH-AUT-Alt)	.53	S	**Cluster B (ACH-Com)**	.39	L
Architect	.70	S	Bricklayer	.19	L
Dentist	.22	L	Carpenter	.44	L
Family Practitioner (M.D.)	.12	L	Cement Mason	.18	L
Interior Designer-Decorator	.60	S	Elevator Repairer	.38	L
Lawyer	.34	L	Heavy Equipment Operator	.43	L
Minister	.36	L	Landscape Gardener	.42	L
Nurse, Occupational Health	.28	L	Lather	.31	L
Occupational Therapist	.61	S	Millwright	.42	L
Optometrist	.28	L	Painter/Paperhanger	.33	L
Psychologist, Counseling	.50	S	Patternmaker, Metal	.33	L
Recreation Leader	.51	S	Pipefitter	.32	L
Speech Pathologist	.50	S	Plasterer	.23	L
Teacher, Elementary School	.60	S	Plumber	.34	L
Teacher, Secondary School	.63	S	Roofer	.24	L
Vocational Evaluator	.65	S	Salesperson, Automobile	.48	L
Cluster C (ACH-Aut-Com)	.56	S	**Cluster D (ACH-STA-Com)**	.66	S
Alteration Tailor	.47	L	Accountant, Certified Public	.62	S
Automobile Mechanic	.37	L	Airplane Co-Pilot, Commercial	.06	N
Barber	.47	L	Cook (Hotel-Restaurant)	.54	S
Beauty Operator	.67	S	Department Head, Supermarket	.50	S
Caseworker	.59	S	Drafter, Architectural	.69	S
Claim Adjuster	.65	S	Electrician	.50	S
Commercial Artist, Illustrat.	.68	S	Engineer, Civil	.75	S
Electronics Mechanic	.53	S	Engineer, Time Study	.92	S
Locksmith	.37	L	Farm-Equipment Mechanic I	.40	L
Maintenance Repairer, Factory	.49	L	Line-Installer-Repairer (Tel)	.27	L
Mechanical-Engineering Tech.	.74	S	Machinist	.52	S
Office-Machine Servicer	.45	L	Programmer (Bus., Eng., Sci.)	.64	S
Photoengraver (Stripper)	.46	L	Sheet Metal Worker	.56	S
Sales Agent, Real Estate	.57	S	Statistical-Machine Servicer	.46	L
Salesperson, General Hardware	.36	L	Writer, Technical Publication	.69	S
Cluster E (COM)	.14	L	**Cluster F (Alt-Com)**	.30	L
Assembler, Production	.02	N	Airplane-Flight Attendant	.05	N
Baker	.20	L	Clerk, Gen. Ofc., Civil Svc.	.18	L
Bookbinder	.23	L	Dietitian	.46	L
Bookkeeper I	.24	L	Fire Fighter	.23	L
Bus Driver	-.02	N	Librarian	.53	S
Key-Punch Operator	.00	N	Medical Technologist	.25	L
Meat Cutter	-.04	N	Nurse, Professional	.24	L
Post-Office Clerk	-.00	N	Orderly	.08	N
Production Helper (Food)	.33	L	Physical Therapist	.51	S
Punch-Press Operator	.18	L	Police Officer	.29	L
Sales, General (Dept. Store)	.51	S	Receptionist, Civil Service	.43	L
Sewing-Machine Operator, Auto	.10	L	Secretary (General Office)	.49	L
Solderer (Production Line)	.07	N	Taxi Driver	.16	L
Telephone Operator	.05	N	Telephone Installer	.27	L
Teller (Banking)	.06	N	Waiter-Waitress	.20	L

Vocational Psychology Research . . . Department of Psychology
University of Minnesota . . . Minneapolis, MN 55455

Figure 10.2 MIQ Correspondence Report for Client A.

environment and the rewards that work *brings*, rather than pleasures gained from actually doing the work. Extrinsic "concommitants," or characteristics, of the work environment include surroundings, associates, supervisory relations, and variety. The third category of extrinsic rewards includes security, prestige, economic returns, and way of life (meaning the kinds of life styles permitted when pursuing different occupations).

Each of the 15 scales of the WVI is assessed by three items reflective of the work value. The examinee rates the importance of each statement using a five point Likert scale ranging from "very important" to "unimportant." The score for each scale is the sum of the responses to the three scale items. The resulting scores can be ranked, with particular attention to the highest and lowest scores. Percentile norms are provided for students in grades 7 to 12, but no normative data are available for adults.

Although there is some evidence for the reliability of the measure (see Super, 1973b) more reliability data, as well as validity and normative data, are needed. The WVI is another potentially useful means of assessing individuals' work-related values. Further research investigating its psychometric characteristics and applied utility would contribute to its potential. For further information about the WVI see Super (1973b) and a review by Brown (1971).

The Values Scale. The Values Scale (VS) was developed by Super and Nevill (1986) to assess 21 values relevant to career but also to move general life interests. The 21 values include both intrinsic and extrinsic values and include values such as Achievement, Aesthetics, Creativity, Economic Rewards, Lifestyle, Personal Development, Physical Activity, Risk, and Social Interaction. The VS was developed as part of the International Work Importance Study, and

has consequently been translated into several languages. There are norms for Canadian, Yugoslavian, and Portuguese, as well as American, high school and college students and adults.

The VS consists of five Likert-type items measuring each of the 21 scales. Table 10.1 shows the 21 scales and an example of an item measuring each one. Responses (1 to 4) are summed for the five scale items, so scale scores can range from 5 to 20. The *Manual for the Values Scale* (Nevill & Super, 1986) provides some preliminary normative information, but the test authors caution against using norm-based interpretations in counseling until more data are available. For counseling purposes they suggest ipsative interpretation, that is, the individual's higher-versus lower-ranked values rather than the absolute score levels.

The manual for the VS provides evidence for the internal consistency reliability of the scales, ranging from the high 0.60s to the high 0.80s. Test-retest stability coefficients ranged from the low 0.50s to the low 0.80s, but the manual does not report the time interval between testings. Evidence for validity is still scant, and the authors strongly suggest the need for further research on the VS.

MEASURES OF CAREER DEVELOPMENT AND CAREER MATURITY

Current theories and measures of career development and career maturity may be said to have begun with the work of Donald Super (1957), along with Ginzberg, Ginsburg, Axelrad, and Herman (1951), and Tiedeman and O'Hara (1963). These writers may be credited with the development of the theoretical underpinnings for both measures of career development and career maturity and the extensive emphasis on career education

Table 10.1 VS scales and sample statements

VALUE SCALE	SAMPLE STATEMENT
1. Ability Utilization	use all my skills and knowledge
2. Achievement	have results which show that I have done well
3. Advancement	get ahead
4. Aesthetics	make life more beautiful
5. Altruism	help people with problems
6. Authority	tell others what to do
7. Autonomy	act on my own
8. Creativity	discover, develop, or design new things
9. Economic Rewards	have a high standard of living
10. Life Style	live according to my own ideas
11. Personal Development	develop as a person
12. Physical Activity	get a lot of exercise
13. Prestige	be admired for my knowledge and skills
14. Risk	do risky things
15. Social Interaction	do things with other people
16. Social Relations	be with friends
17. Variety	have every day be different in some way from the one before it
18. Working Conditions	have good space and light in which to work
19. Cultural Identity	live where people of my religion and race are accepted
20. Physical Prowess	work hard physically
21. Economic Security	be where employment is regular and secure

Taken from D. D. Nevill and D. E. Super, *Values Scale Manual: Theory, Application, and Research* (1986). Copyright © 1986 by Consulting Psychologists Press, 577 College Avenue, Palo Alto, Calif. Reproduced by permission of the publisher.

in schools and a variety of other settings. Although the reader should consult the many excellent resources on career development theory (e.g., Osipow, 1983) for detailed explanations of these theories, a brief overview of Super's theory is necessary to set the stage for a discussion of measures of career development and career maturity.

The major tenet of Super's theoretical work (for the purposes of this chapter) was the idea that the career focus of people's lives was subject to the same kinds of development, growth, and change over time as were other aspects of people's lives. More specifically, Super postulated that vocational development could be characterized as following the same stages as did other life tasks and followed Charlotte Buehler (1933) in the use of the stages of growth, exploration,

establishment, maintenance, and decline to describe vocational development.

The concept of stages in vocational development had several important related ideas. First, Super (1957) contended that the choice of an occupation should be viewed as a continuous process that extends over many years' time, rather than as a one-time event of making a specific choice, such as engineering or nursing. This view leads to a change in the emphasis of career counseling, from helping the client make a specific, one-time career choice to helping the client learn the skills important to the lifelong process of career decision making and development.

Second, Super postulated that each of the vocational life stages presented one or more vocational tasks or challenges that the individual must be able to successfully negotiate or master in order to progress in his/her career development. More specifically, Super (Super, 1963; Super, Crites, Hummel, Moser, Overstreet, & Warnath, 1957) postulated several major career development tasks important to the growth process: crystallization, specification, implementation, stabilization, and consolidation. Crystallization, which generally occurs in the age range of 14 to 18, requires the individual to begin to develop ideas about the kind of work appropriate for that person—in other words, to begin forming a self-concept and the ability to relate that self-concept to educational and occupational possibilities. Specification, which usually occurs in the age range 18 to 21, is the specification of a vocational preference. And although preliminary implementation steps may be occurring in the specification stage, ages 21 to 24 generally call for the actual implementation of the vocational preference. Stabilization, which occurs between the ages of 25 and 35, is the task of settling down within the occupation, achieving at least a reasonable degree of success and satisfaction. Consolidation occurs during the late 30s and early 40s when the people become firmly established and are secure and comfortable in their vocational position.

The view of career choice as a continuing process, then, and the emphasis on the specific tasks and competencies important at each stage led to the emphasis on the assessment and facilitation of career maturity. *Career maturity* can be very generally defined as the extent to which the individual is, in fact, mastering the tasks important for one's developmental level. Measures of career maturity focus on a specific set of developmental tasks and attempt to assess the individual's mastery of those tasks. Three well-known measures of career maturity— Crites's (1978a) Career Maturity Inventory, Super's Career Development Inventory (Super, Thompson, Lindeman, Jordan, & Myers, 1981), and Westbrook's Cognitive

Vocational Maturity Test (Westbrook & Mastie, 1974)—will be the focus of this section. These three inventories have focused mainly on the assessment of career maturity in adolescents and young adults, the most frequent group of individuals targeted for career counseling and career education programs as well as for the assessment and study of career maturity. Other career maturity inventories will be mentioned in brief.

The Career Maturity Inventory

Crites's (1978a) Career Maturity Inventory (formerly called the Vocational Development Inventory) is based on his *model* of career maturity in adolescence. The Crites model, shown in Figure 10.3, is a hierarchical model of career development. At the top, or most general, level is the degree of overall career development, which can be described or defined by four group factors, two of which describe career choice *content* and two of which describe the *process* of career choices.

The maturity of career choice *content* (the individual's current occupational preferences and/or choices) is defined by the "Consistency of career choices" and by the "Realism of career choices." Consistency refers to how consistent the individual's preferences are over time (such as from one month to the next) and across field (for example, science versus art) and level (for example, professional level versus unskilled work). Realism refers to the "match" between the person's individual characteristics, such as abilities and interests, and the characteristics of the job preferences or choices. Inclusion of the "Realism of career choices" is the means by which Crites's model incorporates the "matching," or trait-factor, approach to career choice.

In addition to defining career maturity in terms of *what* the individual chooses, Crites defines career maturity in terms of *how* the choices are made. The "how," or the "proc-

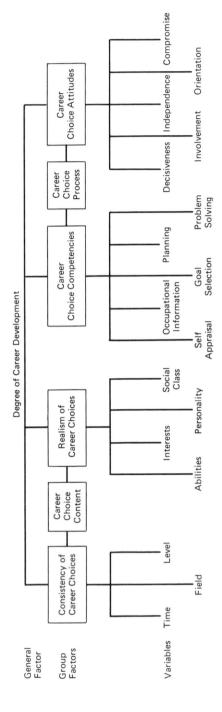

Figure 10.3 Crites's model of career maturity in adolescence. (Reproduced from Crites (1978a) by permission of the publisher, CTB/McGraw-Hill, 2500 Garden Road, Monterey, Calif. 93940. Copyright © 1978 by McGraw-Hill, Inc. All Rights Reserved. Printed in the U.S.A.)

ess," of career decision making is the section of Crites's model incorporating Super's concept of career development tasks and is defined to include two sets of variables, "career choice competencies" and "career choice attitudes" (see Figure 10.3).

Thus, competencies and attitudes describe the quality or maturity of the *process* by which individuals make career choices. Crites's Career Maturity Inventory (CMI) is designed to measure these process variables constituting career maturity and is thus organized into two major sections: the Competence Test, measuring the career choice competencies shown in the figure; and the Attitude Scale, measuring the "career choice attitudes" shown.

The CMI Competence Test. In general, the CMI Competence Test is designed to measure the degree to which the individual possesses the career information and the planning and decision-making skills necessary to make realistic and wise educational and career decisions. More specifically the Competence Test measures five components of effective career decision making. For each component, a technical title and a title by which the test is described to examinees indicate the purpose of the particular subtest. In the description below, the first title is the formal name of the concept or purpose, while the title in parentheses is that provided to examinees.

The first competence test is *Self-Appraisal* ("*Knowing Yourself*"). The first step in both trait-factor and developmental theories of career choice is the acquisition of self-knowledge, awareness of one's abilities, interests, values, and self-concept. More vocationally mature individuals possess greater self-knowledge, and understanding. Operationally, this test requires the examinee to accurately assess the career-relevant capabilities of others. Table 10.2 shows a sample item from this subtest.

Table 10.2 Sample Items from the Five Sections of the Competence Test of the Career Maturity Inventory

Section and Sample Item

Self-Appraisal ("Knowing Yourself")

Duane does a lot of woodshop work at home and also takes shop courses at school. He has made several professional-looking cabinets and has won a prize for one in a citywide contest. He is now trying to decide if he has enough skill to continue with cabinetmaking. What do you think?

F   The work he has done suggests that he has above average cabinetmaking skill and interest.

G   If his friends think he has cabinetmaking skills, he probably does and should continue making cabinets.

H   He should plan carefully, since he may not have enough skill to be a successful cabinetmaker later on.

J   He has skill in making cabinets, and he should also design them.

K   Don't know

Occupational Information ("Knowing About Jobs")

Chuck watched carefully as the huge press ran at top speed, turning out the *Daily Star* evening newspaper. Suddenly, he pushed a button and stopped the press to repair a tear in the roll of paper that was feeding into one of the rollers. He also checked the ink tanks and filled those that were running low. He started the press again and finished the first part of the newspaper. With new plates in place for the remaining parts, he once again started the press and finished the job. What is his occupation?

F   laboratory technician

G   office machine operator

H   printer

J   tool-and-die maker

K   don't know

Goal Selection ("Choosing a Job")

Marty has many interests. He has been in the Debating Club for three years; he has written stories for the school newspaper; he has worked on the school yearbook; and, at the same time, he is one of the best students in the school. He is very good with words and can say exactly what he means. He is also quite persuasive and can often win people to his point of view. Which one of the following occupations would be the best for him?

F   psychologist

G   literary agent

H   insurance agent

J   lawyer

K   don't know

Table 10.2 (Continued)

Planning ("Looking Ahead")

Cindy wants to be a beautician. Three steps she can take to
become one are:
1   find a job as a beautician
2   pass the state licensing tests for beauticians
3   attend a school of beauty culture (cosmetology)
What is the correct order of these steps?

F	1	3	2
G	2	3	1
H	3	1	2
J	3	2	1
K	don't know		

Problem solving ("What Should They Do?")

Paul's father is a doctor and wants him to be a doctor also.
But he is more interested in business as a career. What
should he do?
- F   Be a doctor
- G   Go into business
- H   Try to change his father's mind
- J   Ask a friend what to do
- K   Don't know

SOURCE: Reproduced from J. O. Crites, *Career Maturity
Inventory,* by permission of the publisher, CTB/McGraw-
Hill, 2500 Garden Road, Monterey, CA. 93940. Copyright
© 1978 by McGraw-Hill, Inc. All Rights Reserved. Printed
in the U.S.A.

The second subtest measures *Occupational Information* ("*Knowing About Jobs*"). In addition to knowledge about oneself it is important to possess knowledge about the world of work. Accuracy and extent of job knowledge differentiate the more from the less vocationally mature individuals. Operationally, this test measures the examinee's knowledge of job content, that is, the duties and tasks of various occupations. Table 10.2 provides an illustrative test item.

Third, the CMI measures *Goal Selection* ("*Choosing a Job*"). After acquiring knowledge of both self and the world of work, the vocationally mature individual is able to relate one to the other in the process of career decision making. This aspect of competence in essence attempts to define what Parsons (1909) called "true reasoning" in the process of career decision making. To quote Crites

(1964, p. 329): "The more vocationally mature person not only has greater knowledge about self and work but relates one to the other. . . . He [or she] attempts to 'bridge the gap' between himself [or herself] and the world of work, to achieve a 'synthesis,' as Super (1957) puts it, of the major factors involved in occupational choice." The Goal Selection test assesses the individual's ability to "match" individuals and work environments. The items, a sample of which appears in Table 10.2, require the examinee to correctly match people with jobs.

The fourth test is *Planning* ("*Looking Ahead*"). Once a career decision is made it must of course be implemented. Planning as to how the decided-upon goal is to be achieved is therefore the next logical step in the process of career decision making. As stated by Crites, the concept of planning refers to "the tendency of the individual to think about the means which are necessary to attain a desired end" (1964, p. 328). Major important facets of planning are (1) the time spent in planning, (2) the specificity of planning, (3) the relevance of means to ends in planning, and (4) the ordering of steps in planning. The items of the Planning subtest (see Table 10.2) assess the latter aspect, that is, the ability to properly order steps important in implementing a career decision. Generally these steps include obtaining the appropriate education and/or training, finding employment in the field, and gaining necessary credentials, such as licensing or certification, in the field.

The final Competence Test is *Problem Solving* ("*What Should They Do?*"). The process of making and implementing career decisions is almost never totally problem-free. Rather, problems or obstacles arise along the way and problem solving and coping must occur so that the process of career development may continue. Thus, more career-mature individuals are not only better at initial career decision making and planning, but also are more able to deal effectively with problems that arise. The items in this subtest present various problematic situations related to making and implementing career decisions, such as conflicts with parents, insufficient aptitude for a preferred occupation, and career indecision and unrealism. An example of an item is shown in Table 10.2. The multiple-choice alternatives present several possible solutions to the problem; more career-mature individuals should select more versus less effective solutions.

The subscales of the Competence Test are scored by counting the number of "correct" responses to each of the 20 multiple-choice items. Thus, the subscale scores may range from 0 to 20, while the total score may range up to 100. Responses are defined as "correct" based on a wide variety of occupational information, such as worker trait characteristics and educational and training requirements. The CMI Competence Test is similar in conception to an academic achievement test because it represents a reasonably well-defined domain of knowledge for which correct/appropriate responses can be specified. Thus, the "number correct" score is indicative of the extent to which the individual has mastered that body of content which may be summarized as knowledge of self and occupational environments and career decision making, implementation, and problem-solving skills (Crites, 1981).

The CMI items and keyed responses are also consistent with the notion of career maturity as a *developmental* variable. More specifically, career maturity is postulated to increase with age; therefore, people who are older and/or in higher school grades should on the average earn higher scores on the test. To ensure that the CMI measures a maturational variable, the test items selected were those to which the percentage of correct responses increased systematically with increased age and school grade levels. Thus, the CMI Competence Test utilizes both rational and empirical approaches to test contruction.

Based on the number correct, test scores may be interpreted in terms of standard scores or percentile ranks as a function of school grade. The manual for the CMI (Crites, 1978b) provides standard score and percentile norms for students in grades 6 through 12.

Internal consistency reliability data indicate that the scales of the Competence Test are, in general, relatively homogeneous. Kuder-Richardson-20 values have ranged from 0.72 to 0.90 in samples of sixth through twelfth graders. Only the problem solving scale at the sixth and seventh grade levels is of questionable reliability (KR-20 coefficients of 0.58 and 0.63, respectively). Evidence for criterion-related validity is based on the increase in Competence Test scores with increasing grade level. Evidence for construct validity includes scale intercorrelations of the Competence Test (average values ranging from about 0.53 to 0.68, depending on the test pair and the grade level) and correlations of the attitude and competence scales. Correlations with Westbrook's Cognitive Vocational Maturity Test (CVMT) range from 0.55 to 0.65 for the Competence Test and CVMT and Competence Test total scores. Finally, there is evidence that average scores on the Competence Test increase for individuals receiving career education (Crites, 1981).

The CMI Attitude Scale. The CMI Attitude Scale measures five aspects of the maturity of a person's *attitudes* toward careers and career choices. These five aspects of career maturity, shown in the model of career maturity depicted in Figure 10.3, under "career choice attitudes," are further defined in Table 10.3. Given the definitions provided in Table 10.3, it may be noted that maturity in career choice *attitudes* is defined by Crites as (1) greater decisiveness in mak-

Table 10.3 Variables in the Attitude Scale of the Career Maturity Inventory

Dimension	Definition	Sample Item
Decisiveness in career decision making	Extent to which an individual is definite about making a career choice	"I keep changing my occupational choice."
Involvement in career decision making	Extent to which individual is actively participating in the process of making a choice	"I'm not going to worry about choosing an occupation until I'm out of school."
Independence in career decision making	Extent to which individual relies upon others in the choice of an occupation	"I plan to follow the line of work my parents suggest."
Orientation to career decision making	Extent to which individual is task- or pleasure-oriented in his/her attitudes toward work and the values he/she places upon work	"I have little or no idea of what working will be like."
Compromise in career decision making	Extent to which individual is willing to compromise between needs and reality	"I spent a lot of time wishing I could do work I know I can never do."

SOURCE: Reproduced from J. O. Crites, *Career Maturity Inventory: Theory and Research Handbook* (2nd Ed.), by permission of the publisher, CTB/McGraw-Hill, 2500 Garden Road, Monterey, CA. 93940. Copyright © 1978 by McGraw-Hill, Inc. All Rights Reserved. Printed in the U.S.A.

ing a career choice, (2) greater active involvement in the process, (3) greater independence in decision making rather than reliance on others, (4) ability to accept certain realities about work, such as the reality that work isn't always a lot of fun; and (5) the ability to compromise between one's needs/wants and reality. For each attitudinal dimension, a sample item, to which examinees give an answer of "true" or "false," is provided.

There are currently two forms of the CMI Attitude Scale, a 50-item Screening Form (Form A-2; Form A-1 was the original screening form superseded by Form A-2) and a 75-item Counseling Form (Form B-1). The Screening Form provides an overall score indicating attitudinal maturity across the entire 50-item scale, while the Counseling Form provides subscores for each of the five attitudinal dimensions as well. Like the Competence Test, the Attitude Scale is scored by counting the number of "keyed" responses. Determination of the direction of item scoring—that is, the response indicative of more rather than less mature career-related attitudes—was made in accordance with the re-

sponses of a majority of twelfth grade students in the standardization sample. Thus, if 51 percent or more of twelfth graders answered "true" to a given attitudinal statement, then "true" would be designated as the correct or keyed response. It should be noted that in a study by Hall (1962), obtaining the opinions of 10 counseling psychologists regarding the more vocationally mature response, the expert judges failed to agree with the empirically determined keyed response in 26 of the 100 items. Another problem with the scoring key is that 47 of the 50 items on the Screening Form and 60 of the 75 items on the Counseling Form are keyed "false." Thus, the scale may be open to problems of faking and response bias. Students may figure out that "false" responses predominate and respond "false" more often than they would otherwise, thus artificially inflating their maturity scores. Students who have a general tendency to respond with "false" ("naysayers") would also inflate their maturity scores.

Reliability and validity data for the CMI Attitude Scale have been obtained for the Screening Forms (A-1 and A-2), but considerably less so for the Counseling Form (B-1). The internal consistency reliability (KR-20) of Form A-2 of the Attitude Scale averaged 0.74 across grade levels. Since the total score combines scores from five related but not identical attitudes, this relatively low figure is not surprising. However, the sub-scale scores are not particularly internally consistent either, ranging from 0.50 (Compromise) to 0.72 (Orientation), with 0.62 for Involvement, 0.67 for Decisiveness, and 0.71 for Independence. Test-retest reliability would also be expected to be somewhat low to allow maturational variance, yet high enough to ensure that the variable is being measured systematically. The stability of Form A-1, $r = 0.71$ over a one-year interval, is in this range.

Evidence for the content validity of the CMI Attitude Scale comes primarily from the fact that item content was derived from central concepts and ideas in the career development literature. Evidence for the criterion-related validity of the scale is discussed in the theory and research handbook for the CMI (Crites, 1981). In brief, the maturity of attitudes has been shown to be related to such variables as the realism of occupational aspirations (Bathory, 1967; Hollender, 1964; Crites, 1978c), career decisiveness (Carek, 1965), certainty and commitment to career choice (Graves, 1974), and congruence of Holland code and students' career choices (Capehart, 1973; Walsh & Osipow, 1973). Although most of the correlations found in these studies are small in magnitude, their consistency with theoretical prediction is encouraging. Correlations with other measures of career maturity are relatively small, such as 0.30 to 0.38 with Gribbons and Lohnes's Readiness for Vocational Planning scales.

In terms of construct validity and explication, scores on the CMI Attitude Scale do seem to be related to general intellectual ability or scholastic aptitude. Correlations of Attitude Scale scores with intellectual ability average about 0.40 in high school students and are somewhat lower in college samples. Thus, verbally expressed career attitudes are related to more general verbal intelligence or aptitude. Scores also appear to be related to better general personality adjustment—for example, greater assertiveness, persistence, goal orientation, and independence—and better vocational adjustment as represented by variables such as persistence in college, success in vocational training, and educational achievement. Finally, career counseling and education programs have been found to positively affect career maturity as reflected in CMI Attitude Scores.

Using the CMI. Figure 10.4 shows a sample CMI profile providing scores on both the Attitude Scale and the Competence Test. This examinee, Karen, who was seeking vocational counseling, took the Screening Form of the Attitude Scale, and thus a total score but not subscores are yielded. For each scale, the raw score, the standard score, and percentile rank for a twelfth grade student, plus a graphic portrayal of the percentile score, are provided. Karen appears to possess very mature career attitudes (93rd percentile), but her scores on the Competence Test indicate some weak areas. Karen appears quite competent in Problem Solving (90th percentile), seems reasonably mature in her mastery of Occupational Information, Goal Selection, and Planning (66th, 66th, and 69th percentiles respectively), but is very weak in Self-Appraisal (16th percentile). Her low score on self-appraisal is particularly noteworthy, given her otherwise reasonably high levels of maturity. A counselor working with Karen would be alerted by the CMI profile to focus time on Karen's apparent problems with self-assessment/self-knowledge. Perhaps personal conflicts or problems—for example, low self-esteem or reliance on others' judgments of her—prevent this otherwise rela-

CAREER MATURITY PROFILE

Published by CTB/McGraw-Hill, Del Monte Research Park, Monterey, California 93940. Copyright ©1978 by McGraw-Hill, Inc. All Rights Reserved. Printed in the U.S.A.

Name ▶ KAREN
Teacher ▶
School ▶

Test Date ▶
Birth Date ▶
City ▶

Grade ▶ 12
Age ▶ 17

Batch ▶
Group ▶
Run Date ▶

These scores are derived from
X national or
local
interpretive frequency distributions.

HOME REPORT

94594

Attitude Scale

Rate of Career Maturity
Standard Score and Percentile Rank Scales

	Raw Score	Standard Score	Percentile Rank
X Form A-1 Screening Form A-2 Counseling Form B-1	42 of 50	65	93
1 Decisiveness in Career Decision Making	of 10		
2 Involvement in Career Decision Making	of 10		
3 Independence in Career Decision Making	of 10		
4 Orientation to Career Decision Making	of 10		
5 Compromise in Career Decision Making	of 7		

Competence Test

	Raw Score	Standard Score	Percentile Rank
Part 1 Knowing Yourself (Self-Appraisal)	10 of 20	40	16
Part 2 Knowing About Jobs (Occupational Information)	18 of 20	54	66
Part 3 Choosing a Job (Goal Selection)	15 of 20	54	66
Part 4 Looking Ahead (Planning)	16 of 20	55	69
Part 5 What Should They Do? (Problem Solving)	15 of 20	63	90

Figure 10.4 Sample profile from the Career Maturity Inventory. (From the *Administration and Use Manual, 2nd Ed.*) Reproduced by permission of the publishers, CTB/McGraw-Hill, 2500 Garden Road, Monterey, Calif. 93940. Copyright © 1978 by McGraw-Hill, Inc. All Rights Reserved.

tively mature individual from mature career decision making.

Although not shown on the profile depicted in Figure 10.4, the subscores provided with the Counseling Form of the Attitude Scale may also be very useful in career counseling. Evidence of career immaturity on one or more dimensions may suggest the need to discuss the client's personal concerns. For example, a client whose father wants him or her to be a doctor may have difficulty resisting the father's influence attempts if the client lacks in *independence*. Particularly with women clients, sex-role socialization and reliance on societal expectations of women may lead to a low score on the independence scale, indicating difficulties in career decision making, and home-career conflict (the view that marriage and career are incompatible) may adversely affect *conceptions* of career decision making. An individual who has decided that he or she wants to be an engineer, but who is low in math ability and at the same time unwilling to *compromise* will be in need of additional counseling assistance. Thus, both the level and pattern of attitudinal career maturity can be very important in career counseling.

In addition to their usefulness in individual career counseling, the CMI Attitude Scale and Competence Test are also very useful in the design and evaluation of career education programs. Programs of education may be focused on dimensions in which the performance of a group—a school class, for example—is particularly low in career maturity.

Although the major uses of the CMI have been with high school students, an adult version of the CMI is also available (Crites, 1978c). Designed for use with post-high-school men and women, the inventory uses the same items used in the regular CMI; adult examinees are asked to respond "as if" the items described their situations, even though the items may not appear to have

direct relevance. The major difference between the adult CMI and the regular version of the inventory is that the adult form is designed to be self-administered; the test and instructions are simply provided to the adult respondent.

Some researchers have also questioned the construct validity of both the CMI and the model of career development on which it is based, despite the fact that both are widely used in applied settings. For an extensive and detailed review of these concerns, see Betz (1989).

The Career Development Inventory

The Career Development Inventory (CDI), developed by Donald Super and his colleagues at Teachers College of Columbia University, is designed to accomplish the same general purposes as the Career Maturity Inventory (Super, Thompson, Lindeman, Jordan, & Myers, 1981). Like the CMI, the CDI scales are organized roughly into a knowledge component, similar to the CMI Competence Test, and an attitude component, similar to the CMI Attitude Scale. The scales of the CDI are as follows:

1. *Career Planning* (CP), assesses the degree to which the student has engaged in career planning and also contains questions concerning students' knowledge of the kind of work they would like to do. The scale contains 20 items. Table 10.4 provides an example of the types of items contained in the Career Planning scale.

2. *Career Exploration* (CE) attempts to measure the quality of exploratory attitudes by asking the student to rate the quality of various possible sources of occupational information—such as friends, professors, counselors, books, and TV shows—and to indicate how much useful information he or she has obtained from each of those sources. The CE scale contains 20 items, several of which are provided in Table 10.4.

3. *Decision Making* (DM) measures the ability to apply knowledge and insight to the prob-

lems of career planning and decision making. The 20 items involve hypothetical people making career decisions or needing to solve some career-related problem (see Table 10.4). The scale is viewed as primarily measuring a cognitive rather than an attitudinal component of career maturity.

4. *World-of-Work Information* (WW) assesses knowledge of the tasks of Super's (1957) exploratory and early establishment stages and knowledge of specific occupations. Like the other subtests, WW contains 20 items of the type shown in Table 10.4.

5. *Knowledge of Preferred Occupational Group* (PO) presents 20 occupational groups (shown on the back of the CDI answer sheet, as shown in Figure 10.5). The groups include, for example, "Biological and Medical Science," "Social Science: Research," and "Social Science: Teaching/Social Service." Students are asked to select a preferred occupational group and then to answer 40 multiple-choice questions pertaining to that group. (To help students identify their group, a modified version of the DAT Career Planning Questionnaire [Psychological Corporation, 1972] is provided.) Scoring of the test items is based on the extent to which the student is able to correctly identify the types of duties, abilities, interests, values, and other characteristics involved in the pursuit of an occupation in one's preferred group. Students who are aware of what is actually involved in the pursuit of their occupational preferences are of course more career mature than are those possessing less awareness of such characteristics.

In addition to the five specific scales, the CDI provides three combined scores: Career Development-Attitudes (CDA) is the sum of the CP and CE scores: Career Development-Knowledge and Skills (CDK) combines DM and WW; and Career Orientation Total (COT) combines CP, CD, DM, and WW and is thus a composite measure of several important aspects of career maturity.

The CDI is available in both a School Form (Form S), designed for use in junior and senior high schools, and a College and University Form (Form CU), for use in higher education. The forms are similar in rationale and structure, but the item content differs in order to ensure its appropriateness to younger versus older students. The CDI scores are provided as standard scores having a mean of 100 and a standard deviation of 20. Percentiles are also provided. The standardization group for the School Form consisted of a nonrepresentative sample of 5,039 students distributed across grades 9 through 12. Norms for the College and University Form were based on 1,345 students from several colleges and universities, including community colleges.

Internal consistency reliability data (Cronbach's α) for grades 9 through 12 indicate that the reliability of the combined scores (CDA, CDK, and COT) and the CP, CE, and WW subscales is moderate but sufficient, with medians ranging from 0.78 to 0.89 across grades. The median reliability coefficients for DM and PO, however, are respectively 0.67 and 0.60. Thus, DM and PO should be used only with great interpretive caution. On the CU Form, the average values of alpha range from 0.75 to 0.90 for the three combined scores and from 0.61 to 0.91 for the subscales; the reliabilities of DM (0.62), WW (0.67), and PO (0.61) are insufficient, again implying the necessity of great caution when the CDI is used in individual counseling.

Assumptions regarding the content validity of the CDI derive from the construction of the test, based on prior work on the nature and assessment of career maturity, and from the use of experts in the area to develop items related to each of the dimensions or subscales to be assessed. Statements concerning the construct validity of the CDI are based on the increases in some test scores as a function of age (e.g., from a mean of 95.4 in grade 9 to one of 106.8 in grade 12 for CDA; from 94.9 to 101.4 for CDK; and from 93.8 to 104.9 for COT), on the reasonable correspondence of data regarding

Table 10.4 Sample Items from the First Four Scales of the Career Development Inventory

A. Career Planning

How much thinking and planning have you done in the following areas? For each question below choose the answer that best tells what you have done so far.

1. Finding out about educational and occupational possibilities by going to the library, sending away for information, or talking to somebody who knows.
   A. I have not yet given any thought to this.
   B. I have given some thought to this, but haven't made any plans yet.
   C. I have some plans, but am still not sure of them.
   D. I have made definite plans, but don't know yet how to carry them out.
   E. I have made definite plans, and know what to do to carry them out.

B. Career Exploration

Questions 21 through 30 have four possible answers. Choose the *one best* answer for each question to show whether or not you would go to the following sources for information or help in making your plans for work or further education.

21. Friends
    A. Definitely not
    B. Probably not
    C. Probably
    D. Definitely

22. Dormitory or residence hall counselors
    A. Definitely
    B. Probably not
    C. Probably
    D. Definitely

Questions 31 through 40 also have four possible answers. This time choose the *one best* answer to show how much useful information the people or sources listed below have already given you or directed you to in making your plans for the future.

31. Friends
    A. No useful information
    B. Some useful information
    C. A good deal of useful information
    D. A great deal of useful information

32. Dormitory or residence hall counselors
    A. No useful information
    B. Some useful information
    C. A good deal of useful information
    D. A great deal of useful information

C. Decision-making

What should each of the following students do? Choose the one best answer for each case.

41. E. R. took some tests that suggest some promise for accounting work. This student says, "I just can't see myself sitting behind a desk for the rest of my life. I'm the kind of person who likes variety. I think a traveling job would suit me fine." E. R. should:
    A. disregard the tests and do what he or she wants to do.
    B. do what the test say since they know best.
    C. look for a job that requires accounting ability but does not pin one to a desk.
    D. ask to be tested with another test since the results of the first one are probably wrong.

D. World of Work Information

Choose the one best answer to each of the following questions about career development and the world of work.

Lawyers usually learn their jobs in:

A. on-the-job training
B. community colleges
C. four-year colleges or universities
D. graduate or professional schools

SOURCE: Super, Thompson, Lindeman, Jordan, & Myers (1981). Reproduced with permission. Copyright 1981 by Consulting Psychologists Press.

sex differences to theoretical prediction, on score differences across high school curricula (e.g., students in college preparatory and business programs tend to obtain higher means on the cognitive scales than do students in general and vocational programs), and on the correspondence of the obtained factor structure to theoretical prediction. Similar types of evidence are provided for Form CU. Evidence for the criterion-related validity of the CDI is lacking, however.

Figure 10.6 provides a sample profile

OCCUPATIONAL GROUP PREFERENCE FORM

This form is designed to help you locate your current work interests.

STEP ONE: Read through the following twenty lists of occupations and check all those which you might like to be when you go to work.

Then add, in the blank spaces, any occupations not listed which you are particularly interested in. Put them in the group or groups where they seem to fit best.

GROUP A	GROUP B	GROUP C	GROUP D
PHYSICAL SCIENCE: RESEARCH	**PHYSICAL SCIENCE: APPLIED**	**BIOLOGICAL AND MEDICAL SCIENCE**	**SOCIAL SCIENCE: RESEARCH**
☐ Chemist	☐ Architect	☐ Dentist	☐ Anthropologist
☐ Geologist	☐ Engineer (all types)	☐ Medical Doctor	☐ Economist
☐ Mathematician	☐ Geographer	☐ Pharmacist	☐ Market Research Analyst
☐ Physicist	☐ Industrial Engineer	☐ Scientific Farmer	☐ Social Psychologist
☐ Statistician	☐ Systems Analyst	☐ Veterinarian	☐ Sociologist
☐ _____	☐ _____	☐ _____	☐ _____

GROUP E	GROUP F	GROUP G	GROUP H
SOCIAL SCIENCE: TEACHING/SOCIAL SERVICE	**WRITING AND LAW**	**ART AND MUSIC**	**PUBLIC PERFORMANCE**
☐ Guidance Counselor	☐ Editor	☐ Art Director	☐ Actor/Actress
☐ Marriage Counselor	☐ Lawyer	☐ Commercial Artist	☐ Announcer (radio/TV)
☐ School Psychologist	☐ Librarian	☐ Dress Designer	☐ Dancer
☐ School Teacher	☐ Reporter	☐ Interior Decorator	☐ Musical Entertainer
☐ Social Worker	☐ Script Writer	☐ Musician	☐ Professional Athlete
☐ _____	☐ _____	☐ _____	☐ _____

GROUP I	GROUP J	GROUP K	GROUP L
BUSINESS: FINANCIAL	**BUSINESS: MANAGEMENT**	**BUSINESS: SALES/PROMOTION**	**BUSINESS: OFFICE/CLERICAL**
☐ Auditor	☐ Sup't of Bldgs & Grounds	☐ Advertising Manager	☐ Bank Teller
☐ Bursar/Controller	☐ Bank Manager	☐ Broker/Account Executive	☐ Bookkeeper
☐ Computer Analyst	☐ Hotel Manager	☐ Buyer	☐ Clerk/Typist
☐ Cost Accountant	☐ Personnel Manager	☐ Public Relations Manager	☐ Postal Clerk
☐ Credit Analyst	☐ Store Owner/Manager	☐ Sales Manager	☐ Stenographer
☐ _____	☐ _____	☐ _____	☐ _____

GROUP M	GROUP N	GROUP O	GROUP P
BUSINESS: MERCHANDISING	**TECHNICAL: PHYSICAL SCIENCE**	**TECHNICAL: HEALTH SERVICE**	**TECHNICAL: CRAFTS**
☐ Car Rental Clerk	☐ Air Traffic Controller	☐ Dental Hygienist	☐ Auto Mechanic
☐ Department Store Salesperson	☐ Electronic Technician	☐ Dietician	☐ Dress Maker
☐ Life Insurance Agent	☐ Photoengraver	☐ Nurse (Registered)	☐ Electrician
☐ Real Estate Agent	☐ Surveyor	☐ Occupational Therapist	☐ Jeweler
☐ Retail Salesperson	☐ Weather Analyst	☐ Optician	☐ Printer
☐ _____	☐ _____	☐ _____	☐ _____

GROUP Q	GROUP R	GROUP S	GROUP T
TECHNICAL: OUTDOOR	**TECHNICAL: MECHANICAL**	**PERSONAL SERVICE**	**MANUAL/ PHYSICAL**
☐ Dairy Farmer	☐ Appliance Repair	☐ Beautician	☐ Gas Station Attendent
☐ Fish/Game Warden	☐ Bulldozer Operator	☐ Hospital Attendant	☐ Parking Lot Attendent
☐ Flower Grower	☐ Bus Driver	☐ Host/Hostess	☐ Porter
☐ Grain Farmer	☐ Dry Cleaner	☐ Receptionist	☐ Radio Assembler
☐ Landscape Gardener	☐ Sewing Machine Operator	☐ Waiter/Waitress	☐ Stevedore
☐ _____	☐ _____	☐ _____	☐ _____

NCS Data-Reflex W 1618-5432

STEP TWO: Go back over the occupations you have checked (or added) above. Then decide which ONE of the GROUPS you like best. On the line below, encircle the letter of that GROUP. Note: put a circle around only one letter.

GROUP liked best: A B C D E F G H I J K L M N O P Q R S T

STEP THREE: Turn to the other side and mark the letter you circle in the space provided.

Figure 10.5 Occupational group preference form from the Career Development Inventory by Super et al. (1981). (Reproduced by permission of Consulting Psychologists Press. © 1980 by Consulting Psychologists Press, Inc.)

Case 1: A High School Senior

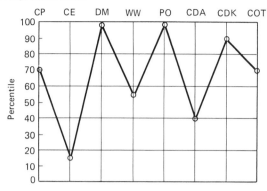

Case 2: Amy

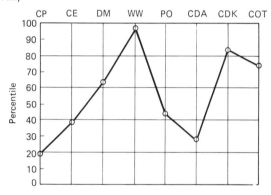

Figure 10.6 Sample profiles from the Career Development Inventory. (Reproduced by permission of Counseling Psychologists Press. Copyright © 1982 by Consulting Psychologists Press, Inc.)

of a student who took the CDI (Form S) as a high school senior. This student's career plans were fairly well-specified when she took the CDI: She was planning to follow in her father's footsteps and become a lawyer. Her high score on PO is most likely due to the specificity of her plans and the care with which she had investigated the occupation of lawyer. However, her focus on the occupation of lawyer and her lack of consideration of other occupations probably contributed to her low scores on CE (Career Exploration) and WW (World-of-Work Information). As a result of taking the CDI, this student might be advised to engage in some occupational exploratory activities and

to attempt to gain greater knowledge of the occupational world. In this way, the student's ultimate career choice, whether or not it was the law, would be a more informed choice and therefore more likely a *good* choice.

The case of Amy, also shown in Figure 10.6, provides an example of how administration of a measure of career maturity can facilitate interpretation of an interest inventory such as the Strong-Campbell Interest Inventory. In this case, the student's SCII profile was relatively flat, in that all Holland theme and Basic Interest scores were average, except for scores in Artistic areas, which were low. The fact that her profile suggested she could eliminate occupations in artistic fields was not particularly helpful to this college student. Her CDI profile, however, indicated that she was having problems in certain areas of her program in career development, particularly in CP, CE, and PO; these low scores were even more problematic in light of her high score (96 percent) on WW. It seemed that while Amy had obtained a lot of occupational information, she was unable to apply it to herself and had not taken steps to engage in career planning or the exploration of careers beyond library materials such as the *Dictionary of Occupational Titles*. For this client, something was blocking her in her career planning and her ability to apply occupational information to her own characteristics. Blocks such as fear of commitment to a decision, fear of success or failure, home-career conflict, or external pressures might be hypotheses to be explored in career counseling. Note that the CDI, as used herein, is helpful in understanding the reasons for a relatively flat SCII profile and assists in the understanding of career indecision in a college student. And, like the CMI, the CDI is very useful in planning and evaluating career guidance and career education programs as well as in career counseling.

The Cognitive Vocational Maturity Test

The Cognitive Vocational Maturity Test (CVMT; Westbrook & Mastie, 1974) differs from the CMI and the CDI in its emphasis on *only* the cognitive, rather than the cognitive and attitudinal, dimensions of career maturity and in its appropriateness for somewhat younger students—those in grades 6 through 9, rather than high school and/or college students.

The underlying assumption guiding the construction of the CVMI is the central importance of occupational information in making good career choices. According to

Westbrook and Mastie (1974), knowledge of the world of work is as crucial as is self-knowledge to the process of finding occupations likely to lead to success and satisfaction. Thus the CVMT is designed to assess the degree to which students know and can begin to use occupational information. The six subtests of the CVMT are as follows (sample items are shown in Table 10.5):

1. *Fields of Work:* Knowledge of the occupations that are available in various fields of work.
2. *Job Selection:* The ability to choose the most realistic occupation for a hypothetical student who is described in terms of his/her abilities, interests, and values.
3. *Work Conditions:* Knowledge of work schedules, income level, physical conditions, job locations, and so forth.
4. *Education Required:* Knowledge of the amount of education generally required for a wide range of occupations.
5. *Attributes Required:* Knowledge of the abilities, interests, and values generally required for various occupations.
6. *Duties:* Knowledge of the principle duties performed in a wide range of occupations.

The entire CVMT contains 120 items. With the exception of Job Selection, containing 15 items, and Duties, containing 25 items, the scales contain 20 items each. The CVMT was standardized in a sample of over 7,000 sixth through ninth graders enrolled in a North Carolina career exploration program. Scores are provided as a simple "number of correct responses" for each subscale. A total score, having a possible maximum of 120, is also provided.

Reliability data for the CVMT (KR-20) indicate values generally in the 0.80s for all but the Job Selection scale, where reliability coefficients ranged from 0.67 to 0.71. Data regarding the validity of the CVMT are inadequate. One criterion-related validity study cited in Westbrook and Mastie (1974) indi-

Table 10.5 Sample Items From the Cognitive Vocational Maturity Test

Subtest	Sample Item
Fields of Work	Which of the following is not in the field of construction? a) Surveyor; b) Architect; c) Carpenter; d) Lawyer; e) I don't know.
Job Selection	Mike had some vocational training in high school and worked hard to graduate. He is physically strong and prefers outdoor work. He is good at doing things with his hands, is dependable and cooperative. He likes to be around other people and has a cheerful personality. Which one seems to be the most likely one for him to be in? a) Payroll Clerk; b) Truck Driver; c) Bricksman; d) Night Watchman; e) I don't know.
Work Conditions	Which one of the following does not have to work with tools? a) Barber; b) Mechanic; c) Carpenter; d) Milkman; e) I don't know.
Education Required	A college education is not required to be a: a) Chemist; b) Architect; c) Agronomist; d) Mechanic; e) I don't know.
Attributes Required	Imagination is most important in which occupation? a) Advertising Artist; b) Electrician; c) Social Worker; d) Librarian; e) I don't know.
Duties	Which one fills prescriptions for drugs and medicine? a) Chemist; b) Physicist; c) Pharmacist; d) Pharmacologist; e) I don't know.

SOURCE: Westbrook and Mastie (1974). Reproduced with permission.

cated that ninth grade students currently making career choices consistent with their aptitudes and interests obtained higher scores on the CVMT than did students making unrealistic choices. In this study, however, only 26 of 249 students in the criterion sample were making career choices consistent with *both* their aptitudes and their interests, while the choices of 117 were incongruent with *both*. Thus, the significant findings of greater career maturity were based on an *N* of 26. More evidence regarding the validity of the instrument is clearly needed.

Another problem with the CVMT is its strong relationship with general intelligence. Correlations of CVMT scores with the IQ score from the California Test of Mental Maturity range from 0.53 (Work Conditions) to 0.69 (Duties). In addition, intercorrelations of the six CVMT scales range from 0.67 to 0.84; factor-analytic research is needed to clarify the basic dimensions assessed by the instrument.

The CVMT may be used as a screening device to assess students' readiness to make vocational decisions and to identify students in most need of counseling assistance. Like the CDI and the CMI, it may be used for diagnostic purposes or to design and evaluate career education programs.

Summary. In summary, a variety of instruments designed to assess aspects of career development and career maturity are available. In a content analysis of five major career maturity inventories, Westbrook (1974) reported that the content of the tests could be summarized according to three major categories: the cognitive (what students know about self, the world of work, and career decision making, planning, and problem solving); the psychomotor (what students have done in terms of, for example, career exploration and planning activities); and the affective (e.g., attitudes and preferences). Since different inventories differently assess these domains, selection of an instrument should take into account the specific purposes and, of course, age groups for which test results are needed. Knowledge of the level and pattern of an individual's or group's career maturity can be very useful to the design and delivery of services and programs facilitative of career development.

MEASURES OF CAREER INDECISION

Much attention in the area of career development has been directed toward assessment of the individual's acquisition of mature career decision-making skills, attitudes, and competencies. Another major focus of attention has been the person who has not yet mastered one of the major career development tasks important in Super's (1963) developmental framework, that of making a specific vocational choice. The focus on such individuals, often called "career-undecided," probably stems from at least three factors. First, making a career choice in an effective, timely manner is important because the important tasks of career implementation, such as obtaining necessary education and training, tend to be delayed until tentative career choices are made. Decisions about subsequent education and training are frequently necessary—for example, decisions about school coursework, college majors, work experience, and post-high-school pursuits. Such decisions are difficult to make without at least some tentative career direction. Second, a large number of counseling clients have problems with indecision about their careers. Third, given generally limited resources, the "career-undecided" are a particularly important group toward which to focus counseling and educational interventions. For these reasons, as well as others, knowledge of the factors contributing to career indecision, and methods by which the influence of these factors for individuals can be assessed, are important to the overall facilitation of career development.

The concepts of vocational decision and indecision have been discussed and defined by, among others, Crites (1969) and Osipow (1980). As noted by Crites (1969), "indecision" in career choice refers to the inability of an individual to select and/or commit oneself to a career direction. Various writers have proposed a variety of *reasons* for indecision.

For example, Tyler (cited in Crites, 1969, p. 305) refers to pressures from family and friends *toward* occupations the individual does not prefer or *away* from occupations one does prefer, the fact that a given preferred occupation probably has undesirable as well as desirable aspects, equipotentiality (the inevitable need to choose among two or more attractive alternatives), and limitations imposed by circumstances.

Although suggestions such as Tyler's have contributed to our understanding of some of the reasons for career indecision, a more recent focus of research on career indecision has involved the development and evaluation of instruments assessing the components of antecedents of indecision in high school and college students. Probably the major instrument of this type, the Career Decision Scale, will be the focus of the subsequent discussion. In addition, an instrument called My Vocational Situation will also be described.

The Career Decision Scale

The Career Decision Scale (CDS; Osipow, Carney, Winer, Yanico, & Koschier, 1976) is an 18-item scale designed to measure both the extent and the nature (i.e., the antecedents) of career indecision in college students. The first two items of the CDS ask the respondent to indicate whether or not he or she has made a definite choice of a college major (item 1) and a career (item 2). The composite of scores on items 1 and 2 is an index of vocational/educational certainty.

Items 3 through 18 of the CDS assess various possible causes or antecedents of career indecision. These antecedents may be organized roughly into four factors. The first factor, "lack of structure and confidence," consists of eight items—for example "I know I will have to go to work eventually, but none of the careers I know about appeal to me" and "I can't make a choice right now because

I don't know what my abilities are." The second factor, "Approach–approach conflict," includes five items suggesting the existence of several possible good career options among which the student is having difficulty deciding—for example, "Several careers have equal appeal to me. I'm having a difficult time deciding among them." The third factor, "external barriers to one's preferred choice," consists of four items such as "I thought I knew what I wanted for a career, but recently I found out that it wouldn't be possible for me to pursue it. Now I've got to start looking for other possible careers." Finally, the fourth factor, "personal conflict," is represented by the item "I'd like to be a _____, but I'd be going against the wishes of someone who is important to me if I did so. Because of this, it's difficult for me to make a career decision right now. I hope I can find a way to please them and myself." In order to capture unique barriers to the career decision, beyond those assessed by the 16 indecision items, an open-ended question was added at the end of the CDS.

Responses to the CDS are obtained using a four-point Likert scale with response alternatives ranging from "exactly like me" (scored 4) to "not at all like me" (scored 1). A total indecision score is calculated as the sum of responses to items 3 through 18. Indecision scores may range from 16 to 64, with higher scores indicating greater degrees of vocational indecision. Normative data in the form of percentile equivalents of raw scores are provided in the manual (Osipow, 1987). Percentile equivalents of indecision scores for male and female college students, freshman through senior, are based on 135 male and 126 female Ohio State University freshmen and over 400 Pennsylvania State University students in their freshman through senior years; sample sizes in the latter group range from 31 male freshmen to 76 male juniors. Normative data (also percentiles) for high school students include approximately 1,500 students across grades 9 through 12; sample sizes ranged from 132 (twelfth grade males) to 251 (ninth grade males). Finally, normative data for 81 adult students seeking continuing education and 67 women returning to college are provided.

Test-retest reliability data for the CDS indicate that it is reasonably stable over time. Osipow, Carney, and Barak (1976) reported two-week test-retest correlations of 0.90 in one study and 0.82 in a second study. Slaney, Palko-Nonemaker, and Alexander (1981) reported a six-week stability coefficient of 0.70. Validity data for the CDS are summarized in the excellent manual (Osipow, 1987).

A central focus of validity studies has been the extent to which indecision scores decrease following career counseling interventions. In other words, if the CDS assesses career indecision, then its scores should decrease following interventions designed to assist an individual in making a good career decision. Evidence for greater decidedness (lower indecision scores) following career interventions was reported in studies by Osipow, Carney, and Barak (1976), among others. Other validity evidence is provided by the data indicating generally decreasing indecision scores with higher grade in school, through high school and through college.

The CDS can be used for purposes of both individual and group assessment and for the evaluation of career education programs and career counseling interventions. The *level* of the indecision score indicates the degree to which the individual is undecided about his or her career, and the specific item responses can be used to stimulate discussion of the factors the individual sees as preventing a good career choice. For group interventions, the CDS scores can be used to obtain an approximate assessment of the degree to which career undecidedness is a problem and, if so, some of the more common barriers/problems characterizing the group. Finally, the CDS can be used to evaluate the effectiveness of career counseling interventions or career education programs. As stated in Osipow, Carney, and Barak (1976), the scale "has potential for diagnostic, criterion, and conceptual purposes related to career indecision" (p. 233).

My Vocational Situation Scale

Somewhat similar to the CDS is Holland, Daiger, and Power's (1980) My Vocational Situation Scale, or MVS. The MVS is an experimental scale for the diagnosis of difficulties in vocational decision making. The MVS is based on the assumption that most difficulties in vocational decision making stem from problems of vocational identity, lack of information about jobs or training, and environmental or personal barriers. These three dimensions are defined by Holland, Daiger, and Power (1980) as follows:

1. The *Vocational Identity* category indicates the degree to which a client possesses a clear and stable picture of his or her goals, interests, personality, and talents. Strong vocational identity leads to relatively untroubled decision making and confidence in one's ability to make good decisions in the face of inevitable environmental ambiguities.
2. The *Occupational Information* category provides a client the opportunity to indicate a need for vocational information, most of which is available in printed form; the counselor can quickly direct the client to the appropriate materials.
3. The *Barriers* category invites the client to indicate perceived external obstacles to a chosen occupational goal. A "yes" response to one or more of the items or the listing of an idiosyncratic obstacle may enable the counselor to focus promptly on a significant problem area.

The first 18 MVS items, all of which are scored true/false, constitute the Vocational Identity scale. Items include "I am uncertain about the occupations I could per-

form well" and "I am confused about the whole problem of deciding on a career." The Vocational Identity score is the number of "false" responses, and higher scores indicate greater certainty and a more positive vocational identity. Four questions pertaining to the need for additional occupational information and four pertaining to barriers to choice constitute the second and third sections of the instrument. In each case, the number of "no" responses is the score, and a higher number of nos is a more positive indication of decision-making status.

Reliabilities (Kuder-Richardson-20 coefficients) for the three scales indicate that the Vocational Identity scale possesses adequate internal consistency (0.86 to 0.89 across samples), but that the Occupational Information and Barriers scales, because of their unacceptable levels of internal consistency, should be viewed as checklists rather than as scales. Other serious weaknesses of the MVS are the lack of validity evidence and the lack of carefully collected normative data. Because of these weaknesses, both Lunneborg (1985) and Westbrook (1985) recommend that use of the MVS be limited to research purposes rather than counseling uses until more information regarding its interpretation (norms) and Psychometric quality is available.

Note that the CDS and the MVS have considerable overlap in content, in that both reflect a lack of confidence in decision-making skills and a lack of information about both the self and the environment.

In summary, models and measures of career indecision can be very useful in assisting counselors in making diagnostic statements or in developing hypotheses about an individual's particular problem in making a career decision, can enhance the effectiveness of counseling or educational interventions by serving as a basis for their design, and can provide criteria by which intervention efforts can be evaluated.

CAREER PLANNING SYSTEMS

Assessment methods in the process of career decision making also make important contributions to larger educational/career guidance programs designed to assist people in career planning and decision making and thereby facilitate their career development. These "career planning systems" provide counselors, and often students and parents, ways of integrating and synthesizing information from a variety of assessment methods and sources of occupational information.

The following section will briefly describe representative "systems" of two major types. The first type includes systems designed to enhance the utility of large-scale aptitude or interest test batteries. Examples of this kind of system include the DAT Career Planning Program and the ACT Assessment. These programs have as their basis at least one widely used test of vocational aptitudes or interests, and all attempt to combine information obtained from scores on an aptitude or interest test with other information obtained in the program.

The second major type of system is the computerized interactive career guidance system that integrates computer-administered (via individual computer terminal) methods of self-assessment and occupational exploration to assist the individual in making career decisions. Two examples of such systems, the System of Interactive Guidance and Information and DISCOVER, will be briefly described.

Large-Scale Systems

The DAT Career Planning Program. The DAT Career Planning Program (CPP) was introduced in 1973 and has as its basis the Differential Aptitude Tests, described in detail in Chapter 7. Along with administration of the DAT, the CPP program consists of two parts: (1) a Career Planning Questionnaire (CPQ), and (2) a Career Planning Report. The system is made available by the Psychological Corporation. The CPQ measures interest in 94 activities, including school subjects, and 100 occupations. The CPQ also includes questions about educational plans (designed to yield an index of Level of Aspiration) and academic performance (grades).

The Career Planning Report is designed to integrate the results of DAT performance with interests and aspirations. In a narrative section of the report, a discussion of the appropriateness of the student's choices relative to his or her measured abilities and interests is provided. If choices are inappropriate, more appropriate alternatives are suggested.

More specifically, the major function of the integrative aspect of the program is to determine and indicate the extent to which students' educational and career plans and preferences are congruent with their measured aptitudes and interests and to suggest to a student additional possible career options based on those aptitudes and interests. The bases upon which statements concerning correspondence were made were a variety of occupational information sources, in particular the occupational classification system from the *Dictionary of Occupational Titles* (DOT), including occupational aptitude requirements (in relationship to the General Aptitude Test Battery) and classification of occupations according to related school subjects and required educational level.

For each occupational group, the General Aptitude Test Battery requirements were transformed to comparable DAT aptitude requirements. The approximate minimum DAT aptitude scores in percentile terms were collapsed into a five-point scale for use in the interpretive materials supplied with the CPP. For each occupation a student chose or was interested in, the extent to which the student possessed the necessary aptitudes was determined by reference to the minimums for that occupation. The computer program also compares the student's stated educational goals to the amount of education required for his or her occupational preferences.

The DAT Career Planning Program report has several very useful features. First, students whose occupational preferences are unrealistically high relative to their abilities are provided with alternative suggestions more correspondent *with* their abilities; no student's DAT scores are so low that at least one occupational group cannot be recommended. On the other hand, students whose occupational aspirations are unrealistically *low* relative to their abilities are encouraged to consider higher-level educational and occupational goals and, thereby, the program attempts to strengthen their academic self-concepts. Thus, the DAT Career Planning Program attempts to assist students to make *realistic* career choices. Taylor (1988) does note one disadvantage of the CPP's provision of occupational alternatives *only* for students whose choices are incongruent with their abilities and interests, rather than also for those who are making congruent choices. Even if students are making a "good" choice, use of the CPP may thus prematurely narrow examination of other viable career alternatives among the latter group of students.

The manual for the DAT Career Planning Program (Super, 1982) suggests several uses for the program. The major use is in individual counseling with high school students and their teachers and parents. Because test score profiles and reports contain much technical information and in some cases contain sensitive information that may be misunderstood, the information should never be given to students and parents prior to an individual conference with a skilled counselor. Score reports from the DAT program can also be effectively used as part of group counseling with students. Group use of the scores may work particularly well if the students in the group have similar types of *problems*—for example, aspirations that are unrealistically high relative to their aptitudes or aspirations that are unrealistically low relative to their abilities. Finally, reports from the DAT Career Planning Program can be used in program planning and curriculum development. They may also be used effectively in combination with measures of career maturity. For example, the realism/unrealism of students' occupational preferences can be assessed and related to components of career maturity/immaturity.

Although there are many potential uses for the program, further research concerning its technical adequacy, as well as research on the effects of such systems on students and on their parents, is necessary. While the system has intuitive appeal, the reactions of students and parents to it and the differential effectiveness of various approaches to its use (e.g., in individual versus group counseling sessions) should receive further empirical study.

The ACT Assessment Program

Like the DAT Career Planning Program, the ACT Assessment Program (AAP) is built around a well-known aptitude test, the ACT, as discussed in Chapter 7. In addition to administration of the four tests of the ACT, the AAP includes: (1) a questionnaire about high school courses and grades, (2) a questionnaire pertaining to educational and career aspirations, and extracurricular activities, and (3) the ACT Interest Inventory. The ACT Interest Inventory is a 90-item instrument assessing interests in six comprehensive career areas: Science, Arts, Social Service, Business Contact, Business Operations, and Technical. The results of the questionnaires and inventory are reported along with the scores on the ACT tests of educational development, as shown in Figure 7.1. The interest inventory results are summarized as a referral of the student to one or more sections of what is known as the World of Work Map, shown in Figure 10.7. The map is contained on the back of the student's score report; the interests of the student shown in Figure 7.1 led to the suggestion of occupations in map regions 11 and 12. Social Service and the Arts were the student's two highest interests; college majors in regions 11 and 12 include Journalism, Advertising, and Radio/TV Broadcasting (career family S) and Nursing, Occupational Therapy, and Dental/Medical Assisting (career family T). (It should be noted that the ACT Interest Inventory, as well as the ACT tests of educational development, is well constructed and highly reliable. (See the 1988 *Technical Manual* for the ACT Assessment Program for further details.)

Two other career guidance systems offered by ACT are the Career Planning Program (CPP) and VIESA. The CPP is an assessment system that collects information on interests, work-related experiences, career-related abilities and skills, educational plans, and needs for help. The system is designed as a group-administered alternative to individual assessment and career counseling. Participants are assisted to understand their results in terms of the World of Work Map and a Career Guidebook cross-referenced to both the map and the *Occupational Outlook Handbook*. Finally, VIESA is an abbreviated and self-scored version of the CPP (see ACT's *Resources for Educators*, 1988).

Other Paper-and-Pencil Programs

Although other programs can only be mentioned, Taylor (1988) has provided a more extensive review of such paper-and-pencil (as opposed to computer-administered) career planning systems. They include the package published by Edits, including the Career Occupational Preference System (COPS), the Career Ability Placement Survey (CAPS), and the Career Orientation Placement and Evaluation Survey (COPES): Such systems also include Harrington and O'Shea's Career Decision-Making System (COM), CareerWise, published by National Computer Systems, and Planning Career Goals, published by CTB/McGraw-Hill. Actually, almost every major test publisher, and most of the smaller publishers, now produce some type of career planning program or system. This trend strongly suggests that career planning has become "big business." Users should carefully evaluate the quality of any such program they are considering for use, since a publisher's haste in getting a package "on the market" to stay competitive with other publishers may not be conducive to careful, systematic construction and evaluation of the assessment methods.

Computer-Assisted Career Guidance Programs

Computer-assisted career guidance programs (CAGS) are one of the fastest growing developments in assessment and counseling. There are several advantages of computer-assisted programs. First, administration and scoring are done by the computer. Second, the administration is interactive, with the student providing responses by keyboard as questions are shown on the screen; this means that the administration can be adapted specifically to the needs of the examinee as they emerge through the testing process. (See the discussion of adaptive ability testing and its advantages in Chapter 3). Third, the computer makes possible access to the massive amounts of occupational information that no individual career counselor could ever memorize. As an example of the utility of an interactive or adaptive capacity, a computerized career guidance system could ask the examinee to indicate which of a list of oc-

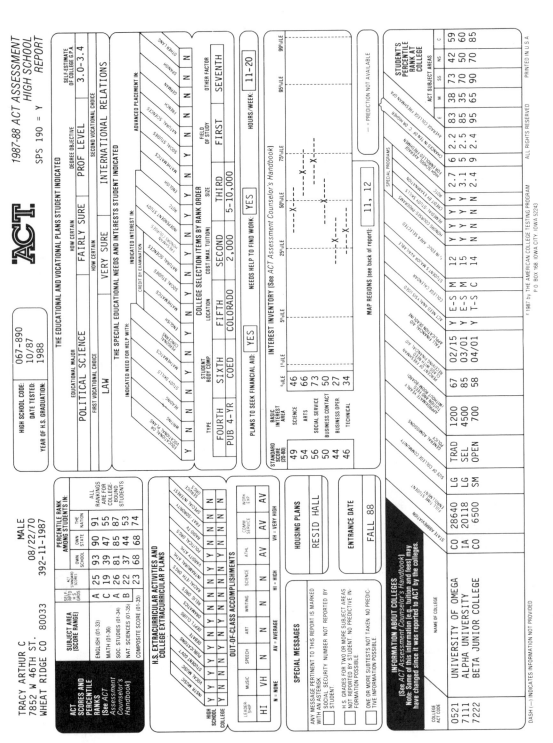

Figure 10.7 World of Work Map, as shown on the back of the Student Profile from the ACT Assessment Program. Copyright © 1987 by The American College Testing Program. Reproduced by permission of the publisher.

CAREER OPTIONS (For Student Use)

The World-of-Work Map arranges Career Families (groups of similar jobs) into 12 regions. The location of a Career Family shows how much it involves working with PEOPLE, THINGS, DATA, and IDEAS. Arrows indicate that work tasks often heavily involve both PEOPLE and THINGS (↔) or DATA and IDEAS (↕). Although the locations of jobs in a family differ, most are near the point shown. Your location on the World-of-Work Map is based on the 90 activity preferences you reported on the ACT Interest Inventory. To identify career options and related college majors, see the steps below the map.

WORLD-OF-WORK MAP (2nd Edition)

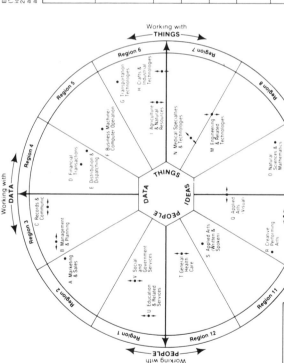

MAP REGIONS:

HOW TO USE THE MAP:

1. Find your map regions in the Interest Inventory section on the reverse side of this report and enter them in the box above. (If "Region 99" is reported, your activity preferences did not indicate particular map regions to explore.)

2. Find your region numbers on the map and circle them. Note the work tasks (working with PEOPLE, THINGS, DATA, IDEAS) shown for your map regions. Then, look over the Career Families in or near the regions you circled.

3. If you wish to consider college majors related to those Career Families, see the list to the right. If you wish to consider job options, ask for ACT's Career Family List, which lists 170 jobs by Career Family. The Career Family List appears on the back of your Student Report.

CAUTION! Map regions (like other test scores) are estimates. They provide suggestions, not decisions. Also, your interests and abilities may differ. Both need to be considered in career planning.

EXAMPLES OF COLLEGE MAJORS AND PROGRAMS

Examples of college majors and programs of study related to each Career Family are listed below. (Your counselor or advisor may have additional examples.) Colleges offering various programs are identified in ACT's *College Planning/Search Book.* Programs are designated (2) if they appear in the 2-year College Search Section, and (4) if they appear in the 4-year College Search Section. Programs appearing in both sections of the *College Planning/Search Book* are designated (2 & 4). However, actual educational requirements for jobs will differ among employers.

A. Marketing and Sales Career Family: Recreation and Tourism (2). Agribusiness (2 & 4). Clothing and Textiles (2 & 4). Food Service (2). Marketing and Purchasing (2 & 4). Real Estate and insurance (2 & 4). Specialized fields (e.g. computers) related to sales (2 & 4).

B. Management and Planning: Farm Management (2). Hotel/Restaurant Management (2). Banking and Finance (2 & 4). Business Management (2 & 4). Community and Regional Planning (2 & 4). Marketing/Purchasing (2 & 4). Office Management (2 & 4). Economics (2 & 4). Institutional Management (4).

C. Records and Communications: Medical Office Assisting (2). Secretarial Studies (2 & 4) including several specializations.

D. Financial Transactions: Bookkeeping (2). Accounting (2 & 4). Business Management Banking, and Finance (2 & 4).

E. Distribution and Dispatching: On-the-Job Training, Apprenticeships and/or Special Schools (e.g. Air Traffic Control)

F. Business Machine/Computer Operation: Computer Operating (2 & 4). Data Processing Technology (2 & 4). Secretarial Studies (2 & 4).

G. Transportation Technologies: Aeronautical/Aviation Technology (2). Auto/Diesel etc. Mechanics (2). Engineering Technology–Automotive (2). Special Schools (e.g. Pilot. Merchant Marine)

*H. Crafts and Industrial Technologies: Appliance and Radio/Tv Repair (2). Business Machine Maintenance (2). Engineering Technologies (2). Heavy Equipment Operation Mechanics (2 & 4). Nursing, Metalworking (2). Small Engine Repair (2). Foods and Nutrition (2 & 4).

*Career Family H also includes Career Families that appear in the ACT Occupational Classification System

I. Agriculture and Natural Resources: Agribusiness (2 & 4). Agriculture (2 & 4). Agronomy (2 & 4). Animal Science (2 & 4). Farm Management (2 & 4). Fish Game and Wildlife Management (2 & 4). Forestry (2 & 4). Horticulture (2 & 4).

M. Engineering and Related Technologies: Architecture Technology (2). Data Systems Repair (2). Drafting and Engineering Graphics (2). Engineering Technologies such as electrical, civil, mechanical, etc. (2). Computer Programming/Science (2 & 4). Food Science and Technology (2 & 4). Engineering in fields such as electrical, civil, mechanical, etc (4).

N. Medical Specialties and Technologies: Dental Hygiene (2 & 4). Medical/Lab/X-ray Technology (2 & 4). Biological Sciences (4). Chemistry (4). Predentistry (4). Prepharmacy (4).

O. Natural Sciences and Mathematics: Agronomy (2 & 4). Biology (4). Chemistry (4). Mathematics (4). Oceanography (4). Physics (4). Zoology (4).

P. Social Sciences: Child Development (2 & 4). Anthropology (4). Economics (4). Psychology (4). Sociology (4).

Q. Applied Arts (Visual): Applied Design (2 & 4). Architecture Technology (2 & 4). Art Painting/Drawing (2 & 4). Clothing and Textiles (2 & 4). Photography/Cinematography (2 & 4). Architecture (4).

R. Creative/Performing Arts: Arts (2 & 4). Dramatic Arts (4). Dance (4). Creative Writing (4). Music (4). Special Schools (e.g. Drama. Ballet. etc.)

S. Applied Arts: Journalism (2 & 4). Radio/TV Broadcasting (2 & 4). Advertising (4). English Literature (4). Foreign Languages (4). Humanities (4). Speech (4).

T. General Health Care: Dental/Medical Assisting (2 & 4). Nursing. Rn/Lpn (2 & 4). Occupational Therapy (2 & 4). Physical Therapy (2 & 4). Premedicine (4).

U. Education and Related Services: Teacher Assisting (2). Education including Elementary. Science. Special. Vocational. etc. (4)

V. Social and Government Services: Social Work Assistance (2) Family Relations and Child Development (2 & 4). Foods and Nutrition (2 & 4). Law Enforcement and Corrections (2 & 4). Parks and Recreation Management (2 & 4). Social Work (4)

Figure 10.7B

cupations he or she would like more information about. It could then search its bank for information about the preferred occupations. In an even more sophisticated manner, the computer could administer tests of abilities, vocational interests, and work needs and then immediately generate a list of occupations congruent with one, two, or all three of those sets of characteristics.

There are now numerous computer-assisted guidance systems. Among the earliest developed and now well-known systems are SIGI and SIGI Plus, developed and published by the Educational Testing Service, and Discover, now published by ACT.

SIGI and SIGI Plus

The computer-administered System of Interactive Guidance and Information (SIGI; Katz, 1975) was developed by the Educational Testing Service to assist students either planning to enter or enrolled in institutions of higher education in their process of educational and career planning. The SIGI system, in which each student goes through the program at an individual computer terminal, involves six subsystems. The six subsystems take the student systematically through the assessment of work values and probabilities of success in preparing for different occupations, based on locally available information such as aptitude test scores. The program provides detailed occupational information and plans for implementing occupational choices and helps the student integrate personal and occupational information in evaluating occupational alternatives. SIGI PLUS is a nine-module system originally designed for adults. However, its greater scope and interactive capabilities relative to SIGI have led to its widening use with younger age groups as well.

DISCOVER

DISCOVER and DISCOVER for Adult Learners are made available by The American College Testing Program and, not surprisingly, have some features in common with the ACT Assessment Program described earlier. Like other computer-assisted guidance programs, DISCOVER helps the examinee to integrate the results obtained from self-assessment modules with educational and occupational information. The program contains four modules: Learning About Yourself, Searching for Occupations, Learning About Occupations, and Educational Information. From Part I, the results of the ACT Interest Inventory (UNIACT) are used to suggest job families from the World of Work Map, as shown previously in Figure 10.7 in the discussion of the ACT Assessment Program. Part II of DISCOVER provides the opportunity to search for occupations congruent with other interest or aptitude test scores. Parts III and IV contain occupational and educational information, respectively. Part III can teach the World of Work Map as an organizational framework for understanding the work world and provides brief descriptions of job families. In Part IV, information about several thousand colleges and universities is available.

DISCOVER, SIGI, and SIGI PLUS, as well as the many other developing computer-assisted guidance systems, are constantly being revised and updated as new developments in assessment and information data bases occur. In other words, because the technology is relatively new, it is still in a state of rapid growth and change.

DISCOVER, developed by the DISCOVER Foundation (1977) in Westminister, Maryland, is a computerized career guidance system designed for use in grades 7 through 12 and in two-year and four-year colleges. The system contains several separate modules:

1. *Entry* describes the DISCOVER system.
2. *Clarifying Values* and *Values and Occupations* help students match their values to occupations.
3. *Effective Decision Making* and *Decision Making in Careers* teach decision-making skills.
4. *Organization* of occupational world, *Browsing* occupations, *Reviewing* interests and strengths, *Making* a list of occupations to explore, *Getting* information about occupations, and *Narrowing* a list of occupations, all assist the student in generating and learning about occupational alternatives.
5. *Exploring Specific Career Plans* assists students in identifying the next appropriate step in their process of career decision making, for example, finding a job, getting an apprenticeship, entering a community or a junior college versus a four-year college, or entering the military.

To summarize, integrative career planning systems like those described probably do have utility in facilitating career exploration and planning. However, the extent to which these instruments actually achieve their purposes is largely unknown (e.g., Johnson, 1978b). Further research on the responses to and effects of these instruments with respect to students themselves and their parents and teachers is needed, as is research on their effectiveness in individual and group counseling. For further information describing computerized career guidance systems see Zunker (1981).

SUMMARY

The present chapter has discussed a variety of assessment methods important in helping individuals make and *learn how to make* good educational and career decisions. Instruments such as those discussed here have utility for the development and evaluation of career education programs as well as for individual and group counseling. The understanding and assessment of concepts such as vocational interests and values, career development and maturity, and career indecision have contributed greatly to the breadth and richness of interventions designed to facilitate educational and career planning and decision making. Integrative systems such as those described also show promise of assisting in the synthesis of rich information about individuals and information describing the increasingly complex world of work.

11

Environmental Assessment

INTRODUCTION

The idea that environmental factors influence behavior, attitudes, and moods is a recurrent one in psychology. As far back as 1924, J. R. Kantor was distinguishing between the physical and the psychological environment. For the physical environment Kantor used the term *biological environment*, which he defined as the surroundings of the organism, such as the geographical region, temperature, and general ecological conditions. He defined the psychological environment somewhat more ambiguously and did not link it to the individual's perception of the physical environment. Instead, Kantor defined the psychological environment behaviorally, within the context of a stimulus response model. Thus, the focus of Kantor's work was on the physical environment and the individual's response (psychological environment) to the physical environment.

Independently of Kantor's work, K. Koffka (1935), in his Gestalt psychology, distinguished between the physical and the psychological world. Koffka made a clear distinction between the geographical (physical) and behavioral (psychological) environment and suggested that the psychological environment was a function of the interaction between the physical environment and the organism. Koffka believed that the geographical environment produced a behavioral environment that affected behavior and perceptions.

Also in 1935, Kurt Lewin introduced his field theory, which emphasized the distinction between the physical and the psychological environment and clearly indicated the necessity of taking into account the psychological environment. Lewin believed that in psychology we can begin to describe the whole situation by roughly distinguishing the person and the environment. Every psychological event depends upon the state of the person and at the same time the state of the environment (Lewin, 1935). Tolman's (1935) theory was similar to Lewin's in proposing that behavior is a function of intrinsic and extrinsic variables. More specifically, he suggested that behavior was a function of the stimulus setup, heredity, training, and the individual's physiological state. A big difference between Tolman's approach and Lewin's was that Tolman argued for a description of the environment in physical terms and Lewin used psychological variables. Thus, Tolman's approach was fairly behavioristic, and Lewin's was somewhat more cognitive-perceptual in orientation.

Very much influenced by Koffka and Lewin, Henry Murray (1938) suggested that the behavior of an individual cannot be formulated without a characterization of each confronting situation, physical and social. According to Murray, the environment must be defined when describing an organism's behavior, and it is important to distinguish between the physical and the psychological aspects of the environment. To do this Murray coined the terms "alpha press" and "beta press." The alpha press defined the environmental situation as it exists in reality (physical environment). The beta press defined the environmental situation as it is perceived by the individual (psychological environment).

Thus, these early classical theorists represented the beginnings of environmental psychology and environmental assessment. In general, these classical theorists saw a need to focus on behavior as a function of not only the person, but also the physical and perceived environments. As we have noted, many of the theorists made a concerted effort to differentiate between the physical environment and the psychological environment. In addition, how individuals tended to perceive environments—the meaning of the situation to the individual—began to develop as an important variable. As noted by Mischel (1968), any assessor who tries to predict the future without information about the environmental conditions influencing the individual's behavior may be more engaged in the process of hoping than of predicting.

Definition of Environment

The early classical theorists recognized that environment plays an important role in determining behavior, and in their discussions they distinguished between two types of environments, the physical and the psychological. The theorists discussed above used different terms with somewhat different meanings. In an effort to integrate these conceptual differences, Endler and Magnusson (1976b) proposed that the main conceptual distinction with respect to type of environment was between the objective outer world (physical and social variables) as it influences the individual, and the subjective world (psychological variables), or the environment as the individual perceives and reacts to it. Endler and Magnusson further distinguished between the physical environment, which may be described on a molar level (buildings, parks, lakes, homes, streets, etc.) or on a molecular level (single objects or single stimulus variables). Similarly the social environment may be discussed on two levels. The macro social environment may be defined by the laws, norms, and values that are common to a whole society or culture. The micro social environment may be defined by the norms, attitudes, and habits of the specific groups with which an individual interacts directly, for example, at home or at school. Endler and Magnusson pointed out that the macro social environment may be regarded as fairly common to most members of society. On the other hand, the micro social environment is to some extent unique for each individual. Thus, the objective outerworld environment is described in terms of physical factors, social factors, or some combination of physical and social factors. An attempt is made to define the environment as it is, independent of the interpretations made by the individuals responding to it.

The subjective world focuses on psychological variables and attempts to describe the psychological significance of the environment to the individual. To investigate the psychological significance of the environment Endler and Magnusson (1976b) suggested studying the individual's perception of the situation (the meaning the person assigns to the situation) and the individual's reaction or response to the situation. Thus, the subjective approach has underlined the importance of the psychological significance of situations as a determinant of behavior.

The subjective approach emphasizes how individuals interpret situations and assign meaning to them. The focus is on the perception of the situation and the psychological meaning of the situation to the individual.

More recently, Magnusson (1981a) and Craik (1981) have returned to an older conceptualization of environment (the environment as it is and as it is perceived), primarily, as noted by Craik, because of the ambiguity associated with the terms *objective environment* and *subjective environment*. Craik (1981) in particular noted that the objective term may be used in a variety of ways, thus complicating the measurement issue. Given this limitation, Magnusson (1981a) recommended a return to the old division of environment into the world as it is (the *actual environment*) and the world as it is perceived and construed in the minds of individuals (the *perceived environment*).

Magnusson (1981a) tends to believe that it is in actual situations that we meet the world, form our conceptions of it, and develop specific behaviors for coping. Within this context Magnusson suggests that there are three main kinds of actual environmental variables that need to be distinguished: physical-geographical, biological, and social-cultural. The physical-geographical environment is defined by the physical characteristics in terms of furniture, books, flowers, and so forth. The biological environment is defined by the people in the physical-geographical environment in terms of their characteristics, such as number, age, and sex. To the physical and biological properties of places (churches, clubs, ballrooms, classrooms) we must attach the social-cultural factors of norms, rules, and roles that contribute to a more complete definition of the actual situation. As noted by Magnusson (1981a), separately and in combination these three types of properties may be used for descriptions of actual environments and situations. The perceived situation is defined as an actual situation as it is perceived, interpreted, and assigned meaning in the mind of a participant. The real world in which we experience, think, and act is the world as we perceive it. Thus, if we define situations as real, they are real in their consequences. Magnusson (1981a) and Magnusson and Endler (1977a) suggest that if we have some idea how an individual interprets and perceives a situation and some idea of how an individual behaves in that kind of situation, we should be able to understand and predict the individual's behavior in that kind of situation.

An important task remaining for psychology is to investigate the relation between perceived and actual environments. This means that we must continue to analyze actual environments and situations, as is being done by sociologists, anthropologists, and more recently by environmental psychologists. These and other professionals deal with environments and situations in terms of actual physical properties and their impact on behavior. In addition, psychology must analyze perceived environments and situations. In this type of analysis, environments and situations are described and classified in terms of person variables such as perceptions, needs, motives, and reactions. Magnusson (1981a) and others have suggested that one of the most important tasks in psychology may be to explain how an individual's perceptions of the outer world are developed in interaction with different actual environments and how they function in relation to the specific actual properties of situations.

APPROACHES TO ENVIRONMENTAL ASSESSMENT

As stated many times throughout this text, any assessment of the person is, in our opinion, incomplete without some assessment of the environment in which the person's thought and behavior occur. Craik (1971) and Moos (1975) suggest that the aim of environmental assessment is the development and application of techniques for the systematic description and evaluation of physical and social environments. We think, similar to Moos's (1976a) theory, that the way one perceives one's surroundings influences the way one behaves in that environment. Thus, in environmental assessment we want to describe and evaluate the physical and social environments, but in addition, and perhaps more important, we want to size up and understand how the individual's perceptions of the environment tend to influence the way that person behaves in that environment. Thus, the individual is not a passive agent for environmental forces, but rather an active agent in a continuous ongoing person-situation process. The person seeks out some situations and avoids others. An individual is influenced by situations in which he or she interacts, but also affects and changes situations in which he or she is interacting. The process is continuous, suggesting that how individuals tend to perceive situations and environments influences the way they behave in these situations and environments.

The environmental context of human behavior may be assessed in a variety of different ways. As noted by Craik (1971), there are at least five different approaches to environmental assessment.

One approach to environmental assessment focuses on the *physical spatial properties of places*. For example, Kasmar (1970) developed the Environmental Descriptor Scales, and Shafer and Thompson (1968) related 40 descriptive dimensions of Adirondack camp sites to how frequently the sites were used. Thus, the emphasis in this approach is on the physical and spatial characteristics of environments and how they tend to subsequently influence behavior.

A second approach to environmental assessment is concerned with the *organization of material artifacts in places*. For example, Laumann and House (1970) developed the Living Room Checklist to assess the contents of living rooms. Through subsequent data analysis they identified a traditional-versus-modern stylistic dimension and a social class dimension. Another example of this approach is the Home Index (Gough, 1974), which is a brief objective inventory for assessing social-economic factors in home and family environments.

A third approach involves assessing the *traits of environments or situations* by means of human observers. Craik (1971) notes that a variety of different adjective checklists, bipolar rating scales, and cue-sort decks are being developed to permit observers to record their impressions of environments in rather rapid, comparable, and comprehensive ways. An example here is the Environmental Assessment Technique, which simply involves counting the number of individuals in a given environment who exhibit certain traits or characteristics. The idea behind this technique is that the dominant psychological features of any particular environment or situation depend on the typical characteristics or traits of its members. Thus, knowledge about the kind of people that constitute a group could tell us something about the climate created in the group.

A fourth approach focuses on assessing the *behavioral attributes of environments* or behavior settings. An analysis of behavior patterns can yield a comparison of environments on the basis of the relative frequency and duration of types of behaviors within those environments or behavior settings. To analyze the behavior patterns in environments, Barker (1965) developed the Behavior Setting Survey, which is able to identify behavior settings, describe behavior settings, and analyze the behavioral stream occurring in the behavior setting.

A fifth approach focuses on the assessment of *institutional attributes of environments*. Here perceived group consensus is used to provide formal measurement of psychological properties of environments. These are properties such as value, beauty, social climate, press, satisfaction, and preferability, all of which tend to have an evaluative as well as a descriptive component. Thus, the focus here is on how different groups of people (staff, residents, participants, observers, personnel people, patients, students, faculty, administrators) tend to perceive the environment and, subsequently, how these perceptions tend to influence their behavior. Examples of assessment techniques based on this approach include the Stern Environmental Indexes and the Moos Social Climate Indexes.

Against this background, most of the tests and inventories described in this chapter will focus on environments and situations as described in terms of person or personality variables such as the individual's perceptions, needs, motives, reactions or behaviors. Two of the other approaches (organizational and situational traits) are represented by the Home Index and the Environmental Assessment Technique, respectively. And some behavioral techniques for assessing the behavioral attributes of environments are presented in Chapter 5's discussion of projective and behavioral measures of personality.

The Stern Environmental Indexes

The College Characteristics Index, the High School Characteristics Index, the Evening College Characteristics Index, and the Organizational Climate Index were developed to assess the perceived environment, or the "consensual beta press." The concept of consensual beta press is derived from the theorizing of Murray (1938) and of Stern, Stein, and Bloom (1956) and is primarily concerned with assessing the environment as it is consensually perceived by the people actually interacting in that environment. In essence, Stern believed that environmental pressures could be inferred from self-reported perceptions of the resources, expectancies, and behaviors likely to be characteristic of others in a given environment or situation. Hence, the approach is perceptual and phenomenological in nature. (See Chapter 12's discussion of person-environment psychology and assessment for additional information on the Murray and Stern Theory.)

The first environmental index to be constructed was the College Characteristics Index (CCI; Pace & Stern, 1958). The basic rationale behind the development of the CCI was that the press (environmental pressures) may be inferred from the collective perceptions or interpretations of the environment. If a consensus of people endorses activities and events associated with a particular press on the CCI, a particular environmental situation potentially capable of shaping a certain pattern of responses may be expected. To develop the CCI, the Stern Activities Index (AI) was used as a model. Each of the 30 personality-need scales of the AI was reformulated in a parallel version reflecting a college environment. Thus, for each of the 30 need scales assessed by the AI there were now 30 press scales assessed by the CCI. Initially Stern thought that the CCI and the AI should be used in tandem in order to explore need-press interactions and the subsequent impact on behavior. In theory this notion made considerable sense, but in practice it did not prove to be very operational.

The present form of the CCI contains 300 items about the specific environment and is organized into 30 scales (see Table 11.1), each of which has 10 items. Each of the items is to be answered "True" or "False." The CCI is a self-administering questionnaire requiring about 15 minutes of response time. CCI norms are based on a sample of 1,993 students in 32 colleges, but a limitation is that these data were collected before 1961. Kuder-Richardson-20 reliability coefficients computed for the 30 CCI scales on a sample of 1,076 students from 23 institutions, ranged from a low of 0.34 to a high of 0.81.

A factor analysis by Saunders (1969) of the CCI produced 11 common factors. In a second-order factor analysis, the 11 CCI first-order factors were found to be underlayed by three second-order significant dimensions: Intellectual Climate, Nonintellectual Climate, and Impulse Control. This analysis suggests that there is considerable scale overlap among the 30 CCI scales.

Considerable validity data are reported in Stern's (1970) book *People in Context*. The rather elaborate validity data presented in Stern's text suggest that the CCI scales seem

TABLE 11.1 The Scales in Stern's Activities Index and Environmental Indexes

Scale Definitions

1. Aba Abasement—Ass Assurance: Self-depreciation and self-devaluation as reflected in the ready acknowledgment of inadequacy, ineptitude, or inferiority, the acceptance of humiliation and other forms of self-degradation versus certainty, self-confidence, or self-glorification.
2. Ach Achievement: Surmounting obstacles and attaining a successful conclusion in order to prove one's worth, striving for success through personal effort.
3. Ada Adaptability—Dfs Defensiveness: Accepting

Scale Definitions

criticism, advice, or humiliation publicly versus resistance to suggestion, guidance, direction, or advice, concealment or justification of failure.
4. Aff Affiliation: Gregariousness, group-centered friendly, participatory associations with others versus social detachment, social independence, self-isolation, or unsociableness.
5. Agg Aggression—Bla Blame Avoidance: Indifference or disregard for the feelings of others as manifested in hostility, either overt or covert, direct or indirect, versus the denial or inhibition of such impulses.

TABLE 11.1 (Continued)

Scale Definitions

6. Cha Change—Sam Sameness: Variable or flexible behavior versus repetition and routine.

7. Cnj Conjunctivity—Dsj Disjunctivity: Organized, purposeful, or planned activity patterns versus uncoordinated, disorganized, diffuse, or self-indulgent behavior.

8. Ctr Counteraction: Persistent striving to overcome difficult, frustrating, humiliating, or embarrassing experiences and failures versus avoidance or hasty withdrawal from tasks or situations that might result in such outcomes.

9. Dfr Deference—Rst Restiveness: Respect for authority, submission to the opinions and preferences of others perceived as superior versus noncompliance, insubordination, rebelliousness, resistance, or defiance.

10. Dom Dominance—Tol Tolerance: Ascendancy over others by means of assertive or manipulative control versus nonintervention, forbearance, acceptance, equalitarianism, permissiveness, humility, or meekness.

11. E/A Ego Achievement (derived from Exocathection-Intraception): Self-dramatizing, idealistic social action, active or fantasied realization of dominance, power, or influence achieved through sociopolitical activities in the name of social improvement or reform.

12. Emo Emotionality—Plc Placidity: Intense, open emotional expression versus stolidness, restraint, control, or constriction.

13. Eny Energy—Pas Passivity (derived from Energy-Endurance—Psychasthenia): High activity level, intense, sustained, vigorous effort versus sluggishness or inertia.

14. Exh Exhibitionism—Inf Inferiority Avoidance: Self-display and attention-seeking versus shyness, embarrassment, self-consciousness, or withdrawal from situations in which the attention of others might be attracted.

15. F/A Fantasied Achievement (derived from Ego Ideal): Daydreams of success in achieving extraordinary public recognition, narcissistic aspirations for fame, personal distinction, or power.

16. Har Harm Avoidance—Rsk Risktaking: Fearfulness, avoidance, withdrawal, or excessive caution in situations that might result in physical pain, injury, illness, or death versus careless indifference to danger, challenging or provocative disregard for personal safety, thrill-seeking, boldness, venturesomeness or temerity.

17. Hum Humanities, Social Science (derived from Endocathection-Extraception: Social Sciences and Humanities): The symbolic manipulation of social objects or artifacts through empirical analysis, reflection, discussion, and criticism.

18. Imp Impulsiveness—Del Deliberation: Rash, impulsive, spontaneous, or impetuous behavior versus care, caution, or reflectiveness.

19. Nar Narcissism: Self-centered, vain, egotistical, preoccupation with self, erotic feelings associated with one's own body or personality.

20. Nur Nurturance: Supporting others by providing love, assistance, or protection versus disassociation from others, indifference, withholding support, friendship, or affection.

21. Obj Objectivity—Pro Projectivity: Detached, nonmagical, unprejudiced, impersonal thinking versus autistic, irrational, paranoid, or otherwise egocentric perceptions and beliefs—superstition (Activities Index), suspicion (Environment Indexes).

22. Ord Order—Dso Disorder: Compulsive organization of the immediate physical environment, manifested in a preoccupation with neatness, orderliness, arrangement, and meticulous attention to detail versus habitual disorder, confusion, disarray, or carelessness.

23. Ply Play—Wrk Work: Pleasure-seeking, sustained pursuit of amusement and entertainment versus persistently purposeful, serious, task-oriented behavior.

24. Pra Practicalness—Ipr Impracticalness (derived from Exocathection-Extraception and Pragmatism): Useful, tangibly productive, business-like applications of skill or experience in manual arts, social affairs, or commercial activities versus a speculative, theoretical, whimsical, or indifferent attitude toward practical affairs.

25. Ref Reflectiveness (derived from Endocathection-Intraception): Contemplation, Intraception, introspection, preoccupation with private psychological, spiritual, esthetic, or metaphysical experience.

26. Sci Science (derived from Endocathection-Extraception: Natural Sciences): The symbolic manipulation of physical objects through empirical analysis, reflection, discussion, and criticism.

27. Sen Sensuality—Pur Puritanism (derived from Sentience): Sensory stimulation and gratification, voluptuousness, hedonism, preoccupation with aesthetic experience versus austerity, self-denial, temperance, or abstinence, frugality, self-abnegation.

28. Sex Sexuality—Pru Prudishness (derived from Sex-Superego Conflict): Erotic heterosexual interest or activity versus the restraint, denial, or inhibition of such impulses, prudishness, asceticism, priggishness.

29. Sup Supplication—Aut Autonomy: Dependence on others for love, assistance, and protection versus detachment, independence, or self-reliance.

30. Und Understanding: Detached intellectualization, problem-solving analysis, theorizing, or abstraction as ends in themselves.

to be meaningful and at least to some extent useful in the assessment of college environments. For example, the scales are able to differentiate among different college climates as perceived by students actually participating in those environments. However in spite of considerable validity data, the CCI scales and the other Stern environmental indexes are waning in use. One major reason for this decline as noted by Layton (1972) and Skager (1972) is that an up-to-date test manual is not available. A preliminary manual was published in 1959, but since that time there has been no concise and organized statement of the description, scoring, and technical information associated with the environmental indexes. In addition, some of the items on the inventories and the norm groups are becoming badly outdated.

The High School Characteristics Index (HSCI; Stern, 1970) was developed from the College Characteristics Index and was designed to measure the environmental press of educational settings different from colleges and universities. As with the CCI, the basic assumption underlying the HSCI is that the environment may be appropriately defined in terms of the press inferred from the collective perceptions of its inhabitants.

The HSCI is a measure of 30 kinds of press, again parallel to the need scales of the Activities Index. The HSCI contains 300 items about the environment, grouped into 30 scales of 10 items each, to be answered "True" or "False." Like the CCI, it is self-administering and requires about 15 minutes of response time. Normative data on the HSCI are reported in *People in Context* (Stern, 1970) and were collected in the early 1960s on 947 students in 12 high schools. The factor structure of the HSCI was explored using the above students, which resulted in the extraction of seven first-order factors, which were further combined into three second-order factors (Developmental Press, Orderliness, and Practicalness).

The scale reliabilities for the HSCI have been estimated by means of the Kuder-Richardson-20 coefficients for 739 students from nine high schools. The reliabilities ranged from a low of 0.28 to a high of 0.77. Validity data (Stern, 1970) suggest that the HSCI scales successfully differentiate between different types of high schools. In general, reliability and validity data on the HSCI are limited.

The third environmental index, the Evening College Characteristics Index (ECCI; Stern, 1970), like the HSCI was rationally derived from the CCI. In essence, it was developed to assess the press of the nonresidential college, the community college, or the two-year junior college. Items were included in the ECCI that represented either the day school or the evening college. However, the ECCI is still quite similar to the CCI in item content; and it is also similar to the other three indexes in terms of the basic rationale.

Like the other indexes, the ECCI is a measure of 30 kinds of press analogous to the need scales of the Activities Index. In structure the ECCI is composed of 300 items grouped into 30 scales of 10 items each, and again the response format is "True" or "False." The ECCI is self-administering and requires about 15 minutes of response time. Similar to the CCI and the HSCI, the recommendation is for research use only.

Norms and reliabilities for the ECCI are not reported in *People in Context* (Stern, 1970). However, one validity study suggests that the ECCI scales are able to differentiate effectively among groups within one environment. Clearly much work needs to be done if the ECCI is to become a meaningful and useful environmental index.

The initial impetus behind the Organizational Climate Index (OCI; Stern, 1970) was to develop an instrument that would be used to measure the press experienced by staff in elementary and secondary education. However, measurement of general organizational climates seemed more practical. Therefore, the OCI was operationalized to accomplish this purpose. In its current form the OCI is a general instrument that may be used to measure formal administrative structures. The current form of the OCI was rationally derived from an earlier version of the OCI based on the CCI, HSCI, and ECCI. As with the other environmental indexes, the OCI is based on the assumption that the environment may be defined in terms of press inferred from perceptions of the participants in that environment.

The OCI is a measure of 30 kinds of press, each of which is a logical counterpart to a particular need scale for the Activities Index. It is composed of 300 items about the environment, grouped into the 30 scales of 10 items each, to be answered "True" or "False." The OCI is self-administering and requires about 15 minutes of response time. Currently the OCI is recommended for research use in administrative settings.

Reliability of the OCI has been explored using Kuder-Richardson-20 coefficients. Values were computed for the 30 scales of the OCI, and the first-order and second-order factors of the OCI. In general, the reliability estimates are acceptable and comparable to the values for the CCI. Validity data indicate that the OCI is able to differentiate between various organizational environments. For example, all 30 scales of the OCI differentiated between the 63 Peace Corps programs; in a school district sample, all but three scales differentiated the 43 school buildings; and for an industrial sample, 20 of the 30 scales discriminated among the industrial sites. Overall, these validity data suggest that the school environments tended to be the most constrained, the Peace Corps programs the most flexible and spontaneous, and the industrial sites the most competitive. Again, additional reliability and validity data are clearly needed to support the meaning and usefulness of the inventory.

In sum, the environmental indexes were developed by Stern as counterparts to the Activities Index to assess environments as perceived by the people actually in them. The initial rationale for the development of the CCI by Pace and Stern was one of the first major attempts to develop an objective inventory to collect information about the psychological environment. There is no question that over the years, Stern and Pace with the construction of these environmental indexes, have made a major contribution to the area of environmental assessment and person environment psychology. The inventories have to some extent fallen into disuse, probably primarily because of the untimely death of Stern. In any event the inventories themselves and the normative groups, along with reliability and validity data, need to be updated.

College Student Experiences Questionnaire

The College Student Experiences Questionnaire (CSEQ) was initially published in 1979 and revised in 1983 and 1986. The 1983 version of the CSEQ was not compatible with the latest scoring equipment and led to a new version, which was released in 1986. The item content did not change. The purpose of the CSEQ is to assess how students spend their time in using the facilities and opportunities that are intended for their learning and development (Pace, 1984, 1987). The questionnaire is based on the premise that the quality of the college experience is a direct function of the efforts individuals expend on its pursuit. As noted by Pace (1984) once students get to college, what counts the most toward their attainment is what they do. The more effort students put into their college experience the more they get out of it (Pace, 1984). The questionnaire is composed of 14 dimensions of college activities, 8 dimensions of college environments, and

21 estimates of outcomes of college. Three additional sections are devoted to personal background information (17 demographic items), opinions about college (3 items), and reading and writing (2 items). Administration of the questionnaire takes about 35 to 45 minutes (Pace, 1987). Normative data are available based on the responses of 25,606 undergraduates from 74 college and universities obtained during the years 1983 to 1986.

The major part of the questionnaire is the Quality of Effort Scale, which consists of 14 College Activity Scales most of which are made up of 10 items each. On each item students respond on a four-point scale (Very Often, Often, Occasionally, Never). The 14 College Activity Scales include the following: Library experiences; Experiences with Faculty; Course Learning; Art, Music, Theater; Student Union; Athletic and Recreational Facilities; Clubs and Organizations; Experience in Writing; Personal Experiences; Student Acquaintances; Science/Technology; Dormitory or Fraternity/Sorority; Topics of Conversation; and Information in Conversations. The activities on each of the 14 scales represent a coherent universe of content (Pace, 1984, 1987). Stated differently, if the scale is assessing the effort in using the library, then all items or activities refer to using the library. An important characteristic of the Quality of Effort Scales is that the items are arranged in a hierarchy and it is assumed that participation in a high activity is qualitatively different from experiencing a lower activity.

The College Environment Scales include eight one-item rating scales. The first five dimensions reflect the purposes of the environment: Scholarship, Aesthetic Awareness, Critical Analysis, Vocational Emphasis, and Practical Personal Emphasis. Three dimensions describe the Supportiveness of Personal Relationships in the environment (among students, with faculty, and with administration). The CSEQ asks students to rate the environment, based on their experience in it, using a seven-point rating scale from strong emphasis to weak emphasis. Five of the environmental dimensions seem to be concerned with student development and three tend to focus on relationships among people at the college.

The final section (the Estimates of Gain and Progress) of the CSEQ is a list of 21 statements describing goals of undergraduate education or outcomes of undergraduate education. Students are asked to report (Very Much, Quite a Bit, Some, or Very Little) perceived gain or progress on each of the goals.

A factor analysis of the Quality of Effort Scales resulted in four factors: scholarly intellectual factor, informal interpersonal activities, group facilities, and a science factor. Factor 1 (scholarly intellectual factor) was defined by library experiences, experiences with faculty, course learning, and experience in writing. The informal interpersonal activities factor (2) was defined by art, music, theater; personal experiences; student acquaintances; topics of conversation; and information in conversations. The group facilities factor (3) was defined by student union, athletic and recreational facilities, and clubs and organizations. Factor 4 is a science factor defined by the Science Technology Activities Scale.

A factor analysis of the College Environment Scales produced three factors (supportive personal relationships; scholarly, intellectual emphasis; and vocational, practical emphasis). The supportive personal relationships factor (1) is defined by personal relationships in the environment among students, faculty, and administration. The scholarly and intellectual emphasis factor (2) is defined by scholarship, aesthetic awareness, and critical analysis. Factor 3 (vocational and practical emphasis) is defined by vocational emphasis and practical personal emphasis.

The estimates of gain and progress items was also factor analyzed. This analysis produced five factors: personal and social; science and technology; general education, literature and arts; intellectual skills; and vocational preparation.

In general, the results of the factor analyses of the College Activity Scales, College Environment Scales, and the Estimates of Gain are consistent with theoretical perspectives about student life and development. The factor analyses tell us much about college life and about the scales themselves.

Estimates of reliability (coefficient alpha) for the 14 Quality of Effort Scales ranged from a low of 0.79 to a high of 0.90. The reliability coefficients given the length of the scales are certainly acceptable. However, as noted by R. D. Brown (1985) there is a need for test-retest reliability data. Brown also notes that there is little or no information regarding reliability of the College Environment and the Estimate of Gain Scales.

With regard to validity, Pace (1984, 1987) provides some meaningful data between CSEQ scores and a variety of other variables. For example, on the scales of library experiences, experiences with faculty, and science, seniors scored significantly higher than did freshmen. In addition, there are expected differences between seniors and freshmen on the variables of grades, aspirations, and time spent on academic work. Significant differences exist between students who have lived on campus at some time and those who have never lived on campus on scales concerned with cultural facilities, clubs and organizations, the student union, athletic and recreational facilities, personal experiences, and student acquaintances. Other evidence shows significant differences between science majors and humanities majors in the Quality of Effort Scales related to those disciplines. Science majors are more involved in the science lab scale activities. Humanities majors are more involved in cultural facilities and writing and score higher on these scales when compared to the science majors. Other evidence suggests that residents are much more involved in campus activities than are commuters. However, additional validity work is needed.

In summary, the CSEQ is a useful inventory combining a variety of scales assessing students' activities, their perceptions of the college environment, and self-reported measures of gains. As noted by Brown (1985) the College Environment and Estimates of Gain are primarily perceptual and for the most part not behaviorally specific. In particular, in the Estimates of Gain Scales behaviorally anchored items would tend to be more meaningful. The Quality of Effort items (the 14 College Activity Scales) have the advantage of focusing on what the student has behaviorally done. Evidence reported thus far indicates that the scales are reliable and demonstrate some validity. However, as noted above, additional reliability and validity data are needed.

The Moos Social Climate Scales

Moos (1976a, 1987b) has developed a series of nine social climate scales applicable in a variety of different environments. The social climate scales were developed using primarily a rational approach that simply asks people individually about their patterns of behavior in certain environments. The basic rationale behind this approach (which is not unlike that of Murray, Stern, and Pace) is that the consensus of individuals characterizing their environment constitutes an assessment of the environment or social climate (Moos, 1987b). See Table 11.2 for a list of the social climate scales. (See Chapter 12's discussion of person-environment psychology and assessment for additional information on the Moos theory.)

To assess treatment environments Moos developed the Ward Atmosphere Scale

Table 11.2 Overview of Social Climate Scales

SCALE	ENVIRONMENT ASSESSED
	Community Settings
Family Environment Scale (FES; Moos & Moos, 1986)	Families, including single-parent and step-families (90 items, 10 subscales, normed on over 1,100 normal and 500 distressed families)
Work Environment Scale (WES; Moos, 1986c)	Work milieus (90 items, 10 subscales, normed on over 3,000 employees)
Group Environment Scale (GES; Moos, 1986a)	Social, task-oriented, psychotherapy, and mutual support groups (90 items, 10 subscales, normed on 148 groups)
	Educational Environments
Classroom Environment Scale (CES; Moos & Trickett, 1987)	Junior high and high school classes in regular, vocational, and alternative schools (90 items, 9 subscales, normed on 382 classes)
University Residence Environment Scale (URES; Moos, 1987c)	University student living groups, including dormitories, fraternities, sororities, and student cooperatives (100 items, 10 subscales, normed on 168 living groups)

(WAS; 1987c) and the Community-Oriented Programs Environment Scale (COPES; 1988a). The WAS assesses the social climate of hospital-based treatment programs, and the COPES assesses the social environments of community-based treatment programs. Both scales have been used extensively in this country and in the United Kingdom, and norms are available for programs in both countries. The current norms for the WAS are based on 160 American and 36 British programs, and the current American norms for the COPES are based on 54 programs for patients and 32 programs for staff. The WAS and the COPES each have 100 items scored on 10 parallel dimensions.

More recently Moos and Lemke (1987) developed the Sheltered Care Environment Scale (SCES) to assess specialized living groups for older persons, including congregate apartments, residential care facilities, and nursing homes. The scale consists of 63 items, seven subscales, and is normed on 323 living settings. This scale was initially developed as part of the multiphasic environmental assessment procedure instruments that are discussed later in this chapter.

To assess total institutions Moos developed the Correctional Institutions Environment Scale (CIES; 1987a) and the Military Company Environment Inventory (MCEI; 1986b). The CIES is used to describe the social climate of juvenile and adult correctional programs. The MCEI was developed to assess the social climate of military companies. For the CIES, normative groups

Table 11.2 (continued) Overview of Social Climate Scales

SCALE	ENVIRONMENT ASSESSED
	Residential Care and Treatment Settings
Ward Atmosphere Scale (WAS; Moos, 1987d)	Hospital-based treatment programs, including alcoholism and substance abuse programs (100 items, 10 subscales, normed on 193 programs)
Community-Oriented Programs Environment Scale (COPES; Moos, 1987a)	Community-based treatment programs, including board and care homes, sheltered workshops, and halfway houses (100 items, 10 subscales, parallel to WAS's, normed on 74 programs)
Sheltered Care Environment Scale (SCES; Lemke & Moos, 1987; Moos & Lemke, 1987)	Specialized living groups for older persons, including congregate apartments, residential care facilities, and nursing homes (63 items, 7 subscales, normed on 323 living settings)
	Other Institutions
Military Environment Inventory (MEI; Moos, 1986b)	Military units, including those in the Army, Navy, Air Force, Marine Corps, and National Guard (84 items, 7 subscales, normed on 32 military companies)
Correctional Institutions Environment Scale (CIES; Moos, 1987b)	Juvenile and adult correctional facilities (90 items, 9 subscales, normed on 112 juvenile and 83 adult units)

Source: Reproduced with permission from *The Social Climate Scales: A User's Guide* by R. H. Moos (1987), pp. 3, 4. Copyright © 1987 by Consulting Psychologists Press, Palo Alto, Calif.

are available for 112 juvenile correctional units for residence and 96 juvenile correctional units for staff. The adult normative sample includes 51 correctional units for males and 32 units for females. The CIES has 90 items scored on nine dimensions. On the MCEI current norms are based on 32 military training companies. The inventory has 84 items, which fall into seven dimensions.

The University Residence Environment Scale (URES; Moos, 1988b) and the Classroom Environment Scale (CES; Moos & Trickett, 1987) were developed to describe educational environments. The URES is used to describe the social climate of university student living groups such as dormitories, fraternities, and sororities. The norms are based on 168 university living groups from 16 colleges and universities throughout the country. The scale has 100 items scored on ten dimensions. The CES assesses the social climate of junior and senior high school classrooms. The current norms are based on 382 classrooms sampled from large and small public schools and vocational schools. The CES has 90 items scored on nine dimensions.

Finally, to assess community settings, three scales have been developed: the Group Environment Scale (GES; Moos, 1986a); the Work Environment Scale (WES; Moos, 1986c); and the Family Environment Scale (FES; Moos & Moos, 1986). The GES measures the social climate of task-oriented, social, and therapeutic community groups. Norms are based on 148 groups, and the inventory itself consists of 90 items scored on 10 dimensions. The WES describes the social climate of industrial or work environments. The scale consists of 90 items scored on 10 dimensions, and the preliminary norms are based on over 3000 employees. The FES assesses the social climate of all types of families. This scale has 90 items scored on 10 dimensions, and the preliminary norms are based on over 1,100 normal and 500 distressed families. In total, as we previously mentioned, 10 social climate scales are available for use.

Each of the above social climate scales has three forms. The Real Form (Form R) asks people to report their perceptions of the current social environment. The Ideal Form (Form I) asks people to indicate how they conceive of an ideal social environment. The Expectations Form (Form E) asks people to indicate what they expect the environment they are about to enter will be like. In addition, there is a Short Form (Form S) for each social climate scale which has been developed for use primarily by people who wish to obtain rapid or rather frequent assessments of a social environment. All items on all scales are in a "true/false" format, and these scales take about 15 to 20 minutes to complete.

Reliability and validity data for the nine social climate scales are not abundant. In terms of reliability, the social climate scales at minimum have subscale internal consistency coefficients calculated using the Kuder-Richardson-20. In the main, the subscale internal consistencies are acceptable. However, more specific and penetrating reliability data do exist for some of the social climate inventories. For example, test-retest data on the URES indicate that residents tend to perceive their environments in similar ways both one week and one month after initial testing.

The subscale correlations ranged from 0.66 to 0.77 after one week and from 0.59 to 0.74 after one month (Moos, 1988b). Test-retest data on the FES were calculated on 47 family members in nine families who took the FES twice within an eight-week interval between testings. The subscale test-retest correlations vary from a low of 0.68 to a high of 0.86 (Moos & Moos, 1986).

Another aspect of reliability is the stability of the profile for the living group as a whole over some period of time. For example, profile stabilities of over 0.90 have been obtained in two-week test-retest administrations of the CES, and profile coefficients averaging over 0.90 have been obtained in one-month test-retest administrations of the URES. Other data indicate that social environments of psychiatric and correctional programs remain rather stable, with profile coefficients averaging about 0.75 for one- to three-year intervals. In general, the existing work suggests that the underlying characteristics of social environments tend to remain rather stable over time (Moos, 1987b).

The validity data on the social climate scales are limited. In general, the scales tend to discriminate effectively among the relevant environmental units and/or living groups and are only minimally related to the personality characteristics of respondents—or, as Moos would say, the social climate scales discriminate among environments about as well as personality tests discriminate among people. More specifically, for example, Moos (1979) found that all 10 scales of the URES differentiated among 13 living groups as well as among fraternities and various other living units on the same and on different campuses. In terms of concurrent validity on the URES, Moos (1979) studied 52 living groups and found that students in units high on Emotional Support reported more supportive interactions (like listening to a friend's personal problems and studying with other people). Also, students in units high on Intellectuality reported engaging in more cultural activities (such as attending an art exhibition, visiting a museum, or attending a play). Another example of concurrent validity has been found on the CES. Here students who work in small groups tend to perceive their classes as high in affiliation. On the FES, concurrent validity data suggest that there is a general tendency for Cohesion and Expressiveness to decrease and for Conflict to increase with an increasing family size. There is also a tendency for the emphasis on FES Independence to decline somewhat with family size. Again, on the FES children in low-drinking families perceived more emphasis on Cohesion, Expressiveness, Achievement Orientation, and Organization than did the children in high-drinking families. On the other hand, the children from higher-drinking families perceived more emphasis on Intellectual Cultural Orientation. Other validity data (primarily content and concurrent validity) do exist and may be found in the manuals. However, much needs to be done with the social climate scales in the area of validity.

A very important finding of the Moos work (1976a, 1979, 1987b) and others is that the nine vastly different social environments may be described by some common sets of dimensions associated with three somewhat global categories. These broad categories are the relationship dimensions, personal growth or goal orientation dimensions, and system maintenance and change dimensions. The specific dimensions included in the relationship and system maintenance and change domains are fairly similar in most settings although some environments impose unique variations (Moos, 1979, 1987b). The personal growth dimensions measure the underlying aims of the environment and consequently vary much more from setting to setting (Moos, 1979, 1987b). See Table 11.3 for the three domains of social climate dimensions. The significant feature of iden-

tifying some common dimensions across different social environments is that such environments may now be compared and attempts may be made to explore why an individual does well in one environment and not so well in another. In general, the most profound research findings using these three dimensions, and the social climate scales suggest that people tend to be more satisfied and comfortable, less depressed and irritable, and more likely to report beneficial effects on their self-esteem in environments they perceive to strongly emphasize the relationship dimensions.

As noted by Moos (1987b) one of the most obvious uses of the social climate scales is to provide information about how various participants in a social environment view that environment. These scales may be used to compare the perceptions of different groups of program participants, for example, patients and staff in treatment programs, and students and teacher in classrooms. They may be used to compare different social environments. For example, one treatment program may be compared to another treatment program, or one classroom environment may be compared to another classroom environment. The scales may also be used to assess the degree of perceived change in a social environment when some major program change has been instituted. For example, as noted by Moos, to what extent does the treatment environment of a psychiatric ward change when staff are trained in group therapy techniques? A variety of other uses are reported in the manuals and in the social climate scales overview booklet (Moos, 1987b).

The Multiphasic Environmental Assessment Procedure

More recently Moos and his colleagues have developed the Multiphasic Environmental Assessment Procedure (MEAP; Moos & Lemke, 1979) in order to assess, measure,

Table 11.3 Common Social Climate Dimensions Across Environments

TYPE OF ENVIRONMENT (SCALE)	RELATIONSHIP DIMENSIONS	PERSONAL GROWTH DIMENSIONS	SYSTEM MAINTENANCE & CHANGE DIMENSIONS
COMMUNITY SETTINGS			
Families (FES)	Cohesion Expressiveness Conflict	Independence Achievement Orientation Intellectual-Cultural Orientation Active Recreational Orientation Moral-Religious Emphasis	Organization Control
Work milieus (WES)	Involvement Peer Cohesion Supervisor Support	Autonomy Task Orientation Work Pressure	Clarity Control Innovation Physical Comfort
Social, task-oriented, & therapeutic groups (GES)	Cohesion Leader Support Expressiveness	Independence Task Orientation Self-Discovery Anger & Aggression	Order & Organization Leader Control Innovation

and describe sheltered care settings, such as skilled nursing facilities and a variety of senior citizen housing facilities. According to Moos and his colleagues such information makes it possible to review the quality of the environment, to assess the impact of specific features on programs, and to explore the interaction between resident and environmental characteristics (Lemke, Moos, Mehren, & Gauvain, 1979).

Moos and Lemke (1979) note that the MEAP is structured to reflect four conceptual approaches that have been used in characterizing human environments: the physical and architectural features, the policies and procedures, the human aggregate or the characteristics of residents and staff in the setting, and the social climate. These approaches represent four of the instruments that have been developed to assess, characterize, and describe the human environ-

ments. A fifth instrument (a rating scale) has also been developed to assess outside observations of the human environments. A brief description of each instrument is presented below.

The Physical and Architectural Features checklist (PAF) assesses nine dimensions (see Table 11.4) of the physical and architectural resources of a facility. The PAF includes questions about the facility's location, its external and internal physical features, and its space allowances. This is relatively objective information about the facility that probably will be collected by interview with an administrator or a staff member. Generally an hour is sufficient time to complete the PAF.

The Policy and Program Information Form (POLIF) assesses 10 dimensions (see Table 11.4) of the organization, services, and policies of the facility. More specifically, the

Table 11.3 (continued) Common Social Climate Dimensions Across Environments

TYPE OF ENVIRONMENT (SCALE)	RELATIONSHIP DIMENSIONS	PERSONAL GROWTH DIMENSIONS	SYSTEM MAINTENANCE & CHANGE DIMENSIONS
EDUCATIONAL			
Junior high and high school classes (CES)	Involvement Affiliation Teacher Support	Task Orientation Competition	Order & Organization Rule Clarity Teacher Control Innovation
University student living groups (URES)	Involvement Emotional Support	Independence Traditional Social Orientation Competition Academic Achievement Intellectuality	Order & Organization Student Influence Innovation
RESIDENTIAL CARE AND TREATMENT			
Hospital and community programs (WAS & COPES)	Involvement Support Spontaneity	Autonomy Practical Orientation Personal Problem Orientation Anger & Aggression	Order & Organization Clarity Control
Sheltered·care settings for the elderly (SCES)	Cohesion Conflict	Independence Self-Exploration	Organization Resident Influence Physical Comfort
TOTAL INSTITUTIONS			
Military units (MEI)	Involvement Peer Cohesion Officer Support	Personal Status	Order & Organization Clarity Officer Control
Correctional facilities (CIES)	Involvement Support Expressiveness	Autonomy Practical Orientation Personal Problem Orientation	Order & Organization Clarity Control

items cover the financial and entrance arrangements, the types of rooms or apartments available, the way in which the facility is organized, and the services provided for the residents. Again, this is relatively objective information about the facility that may be obtained by interview method from an administrator or staff member. The POLIF requires about an hour to complete.

The Resident and Staff Information Form (RESIF) assesses nine dimensions (see Table 11.4) describing the residents and staff in the facility. For example, questions include the residents' social backgrounds and functional abilities, types of activities in which residents participate, and the characteristics of staff and volunteers. With the help of the administration and staff, these data may be obtained from a variety of records such as social histories, medical records, records of activities, and staff records in general. The number of residents tends to determine how much time is needed to complete the RESIF. For example, the scoring manual (Lemke, Moos, Mehren, & Gauvain, 1979) suggests that for 100 residents one should allow about three hours to locate and tabulate this information.

The Rating Scale (RS) assesses the experimenters' or other observers' perceptions of the physical environment and resident and staff functioning. Thus, the RS focuses on the observers' judgments about a facility on four dimensions (see Table 11.4). The first three parts of MEAP provide relatively objective information about a facility obtained from observations, administrators and staff,

and facility records. The RS, however, is based on the observers' judgments (perception) of the physical attractiveness of the facility. The RS is completed (or data for the RS are collected) by the observer or experimenter or evaluator while the other MEAP instruments are being completed. The scoring manual (Lemke, Moos, Gauvain, & Mehren, 1979) notes that most of the items on the RS may be filled out while gathering information for the PAF.

The Sheltered Care Environment Scale (SCES; Lemke & Moos, 1987; Moos & Lemke, 1987) assesses residents and staff members' perceptions of seven dimensions (see Table 11.4) of a facility's social climate or environment. This is a 63-item "yes/no" questionnaire designed to assess the three social climate dimensions of relationship, personal growth, and system maintenance and change. In general, the residents and staff are asked to report their perceptions of the social climate at a given facility. Similar to a number

TABLE 11.4 Subscales of the Multiphasic Environmental Assessment Procedure Instruments

Physical and Architectural Features Checklist	Policy and Program Information Form	Resident and Staff Information Form	Rating Scale	Sheltered Care Environment Scale
Physical amenities	Selectivity	Staff richness	Physical attractiveness	Cohesion
Social-recreational aids	Expectations for functioning	Resident social resources	Environmental diversity	Conflict
Prosthetic aids	Tolerance for deviance	Resident heterogeneity	Resident functioning	Independence
Orientational aids	Policy clarity	Resident functional abilities	Staff functioning	Self-exploration
Safety features	Policy choice	Resident activity level		Organizations
Architectural choice	Resident control	Resident integration in community		Resident influence
Space availability	Provision for privacy	Utilization of health resources		Physical comfort
Staff facilities	Health services	Utilization of daily living assistance		
Community accessibility	Daily living assistance	Utilization of social-recreational activities		
	Social-recreational activities			

of the other Moos inventories, the SCES has a Real Form, an Ideal Form, and an Expectations Form. The SCES requires about 15 to 20 minutes to complete.

Four steps were involved in developing the MEAP instruments. First, a form was constructed using the four conceptual approaches of physical and architectural features, policies and procedures, the human aggregate, and the social climate. Items were identified through interviews with residents and staff, interviews with facility administrators, discussions with state and local government inspectors, a search of the literature, and items based on observations. After the items were pretested, these procedures resulted in the initial form of the MEAP, which was administered to 93 different facilities. A working scoring key was constructed, and the MEAP dimensions were then developed using a set of six conceptual and empirical criteria: meaningfulness, applicability, item distribution, item discrimination, item interrelatedness, and subscale independence. In general, the items in the PAF, POLIF, and SCES are scored dichotomously. The items on the RESIF are scored either dichotomously or in terms of the proportion of residents who have certain background characteristics or who participate in the activities or use the services offered in the facility. The RS items are rated and scored on a four-point scale. For four of the instruments (PAF, POLIF, RESIF, and RS) raw scores are reported in terms of percentage scores. The SCES uses a standard score procedure.

As noted in the manual (Moos & Lemke, 1979) data on the MEAP have been gathered from a sample of 93 sheltered care settings for the elderly. The sample includes 43 skilled nursing facilities, 28 residential care facilities, and 24 apartment facilities. These facilities are all in several counties in California. These data and some revisions are discussed in the new final manual for the MEAP (Moos & Lemke, 1984).

In terms of reliability, the new manual (Moos & Lemke, 1984) reports internal consistency coefficients (Cronbach's Alpha) for all five instruments that range from a low of 0.56 to a high of 0.95. For four of the instruments (PAF, POLIF, RESIF, and RS) the manual reports test-retest coefficients for a 9- to 12-month interval that range from a low of 0.34 to a high of 0.99. Currently no test-retest reliability data are available for the SCES.

Concurrent validity data reported in the manual (1984) indicate that the scales of the various instruments are able to effectively discriminate between different facilities. For example, Figure 11.1 describes the physical and architectural resources profiles for two skilled nursing facilities. However, without question, considerable additional validity data are needed.

The manual reports a number of applied uses of the assessment procedures, which include environmental description, comparing and contrasting environments, evaluating environmental change, evaluating environmental change, evaluating environmental impact, determinants of social climates, maximizing environmental information, cross-cultural comparisons, and facilitating change. More individually oriented uses of the MEAP scales include enhancing clinical case descriptions and increasing person environment congruence. Moos and his colleagues have clearly made a bold attempt to develop environmental assessment procedures that may be used effectively and meaningfully with elderly populations and facilities. However, additional validity data are needed in order to verify and support the use of the MEAP scales in a meaningful way. Thus, until these data are accumulated, the scales remain preliminary, in many ways noted by the author.

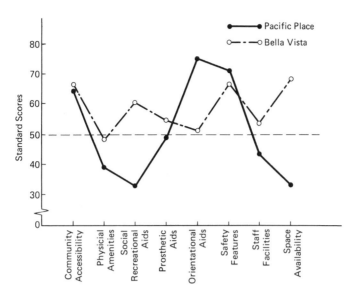

Figure 11.1 Physical and architectural resources profile for two nursing homes. (Reproduced with permission from the *Multiphasic Environmental Assessment Procedure (MEAP) Manual* by R. H. Moos and S. Lemke, p. 22. Copyright 1984 by the Social Ecology Laboratory, Stanford University School of Medicine, Palo Alto, Calif.)

The Environmental Response Inventory

The Environmental Response Inventory (ERI; McKechnie, 1974) is a psychological assessment instrument developed to measure environmental dispositions. McKechnie defines environmental dispositions in terms of the individual differences in the ways people think about and relate to the everyday physical environment. That is, as noted in the manual (McKechnie, 1974), the ERI represents an extension of the rationale and techniques of personality assessment to the study of people-environment relations. Although the instrument was developed for the interdisciplinary study of people and the environment, it is currently only recommended for research use.

The ERI consists of 184 items of the objective personality inventory type. Respondents indicate the extent to which each statement applies to them, using a five-point scale ranging from "Strongly agree" to "Strongly disagree." From these 184 responses, eight environmental disposition scores and one validity score are derived as reported in Table 11.5. The development of the scales involved a rather complex process of test construction that included the development of an initial item pool, an exploratory factor analysis, preliminary scale construction, item analysis, scale refinement and shortening, and a confirmatory factor analysis. Although a number of methods of scale construction were employed, factor analysis seemed to be the central procedure. The ERI has been used in research testing with high school students as young as 15 years of age and with adults as old as 70 years of age. Testing time is about 25 to 30 minutes, and scoring may be done by hand, but it is somewhat cumbersome. Hand-scorable answer sheets are available, along with scoring keys. Normative data, although somewhat fragmentary, are reported in the manual for col-

TABLE 11.5 Environmental Response Inventory (ERI) Scales

High Scorers Are Often Described as:	Scale and Major Themes:	Low Scorers Are Often Described as:
Aesthetic, affectionate, complicated, distractible, outspoken, progressive, rebellious, unconventional, unpredictable, selfish.	PA (Pastoralism). Opposition to land development; concern about population growth; preservation of natural resources, including open space; acceptance of natural forces as shapers of human life; sensitivity to pure environmental experiences; self-sufficiency in the natural environment.	Apathetic, conscientious, conservative, conventional, deliberate, dependable, friendly, honest, practical, self-controlled.
Critical, skeptical, responsive to urban aesthetics, highbrow, concerned with philosophical problems in life, valuing intellectual activity, managerial interests.	UR (Urbanism). Enjoyment of high density living; appreciation of unusual and varied stimulus patterns of the city; interest in cultural life; enjoyment of interpersonal richness and diversity.	Conscientious, conventional, friendly, generous, nonverbal, opportunistic, robust, simple, unselfish.
Autocratic, condescending, conservative, efficient, enterprising, extroverted, hard-headed, mannerly, methodical, power and money oriented, judgmental, aesthetically unresponsive.	EA (Environmental Adaptation). Modification of the environment to satisfy needs and desires, and to provide comfort and leisure; opposition to governmental control over private land use; preference for highly designed or adapted environments; use of technology to solve environmental problems; preference for stylized environmental details.	Artistic, awkward, compassionate, curious, distractible, idealistic, introspective, moody, nonconforming, sensitive, sensuous, worrying, forthright.
Adventurous, disorderly, distractible, dreamy, easy-going, immature, impulsive, progressive, unconventional, undependable.	SS (Stimulus Seeking). Interest in travel and exploration of unusual places; enjoyment of complex and intense physical sensations; breadth of interests.	Conscientious, conservative, fastidious, practical, responsible, rigid, severe, stingy.
Capable, competent, diligent, efficient, helpful, ingenious, resourceful, stable, thorough, tolerant, well-adjusted.	ET (Environmental Trust). General environmental openness, responsiveness, and trust; competence in finding one's way about the environment vs. fear of potentially dangerous environments; security of home; fear of being alone and unprotected.	Bitter, cold, coarse, dissatisfied, distrustful, intolerant, moody, prejudiced, spendthrift, unkind.
Affectionate, artistic, changeable, dependent, dreamy, emotional, forgiving, idealistic, introspective, aesthetically reactive, warm.	AN (Antiquarianism). Enjoyment of antiques and historical places; preference for traditional vs. modern design; aesthetic sensitivity to man-made environments and to landscape; appreciation of cultural artifacts of earlier eras; tendency to collect objects for their emotional significance.	Coarse, cool, conservative, deliberate, mischievous, moralistic, practical, sly, stolid, unemotional.
Aloof, arrogant, autocratic, bitter, cold, formal, hard-hearted, sulky, polished, resentful, stubborn.	NP (Need for Privacy). Need for physical isolation from stimuli; enjoyment of solitude; dislike of neighboring; need for freedom from distraction.	Appreciative, cooperative, easy-going, friendly, seeking reassurance, warm, seeks acceptance, lacks confidence, introverted.

TABLE 11.5 (cont.) Environmental Response Inventory (ERI) Scales

High Scorers Are Often Described as:	Scale and Major Themes:	Low Scorers Are Often Described as:
Arrogant, conceited, egotistical, hard-hearted, masculine, self-seeking, inflexible, sociable, manipulative.	MO (Mechanical Orientation). Interest in mechanics in its various forms; enjoyment in working with one's hands; interest in technological processes and basic principles of science; appreviation of the functional properties of objects.	Affectionate, feminine, generous, sincere, understanding, submissive, sympathetic, warm.
Calm, civilized, initiatory, mannerly, patient, tactful, trusting, rule-following.	CO (Communality). A validity scale, tapping honest, attentive, and careful test-taking attitude; response to items in statistically modal manner.	Hard-headed, flirtatious, good looking, immature, opportunistic, versatile, witty, independent-minded, psychologically complex.

SOURCE: Reproduced with permission from the *Manual for the Environmental Response Inventory,* by G. E. McKechnie (1974), p. 2. Copyright 1974 by Consulting Psychologists Press, Palo Alto, California.

lege students and adults (McKechnie, 1974). The adult group ($N = 1565$) includes two area-wide samples from a northern California county, with quotas for age, sex, and geographical location. The college student sample ($N = 939$) represents 11 institutions of higher learning geographically dispersed across the United States and Canada. The ERI profile sheet provides norms for males and females on opposite sides of the sheet, based upon the adult samples only. The profile is constructed so that raw scores are displayed on the profile sheet as standard scores having a mean of 50 and a standard deviation of 10. Thus, an above-average score on a given scale would tend to be a standard score of 60 or higher. As noted in the manual (McKechnie, 1974), ERI answer sheets containing more than eight unanswered items are suspect, and records containing more than 16 omissions should not be scored. The Communality scale of the ERI, as noted in Table 11.5, was constructed to help identify profiles that are invalid for reasons other than response omissions. Random response to the items on this scale will produce a score that is very low.

In their reviews of the ERI, Richards (1978) and Stricker (1978) suggest that the reliability of the scales is adequate. More specifically, split-half reliabilities for the scales range from 0.65 to 0.87 for an adult sample ($N = 255$) and from 0.70 to 0.86 for a college sample ($N = 939$). Test-retest stability coefficients were obtained on the ERI scales for a sample of 130 residents of Vancouver, British Columbia, who completed the ERI twice, with a two-week interval between administrations (McKechnie, 1974). Test-retest coefficients obtained from these data ranged from a low of 0.81 to a high of 0.90. McKechnie (1974) notes that although these reliability data are acceptable, a need still exists for long-term (one year or more) stability information.

Validity data are available for two samples, and these data are reported in the manual (McKechnie, 1974). One sample consists of 255 adults (118 males and 137 females) from Marin County, California. Personality data come from a sample of 50 individuals (25 males and 25 females) drawn from the above sample of 255 adults. Rather extensive validity data are presented in the form of correlations with standard personality tests for this sub-sample of 50 adults. The personality tests used in this correlational analysis to explore concurrent validity of the ERI included the Leisure Activities Blank, the Adjective Check List, the Strong Vocational Interest Blank, the California Psychological Inventory, the Minnesota Multiphasic Personality Inventory, the Study of Values, and the Myers-Briggs Type Indicator. In general, some of these correlations support the validity of the ERI scales, and others tend to raise questions about the validity of the scales. Additional validity work with the ERI is needed to document the meaning of the scales.

A principal goal in the development of the ERI noted by McKechnie (1974), was to produce an assessment instrument having value for interdisciplinary study of people and the environment. However, in its current state of validation the ERI is intended primarily for research use only to obtain information on how a person or group of persons thinks about, and relates to, the everyday physical environment. Other research applications suggested in the manual include response to residential and institutional architecture, adjustment to geographic migration, response to urban stress, study of environmental attitudes, and urban and suburban design preferences. A basic question of interest to McKechnie (1978) is to what extent individual differences in environmental dispositions relate to significant environmental behaviors. Unfortunately, little data are available addressing this issue. Figure 11.2 presents four environmental professions on the ERI scales suggesting how the instrument may be used to describe environmental dispositions.

In summary, the ERI has set out to measure some interesting variables in the domain of environmental psychology. It has attempted to combine personality traits, attitudes, and interests in order to assess en-vironmental dispositions. As noted by Stricker (1978), the ERI's validity is spotty, but because of the scarcity of measures designed for environmental psychology the inventory needs to be considered for research use in this area.

The Institutional Functioning Inventory

The Institutional Functioning Inventory (IFI; Peterson, Centra, Hartnett, & Linn, 1983) was developed in 1968 by the higher education research group at the Educational Testing Service and subsequently revised in 1978. Initially, the IFI grew out of a study of institutional vitality supported by the Kettering Foundation and directed by Earl J. McGrath, then at the Institute of Higher Education, Teachers College, Columbia University (Peterson, Centra, Hartnett, & Linn, 1983). The IFI is designed to describe the perceived climate of institutions of higher education. Primarily developed to assess faculty members' perceptions about their institutions, the IFI may be used with administrators, students, and other groups acquainted with the institutional environments. Thus, the primary purpose of the IFI is to help institutions understand how their members (faculty, administrators, students, trustees, and a variety of other groups) perceive important aspects of the college environment.

In its present form the IFI consists of 132 short statements divided equally among the 11 dimensions described in Table 11.6. Forty-eight of the items are regarded as factual and responded to in terms of "Yes," "No," or "Don't Know." The remainder of the items are regarded as opinions responded to by "Strongly agree," "Agree," "Disagree," or "Strongly disagree." Each scale is composed of 12 items. About 20 to 30 minutes are required to complete the entire inventory.

Scales were rationally constructed from a larger item pool. In the beginning 20 items

TABLE 11.6 Definitions of the Scales of the Institutional Functioning Inventory (IFI)

Brief Descriptions of the Eleven Scales of the Institutional Functioning Inventory

1. **Intellectual-Aesthetic Extracurriculum** (IAE): the extent to which activities and opportunities for intellectual and aesthetic stimulation are available outside the classroom.
2. **Freedom** (F): the extent of academic freedom for faculty and students as well as freedom in their personal lives for all individuals in the campus community.
3. **Human Diversity** (HD): the degree to which the faculty and student body are heterogeneous in their backgrounds and present attitudes.
4. **Concern for Improvement of Society** (IS): the desire among people at the institution to apply their knowledge and skills in solving social problems and prompting social change in America.
5. **Concern for Undergraduate Learning** (UL): the degree to which the college—in its structure, function, and professional commitment of faculty—emphasizes undergraduate teaching and learning.
6. **Democratic Governance** (DG): the extent to which individuals in the campus community who are directly affected by a decision have the opportunity to participate in making the decision.
7. **Meeting Local Needs** (MLN): institutional emphasis on providing educational and cultural opportunities for all adults in the surrounding communities.
8. **Self-Study and Planning** (SP): the importance college leaders attach to continuous long-range planning for the total institution, and to institutional research needed in formulating and revising plans.
9. **Concern for Advancing Knowledge** (AK): the degree to which the institution—in its structure, function, and professional commitment of faculty—emphasizes research and scholarship aimed at extending the scope of human knowledge.
10. **Concern for Innovation** (CI): the strength of institutional commitment to experimentation with new ideas for educational practice.
11. **Institutional Esprit** (IE): the level of morale and sense of shared purposes among faculty and administrators.

SOURCE: Reproduced with permission from the *Institutional Functioning Inventory Profile Sheet.* Copyright 1970 by Educational Testing Service, Princeton, New Jersey.

were written for each scale, and this set was administered to faculty samples at 67 colleges and universities. An extensive item analysis was then used to reduce the number of items to 12 for each scale. The norm group is made up of responses of faculty members of 37 colleges and universities. These 37 were selected to represent the population of four-year American colleges. The norms based on faculty perceptions do not include the perceptions of students, administrators, or other significant groups.

Interscale correlations reported in the technical manual suggest some relatively high relationships. For example, eight of the 55 coefficients were 0.60 or higher, and an additional seven were in the 0.50s. As reported in the technical manual a more comprehensive view of these patterns of scale relationships was obtained through factor analysis of the 37 college means (Peterson, Centra, Hartnett, & Linn, 1983). These data suggest that four factors tend to explain the faculty-perceived climates that tend to distinguish among four-year higher education institutions. Factor one, the Liberal Orientation, is characterized by a concern for freedom, human diversity, and improving society. Factor two suggests a Community dimension characterized by high faculty esprit de corps, interested groups in the institution involved in governance and planning, and a concern for continuous innovation. The third factor, Intellectual Climate, suggests an emphasis on research and intellectual and artistic extracurricular interests. Factor four, the Ivory Tower Orientation, suggests an emphasis on undergraduate learning and lack of concern for meeting local community needs. Against this background, the evidence does suggest that there is substantial overlap among the 11 scales of the IFI. In spite of the apparent overlap, the technical manual argues that the preliminary nature of the IFI and the conceptual distinctness of the scales favor the retention of the current format.

In terms of reliability, the internal consistency coefficients for faculty members at 37 colleges and universities range from a low

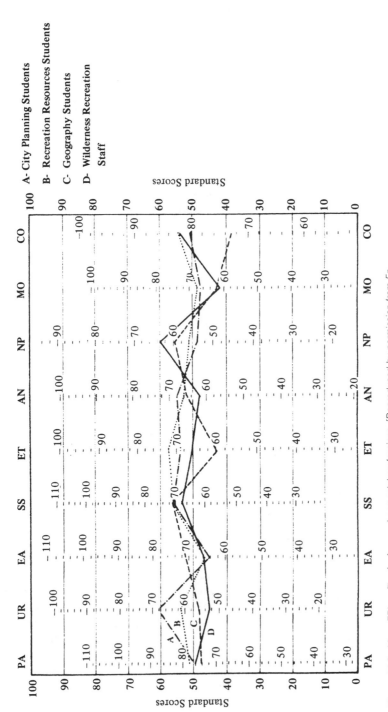

Figure 11.2 Mean ERI profiles for four environmental professions. [Reproduced by permission from *Environmental Dispositions: Concepts and Measures* by G. E. McKechnie, p. 168. In McReynolds, P. (ed.), *Advances in Psychological Assessment, Vol. 4.* (San Francisco: Jossey-Bass, Inc.). Copyright 1977 by Consulting Psychologist Press, Palo Alto, Calif. 94306.]

A- City Planning Students
B- Recreation Resources Students
C- Geography Students
D- Wilderness Recreation Staff

of 0.86 to a high of 0.96, with a median internal consistency coefficient of 0.92. Internal consistency reliabilities for students are based on data from 17 institutions and range from a low of 0.87 to a high of 0.96. Reliabilities for administrators based on data from 22 institutions range from a low of 0.83 to a high of 0.94. In general, as noted in the technical manual, the IFI scales appear to be quite reliable when defined in terms of internal consistency. However, there are no data pertaining to the overall profile stability of colleges and universities over some period of time.

The issue of validity as noted by Dressel (1972) is not easily determined for an instrument like the IFI. The technical manual provides correlates of the IFI scales with relevant published institutional data, student perceptions of their college environment, and a national study of student protest. The IFI scales as responded to by faculty have been correlated with the above three kinds of information. As suggested by Lunneborg (1972) many of these correlations are consistent with the IFI scale definitions, but others tend to raise interesting questions. In the technical manual itself the correlational data from all sources are presented and discussed on a scale by scale basis (Peterson, Centra, Hartnett, & Linn, 1983). Additional validity data certainly would be of value.

The IFI was initially developed to assess the perceived climate of institutions of higher education and contribute to institutional self-study and research. Within this context it is suggested that the IFI might be used to assess college functions and goals; compare the perceptions of faculty subgroups; compare the views of faculty, administrators, and students; and compare the perceptions of a variety of other campus groups. Figure 11.3 reports the perceptions of faculty at an armed service academy and the perceptions of faculty at a selective liberal arts college across the 11 scales of the IFI. Faculty perceptions in these two academic environments tend to differ substantially. The armed service academy tends to score high on the Institutional Esprit and Self-Study in Planning dimensions. The well-known liberal arts college has high scores on Freedom, Undergraduate Learning, Democratic Governance, and the Innovation dimension. For the liberal arts college all reported perceptions tend to be fairly consistent with public image. These and other examples are reported in the technical manual.

In summary, the IFI is an experimental inventory primarily concerned with institutional self-study and research. The approach is perceptual, and the environmental data are derived from the perceptions of the individuals actually interacting in the setting. In time, additional validity and normative data will contribute to the meaning and usefulness of the scales.

The Work Environment Preference Schedule

The Work Environment Preference Schedule (WEPS; Gordon, 1973) attempts to identify individuals who are likely to be adaptable to bureaucratic settings. As noted in the manual (Gordon, 1973), the WEPS is designed to assess a personality construct, bureaucratic orientation, which reflects a commitment to the set of attitudes, values, and behaviors that are characteristically rewarded by bureaucratic organizations. Thus persons scoring high on the WEPS tend to accept authority and to prefer specific rules and guidelines to follow, impersonalized work relationships, and the security of organizational and in-group identification.

The WEPS is made up of 24 items and is self-administering. There is no time limit, and most individuals are able to complete the inventory in about 10 minutes. It is suggested that the inventory is appropriate for grades 11 through 16 and for adults. The

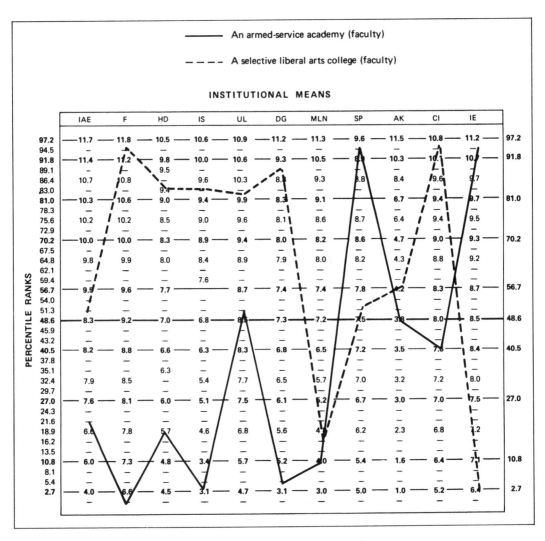

Figure 11.3 Mean Score Profile. (Reproduced with permission from the *Institutional Functioning Inventory Preliminary Technical Manual* by R. E. Peterson et al, p. 31. Copyright 1983 by Educational Testing Service, Princeton, N.J.)

manual does not comment on this issue. The WEPS is easily scored by hand counting two points for "Strongly agree" or "Agree" responses, one point for "Undecided" and "Disagree" responses, and 0 points for "Strongly disagree" responses. The maximum score is 48. Only a single total score is obtained for the WEPS. The manual suggests that a reasonable score estimate may be obtained if four or fewer items have been omitted. A copy of the inventory is shown in Table 11.7.

The WEPS was rationally constructed by initially writing items to fit four descriptive categories of individual characteristics: Self-Subordination, Impersonalization, Rule Conformities, Traditionalism, and Compartmentalization. The manual (Gordon, 1973) says very little about item content specification or the number of items initially writ-

TABLE 11.7 Work Environment Preference Schedule

WORK ENVIRONMENT PREFERENCE SCHEDULE (WEPS)
Leonard V. Gordon

In most organizations, there are differences of opinion as to how the organization should be run, or how people should conduct themselves. Following are a number of statements concerning these matters. You are asked to give *your own* personal opinion about each statement.

Specifically, this is what you are asked to do. Examine each statement and, using the key provided below, decide on the extent to which *you* agree or disagree with the statement. Then blacken the space under the appropriate symbol, on the line next to that statement.

Now look at the example below. Suppose that you *strongly disagree* with the statement "Safety rules are made to be broken." First, you would notice that SD stands for Strongly Disagree on the key. Then, you would blacken the space under SD on the line next to the statement. Notice that this has been done for you.

RAW SCORE **PERCENTILE** **NORMS GROUP**

> **Key: SA—Strongly Agree**
> **A—Agree**
> **U—Undecided**
> **D—Disagree**
> **SD—Strongly Disagree**

Example:

	SA	A	U	D	SD
Safety rules are made to be broken	══	══	══	══	▬▬

You may find yourself agreeing strongly with some of the statements and disagreeing just as strongly with others. In each instance, blacken the space under the symbol that comes closest to representing *your own opinion*. Whether you agree or disagree with a particular statement, you can be sure that many other people feel the same way you do. Be sure to make one choice, and only one choice, for each statement and do not skip any. Now, go ahead.

GRADE or OCCUPATION

(First)   SCHOOL or FIRM

(M or F)

SEX   (Last)

PRINT NAME   DATE

	SA	A	U	D	SD
1. People at higher levels are in the best position to make important decisions for people below them	══	══	══	══	══
2. Relationships within an organization should be based on position or level, not on personal considerations	══	══	══	══	══
3. In dealing with others, rules and regulations should be followed exactly	══	══	══	══	══
4. A person's expressions of feeling about his organization should conform to those of his fellows	══	══	══	══	══
5. A person's first real loyalty within the organization should be to his superior	══	══	══	══	══
6. Formality, based on rank or position, should be maintained by members of an organization	══	══	══	══	══
7. A person should avoid taking any action that might be subject to criticism	══	══	══	══	══
8. Outsiders who complain about an organization are usually either ignorant of the facts or misinformed	══	══	══	══	══
9. In a good organization, a person's future career will be pretty well planned out for him	══	══	══	══	══

Please turn the page and continue.

Reproduced by permission from the *Work Environment Preference Schedule* by Leonard V. Gordon. Copyright © 1973, The Psychological Corporation, New York, N. Y. All Rights Reserved. Address inquiries to the author, P. O. Box 669, Guilderland, N. Y. 12084.

TABLE 11.7 *(Cont.)*

> Key: SA—Strongly Agree
> A—Agree
> U—Undecided
> D—Disagree
> SD—Strongly Disagree

10. A person should think of himself as a member of the organization first, and an individual second

    SA   A   U   D   SD

11. People are better off when the organization provides a complete set of rules to be followed

    SA   A   U   D   SD

12. Within an organization, it is unwise to question well-established ways of doing things

    SA   A   U   D   SD

13. A superior should expect subordinates to carry out his orders without question or deviation

    SA   A   U   D   SD

14. Within the organization, it is better to maintain formal relationships with other people

    SA   A   U   D   SD

15. There is really no place in a small organizational unit for the nonconformist

    SA   A   U   D   SD

16. Pins, written commendations, ceremonies, etc. are all signs of a good organization

    SA   A   U   D   SD

17. The most important part of a superior's job is to see to it that regulations are followed

    SA   A   U   D   SD

18. In general, a person's rank or level should determine his relationships toward other people

    SA   A   U   D   SD

19. Job security is best obtained by learning and following standard work procedures

    SA   A   U   D   SD

20. A person should defend the actions of his organization against any criticism by outsiders

    SA   A   U   D   SD

21. A person should do things in the exact manner that he thinks his superior wishes them to be done

    SA   A   U   D   SD

22. Within an organization, a person should think of himself as a part in a smoothly running machine

    SA   A   U   D   SD

23. It is better to have a complete set of rules than to have to decide things for oneself

    SA   A   U   D   SD

24. Length of service in an organization should be given almost as much recognition as level of performance

    SA   A   U   D   SD

$$2 \times \boxed{} = \boxed{} + \boxed{} = \boxed{}$$

ten. The selection of the final six items for four of the categories (Self-Subordination, Impersonalization, Rule Conformity, and Traditionalism) was based on magnitude of correlations of items with category totals. The Compartmentalization items were found to be unrelated or negatively related to those of the other four categories. The manual notes that this category was eliminated from the final form because the retention of Compartmentalization items would have required differential scoring for upper level positions. Thus, the WEPS consists of 24 items producing a single total score. The items and categories are so highly related that the manual recommends not attempting to generate separate subscales or subscores.

Normative data are provided for large groups of high school and college students. Data are also presented for a group of army ROTC students and for eight occupational groups (warehouseworkers and delivery people, corporation supervisors, salespeople, service personnel, supervisory nurses, high school principals, school superintendents, and high school administrators), but the sample groups are very small. In fact, the manual refers to these groups as illustrative and not really representative of the occupations in question.

In general, the reliability of the WEPS does seem to be adequate. Internal consistency coefficients were found to be 0.91, 0.89, 0.84 and 0.83, respectively, for samples of Peace Corps volunteers, guidance counselors, business administration students, and military academy seniors. The test-retest coefficient obtained for a sample of high school students over a three-month period of time was 0.82. The stability of the WEPS was further assessed by administering the instrument twice to a sample of Army ROTC students, with a 16-month interval between testings. The test-retest coefficient was 0.65.

The manual (Gordon, 1973) reports correlations between the WEPS scores and a variety of other inventories (i.e., the Study of Values, the California F. Scale, the Rokeach Dogmatism Scale, the Religious Conservatism Scale, the Internal-External Control Scale, and others). The manual then subsequently suggests that these correlational relationships may be drawn upon to describe the personality characteristics of high scorers on the WEPS. This interpretive procedure has been very much criticized in reviews by Demaree (1978) and Rogers (1977). Other validity data have explored the person-environment congruence hypothesis, which in essence suggests that people in environments consistent with their personality will tend to be more satisfied and productive. For example, the manual reports studies using samples of ROTC cadets at two Catholic colleges. The findings in these studies show that significant WEPS score differences were found between cadets remaining in the military program (high mean scores) and those dropping out. The results were similar on the variable of career motivation for a sample of West Point graduating students. Three studies, one in Japan and two in India, were designed to relate WEPS scores to employees' feelings of satisfaction with aspects of their work environments. These studies revealed significantly higher WEPS scores for industrial workers and school teachers who were most satisfied with their jobs. Furthermore, the manual reports high mean scores for individuals who have adapted very well to Veterans Administration hospital work environments, navy hospital work environments, and mental hospital work environments. However, as noted by Demaree (1978) none of these validity studies looking at person-environment interaction measured organizational or work-setting variables. It was simply assumed that these work environments were bureaucratic in nature. Thus, it seems that no real link between person-environment variables and subsequent satisfaction and performance has been made.

In terms of suggested uses, the manual mentions that the instrument was designed for counseling the non-college-bound student and the socially disadvantaged. Demaree (1978) and Rogers (1977) raise some question about this as a use of the inventory and further suggest that the WEPS may be more appropriate with middle class and professional workers. In any event, given the current state of the validity data the inventory is probably most realistically appropriate for research use only.

School Environment Preference Survey

The School Environment Preference Survey (SEPS) (Gordon, 1978) was designed to assess work-role socialization as it occurs in the school environment. The survey is intended to assess the individual's level of commitment to the set of attitudes and behaviors that are characteristically rewarded in the school environments (Gordon, 1978). These attitudes, values, and behaviors include an acceptance of authority, an identification with the institutional subculture, a close adherence to rules of conduct, and a disinclination to question what is taught. There is one overall scale, titled Structured Role Orientation, and four subscales (Self-Subordination, Traditionalism, Rule Conformity, and Uncriticalness). The Self-Subordination Scale assesses a desire to comply with the wishes of and to please one's teacher. Traditionalism assesses the need to identify with one's school and to conform to the general student norm. The Rule Conformity Scale assesses the desire for the security that following rules and regulations affords. The Uncriticalness Scale assesses the tendency to accept expert judgment. High scores on the overall scale (Structured Role Orientation) typify students who are accepting of and acquiescent to authority. In addition, these students tend to seek the security of institutional and group identification, prefer to have specific rules to follow, and are disinclined to question their teachers.

The SEPS consists of 24 items presented in Likert response format. Six items are related to each of the four subscales and all 24 items provide a measure of the Structured Rule Orientation Scale. The instruments can be taken in 10 to 15 minutes and hand-scored in approximately one minute. The manual (Gordon, 1978) indicates that the SEPS is appropriate for use from the fourth through the twelfth grade levels. Norms provided in the manual have been prepared for grades 5 through 12. Testees respond to the 24 items on a five-point Likert scale ranging from "Strongly agree" to "Strongly disagree."

The SEPS is unique in that the variables measured at the school level were originally derived directly from the World of Work Map. A measure of Work Role Socialization, the Work Environment Preference Schedule (WEPS: Gordon, 1973), was initially developed for use with adults. The School Environment Preference Schedule was a parallel measure designed to assess the same characteristics for use in the schools.

A review of the technical aspects of the SEPS shows some reliability and validity. Test-retest reliability coefficients reported in the manual range from 0.64 to 0.75. The test-retest interval was one year in the first instance and nine weeks in the second.

The SEPS has been found to be related to indices of school achievement and adjustment, both attitudinal and behavioral (Gordon, 1978). For example, Haipt (1972) found that the more highly structured role-oriented student tends to perceive one's school as promoting greater student growth. Other research (Gordon, 1978) using the SEPS suggests that the student who is less able to cope intellectually tends to be more inclined to accept authority. These students also seem to have difficulty in problem-solving situations.

In summary, the SEPS is an attempt to assess person-environment fit within the context of a school setting. The interrelationships among student, environment, and teacher are assessed primarily on variables of authority. The goal of the developer of the SEPS was to assess students' progress in socialization in terms of the authority variables. A review of the SEPS (Price, 1984) is recorded in Test Critiques.

The Fear Survey Schedule

The manual indicates that the Fear Survey Schedule (FSS) was developed by Wolpe and Lange (1977) to identify and quantify maladaptive anxiety responses to a variety of fear-producing stimuli. The stimulus situations that make up the inventory are situations to which it is unadaptive for a person to have more than mild anxiety.

The present FSS (Wolpe & Lange, 1969) is an extension of the earlier FSS (Wolpe & Lange, 1964). The 1969 FSS lists 108 common fears (example items shown in Table 11.8), and individuals are asked to report their unpleasant feelings on a Likert-type scale from "none at all" to "very much." Response time is about 15 minutes, and the FSS is to be used primarily with college students and adults.

Item norms are reported for 115 female and 141 male university students for the most recent form of the FSS. Ages for males ranged from 17 to 46, with a mean of 23.14 years, and ages for females ranged from 16 to 68, with a mean of 22.66 years. Means and standard deviations for each item were calculated separately for men and women. Larger and more diversified normative data are certainly needed.

Suinn (1969a) explored the test-retest reliability of the FSS using a group of 82 college students. He found a stability coefficient of 0.72 for a five-week time interval. Tasto and Suinn (1972) found a test-retest reliability of 0.67 in twice administering the FSS to 27 male and 46 female students with a 10-week interval between testings. In general, the stability coefficients seem adequate, but information from Suinn (1969a) suggests that retest scores on the FSS tend to decrease. As noted in the manual (Wolpe & Lange, 1977), this point needs to be taken into account when interpreting FSS scores.

Some studies relate to the validity of the FSS. For example, Fazio (1969) found that 70 college students reporting fear of insects in fact scored significantly higher on insect items of the FSS than on other items. Geer (1966) used the FSS to classify 32 female subjects as "high fear" with respect to spiders. When the subjects were shown slides of spiders, the galvanic skin response was significantly more elevated for this high-fear group than for the control group. Other data (Lang & Lazovik, 1963) show a significant positive correlation ($r = 0.80$) between the FSS and the Manifest Anxiety Scale using phobic patients as subjects. Grossberg and Wilson (1965) found a correlation of 0.46 between the FSS and the Manifest Anxiety Scale for a normal undergraduate sample. Suinn (1969a) found a similar correlation (0.49) for a sample of 67 college students between the FSS and the Sarason Test Anxiety Scale. Finally, a number of studies have explored the factor structure of the FSS. In general, these data suggest that the largest factor accounting for most of the variance is a fear of being socially unacceptable. In sum, the limited validity data are to some extent supportive, but clearly additional work needs to be carried out to validate the meaning of the FSS.

As noted by Spielberger (1978), it is difficult to evaluate the FSS because of the limited psychometric data reported in the preliminary manual (Wolpe & Lange, 1977). For example, no information about how the

TABLE 11.8 The Fear Survey Schedule

FEAR SURVEY SCHEDULE

by

Joseph Wolpe and

Peter J. Lang

NAME _____

OCCUPATION _____ AGE _____ SEX _____

ADDRESS _____

The items in this questionnaire refer to things and experiences that may cause fear or other, related unpleasant feelings. Read each item and decide how much you are disturbed by it. Then mark your booklet according to the following scale:

If going boating generally leads you to feel no fear, blacken in space (0) (not at all). If you would feel a little fear, check number (1) (a little). If you feel more afraid mark a higher number — (2) (a fair amount), (3) (much), or (4) (very much), depending on your response to the item. Remember to blacken in only one of the spaces after each. Answer all the items. Please work rapidly and do not spend too much time on any one statement.

	0	1	2	3	4
0. Not at all	∎	∷	∷	∷	∷
1. A little	∷	∎	∷	∷	∷
2. A fair amount ...	∷	∷	∎	∷	∷
3. Much	∷	∷	∷	∎	∷
4. Very much	∷	∷	∷	∷	∎

PUBLISHED BY EDUCATIONAL AND INDUSTRIAL TESTING SERVICE
SAN DIEGO, CALIFORNIA 92107

PRINTED IN U.S.A.

Reproduced with permission from *The Fear Survey Schedule* by J. Wolpe and P. J. Lange. Copyright 1969 by the Educational and Industrial Testing Service, San Diego, California.

TABLE 11.8   *(Cont.)*

	0	1	2	3	4		0	1	2	3	4
1. Noise of vacuum cleaners	::	::	::	::	::	28. Flying insects	::	::	::	::	::
2. Open wounds	::	::	::	::	::	29. Seeing other people injected	::	::	::	::	::
3. Being alone	::	::	::	::	::	30. Sudden noises	::	::	::	::	::
4. Loud voices	::	::	::	::	::	31. Journeys by car	::	::	::	::	::
5. Dead people	::	::	::	::	::	32. Dull weather	::	::	::	::	::
6. Speaking in public	::	::	::	::	::	33. Crowds	::	::	::	::	::
7. Crossing streets	::	::	::	::	::	34. Cats	::	::	::	::	::
8. People who seem insane	::	::	::	::	::	35. One person bullying another	::	::	::	::	::
9. Being in a strange place	::	::	::	::	::	36. Tough looking people	::	::	::	::	::
10. Falling	::	::	::	::	::	37. Birds	::	::	::	::	::
11. Automobiles	::	::	::	::	::	38. Sight of deep water	::	::	::	::	::
12. Being teased	::	::	::	::	::	39. Being watched working	::	::	::	::	::
13. Dentists	::	::	::	::	::	40. Dead animals	::	::	::	::	::
14. Thunder	::	::	::	::	::	41. Weapons	::	::	::	::	::
15. Sirens	::	::	::	::	::	42. Dirt	::	::	::	::	::
16. Failure	::	::	::	::	::	43. Journeys by bus	::	::	::	::	::
17. Entering a room where other people are already seated	::	::	::	::	::	44. Crawling insects	::	::	::	::	::
18. High places on land	::	::	::	::	::	45. Seeing a fight	::	::	::	::	::
19. Looking down from high buildings	::	::	::	::	::	46. Ugly people	::	::	::	::	::
20. Worms	::	::	::	::	::	47. Fire	::	::	::	::	::
21. Imaginary creatures	::	::	::	::	::	48. Sick people	::	::	::	::	::
22. Receiving injections	::	::	::	::	::	49. Being criticized	::	::	::	::	::
23. Strangers	::	::	::	::	::	50. Strange shapes	::	::	::	::	::
24. Bats	::	::	::	::	::	51. Being touched by others	::	::	::	::	::
25. Journeys by train	::	::	::	::	::	52. Being in an elevator	::	::	::	::	::
26. Feeling angry	::	::	::	::	::	53. Witnessing surgical operations	::	::	::	::	::
27. People in authority	::	::	::	::	::	54. Angry people	::	::	::	::	::

FSS should be scored is provided in the manual. In addition, most of the validity studies have been carried out on the earlier 1964 version of the FSS. Thus, as noted by Spielberger (1978) and Demaree (1972), an expanded test manual is very much needed. In spite of limitations, the FSS in an applied sense is a practical and useful way of collecting information about an individual's unpleasant feelings and responses to environmental situations and conditions. It is a self-report inventory that asks individuals to report their unadaptive responses and feelings and perceptions about various environmental situations. The FSS is frequently used in behavior therapy to identify unadaptive responses that subsequently may be treated using some form of counterconditioning (the use of a competing response to inhibit the anxiety that a particular stimulus tends to evoke). The technique used most frequently in behavior therapy is desensitization.

The Environmental Assessment Technique

To assess environments, Astin and Holland (1961) developed the Environmental Assessment Technique (EAT). The EAT is really not a test or inventory, but rather a technique that uses eight objectively determined indices to assess the environment. The rationale for the development of the technique was based on the assumption that a major portion of environmental forces is transmitted through other people. This assumption implies that the dominant features of any particular environment depend on the typical characteristics of its members. Thus, it makes sense that knowledge about the kind of people that constitute a group should reveal something about the climate created in the group. For example, a setting inhabited primarily by social workers would be expected to have a different psychological atmosphere than would a setting occupied primarily by chemists or accountants.

Because the EAT characterizes an environment by assessing its population, the measurement technique used entails a census of such things as self-reported vocational preferences, academic majors of college students, and occupations of members of a population. Although, according to Holland (1985a), the population may be a college, a hospital, a bank, or the like, the major use of the EAT to date has been to characterize college and university environments.

The form of the EAT that has been used to assess college environments is composed of eight variables: the total number of students in the college, the average intelligence of the students, and the six model environments. The six environments are described in Table 11.9. Institutional size is simply the total enrollment (N) at the institution. The intelligence level of the student body may be estimated by using the scores on the National Merit Scholarship Qualifying Test, the College Entrance Examination Boards Scholastic Aptitude Test, or the American College Testing Program Assessment.

The remaining six variables (environmental models) correspond to Holland's (1985a) six personality types. (See Chapter 12's discussion of person-environment psychology and assessment for additional information on Holland's theory.) Vocational preferences or actual major fields or occupations are classified into one of the model environments. The six scores are calculated by simply counting the number of students who have expressed vocational preferences or are in college majors consistent with a particular environmental model and/or personality type. The assignment to particular categories is accomplished by using a psychological classification scheme for vocations and major fields developed by Holland. For example, a social worker would be classified

TABLE 11.9 Descriptions of Six Model Environments

The *Realistic environment* is characterized by demands for explicit, physical, concrete tasks. Expected and frequent behaviors include mechanical responses, persistence, and a variety of physical movements in outdoor settings. Tasks usually call for immediate behavioral action. Therefore reinforcement generally follows the successful completion of a task. Pressure does not exist for interpersonal skills and for close interpersonal relationships.

The *Investigative environment* is characterized by tasks that require thinking responses that are not only abstract in nature but also require the use of creativity and imagination. In this environment, work involves ideas and things rather than other people. A minimal pressure for social skills exists, therefore, relationships with others are usually superficial rather than close. Laboratory equipment is frequently used, but the occupational requirements are usually not physically demanding (talking, reading, writing, and ideational learning). As might be expected, the work setting is usually indoors.

The *Social environment* requires the ability to interpret as well as to modify human behavior. There is pressure to be interested in communicating with and helping others. Work situations such as teaching, lecturing, social work, and other forms of helping generally demand verbal facility with people rather than facility with things. The work environment fosters prestige, but reinforcements tend to be delayed.

The *Conventional environment* is characterized by tasks that require systematic, concrete, and routine responses. Minimal physical strength is required and the activities are carried out indoors. Because work in this environment is mainly with things and materials, pressure for interpersonal skills is not high.

The *Enterprising environment* is characterized by tasks requiring verbal responses meant to influence other people. Pressure exists to assume persuasive and supervisory roles. Work situations require behaviors such as directing, controlling, and planning the activities of others. The environment demands an interest in people and things. Social skills are needed because many work situations are people oriented. The environment does not call for the ability to form close relationships, however.

In the *Artistic environment*, tasks generally require the use of imagination as well as personal interpretation of feelings, ideas, or facts. Personal interpretations are usually evaluated against sensory or judgmental criteria. Although excellence is valued, the standards of excellence are often defined ambiguously. Work situations usually require intense involvement for long periods of time and draw upon a person's total resources. Some work situations (such as drama) involve close interpersonal relationships, other work situations (such as painting) are completed in isolation.

into the Social environment and an engineer would be classified into the Realistic environment. After assignment to particular categories, each score is expressed as a percentage of the total number of classifiable majors. For example, a small private college of 1,000 students might be classified into the environmental models given in Table 11.10.

In the example in Table 11.10, the environmental code would be represented as 345216. That is, the dominant type in this environment is Artistic, followed by Social, Enterprising, Investigative, Realistic, and Conventional. Thus, this environment would be expected to emphasize self-expression, creativity, and social expression. Work tasks frequently would involve personal interpretation of feelings and ideas. Excellence would be valued, but standards would be vaguely defined. In general, the environment would tend to reward insightful, original, emotional, and understanding behaviors.

Astin and Holland (1961) studied the test-retest reliability of the six EAT variables for intervals of one, three, and six years, using a sample of 31 institutions. Scores on the six variables were obtained for the graduation years of 1952, 1955, 1956, and 1958. The coefficients of stability indicated high retest reliability over a one-year interval. The coefficients ranged from 0.81 to 0.99. In addition, the coefficients for the three-year and six-year periods suggested high retest reliability for all but the Investigative variable. These data at least tentatively suggest that curricular differences among institutions (environments) tend to be quire stable from one year to the next.

Initial data on the EATs concurrent validity (Astin 1963; Astin & Holland, 1961) were gathered using the College Characteristics Index (Pace & Stern, 1958). EAT profiles of 335 colleges were obtained. Scores on all eight EAT measures were correlated with the ratings of these same colleges by other groups of students, as indicated by

TABLE 11.10 Environmental Assessment Technique

Environment Number	Environment	Number of People	Percentage
1	Realistic	40	4
2	Investigative	80	8
3	Artistic	550	55
4	Social	200	20
5	Enterprising	100	10
6	Conventional	30	3
		1000	100

scores on the 30 scales of the CCI. In general, the findings supported the validity of the EAT. Of the 240 correlation coefficients, 23 percent were significant at the 0.01 level and 39 percent at the 0.05 level. And these correlations tended to make sense. For example, colleges and universities with large percentages of Investigative students tended to be rated low on Deference, but high on Fantasized Achievement, Objectivity, and Understanding. Thus, Investigative environments seem to reward independence of thought and action, the need to achieve, and the need to analyze and understand.

Another interesting study focused on identifying institutional differences using the EAT scales and other variables. The sample consisted of 335 accredited, four-year, degree-granting institutions. In sum, the evidence suggested that the census of a college provided by the EAT in effect gives information about a variety of institutional characteristics. Indeed, in two books Astin (1965, 1968) has shown that the EAT variables are related to a broad range of student, as well as institutional, characteristics.

In summary, the few existing validity studies do tend to support the concurrent and construct validity of the EAT. In essence, these studies suggest that a census of the kinds of people found in college environments provides a certain amount of information about the environmental climates of colleges—that is, a census of the kinds of people found in an environment suggests

something about the climates they have created. Thus, as we previously noted, the EAT is not a test or an inventory, but rather a technique that may be used in research or in an applied sense to describe the psychological characteristics of an environment. An interesting point from an assessment perspective is that this counting (census) technique may be used with a variety of traits or characteristics to size up the psychological environment. The technique is simple, straightforward, economical, and meaningful, within limits.

The Home Index

The Home Index (Gough, 1949) is an objective inventory for assessing social-economic factors in the home and family environment. The Home Index is intended primarily to be used with grade school, junior high school, and high school students. In its original version (Gough, 1949) it contained 21 items inquiring about material possessions, education of parents, and participation in community and other affairs. The current edition of the index (Gough, 1974), contains 22 items. A copy of the Home Index is shown in Table 11.11. The index may be administered in five minutes or less, and scoring is quite rapid. The items are fairly simple and straightforward and may be read and understood by individuals with reading ability of fourth-grade level or better.

TABLE 11.11 The Home Index

THE HOME INDEX

Name.., Date...
     (PLEASE PRINT) last,   first   initial

Age................. Sex............................ Education...
                                       (if now in school, present grade)

Place of testing..
         (name of school or agency)   (city)   (state)

What is (or was) your father's occupation?...

What is (or was) your mother's occupation?..

What is your occupation (or intended occupation)?...

Directions: Mark your answer by putting an X in the proper box. For example, on the question "Does your family have a car?" put an X in the box under YES if your family does have a car, and under NO if it does not. Be sure to answer all of the questions.

	YES	NO		YES	NO
1. Did your mother go to high school?	☐	☐	13. Does your family have a car?	☐	☐
2. Did your mother go to a college or university?	☐	☐	14. Does your family have a phonograph (record player)? . . .	☐	☐
3. Did your father go to high school?	☐	☐	15. Do you have your own room at home?	☐	☐
4. Did your father go to a college or university?	☐	☐	16. Does your family own its home?	☐	☐
5. Do you have a fireplace in your home?	☐	☐	17. Does your mother belong to any clubs or organizations, such as study, art, or civic clubs?	☐	☐
6. Does your family have any servants, such as a cook or maid?	☐	☐	18. Does your father belong to any civic, study, service, or political clubs, such as the Chamber of Commerce, the Lions Club, etc? . . .	☐	☐
7. Does your family leave town every year for a vacation?	☐	☐			
8. Does your family have more than 500 books?	☐	☐	19. Do you belong to any club where you have to pay dues?	☐	☐
9. Is there an electric or gas refrigerator in your home? . . .	☐	☐	20. Does your family subscribe to a daily newspaper?	☐	☐
10. Is there a telephone in your home?	☐	☐	21. Do you have a piano in your home?	☐	☐
11. Do you have a bathtub in your home?	☐	☐	22. Have you ever had private lessons in music, dancing, art, etc., outside of school?	☐	☐
12. Is your home heated with a central system, such as by a furnace in the basement?	☐	☐			

Reproduced with permission from the Home Index by H. G. Gough, Institute of Personality Assessment and Research, University of California, Berkeley, California.

The prepublication manual (Gough, 1974) says little about the initial development of the Home Index. However, to explore the internal structure of the revised 22-item index a factor analysis was carried out (Gough, 1971a). To gather data for such an analysis, the index was administered to 1,379 high school students (698 males and 681 females) in 14 high schools from 12 states. The factor analysis identified four factors, accounting for 94 percent of the variance. The first factor, Social Status, included the first 8 items of the scale. The second factor, Ownership, was made up of items 9 through 16. Factor three, Social-Civic Involvement, included items 17 through 20. Factor four, Aesthetic Involvement, consisted of items 21 and 22. Gough (1974) notes that the total score based on all 22 items is probably the one that will be used most often, but scores on the other four factors can be easily computed and may be of interest in particular environments.

The normative data for the current version of the scale is based on a sample of 2,267 high school students from 22 communities in 16 states, and in 1970/71 an additional sample was gathered consisting of 2,564 students from grades three through eight in an ethnically representative selection of schools in California. Thus, normative data on the Home Index are based on a total sample of 4,831 students (2,328 males and 2,503 females). The split-half reliability coefficient for 100 male and 100 female protocols was found to be 0.89.

Validity data (primarily concurrent) suggest that scores on the Home Index tend to be significantly associated with high school graduation and college attendance (Gough, 1971b). These results obtained for males and females. Other evidence (Gough, 1974) suggests that total score on the Home Index tends to be modestly related to intellectual ability and to academic performance in high school as indicated by grades. Another source

of data (Mann, 1959), using 290 male college students eight years after graduation, obtained correlations of 0.23 between the index and present salary, 0.41 between the index and Social Civic involvement, and 0.19 between the Status scale and current level of cultural and aesthetic interests. Currently the Home Index is for research use only. However, with additional validity data the index could become a useful tool for exploring the relationships and interactions between the home environment and behavior.

The Home Observation for Measurement of the Environment

The Home Observation for Measurement of the Environment (HOME), revised in 1984, is an inventory designed to assess the extent to which the child's home environment supports and fosters cognitive development (Caldwell & Bradley, 1984). Thus, HOME is an environmental process measure that attempts to assess patterns of nurturance and stimulation provided to children in their homes. The assessment process for HOME involves direct observation of children's home environments. Items on the inventory are scored according to what the observer actually sees. However, some items require scoring based on the verbal self-report of the mother obtained through an interview during the home visit.

The HOME actually consists of three inventories. The HOME Inventory for Families of Infants and Toddlers (birth to age three) consists of six subscales. The HOME Inventory for a Family of Preschool Age Children (age three to six) consists of eight subscales. A third form for elementary school children (age six to ten) is still in an experimental stage. The form for infants and toddlers (birth to age three) is made up of 45 items organized into the following six scales: Emotional and Verbal Responsivity of Parent, Acceptance of Child's Behavior, Organization of Physical and Temporal Environment, Provision of Appropriate Play Materials, Parent Involvement with Child, and Opportunities for Variety in Daily Stimulation. The current version of the form for preschoolers consists of 55 items representing the following eight scales: Learning Stimulation, Language Stimulation, Physical Environment, Affection and Warmth, Academic Stimulation, Modeling and Encouragement of Social Maturity, Variety in Experience, and Acceptance and Physical Punishments. The form for elementary school children consists of 59 items representing seven scales: Emotional and Verbal Responsivity, Encouragement of Maturity, Emotional Climate, Growth-Fostering Materials and Experiences, Provision for Active Stimulation, Family Participation in Developmentally Stimulating Experiences, and Aspects of the Physical Environment. In general, as noted above, each item refers to behaviors in which the parent may or may not engage and types of activities that may or may not be available to the child.

On the HOME Inventory for Families of Infants and Toddlers, test-retest reliability, based on a study of 91 families assessed on three occasions (six months, 12 months, and 24 months), indicated moderate stability (coefficients of 0.27 to 0.77 for scales and 0.62 to 0.77 for the total score) (Caldwell & Bradley, 1984). Concurrent validity data reported by Caldwell and Bradley (1984) show moderate relationships between HOME subscales and mother's and father's education, father's occupation, and crowding ratio. In addition, the HOME was able to correctly classify children with IQ scores below 80 about 71 percent of the time, but was less effective in predicting retarded development (43 percent) (Caldwell & Bradley, 1984).

Information pertaining to the reliability and validity of the HOME Inventory for use with preschool children is more limited. A test-retest reliability study carried out with 33 families when their children were 3 and 4½ years of age produced coefficients that were low to moderate over time, ranging from 0.05 to 0.70. Concurrent validity data suggest significant relationships between HOME subscale scores and SES variables, mother's and father's education, and crowding ratio. In addition, HOME scores obtained at three years were significantly related to IQ scores at ages 3 and 4½ (Caldwell & Bradley, 1984). Finally, correlations between HOME scores at age five and SRA Achievement Test Scores tend to support the validity of the inventory (Caldwell & Bradley, 1984).

In summary, as noted by Boehm (1985) and Procidano (1985) the HOME Inventories are useful and well researched tools for assessing stimulation aspects of the home environment and to some extent related to later cognitive functioning. In general the reliability and validity data support the use of the HOME Inventories for clinical and educational assessment and for research.

Other Environmental Assessment Inventories

A variety of other environmental assessment inventories and techniques have not been discussed here. For example, as noted by Craik (1981), for the physical environment there are Kasmar's (1970). Environmental Descriptor Scales and Craik's (1975) Landscape Adjective Checklist, as well as Craik's (1975) more comprehensive Environmental Adjective Checklist. Laumann and House (1970) used a Living Room Checklist to record a physical description and inventory of objects for a sample of 897 living rooms. Objects recorded included things such as fireplace, wall mirror, trophies, and stuffed furniture. The subsequent space analysis yielded two dimensions, one related to modern-versus-traditional style of decor and the other related to the social status of the owners.

In order to assess two fundamental dimensions of personality Little (1973) developed the Person Orientation and Thing Orientation Scales. These scales in essence assess the extent to which the individual relates to the social and physical environments. The Environmental Cue Set (Block, 1961) was developed for describing childhood family context and subsequent behaviors.

For work environments as noted by Craik (1981) a number of instruments for assessing organizational climate have been developed. Some of these include the Organizational Climate Description Scales (George & Bishop, 1971), the Executive Climate Questionnaire (Tagiuri, 1968), the Agency Climate Questionnaire (Schneider & Bartlett, 1970), the Organizational Climate Questionnaire (Litwin & Stringer, 1968), and the Group Dimensions Description Questionnaire (Pheysey & Payne, 1970). In addition, Payne and Pugh (1976) have developed instruments for observer based estimates of organizational structure.

Some other more traditional measures of personality also appear to relate to everyday environmental behaviors (Craik, 1969). Included among these are several measures of stimulus or arousal seeking behavior that have emerged in the work of Mehrabian and Russell (1973). Closely related are the Need Change Scale of the Adjective Checklist (Gough & Heilbrun, 1965) and the dichotomous scales of the Myers-Briggs Type Indicator (Myers, 1962), which is based on Jung's theory of types (Extroversion, Introversion, Sensation, Intuition, Thinking, Feeling, Judging, and Perceiving).

An entire issue of the *Journal of Environment and Behavior* by Craik and McKechnie (1977) was devoted to research on environmental dispositions. There is no question that a variety of research and measurement scales are emerging in the area of environmental assessment. Psychologists more and more are realizing that any assessment of a person is incomplete without some assessment of the environment with which that person is interacting.

SUMMARY

In environmental assessment we want to describe and evaluate the physical and social environments, but in addition we want to size up and understand how the individual's perceptions of the environment tend to influence the way the person behaves in that environment. Thus, the individual is not a passive agent for environmental forces, but rather an active agent in a continuous ongoing person-situation process. Individuals are influenced by situations in which they interact, but also affect and change situations in which they are interacting. The environmental context of human behavior may be assessed in a variety of different ways. One approach to environmental assessment focuses on the physical spatial properties of places. The emphasis is on the physical characteristics of the environments and how they tend to influence behavior. A second approach to environmental assessment is concerned with the organization of material artifacts in places. A third approach involves assessing the traits of environments or situations by means of human observers. A variety of different adjective checklists, counting techniques, bipolar rating scales, and Q sort decks are being developed to permit observers to record their impressions of environments. A fourth approach focuses on assessing the behavioral attributes of environments or behavior settings. An analysis of behavior patterns can yield a comparison of environments on the basis of the relative frequency and duration of types of behaviors within those environments or behavior settings. The final and perhaps the most popular approach focuses on the assessment of institutional attributes of environments. Here perceived group consensus is used to provide formal measurement of psychological properties of environments.

Representing the different approaches to environmental assessment we discussed the Stern Environmental Indexes, the College Student Experiences Questionnaire, the Moos Social Climate Scales, the Multiphasic Environmental Assessment Procedure, the Environmental Response Inventory, the Institutional Functioning Inventory, the Work Environment Preference Schedule, School Environment Preference Survey, the Fear Survey Schedule, the Environmental Assessment Technique, the Home Index, the Home Observation for Measurement of the Environment, and a few other environmental assessment inventories. There is no question that a variety of research and measurement scales are emerging in the area of environmental assessment and that environmental variables need to be taken into account in the assessment process.

12

Person-Environment
Psychology and Assessment

INTRODUCTION

Probably the most popular and common way of dealing with historical events is through the eyes of individuals who have made significant contributions over the years. Person-environment psychology is no exception. As an historical review, Ekehammar (1974) suggests that the numerous psychologists who have made important contributions to the person-environment model fall into two major groups: the classical interactionalists and the more contemporary, or modern, interactionalists. The classical people were predominantly theorists, while the more contemporary people are more empirically oriented and committed to data-based research.

J. R. Kantor (1924) made one of the earliest contributions to person-environment psychology. This "classical interactionalist thought that the study of psychology should focus on the personenvironment unit. He viewed psychology as interbehavioral and emphasized the reciprocal interplay between person and environment. Implicit in Kantor's theory was the suggestion that the person is a function of the environment and the environment is a function of the person, two perspectives that in time were to be relevant in other person-environment models.

In 1935 Kurt Lewin made a very profound contribution to the person-environment area by more explicitly suggesting that a person's behavior is a function of the person *and* of the environment. Lewin's idea that the environment is as important as the individual, and that both must be analyzed to assess and understand behavior, continues to be a theoretical base for person-environment psychology today. In essence, Lewin believed that behavior is a function of the whole situation and that the whole situation must take into account interactions between person and environment. Lewin's theory had an enormous impact on the field of person-environment psychology and assessment for years to come.

About the same time, Kurt Koffka (1935), whose primary interest was in perception, suggested that as psychologists we must be concerned with both the physical environment and the psychological environment. Koffka, much like Kantor and Lewin, made a clear distinction between the two types of environment (as we noted in Chapter 11 on environmental assessment). Koffka further thought that the psychological environment is a function of the interaction between the human organism and the physical environment.

In 1938 Henry Murray, very much influenced by Koffka and Lewin, expanded on the notion of person-environment interaction by suggesting that behavior is a function of the individual's personality needs and perceived environmental "presses," or pressures. Murray viewed the environment from a somewhat objective perspective, which he labelled the "alpha press," and from a psychological perspective, which he labelled the "beta press." Murray thought the beta press, or how individuals tend to perceive environments in which they are interacting and responding, was the more important of the two. Thus, according to Murray, the perceived pressures in a given environment tend to stimulate certain needs and ultimate behaviors. Murray, like Lewin, had a profound impact on the person-environment area of psychology and was probably the first to attempt to operationalize person-environment concepts in an applied and meaningful way, through use of his Thematic Apperception Test.

In 1935 Tolman, another classical theorist, suggested that a person's behavior is a function of the stimulus condition and of the person's heredity, past training, and physiological state. He further hypothesized that these variables are fairly independent, rather than interdependent, as suggested by Kantor, Lewin, and Koffka. In 1941 Angyal introduced his notion of "biosphere," suggesting that we must take into account how the biological, sociological, and psychological variables tend to affect the person-environment unit. Murphy (1947) continued the person-environment tradition by introducing a "biosocial" theory suggesting that the personality is the product of the biological organism and its social environments. Rotter's (1954) "social learning theory" reinforced the person-environment connection. Brunswik (1952) and Helson (1959) both focused on the environmental or situational components of interactionalism.

In summary, these classical theorists represented the beginnings of the person-environment field in psychology, and their work had profound implications for the assessment process. They saw a need to focus on behavior as a function of not only the person, but also the actual and perceived environments. Many of the classical theorists made a concerted effort to differentiate between the physical environment and the psychological environment—the environment as it actually is and the environment as it is perceived to be. They began to develop as an important variable in human behavior the meaning of a situation to an individual. As a result of their work, behavior as a function of the whole person-environment context became an important theoretical model.

The more contemporary formulations of the person-environment model cover the period of time from the 1960s to the present, tend to be less theoretically based, focus considerable attention on assessing the situation or the environment, and tend to be more empirical in nature. Sells (1963) continued the interactional emphasis by suggesting that the total variance of any response can be accounted for only in part by the individual differences of persons. Endler and Hunt (1966) followed up on Sell's notion by focusing on the situational variance contributing to person-environment interactions. Within this stream of thought, Barker (1965) developed his theory of "behavior settings," based on the idea that human environments have a coercive influence on human behavior. The work of Cronbach (1957b), Meltzer (1961), Abelson (1962), Cattell (1963a), and Allport (1966) all seems to focus on the serious neglect of situational variables in personality assessment and research. The message of these researchers in essence was that actual and perceived situations and environments do tend to influence behavior.

An important happening in the late 1960s involved Lawrence Pervin's (1968) focus on the transactional mode, which was an important contribution to the field. Pervin, who had been influenced by Lewin and Murray, suggested that transactionalism involves the continuous and reciprocal influence of person and environments, and he subsequently developed a theoretical framework to organize this perspective. In 1973 Bowers suggested that the major determinant of behavior is the individual's perception of the situation and not necessarily the environment per se. In that same year Mischel (1973) enhanced the person-environment field by introducing his cognitive social learning theory, and Walsh (1973) reviewed five theories of person-environment interaction in terms of how they assess and influence the individual.

A number of others have made important contributions to the person-environment model (e.g., Wachtel, 1973; Bem, 1972; Ekehammar, 1974; Raush, Dittmann, & Taylor, 1959; and Moos, 1973. Endler and Magnusson's two books *Interactional Psychology and Personality* (1976a) and *Personality at the Crossroads* (Magnusson & Endler, 1977b) have made an effort to define interactional psychology and look at meaningful person environment variables. *Perspectives in Interactional Psychology*, edited by Pervin and Lewis (1978), takes an up-to-date look at theory and data in the person-environment field. And Magnusson's *Toward a Psychology of Situations: An Interactional Perspective* (1981b) focuses on the psychology of situations—the environment as it is and the environment as it is perceived.

More recently, the *Journal of Vocational Behavior* published a special issue (Spokane, 1987) that focused on the conceptual and methodological issues in person-environment research. The special issue consolidates a number of conceptual, methodological, and data-based contributions on the role of fit or congruence in the field of person-environment psychology. In 1988 David Magnusson published the first volume of a longitudinal study (*Individual Development from an Interactional Perspective*) that he has been working on for some time. The purpose of the project is to explore how person-environmental factors operate and influence the course of individual development from childhood to adulthood. Finally, Bruce Walsh, Ken Craik, and Richard Price are editing a volume titled *Person-Environment Psychology: Models and Perspectives* that is scheduled for publication in 1991. The main focus of this work is to present models and perspectives that make some sensible predictions concerning the individual and the environment using the person-environment relationship. This should be a very contemporary and timely volume presenting the most current theoretical and research information in the field.

Person-Environment Psychology and Assessment

The person-environment interactional and transactional models assume that human behavior tends to be influenced by many determinants both in the person and in the situation. The models emphasize the effects of person-situation interactions or personality and suggest that behavior involves a continuous interaction between individuals and situations (Endler & Magnusson, 1976b). Behavior is thought to be inter-outer directed and variable across persons and situations. To collect data, interactionalists have developed tests and questionnaires and use observational methods. However, a host of measurement problems are introduced when we attempt to develop inventories that take into account individuals, responses, and situations simultaneously. Suffice it to say that the interactional model has been difficult to apply, but it does hold considerable hope for the future. As we have noted previously, mounting evidence suggests that behavior is much more a function of person-situation interactions than it is of person variables or situation variables.

A number of theories of person-environment psychology have developed over the years in an attempt to understand behavior in terms of person and environment variables. In general, the theories that have emerged have implications for helping people organize and understand their behavior and their social environments. We think the theories help people assess themselves and their environments in order to cope more effectively and interact in social environments consistent with their personality styles.

In attempts to assess and understand behavior, the various theories of person-environment psychology discussed below have in general mirrored the interactional perspective. However, within this perspective some of the theoretical frameworks have emphasized or highlighted different concepts and variables. For example, the theories of Holland (1985a), Stern (1970), and Pervin (1968) assume that behavior is a function of the person and the social environment and attempt to consider aspects of both. The theories of Moos (1984) and Barker (1968) tend to emphasize environmental or situational variables as the primary influences on behavior, with the individual's behavior tending to vary from one context or social environment to another. The theoretical frameworks of Roe (1957) and Freud (1964) emphasize person variables and suggest that personality characteristics tend to link the individual to different environments. In general, these theoretical frameworks view individuals as having characteristic levels on various personality dimensions that are fairly constant (or at least stable in rank order) from one context to another. There are other perspectives and ways of viewing the theories of person-environment psychology, but the above seem most meaningful here.

This chapter focuses on the field of person-environment psychology as it reflects the convergence of theory, assessment, and research. Thus, we consider selected theories of person-environment psychology that have implications for assessment and application.

THE INTERACTIONAL PERSPECTIVE

Endler (1976) has defined interactional psychology as the scientific investigation of a complex interplay of situations and persons in determining behavior. Endler and Magnusson (1976b) further suggest that there are four basic elements of the person-situation interactional model. The first basic element suggests that behavior is a function of a continuous process of multidirectional interaction between the individual and the situations he or she encounters. Second, the individual is an intentional, active agent in this interactional process. Third, on the person side of the interaction, cognitive and motivational factors are essential determinants of behavior. Fourth, on the situation side, the psychological meaning of situations for the individual is the important determining factor. The interactional perspective may also be expressed as $B = f(P, E)$, where B stands for behavior, f for function, P for person, and E for the environment or situation. Thus, in many respects the interactional perspective may be viewed as a synthesis of person and environment in which the interaction of the two is the main source of behavior. Some theories mirroring this perspective are Holland's Personality Types and Model Environments, Stern's Need/Press Culture Theory, and Pervin's Person-Environment Theory.

Holland's Theory of Personality Types and Model Environments

John Holland's (1985a) theory of personality types and model environments is a theory of vocational psychology, personality, and, from our perspective, a theory of person-environment psychology. Holland's theory as viewed by Helson and Mitchell (1978) is tough, practical, and useful. The theory is operational and has collected a wide range of data that tends to be supportive in nature.

In essence, the theory suggests that behavior is a function of the complementary match or congruence between the individual's personality style and the psychological environment. Holland suggests that individuals enter environments because of their personalities and remain in those environments because of the reinforcements and satisfactions obtained through the interactions in that environment.

Holland's (1985a) theory is based on the notion that behavior is a function of personality and social environment. The theory emphasizes interests and personality, since to Holland the choice of an occupation is an expression of personality; thus, interest inventories become personality inventories. The environmental component of the theory is linked to the notion that people in a particular environment tend to have similar personalities and histories of personal development. Because people in a given environment have similar personalities, Holland believes they tend to cope in similar ways. In general, Holland holds that complementary person-environment links are reinforcing and satisfying and contribute to persistence in those environments. On the other hand, he views incongruent person-environment links as not being reinforcing and thus suggestive of a need for change.

More specifically, Holland attempts to explain behavior by using a few well-defined ideas. These ideas or assumptions of his theory tend to be fairly practical, simple, straightforward, and very operational in terms of data-collection procedures. The first of these assumptions is that people learn to be one or more personality types. A type is defined as a cluster of personal attributes that may be used to assess the person. Holland's six personality types are described below.

The *Realistic* (R) type likes realistic jobs such as automobile mechanic, farmer, or electrician. R's have mechanical abilities and tend to be conforming, honest, materialistic, natural, persistent, practical, modest, and stable.

The *Investigative* (I) type likes investigative jobs such as chemist, physicist, biologist, or geologist. I's have mathematical and scientific ability and are described as analytical, independent, intellectual, introverted, methodological, and rational.

The *Artistic* (A) type likes artistic jobs such as musician, writer, or actor. A's have writing, music, and/or artistic abilities and are described as complicated, emotional, expressive, imaginative, impulsive, nonconforming, and original.

The *Social* (S) type likes social jobs such as teacher, counseling psychologist, clinical psychologist, or speech therapist. S's have social skills and are described as cooperative, friendly, helpful, insightful, responsible, sociable, and understanding.

The *Enterprising* (E) type likes enterprising jobs such as salesperson, manager, or business executive. E's have leadership and verbal abilities and are described as ambitious, domineering, pleasure seeking, self-confident, and sociable.

The *Conventional* (C) type likes the conventional jobs such as bookkeeper, banker, or tax expert. C's have clerical and arithmetic ability and are described as conformfing, conscientious, orderly, persistent, practical, and self-controlled.

A person's resemblance to each of the personality types is assessed by the use of the Vocational Preference Inventory (VPI), the Self-Directed Search (SDS), and the Strong-Campbell Interest Inventory (SCII), which were discussed in Chapter 9. All of these inventories are objective in nature and collect interval kinds of data that may be used in a variety of research settings. Practically all of the research on Holland's theory has used one of these instruments in a field research setting.

A second idea used by Holland to explain behavior is that environments in which people live and work may be characterized by their resemblance to one or more model environments. Holland suggests six model environments corresponding to the six personality types (See Chapter 11) and believes that people tend to move toward environments congruent with their personality types: Realistic types tend to move toward Realistic environments. Enterprising types tend to move toward Enterprising environments, and so forth. To assess environments Holland and Astin developed the Environmental Assessment Technique discussed in Chapter 11 (Astin & Holland, 1961). This assessment technique simply makes a count or a census of the number of different personality types existing or interacting in a given environment. The personality type occurring most frequently in a given environment is thought to be dominant in that environment and to have a psychological influence in that specific environment. In sum, Holland defined the environment psychologically according to the people who were actually interacting in it. Or, as he would say, people define the environment. Thus, although the environment is determined by a count, the influence is thought to be psychological in nature.

A third idea used by Holland is that person-environment congruence tends to be associated with satisfaction, productivity, personal stability, vocational stability, and satisfaction. The thought is that, for example, a Realistic type in a Realistic environment would tend to be more productive, more satisfied, more stable, and more vocationally satisfied. Complementary person-environment links are reinforcing and satisfying. Uncomplementary or incongruent person-environment links are punishing and contribute to change. This is not to say that congruence is good and incongruence is bad but suggests that a state of incongruence may be part of the learning and developmental process. Thus, there may realistically be periods of incongruence in an individual's life span that need to be worked through in order to pursue ultimate personal and vocational goals.

Based on his six personality-environment types Holland further suggests that the relations among types, among environments, and between types and environments tend to be hexagonal in nature (see Chapter 9, Figure 9.4). Types and environments that are in closest proximity in the hexagon figure are more psychologically related. Types and environments that are further removed from one another are more psychologically different. For example, an Artistic person in an Artistic environment is in a more congruent situation than an Artistic person in a Social environment. An Artistic person in a Conventional environment is in the most incongruent situation possible. In this way, the hexagonal model may be used to obtain and estimate different degrees or levels of person-environment congruence. The unique and clever hexagonal model for the six personality types and environments has also been used to identify individuals in vocational or personal conflicts, to compare different tests and inventories, to organize occupational environments, and to guide the layout of the Strong-Campbell Interest Inventory. In general, the research based on Holland's ideas supports the existence of the personality types and model environments. Evidence indicates that individuals tend to choose, enter, and persist in college major environments and occupational environments consistent with their personality types. For example, Enterprising people tend to choose, enter, and remain in Enterprising occupational environments.

A few studies have attempted to explore the development of the personality types. For Holland (1985a), an individual's personality type is a product of his or her life history (heredity, past and current cultural and personal forces, and the past and current physical environments) and is in many ways learned. Holland further comments that in his opinion the social pressures in early adolescence and childhood experiences with parents are particularly important to the development and learning of a personality type. The very limited evidence (Grandy & Stahmann, 1974; DeWinne, Overton, & Schneider, 1978) suggests that offspring tend to emulate or learn from their parent types; other data (Grotevant, Scarr, & Weinberg, 1977) suggest that biologically related family members resemble each other on measures of Holland's interest styles more than do adoptive family members. The data here are clearly limited and tentative, but to some extent do suggest that personality types are the product of life history and in many ways learned.

In general, as we have noted, the findings rather clearly indicate that to some extent individuals tend to choose and enter environments consistent with their personality types. For example, Enterprising types tend to enter and remain in Enterprising kinds of environments. Furthermore, the evidence suggests that congruent person-environment interactions are conducive to personal and vocational stability and satisfaction, and, to a lesser extent, actual achievement. More specifically, the pattern of findings (Spokane, 1985) suggests to some extent that person-environment congruence is related to measures of personal and vocational adjustment, satisfaction, integration, vocational maturity, and planning ability, but not necessarily to measures of decision making, sociability, and problem-solving ability. In addition, meaningful data about adolescents and adults imply that person-environment congruence and job satisfaction may increase with age. Thus, it seems that people in congruent work situations will probably change little, since their expression of interests, abilities, and personality is rewarded. Persons in incongruent work environments will probably change the most, since they tend to be ignored and punished (Holland & Gottfredson, 1976). This work, then, indicates that students and workers who tend to be functioning in environments consistent with their personal characteristics probably are psychologically healthier and more satisfied when compared to people in incongruent situations.

In summary, in Holland's theory behavior is viewed as a function of person-environment interactions, and from this perspective person-environment congruence becomes a very important concept. Thus, Holland suggests, and the data tend to support, the notion that people in environments congruent with their personality types tend to be happier, more satisfied and more productive than are people in incongruent environments. Their behavior tends to be rewarded. Person-environment incongruence suggests some kind of imbalance that may contribute to misperceptions and eventually to inappropriate behavior. In any event, the concept of congruence (person-environment fit) is a significant one and, as we shall see, important to all the theoretical frameworks discussed here.

Stern's Need/Press Culture Theory

The foundation of Stern's (1970) work is based on the Murray need/press interactional model (1938), which is firmly couched in Lewin's (1935) dictum that behavior is a function of the person and the environment. At the time Lewin stated his interactional position there were no existing person-environment models. Henry Murray's need/press model, the first interactional model presented, permitted the Lewin theory of person and environment interaction to be represented in common conceptual terms (see Figure 12.1). Stern operationally defined the important concepts of Murray's/Model; the empirical procedures developed by Stern and others are elaborately presented in *People in Context* (Stern, 1970).

Three ideas underlie the Murray-Stern assessment of people in context. The first,

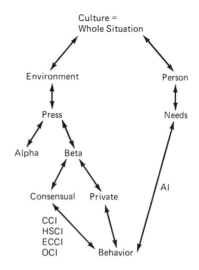

AI   = Activities Index
CCI = College Characteristics Index
HSCI = High School Characteristics Index
ECCI = Evening College Characteristics Index
OCI = Organizational Climate Index

Figure 12.1 The Need/Press Model

most basic idea drawn from Lewin is that behavior is a function of the relationship between the individual (needs) and the perceived environment (presses). Murray (1938) stressed the reciprocal nature of needs and presses in determining behavior. He thought that the environment must be defined when describing an organism's behavior and that the unit of study for psychology should be need/press interactions. To Murray the relevant characteristics of the person were expressed in terms of needs, and the relevant characteristics of the environment were expressed in terms of perceived pressures or presses. The person-environment interaction in Murray's theory was manifested in the need-satisfying or need-frustrating potential of the environment (press). Thus the need/press interaction in Murray's theory tends in some respects to reflect a reward/punishment model.

The second basic idea is that the psychological significance of the person-component of person-environment interaction may be defined in terms of needs inferred from self-reported behavior. Thus, the relevant characteristics of a person are defined in terms of needs identified from the individual's self-reported behavioral preferences. A need state is characterized by the tendency to perform actions of a certain kind. Stern operationally defined 30 of Murray's needs, forming the Activities Index. (The 30 needs—achievement, adaptability, dominance, and so forth—measured by the Activities Index are noted and defined in Chapter 11, Table 11.1). Stern thought that an individual's responses to certain environments can be anticipated in terms of the person's preferences for activities associated with a particular need orientation. The person's self-reported preferences presumably say something about the individual's personality.

The third idea basic to the Murray-Stern concept of person-environment interaction is that the psychological significance of the environment may be inferred from a person's perceptions of that environment. In the need/press model, the environment is defined in terms of presses inferred from self-reported perceptions of the environment. Murray defined press as the characteristic demands or features of the environment as perceived by those who live in the environment. Thus, the environment is defined as it is collectively perceived and reported by its participants. To assess the environment, Stern developed four indexes: the College Characteristics Index, the High School Characteristics Index, the Evening College Characteristics Index, and the Organizational Climate Index (see Chapter 11). The press concept provides an external parallel to the internalized personality needs; for each personality need there is a related press.

Stern (1970) described and hypothesized a congruent/dissonant dimension he believed to be quite important. A relatively congruent person-environment relationship (a stable or complementary combination of needs and presses) Stern thought would probably produce a sense of satisfaction and fulfillment for the participant. Stated in an over simplified form, Stern thought, for example, that an individual with a high need for achievement would probably be most happy and productive in an environment where there existed a high press for achievement. On the other hand, a relatively dissonant person-environment relationship (an unstable or uncomplementary need/press combination) would tend to produce discomfort and stress for the participants. Unfortunately, the studies exploring this need/press congruence hypothesis for individuals (e.g., have not been that supportive), (Herr & Moore, 1968; Lauterbach & Vielhaber, 1966) for a number of reasons. One such reason is that the need/press concepts are not necessarily as reciprocal as Murray and Stern had hoped and hypothesized. For example, the need for achievement involves the maximization of striving for success through personal effort. An environmental press for achievement is one in which opportunities for achievement behaviors are optimized. However, it may not be assumed that persons manifesting a high need for achievement will exhibit achievement-oriented responses in all situations. Nor may we assume that a strong press for achievement will stimulate achievement-oriented behavior from all people in the environment. The perceived press is potentially capable of influencing behavior, but it need not be responded to or even perceived by a participant in that environment. In any event, in spite of problems, Stern in time was able to show some meaningful relationships among need and press variables.

Thus, when Stern started out he was searching for a way of relating personal needs to environmental presses in order to make more effective and precise predictions about future behavior for individuals. Stern hypothesized that need/press congruence would tend to be associated with achievement, satisfaction, and a variety of other variables. He thought that if we could understand the need/press congruence concept more clearly we would be able to make more precise statements about the future behavior of individuals. In general, the indexes Stern and others developed for describing the need and press concepts had problems, but at the same time a modest amount of reliability and validity. However, in spite of their common conceptual scheme, these instruments remained relatively inaccessible to one another. The need measures and press measures could not be reconciled with one another on a simple scale for scale correspondence of variables of the same name. Or, stated more simply, the research exploring need/press congruence for individuals had not been that productive. The findings did not suggest that achievement, satisfaction, and attrition behaviors were functionally related to the person and the environment.

In view of these findings (Stern, 1970; Walsh, 1973) Stern could tell that this need/press congruence strategy was not all that productive. Theoretically, Stern believed that the need/press congruence concept was sound, but in the face of the negative findings for individuals he was motivated to search out a more effective research strategy. Such a strategy presented itself when Stern was reviewing a need/press correlation matrix across a number of different colleges and universities. Clearly some of these correlation coefficients were sizable and suggested meaningful need/press relationships across different college environments. Thus, Stern could see that when need/press scale or factor means across environments rather than persons were related, the resulting intercorrelations were far more interesting and meaningful. In addition, he reasoned that factor analysis could probably be used to ro-

tate out clusters of related need/press transactions. The most recent research of Stern and his students has applied this research strategy with some success (Cohen, 1966). In other words, the recent research using need and press scale factor means across colleges rather than persons suggests some congruence between the average level of student needs and environmental presses. This work is discussed below.

Other relevant research suggests some congruence between student needs and environmental presses. Using the Activities Index and the College Characteristics Index to assess needs and presses, Cohen (1966) conducted a factor analysis across 55 colleges and universities, which produced five college cultures (similar, at least in name, to Holland's personality types and model environments): Expressive (Artistic), Intellectual (Investigative), Protective (Conventional), Vocational (Realistic), and Collegiate (Social/Enterprising). A college culture is defined as a composite of the environmental press and the needs of its inhabitants. These findings indicate that students characterized by a certain need pattern tend to be found at institutions with appropriate press. Thus the results indicate that behavior may to some extent be functionally related to needs and perceived environmental pressures. Stern (1970) further suggests that, in his opinion, in some settings press variables may be stronger than need variables, but in other settings need variables may be stronger than press variables. Stated more simply, in some settings the environment tends to shape behavior, but in other settings the individual is the prime determinant of behavior.

A next logical step is to extend the findings to a variety of other environments, an idea that Stern had in mind before his untimely death. In any event, the evidence to some extent implies that individuals characterized by a certain need pattern may be found in environments with appropriate pressures. Thus, the implication is that people tend to move toward environments consistent with their personality styles. In terms of the Stern need/press congruence concept, additional work is clearly needed to explore the congruence hypothesis and achievement and satisfaction. There is no question that the Murray-Stern model has problems, but the evidence does indicate that the press toward environmental congruence is fairly strong.

Pervin's Person-Environment Theory

Pervin developed the first stage of his person-environment theory in about 1968 and called it the "transactional approach." In operational terms the transactional approach defined the individual and the environment according to the individual's self-reported perceptions and his or her reactions to these perceptions. The approach attempted to focus on the reciprocal relationships that occur between the individual and the environment. In 1975 Pervin developed the second stage of his theory, which he labelled the "ideographic approach to person-environment psychology" (Pervin, 1977). The ideographic approach used a free-response technique to analyze person and situation variables. In this work Pervin explored individual stability and variability as a function of situational characteristics and the nature of these characteristics.

The transactional stage of Pervin's theory was clearly influenced by Lewin and Murray. Lewin (1935) had planted the transactional seed by suggesting that behavior was a function of the whole situation and that the whole situation must take into account the person and the environment. Pervin draws much from Murray's (1938) notion of press in the second, "ideographic" stage of his theory.

The theoretical rationale behind Pervin's transactional approach (1968) was that human behavior can best be understood in terms of the transactions (reciprocal relationships) between the individual and the environment. To Pervin, for each individual there are environments that tend to match or to fit the individual's personality characteristics. Pervin thought that a match between individual and environment would probably contribute to a higher degree of performance and satisfaction. Thus, he hypothesized that individuals tend to show higher performance, more satisfaction, and reduced dissonance in environments that are congruent with their personality characteristics (i.e., environments that tend to move them from their perceived self toward their perceived ideal self).

In the main, Pervin's transactional approach focuses on the discrepancies between the individual's perceived self and ideal self, based on the notion that people tend to dislike unpleasant stages or cognitive imbalance. Thus, Pervin holds that there is a basic tendency for individuals to attempt to reduce imbalanced or unpleasant states such as cognitive dissonance. Consequently, the most important hypothesis that he pursues in this first stage of his person-environment theory suggests that high performance and satisfaction tend to be associated with perceived environments that reduce the discrepancies between the individual's perceived self and ideal self. Pervin thought that people in environments congruent with their personality characteristics would tend to be more satisfied and productive.

Against this backdrop Pervin suggests three basic assumptions that underlie the transactional approach. The first of these assumptions is that individuals find painful and unpleasant large discrepancies between their perceived selves and their perceived ideal selves. The second assumption is that individuals tend to be positively attracted toward people, objects, or ideas in the perceived environment that hold potential for moving them toward their ideal selves and are negatively disposed toward stimuli that may move them away from their ideal selves. The third assumption is that people with small discrepancies between perceived self and perceived ideal self are psychologically healthier, more open to personal growth, better choosers, and probably have more self-esteem.

The main thrust of Pervin's transactional approach has focused on the way students as individuals perceive the environment and themselves. In order to investigate the student-environment fit Pervin used a semantic differential called the Transactional Analysis of Personality and Environment (TAPE; Pervin & Rubin, 1967). The important concepts of Pervin's transactional approach have been operationally defined in the TAPE questionnaire, which uses an 11-point semantic differential technique. Individuals are defined in terms of their own self-reported perceptions using the TAPE. Pervin also conceptualizes the environment in terms of perceptions, again using the TAPE, and suggests that an interpersonal environment be defined in terms of the perceptions of its members. On the TAPE subjects are asked to rate their self-concepts, their ideal self-concepts, and the college environment on various semantic differential scales. Some examples of the polar adjective sets are: "religious/secular," "artistic/pragmatic," "conforming/rebellious," "materialistic/idealistic," and "theoretical/practical." The direction and distance between the self-concept and the perceived environment in relation to the ideal self-concept are then related to various ternal variables. The test-retest reliabilities for a one-month interval for college, self, and students were found to be high, ranging from a low of 0.95 to a high of 0.99.

The limited research conducted on this first stage of Pervin's theory suggests only partial support for the transactional approach, and most of the work has focused on the congruence-satisfaction hypothesis. In general, the research suggests that self-environment congruence (low self-environment discrepancy) is associated with self-reported satisfaction. Or, stated differently, the findings suggest that a high self-college discrepancy score tends to be associated with reported dissatisfaction with primarily academic life. Thus, the limited evidence does at least suggest that self-environment similarity (person-environment congruence) does tend to be associated with self-reported satisfaction. Again, the applied implication is that complementary person-environment links tend to be reinforcing and satisfying. Uncomplementary person-environment links tend to be dissatisfying. Another applied implication of the above research was that now more than ever Pervin believed that how individuals perceive self and environment has an important impact on behavior. Thus, the above research and Pervin's convictions led to the second stage of his theory.

Pervin developed in the second stage of his theory of person-environment psychology a conceptual scheme to explore questions concerned with why people remain stable in their behavior and/or vary their behavior according to situational characteristics. Consistent with the first stage of his theory, the second stage suggests that perceiving individuals are the prime creator of their world of episodes and as such the most important variable in social episode perception. With this in mind Pervin developed a model for any one instance of a person-situation interaction. The model suggests that the basic considerations of a person-situation process are an objectively defined situation, a perceived situation, an affective or emotional response and evaluation of the potential consequences of various responses, and a behavioral response. The model is graphically displayed in Figure 12.2. The use of the presses is drawn from the Murray work and, as indicated, suggest a more ob-

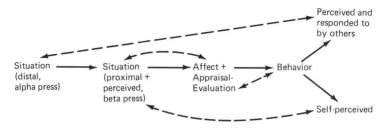

Figure 12.2 Descriptive analysis of the process of person-situation interaction. (Reproduced with permission from L. A. Pervin, "The Representative Design of Person-Situation Research," in D. Magnusson and N. S. Endler (eds.), *Personality at the Crossroads: Current Issues in Interactional Psychology* [Hillsdale, N.J.: Lawrence Erlbaum Press, 1977], p. 375. Copyright 1977 by Lawrence Erlbaum Associates, Inc.)

jectively defined environment and a perceived environment. Pervin viewed the linkages among the parts as complex and not always unidirectional (Pervin, 1977). He further noted that the model seemed to be suggesting that emotions may serve as the intervening link between situations and behavior. This clearly was a notion that was not data-based at the time.

To operationalize this model Pervin used a free-response ideographic descriptive approach to the analysis of person-situation variables. He wanted to study an individual's perception of life situations and perceived pattern of behavior in relation to those situations. The subjects in the study (Pervin, 1976, 1977) were four Rutgers University undergraduates (two male and two female). The students were told that the purpose of the study was to explore their current life situations, how they perceived these situations, and how they tended to respond in these different situations. Each student was first asked to list current life situations. A situation was described as involving a specific place, which in most cases involved specific people, a specific time, and specific activities. Current life was defined to include the past six months. Second, students were asked to describe each situation using adjectives, traits, and/or phrases, in order to generate a list of situational traits. Third, students were asked to describe their feelings

in each situation in order to generate a list of feelings relevant to the individual. Finally, students were asked to indicate their behavior in each situation. Thus, this free-response ideographic procedure produced a list of life situations, a description of each situation, a description of feelings in each situation, and a description of behaviors in each situation. The data then were subsequently factor-analyzed for each student in order to determine those feelings and behaviors that the students perceived to be associated with specific situations.

The findings were interesting to say the least. First, the evidence indicated that the number of situations listed by each student was fairly similar, ranging from 23 to 29. In addition, the situations seemed to cluster into a few homogeneous categories—home/family, friends/peers, relaxation/recreation, work/school, and alone. Another striking finding noted by Pervin (1976) is the extent to which situations were described in terms of emotional reactions (e.g., threatening, warm, interesting, dull, tense, calm, rejecting). In other words the same affectively toned word may be applied to the situation, to the self experiencing the situation, and to the self behaving in the situation. Thus, these findings do tend to indicate the importance of affects in influencing how we tend to organize and perceive-situations as well as respond and behave in them (Pervin, 1977).

Four affective dimensions appear to be the most salient in the ratings of situations: friendly/unfriendly, calm/tense, interesting/dull, and free/constrained (Pervin, 1976). An applied implication here is that people in situations perceived to be more friendly, calm, interesting, and free may tend to report being more happy, satisfied, and productive. This tends to be consistent with some of the work of Moos (1976a) suggesting that people tend to be more satisfied and comfortable in environments that they perceive to be relationship oriented. Another applied implication already mentioned is that situations appear to be distinguished much more in terms of feelings aroused by them than in terms of some cognitive perceived set of variables (Pervin, 1977). Thus, Pervin's person-environment model and the limited data reported here tend to suggest that emotions may serve as the intervening link between situations and behavior. However, we must keep in mind that the empirical research generated by Pervin's theory has not been extensive. In sum, a much wider data base is needed to effectively evaluate the contribution of Pervin's work on both the transactional stage and the ideographic stage of his theoretical framework.

THE PERSON PERSPECTIVE

Person-environment theories developed from the person perspective focus upon the individual as the crucial variable in the development process. The individual's traits, psychic structures, self-concept, and inner disposition are viewed as the main determinants of behavior, and, in general, environment is viewed as additive rather than interactive. This perspective may be expressed as $B = f(P)$, where B stands for behavior, f for function; and P for person. The psychoanalytic approach and Roe's person-

ality approach adhere to this person's emphasis.

The Psychoanalytic Approach

The psychoanalytic approach is primarily concerned with the motives involved in the development process. From our person-environment perspective, a basic assumption is that individuals tend to move toward environments that permit the expression and satisfaction of preferred ways of seeking gratification and some protection from anxiety. In the psychoanalytic tradition, of course, the emphasis is on the internal needs and factors as the most significant ones in the development process.

The main idea behind the psychoanalytic stance is that individuals tend to adjust to social expectations by entering environments that facilitate the sublimation of their impulses. Or, more simply, we tend to move toward environments that facilitate the transfer of our impulses into socially acceptable activities through social contacts and work. Through the socialization process we learn to satisfy internal needs in a way that meets the approval of parents, friends, teachers, and society. In addition, the identification with significant others such as parents and friends has personal vocational development implications and presents us with some personal and vocational models. To cope with personal vocational stress the individual develops ego strength, which assists the personality in delaying gratification, compromising, and reality-testing his/her perceptions and abilities.

To assess psychoanalytic concepts Dombrose and Slobin (1958) developed the Id, Ego, Superego Test (IES). The IES was constructed to assess the relative strengths of impulse, ego, and superego forces. The test is entirely pictorial and provides a group of standard situations designed to elicit impulse, ego, and superego behavioral responses that are quantifiable. In some respects the IES asks individuals to report how they would respond in different situations. The IES has four subtests: The Picture Title Test assesses the degree to which an individual can accept his or her impulse and superego demands, the Picture Story Completion Test is a measure of reality contact, the Photo Analysis Test assesses how the individual would like to function in a situation, and the Arrow Dot Test assesses the individual's probable behavior in real life. The four subtests require a total of about 30 minutes to administer and provide both quantitative and qualitative data of a projective nature. Test-retest reliability coefficients for a 30-to-60-day period across the four subtests for 30 male patients receiving outpatient psychotherapy ranged from a low of 0.35 to a high of 0.83. Mean scores and standard deviations on the four subtests are available for 161 children, 33 adolescents, and 183 male adults. Scores of normal adult males are compared with those of a variety of other age and patient groups to provide both developmental data and information as to assessing potential problems. In general, the limited validity data (Dombrose & Slobin, 1958) suggest that the subtests of the IES are able to differentiate effectively among a number of different groups, such as normal adults, children of the latency period, adolescents, constricted neurotics, paranoid-schizophrenics, and geriatric groups. The concurrent validity evidence indicates that differences among these groups in comparison rankings were correctly predicted a significant number of times. As a clinical and research tool the IES does seem to hold some promise for the assessment process, primarily from a psychoanalytic perspective. In addition, as we noted previously, the test does make an effort to assess how individuals tend to respond in different situations using a projective approach.

The main concern of the psychoanalytic approach is with motives or internal motivation (nonobservable) kinds of variables, which in some respects limits the applied features of the approach. However, the Id, Ego, Superego Test is one instrument that has made an attempt to operationalize and make more applied some of these concepts and variables. In any event, there are some applied features of interest. In general, the evidence (Osipow, 1983) suggests that psychoanalytic concepts have some utility in identifying relationships among childhood experiences, personality differences, and ultimate vocational choices. For example, in exploring the early experiences of lawyers, dentists, and social workers, researchers found that aggressive impulses were more accepted in the families of lawyers and social workers and repressed in the families of dentists. In the families of lawyers and dentists, the fathers were more dominant and "masculine," fairness being emphasized in the lawyers and obedience to authority in the dentists. For families of social workers, the mother was stronger and more dominant, the father was either weaker or absent, and the discipline was less "masculine." The home atmosphere of lawyers was warmer compared to dentists, in which propriety and conventionality were more dominant. The early experiences of social workers included some kind of trauma and concern for the feelings of others. Other research indicates that parental identification seems to be associated with predictable interest patterns and eventual vocational choice. In addition, findings indicate some relationships between interest patterning and ego strength. All in all, the evidence suggests that the psychoanalytic concepts need to be kept in mind during the person-environment assessment process. The psychoanalytic data do seem to give us some information about the environments that people tend to enter in order to facilitate the expression and satisfaction of their motives.

Roe's Person-Environment Theory

Anne Roe's person-environment theory (Roe, 1957; Roe & Klos, 1969; Roe & Siegelman, 1964; Medvene & Shueman, 1978) is based on a series of studies exploring the personalities of male research scientists in different fields. The findings of these studies demonstrated differences in the personality characteristics and childhood experiences of men in different fields and environments. Roe further concluded that a major distinction among the scientists was on a dimension of interest toward persons or not toward persons (interest toward things). Based on this data, Roe surmised that the work environment entered was related to personality development that was an outgrowth of early parent/child interactions.

Roe attempted to link person-environment interactions (parent/child interactions) to various types of personal orientations by hypothesizing that the extent to which individuals are rewarded or punished in dealing with people or things will determine the environments to which they are attracted. She thought that preferences for people activities or for thing activities were probably a function of the reward or punishment pattern that developed during early parent/child interactions. For example, an individual reared in a warm and "accepting" family environment, in the main, has had people activities rewarded and is therefore attracted to and moves toward environments involving frequent contact with people. On the other hand, the person raised in a cold and "avoiding" family environment has not been rewarded for people contacts and therefore moves toward environments involving minimal contact with people. Person-oriented environments are general-cultural, arts and entertainment, services, and business contacts. Nonperson-oriented environments are science, outdoor, technological, and organizational.

The environmental groups are distributed, as shown in Figure 12.3, along two dimensions: orientation to purposeful communication to resourceful utilization, and orientation to interpersonal relation to natural phenomena. The environmental level (professional and managerial to unskilled) aspired to is based on ability and determines the amount or degree of the individual's job responsibility. The two groups of variables (environmental fields and levels) are then linked together in conical shape with the unskilled environments in each field at the bottom of the cone, indicating that they tend to be more psychologically similar than higher-level environments. The professional and managerial environments in each field are at the open and wide end of the cone, suggesting that such environments tend to be more psychologically different. For example, the mechanical engineer and the actor live in very different psychological environments.

For years no attempts were made to produce within Roe's framework an empirical test or inventory for use in assessing interests or psychological environments. More recently, however, a number of experimental inventories have been developed. Based on Roe's classification of occupational environments by fields and by levels, the inventory called "Ramak" ("a list of occupations" in Hebrew) was constructed (Meir & Barak, 1974). This is a list of 72 occupational environments that produces 24 occupational field and level scores (eight fields and three levels within each field). The Career Occupational Preference System Interest Inventory (COPS, Revised Edition; Knapp & Knapp, 1980a) was developed through factor analysis of interest activity items written to reflect Roe's groups and levels classification. The COPS, Form R, is a self-contained unit that is essentially self-administering, with items written at the sixth grade level. The inventory booklet consists of 168 job envi-

Figure 12.3 Occupational groups ordered by role performer's orientation to people, by date, and natural phenomena. (From A. Roe and D. Klos, "Occupational Classification." *The Counseling Psychologist*, 1(3), 92 [1969]. Copyright 1969. Reprinted with the permission of Sage Publications, Inc.)

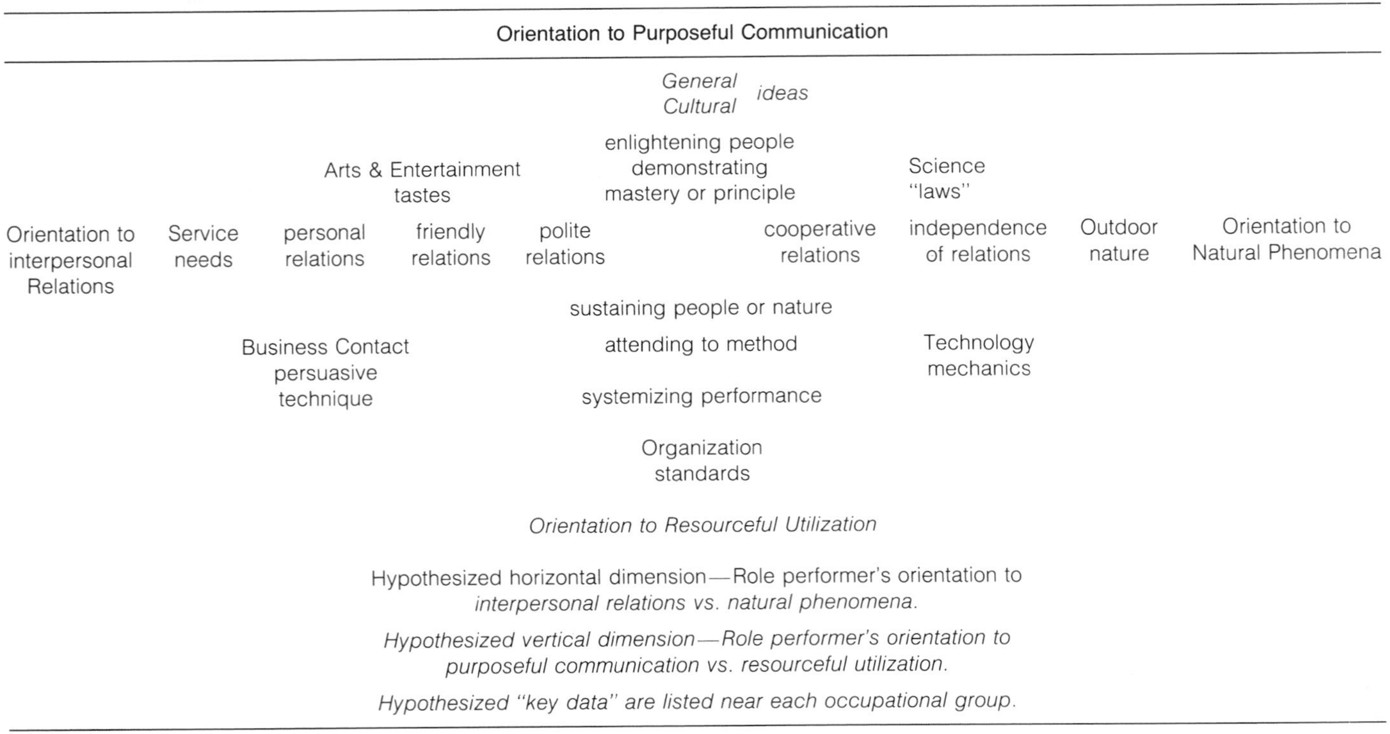

Orientation to Purposeful Communication

Orientation to interpersonal Relations

General Cultural ideas

Service needs

personal relations

Business Contact persuasive technique

Arts & Entertainment tastes

friendly relations

polite relations

enlightening people demonstrating mastery or principle

sustaining people or nature

cooperative relations

attending to method

systemizing performance

Organization standards

Science "laws"

independence of relations

Technology mechanics

Outdoor nature

Orientation to Natural Phenomena

Orientation to Resourceful Utilization

Hypothesized horizontal dimension—Role performer's orientation to interpersonal relations vs. natural phenomena.

Hypothesized vertical dimension—Role performer's orientation to purposeful communication vs. resourceful utilization.

Hypothesized "key data" are listed near each occupational group.

ronment descriptions reflecting work performed in a wide variety of occupations. Based on Roe's (1956) classification of occupations into groups and levels within each group, the COPS, Form R, is scored on five major groups (arts, service, science, technology, and business) at two levels each (professional and skilled), plus four other groups of scales (consumer economics, communication, clerical, and outdoor). The Hall Occupational Orientation Inventory (Hall, 1976) is based on the development of psychological needs in occupational terms. This inventory samples needs, job characteristics, and worker traits. The items are empirically assigned to three kinds of scales: 13 directional scales reflecting values and needs; the data, people, things orientations of the *Dictionary of Occupational Titles*; 8 degree scales that assess the person's concerns about job factors such as co-workers and vacations; and a verification scale that assesses a defensive response. Although these inventories are in need of additional reliability and validity data, they do offer promise for the future of Roe's person-environment formulations and assessments.

Research (Osipow, 1983) indicates that the psychological assumptions underlying Roe's occupational environment system are basically solid. On a more subjective basis, her classification of environmental groups is very similar to Holland's derived hexagon model of environments. Both Roe and Holland support with data the notion that adjacent occupational environments are more closely related psychologically than distant ones. Other research (Roe & Siegelman, 1964) rather clearly indicates that early social activity and experiences tend to be associated with later person orientation. Evidence shows that person-oriented students more frequently come from families where there was acceptance of or an emotional concentration on the child than do nonperson-oriented students. Work by Medvene and Shueman

(1968) further supports the above findings. These authors found that engineering students in general tend to describe their dominant parent as "avoiding" than as either "accepting" or "concentrating." In addition, Medvene and Shueman discovered that students choosing a sales and technical service job function (defined as person-oriented) were more likely to describe their dominant parent as "accepting," while those in the other three functional groups (basic research, applied research, and product and process engineering) defined as nonperson-oriented were more likely to describe their dominant parent as "avoiding." These findings again support Roe's theory that individuals reared in families where the dominant parent is perceived as primarily "avoiding" developed spheres of interest centered around non–person-oriented environments. Thus, in summary, Roe's most profound applied finding is that individuals tend to vary on a person-oriented to nonperson-oriented dimension in their interests and personalities, and that their orientation influences to some extent the environments they choose to enter.

THE ENVIRONMENTAL PERSPECTIVE

This position views behavior as mainly a function of environmental or situational factors. This perspective may be expressed as $B = f(E)$, where B stands for behavior, f for function, and E for the environment or some part of the environment. Adhering to this environmental or situational emphasis and discussed here are the Moos social ecological approach and Barker's behavior setting theory.

Moos's Social Ecological Approach

Moos work (1976a, 1979, 1984, 1987d) was probably most profoundly influenced by Murray (1938) and Pace and Stern (1958), who were clearly very interested in the beta press, or how environmental perceptions tend to influence behavior. However, like many other theorists, Kantor, Lewin, and Koffka also influenced the Moos approach. Kantor as early as 1924 emphasized the reciprocal interplay between man and environment. Lewin suggested that behavior was a function of the person and the environment. And Koffka placed his emphasis on perception and the psychological environment.

The Moos social ecological perspective is based on the general principle that the way one perceives the environment tends to influence the way one will behave in that environment. Thus, Moos focuses on the social climate (the personality of the environment) by suggesting that environments, like people, have unique personalities. Just as some people are more supportive and nurturant than others, so are some environments more supportive and nurturant than others. According to Moos we should be able to describe and characterize an environment just as we describe an individual's personality. The Moos approach has been unveiled in two stages, by two books: *The Human Context* (1976a) and *Evaluating Educational Environments* (1979). The second stage has been elaborated in two recent publications (Moos, 1984, 1987d).

The first stage of the Moos perspective has been based on two assumptions. The first is that social climate may be inferred from behavioral perceptions. Thus, Moos describes environments as perceived by the people in them. This notion without question is very similar to the Murray beta press and the follow-up work done by Stern focusing on environmental perceptions. The second assumption made by Moos is that the way we perceive surroundings influences the way we behave in that environment. Stated more simply, our perceptions of the environment influence our behavior. How the environment is perceived exerts a direc-

tional influence on behavior. Thus, according to Moos, the perceived social climate tends to shape behavior and people. Or, stated differently, the perceived social climate in which we live and work tends to have a significant impact on attitudes, behavior, and physical and psychological well-being.

The theoretical assumptions stated in the second stage of the Moos approach seem to be sharper and somewhat more specific than those stated in the first stage. The first assumption is that one can distinguish different dimensions of social environments. Moos has been able to do this conceptually and empirically. The second assumption indicates that these dimensions or social environments have distinct influences on people. Again, at least so far, the data tend to support this assumption. The third assumption is that the social influences tend to differ from one person to another. This assumption seems to be reasonably sensible and consistent with the notion of individual differences. Based on these assumptions, Moos then developed a conceptual framework suggesting theoretically that people and environments reciprocally influence each other. Operationally, however, the Moos approach is primarily concerned with how our perceptions of environments tend to influence our behavior. The main emphasis is on the environmental perspective, with rather weak emphasis on the person-environment process. This is a limitation, but without question Moos has made some very positive contributions with his work.

In order to operationalize the social-climate concept, Moos and a number of his colleagues have developed a variety of inventories (Moos, 1987b). The social-environment inventories have been developed using primarily a rational approach that simply asks people individually about the patterns of behavior in certain environments. The basic logic behind this approach is that the consensus of individuals characterizing their environment constitutes a measure of environment or social climate. For a more elaborate review of these inventories and their reliability and validity see Chapter 11's discussion of environmental assessment. The inventories reviewed in Chapter 11 include the Ward Atmosphere Scale, the Community-Oriented Program Environment Scale, the Sheltered Care Environment Scale, the Correctional Institutions Environment Scale, the Military Company Environment Inventory, the University Residence Environment Scale, the Classroom Environment Scale, the Group Environment Scale, the Work Environment Scale, and the Family Environment Scale. More recently Moos and his colleagues have developed the Multiphasic Environmental Assessment Procedure in order to assess, measure, and describe sheltered care settings. This assessment procedure is also discussed in Chapter 11.

An important finding of the Moos work (1976a, 1979, 1984, 1987d) is that very different social environments may be described by some common sets of dimensions associated with three somewhat global categories. In other words, different social climates may be characterized by common or similar kinds of dimensions. These broad categories are the relationship dimensions, personal growth or goal orientation dimensions, and system maintenance and change dimensions. In general, the relationship dimensions assess the degree to which people are involved in the setting, the degree to which they support and help one another, and the extent to which they express themselves freely and openly. The personal growth dimensions assess basic goals of the setting and the areas in which personal development and self-enhancement tend to occur. The system maintenance dimensions measure the degree to which the environment is orderly and clear in its expectations, maintains control, and responds to change. Again, these dimensions are more elaborately discussed in

Chapter 11. An important reason for identifying some common dimensions across different social environments is that such environments may now be compared and attempts may be made to explore why an individual does well in one environment and not so well in another.

In terms of the research, the findings clearly have implications for person-environment assessment. The most profound and consistent finding about the impact of social climates has to do with the human relationship dimensions. The evidence indicates from a wide range of research (Moos, 1974, 1984, 1987b, 1987d) that the relationship dimensions appear to have a positive effect across different kinds of environments. For example, evidence indicates that the quality of personal interaction with supervisors in work environments is associated with job satisfaction and performance. Workers who perceived their work environments as supportive were rated more favorably by their supervisors on dimensions of competence, friendliness, and conscientiousness. In educational settings, students reported greater satisfaction, showed more interest in their course material, and engaged in more course relevant activities in classes perceived to be high on human relationship dimensions (Moos, 1976a, 1987b, 1987d). In psychiatric treatment settings, the evidence (Moos, 1976a) shows that the qualities of the relationships in individual and group therapy are highly related to positive evaluation of treatment and to positive personality change. In general, the evidence indicates that people tend to be more satisfied and comfortable, less depressed and irritable, and more likely to report beneficial effects on their self-esteem in environments that they perceive to strongly emphasize the human relationship dimensions.

In another research area of interest to Moos, some evidence (Moos, 1976a, 1987b, 1987d) suggests that the perceived social environment has important physiological and health-related effects. More specifically, perceived work pressure and too much responsibility tend to be associated with higher heart rates and heart problems. The coronary-prone pattern is particularly descriptive of the type-A person, who may be characterized as extremely aggressive, competitive and ambitious, with accompanying feelings of restlessness, and a sense of time urgency. In general, the evidence suggests that people who are satisfied in jobs have a much better chance of remaining healthy than those who are not.

Over all, the evidence does suggest that social environments do tend to shape behavior. How we as individuals tend to perceive our social environments has important affects on our satisfaction, learning, and personal growth. The clearest and most profound research finding across a number of studies and a number of different social environments is that satisfying human relationships facilitate personal growth and development. In the main, people tend to be more satisfied and more productive in environments that are perceived to be relationship oriented. The evidence to date indicates that perceived environments have impact on coping behavior, psychological well being, and physiological health.

Barker's Behavior Setting Theory

The Barker (1965, 1968) work was probably most profoundly influenced by Brunswik's (1952, 1956) thinking. Brunswik's conceptual framework has not been classified as interactional primarily because of his neglect of the person variables, but his emphasis on the situation has been of great importance. Brunswik proposed that it might very well be meaningful to sample situations rather than individuals. In fact, he suggested that the sampling of situations and problems may in the end be more important than proper

sampling of subjects (Brunswik, 1956). Brunswik defined the situation in objective terms independently of the responses of the person acting in the situation. Barker (1965, 1968) without much question belongs to this group of psychologists interested in the nonpsychological environment. Barker's approach to the analysis of situations was to primarily use social physical characteristics and to describe the situation in terms of so-called behavior settings. In the main, Barker (1968) believed that behavior settings (a stable pattern of activities associated with the surrounding environment) tend to shape the behavior of people who inhabit them. To Barker, behavior settings actually link actions and environments by structuring behavioral rules for specific environments or situations. The basic assumption is that people will tend to be influenced by the imposed behavioral rules of a setting, particularly if they obtain certain satisfaction from the setting. The thought is that in order to understand behavior, it is important to know the specific environment in which people are interacting or working. Thus, to Barker the ecological psychologist seeks to understand human behavior and environments by unobtrusively observing events that he or she has not constrained in any significant way (Barker, 1968).

The primary means of assessment used by Barker and his associates over the years has been the observation of people in real life. Here the assessment task involves observing the behavior of people in ongoing real life situations or environments. To Barker, observational assessment of people in simulated or laboratory settings tends to disturb the environment and thus distort people's behavior. Based on the naturalistic everyday observations of children's behavior, Barker noted that as children go from one place to another (from spelling class to recess) their behaviors change substantially. In addition, he noted that within the same situation, different children behave quite similarly. The children act in ways that are compatible with the predominant activity. Barker concluded that environmental influences on behavior are not restricted to inputs from one or a few people. According to Barker (1965), more than people are involved in the mutual causal relations between the environment and behavior.

In general, the research to date has mainly focused on the differences between small settings and large settings. Settings in small organizations are assumed to be "underpersoned" and those in large organizations are assumed to be relatively "overpersoned" (there are more persons than can be accepted given the capacity of the setting). Small settings (underpersoned) have fewer people but the same standing patterns of behavior as the large overpersoned settings. Therefore people in small, underpersoned settings are involved in more actions, stronger actions, and more varied actions in order to maintain the behavior setting. The people tend to be busier, more vigorous, more versatile, and more involved in the setting. The research (Barker, 1968; Walsh, 1973) tends to support this notion.

Wicker (1979) has suggested some amendments to Barker's theory. He has proposed that the level of "manning" be regarded as a continuum having three critical regions: "undermanning" (underpersoned), adequate (or optimal) "manning," and "overmanning" (overpersoned). The conceptual separation of "overmanning" from adequate or optimal "manning" was a distinction not clearly made previously by Barker. Wicker further suggested that "manning" should be calculated separately for people who have responsible positions in a setting (workers or staff) and those who are members, clients, or onlookers. For example, as noted by Wicker, a crowded physician's office would be underpersoned at the staff level and overpersoned at the patient level. Thus, settings can be understaffed, adequately staffed, or overstaffed, and they can be underpopulated, adequately populated, or overpopulated by clients. In general, the evidence indicates that people in overpersoned conditions tend to report less involvement than do people in underpersoned conditions.

We find that this theory and some of the research has meaning for a broad range of environments and for person environment assessment. Research findings (Walsh, 1973) indicate, for example, that people working or interacting in small settings in comparison with people working in large settings are absent less often, report more satisfaction, are more productive, and evidence less turnover. In addition, people in small settings reported more group cohesiveness, greater frequency of social interaction, and easier communication than did the people in large settings. Other findings show that the smaller the work setting, the higher the morale. In small settings work activity is reported by employees as being more meaningful, and workers perceive themselves as important to the work setting. Thus, the evidence suggests in general that work settings do influence worker attitudes and behavior. People in small settings tend to be more productive, involved, and satisfied than do people in large settings. In summary, the evidence suggests that people tend to enter and remain in behavior settings that they view (perceive) to be satisfying and congruent. In general, people want these behavior settings to endure.

SUMMARY

This chapter has been devoted to some discussion of various theoretical perspectives of person-environment psychology that people may use to assess and organize information about themselves. The theories assuming an interactional perspective have suggested that development is a function of the person and the environment; their notion is that assessment of the person is incomplete without some assessment of the environment. Theories assuming the person perspective have focused on the individual's personal characteristics as the primary determinant of behavior; individual personality links the person to an environment or situation. The environment perspective suggests that behavior is a function of environment or situational variables; the context or situation is the determining variable, and the individual's behavior tends to vary from one context or environment to another. Within these three perspectives, the theories discussed seem to be the most meaningful for helping people assess, organize, and understand information about themselves and their social environments.

13

Human Development and Assessment

INTRODUCTION

Human development is complex. No one theory has yet been developed that encompasses all aspects of human development. At best, we have a number of partial theories, most of which are very age-specific; probably the most traditional approach to describing and classifying human behavior is according to chronological age (Schuster, 1980). As one becomes more knowledgeable about norms of behavior, one is able to make more effective predictions. However, the chronological-age approach to human development says little about the normal variations that exist among individuals and, in addition, is not very informative about the cultural and biological factors that influence the predicted behaviors.

Current theorists of human development go beyond the age-specific description of behavior by attempting to identify meaningful relationships among behaviors: Complex behaviors are reduced to core problems, tasks, or accomplishments for each phase of life. In general, the human development theorists tend to differ in two major ways. One difference concerns the focus on heredity versus environmental influences. To this very day this issue continues to stimulate considerable controversy in theory development. The second major issue concerns how the theorists attempt to explain the nature of developmental changes over time. Most theorists recognize orderly sequential changes from simple to more complex kinds of behaviors. However, some theorists suggest that these changes occur in a continuous pattern, in which earlier skills lead to the development of later skills; while other theorists suggest rather abrupt changes in behavior patterns, indicating that many behaviors change simultaneously and thus introducing a new level of cognitive, biophysical, and/or psychosocial functioning.

Theories of human development are more or less adequate and more or less general. They examine different developmental phenomena, often at different levels of abstraction: Some theories of human development conceptualize thinking phenomena, while others explore feeling or behavioral phenomena. Finally, human development usually does not occur quickly. Fundamental changes take years to accomplish and thus precise descriptions of how changes occur tend to be problematic.

In general, then, we may think about human development as including changes in physical abilities, cognitive structure, intellectual ability, behavior, roles, social interactions, attitudes, and a variety of other variables. Just about any characteristic or aspect of the individual that changes with the passage of time and life experiences may probably be thought of as some aspect of human development. In addition, these changes in human development tend to occur throughout the life span and may be a function of physical maturation, environmental influences, or person-environment interactions. We believe that human development and changes in cognitive structure, physical abilities, personality, and behavior need to be included in the assessment process. Symptoms of arrested development, accelerated development, or problematic development

realistically have implications for the individual's psychological health and well-being.

In this chapter we will focus on theories of human development and how these concepts of human development are assessed. More specifically, we will review four theories of cognitive development (by Piaget, Kohlberg, Perry, and Loevinger) and three psychosocial theories of development (by Erikson, Chickering, and Levinson). A basic point of this chapter is that information about the human development process is important in assessing people and environments. Thus, people and environments need to be viewed from a developmental perspective in the assessment process.

COGNITIVE DEVELOPMENTAL THEORY

As noted by Rodgers (1980), Parker (1978), and Hansen (1982) the cognitive developmental theories are primarily concerned with how we reason, think, or make meaning of our experiences. For our purposes and from an assessment perspective, it makes sense that learning, understanding, and problem solving are influenced by the nature of the reasoning pattern an individual holds. Within this context the basic element in cognitive developmental theory is a *structure*. A structure essentially defines how an individual will tend to perceive, organize, and evaluate experiences and events. Stated differently, a structure is a total way of thinking, not an attitude toward a particular situation (Rodgers, 1980). The basic structures of reasoning are called *stages*. For most cognitive developmental theorists, stages have the following characteristics (Rodgers, 1980). First of all, stages are sequential (invariant sequences), which means that persons develop through them one at a time and in the same order. This means that no one can skip or jump over stages. Second, stages are hierarchical. The structure of each successive stage is more differentiated and integrated and incorporates the critical aspects of the preceding stages into its more complex mode of reasoning. Third, some theorists suggest that stages are universal, that individuals move through certain stages regardless of cultural conditions and that some sequences of cognitive development may occur in any culture (e.g., Kohlberg, 1969). Fourth, stages are qualitatively different. Thus, successive stages are not adding more of the same thing but are changing to a different thing: Stage shifts are changes from one way of thinking about experiences to another way of thinking about experiences. Finally, stages are structures of how we think, not of what we think. Theories of cognitive development are only concerned with the "how" not with the "what."

Another significant question we need to ask is, How does developmental change take place? In general, cognitive developmental theory suggests that developmental change results from encountering cognitive conflict. An individual's current way of thinking is challenged by a different and structurally more advanced way of reasoning (Rodgers, 1980). The result is cognitive conflict. This is the beginning of developmental change, in order to understand it we need to review three concepts: equilibration, assimilation, and accommodation.

According to Rodgers (1980) *equilibration* is essentially a balancing process. Here, an individual's current stage of reasoning is working, or is in balance, with the individual's experiences. The individual is in equilibrium. However, if an individual's existing structure is inadequate to deal with events encountered, the resulting disequilibrium or conflict could lead to an *assimilation* or an *accommodation*. Remember, as we mentioned above, that cognitive conflict exists when the structure of a person's stage of reasoning is

in conflict with the structure of the environment. Given cognitive conflict, if a person assimilates, conflict and confusion are handled by forcing the environmental challenge to fit the person's current stage of reasoning (Rodgers, 1980). When a person accommodates, conflict and confusion are resolved by changing the current structure to accommodate a new way of thinking and making meaning out of things. Thus accommodation involves developmental change.

In terms of the assessment process, cognitive developmental theory is primarily concerned with sizing up or determining how far a person has progressed along a sequence of stages. Thus, the assessment task is to obtain a representative sample of a person's thinking and then to match the sample with descriptions of the sequence of stages. Samples of thinking are obtained in basically two ways (Rodgers, 1980). First, persons respond to open-ended essays and incomplete stories. In order to fit the sample with the stages, trained raters judge the responses, generally using a scoring manual with structured protocols and examples. Second and less common, an objective instrument containing examples of thinking for all of the stages in a sequence may be constructed. On such an instrument subjects are asked to review the examples of thinking and to select the reasoning most preferable to or descriptive of themselves. Here, as noted by Rodgers (1980), subjects are asked to recognize structures and not to create them. The assumption is that their preferences will tend to reveal stage preferences. Raters and scoring manuals tend not to be used.

In sum, given the above general conceptualization of structure, stage, and how change takes place, it is important to remember that cognitive developmental theory is primarily concerned with how we reason, think, or make meaning of our experiences. Keeping this in mind, let's move to a discussion of some of the specific theoretical frameworks.

Piaget's Cognitive Developmental Theory

The central themes of cognitive developmental theory have come from the work of Piaget (1952, 1965). His work on logical mathematical and moral development and his conceptualization of the characteristics of the stages and equilibration previously discussed are the basis for many theories of cognitive development.

Piaget believed that mental development is a process that begins the day the infant is born. He further theorized that the stream of cognitive development is the same for all people, although they progress at different rates. From his early work in biology, Piaget believed that biological responses as well as intellectual responses were primarily concerned with adaption to the perceived environment. Piaget thought that an individual's primary goal is to learn to master the environment. The pleasure received from mastering the environment stimulates curiosity, problem solving, imitation, practice, and play activities. In the main, Piaget assumed that human nature is rational (Schuster, 1980).

The stream of cognitive development that begins at birth is the same for all people, according to Piaget, and is divided into four developmental periods: the *sensory motor period* (birth to age two), the *preoperational period* (two to seven years), the *concrete operational period* (seven to eleven years), and the *formal operations period* (11 to 15 years). In the sensory motor period development moves from the reflexive activities to the sensory motor solution to problems. The ability to use language enables the child of the preoperational period to solve simple motor problems internally through the use of language. In the concrete operational period the child is able to provide logical solutions to concrete problems. In the formal operations period abstract thinking processes begin to develop. After this period Piaget suggests that quantitative, but not qualitative, changes in intellectual functioning and development occur (Schuster, 1980).

Parallel to a child's mental development, Piaget identified two broad stages of moral development. The earlier stage, lasting from approximately age 3 to age 11, he called a "morality of restraint." During this stage the rules are viewed as sacred by the child primarily because they are handed down by dominant adults. According to Garsee (1980), the rules are sacred, morality is imposed primarily by outside forces, and punishment is vengeful or compensatory. From a child's perspective everyone must play by the rules.

For Piaget a "morality of reciprocity" describes the older child of 12 years and above. The development of abstract thought enables the young person to internally regulate value responses. According to Garsee (1980), in the later stages a child develops the ability to be more forgiving. But it is the interaction with peers, according to Piaget, that is the significant element from which rational morality develops.

Piaget's techniques of inquiry have been primarily clinical (Ashburn, 1980). His method was to observe a child's behavior in an environment, to develop a hypothesis concerning the structure that underlies the child and the environment, and then to test the hypothesis by altering the environment to some extent. His more recent work (Piaget, 1972) suggests that individual differences in cognitive development among adults are influenced more by experiences than by the general characteristics determining the individual's type of formal thinking (Ashburn, 1980). Thus, to some extent Piaget did recognize the role of experience and social interaction on cognitive development. Much of Piaget's work is criticized because of the small sample size and the nonexperimental methodology, but it has had a profound impact in stimulating the development of theory in this area.

Hunt (1961) became particularly interested in Piaget's work on the growth of intelligence in children. Hunt believed that environmental stimulation can significantly raise a young child's intelligence. Based on this notion Hunt saw the need to accumulate better information from existing programs through more precise and accurate measures of young children's specific skills. Thus, Hunt and Ina Uzgiris produced a series of films demonstrating the steps on their scales of infant development (Uzgiris & Hunt, 1975). They next used the scales to assess the progress of babies in the Teheran (Iran) orphanage.

The scales attempt to identify an infant's developmental level for each of six highly specific cognitive functions (the development of visual pursuit and the permanence of objects; the development of means for obtaining desired environmental events; the development of imitation; the development of operational causality; the construction of object relations in space; and the development of schemes for relating to objects). Items consist of situations chosen for their ability to reveal the dominant aspects of successive steps in a developmental sequence. An infant's cognitive development is inferred from behavioral observations. The scales are recommended for the purpose of discovering differential rates of development associated with the various child-rearing practices. The idea is that levels of development may be fostered by environmental manipulations. Presently, additional reliability and validity data are needed, but the scales do promise to help us understand what kinds of experiences are probably most productive for various groups of children at different stages. Rosenthal (1985) in a review of the scales indicates that they serve a highly specific function not previously captured by traditional tests of infant development. She further notes that the authors seek to obtain empirical evidence for constructs typically evaluated in a qualitative way.

Loevinger's Theory of Ego Development

In over 14 years of research Jane Loevinger and her associates have developed a cognitive developmental theory of ego (personality) development (Loevinger, 1966, 1976; Loevinger & Wessler, 1970). Loevinger and Wessler (1970) trace the use of the term *ego development* to Alfred Adler's concept of style of life. To Loevinger, ego development is not just a personality trait but a master trait second only to intelligence in determining an individual's pattern of responses to situations (Weathersby, 1981).

Loevinger (1976) suggests that ego development is marked by a succession of stages identifying milestone sequences (patterns of personality change) in the areas of impulse control (character development), interpersonal style, conscious preoccupation, and cognitive style. To Loevinger (1976) ego development is one dimension made up of those four interwoven areas. She names her stages as follows: presocial (birth to one year), symbiotic (two to three years), impulsive (four to five years), self-protective (six to seven years), conformist (eight to 11 years), self-awareness (transition stage), conscientious (12 to 14 years), individualistic (transition stage), autonomous (15 to 18 years and older), and integrated adult.

The early stages of development are generally viewed by Loevinger as childhood stages, and adults who remain in them are often viewed as marginal to society. A significant step in ego development according to Loevinger is movement from the self-protective stage to the conformist stage, in which individuals with increasing self-awareness tend to identify with social rules and society in general. In the transition from the conformist stage to the conscientious stage, or what is known as the self-awareness stage, an individual develops an increasing self-awareness and the ability to think in terms of alternatives. Individuals at this stage, Loevinger suggests, are sometimes painfully aware of their separateness in relation to social groups. In the conscientious stage the individual lives according to self-evaluated standards. Individuals at this stage are concerned about responsibility and mutuality in relationships and view life as offering real choices. The individualistic stage, which is a transition between the conscientious stage and the autonomous stage, is characterized by a respect for individuality and a concern for development. Here an attempt is made to differentiate between one's inner and outer life. In moving to the autonomous stage the individual develops the ability to acknowledge inner conflict, develops tolerance for self and others, and respects the autonomy of others as well as one's own. People tend to have an expanded view of life, to be objective about self and others, and to have a complex cognitive style with a high tolerance for ambiguity. The integrated stage, the highest stage of ego development, accentuates the autonomous stage and adds the reconciliation of inner conflicts. In this stage identity is a conscious preoccupation and interpersonal relations reflect a value for individuality. However, according to Loevinger this stage is rare and thus difficult to study. Weathersby (1981) notes that this stage is similar to Abraham Maslow's description of the "self-actualizing person."

Although Loevinger's stages are structural, she has not explicitly defined or suggested an interventional environment that would nurture and foster such development. Loevinger (1976) is clear to point out that ego development is not an easily accomplished personality change. Erikson (1968) suggests that ego development is fostered through meaningful achievement in our culture. Sanford (1962) suggests that ego development is fostered by personal experience, new responses, and through the making of role decisions. In general, as noted by Weathersby (1981), there seem to be three basic conditions that foster ego development: very direct experiences and roles, meaningful achievement, and relative freedom from anxiety and pressure.

Loevinger's theory has stimulated a reasonable amount of research. She and her students have done cross-sectional and longitudinal studies in attempts to refine the theory and improve the instrumentation. Evidence to date indicates that at least across three cultures (the United States, Japan, and Curaçao) there seems to be a uniform sequence of stages of ego development. In addition, comparative studies correlating ego development and other cognitive developmental theories have been carried out (Rodgers, 1980).

For assessment purposes Loevinger uses the Sentence Completion Test (SC; Loevinger & Wessler, 1970). The SC assumes that there are coherent meanings in experience. Thus, operationally, the SC is primarily concerned with identifying qualitative differences in ego level. In this context the test consists of 36 incomplete sentence stems. The subject is asked to complete the sentence, and testing time is about 15 to 30 minutes. A variety of forms for girls, women, boys, and men are available in Loevinger and Wessler (1970). The test may be administered to groups, and the age range is from 11 through adulthood. The SC was developed with women, and a scoring manual is available for females. Scoring of the test requires two trained raters, and a self-training program is available in Loevinger and Wessler (1970). Norms are available for a cross section of females ranging in age from 11 to 50. Loevinger and Wessler indicate that the norms are fairly representative in terms of race, marital status, and educational and socioeconomic status. Norms and a scoring manual for males have not been published, but Loevinger and Wessler (1970) tentatively suggest adapting the scoring rules for females until a manual for males is published.

Information on the reliability and percentage agreement of raters on the total protocol ratings is reported extensively in Loevinger and Wessler (1970). In general, the interrater reliability and agreement and the internal consistency of the SC are reasonable. In addition, a highlight of the Loevinger and Wessler (1970) interrater agreement and reliability data is the performance of the self-trained raters. The median correlations for four self-trained raters with a composite trained rater were 0.78, 0.79, 0.85, and 0.76.

In terms of validity, the limited evidence suggests that the SC appears to measure a unitary dimension structure (Mines, 1982). A factor analysis (Loevinger and Wessler, 1970) indicates that the first factor correlates at 0.999 with the sum of the item ratings. In general, the cross-sectional studies suggest progressive age differences across the ego levels (Mines, 1982).

The SC is usable in assessment, evaluation, and research projects, although it has clear limitations and additional reliability and validity data are needed. As noted by Rodgers (1980), Mines (1982), and Williams and Vincent (1985) the availability of trained raters may be a problem, and the scoring task in and of itself is time consuming. Thus, refining the scoring rules would be an important advancement. In addition, change in ego development is a slow process complicating the assessment task. Finally, the conceptualization of the theory and of ego development is so broad that the instrument may not be sensitive to a variety of different variables.

Kohlberg's Theory of Moral Reasoning

Kohlberg's cognitive developmental theory of moral reasoning (1969, 1971) is an extension of Piaget's work and has stimulated considerable interest and research in moral development over the past 15 years. Kohlberg's stages of development are an invariant sequence (stages cannot be skipped) of cognitive structures (ways of thinking about things and organizing perceptions) used in analyzing and judging courses of action in moral situations. In essence, the stages represent qualitatively different ways of resolving competing claims—that is, qualitatively different organized systems of thought. Like Piaget, Kohlberg emphasizes cognitive structure rather than behavior. However, Kohlberg claims that some implications about behavior can be drawn from a person's moral reasoning. For example, the person who understands justice is more likely to practice it. Kohlberg's stages of moral reasoning are as follows (Colby, Kohlberg, Speicher, Hewer, Candee, Gibbs & Power, 1987):

1. The *heteronomous* stage: Right is blind obedience to rules and authority. The individual does right to avoid punishment and respect for authority means obedience.

2. *Individualism and instrumental purpose and exchange:* Right involves pursuing one's own and sometimes others' needs and making fair deals in terms of a concrete exchange. What is right is following rules, but when someone's immediate self-interest is involved right is acting to meet one's own interests. The thought is that other people should do the same.

3. *Mutual interpersonal expectations, relationships, and interpersonal conformity:* Right is living up to what is expected by people close to you. Being good or nice is important and means having good motives. Important characteristics in this stage are trust, loyalty, respect, and gratitude.

4. The *social system* stage: Right is doing one's duty in society, upholding the social order, and upholding the welfare of society.

5. The *social contract* stage: Right involves upholding the basic rights, values, and legal contracts of society, even when they conflict with concrete laws of one's group. This attitude is based on increased awareness of the relativity of social standards, values, and laws.

6. *Universal ethical principles:* Right involves using universal ethical principles, such as the Ten Commandments, which all humanity should follow. The equality of human rights and respect for the dignity of human beings as individual persons are particular principles of justice that should be used to generate decisions.

As individuals move through these stages they tend to reflect different orientations. The first developmental orientation is toward conformity to the requirements of social approval and the maintenance of authority. The second orientation is toward contractual obligation and the welfare of others. And the third orientation reflects the intrinsic rightness or wrongness of an act. As noted by Garsee (1980), there is no guarantee that an individual will arrive at a more advanced moral stage simply because the person reaches a certain age. Many adults continued to function in the early morality stages. The thought is that many factors in the social environment have a bearing on progression through the stages.

Kohlberg, like Piaget, suggests that the stages in the development of moral reasoning are fixed in number and order and that the stages are entered in invariable sequence. Kohlberg (1971) further suggests that the movement from one stage to the next can be encouraged through creating cognitive disequilibrium or conflict by challenging an individual with moral problems. Kohlberg believes that new ways of thinking are facilitated if the environmental challenge is one stage above the person's current stage of reasoning. In addition, the Piaget and Kohlberg perspectives suggest that social interaction and social experience are significant determinants of progression from one stage to another. The thinking is that educators, parents, and significant others can markedly accelerate advancement through the stages if they know what the stages are and what cognitive responses are appropriate for the different stages.

In general, Kohlberg suggests that the stages of moral reasoning tend to be valid across many different cultures. Evidence (Kohlberg & Wasserman, 1980) supporting this claim comes from a 20-year study of 50 Chicago-area boys, middle class and working class, initially interviewed at ages 10 through 16. This sample has been reinterviewed at three-year intervals thereafter. Other evidence (Kohlberg & Wasserman, 1980) comes from a six-year longitudinal study of Turkish village and city boys of the same age. Additional studies in the United States, Canada, Britain, Israel, Taiwan, Yucatan, Honduras, and India have to some extent supported the universal claim of the theory.

To assess moral development a variety of different tests have appeared in the literature. Colby, Kohlberg, Speicher, Hewer, Candee, Gibbs, and Power (1987) present the most recent edition of the Moral Judgment Interview (MJI). This test is a production task (oral interview) measure of stage level of moral development. The interview involves a minimum of 21 questions inquiring about the subject's reasoning regarding three moral dilemmas. An example is a man who must decide whether to break the law and steal a high-priced drug in order to save his dying's wife's life. The two standard issues pertaining to this dilemma are law and life. These samples of a person's reasoning are then rated by matching each score unit against stage criteria in a rater's manual. As noted by Rodgers (1980) the procedure is technical, difficult, and time-consuming and requires raters to be trained to conduct the interviews and rate the responses using the manuals. Rodgers (1980) suggests that it would be difficult and not very economical to use this method with large samples.

Gibbs, Widaman, and Colby (1982) developed a group administration version of Kohlberg's Moral Judgment Inventory. Like the MJI, the Social Moral Reflection Measure (SRM) is a production task assessment of moral reasoning whereby subjects express their thinking about various moral dilemmas. However, certain modifications in format and organization have been made in the SRM in order to make feasible the convenience of group administration for data collection and self-training. Evidence indicates that the SRM has acceptable concurrent validity with the MJI, as well as high levels of construct validity and reliability (interrater, test-retest, parallel forms, and internal consistency). Recently Gibbs and Basinger (1990) have revised and developed a short form of the Social Moral Reflection Measure.

Another method of assessment that has gained some prominence is the Defining Issues Test (DIT) developed by Rest (1979a,b). The DIT is a paper-and-pencil instrument that collects a different kind of data from the data obtained through Kohlberg's methods. Kohlberg's method of assessment has a person spontaneously create a sample of thinking, while the DIT has a person recognize preferred ways of thinking from a sample of responses. As noted by Rodgers (1980) it may be easier to recognize a form of reasoning than to create it. Thus, the DIT perspective suggests that a subject whose top rankings consistently go to high-stage considerations can be inferred to be developmentally more advanced in moral judgment than an individual whose top rankings go to lower-level considerations.

The DIT consists of a long form (six stories) and a short form (three stories) and may be administered to students in the ninth grade or above. Administration time for the long form is about 50 minutes and for the short form is 15 to 30 minutes. The DIT is an objectively scored inventory and may be hand scored in just a few minutes. In terms of reliability, the manual (Rest, 1979b) reports test-retest reliabilities in the 70s and 80s. However, the reliability coefficients for the specific stage scores are lower and mainly in the 50s and 60s. Validity data (Rest, 1979a,b, 1981) indicate a consistent relationship between higher levels of moral reasoning and educational level. Of interest is the fact that the correlation between moral judgment scores and education has been consistently higher than the correlation between moral reasoning and age (Kitchener, 1982). Rest (1981) also found that students who do not live at home show larger increases in moral judgment scores than do those who remain at home while attending college. Other data show that the DIT and the MJI have correlated 0.68 with a heterogeneously aged population and 0.57 with an adult sample. In addition, the DIT has correlations of 0.20 to 0.50 with measures of cognitive development and intelligence. In summary, the reliability and validity data suggest that the DIT is a solid measure of moral reasoning. However, as noted by Rodgers (1980) and Mines (1982) there are advantages and disadvantages. Clear advantages are that the DIT may be group administered and computer or hand scored. Hence, individual interviewing and assessment training are not necessary. On the other hand, the DIT, like many of the cognitive stage instruments, has difficulty assessing the specific stage characteristics related to moral reasoning. The development of assessment techniques that reflect these stage-specific changes are needed to effectively evaluate social cognitive stage change (Mines, 1982). Whether or not the DIT responses can be used as an adequate substitute for a spontaneously created moral reasoning response remains an empirical question. In any event, as noted in reviews by McCrae (1985) and Moreland (1985) the DIT is the result of careful thought both about moral development and test construction. It is supported by solid construct validity studies, and it shows promise of playing a significant role in the investigation of moral development.

Other assessment methods being developed include the Ethical Reasoning Inventory (ERI; Page & Bode, 1980). This is a paper-and-pencil instrument that consists of the six standardized dilemmas published in Kohlberg's scoring manuals. Each question is followed by two responses and sets of reasons for supporting those responses. The supporting reasons represent various stages of Kohlberg's theory. The ERI takes about 50 minutes to administer and may be used in group situations.

Perry's Theory of Cognitive Development

Of interest for individuals working with college populations is Perry's (1970) theory of cognitive development. It is based upon interview data acquired from Harvard University undergraduates from 1954 to 1968 In essence, Perry and his colleagues traced the changes in students' ways of perceiving knowledge and values during the college years. Like Kohlberg and Loevinger, Perry focuses upon the students' internal cognitive structure in his description of development. The theory conceptualizes nine internal structures, which Perry calls "positions" rather than "stages" and which tend to influence how the individual will perceive, organize, and evaluate events and activities in the environment. Perry views intellectual development as occurring for the most part in an irreversible sequence of positions in which each position represents a qualitatively different structure for perceiving the meaning of knowledge in situations. The thinking is that individuals who are at different positions will reflect those differences in their approaches to learning.

According to Perry (1970), the nine positions may be grouped into three general categories: dualism, relativism, and commitment. Each category consists of three positions. The three positions in "dualism" and the three positions in "relativism" are considered to be primarily structural positions. The three positions in "commitment" are more affective kinds of positions that reflect the process of living through commitment. Perry suggests that students pass through the nine major positions in their intellectual and ethical developments. In the main, students move from a simplistic view to a more complex perspective. The scheme is summarized below.

The dualistic perspective (positions 1, 2, and 3) represents people who assume that all information can be classified as either right or wrong and that uncertainty or ambiguity is an error of some sort. Students at these positions view learning as a matter of finding the right answers. All information is either right or wrong. Individuals developmentally located at position 2 have a similar perspective and in addition view uncertainty as an error committed by a wrong authority. Individuals at position 3 again view all information as either right or wrong, but uncertainty is acceptable in areas where experts do not yet know the answers. The belief held here at this position is that some day the right answer will be found.

The next three positions (4, 5, and 6) represent a relativistic structure for viewing knowledge and values. As the individual moves through these positions absolute right-or-wrong conceptions of knowledge and values are modified. Uncertainty becomes legitimate and knowledge is seen as uncertain or valid only within a context. However, students may continue to ask, "How do I live if there are no right answers?" More specifically, individuals at position 4 tend to view knowledge as pervasively uncertain. Ideas are of equal value, opinions are important, but no one has the right answers. Individuals at position 5 tend to view knowledge as contextual or situational. If this is the case, people ask, "What am I to be, to do, and to value?" In position 6 personal commitment becomes more important. The individual views life and values as emerging as commitments are made.

Positions 7, 8, and 9 make up the commitment category. The changes in these last three positions are affective rather than structural. Thus, the individual's assumption about knowledge is and continues to be relativistic. During the commitment process Perry found two different dimensions, one involving selecting a career and the other involving defining a style of identity. For example, in position 7 the individual makes a commitment in some area or career. In position 8 the individual realizes that commitment involves responsibility. In defining identity one must assume the responsibility for that identity. In position 9 the individual experiences an affirmation of identity and responsibility and further realizes that commitment is an ongoing process of expressing life style.

In general, Perry's views on cognitive development are consistent with the cognitive developmental orientation. Although the theory was developed using only Harvard students, extensions of this work, according to Rodgers (1980), have now been carried out at the University of Maryland, Ohio State University, and the University of Minnesota. More recently, Perry and others have explored the processes of developmental change and found that the variables fostering transition to a new position may be position-specific. Perry (1970) found that the advancement of dualists resulted from outright confrontation with diversity. However, relativists needed a sense of community support in moving to commitment. Widick, Knefelkamp, and Parker (1975) identified some general environmental design varia-

bles for generating development for dualists and relativists. They found that dualistic-thinking students tended to be supported by environments that were highly structured and that had limited degrees of freedom and warm personal atmospheres. In addition, dualistic students seem to be challenged by environments that introduced moderate diversity and emphasized experiential learning. Relativistic-thinking students showed more growth in environments with extensive degrees of freedom, less structure, and genuine and warm interpersonal relationships. These students seemed to like diversity, commitment, and indirect vicarious learning experiences.

For assessment purposes King (1978) points out that over eight different assessment methods have been used to determine the cognitive development position scores corresponding to Perry's theory. The original interview method continues to be used to extend Perry's work, but it is time consuming, particularly in applied kinds of situations.

A more practical solution to the assessment problem is the paper-and-pencil measure introduced by Knefelkamp (1974) and Widick (1975). Their instrument is called the Measure of Intellectual Development (MID) and focuses on the intellectual assets of the Perry model (positions 1 through 5). The MID, as noted by Mines (1982), is designed to assess cognitive stage level in decision making, careers, and classroom learning. The instrument samples a person's thinking and position through responses to five sentence stems and two of three possible essays. Responses are then scored by trained raters using a written set of protocols and examples. Standardized normative data are not currently available, but the instrument has been used with a variety of different groups.

Reliability studies have correlated the MID with interview ratings and external experts' responses. Interrater reliability data are also available. Correlations are moderate and in general range from a low of 0.42 to a high of 0.93. Validity evidence correlating the MID with the Defining Issues Test is not clear. Meyer's (1977) work found a correlation of 0.45, but the work of Wertheimer (1980) found a correlation of 0.13. The MID correlated 0.30 with a measure of ego development (Wertheimer, 1980). Findings from some general cross-sectional studies (Mines, 1982) indicate that freshmen tend to be largely in transition between positions 2 and 3 and juniors and seniors tend to be in transition between positions 3 and 4. In addition, work summarized by Moore (1982) indicates expected freshmen/senior differences predicted by the Perry model.

Finally, experimental studies summarized by Mines (1982) found that the MID successfully identified differential gains in the theoretically predicted direction as a result of developmentally designed classroom experiences. In summary, the MID produces essay responses that are rich data and that can be consistently scored by trained raters with a reasonable percentage of agreement (Mines, 1982). Furthermore, the MID may be administered in a group situation. However, major liabilities of the instrument are its scoring system and the time and expense of learning to use the scoring system (Mines, 1982; Rodgers, 1980).

In addition, as noted by Mines (1982) the scoring system does not seem to represent the complexity of stage interaction. In spite of limitations, the MID does seem to be a more efficient method for collecting data in applied settings within the Perry theory. However, additional validity work is needed.

Another assessment technique partially based on the Perry model is the Reflective Judgment Interview (RJI) developed by Kitchener (1977) and King (1977). The Kitchener and King RJI is a semistructured interview producing responses that provide a description of the subject's intellectual stage functioning. The interview takes about one hour and involves verbally presenting four social dilemmas while the subject follows along on an identical written copy. After each dilemma is read the interviewer asks a series of standard probe questions. It is recommended that the subject's responses be tape-recorded, transcribed, and subsequently rated by blind (independent and unknowing) certified raters. Kitchener and King insist that individuals using the RJI have certified interviewers and raters in order to assure comparability of results across different studies.

The RJI has been developed using high school, college, and graduate student populations, but currently no normative data have been made available. In terms of reliability, the evidence generally suggests that the RJI has adequate reliability and good interrater agreement. Overall interjudge reliability across five studies varies from a low of 0.53 to a high of 0.96. In terms of validity, cross-sectional work by Kitchener and King (1981) found support for the age and education trend in the theoretically predicted direction. A longitudinal study by King, Kitchener, Davison, Parker, and Wood (1982) revealed stage changes in the appropriate direction. However, additional validity data are clearly needed. Limitations noted by Rodgers (1980) and Mines (1982) include the need for trained raters and a fairly cumbersome scoring system.

In addition, according to Rodgers (1980) to date there are no studies correlating to RJI and the MID. Such a correlation study may be informative about these assessment techniques and the Perry model. As noted by Mines (1982) no objective measure of reflective judgment currently exists. However, two groups of researchers at the University of Minnesota and Bowling Green State University are attempting to develop objective format tests.

Finally, additional reliability and validity data on the RJI would seem to be of value. The RJI does have heuristic value, but probably what is needed is an instrument that is capable of assessing stage specificity in a reliable and valid manner.

The Parker Cognitive Development Inventory (PCDI) (Parker & Hood, 1986) was developed to produce an objectively scored measure of cognitive development according to the Perry theory. Initially the plan was to develop an inventory that would assess each of the Perry nine positions. However, reliability estimates (alpha coefficients of internal consistency) were quite low for a number of the positional subscales and this strategy was abandoned. Because of the low reliability estimates for a number of the subscales, the decision was made to reorganize the subscales into the three more general positional groupings described by Perry: Dualism (positions 1, 2, 3), Relativism (positions 4 to 6), and Commitment in Relativism (positions 7 to 9). Alpha coefficients for the three positional subscales and the three content scales (Education, Career, and Religion) ranged from a low of 0.81 to high of 0.92. The current form of the PCDI consists of 144 items. The PCDI contains items in three different content areas (Education, Career, and Religion), and according to Perry's theory, an individual's cognitive developmental position (Dualism, Relativism, and Commitment) should be fairly similar across content areas (Parker & Hood, 1986).

Perry's scheme does seem to be useful in the designing of learning environments in a variety of content areas. For example, the scheme would seem to be useful in designing interventions for choice of career, conflict management, commitments to life style of values, and college orientation. However, without question we need to identify behavior patterns that are indicative of different developmental positions. The behavior of students and individuals in a variety of situations needs to be observed and described. Knowledge of the internal characteristics and behavioral patterns associated with the different positions would add significantly to the reliability and validity of assessing the developmental process.

PSYCHOSOCIAL THEORY

The cognitive development theories discussed above are primarily concerned with the "how," or processes, of development. The psychosocial theories to be discussed in this section, on the other hand, are concerned with the "what," or content, of development. Whereas cognitive developmental theory examines our structures for making meaning of our experience, psychosocial theory integrates feelings, behavior, and thinking into a complex picture of the life span (Hansen, 1982; Rodgers, 1980; Parker, 1978). Thus, psychosocial theory examines the various personal preoccupations of the life cycle, such as "Who am I? Who am I to love? What am I to believe?"

Like the cognitive developmental theories, the psychosocial theories use some basic concepts that need discussion. These concepts include *stage, developmental crisis, developmental task,* and *developmental coping skills.* A *stage* is defined as a period of time during which the individual faces and resolves (either adequately or inadequately) a *developmental crisis* and its *developmental tasks.* A stage starts when an internal change (psychological in nature, physiological in nature, or both) triggers an internal crisis for a person. This internal crisis must now deal with an external societal demand causing a developmental crisis. In order for the person to get through the developmental crisis, certain developmental tasks must be dealt with. Developmental tasks are the problematic issues that a person needs to resolve in a given stage before the next stage and its tasks may begin.

Or, stated differently, life is in some respects divided into periods (stages) that are marked by a concern with, and a need to accomplish, certain tasks. These tasks (such as developing new attitudes and skills) become important because of physiological maturation and social expectations.

For example, the college student asking "Who am I?" must resolve the problematic issues of identity—career, values, and life style. An adequate resolution of this developmental task is a favorable balance toward an identity and will help one cope with tasks in future stages. An inadequate resolution of this task is a balance in favor of role confusion. Thus, an adequate resolution suggests some kind of favorable ratio or favorable balance, rather than an all-or-nothing kind of closure. Inadequate resolutions of developmental tasks tend to lead to inordinate stress, maladaptive behavior, and a decrease in the probability of resolving the tasks of future stages adequately.

Finally, individuals with more highly developed *coping skills* tend to more effectively deal and resolve developmental tasks. For example, our college student with career, value, and life style identity problems will tend to cope with these developmental issues more effectively if the student has learned decision-making skills.

Before reviewing some individual theories of psychosocial development, we need to discuss just how developmental change takes place. To do this we need to discuss three broad concepts of psychosocial change. The first concept is *epigenesis*. This is Erikson's (1968) term for the whole process of personality development throughout the life cycle. The second concept is *developmental* or *optimum dissonance*. This term is suggestive of the right amount of tension to produce change. The third concept, *challenge-support*, is primarily concerned with the amount of challenge and support needed to facilitate personality change.

The epigenetic principle states that anything that grows has a ground plan and that out of this ground plan the parts arise, each part having its time of special ascendency, until all parts form a functioning whole (Erikson, 1968). According to Erikson this process operates like an "internal clock," and at the right time each successive stage of development unfolds. Unlike the cognitive developmental changes that have to be stimulated by cognitive conflict, these psychosocial changes supposedly occur automatically at the time of their ascendency. The new stages tend to unfold at their assigned times whether the individual is ready or not. In addition, the ground plan, or the internal clock, has a biological part and a psychological part. In childhood and adolescence, the biological part seems to be dominant. In early and middle adulthood the psychological pressures for change tend to trigger the adult stages.

The concept of developmental dissonance is primarily concerned with the right amount of tension to produce change. Both cognitive developmental theorists and psychosocial theorists suggest that change involves a period of disequilibrium, anxiety, and dissonance that results in the establishment of a new stage. Sanford (1963) further suggests that if there is too much dissonance individuals will tend to regress to an earlier, less adaptive behavior, to harden their current behavior, to escape the dissonance or challenge, or to ignore the challenge. If there is too little dissonance or challenge individuals may feel safe and secure. These conditions are not conducive for psychosocial development. Thus, the goal becomes one of finding the range of developmental dissonance appropriate to the individual.

The challenge-support dimension is primarily concerned with facilitating personality change. Sanford (1963) notes that change is facilitated through the two processes of challenge and support. Psychosocial development or growth is difficult without challenge, and the amount of challenge we can tolerate is a function of the support available. The current thinking is that if solid appropriate support is available, then the amount of challenge or dissonance may be increased. Now let us discuss a few psychological theories of human development and their implications for assessment.

Erikson's Psychosocial Theory

Erikson (1968) laid the groundwork for many of the other psychosocial theories. In essence, Erikson's theory is a refinement and extension of Freud's theory. Erikson viewed psychosocial development in terms of its dependence on the interaction with others. He believed, unlike Freud, that personality continues to develop through the life cycle. He stressed the need for social integration in place of Freud's infantile sexuality, believing that an individual's social view of self is more important than his or her sexual and aggressive urges. Whereas Freud looked for the origin of pathology, Erikson searched for components that were conducive to growth. Erikson argued that personality development does not end with childhood, but continues throughout the life span. From this perspective Erikson recognized eight stages of development that continue into the adult years. However, partial resolution of each of eight psychosocial crises was essential to passing through the eight stages of development. Thus, Erikson proposed a core task for each phase, a basic virtue that developed with successful resolution, and the negative counterpart of unsuccessful resolution.

Each of Erikson's eight stages of growth for humans has a basic task and a negative counterpart. In each stage two opposing forces cause a crisis and demand a resolution. Adequate resolution facilitates the advancement to the next stage. However, unsuccessful or inadequate resolution may be resolved later in life under more favorable conditions. Erikson further believed that a basic virtue developed with the successful resolution of each stage. The eight stages, with their basic tasks, negative counterparts, and basic virtues, are listed below.

> Trust versus mistrust (hope)
> Autonomy versus shame/doubt (willpower)
> Initiative versus guilt (purpose)
> Industry versus inferiority (competence)
> Identity versus identity confusion (fidelity)
> Intimacy versus isolation (love)
> Generativity versus stagnation (care)
> Integrity versus despair (wisdom)

In terms of assessment, Erikson's techniques varied from watching children play with toys to being a participant observer among Native American tribes. For example, he is well known for his psychohistorical approach to prominent people, which involved incorporating other people's perceptions of their own lives into his accounts of them. Marcia (1966) developed an instrument and structured interview for measuring Erikson's stages of identity. This matrix of identity concepts (identity achievement, moratorium, identity foreclosed, and identity diffused), according to Rodgers (1980), may be useful in studying college students. Dignan (1965) also developed a paper-and-pencil instrument for measuring identity called the Ego Identity Scale (EIS). The EIS consists of the items considered to be indicative of aspects of identity. A single score is obtained that suggests favorable or unfavorable resolution of identity tasks. The Inventory of Psychosocial Development (IPD) was developed by Constantinople (1969) for assessing all of Erikson's stages. The IPD consists of 60 items with five positive and five negative responses to assess each stage. Individuals respond to each item on a 1-through-7 Likert-type scale, indicating how characteristic the item is of themselves. The inventory may then be scored for each stage.

Erikson is a very influential psychosocial theorist. His work has been extremely influential in psychology and education. There is no question that Erikson has been the stimulus and inspiration for many other psychosocial theorists who have clarified and made more explicit the developmental stages of the life span.

Chickering's Psychosocial Theory

Chickering's psychosocial theory (Chickering, 1969, 1974) in the main is an elaboration of Erikson's stages of identity and intimacy. Based on his research on college students from 13 liberal arts colleges and the works of others, Chickering developed a theory that made some of Erikson's stages more explicit. His theory focuses on the age range of 17 to 25 and is constructed mainly from his research on college students.

From the ages of 17 to 25, Chickering hypothesized, seven vectors to development ascend in the lives of college students. (What most psychosocial theorists call "developmental tasks" Chickering prefers to call "vectors.") These seven vectors are developing competence, managing emotions, developing autonomy, establishing identity, freeing interpersonal relationships, developing purpose, and developing integrity. According to Chickering, the first three vectors (developing competence, managing emotions, and developing autonomy) tend to ascend simultaneously and before the other four. Chickering further suggests that progress toward the favorable and adequate resolution of these three vectors is necessary before the next vector (identity) can be undertaken in a productive and healthy way. The identity vector serves to integrate the first three vectors in terms of sexual orientation, body acceptance, and knowing the kinds of experiences one prefers. In essence, the individual develops an identity.

Development and progress on the first four vectors lays the groundwork for the last three vectors (freeing interpersonal relationships, developing purpose, and developing integrity), all three of which again tend to occur simultaneously. The individual moves toward the favorable resolution of the vectors as he or she approaches the age of 25 years. Thus, during their junior and senior college years many students are beginning to develop a depth of understanding in relationships with significant others, to integrate their vocational choices and life styles, and to develop a consistency between values and actual behavior. In sum, Chickering's conceptualizations tend to be more explicit than Erikson's and therefore probably more useful in the area of college student development.

In the beginning the Omnibus Personality Inventory (OPI) was used to assess some of Chickering's vectors. Chickering simply had judges identify the OPI scales that seemed to appropriately measure the different vectors. If in the main the judges agreed, the scale was subsequently used for assessment purposes.

Major instrument construction has been carried out by Winston, Miller, and Prince (1979) in their development of the Student Development Task Inventory–2 (SDTI-2). The SDTI-2 focuses on the behavioral aspects of the developmental tasks and at this point in time is probably the most sophisticated data-based inventory for the assessment of some of Chickering's vectors. The SDTI-2 is primarily concerned with the assessment of Chickering's vectors of developing autonomy, developing mature interpersonal relationships, and developing purpose. In context the inventory represents a sample of behaviors that students can be expected to demonstrate when they have satisfactorily achieved certain developmental tasks (Winston, Miller, & Prince, 1979). To assess the three vectors (autonomy, interpersonal relationships, and purpose) 140 items are marked "true" or "false" and scored on three subtasks within each of the three developmental domains. The inventory may be administered individually or in groups and takes about 20 to 30 minutes to complete. The inventory was designed to assess behaviors related to task resolution for individuals between the ages of 17 and 23 years. The idea is that mastery of the behavioral subtasks will supposedly lead to a favorable resolvement of the basic vectors.

Norms are not available, but the authors (Winston, Miller, & Prince, 1979) indicate that the SDTI-2 is to be used primarily with individual students, thus reducing the need for established norms. The manual reports two-week test-retest liability correlations for the scales ranging from 0.85 to 0.93. However, the alpha coefficients for the nine subscales ranged from 0.45 to 0.78, suggesting that the subscales need to be interpreted with caution. Validity data as noted by Winston, Miller, and Prince (1979) and Mines (1982) indicate that correlations between the SDTI-2 scales and the subscales of the College Student Questionnaire (Study Habits, Family Independence, and Peer Independence) tend to be in the theoretically predicted direction.

In addition, the SDTI-2 scales successfully differentiated among active daters, nondaters, joiners, and social isolates living in the residence halls. For example, joiners and active daters scored higher on the Developing Mature Interpersonal Relationships Scale than did the nondaters and social isolates. Finally, scales of the Career Development Inventory (Crystallization, Specification, and Implementation) correlated to some extent (low-moderate) with the Developing Purpose and Developing Autonomy scales of the SDTI-2.

The SDTI-2 underwent a major revision that was published in 1987. The revised inventory is called the Student Developmental Task and Lifestyle Inventory (SDTLI)

(Winston, Miller, & Prince, 1987). Motivation for the revision was based upon a number of factors (Winston & Miller, 1987). Research had called into question the scale structure of the SDTI-2. Furthermore, there were objections about the exclusive emphasis on heterosexual relationships. Finally, experience with the instrument suggested the need to address areas previously not included in the SDTI-2. For example, the SDTI-2 did not include participation in cultural activities, attention to health and wellness issues, and identification of response bias.

In its current form the SDTLI represents a sample of behaviors and reports of feelings and attitudes that students can be expected to demonstrate when they have satisfactorily achieved certain developmental tasks common to young adult college students (Winston & Miller, 1987). The SDTLI is composed of 140 true/false items and requires 25 to 30 minutes to complete. The inventory consists of items characterizing three basic developmental tasks and three scales (Winston & Miller, 1987): establishing and clarifying purpose task, developing mature interpersonal relationships task, developing academic autonomy task, salubrious life style scale, intimacy scale, and response bias scale. Two of the tasks are further defined by subtasks. A subtask is defined as a more specific component of a larger developmental task. The establishing and clarifying purpose task is made up of the following subtasks: educational involvement, career planning, life style planning, life management, and cultural participation. The developing mature interpersonal relationships task is composed of the tolerance, peer relationships, and emotional autonomy subtasks.

In the SDTLI, Winston and Miller (1987) indicate that tasks and subtasks are differentially affected by participation in the Academic Environment, Personality Development, and Person-Environment Transactions. A scale on the SDTLI as noted by Winston and Miller (1987) is the measure of the degree to which students report possessing certain behavioral characteristics and attitudes, but unlike a developmental task may not be directly influenced by participation in the higher education environment. As we noted above a developmental task is defined as an interrelated set of behaviors and attitudes that the culture specifies should be exhibited at a certain age. The idea is that successful achievement of a developmental task allows the individual to acquire the experiential base needed to achieve further developmental tasks (Winston & Miller, 1987).

Normative data were collected from undergraduates (age 17 to 24) enrolled at 20 different colleges in the United States and Canada. As noted above, a characteristic of a developmental task in the SDTLI is that more seniors than freshmen answered each item in the keyed direction (Winston & Miller, 1987). Thus, norms are provided by academic class standing.

The manual reports two-week and four-week test-retest reliability coefficients. Test-retest coefficients clustered around 0.80 with the lowest being 0.70 and the highest being 0.88 for the four-week correlations and 0.74 and 0.89 for the two-week correlations (Winston & Miller, 1987). Alpha coefficients were somewhat more variable and ranged from a high of 0.90 for the establishing and clarifying purpose task to a low of 0.50 for the five-item response bias scale. A number of validity studies are noted in the manual (Winston & Miller, 1987) and are organized and discussed according to the three developmental tasks and the three scales. In general, these studies suggest that the developmental tasks and scales demonstrate reasonable concurrent validity.

A number of instruments focusing on Chickering's theory have been developed at the University of Iowa and are summarized in a volume by Albert Hood (1986). The University of Iowa instruments (the Iowa Student Development Inventories) are in many respects in the preliminary stages of development, but they do show considerable promise.

The Developing Competency Inventory (Hood & Jackson, 1986a) is made up of three subscales: Self Confidence, Competence in Math, and Competency in Writing. High alpha reliabilities were found for each of the subscales and for the total inventory ranging from 0.91 to 0.96 (Hood & Jackson, 1986a). The total inventory is made up of 70 items.

The Iowa Managing Emotions Inventory (Hood & Jackson, 1986c) contains 60 items and is made up of five subscales of 12 items each. Each subscale deals with a particular type of emotion: Depression, Anger, Frustration, Happiness, and Attraction. The alpha reliability for the total inventory of 60 items was 0.95 (Hood & Jackson, 1986c). Hood and Jackson (1986c) further note that the subscales on the Managing Emotions Inventory are measuring essentially the same factor and that little is gained by separating out the individual subscales.

The Iowa Developing Autonomy Inventory (Hood & Jackson, 1986b) is made up of 90 items divided into six 15-item subscales: Mobility, Time Management, Money Management, Interdependency, Emotional Independence Regarding Peers, and Emotional Independence Regarding Parents. The total inventory had an alpha reliability coefficient of 0.94. The total score on the inventory correlated 0.50 with student age and 0.43 with a student's class in college (Hood & Jackson, 1986b). These correlations suggest that students tend to become more autonomous as they get older and move through the college years.

The Erwin Identity Scale (Erwin, 1979; Hood, 1986) attempts to measure identity through three subscales (Confidence, Sexual

Identity, and Conceptions About Body and Appearance). The inventory is made up of 58 items. However, as noted by Rodgers (1980), an analysis of the conceptual content of the subscales indicates that they may be measuring parts of four different vectors as conceptualized by Chickering. White (1986) reported alpha reliability coefficients of 0.80 to 0.85 for the subscales and 0.91 for the total scale. For 55 students retested during the first semester of their freshmen year, a significant increase was found on the Confidence subscale and a significant decrease on the Conceptions About Body and Appearance subscale (White, 1986).

The Mines-Jensen Interpersonal Relationships Inventory (Mines, 1978; Hood & Mines, 1986) is an attitudinal measure of Chickering's freeing interpersonal relationships vector. The inventory consists of 42 items that represent four content areas (Peers, Adults, Friends, and Significant Others) on two scales (the Tolerance scale and the Quality of Relationships scale). The Tolerance scale consists of 20 items and the Quality of Relationships scale contains 22 items. The items on the two scales seem to reflect reasonably and accurately Chickering's conceptualizations. Alpha reliabilities for 168 freshmen were 0.65 for the tolerance scale and 0.68 for the Quality of Relationships scale.

The Developing Purposes Inventory (Barratt & Hood, 1986) is primarily concerned with assessing Chickering's vector of developing purpose. The current form of the inventory contains three 15-item scales designed to measure each of the three subvectors of developing purpose: a Vocational/Recreational Purpose, Vocational Purpose, and Style of Life. The items seem appropriate, and the inventory has been used with some success on college freshmen and seniors. Additional reliability and validity data are needed, however.

In summary, the essence of Chickering's work is that what goes on during the college years in terms of human development is important. In addition, Chickering is interested in exploring the relationship between college-environment conditions and human development, which he considers significant.

Levinson's Theory of Adult Male Development

Since 1974 a number of theories of adult development have appeared. Levinson, Darrow, Klein, Levinson, and McKee (1978) focus on the development of men across cultural and social economic types. They have conducted a series of longitudinal studies using the Thematic Apperception Test (TAT) and a biographical interview assessment method. Levinson and his colleagues are primarily interested in what are called "life structures." A life structure is an underlying pattern of life made up of career, love relationships, marriage and family, relationships with self, uses of solitude, roles in social context, and relationships with individuals, groups, and institutions. In general, life structures are concerned with relationships between the self and the world.

The adult years from age 17 to post-70 have been the field of study for Levinson. According to Levinson, this major portion of the male life span is made up of a sequence of transitional periods that last four to five years and stable periods that last five to ten years. The transitional periods are times when existing life structures are reviewed and evaluated and new possibilities and options are explored. The outcomes of transition are the commitments or choices that are made during that time period. Periods of stability, then, are times for consolidating a new life structure and pursuing goals and values within that structure. According to Levinson, the traits of transition periods and stable periods are functions of a variety of developmental tasks that are fairly common to most men in our culture. However, these developmental tasks are experienced in a variety of different ways by adult males and may be resolved either positively or negatively.

The names of Levinson's transitional and stable periods are summarized below: early-adult transition or leaving the family, ages 17 to 22; entering the adult world, ages 23 to 28; age-30 transition, ages 29 to 33; settling down, ages 34 to 40; midlife transition, ages 41 to 45; entering middle adulthood, ages 46 to 50; age 50 transition, ages 51 to 55; culmination of middle adulthood, ages 56 to 60; late-adult transition, ages 61 to 65; and 70-plus. These transitional and stable periods are in need of substantial study in order to be more informative about the male life span and adult development process. Assessment to date has been primarily through the interview method. Clearly other assessment techniques need to be developed.

SUMMARY

This chapter has reviewed the cognitive developmental and psychosocial theories of human development. The cognitive developmental theories are primarily concerned with how we make meaning from our experience. On the other hand, psychosocial theories tend to focus on the content of experience and the developmental tasks of the life span. Both groups of theories tend to emphasize stress or conflict when they consider developmental change. If the individual does not experience conflict, dissonance, or incongruent situations that are difficult to cope with, then the individual will probably not grow and develop. Conflict and dissonance (but not too much and with support) are needed to challenge the cognitive and psychosocial human development process. In general, then, the theories discussed in this chapter are primarily concerned with the development among young and old of increasingly complex concepts of logic, knowledge, self, relationships, and morality. These conceptual systems, as noted by Kitchener (1982), are very meaningful because they provide the framework through which the individual understands the world, the self, relationships with others, and the nature of problem solving.

14

Professional and Ethical Standards and Social Issues in Assessment

INTRODUCTION

Educational and psychological testing and assessment represent one of the most important contributions of behavioral science to the understanding and solution of applied problems. As described in previous chapters of this book, the significant uses of psychological tests and assessments are many—from assisting individuals in the process of educational and vocational decision making to helping schools and businesses in the effective selection and placement of new students and employees. Tests and assessments have had tremendous utility for individuals, for organizations, and for a society concerned with the development and nurturance of individual potential and the facilitation of productivity and high quality of life.

Although the various tests described in this book have tremendous applied utility, there are potential dangers as well as benefits in the use of tests, just as there are in other types of sophisticated knowledge and technology. As an example, consider the relatively new field of genetic engineering: Knowledge in this field could be used in very positive ways—in the cure of cancer or the elimination of birth defects, for example—or it could be used in negative ways—perhaps, to make all people alike. Similarly, advanced computer technology has untold numbers of positive uses but has also been used in sophisticated computer thefts of both money and high technology. Thus, science and technology in general and psychology and psychological tests in particular can be used both wisely, to the overall benefit of people, and unwisely, in ways that do not contribute to the overall welfare of the individuals involved.

Psychologists and other test specialists have long been aware of the possibility of misuse of tests and test scores and have therefore formulated ethical and professional standards designed to ensure that tests are used appropriately, effectively, and fairly. First, the ethical principles of the American Psychological Association (APA) were originally developed in 1953 to ensure the ethical practice of psychology and the protection of the rights and welfare of the individual consumer of psychological services (American Psychological Association, 1981). Many of these ethical principles pertain to the use of psychological tests and assessments. Second, although a general set of ethical statements concerning test use was thus available,

the American Educational Research Association (AERA), the APA, and the National Council on Measurement in Education (NCME) have formulated a much more specific set of professional *Standards for Educational and Psychological Testing* (AERA, 1985), by which the *quality* of psychological tests and assessments may be evaluated and by which the *effectiveness* and *fairness* of test use in specific situations may be judged. Because these standards were developed specifically to control the quality of tests and the care with which tests are used, they offer essential information beyond that provided by the more general ethical principles.

In the first part of this chapter, ethical and professional considerations in the selection and use of psychological tests and assessments will be discussed. For each area of consideration discussed here, the relevant APA ethical principles and APA/AERA/NCME test standards will be described, along with additional considerations based on sound professional judgment and respect for individuals.

The second part of this chapter addresses issues involved in the use of tests for specific purposes and with specific types of people. The issues addressed include cultural and racial biases, sex bias, the use of tests for employment selection, scholastic aptitude testing, and educational classification and placement, and minimum competency testing.

ETHICAL AND PROFESSIONAL STANDARDS FOR TESTS AND TEST USE

Quality of Tests and Test Materials

The first and most fundamental consideration in using tests and assessments is that the tests and assessment devices be of high technical quality and be accompanied by enough information that a test user can effectively evaluate, administer, use, and interpret them. Concern about the quality of tests and accompanying test materials dates back to 1895, when the first APA committee on mental measurements was formed. Table 14.1, adapted from a review by Novick (1981), details several key events in the development of professional standards for tests and test use. Among other things, this development included the growth and maintenance of an effective cooperation among several professional organizations involved in the development and use of educational and psychological tests, the APA, the AERA, and the NCME.

Thus, a major purpose of the test standards was to provide guidelines for the *quality* of tests and test materials. Standards for test quality must be observed by test developers in constructing the test, by test publishers before distributing the test, and by test users in evaluating and selecting tests. There are a number of dimensions along which test quality may be evaluated. Adhering to the test standards (AERA, APA, NCME, 1985), the following dimensions of quality may be addressed: (1) reliability and measurement error; (2) test validation; (3) test development and revision; (4) norming, scaling, test comparability, and equating; (5) test publication, technical manuals, and user guides; and (6) test administration, scoring, and use.

In stating the criteria by which to evaluate test quality, the authors of the standards have classified them as either *primary standards* or *secondary standards*. Primary standards are those that should be met by *all* published or marketed tests; the only tests exempt from these standards would be teacher-made tests or tests used only in research. Secondary standards are those which are desirable in some testing situations but may not be feasible to require in other testing situations.

Elaborating on the dimensions of test quality, the concept of *reliability* and its importance as a criterion for a good test were discussed extensively in Chapter 3. The test standards themselves emphasize that, if possible, the establishment of the reliability of a test should include all the methods of studying reliability that were discussed in

TABLE 14.1 Key Events in the Development of Testing Standards Within Psychology and Education

1895	The American Psychological Association (APA) formed the first committee on mental measurement to facilitate standardization in measurement.
1906	An APA committee on measurements was appointed to standardized testing techniques.
1916, 1921	Symposia published in the *Journal of Educational Psychology* urged care and caution in the use of intelligence tests.
1938	First edition of O. K. Buros's *Mental Measurements Yearbook* provided extensive information for the selection, evaluation, and use of tests.
1954	*Technical Recommendations for Psychological Tests and Diagnostic Techniques,* prepared by the APA, provided initial guidelines concerning the evaluation of tests (e.g., validity, reliability, use of scales and norms) and stressed the importance of an informative manual accompanying a test.
1955	*Technical Recommendations for Achievement Tests,* prepared by the American Educational Research Association (AERA) and the National Council on Measurement in Education (NCME).
1966	*Standards for Educational and Psychological Measurement,* prepared by the APA, the AERA, and the NCME, improved the technical basis for studies of validity and reliability.
1974	*Standards for Educational and Psychological Tests,* prepared by the AERA, the APA, and the NCME, responds to 1970 United States Equal Employment Opportunity Commission guidelines and other concerns of test misuse and bias and race and sex discrimination. (The current edition of these standards was published in 1984.)
1985	*Joint Technical Standards for Educational and Psychological Testing*

SOURCE: Compiled from Novick, *American Psychologist,* 36 (1981), 1035–46.

Chapter 3—alternate forms, internal consistency, and test-retest stability. All of these methods of estimating reliability are important to supporting a test's reliability for applied purposes. In addition to evidence for reliability, information regarding the standard error of measurement should be reported in enough scope and detail to enable the test user to judge whether scores are sufficiently dependable for the intended uses of the test.

Along with evidence for its reliability, a test should be shown to possess validity for the intended uses. As was discussed in Chapter 3, several different kinds of evidence are pertinent to the establishment of a test's validity; the three basic types of validity evidence are construct validity, content validity, and criterion-related validity. The test standards emphasize the importance of all three types of validity and of studying the validity of a test within the context of theory development and explication. Therefore the standards, like the present text, emphasize the importance of viewing psychological tests and assessment instruments as occurring within the context of psychological theory. The standards emphasize that all three components of validity are important and that, ideally, evidence for a test's validity should include evidence from all three types of validity.

Standards pertaining to test development and revision are designed to ensure that test developers use both expertise and care in their methods of test construction and that they revise their tests periodically to ensure that test content continues to be relevant and appropriate for the purposes for which the test is used. In addition, these standards specify that the test developers and publishers are responsible for the provision of a test manual describing the methods of construction and revision, data regarding reliability and validity, and other informa-tion needed for effective and accurate test interpretation.

Another dimension of test quality pertains to the available of scales, norms, and other means of interpreting test scores. Methods of scoring the test should be carefully described, and normative, criterion-referenced, or other methods of comparative interpretation of test scores should be provided. In addition, as new forms of a test are developed, information concerning methods of comparing or equating scores across forms may be necessary. The normative data provided should be clearly described in terms of the population from which they come and should be the same groups of people with whom the test is designed to be used.

Standards regarding test publication, technical materials, and user guides emphasize the importance of published, or at least widely available, information about a test. Further, that information should provide a clear description of to what extent and in what manner the test has met the other test standards. The importance of information is based on the idea of *informed consent*—that is, anyone interested in using a test should be provided with complete information by which she or he can evaluate its quality and potential utility. This complete information is best provided in a manual for the test; the manual should be revised as new data regarding the test's reliability, validity, norms, and use become available. Test information should not only be adequate to evaluate the test's quality; it should also provide detailed instructions for procedures of administration and scoring of the test. These instructions should be provided in such detail that the test user is able to duplicate the administrative conditions under which the normative data were obtained; test users should be warned that failure to follow the correct procedures for test administration and scoring will generally invalidate the resulting assessment data.

To summarize briefly, the AERA/APA/NCME technical standards describe the criteria for test reliability, test validation, procedures in test development and revision, norming of tests, test manuals and guides for users, and standards for test administration, scoring, and use. These standards specify that assessment methods should be of adequate reliability and validity; should have been developed in appropriate and knowledgeable ways; and should be accompanied by normative or other comparative information, by adequate information concerning the development, quality, and use of the tests, and by information that will ensure that test administration and scoring are efficient, uniform, and fair to all individuals tested.

Ideally, these dimensions of test quality should be addressed *before* the test is distributed for use. More realistically, however, test manuals are expected to provide information by which the user can evaluate the extent to which the standards *have been* met, to mention areas in which technical support is lacking, and to describe the current research efforts that will increase the base of technical support for the quality of the instrument. Test manuals should also make it clear that extra caution in test use and interpretation is necessary in cases where there is as yet insufficient evidence supporting the test's quality. Also, tests not yet meeting quality standards should be probably be reserved for needs for which there are no better alternative tests or assessment devices.

Finally, though, it should be emphasized that because test use occurs in the context of a specific applied problem, the ultimate bases for judging the necessity of a particular standard include both the individuals and organizations involved and the particular uses to which the test is to be put.

The good judgment, sound knowledge, and professional integrity of the test user are therefore essential.

Test User Competence

It is essential not only that *tests* be of high quality but also that *test users* be qualified to use them. Tests are sophisticated psychological tools that can be used in harmful and/or ineffective as well as helpful ways. They should be used only by qualified, informed individuals who will make sure that they are used and interpreted effectively and correctly. Accordingly, a major principle of the APA ethical code is that psychological knowledge and techniques are used only by those *qualified* to use them and, conversely, that test users operate only within the bounds of their own knowledge and competence. According to the APA code it is important that psychologists who use test results have an understanding of psychological measurement, problems of test validation, and test research (American Psychological Association, 1981). Therefore it is important to ensure that tests and test scores are used by people qualified to use them.

Qualifications for test use vary according to the types of tests in question, but in general are stricter with tests having greater potential for harm and misinterpretation. One of the earliest systems by which user qualifications were specified, provided by the first APA test standards, has classified tests according to three levels of complexity (American Psychological Association, 1954, pp. 146–148).

Level A tests are those that can be administered, scored, and interpreted by responsible nonpsychologists who have carefully read the test manual and are familiar with the overall purposes of testing. Educational achievement tests fall into this category.

Level B tests require technical knowledge of test construction and use and appropriate advanced coursework in psychology and related courses (e.g., statistics, individual differences, and counseling). Vocational interest inventories, group intelligence and special aptitude tests, and some personality inventories are generally considered Level B tests. For example, Consulting Psychologists' Press limits purchase of tests such as the Strong-Campbell Interest Inventory, the State-Trait Anxiety Inventory, the Myers-Briggs Type Indicator, and the Bem Sex Role Inventory to people who have completed university courses in tests and measurements or equivalent training. Similar requirements for access to tests such as the Jackson Vocational Interest Inventory, the Personality Research Form, and the Jackson Personality Inventory are stated by their publisher, Research Psychologists Press.

Level C tests require at least an advanced degree in an appropriate profession and/or membership in an appropriate professional association, state licensure, or national or state certification. Level C tests generally include individually administered intelligence tests and personality tests, (e.g., the Stanford-Binet Intelligence Scale, the Wechsler Adult Intelligence Scale, and the Minnesota Multiphasic Personality Inventory). Graduate students may be qualified to purchase and use Level B or Level C tests if they are being supervised in that work by someone who does possess the appropriate user qualifications.

Although the Level A, B, C system has some face validity, it has never been widely and consistently adopted nor, more importantly, have specific guidelines for defining test user qualifications been addressed in either the APA Ethical Principles or Test Standards. In a recent attempt to discern if and how test publishers were restricting the sale of tests, the Test User Qualifications Working Group (TUQWOG) of the Scientific Affairs Office of the APA conducted a study of test publishers (see Eyde, 1986). All of the 13 major test publishers placed some restriction on the sale of tests to individuals based on their professional qualifications, but there was wide variability in the nature and extent of the criteria used to screen potential test buyers. In response to this lack of uniformity, the TUQWOG has been working on defining essential qualifications needed by purchasers of various types of tests. Until a set of uniform guidelines becomes available, the rough guidelines of the Level A, B, C system and the specific criteria stated in test publishers' catalogues may be used to determine necessary user qualifications.

Ensuring that test users are competent is also the responsibility of the administrators of any organization or agency using tests (e.g., schools and businesses), of test developers who should make available complete information about the technical adequacy and use of the test, and of test users themselves, who, even after earning the appropriate degrees, must engage in continued study of testing research and techniques in order to be competent in their use. A "qualified" test user not only possesses the necessary education, training, and experience, but is familiar with the technical, psychometric characteristics of the test to be used, is able to defend the use of the particular test selected rather than alternative tests, is knowledgeable about both administration and interpretation of the test, and is aware of the potential misuses of the test and of circumstances and/or types of individuals with whom particular care must be taken.

Privacy and Confidentiality

Principle 5 of the APA ethical code describes psychologists' obligations in maintaining the confidentiality of information obtained from individuals through testing or any other formal or informal means of gathering information (American Psychological Association, 1981). The maintenance of confidentiality means protecting the individual's right to privacy and involves the principles of informed consent, constraints on the provision of individual information to other parties, and care in the storage and disposal of information.

The first responsibility of the test user is to minimize, as far as possible, the extent to which testing may threaten a person's right to privacy. The extent to which the use of tests constitutes an invasion of individual privacy is a complex issue involving a number of considerations. It should be noted that test data are no more invasive of privacy than are other kinds of information obtained about people. With any kind of personal information, *including* test data, the use of the data should be characterized as far as possible by the principles of *relevance* and *informed consent* (Anastasi, 1982).

The concept of *relevance* means that test scores are collected and used only if they are relevant to some valid set of purposes; collecting a set of test scores for no other purpose than "curiosity" would constitute an unnecessary invasion of an individual's privacy. Similarly, asking a person's height and weight would be appropriate only if related to the purpose at hand. The principle of *informed consent* means that, as far as possible, the individual is informed about both the nature of the information collected and the purposes for which the information will be used. This principle does not imply that test takers (or their parents) necessarily have a right to information that would invalidate the use of the test or that is beyond the sophistication of the consumer (e.g., test items or methods of scoring), but does require that the test taker be informed as fully as possible about the nature and uses of the test scores.

Although the principle of informed consent is intended to provide to the test taker at least some opportunity for *choice* in

the matter of how much information to reveal and in the uses to which that information will be put, the extent to which the individual actually *does* have a choice varies across different situations. For a client in counseling, revealing personal information is important to the process of getting help; unwillingness to be open with the counselor or therapist may make treatment very difficult and client improvement less likely. As an extreme example, a client wishing help with vocational decision making who refused to talk about his/her vocational interests or take a vocational interest inventory would be very difficult for a counselor to help.

When tests are used for *institutional* (rather than individual) purposes and decisions the individual may choose *not* to reveal the requested information, but that choice may be costly in terms of an educational or job opportunity. For example, an individual who chooses not to take the Scholastic Aptitude Test (SAT) might forfeit his or her opportunity to go to certain colleges and universities.

Where tests are being used in research, the principle of informed consent is to give the individual an opportunity to choose *not* to participate in the research. A particularly important principle in the research use of test scores is anonymity of results. This principle means that where the identity of research participants is unnecessary to the purposes of the research the participants' anonymity should be preserved so that the invasion of privacy is minimized.

Finally, cases in which test takers are minors involve special informed-consent concerns. Although minors should be informed as far as possible and at a complexity level that will facilitate their comprehension, parental or guardian consent may be necessary in some circumstances. Guidelines for the collection and use of test data with minors (e.g., Russell Sage Foundation, 1970) should guide the use of tests in these situations.

In essence, the issue of invasion of privacy means finding a compromise between the *need* for meaningful, relevant information to guide problem solving in applied situations and the individual's *right* to personal privacy and freedom of choice. This compromise is best achieved when respect for the individual is combined with sound professional judgment concerning the kinds of information needed for the purposes at hand.

Confidentiality issues pertain to decisions about access to test results on the part of those other than the original test user. For example, a school system may have collected achievement test data that are later requested by a potential employer of the student. Or a psychologist may have given a client a Minnesota Multiphasic Personality Inventory (MMPI), scores from which are later requested by another psychologist or the school system. Ethical and test standards mandate that, in general, the confidentiality of test results is to be protected by the *original test user* unless the test taker gives consent for test results to be provided to someone else. The original informed consent should have covered all intended test uses, and *additional consent* is necessary for any use beyond those originally agreed to. In the examples given, the student would need to release achievement test scores to the potential employer, and the client would need to release his or her MMPI scores to the second psychologist or to the school system.

A final responsibility of test users involves the secure storage of test results and, when test results are too old to be useful, the permanent disposal of test data. Keeping test results in places where they are accessible to anyone but the original test user is irresponsible, as is disposing of test scores in such a way that they could be easily retrieved by unauthorized individuals. And the test user is responsible for judgments concerning the continued utility of test results collected previously. According to the AERA/APA/NCME standards, test scores should be kept in a person's file only as long as they serve a useful purpose.

To summarize, issues of privacy and confidentiality require respect for the individual client or test taker and the person's rights to privacy and informed consent, as well as care in the release, storage, and disposal of test data and other types of personal information.

Assessment Techniques: Use and Interpretation

One entire principle of the APA ethical code is devoted to the use of assessment techniques. As stated in Principle 8, "Assessment Techniques" (American Psychological Association, 1981):

> In the development, publication, and utilization of psychological assessment techniques, psychologists make every effort to promote the welfare and best interests of the client. They guard against the misuse of assessment results. They respect the client's right to know the results, the interpretations made and the bases for their conclusions and recommendations. Psychologists make every effort to maintain the security of tests and other assessment techniques within limits of legal mandates. They strive to assure the appropriate use of assessment techniques by others.

Note that this principle reiterates several issues mentioned previously—that is, issues of promotion of client welfare, protecting the security of test results, and ensuring the client's right to be informed about test procedures and results.

In addition to these issues, this principle introduces the necessity of care in the interpretation of test results and in their communication to clients. Although a detailed discussion of *counseling techniques* involved in test interpretation is beyond the scope of this book (but see, for example, Goldman, 1971; Maloney & Ward, 1976), several general recommendations for methods of test interpretation can be made.

First of all, communication and interpretation of test results should always be done in ways that will best serve the original purposes for which test data were collected. For example, the interpretation of personality test data collected in counseling and therapy should be used with the goal of better understanding and helping the client. Test data collected for use in revising school curricula should be interpreted with that end in mind.

Second, the individual interpreting a test should be considerate of the needs of the test taker. As far as possible, test interpretation should occur within the context of an interpersonal situation or relationship. The test user should be prepared to be supportive of emotional reactions from the test taker, particularly when test information may be sensitive or in some way negative. Test interpretation should utilize language that is understandable to the test taker and should avoid too much technical terminology or jargon. Simple respect for the individual test taker and for the person's rights and welfare, in combination with knowledge and skill, will help to ensure responsible test interpretation.

Third, test results should, as far as possible, be communicated *descriptively* rather than as numbers and labels, and ideally should provide both a current understanding of the person and constructive suggestions for facilitating the person's development. For example, interpreting intelligence and/or scholastic aptitude test scores in terms of expected levels of educational performance and including suggestions for potentially facilitative educational interventions would generally be preferable to the use of a numerical IQ score or a label such as "retarded" or "genius."

The use of categories or labels based on test scores has been the subject of much justifiable criticism. Too often labels tend to stick with, and consequently stigmatize, a person, even when they're no longer appropriate. For example, ridding oneself of the labels "retarded," "ex-convict," or "alcoholic" may prove extremely difficult. Lay persons often assume an erroneous "fixity," an unchangingness in the human personality. Although there is much about us that doesn't change, human beings are capable of much growth, change, and flexibility. Current behavioral description rather than labeling is more consistent with this great potential for growth and change.

Another problem with labeling is that it can influence our views of ourselves and others' views of us and thus how we actually behave or are *seen* to behave. The phenomenon of the "self-fulfilling prophecy" refers to the fact that our expectations of events or people can influence what actually happens. The label "mentally retarded" may cause both teachers and the child so labeled to have very low expectations of performance and potential. The child may receive less encouragement and attention from teachers than do "normal" children. Worse, a child who learns to think of himself or herself as retarded may "give up" before ever testing his or her potential. Thus, whether or not a label like "retarded" or "delinquent" is initially justified, it may adversely influence the development of the individual.

Although labels have dangers, they can also be useful for some purposes. Labels often serve to efficiently summarize and communicate a great deal of information and should always be accompanied by some suggestions for treatment or positive intervention. The AERA/APA/NCME test standards require that if labels or categories are used the categories chosen should be based on careful criterion, content, and/or construct validation, as appropriate. Furthermore, the *least stigmatizing* label should always be assigned. Ultimately, the knowledge and good judgment of the test user are needed to control the use that will be made of psychological labels and diagnostic categories and to decide when the potential risks of assigning labels outweigh the benefits in terms of the facilitation of understanding.

A final point in test interpretation, and probably the most important one, is that the communication, interpretation, and use of test/assessment results should always occur within a context that includes and considers all relevant information about a person (e.g., Maloney & Ward, 1976). Historical and demographic data and information from interviews and naturalistic observation serve to provide a framework from which to make any kind of test/assessment data richer, more meaningful, and more useful. It is inappropriate to interpret a scholastic aptitude or achievement test score without reference, among other things, to a person's cultural and socioeconomic background and educational opportunities and experiences. Similarly, a score on a vocational interest inventory must be interpreted in a context that includes the person's sex, racial and ethnic heritage, and other background characteristics. Given the present text's view of the purposes of person and environmental assessment, it is logical and essential to view assessment in the broad context of the compilation and integration of a variety of data, test and otherwise, for the purposes of understanding and solving applied problems.

Summary

The ethical and professional standards for tests and test use are designed to ensure that tests and assessment devices themselves are of high technical, informative, and interpretive quality and that they are used by qualified, knowledgeable, ethical people who care deeply about the rights and welfare of the individuals they serve. High-quality, effective, and fair test use is dependent on the quality of both the tests and the users. Even the highest-quality test can be misused by an unqualified or careless person, and the most highly skilled test user in the world is ineffective without carefully developed, well-standardized, reliable, and valid tests. As test users, therefore, we are responsible for ensuring both our own competence and the quality of the tools we use. Ethical test use is knowledgeable, informed, careful, and critical test use.

SOCIAL ISSUES IN TESTING

Background

Although the testing profession has long had both ethical standards and standards regarding test quality, recent years have witnessed increasing public concern and controversy over particular kinds of test use. These areas of controversy have involved important social issues and have had far-reaching legal, legislative, and public policy implications.

The test uses that were most subject to scrutiny in past years have been those involving what we might call "special groups" of individuals. Although the issues regarding test use differ depending on the type of test involved (e.g., intelligence and aptitude tests, vocational interest inventories, personality inventories) and on the "special group" with which the test is to be used (e.g., women, racial and/or ethnic minorities, the disabled, etc.), there are some common bases for concerns about using tests in special groups.

At the most fundamental level is the

fact that tests are, to at least some extent, culture bound. It is impossible to construct a test independently of a cultural context because, as so well stated by Anastasi (1988), human behavior itself occurs within a cultural context. To assume that tests can be made culture-free is as erroneous as to assume that behavior, attitudes, etc., can be made culture-free. For example, a test of verbal aptitude is constructed in a given language and is based on what may well be culture-specific item content. Most intelligence and aptitude tests in use were constructed in the context of a white, middle-class value system. Thus, nonwhite or lower-class examinees would possibly be less familiar with the test content than would examinees representing the white middle class. A picture of a deciduous tree on a picture vocabulary test of intelligence for children would be an unfair item for a Navaho child raised in the Arizona desert. An item representing a farm animal might be unfamiliar to a black child raised in a ghetto.

The issue of test item familiarity affects interest measurement as well as ability measurement. For example, basic dimensions of vocational interest have been measured using content differentially characteristic of the experiential backgrounds of males versus females. To ask a female whether she's interested in auto mechanics when she's never had the chance to experience activities related to it is an example of how item content can be sex-biased. The use of sexist occupational titles (e.g., policeman, cleaning woman) or, as was the case in one inventory for children, pictures of whites in higher-status and blacks in lower-status occupations, provide further examples of content bias.

Finally, when measuring dimensions of personality, cross-cultural differences in the perceived appropriateness of different behaviors may affect measurement. For instance, the sometimes conflicting values of cooperation/community vs. competition/individuality are differentially valued in different cultures. In some cultures, for example the Japanese, assertiveness with one's elders may be viewed as a sign of disrespect and, therefore, as highly inappropriate. In some cultures men are free to express affection publicly to other men, whereas in other cultures such displays would be frowned upon. Different views of social appropriateness cannot help but influence self-reports of behavior and personality.

In addition to the cultural relativity of test item content is the nature of the standardization or norm groups. A basic principle of test interpretation is that test scores should be interpreted with reference to *appropriate* norm groups, that is, norm groups consisting of individuals comparable to the individual being tested. If norm groups are predominantly or totally white, the scores of a black or Hispanic person are of reduced interpretability. Similarly, using a test cross-culturally is unwise until both necessary translations of the test and collection of norms in the new population have been accomplished.

Thus, responsible test constructors and test users no longer automatically assume the usefulness of a test for any examinee. Thanks to this widespread criticism of possible biases in test content and of the predominance of whites or, in some cases, white males only in norm groups, revisions in tests and collection of new, more diverse normative samples have taken place. However, differences in the *outcomes* of testing still occur. That is, even after revisions to both test content and normative procedures have been undertaken, group differences, such as race differences in intelligence and some abilities, continue to occur. What to do about differences in test *outcomes* is a social policy issue rather than a measurement issue, as will be further discussed in the next section.

ISSUES IN USING TESTS WITH RACIAL/ETHNIC MINORITIES

Introduction

The fundamental issue in using tests with racial/ethnic minority groups is interpretation and use of ability and intelligence test scores that are, among blacks and other American minorities, consistently lower on the average than are the average scores of white individuals. Bringing this issue to widespread public and professional attention was Arthur Jensen, who in 1969 published an article entitled "How Much Can We Boost IQ and Scholastic Achievement?" in the *Harvard Educational Review*. In this article, Jensen asserted that genetic factors were the cause of observed differences between blacks and whites in performance on standardized intelligence tests. Research data had fairly consistently indicated that on standardized tests of intelligence, the performance of whites as a group generally exceeded the performance of blacks as a group. To illustrate, the mean IQ of whites on a given intelligence test might be 105, in contrast to a mean IQ of 95 for a group of blacks. Jensen took this *observed* difference in intelligence test performance and attributed that difference primarily to heredity rather than to environment. In other words, it would be possible to interpret this score difference as the result of some inherent differences between blacks and whites, and/or it would be possible to attribute the difference to the fact that in American society, blacks are disadvantaged relative to whites in terms of their socioeconomic status, their educational and occupational opportunities, and so on. So although the *existence* of the test score difference was not necessarily being debated, the *reasons* for this difference were an important focus of controversy.

Jensen's article led to widespread public outrage and to numerous alternative explanations. First of all, there is no question that blacks and whites in this country grow up in drastically different environments—black people have been of generally lower socioeconomic status than have white people and have in general been culturally disadvantaged. Any group that suffers cultural disadvantage may be expected to perform less well on tests that are constructed within and reflect the majority culture or middle-class society. Thus, any discussion of race differences in IQ test performance must account for the fact that blacks and white develop in drastically different socioeconomic, cultural, and educational environments. Second, it is always essential to recall the point that even if we observe group differences in intelligence, we cannot make any statements about the performance of a given individual.

Probably the most frequently offered argument, and that which has been the subject of most *current* controversy, is that intelligence and aptitude tests are by their nature and their content biased against blacks and other individuals not representative of the "majority" culture. This argument suggests that because blacks and others represent a cultural as well as economic minority, tests constructed by and for the cultural majority (i.e., the white middle class) are simply inappropriate and unfair. This section begins with a brief review of the issue of potential racial bias in testing and goes on to discuss the problems of using tests with minority groups.

Cultural Bias in Testing

As has been mentioned, one major possible explanation for the generally poorer performance of blacks and other minority groups on standardized aptitude and intelligence tests is that tests discriminate against minority groups through cultural bias. This argument is based on the charge of cultural bias in both the nature and the content of intelligence and aptitude tests. It is assumed that tests developed by and for the white middle class stress white, middle-class values and areas of knowledge, rather than the values and areas of knowledge within the black or other minority cultures. Cultural bias has been postulated to be manifested in tests themselves in one of three ways: content bias, bias in internal structure, and selection bias.

Content bias is probably the best-known and most easily understood type of bias. Very simply, content bias refers to a test that contains content more familiar to white, middle-class examinees than to members of other racial or socioeconomic groups. Specifically, content bias may involve *test questions* that would be more familiar to one cultural group than to another.

Test constructors have addressed the problem of content bias by obtaining expert judgments of the degree to which item content is culturally loaded and by soliciting item contributions from test professionals representing other cultural groups. The construction of most scholastic aptitude and achievement tests is now done by panels of experts that include the representation of women, blacks, Hispanics, and so on and members of lower socioeconomic status groups. These panel members both contribute items and evaluate the item pool with the objective of minimizing gender, race, cultural, and class bias. Tests not originally constructed in this manner should be revised to remove content bias as far as possible. Test users should include in their evaluations of tests the extent to which issues of gender and cultural diversity were incorporated into test development.

As a result of concerns about race and sex bias in content, most ability and achievement tests constructed or revised in the 1980s were subjected to a careful screening for such bias by review panels consisting of women and representatives of racial minority, handicapped, and otherwise disadvantaged

groups. For example, a review of the SAT in the *Ninth Mental Measurements Yearbook* (Cohn, 1985b) applauded the constructors of the SAT for careful attention to the removal of cultural bias, sexist language, and language potentially offensive to particular subgroups.

A second type of test bias postulated is that in the *internal structure* of the test. If the internal or factor structure of a test and/or the behavior of items in relationship to each other (i.e., internal consistency) are found to differ across cultural groups, then the test is measuring different things across groups. In other words, factor structure and item interrelationships contribute to the explication of the construct being measured by the test, and tests should not be used for the same purposes in different groups unless they are measuring the same construct as well.

Accordingly, test developers and publishers have done research investigating and comparing factor structure and item characteristics across groups. In general, available studies of factor structure (e.g., Humphreys & Taber, 1973; Jensen, 1980) have reported similarity across groups in factor structure and patterns. Studies of such characteristics of individual test items as item difficulty, item total score correlations, and item characteristic curves have generally shown at least some group differences. However, consistent patterns of difference that would contribute to test revisions designed to eliminate bias have not yet been found (see Cole, 1981). More research comparing tests' internal structural characteristics across groups is needed.

The final type of test bias postulated is a large category of bias which can be summarized as *selection bias*. Selection bias would be a bias caused when a test has different predictive validity across groups. For example, just because a scholastic aptitude test predicts the performance of white, middle-class students doesn't mean that it predicts the performance of blacks or lower-class individuals. It is erroneous to assume that what we know about predictive validity in one group also characterizes other groups, and if a test does not predict well for blacks or members of other groups then it shouldn't be used for that purpose in those groups.

Selection bias is examined through the comparison of regression equations and regression lines obtained within different groups. If the regression lines differ significantly across groups, then some type of selection bias is occurring (Cole, 1981). Differences in the regression lines can be either in the *slope* of the regression line ("slope bias") or in the *interception* of the line with the Y axis ("intercept bias").

When both the predictor and the criterion scores are expressed in standard score units, the *slope* of the regression line ("line of best fit") is equal to the correlation (*r*) between predictor and criterion (Cole, 1981). If the value of the correlation in one group differs significantly from the value in another group (thereby resulting in different slopes), then the test is differentially valid in predicting the criterion. Critics of standardized testing have postulated that tests that are significant predictors in white samples

may not predict as well or at all in black samples.

Figure 14.1 shows several sample regression lines that together help illustrate how slope bias is postulated to operate. In this example, scores on hypothetical Text X, which may range from 0 to 60, are to be used to predict grade-point averages (GPAs) at hypothetical College Y. Assume that the line intermediate between the other two is the regression line characterizing the group as a whole (which is assumed to be predominantly white middle class) and that users of the test wish to select only those individuals predicted to achieve a GPA of at least 2.0. The dotted lines connecting the large group regression line with the horizontal or X axis show that a cut-off score of 32 on the test would select individuals predicted to obtain a GPA of 2.0. Therefore, students scoring 32 or better would be selected, while those scoring 31 or less would be rejected. Charges of selection bias are based on the possibility that, within a subgroup, for example, a sample of blacks, a regression line like that shown for Subgroup 1 would be found, indicating that the same *test score* predicted a higher criterion GPA. In the upper line labeled Subgroup 1, a score of 28 represents the

Figure 14.1 Illustration of slope bias in a hypothetical case involving the use of test scores (X) to predict the criterion of grade point average or GPA (Y).

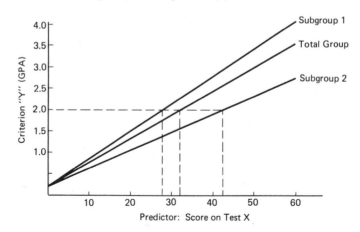

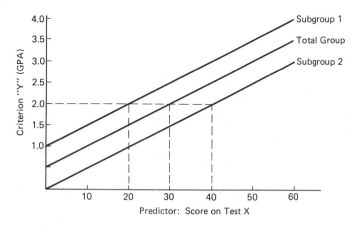

Figure 14.2 Illustration of intercept bias in a hypothetical case involving the use of test scores (X) to predict the criterion of grade point average or GPA (Y).

intersection of the line with the Y axis at 2.0. The difference in slope between the large group and the line for Subgroup 1 represents a case where even though blacks didn't do as well as whites did on the test, they did as well on the criterion with lower predictor scores, so a lower cutoff should be used in a black rather than in a white sample. This is a case where test scores "underpredict" the criterion.

The line labeled Subgroup 2 in Figure 14.1 shows a situation exactly opposite that of "underprediction." With the line shown for Subgroup 2, a given test score is related to *lower* criterion performance in group 2 than in the total group—for example, a test score of 42 is needed before a GPA as high as 2.0 is predicted. In this case, use of the overall regression line with Sub-group 2 members leads to *overprediction* of their criterion scores. Slope bias discriminates *against* the group with the steeper regression line (Subgroup 1) and *in favor of* the group with the flatter line (Subgroup 2).

Studies of slope bias suggest that the majority of tests predict about as well for minority group members as they do for majority group members. If anything, use of the overall regression lines leads to overprediction rather than underprediction of

the criterion performance of minority group members (Cole, 1981; Hunter, Schmidt, & Hunter, 1979; Breland, 1979).

Figure 14.2 shows how intercept bias might occur using the same hypothetical situation. In intercept bias, the slopes of the different regression lines are equal, but the points at which the lines intersect the vertical, or Y, axis (the criterion, GPA) differ. Note that the three lines shown in Figure 14.2 have the same slope but cross the Y axis at different points. If our criterion for selecting students continues to be a predicted GPA of 2.0, a score of 30 is the minimum necessary using the total group regression equation. If the equation shown for Subgroup 1 were used, a score of only 20 would lead to a predicted GPA of 2.0. This is a case of underprediction, which is like that postulated by test critics to describe the situation of blacks. In contrast, the equation found to describe Subgroup 2 would require a test score of 40 before a predicted GPA of at least 2.0 would be expected. This illustrates a case of overprediction. Intercept bias discriminates *against* the group with the higher or larger intercept (Subgroup 1) and *in favor of* the group with the lower or smaller intercept (Subgroup 2).

As with slope bias, well-controlled studies of intercept bias have found either no significant differences in the intercepts of the lines characterizing different groups or lower intercepts among blacks, discriminating in favor of blacks when the common regression line is used. In general, findings that the use of overall group regression lines benefits blacks are also true for lower SES groups and, in general, for groups obtaining lower *mean* test scores. (See Linn, 1982, for a review of pertinent research.) Thus, there is little, if any, evidence that psychological tests discriminate against blacks in a predictive sense, and in fact the use of total group regression lines is likely in some cases to benefit the black applicant.

Over all, charges of test bias have been met by many constructive changes in methods of test construction designed to remove content bias as far as possible. Research investigating selection bias and bias in internal structure has not led to much evidence for either the existence or the effects of these biases.

Unfortunately, trying to correct at least some of the biases in tests themselves has not, nor will it ever, ameliorate the problem of the negative impact that testing has on blacks and members of other minority groups. In other words, a test can be valid and relatively free of bias yet still produce scores having negative results for blacks, scores that lead, for example, to the rejection of proportionately more black than white applicants for a college or a job. The *quality of a test* and the *uses of test scores* are two separate issues.

As so well discussed by Messick (1975), Cronbach (1980), and Cole (1981), the existence of bias in tests is a *psychometric* issue, involving the concern about how tests themselves are constructed and evaluated. On the other hand, questions concerning whether or not tests should be used at all or used only for certain kinds of purposes are *social* issues. A test may be of high psychometric quality, yet because of social policy concerns we may choose not to use it, even for purposes for which it was designed.

It is erroneous to assume that answers to validity and test bias questions will or should provide answers to social policy issues. Valid tests may be used in ways that society perceives as negative or undesirable. It is the job of psychometricians and other test professionals to produce tests that are high in technical quality and low in bias, but it is the job of society, which includes the educational system, the legislative and legal systems, and anyone who is a user or consumer of assessment technology, to determine how, with whom, and for what purposes tests should be used.

The development of educational and social policies with respect to the *use* of tests has to date been concerned with several controversial uses of tests. These controversial uses, which include the use of tests in employment selection, educational classification and placement, the establishment of minimum educational competencies, and educational admissions, are discussed in the next sections.

Social Policy Issues

Tests in Employment Selection. The controversy surrounding the use of tests in employment selection may be summarized as the problem of *adverse impact*. Adverse impact means that even when standardized tests are not used with *intent* to discriminate against minorities, their use has led to the hiring of proportionately fewer minorities. Thus, whether or not discrimination was intended, the impact of using standardized tests in employment selection has been negative or adverse in terms of the representation of minorities.

Race and sex discrimination in employment selection, regardless of how it occurs (e.g., from outright refusal to consider black or female applicants to selection procedures that make it difficult or impossible for blacks or women to qualify and compete) has been an important, indeed crucial, civil rights issue, which was first addressed by federal legislation beginning in 1964. The Equal Employment Opportunity Act, based on Title VII of the 1964 Civil Rights Act, prohibited discrimination on the basis of race, color, religion, sex, or national origin in selection procedures leading to employment decisions within employers (both private or governmental), labor organizations, employment agencies, and licensing and certification boards. The United States Equal Employment Opportunity Commission (EEOC) was formed to implement and enforce the act, and in 1970 the EEOC developed a set of guidelines for that purpose.

These guidelines developed by the EEOC specified, among other things, that properly validated and standardized employment selection procedures can *contribute to*, rather than detract from, fair personnel practices through their objectivity and "blindness" to someone's race, gender, national origin, and so on. The guidelines also stated, however, that tests that adversely affect the hiring, promotion, and advancement of protected groups such as racial minorities and women must be shown to possess validity for the selection and the employer must demonstrate that alternative selection procedures not having adverse impact are not available. In 1978 a revised and simplified set of guidelines, the *Uniform Guidelines on Employee Selection Procedures*, was issued by the EEOC.

The major concept currently underlying the justification for using tests or other selection methods that have adverse impact on certain groups is *job-relatedness*—that is, the biased tests or selection procedures are claimed to be related to job performance. Often the supposed job-relatedness of certain tests and procedures is highly questionable. If a test or selection requirement has

little or nothing to do with job performance, its use is obviously unfair and is illegal. For example, imagine how unfair it would be if only tall people were admitted to colleges or accepted for jobs as computer programmers or management trainees. We would surely protest such a criterion based on its lack of relevance to doing well in college or in computer programming or management. A test's content should have some relationship to the requirements of the job!

A classical legal case related to the concept of job-relatedness is that of *Griggs* v. *Duke Power Company*, in which the United States Supreme Court ruled that the use of a general intelligence test, a mechanical aptitude test, and the requirement of possessing a high school diploma were illegal in the selection of common laborers, as they resulted in the selection of far fewer blacks than whites and *were not job-related*.

Although paper-and-pencil aptitude and intelligence tests most often result in adverse impact on blacks, performance tests, such as those required for selection into the police and fire services, more often affect female candidates adversely and, again, job-relatedness must be demonstrated. For example, if a height of, for example, 5'8" were required for selection as a police officer (a selection criterion that would have adverse impact for women rather than for men as a group), that requirement would have to be shown as necessary for adequate job performance. As an example of the possible invalidity of height requirements, consider the following: A discriminatory height requirement for selection as a police officer in New York was stated to be necessary so that officers could stand and fire guns over the tops of their police cars. The court ruled that this requirement was illegal because the "performance" for which height was supposedly needed (firing over the top of the car) was actually *contrary* to established police procedure in the state!

Although the concept of job-relatedness seems like a reasonable basis on which to justify the use of tests or other selection devices, the continuing problem in court cases centers around the definition of "job-relatedness" (Bersoff, 1981). Job-relatedness can be interpreted to mean content similarity, that is, the similarity of the test's content to the job itself. As an example, a test of typing speed and accuracy has obvious relatedness to the job of a typist or secretary. In contrast, a test of intelligence would be less obviously related to the job duties, so its use would have to be justified. Using requirements related to physical attributes—height, weight, body build—to select secretaries would be clearly discriminatory and therefore illegal, since employers would be hard-pressed to show how these were related to job content.

Job-relatedness can also be interpreted in terms of criterion-related validity, that is, the correlation between test performance and some gauge of the quality of job performance. For example, if scores on a test of finger dexterity are positively related to the number of "widgets" the employee can produce per hour, then the test has criterion-related validity.

A significant set of research findings regarding the validity of tests for employment selection is that from research on "validity generalization." A variety of research evidence—summarized, for example, by Schmidt and Hunter (1977, 1981) and Schmidt, Hunter, Pearlman, and Shane (1979) suggests that cognitive ability tests (including tests of verbal, quantitative, spatial and mechanical ability, perceptual speed, reasoning abilities) are valid predictors of performance both on the job and in training across a *variety* of jobs and job settings and are equally valid for majority-group and minority-group applicants.

The implications of research on "validity generalization" and other research on the use of tests in selection are that the use of most tests of cognitive abilities, no matter how valid, "job-related," and so forth, will continue to have adverse impact on blacks and other minorities in employment selection. In other words, although federal legislation has undoubtedly had tremendous positive effects in terms of reducing the use of discriminatory or adverse selection procedures, the possibility of adverse impact simply cannot be totally eliminated unless it is decided to "outlaw" tests *and* any other valid selection criteria that also have adverse impact. The basic issue is not the validity of tests but how selection decisions should be made. As concluded by a panel formed by the National Academy of Sciences (NAS) to study ability testing practices, "tests should not be required to do things they cannot do, such as guarantee that distributions of scores will not differ for different racial or ethnic groups" ("NAS calls," 1982, p. 4). The issue really is the *criteria* that should be used to select people for jobs.

Originally, employee selection procedures were designed to allow the selection of people predicted to be most productive and successful on the job, with the intent of maximizing organizational productivity, efficiency, and profit. And such methods have worked. For example, Schmidt and Hunter (1981) estimate that the use of cognitive ability tests for selection in hiring saves tremendous amounts of money—$18 million per year (in 1980 dollars) for the 5,000-member Philadelphia police department and $16 billion per year (in 1981 dollars) for a large employer like the federal government. There is no question that the use of such tests saves money. The question, of course, pertains to the *social costs* of selection procedures that greatly improve employee productivity and therefore greatly reduce employer costs. Hunter and Schmidt (1981) calculate on the basis of *conservative* statistical assumptions that the United States gross national product (GNP) could be increased by $80 billion to $100 billion dollars a year (in 1981 dollars) if improved selection procedures were implemented throughout the country.

The use of tests and other *objective* methods of employee selection was also originally thought to represent an improvement over selection based on family background and connections, race, religion, and other biased factors. In other words, the concept of a "meritocracy," which rewards the most intellectually talented and enterprising people, was seen as the best avenue to equal opportunity by giving people the chance to develop their individual talents, abilities, and interests.

Now, however, it is clear that the use of selection models based only on the traditional concept of a meritocracy is inconsistent with current ideals of equal opportunity. Rather, methods of selection must increasingly seek a trade-off between economic goals and social goals such as proportional minority representation in the occupational structure. Preferential selection systems that hire the highest-scoring applicants within various subgroups can increase minority representation (Schmidt & Hunter, 1981) without throwing out tests or other objective selection criteria altogether. Decision-theoretical models, in which the quality of a decision is gauged by its overall utility, provide methods by which social values and goals may be explicitly incorporated into decision rules and selection criteria (Messick, 1980). Thus, test scores may be used along with other kinds of information in selection procedures that formally or informally take into account, and work to *counteract*, the effects of socioeconomic disadvantage upon performance and that incorporate the values of equal opportunity and the desirability of human diversity within all settings. See Gottfredson (1986) and Gottfredson and Sharf (1988) for reviews of the issues in using cognitive ability tests in employment selection.

Finally, the ethical and professional responsibilities of test users should be noted. The AERA/APA/NCME test standards emphasize the necessity for evidence regarding a test's validity and a sound rationale for why particular kinds of validity evidence are appropriate. In addition, Bray (1982) reiterates the principle of informed consent, in this case the right of the person evaluated to receive complete information about the basis of the selection decision or recommendation. And, above all, the psychologist or other test professional is responsible for making sound, well-thought-out decisions that will allow the utilization of the advances made possible by the science and technology of psychological tests and assessment, as well as the protection of individual rights and opportunities

Educational Classification and Placement. Another area in which charges of race discrimination have been filed is that of the use of intelligence tests, such as the Wechsler Intelligence Scale for Children and the Stanford-Binet Intelligence Scale, to place children in tracks within a school system. Two main issues have characterized the controversy: the overrepresentation of blacks in special education programs and the cultural bias in IQ tests that is suggested to underlie this overrepresentation. In essence, these programs have tended to classify far more black than white children as mildly retarded (using the term "educable mental retardation," or EMR) and/or in need of special education. Critics view IQ tests as the cause of such differential classification.

This area of concern has been particularly prominent in the courts (see Bersoff, 1981), as well as in numerous books and articles (e.g., Reschly, 1981; Bernal, 1975; Cleary, Humphreys, Kendrick, & Wesman, 1975; G. Jackson, 1975; Prasse, 1978). Two major legal cases were *Larry P.* v. *Riles*, and *PASE* (Parents in Action on Special Education) v. *Hannon*. In both of these cases the crucial aspect of the ruling derived from the judge's conceptualization of cultural bias in testing.

In the 1980 California case of *Larry P.* v. *Riles*, the judge ruled that the tests were inherently culturally biased and, therefore prohibited the use of standardized tests for the EMR identification, classification, or placement of black children without court approval. The decision also made it almost impossible to restore use of the tests by removing the cultural biases thought to be present, because these biases were judged as inherent to the form and content (e.g., verbal skills) of the test. In essence, the judge's ruling implied that any test showing group differences in scores is biased until those differences are eradicated, thus essentially invalidating the notion of individual differences. In 1986, the judge reissued his ruling, forbidding personnel in California schools from using IQ tests to assess black children for placement in special education classes ("Judge Reiterates IQ Test Ban," 1986).

In contrast, the judge in the 1980 Illinois case *PASE* v. *Hannon* ruled that psychological tests are not inherently culturally biased when used in the context of an overall plan of psychoeducational evaluation. Although this decision was more favorable in terms of the continued use of psychological tests, the judge based his decision regarding its bias on *his own* examination of the test content. Not only was this a naive, unprofessional approach to the question of cultural bias, but it had the effect of placing WISC-R and Stanford-Binet questions and answers in the court record, thereby seriously compromising test security.

Cases in this area will probably continue to be examined in the courts. Because decisions to date have been based heavily on the judge's *opinion* of what makes a test culturally biased, it is hoped that the legal profession will be responsive to the technical knowledge of psychologists in the definition and understanding of test bias and will respect psychologists' concern about, and suggestions concerning, the obvious social and values questions involved. In some ways it is not helpful to lay the entire burden of blame on the so-called cultural bias of tests when much of the problem may stem from socioeconomic disadvantage and centuries of discrimination against blacks and other minorities, the effects of which have probably accumulated. Blaming test bias detracts from efforts to address the problems of educational disadvantage in more constructive ways.

One constructive response to the problem of EMR placement was taken by the formation by the Panel on Selection and Placement of Students in Programs for the Mentally Retarded set up by the National Research Council upon the request of the Department of Education's Office of Civil Rights. In its summary report this panel concluded that the disproportionately higher number of black children in special classes was not a problem unless the educational needs of the children were not being met by those classes ("Less Labeling, More Help," 1982). The panel recommended that assessment focused on the child's educational needs—that is, tied as closely as possible to the design and delivery of educational interventions—would help minority children obtain the quality education needed to address previous disadvantage. The panel also recommended that labels like EMR be used *only* if they lead to differential programs of instruction and that students should be reassessed annually and returned to regular classrooms as soon as possible. The most important goal implied here is that of improving the child's educational skills as effectively and quickly as possible; IQ tests, other types of assessment, and labels should be used with *that goal* in mind (see also Reschly, 1981).

In addition to the panel's recommendation (see Cordes, 1982), Reschly (1981) suggests that our assessment methods should put greater emphasis on adaptive behavior (e.g., interpersonal skills, daily functioning), on behavioral assessment, and on criterion-referenced testing, rather than on the concept of IQ alone, and that we need to better understand the EMR label. This classification includes children whose performance and functioning are essentially normal except for lower academic aptitude and lower classroom achievement than children having IQs in the normal range. Yet because of the label "retarded," such children are perceived as deficit in many more ways than are intended to be implied, leading to widespread misunderstanding and, often, to maltreatment on the part of teachers, parents, and peers. "Retarded" is a degrading, humiliating label that, as already mentioned, may become a self-fulfilling prophecy.

Test administrators should also take special care in the administration of tests to minority children. It is essential to be aware of the possibility that, in contrast to the white, middle-class examinee, the minority child (or any culturally different person) may have had less previous experience in taking tests, may be less motivated to perform well in the situation, or may be alienated by test content emphasizing white, middle-class values. It is the responsibility of the test administrator to build rapport with the culturally different examinee and, as far as possible, to ensure that the level of familiarity with testing materials and of motivation are as similar as possible to conditions that prevail when white, middle-class examinees are tested.

Finally, it is especially crucial in testing for educational classification and placement to ensure that the parents are informed concerning the meaning of test scores. Test users should view test scores as only one part of the data used to make classification decisions and should therefore interpret scores in the context of other information about the child. And, finally, reassessment leading to the reconsideration of earlier decisions should be systematically incorporated into the program of classification and placement.

Minimum Competency Testing. Minimum competency testing is another area where the use of tests has potentially great benefits, but not without some costs to individuals. The minimum competency testing movement usually refers to the requirement that individuals who've completed high school must pass a test of competency in the basic educational skills before being awarded a diploma. The movement supporting minimum competency testing gained impetus with increasing evidence concerning the failure of a high school education to guarantee even the most basic skills of reading and using arithmetic.

Based on research data provided by the National Assessment of Educational Progress (1976; see also Lerner, 1981), it has been estimated that about 13 percent of American high school graduates could be classified as illiterate, and another 44 percent as semi-literate, leaving a shocking figure of only 43 percent qualifying as functionally literate. Among black students, the illiteracy rate was 40 percent, and only 20 percent qualified as functionally literate. Even worse, these data did not include the 20 to 25 percent of American high school students who drop out before age 17, so they undoubtedly underestimate actual illiteracy rates in this country. A recent estimate from the U.S. Department of Education ("Losing the War of Letters," 1986) is that between 17 million and 21 million adult Americans are illiterate. Also widespread is what may be termed "functional anumeracy," or the inability to perform simple arithmetic functions such as adding and multiplying. The importance of basic skills and the seriousness of the problems of illiteracy and anumeracy for society and for individuals are suggested, for example, by Lerner (1981), who states that "functional literacy and/or numeracy is an essential prerequisite for the competent performance of almost all skilled jobs, blue collar or white collar, in the United States or in any other developed nation in the world today" (p. 1059).

As a result of these concerns, many states began to institute competency testing programs. In such programs, individuals were not to receive a high school diploma until they could demonstrate at least minimal ability to read and to use arithmetic. As of 1980, 38 states used minimum competency testing in the schools.

Unfortunately, the failure rate on minimum competency tests was much higher among black students than among white students, meaning that proportionately more blacks were denied high school diplomas on the basis of test scores. A number of charges of race discrimination were filed. For example, in the case of *Debra P*. v. *Turlington*, Florida's minimum competency requirement was contested, based on the fact that, if enforced, it would have served to deny diplomas to 29 percent of the state's black high school students, versus only 2 percent of the whites. On the first testing, 78 percent of blacks, versus only 25 percent of whites, failed. Arguments concerning the test's validity and the inferior quality of the education received by blacks were among those used to place a moratorium on minimum competency testing in Florida that lasted until 1982.

Although minimum competency testing is under continued scrutiny, several arguments in its favor, as well as against it, should be noted. First of all, minimum competency testing was intended to have, in the long run, a beneficial effect on students' educational and occupational attainments. An external requirement, such as a test of basic educational skills, is designed to have the effect of increasing time and effort on these basic skills on the part of both teachers and students. It has been hoped, therefore, that in the long run minimum competency testing will reduce rates of illiteracy and increase students' mastery of educational skills. In turn, students should later find greater occupational and economic success as well as the personal rewards from something so basic in this society as knowing how to read.

Another type of argument concerns the role of the federal government in matters of educational policy, including policy regarding minimum competency testing. Lerner (1981) argues that such policy decisions are more appropriately left to state and local governments. However, these cases are brought into the federal judicial system when plaintiffs attempt to redefine them (with judges' cooperation) as constitutional questions of due process and equal protection under the Fourteenth Amendment. Lerner argues persuasively that the Fourteenth Amendment does not prohibit minimum competency testing programs or guarantee high school diplomas as a constitutional right.

But even as minimum competency testing is designed to have positive effects and *should* be considered a matter of educational policy rather than civil rights, it *does* adversely affect blacks' ability to receive a high school diploma. Assuming evidence for content validity with reference to the instruction offered, until the quality of the education received by blacks is more consistently comparable to the quality of that received by whites and unless students and teachers are given time to prepare themselves for the *fact* of competency examinations, it may not be fair to deny diplomas on the basis of testing. Yet the alternative, which is to allow the serious problem of illiteracy to continue without the multifaceted attention that would include testing, does not sound appealing either. Again, there are no totally costless approaches to the problem.

Scholastic Aptitude Testing. One of the bitterest educational controversies has involved criticisms of the use of scholastic aptitude tests. In a widely read and commented-upon 1980 report (*The Reign of ETS: The Corporation That Makes up Minds*, authored by Allen Nairn and often called the "Nairn/Nader report"), Ralph Nader's research group charged that scholastic aptitude tests like the Scholastic Aptitude Tests (SAT) and the Law School Admission Test (LSAT) are not only biased against minority-group and lower-income students but are not *helpful*, because they do not predict success in college, not to mention success in pursuits following completion of formal education. Scores, the group contended, reflect family income rather than scholastic potential (Nairn, 1980). Furthermore, scores are not valid because they can be boosted significantly by coaching. The report was particularly critical of the Educational Testing Service (ETS), the publisher of many widely used scholastic aptitude tests, and implied that ETS's only concern was the profits that could be gained through scholastic aptitude testing, not with either the educational utility of testing or the scientific basis or social implications of testing. As may be expected, the Nairn/Nader report elicited considerable reaction and many responses to the charges from the testing and assessment community.

In response to charges questioning the quality of the SAT and tests like it, psychometricians have stressed that the SAT is, psychometrically, one of the most impressive tests available (Kaplan, 1982). It is highly reliable (values of Kuder-Richardson-20 coefficients average 0.91 for the SAT-V and 0.92 for the SAT-M) and possesses a respectable degree of validity for predicting grades in the first year of college. Although validity coefficients vary across academic majors, they range from the 0.10s to the 0.60s, and for liberal arts students average in the mid 0.40s for women and the 0.30s for men (Kaplan, 1982).

With respect to the alleged *lack* of predictive validity of these tests, the Nairn/Nader report's conclusions were based on frequent misinterpretation of validity data, for example, regression coefficients. In addition, the Nairn/Nader report failed to acknowledge the effects of restriction in range of aptitude test scores (because samples were constituted by individuals whose aptitude test scores were high enough to be selected) in reducing the maximum possible size of regression coefficients and of the less-than-perfect reliability and validity of the criterion itself, that is, grades during one's freshman year in college. Anyone who's been a freshman in college can attest to the challenges of adjustment and their potential effect on performance in classes. Given these considerations, the SAT and tests like it do a rather impressive job of prediction. And, in fact, Schrader's (1977) review of studies of the relationship of LSAT scores to grades in law school showed a strong positive relationship between the *variability* in students' LSAT scores and the obtained validity coefficient: the more variable, that is, the *less* restriction in range, the higher the predictive validity coefficient.

In its challenge of racial bias, the Nairn/Nader report defined a biased test as any test that results in a disproportionate selection of minorities—in other words, causes what has been referred to as "adverse impact." As has been mentioned, adverse impact is difficult to eradicate without throwing out tests altogether, and it *can* be addressed by simply including race as a variable in selection decisions. As long as there are group differences on standardized tests of cognitive abilities, any selection procedure not explicitly taking race into account will lead to the disproportionate selection of minority applicants.

Charges that SAT scores reflect primarily family wealth were based on inaccurate data. The correlation of SAT scores with family income has ranged between 0.23 and 0.29 (rather than 0.965, as reported by Nairn), and there is huge variability in family income at a *given* SAT score level. In actuality, family income is more closely related to first year grades than it is to test scores. Furthermore, high school grades, which the Nairn/Nader report said should be used *instead of* test scores to make admissions decisions, are almost as discriminatory against blacks as are test scores.

Other recommendations of the Nairn/Nader report restated guidelines already stated in the SAT manual (College Entrance Examination Board, 1986). For example, the Nairn/Nader report insisted that SAT scores should not be the only factor in selection, but the SAT manual has *always* recommended against such practices. Any selection policy based solely on one test score would be inappropriate and irresponsible. Even as scholastic aptitude tests are excellent predictors of both grades and persistence in higher education, it is essential to remember that there are a number of other important variables that scholastic aptitude tests simply do not measure. Variables such as motivation, social skills, common sense, perseverance, sense of humor, sensitivity and caring, and talent in a variety of areas are not measured by these tests. Certainly scholastic aptitude is helpful in terms of achieving goals of higher education, but there are many other personal and motivational qualities that are important to people's ability to be successful in and contribute to our society.

The responsibility of ETS, which has been met, is to continue to ensure correct use through the manual's clear and detailed guidelines concerning use and interpretation of test scores. It is the responsibility of college and university personnel to ensure that testing practices follow these guidelines, but, beyond that, it is not the responsibility of ETS to ensure that Harvard or Yale, for

example, institute a particular type of *selection* policy. As stated by Kaplan (1982, p. 22), "Psychometricians and test constructors have an ethical responsibility to develop fair selection devices, and with the help of these devices, college administrators have the responsibility to assure that the available spaces are filled in a fair and just manner."

In fact, many colleges and graduate and professional schools clearly are using much more than test scores in admissions decisions. Law schools admit a far higher proportion of blacks than whites at LSAT score levels below 600 (Evans, 1977). For example, 62 percent of black, versus only 27 percent of white, students scoring between 450 and 500 on the LSAT were admitted to at least one law school (Evans, 1977).

Whether or not test scores are used may not even be important to admission to college. Kaplan (1982) and Linn (1982) demonstrate that tests like the SAT have very little effect on whether or not a given individual will go to college. According to Hartnett and Feldnesser (1980), a third of all colleges accept 90 percent or more of those applying, and only 10 percent of schools select fewer than 50 percent of their applicants. Although SATs may be too low for acceptance to Harvard or Princeton they rarely stand in the way of a college education. Furthermore, there are many institutions that selectively accept and reject people without ever using tests at all (Hartnett & Feldnesser, 1980; Linn, 1982). Thus, the hostility of the Nairn/Nader group, even if warranted, is unfairly focused on a single organization (e.g., Linn, 1982).

The Nairn/Nader criticism concerning the "coachability" of scholastic aptitude tests is based on the argument that if such scores as those on the SAT can be significantly increased through a few hours or weeks of "cramming" then they can't be very meaningful either conceptually or in the prediction of college performance. The argument is based on the following three assumptions: that commercial coaching programs significantly improve test performance; that the effects of "coaching," if any, cast doubt on the meaningfulness of the concept of scholastic aptitude; and that coaching reduces the predictive validity of test scores.

With respect to the first assumption, research suggests that the amount of improvement in test scores is related to the time spent in the coaching program. Messick (1980), Linn (1982), and Anastasi (1981) summarize evidence suggesting that 8-to-12-hour coaching programs result in an average 10-point increase in scores. Longer coaching programs are necessary to result in 30-point gains: 45 hours for SAT-M and 260 hours for SAT-V. Increases over 30 points would appear to require coaching as time-consuming as full-time schooling. The relative insignificance of these 10-to-30-point increases is suggested by the fact that a 30-point increase corresponds to only three additional correct items (Anastasi, 1981). Ten to 30 additional SAT points would rarely be significant enough to change a decision of "reject" to one of "accept." Thus, the score increases resulting from coaching programs are, at best, of minimal practical significance.

The effects of coaching cast doubt on the meaning of test scores only if coaching does not address the *developed abilities* of verbal and mathematic reasoning and comprehension (Messick, 1980). The aptitudes measured by the SAT and similar tests are not innate, but rather represent the impact of *years of schooling* on a person with some range of potential intellectual development. To the extent that coaching programs are long enough in duration and include emphasis on the basic cognitive skills in addition to or instead of "cramming" on specific test items, they should enrich the individual's developed abilities and enhance his or her capability of performing well in school. In other words, if coaching programs emphasize the important cognitive skills and abilities, they would be expected to improve both test scores and performance in college. In this way they resemble any effective educational intervention. However, compensating fully for years of inadequate schooling takes years of compensatory education and cannot be expected from the standard coaching programs available, no matter how high in quality.

Finally, evidence regarding the effects of coaching on test validity is sparse and, again, the effects would depend on the nature of the coaching—that is, on the position of the particular program on the "cramming" versus "education" continuum. Research that is available suggests that cramming programs lead to reductions in the predictive validity of test scores (Linn, 1982; Anastasi, 1981).

Hence, in response to the Nairn/Nader report it may be said that score increases due to coaching are of questionable practical significance and are certainly of less significance than implied in the report. However, when score increases do occur they can be viewed positively and as consistent with the concept of scholastic aptitude if the coaching program emphasized the acquisition of important cognitive skills. But the small effects of coaching in general seem insufficient to warrant the attacks of the Nairn/Nader report.

In essence, criticisms of scholastic aptitude testing, like those of other uses of standardized tests of cognitive abilities, are to some extent misdirected. They are phrased as psychometric issues (e.g., test validity, the effects of coaching, and so forth), when in reality they should be phrased as issues of human values. Readers interested in more information and discussion of this controversy may wish to see the ETS response (1980b), Guion (1981), Kaplan (1982), Linn (1982), Hargadon (1981), Anastasi (1981), and the *Harvard Educational Review* articles of Slack and Porter (1980a,b) and Jackson (1980).

Summary of Issues in Cultural Bias

In summary, critics of standardized tests point to the well-established test score differences between blacks and whites and the numerous instances where low test scores have restricted the educational and/or occupational opportunities of blacks and other low-status groups. They contend that standardized tests do not accurately measure the abilities of low-status groups and that they should be used, if at all, only with middle-class groups. Test proponents, on the other hand, counter with psychometric and statistical arguments. They point, for example, to the equivalent predictive validity across racial groups and to the fact that objective, well-standardized tests should be the most "race-blind" selection techniques available. But the dialogue has not led to resolution of the controversy.

Most likely the reason why all the argument, debate, statistical innovations, and research data have neither resolved nor quieted the controversy is that it is not a technical, statistical, methodological controversy nor one that is specific to testing. Rather, it is a *value* controversy, and the values questions concern the merits of traditional methods of selection versus demands for equal opportunity (Gordon & Terrell, 1981). In other words, the issue is really not the tests *used* in selection, but the existence of selection policies that by their very nature and definition select some and reject others.

Testing in education and industry is based on the assumptions and values of a meritocracy, that is, that ability, talent, and achievement should be developed and rewarded regardless of social class, family background, or other background characteristics. And although the idea of a meritocracy has been thought to be a great improvement over status based on wealth, family name and ancestry, or race, it is in principle a problematic concept because measured ability and past opportunity are related. A

true concept of equal opportunity in the future really necessitates some control over opportunity in the past. Blacks and other disadvantaged groups may argue that past inequities in educational and occupational opportunity leave them at a disadvantage in terms of the meritocratic *ideal* of competition for present and future opportunities. Tests, therefore, continue to result in adverse impact when traditional methods of selection are used.

In summary, it seems self-evident that tests should not be the only basis on which to decide access to educational and occupational opportunities in our society. Concerns about past inequities and their possible continuing effects on blacks and other disadvantaged groups must be part of any decision that controls access to opportunities. Test users must familiarize themselves with the technical and interpretive considerations and cautions necessary in testing minority group members and, most important, must confront the reality of inherent contradictions between some aspects of the institutional value system—for example, selection and the societal value of equal opportunity. It probably makes most sense to attempt to develop decision models that can consider and evaluate quantitative data obtained from various assessment procedures in the context of institutional objectives of equal opportunity and affirmative action. Also, where possible, tests should serve a developmental, diagnostic, pedagogical function; they can help clarify in what direction and *how* the individual's talents can be further developed and utilized.

To argue that tests should not be used at all is as extreme and untenable a position as that of total unresponsiveness to issues of discrimination and cultural bias. Rather, tests must be used in ways that, as far as possible, take advantage of the tremendous *utility* of test and other assessment data, while also facilitating optimal understanding and nurturance of a wide range of individual and cultural differences.

TEST INTERPRETATION WITH RACIAL/ETHNIC MINORITIES

One of the most important AERA/APA/ NCME standards for test use, especially when working with an individual from a racial or ethnic minority group, is the following: "A test taker's score should not be accepted as a reflection of a lack of ability with respect to the characteristic being tested without alternative explanations for the test taker's inability to perform on that test at that time" (AERA, APA, NCME, 1985; p. 43).

In interpreting the ability-test scores of a minority group member, the likelihood that the individual has come from a socioeconomically deprived background or a less privileged school system *must be* kept in mind. Consider the following two hypothetical students, each having ACT scores at the 30th percentile.

First, Jill is an 18-year-old white female who has just graduated from the top suburban high school near your city. Because this school is outside of the city school district, it was not subject to busing to alleviate de facto segregation in the city's schools, and middle-class white families moved to this suburb with great haste once busing was enforced in the city district. Not surprisingly, the suburban school's resources are rich, providing students with excellent educational opportunities.

Joan, on the other hand, is an 18-year-old black female who has just graduated from a city high school. She is from a relatively poor family, and the school itself was minimally equipped with books and materials.

Thus, it can be argued that Jill grew up in an "enriched" environment (at least in terms of support for academic pursuits), whereas Joan grew up in a "deprived" en-

vironment. Jill and Joan have the same ACT scores, but it would be reasonable to interpret them differently. Although we don't know if there are other factors that limited Jill's intellectual development, we can assume that Joan's background was not conducive to the full development of her intellectual potential and that, given environmental enrichment, she may be able to do substantially better academically than her current test scores would indicate. Certainly there are many reasons, such as lack of motivation, why students of all races and socioeconomic backgrounds might underutilize their intellectual potential, but minority students usually start with a less advantaged educational background. Thus, experiences that can help to enrich their background are vital.

GENDER ISSUES IN TEST USE

Gender issues in test use focus around the problems of sex restrictiveness in interest inventories and in aptitude batteries, and sex bias in the nature of aptitude test item content.

Sex Restrictiveness in Vocational Interest Inventories

The concept of sex restrictiveness in interest inventories is based on the pervasive and strong influence in our society of gender-role socialization and the continuing existence of *occupational sex segregation* (see Betz & Fitzgerald, 1987). Gender role socialization is the phenomenon by which girls are socialized into traditionally female roles, personality characteristics, competencies, and interests, and, likewise, boys are socialized into traditional male areas of competency and interest. Occupational sex segregation refers to the continuing overrepresentation of women in a small number of "pink-collar" jobs such as waitress and secretary and in the traditionally female professions, including nursing, teaching, social work, etc., and their continuing underrepresentation in traditional male areas such as the sciences, engineering, academia, business management, and the skilled trades.

Vocational interest inventories have, at least until recently, unintentionally emphasized socialized sex differences and, consequently, have perpetuated occupational sex segregation and limited the options of individual men and women. To understand the process by which this has occurred, some background may be helpful.

Historically, the interests of the two sexes were measured separately (Campbell, 1977; Hansen, 1984a, 1984b). The construction of separate forms of the Strong Vocational Interest Blank for Men (SVIB-M; Strong, 1927) and for women (SVIB-W; 1933) was based on the different item responses of men and women and on the marked differences between men and women in the extent and nature of their employment (Campbell, 1977). For decades this system was generally accepted, although career-oriented women were frequently administered the SVIB-M rather than the SVIB-W because of the former's greater utility in suggesting professional level careers (Campbell, 1977).

Although the more recent criticisms of sex bias and restrictiveness in interest inventories have largely eliminated the use of separate forms for males and females (see expanded discussion below), men and women continue to respond differentially to many interest inventory items. Generally, women are more likely than men to indicate interests in social and artistic activities, whereas men are more likely than women to indicate interest in scientific, technical, and mechanical activities.

The existence of sex differences at the item level has resulted in different overall score patterns for the two sexes (Cole & Hanson, 1975). Raw scores on interest tests are computed by simply summing the number of "yes" or "like" responses to the items representing each domain of interest—for example, the six Holland themes measured in the Self-Directed Search. Combined sex norms compare a person's scores on each theme or interest scale to those of a standardization sample consisting of both males and females. Because most interest scales are composed of items differentially reflective of the experiences of males versus females (the items "I like to build things with wood" and "I like to take care of children" are illustrative), it is not surprising that when raw or combined sex norms are used, females obtain higher mean scores on the Social, Artistic, and Conventional themes, whereas males obtain higher means on the Realistic, Investigative, and Enterprising themes (Gottfredson, Holland, & Gottfredson, 1975). Similar findings have resulted using the Vocational Interest Inventory (VII; Lunneborg, 1980), a measure of Roe's eight fields of occupational interest. Findings of sex differences on basic dimensions of vocational interest are most evident and durable for Social and Realistic (Technical) interests. Social interests are far more predominant among females, whereas Realistic interests are found far more frequently among males (e.g., Lunneborg, 1979a, 1980; Prediger, 1980).

One major implication of differential raw score patterns among males and females is that when these scores are taken to the interpretive guides accompanying interest inventories (such as The Occupations Finder accompanying the Self-Directed Search [SDS]; Holland, 1985b), the resulting occupational suggestions tend to reinforce the existing segregation of females and males in our society into traditionally female and traditionally male occupations. High scores on the Social and Conventional themes suggest traditionally female educational and social welfare and office and clerical occupations. In contrast, females' lower scores on the Realistic, Investigative, and Enterprising themes result in less frequent suggestion of traditionally male professions—for example, medicine, engineering, science, and of occupations in management and the skilled trades. Thus, socialized patterns of interest lead to interest inventory results that perpetuate females' overrepresentation in traditionally female occupations and their underrepresentation in occupations traditionally dominated by males.

Such divergent and sex-stereotypic suggestions of occupational alternatives to males and females were the basis for the criticisms of sex bias and sex restrictiveness in interest inventories, extensively documented and discussed in reports funded by the National Institute of Education (Diamond, 1975b; Tittle & Zytowski, 1978). According to this and other discussions of sex bias, the use of separate forms for men and women, sexist language in occupational titles (e.g., policeman versus police officer), and raw scores or combined-sex normative scores, among other things, contributed to the failure of interest inventories to result in fairness in the suggestion of occupational alternatives to males and females. In other words, interest inventories served to maintain and perpetuate the limited range of occupations considered appropriate for and usually pursued by women.

In response to the criticisms of sex bias, many test developers have addressed these issues by combining the men's and women's forms—for example, the Strong-Campbell Interest Inventory—by eliminating sexist language and by discussing issues of sex-role socialization in interpretive materials (Association for Measurement and Evaluation in Guidance, 1977). In revisions of the SDS, sexist occupational titles were changed and items with vastly different endorsement percentages for the two sexes were omitted.

In addition to changes such as those mentioned above, other test developers have focused on reducing the sex restrictiveness of interest inventory scores. The two major approaches to reducing sex restrictiveness in the scores that provided for basic dimensions of vocational interest are the use of same-sex normative scores and the use of sex-balanced items. Same-sex normative scores compare a person's scores on basic dimensions of vocational interest—for example, the Holland themes or the Basic Interest scales of the SCII—to those of persons of the same sex. Thus, women are compared to other women, whereas men are compared to other men. The use of same-sex norms increases the likelihood that the background socialization experiences of the comparison sample are more similar to those of the examinee, and this in turn tends to highlight interests that have developed in spite of the limiting effects of sex-role socialization. The SCII provides same-sex normative scores for both the General Occupational (i.e., Holland) Themes and the Basic Interest Scales (see Hansen, 1984b, 1986 for guidelines regarding their use.)

The second approach to reducing sex restrictiveness in interest inventories is the use of sex-balanced item sets. A sex-balanced inventory scale—for example, one of the Holland themes—would be constructed to include items more likely to characterize male sex role socialization and others more common in female socialization; the desired end result is interest scales on which the sexes obtain similar raw scores. The Unisex Edition of the ACT-IV (UNIACT; Lamb & Prediger, 1981) and the revised version of the Vocational Interest Inventory (VII; Lunneborg, 1980, 1981) are based on this strategy of scale construction, and both result in more equivalent distributions of scores across the six Holland themes (UNIACT) or Roe's eight fields (VII) for the two sexes. Thus, on the UNIACT, for example, the Realistic scale contains items pertaining to sewing and cooking, that is, *content* areas more often emphasized in the backgrounds of females, in addition to items more reflective of males' socialization experiences—for example, the skills learned in high school shop courses.

Use of same-sex normative scores and sex-balanced interest scales is intended to increase the probability that females who could potentially be interested in Realistic, Investigative, or Enterprising occupations will obtain interest inventory profiles suggesting those areas. Thus, such methods of constructing and scoring interest inventories are designed to facilitate females' exploration of the full range of occupational alternatives and to minimize the extent to which women continue to be directed toward traditional female occupations.

Test users are urged to use either same-sex normative scores in interpreting scales such as the Holland themes or to use sex-balanced interest inventories. In essence, use of same-sex norms and sex-balanced interest inventory scales allows test users to be alert for areas in which the client has developed interests *in spite of* sex-role socialization (there seems no good reason why such interests should not be encouraged by suggesting further, or, in some cases, initial opportunities for exploration).

Thus, while attempts to remove sex restrictiveness from interest inventories are important and useful, the more direct solution to the problem of sex-stereotypic vocational interests involves increasing the range of experiences relevant to the development of those interests. Until girls and women have the opportunity to engage in activities relevant to, for example, Realistic and Investigative as well as Social and Artistic interest areas, interests in nontraditional areas will not develop in the majority of women. Encouraging a wider variety of activities and experiences for young girls and, for women, also encouraging involvement in jobs or job-related experiences beyond the limits of socialized interests and experiences are both necessary; women's vocational interests and, consequently, their career choices should derive from a rich background of experience and knowledge rather than from a background exposing them only to stereotypical female areas of activity and interest.

Gender Issues in Aptitude Testing

Regarding employment selection, the major issue facing women has not been that of intelligence testing, as it has been for racial minorities, but physical requirements—for example, height and weight, on which there are sex differences. For instance, there are often height and weight requirements for jobs such as police officer and firefighter. Such requirements can be highly discriminatory against women. Counselors and other test users should have an understanding of federal, state, and local regulations concerning the use of tests in employment selection, and in particular the importance of demonstrating that a physical requirement is job-related if it is to be used in selection.

Test users should also be concerned about the fact that in the areas of aptitude and ability testing, males have often obtained higher scores than females on tests representative of stereotypically male domains—for example, mechanical reasoning, spatial ability, and mathematical ability. Such score differences, when used in educational or occupational planning, may serve to further restrict females' educational and career options.

To some extent, aptitude test score differences, like interest test score differences, are attributable to differential patterns of male and female socialization in society. For example, males have been encouraged to take math, science, and shop courses, and females have been encouraged to take English, home economics, and typing. But tests themselves have worsened the problem through bias in item content and wording. In aptitude tests, for example, use of predominantly male characters in word problems, the use of sexist language, and sex-biased content have frequently been used (see Betz & Fitzgerald, 1987, for numerous examples).

Examples of sex-biased content may be drawn, for instance, from the General Aptitude Test Battery (GATB) Tool Matching Test, which is a measure of the ability of form perception. In the GATB Numerical Reasoning Test, male characters and objects predominate—the word problems focus on amounts of lumber and electrical wire rather than on fabric or recipe ingredients. Tools, lumber, and electric wire are far more common in the background experiences of boys than they are in girls growing up in our society. Test items could be written to use content such as sewing patterns to measure form perception and amounts of food or fabric in spatial test items or in math word problems—this content would probably tap more into the socialization experiences of females and yet be equally appropriate in the measurement of spatial and math abilities.

In an illuminating recent study, Betz and Hackett (1983) measured the perceived self-efficacy expectations or confidence of college women and men with respect to a variety of math tasks and problems. There were 18 math tasks, 16 math-related college courses, and 18 math problems, or a total of 52 items. As predicted, males reported higher expectations of self-efficacy on 49 of the 52 math-related items. There were only *three* out of 52 items on which females reported higher expectations of self-efficacy than males—those three items were as follows: (1) figure out much material to buy in order to make curtains; (2) estimate your grocery bill in your head as you pick up items; and (3) calculate recipe quantities for a dinner for 41 when the original recipe was for 12 people.

Given these data, one wonders what the effects would be of testing math ability, as well as math self-efficacy, using a more balanced set of items. If the sex differences in self-efficacy expectations can be eliminated by asking questions based on content familiar to women, it seems that ability measurement should also be revised. A similar conclusion has been made by Lunneborg and Lunneborg (1986) in their research exploring the experiential bases for the development of spatial ability. (It should be noted that revisions of test content should not be taken as a sufficient answer to the limiting effects of sex-role socialization on the development of both males and females, and it is hoped that broadened childhood experiences for both boys and girls would be facilitated by parents, the schools, the media, etc. But until socialization practices change for the majority of girls and women, testing them using content underemphasized in their background experiences is unfair.)

Even if a test profile is not used in selection, it may be used by clients and counselor to make educational and career decisions. And in this respect it is vital to again recall that we cannot accurately measure an ability, or an interest, if the person's background experience has provided only limited exposure to that domain of competency. The APA standard cautioning against inferences of lack of ability prior to exhausting other explanations should be recalled in this regard as well as with racial minorities. For example, the literature suggests that sex differences in math performance begin to appear only as girls stop taking math, and that the differences disappear when math background is controlled for (see Betz & Fitzgerald, 1987, for an extensive review). Thus, lack of potential must not be inferred in the absence of ample opportunity to develop that potential.

There are several ways to address these issues. First, test users should be well informed regarding the nature and occurrence of sex bias in ability tests. In an important recent study, Selkow (1984) evaluated the extent of bias and sex-role stereotyping in 74 major tests of ability, personality, and school achievement and readiness. Familiarity with the methods and findings of this study would facilitate informed test use.

Second, it is critical that test users, when interpreting differential aptitude test scores—for example, mathematics versus verbal ability—remember that gender-role socialization shapes girls and boys differently, that girls are not encouraged to continue taking math, and that girls may need more help in building confidence and reducing anxiety with respect to math. The amount of math taken in high school and college is strongly related to the degree to which educational and career options remain open or closed to the individual. A counselor examining a pattern of aptitude test scores should not overlook alternative explanations for low scores, particularly in the context of overall high ability.

Finally, use of same-sex norms in interpreting ability test scores, urging test publishers to include test items from the backgrounds of both sexes, and cognizance of the overall tendency of females to underutilize their abilities in educational and career pursuits are among the possible ways of addressing the sex bias in ability-test items.

CROSS-CULTURAL ISSUES IN TEST USE

At least two major issues should be considered in the cross-cultural use of tests. First, when using tests with ethnic minorities or foreign-born examinees in this country, the possible influences of different cultures on both test performance and the meanings of various attributes and behaviors must be considered. As was mentioned earlier, tests of behavioral capabilities and personality may be of particular concern because they inevitably involve assumptions about appropriate or psychologically healthy versus less appropriate or healthy behaviors and characteristics. For example, the behavior of assertiveness in some cultures might be viewed as inappropriate vis-á-vis to at least some other people—for example, one's elders—yet not be considered inappropriate in other cultures.

The second issue regarding the use of tests cross-culturally centers around whether or not a test has been translated into other languages or cultural usages (e.g., making sure that a test developed in America is revised to incorporate language usages common in Great Britain or Australia) and, if it is available in other cultures, assuring that there are data pertaining to the reliability, validity, and utility of the test scores in that culture.

The extent to which a test satisfies these criteria varies markedly across tests, although most tests provide little or no information about cross-cultural usage. It is the responsibility of the test user to make sure that a test to be used in another country or with people from another culture has been supported for those uses. For example, the cross-cultural utility of the SCII has been investigated in a series of studies (Fouad, Cudeck, & Hansen, 1984; Fouad & Hansen, 1987; Fouad, Hansen, & Arias, 1986). In a particularly important study, for example, the utility of the SCII with bilingual Hispanic high school students was investigated (Fouad, Cudeck, & Hansen, 1984). Super's Career Development Inventory (CDI) has also been the subject of considerable cross-cultural research, and several editions for use in foreign countries have been developed. For example, the CDI has been revised for use in such countries in Australia, Portugal, and Great Britain (see also Betz, 1988). Holland (1985b) discusses research investigating the applicability of the SDS in other countries.

Although the SCII and the CDI represent exemplars in this area, most tests have not been examined for cross-cultural uses. At this point three statements can be made with confidence: (1) use of a test that has not been validated in the population in which it is to be used is highly problematic and should be avoided unless no locally validated alternatives are available; (2) there has been very little research investigating the cross-cultural or cross-national utility of well-known U.S.-developed tests (but see Hansen, 1984a for a review of what is available); and (3) additional research in this area is sorely needed and would have the potential of contributing substantially to the utility of tests and assessments.

SUMMARY

Psychological tests and assessments of persons and environments have been shown to have tremendous utility for a wide range of applied problems. They are also excellent tools for facilitating increased understanding through theory development and research. However, they are tools that can be used in harmful, inaccurate, and inappropriate, as well as helpful, appropriate, and effective ways, and it has been the purpose of this chapter to inform the student and potential test user about these potential misuses. Test users must be familiar with, and guide their practices in accordance with, APA ethical principles and the AERA/APA/NCME test standards. In addition, they must be familiar with the possible negative effects of various kinds of test use and with ways in which those effects can be minimized. If tests and assessments are used carefully, knowledgeably, thoughtfully, and ethically, their potential for great benefits and wide practical utility will be fully realized.

References

ABELSON, R. P. (1962). Situational variables in personality research. In S. Messick and J. Ross (Eds.), *Measurement in personality and cognition*. New York: Wiley.

AHMANN, J. S. (1985). Review of SCAT-III. In J. V. Mitchell, Jr. (Ed.), *The ninth mental measurements yearbook*. Lincoln, NE: University of Nebraska Press.

ALLPORT, G. W. (1937). *Personality, a psychological interpretation*. New York: Holt, Rinehart and Winston.

ALLPORT, G. W. (1966). Traits revisited. *American Psychologist, 21*, 1–10.

American College Testing Program. (1987). *College student profiles: Norms for the ACT assessment*. Iowa City, IA: Author.

American College Testing Program. (1988). *Technical manual for the ACT assessment*. Iowa City, IA: Author.

American College Testing Program. (1988). *Resources for educators*. Iowa City, IA: Author.

American Educational Research Association, American Psychological Association, National Council on Measurement in Education. (1985). *Standards for educational and psychological testing*. Washington, DC: Authors.

American Educational Research Association, American Psychological Association, National Council on Measurement in Education. (1985). *Joint technical standards for educational and psychological testing*. Washington, DC: Authors.

American Educational Research Association, National Council on Measurement in Education. (1955). *Technical recommendations for achievement tests*. Washington, DC: Authors.

American Psychiatric Association. (1952). *Diagnostic and statistical manual of mental disorders* (1st ed.). Washington, DC: Author.

American Psychiatric Association. (1980). *Diagnostic and statistical manual of psychiatric disorders* (3rd ed.). Washington, DC: Author.

American Psychiatric Association. (1987). *Diagnostic and statistical manual of mental disorders* (3rd ed., revised). Washington, DC: Author.

American Psychological Association. (1953). *Technical recommendations for psychological tests and diagnostic techniques*. Washington, DC: Author.

American Psychological Association. (1966). *Standards for educational and psychological tests and manuals*. Washington, DC: Author.

American Psychological Association. (1974). *Standards for educational and psychological tests and manuals*. Washington, DC: Author.

American Psychological Association. (1981). Ethical principles of psychologists. *American Psychologist, 36*, 633–638.

American Psychological Association, American Educational Research Association, National Council on Measurement in Education. (1966). *Standards for educational and psychologic measurement*. Washington, DC: Authors.

ANASTASI, A. (1981). Coaching, test sophistication, and developed abilities. *American Psychologist, 36*, 1086–1093.

ANASTASI, A. (1982). *Psychological testing* (5th ed.). New York: Macmillan.

ANASTASI, A. (1985). Review of the Kaufman Assessment Battery for Children. In J. V. Mitchell, Jr. (Ed.) (1985). *Ninth Mental Measurements Yearbook*. Lincoln, NE: University of Nebraska Press.

ANASTASIA, A. (1988). *Psychological testing* (6th ed.). New York: Macmillan.

ANGYAL, A. (1941). *Foundation for a science of personality*. Cambridge, MA: Harvard University Press.

ANSORGE, C. J. (1985). Review of the Cognitive Abilities Test. In J. V. Mitchell, Jr. (Ed.) *Ninth Mental Measurements Yearbook*. Lincoln, NE: University of Nebraska Press.

ASHBURN, S. S. (1980). Selected theories of human development. In C. S. Schuster and S. S. Ashburn (Eds.), *The process of human development* (pp. 897–910). Boston: Little, Brown.

ASHER, H. B. (1976). *Causal modeling.* Beverly Hills, CA: Sage Publications.

Association for Measurement and Evaluation in Guidance. Commission on Sex Bias in Measurement. (1977). A case history of change: A review of responses to the challenge of sex bias in interest inventories. *Measurement and Evaluation in Guidance, 10,* 148–152.

Association of American Medical Colleges. (1977). *New Medical College Admissions Test: Interpretive manual.* Washington, DC: Author.

ASTIN, A. W. (1963). Further validation of the Environmental Assessment Technique. *Journal of Educational Psychology, 54,* 217–226.

ASTIN, A. W. (1965). *Who goes where to college?* Chicago: Science Research Associates.

ASTIN, A. W. (1968). *The college environment.* Washington, DC: American Council on Education.

ASTIN, A. W., and HOLLAND, J. L. (1961). The Environmental Assessment Technique: A way to measure college environments. *Journal of Educational Psychology, 52,* 308–316.

AZRIN, V. B., AZRIN, N. H., and ARMSTRONG, P. M. (1977). The student-oriented classroom: A method of improving student conduct and satisfaction. *Behavior Therapy, 8,* 193–204.

BANDURA, A. (1978). The self system in reciprocal determinism. *American Psychologist, 33,* 344–359.

BARKER, R. G. (1965). Explorations in ecological psychology. *American Psychologist, 20,* 1–14.

BARKER, R. G. (1968). Ecological psychology: Concepts and methods for studying the environment of human behavior. Stanford, CA: Stanford University Press.

BARRATT, W. R., and HOOD, A. B. (1986). Assessing development of purpose. In A. B. Hood (Ed.), *The Iowa student development inventories.* Iowa City, IA: Hitech Press.

BATHORY, M. J. (1967). Occupational aspirations and vocational maturity. Paper presented at the meeting of the American Vocational Association, Cleveland.

BECK, A. T. (1967). *Depression: Clinical, experimental and therapeutic aspects.* New York: Harper and Row.

BECK S. J. (1937). *Introduction to the Rorschach method.* New York: American Orthopsychiatric Association.

BECK S. J. (1944). *Rorschach's test* (Vol. I: Basic Processes). New York: Grune and Stratton.

BECKER, J. M. T. (1977). A learning analysis of the development of peer-oriented behavior in nine-month-old infants. *Developmental Psychology, 13,* 481–491.

BELLAK, J., PARSQUARELLI, B. A., and BRANERMAN, S. (1949). The use of the Thematic Apperception Test in psychotherapy. *Journal of Nervous and Mental Diseases, 110,* 51–65.

BEM, D. J. (1972). Constructing cross-situational consistencies in behavior: Some thoughts on Alker's critique of Mischel. *Journal of Personality, 40,* 17–26.

BENDER, L. (1938). *A Visual Motor Gestalt Test and its clinical use* (Research Monograph No. 3). New York: American Orthopsychiatric Association.

BENNETT, G. K., SEASHORE, H. G., and WESMAN, A. G. (1974). *Manual for the Differential Aptitude Tests.* New York: Psychological Corporation.

BENNETT, G. K., SEASHORE, H. G., and WESMAN, A. G. (1982a). *Administrators handbook for the Differential Aptitude Tests, Forms V and W.* New York: Psychological Corporation.

BENTLER, P. M. (1968). Heterosexual behavior assessments: I. Males. *Behavioral Research and Therapy, 6,* 21.

BENTLER, P. M. (1980). Multivariate analysis with latent variables: Causal Modeling. *Annual Review of Psychology, 31,* 419–456.

BERNAL, E. M., JR. (1975). A response to "Educational uses of tests with disadvantaged subjects." *American Psychologist, 30,* 93–95.

BERSOFF, D. N. (1981). Testing and the law. *American Psychologist, 36,* 1047–1056.

BETZ, N. E. (1988). The assessment of career development and maturity. In W. B. Walsh and S. H. Osipow (Eds.), *Career decision-making* (pp. 77–136). Hillsdale, NJ: Lawrence Erlbaum Associates.

BETZ, N. E., and FITZGERALD, L. F. (1987). *The career psychology of women.* New York: Academic Press.

BETZ, N. E., and HACKETT, G. (1983). The relationship of mathematics self-efficacy expectations to the selection of science-based college majors. *Journal of Vocational Behavior, 23,* 329–345.

BETZ, N. E., and WEISS, D. J. (1973). An empirical study of two-stage ability testing. Research Report 73-4, Psychometric Methods Program, University of Minnesota.

BIJOU, S. W., and PETERSON, R. F. (1971). Functional analysis in the assessment of children. In P. McReynolds (Ed.), *Advances in psychological assessment* (Vol. 2, pp. 63–78). Palo Alto, CA: Science and Behavior Books.

BINGHAM, W. V. D., and MOORE, B. V. (1924). *How to interview.* New York: Harper and Row.

BLOCK, J. (1961). *The Q sort method in personality assessment and psychiatric research.* Springfield, IL: Charles C. Thomas. (Reissued by Consulting Psychologists Press, Palo Alto, CA. [1978].)

BOEHM, A. E. (1985). [Review of the Home Observation for Measurement of the Environment.] In J. V. Mitchell, Jr. (Ed.), *The ninth mental measurements yearbook* (Vol. I, pp. 663–665). Lincoln, NE: The Buros Institute of Mental Measurements.

BOLTON, T. L. (1891–1892). The growth of memory in school children. *American Journal of Psychology, 4,* 362–380.

BORDIN, E. S. (1943). A theory of vocational interests as dynamic phenomena. *Educational and Psychological Measurement, 3,* 49–65.

BORGEN, F. H. (1986). New approaches to the assessment of interests. In W. B. Walsh & S. H. Osipow (Eds.), *Advances in vocational psychology: The assessment of interests, Volume I.* Hillsdale, NJ: Lawrence Erlbaum Associates.

BORGEN, F. H., and HARPER, G. T. (1973). Predictive validity of measured vocational interests with black and white college men. *Measurement and Evaluation in Guidance, 48,* 378–382.

BORING, E. G. (1950). *A history of experimental psychology* (2d ed.). Englewood Cliffs, NJ: Prentice Hall.

BOWERS, K. S. (1973). Situationism in psychology: An analysis and a critique. *Psychological Review, 80,* 307–336.

BRAY, D. W. (1982, May). Job, school choices call for valid tests. *APA Monitor,* p. 4.

BRELAND, H. M. (1979). Population validity and college entrance measures. New York: The College Board.

BROWN, F. G. (1971). Review of Super's Work Values Inventory. *Measurement and Evaluation in Guidance, 4,* 189–190.

BROWN, F. G. (1983). *Principles of educational and psychological testing* (3rd ed.). New York: Holt, Rinehart and Winston.

BROWN, R. D. (1985). [Review of the College Student Experiences Questionnaire.] In J. V. Mitchell, Jr., (Ed.), *The ninth mental measurements yearbook* (Vol. I, pp. 365–366). Lincoln, NE: The Buros Institute of Mental Measurements.

BROWN, W. R., and MCGUIRE, J. M. (1976). Current psychological assessment practices. *Professional Psychology, 7,* 475–484.

BRUNSWIK, E. (1952). *The conceptual framework of psychology.* Chicago: University of Chicago Press.

BRUNSWIK, E. (1956). *Perception and the representative design of psychological experiments.* Berkeley: University of California Press.

BUCK, J. N. (1948). The H-T-P technique, a qualitative and quantitative scoring manual. *Journal of Clinical Psychology, 4,* 317–396.

BUEHLER, C. (1933). *Der menschliche lebenslauf als psychologiches problem. [The human course through life as a psychological problem.]* Leipzig: Hirzel.

BUROS, O. K. (Ed.). (1938). *The nineteen thirty-eight mental measurements yearbook.* Highland Park, NJ: Gryphon Press.

BUROS, O. K. (Ed.). (1961). *Tests in print.* Highland Park, NJ: Gryphon Press.

BUROS, O. K. (Ed.). (1972). *The seventh mental measurements yearbook* (Vol. I). Highland Park, NJ: Gryphon Press.

BUROS, O. K. (Ed.). (1974). *Tests in print: II.* Highland Park, NJ: Gryphon Press.

BUROS, O. K. (Ed.). (1975c). *Vocational tests and reviews.* Highland Park, NJ: Gryphon Press.

BUROS, O. K. (Ed.). (1978). *The eighth mental measurements yearbook* (Vol. I). Highland Park, NJ: Gryphon Press.

BURT, C. (1949). The structure of the mind: A review of the results of factor analysis. *British Journal of Educational Psychology, 19,* 110–111, 176–199.

CALDWELL, B. M., and BRADLEY, R. H. (1984). *Home Observation for Measurement of the Environment.* Little Rock, AR: University of Arkansas at Little Rock, Center for Child Development and Education.

CAMPBELL, D. P. (1971). *Handbook for the Strong Vocational Interest Blank.* Minneapolis: University of Minnesota Press.

CAMPBELL, D. P. (1977). *Manual for the SVIB-SCII Strong-Campbell Interest Inventory* (2nd ed.). Stanford, CA: Stanford University Press.

CAMPBELL, D. P., and HANSEN, J. C. (1981). *Manual for the Strong-Campbell Interest Inventory* (3rd ed.). Stanford, CA: Stanford University Press.

CAMPBELL, D. T., and FISKE, D. W. (1959). Convergent and discriminant validation by the multitrait-multimethod matrix. *Psychological Bulletin, 56,* 81–105.

CAMPBELL, D. T., and STANLEY, J. C. (1966). *Experimental and quasi-experimental designs for research.* Chicago: Rand McNally.

CAPEHART, J. L. (1973). *The relationship of vocational maturity to Holland's theory of vocational choice.* Unpublished doctoral dissertation, University of North Carolina, Chapel Hill.

CAREK, R. (1965). The interrelations between social desirability, vocational maturity, vocational realism, and vocational decision. Unpublished master's thesis, University of Iowa.

CARTER, H. D. (1940). Resources for the consultant: The development of vocational attitudes. *Journal of Consulting Psychology, 4,* 185.

CATTELL, J. M. (1890). Mental tests and measurement. *Mind, 15,* 373–380.

CATTELL, R. B. (1963a). Formulating the environmental situation in behavior theory. In S. B. Sells (Ed.), *Stimulus determinants of Behavior* (pp. 75–105). New York: Ronald Press.

CATTELL, R. B. (1963b). Theory of fluid and crystalized intelligence: A critical experiment. *Journal of Educational Psychology, 54,* 1–22.

CATTELL, R. B. (1971). *Abilities: Their structure, growth, and action.* Boston: Houghton Mifflin.

CATTELL, R. B., EBER, H. W., and TATSUOKA, M. M. (1970). *Handbook for the Sixteen PF.* Champaign, IL: Institute for Personality and Ability Testing.

CATTELL, R. B., EBER, H., and TATSUOKA, M. M. (1980). *Handbook for the Sixteen Personality Factor Questionnaire (16 PF).* Champaign, IL: Institute for Personality and Ability Testing.

CAUTELA, J. R., and KASTENBAUM, R. A. (1967). A reinforcement survey schedule for use in therapy, training, and research. *Psychological Reports, 20,* 1115–1130.

CHASE, W. G., and SIMON, H. A. (1973). The mind's eye in chess. In W. G. Chase (Ed.), *Visual information processing* (pp. 215–218). New York: Academic Press.

CHI, M. T. H., FELTOVICH, P. J., and GLASER, R. (1981). Representation of physics knowledge by experts and novices. *Cognitive Science, 5,* 121–152.

CHICKERING, A. W. (1969). *Education and identity.* San Francisco: Jossey-Bass.

CHICKERING, A. W. (1974). *Commuting versus residence students.* San Francisco: Jossey-Bass.

CHIESI, H. L., SPILICH, G. J., and VOSS, J. F. (1979). Acquisition of domain-related information in relation to high and low domain knowledge. *Journal of Verbal Learning and Verbal Behavior, 18*, 257–273.

CLEARY, T. A., HUMPHREYS, L., KENDRICK, A., and WESMAN, A. (1975). Educational uses of tests with disadvantaged students. *American Psychologist, 30*, 15–41.

COAN, R. W. (1978). [A review of the Myers Briggs Type Indicator.] In O. K. Buros (Ed.), *The eighth mental measurements yearbook* (Vol. 1, pp. 973–975). Highland Park, NJ: Gryphon Press.

COHEN, D. C. (1977). Comparison of self-report and overt-behavioral procedures for assessing agoraphobia. *Behavior Therapy, 8*, 17–23.

COHEN, J. (1957a). The factorial structure of the WAIS between early adulthood and old age. *Journal of Consulting Psychology, 21*, 283–290.

COHEN, J. (1957b). A factor-analytically based rationale for the Wechsler Adult Intelligence Scale. *Journal of Consulting Psychology, 21*, 351–457.

COHEN, R. D. (1966). *Students and colleges: Need-press dimensions for the development of a common framework for characterizing students and colleges* (Ed. 011083). Washington, DC: U.S. Office of Education.

COHN, S. J. (1985a). Review of the GRE. In J. V. Mitchell, Jr. (Ed.), *The ninth mental measurements yearbook.* Lincoln, NE: University of Nebraska Press.

COHN, S. J. (1985b). Review of the SAT. In J. V. Mitchell, Jr. (Ed.), *The ninth mental measurements yearbook.* Lincoln, NE: University of Nebraska Press.

COLBY, A., KOHLBERG, L., SPEICHER, B., HEWER, A., CANDEE, D., GIBBS, J. C., and POWER, C. (1987). *The measurement of moral judgment* (Vol. II). Cambridge, MA: Harvard University Press.

COLE, N. S. (1981). Bias in testing. *American Psychologist, 36*, 1067–1077.

COLE, N. S., and HANSON, G. R. (1975). Impact of interest inventories on career choice. In E. E. Diamond (Ed.), *Issues of sex bias and sex fairness in career interest measurement.* Washington, DC.: National Institute of Education.

College Entrance Examination Board. (1981a). *CLEP: General and subject examinations.* Princeton, NJ: Educational Testing Service.

College Entrance Examination Board. (1981b) *CLEP scores: Interpretation and use.* Princeton, NJ: Educational Testing Service.

College Entrance Examination Board. (1986). *1986–1987 ATP Guide for High Schools and Colleges: SAT and achievement tests.* Princeton, NJ: College Entrance Examination Board.

COMREY, A. L. (1970). *Manual for the Comrey Personality Scales.* San Diego, CA: Educational and Industrial Testing Service.

CONRAD, L., TRISMEN, D., and MILLER, R. (Eds.). (1977). *GRE technical manual.* Princeton, NJ: Educational Testing Service.

CONSTANTINOPLE, A. (1969). An Eriksonian measure of personality development in college students. *Developmental Psychology, 1*, 357–372.

COOK, T. D., and CAMPBELL, D. T. (1979). *Quasi-experimentation: Design and analysis for field settings.* Boston: Houghton Mifflin.

COOPER, J. E. (1976). Comparative impact of the SCII and the Vocational Card Sort on career salience and career exploration of women. *Journal of Counseling Psychology, 23*, 348–351.

CORDES, C. (1982, November). Less labeling, more help, NRC panel tells educators. *APA Monitor*, p. 5.

COTTLE, W. C. (1950). Card versus booklet forms of the MMPI. *Journal of Applied Psychology, 34*, 255–259.

CRAIK, K. H. (1969, September). *Assessing environmental dispositions.* Paper presented at the meeting of the American Psychological Association, Washington, DC.

CRAIK, K. H. (1971). The assessment of places. In P. McReynolds (Ed.), *Advances in psychological assessment* (Vol. II, pp. 40–62). Palo Alto, CA: Science and Behavior Books.

CRAIK, K. H. (1973). Environmental psychology. In P. H. Mussen and M. R. Rosenzweig (Eds.), *Annual review of psychology* (pp. 403–423). Palo Alto, CA: Annual Reviews.

CRAIK, K. H. (1975). Individual-variation in landscape description. In E. H. Zube, R. O. Brush, and J. Fabos (Eds.), *Landscape assessment: Values, perceptions, and resources* (pp. 130–150). Stroudsburg, PA: Dowden, Hutchison, and Ross.

CRAIK, K. H. (1981). Environmental assessment and situational analysis. In D. Magnusson (Ed.), *Toward a psychology of situations: An interactional perspective* (pp. 37–49). Hillsdale, NJ: Lawrence Erlbaum Associates.

CRAIK, K. H., and McKECHNIE, G. E. (1977). Editors' introduction: Personality and environment. *Environment and Behavior, 9*, 155–168.

CRITES, J. O. (1964). Proposals for a new criterion measure and research design. In H. Borow (Ed.), *Man in a world at work.* Boston: Houghton Mifflin.

CRITES, J. O. (1969). *Vocational psychology.* New York: McGraw-Hill.

CRITES, J. O. (1974). Methodological issues in the measurement of career maturity. *Measurement and evaluation in guidance, 6*, 200–209.

CRITES, J. O. (1978a). *Career Maturity Inventory.* Monterey, CA: CTB/McGraw-Hill.

CRITES, J. O. (1978b). *Career Maturity Inventory: Administration and use manual.* Monterey, CA: CTB/McGraw-Hill.

CRITES, J. O. (1978c). *Career Maturity Inventory: Adults.* Monterey, CA: CTB/McGraw-Hill.

CRITES, J. O. (1981). *Career Maturity Inventory: Theory and research handbook* (2nd ed.). Monterey, CA: CTB/McGraw-Hill.

CRONBACH, L. J. (1951). Coefficient alpha and the internal structure of tests. *Psychometrika, 16*, 297.

CRONBACH, L. J. (1957a). *Aptitudes and instructional materials.* New York: Wiley.

CRONBACH, L. J. (1957b). The two disciplines of scientific psychology. *American Psychologist, 12*, 671–684.

CRONBACH, L. J. (1980). Validity on Parole: How can we go straight? In W. B. Schrader (Ed.), *New directions for testing and measurement: No. 5*, San Francisco: Jossey Bass.

CRONBACH, L. J. (1984). *Essentials of psychological testing* (4th ed.). New York: Harper & Row.

CRONBACH, L. J. (1985). Review of the SAT. In J. V. Mitchell, Jr. (Ed.). *The ninth mental measurements yearbook*. Lincoln, NE: University of Nebraska Press.

CURETON, E. E. (1965). Reliability and validity: Basic assumptions and experimental designs. *Educational and Psychological Measurement, 25*, 327–346.

DAHLSTROM, W. G., WELSH, G. S., and DAHLSTROM, L. E. (1972). *An MMPI Handbook, Vol. I, Clinical interpretation*. Minneapolis: University of Minnesota Press.

DAHLSTROM, W. G., WELSH, G. S., and DAHLSTROM, L. E. (1975). *An MMPI Handbook, Vol. II, Research developments and applications*. Minneapolis: University of Minnesota Press.

DARLEY, J. G. (1941). *Clinical aspects and interpretation of the Strong Vocational Interest Blank*. New York: The Psychological Corporation.

DAWIS, R. V. (1987). Scale construction. *Journal of Counseling Psychology, 34*, 481–489.

DELANEY, E. A., and HOPKINS, T. F. (1987). *Examiner's Handbook for the Stanford-Binet Fourth Edition*. Chicago: Riverside.

DEMAREE, R. G. (1972). [Review of the Fear Survey Schedule.] In O. K. Buros (Ed.), *The seventh mental measurements yearbook* (Vol. I, pp. 172–173). Highland Park, NJ: Gryphon Press.

DEMAREE, R. G. (1978). [Review of the Work Environment Preference Schedule.] In O. K. Buros (Ed.), *The eighth mental measurements yearbook* (Vol. I, pp. 1152–1154). Highland Park, NJ: Gryphon Press.

DENNY, D. R., and SULLIVAN, B. J. (1976). Desensitization and modeling treatments of spider fears using two types of scenes. *Journal of Consulting and Clinical Psychology, 44*, 573–579.

DEVITO, A. J. (1985). [Review of the Myers-Briggs Type Indicator.] In J. V. Mitchell, Jr. (Ed.), *The ninth mental measurements yearbook*. (Vol. II, pp. 1030–1032). Lincoln, NE: The Buros Institute of Mental Measurements.

DEWEY, C. R. (1974). Exploring interests: A nonsexist method. *Personnel and Guidance Journal, 52*, 311–315.

DEWINNE, R. F., OVERTON, T. D., and SCHNEIDER, L. J. (1978). Types produce types—especially fathers. *Journal of Vocational Behavior, 12*, 140–144.

DIAMOND, E. E. (1975a). *Career development inventory technical supplement*. Chicago: Science Research Associates.

DIAMOND, E. E. (1975b). Guidelines for the assessment of sex bias and sex fairness in career interest inventories. *Measurement and evaluation in Guidance, 8*, 7–11.

DIAMOND, E. E., COSTELLO, J. M., and MURRAY, A. (1975). *Career Development Program: Program guide*. Chicago: Science Research Associates.

DIGNAN, M. (1965). Ego identity and material identification. *Journal of Personality and Social Psychology, 1*, 476–483.

DISCOVER Foundation. (1977). DISCOVER: A computer-based career development and counselor support system. Westminster, MD: Author.

DOLLIVER, R. H. (1969). An adaptation of the Tyler Vocational Card Sort. *Personnel and Guidance Journal, 45*, 916–920.

DOLLIVER, R. H., IRVIN, J. A., and BIGLEY, S. E. (1972). Twelve-year follow-up of the Strong Vocational Interest Blank. *Journal of Counseling Psychology, 19*, 212–217.

DOMBROSE, L. A., and SLOBIN, M. S. (1958). The IES test [Monograph Supplement 3]. *Perceptual and Motor Skills, 8*, 347–389.

DRESSEL, P. L. (1972). [Review of the Institutional Functioning Inventory.] In O. K. Buros (Ed.), *The seventh mental measurements yearbook* (Vol. I, pp. 189–190), Highland Park, NJ: Gryphon Press.

DUCKWORTH, J., and ANDERSON, W. (1986). *MMPI interpretation manual for counselors and clinicians* (3rd ed.). Muncie, IN: Accelerated Development.

DUNNETTE, M. D. (1966). *Personnel selection and placement*. Belmont, CA: Brooks/Cole.

EBEL, R. L. (1962). Content standard test scores. *Educational and psychological Measurement, 22*, 15–25.

Educational Testing Service. (1980a). *Manual and technical report for the School and College Ability Tests, Series III*. Menlo Park, CA: Addison-Wesley.

Educational Testing Service. (1980b). *Test use and validity*. Princeton, NJ: Author.

Educational Testing Service. (1981). *NTE: Interpreting National Teacher Examination Scores*. Princeton, NJ: Author.

Educational Testing Service. (1987). *GRE 1987–1988 Student Information Bulletin*. Princeton, NJ: Author.

Educational Testing Service. (1988). *Taking the SAT: A Guide to the Scholastic Aptitude Test and the Test of Standard Written English*. Princeton, NJ: Author.

EISLER, R. M., FREDERIKSEN, L. W., and PETERSON, G. L. (1978). The relationship of cognitive variables to the expression of assertiveness. *Behavior Therapy, 9*, 419–427.

EKEHAMMAR, B. (1974). Interactionism in personality from a historical perspective. *Psychological Bulletin, 81*, 1026–1048.

ENDLER, N. S. (1976). The role of person by situation interactions in personality theory. In F. Weizmann and I. C. Uzgiris (Eds.), *The Structuring of Experience* (pp. 60–85). New York: Plenum Press.

ENDLER, N. S., and HUNT, J. M. (1966). Sources of behavioral variance as measured by the S-R Inventory of Anxiousness. *Psychological Bulletin, 65*, 338–346.

ENDLER, N. S., and MAGNUSSON, D. (Eds.). (1976a). *Interactional psychology and personality*. New York: Halstead Press.

ENDLER, N. S., and MAGNUSSON, D. (1976b). Personality and person by situation interactions. In N. S. Endler and D. Magnusson (Eds.), *Interactional psychology and personality* (pp. 1–27). New York: Wiley.

ERIKSON, E. (1968). *Identity, youth, and crisis*. New York: W. W. Norton.

ERON, L. D. (1972). [A review of the Thematic Apperception Test.] In O. K. Buros (Ed.), *The seventh mental measurements yearbook* (Vol. I, pp. 460–462). Highland Park, NJ: Gryphon Press.

ERWIN, T. D. (1979). The validation of the Erwin Identity Scale. (Doctoral dissertation, The University of Iowa, 1978.) *Dissertation Abstracts International, 39*, 4818A.

EVANS, F. R. (1977). Applications and admissions to ABA accredited law schools: An analysis of national data for the class entering in the fall of 1976 (Rep. LSACO77-1). In Law School Admission Council (Ed.), *Reports of LSAC sponsored research: 1975–1977* (Vol. 3). Princeton, NJ: Law School Admission Council.

EXNER, J. (1974). *The Rorschach: A comprehensive system* (Vol. I). New York: Wiley.

EXNER, J. (1978). *The Rorschach: A comprehensive system, current research and advanced interpretation* (Vol. II). New York: Wiley.

EXNER, J. E., JR., and EXNER, D. E. (1972). How clinicians use the Rorschach. *Journal of Personality Assessment, 36*, 403–408.

EYDE, L. D. (1986). Test purchaser qualifications: A proposed voluntary system based on test ethics. In APA (Eds.), *Test purchaser qualifications*. Washington, DC: APA Office of Scientific Affairs.

FAZIO, A. F. (1969). Verbal and overt-behavioral assessment of a specific fear. *Journal of Consulting and Clinical Psychology, 33*, 705–709.

FELDMAN, M. P., and MACCULLOCH, M. J. (1971). *Homosexual behavior: Therapy and assessment*. Oxford, England: Pergamon Press.

FELDT, L. S., FORSYTH, R. A., and ALNOT, A. (1988). *Teacher, Administrator, and Counselor Manual: Iowa Tests of Educational Development*. Chicago: Riverside.

FEUERSTEIN, R. (1979a). *The dynamic assessment of retarded performers: The learning potential assessment device, theory, instruments, and techniques*. Baltimore: University Park Press.

FEUERSTEIN, R. (1979b). *Instrumental enrichment: An intervention program for cognitive modifiability*. Baltimore: University Park Press.

FITTS, W. H. (1965b). *Manual: Tennessee Self-Concept Scale*. Los Angeles, CA: Western Psychological Services.

FITTS, W. H. (1972). *The self-concept and behavior: Overview and supplement (Monograph VII)*. Nashville, TN: Counselor Recordings and Tests.

FITZGERALD, L. F., and HUBERT, L. T. (1987). Multidimensional scaling: Some possibilities for counseling psychology research. *Journal of Counseling Psychology, 34*, 469–480.

FOUAD, N. A., CUDECK, R., and HANSEN, J. C. (1984). Convergent validity of the Spanish and English forms of the SCII for bilingual Hispanic high school students. *Journal of Counseling Psychology, 31*, 339–348.

FOUAD, N. A., and HANSEN, J. C. (1987). Cross-cultural predictive accuracy of the Strong-Campbell Interest Inventory. *Measurement and evaluation in Counseling and Development, 20*, 3–10.

FOUAD, N. A., HANSEN, J. C., and ARIAS, F. G. (1986). Multiple discriminant analysis of cross-cultural similarity of vocational interests of lawyers and engineers. *Journal of Vocational Behavior, 28*, 85–96.

FREUD, S. (1964). *An outline of psychoanalysis* (1938 Standard Edition, Vol. 23). London: Hogarth Press.

FRIEDMAN, P. H. (1971). The effects of modeling and role playing on assertive behavior. In R. D. Rubin (Eds.), *Advances in behavior therapy* (pp. 353–382). New York: Academic Press.

GALTON, F. (1879). Psychometric experiments. *Brain, 2*, 149–162.

GALTON, F. (1883). *Inquiries into human faculty and its development*. London: Macmillan.

GAMBRILL, E. D., and RICHEY, C. A. (1975). An Assertion Inventory for Use in Assessment and Research. *Behavior Therapy, 6*, 550–561.

GARDNER, E. F., RUDMAN, H. C., KARLSEN, B., and MERWIN, J. C. (1982). *The Stanford Achievement Test: Seventh Edition*. New York: Harcourt, Brace, Jovanovich.

GARSEE, J. W. (1980). The development of an ideology. In C. S. Schuster and S. S. Ashburn (Eds.), *The process of human development* (pp. 539–557). Boston: Little, Brown.

GEER, J. H. (1966). Fear and autonomic arousal. *Journal of Abnormal Psychology, 71*, 253–255.

GEORGE, J. R., and BISHOP, L. K. (1971). Relationship of organizational structure and teacher personality characteristics to organizational climate. *Administrative Science Quarterly, 16*, 467–475.

GETTER, H., and WEISS, S. D. (1968). The Rotter Incomplete Sentences Blank Adjustment Score as an indicator of semantic complaint frequency. *Journal of Projective Techniques and Personality Assessment, 32*, 266.

GIBBS, J. C., and BASINGER, K. S. (1990). *Moral maturity: measuring the development of social moral reflection*. Hillsdale, NJ: Lawrence Erlbaum Associates.

GIBBS, J. C., WIDAMAN, K. F., and COLBY, A. (1982). Construction and validation of a simplified, group-administerable equivalent to the Moral Judgment Interview. *Child Development, 53*, 895–910.

GINZBERG, E., GINSBURG, S. W., AXELRAD, S., and HERMAN, J. L. (1951). *Occupational choice*. New York: Columbia University Press.

GLASER, R. (1963). Instructional technology and the measurement of learning outcomes. *American Psychologist, 18*, 519–521.

GLASS, G. V., and HOPKINS, K. D. (1984). *Statistical methods in education and psychology*. (2nd ed.). Englewood Cliffs, NJ: Prentice Hall.

GOLDBERG, P. (1965). A review of sentence completion methods in personality assessment. *Journal of Projective Techniques and Personality Assessment, 29*, 12–45.

GOLDFRIED, M. R. (1982). Behavioral assessment: An

overview. In A. S. Bellack, M. Hersen, and A. E. Kazdin (Eds.), *International handbook of behavior modification and therapy.* New York: Plenum Press.

GOLDMAN, L. (1971). *Using tests in counseling* (2nd Ed.). Englewood Cliffs, NJ: Prentice Hall.

GOODENOUGH, F. (1926). *Measurement of intelligence by drawings.* New York: World Book.

GORDON, E. W., and TERRELL, M. D. (1981). The changed social context of testing. *American Psychologist, 36,* 1167–1171.

GORDON, L. V. (1973). *Work environment preference schedule manual.* New York: Psychological Corporation.

GORDON, L. V. (1978). *School Environment Preference Schedule manual.* San Diego, CA: Educational and Industrial Testing Service.

GOTTFREDSON, G. D., HOLLAND, J. L., and GOTTFREDSON, L. S. (1975). The relation of vocational aspirations and assessments to employment reality. *Journal of Vocational Behavior, 7,* 135–148.

GOTTFREDSON, L. S. (1986) (Ed.). The "g" factor in employment. Special issue of the *Journal of Vocational Behavior, 29* (3).

GOTTFREDSON, L. S., and SHARF, J. (1988). Fairness in employment testing. Special issue of the *Journal of Vocational Behavior, 33* (3).

GOUGH, H. G. (1949). A short social status inventory. *Journal of Educational Psychology, 40,* 52–56.

GOUGH, H. G. (1968). An interpretive syllabus for the California Psychological Inventory. In P. McReynolds (Ed.). *Advances in personality assessment* (Vol. I, pp. 55–79). Palo Alto, CA: Science and Behavior Books.

GOUGH, H. G. (1971a). A cluster analysis of Home Index Status items. *Psychological Reports, 28,* 923–929.

GOUGH, H. G. (1971b). Socioeconomic status as related to high school graduation and college attendance. *Psychology in the Schools, 8,* 226–231.

GOUGH, H. G. (1974). *Manual for the Home Index.* Berkeley, CA: Institute of Personality Assessment and Research.

GOUGH, H. G. (1975). *Manual for the California Psychological Inventory.* Palo Alto, CA: Consulting Psychologists Press.

GOUGH, H. G. (1987). *California Psychological Inventory Administrators Guide.* Palo Alto, CA: Consulting Psychologists Press.

GOUGH, H. G., and HEILBRUN, A. B. (1965). *The Adjective Checklist manual.* Palo Alto, CA: Consulting Psychologists Press.

GRANDY, T. G., and STAHMANN, R. F. (1974).Types produce types: An examination of personality development using Holland's theory. *Journal of Vocational Behavior, 5,* 231–243.

GRAVES, T. D. (1974). A study of vocational maturity and college students' certainty and commitment to career choice. Unpublished doctoral dissertation, University of Northern Colorado.

GROSSBERG, T. M., and WILSON, H. K. (1965). A correlational comparison of the Wolpe-Lang Fear Survey Schedule and the Taylor Manifest Anxiety Schedule. *Behavior Research and Therapy, 3,* 125–128.

GROTEVANT, H. D., SCARR, S., and WEINBERG, R. A. (1977). Patterns of interest similarity in adoptive and biological families. *Journal of Personality and Social Psychology, 35,* 667–676.

GUILFORD, J. P. (1954). *Psychometric methods.* New York: McGraw-Hill.

GUILFORD, J. P. (1965). *Fundamental statistics in psychology and education.* New York: McGraw-Hill.

GUILFORD, J. P. (1967). *The nature of human intelligence.* New York: McGraw-Hill.

GUILFORD, J. P., and FRUCHTER, B. (1978). *Fundamental statistics in psychology and education* (6th ed.). New York: McGraw-Hill.

GUILFORD, J. P., GUILFORD, J. S., and ZIMMERMAN, W. S. (1978). *The Guilford-Zimmerman Temperament Survey: Directions for administering, scoring, and interpreting.* Orange, CA: Sheridan Psychological Services.

GUILFORD, J. P., and ZIMMERMAN, W. S. (1956). Fourteen dimensions of temperament. *Psychological Monographs, 70* (10, Whole No. 417).

GUILFORD, J. S., GUILFORD, J. P., and ZIMMERMAN, W. S. (1976). *Interpretation system for the Guilford-Zimmerman Temperament Survey.* Orange, CA: Sheridan Psychological Services.

GUILFORD, J. S., ZIMMERMAN, W. S., and GUILFORD, J. P. (1976). *The Guilford-Zimmerman Temperament Survey handbook.* Orange, CA: Sheridan Psychological Services.

GUION, R. (1981, January). Kind words for ETS [Letter to the editor]. *APA Monitor,* p. 4.

HAPIT, M. (1972). A study of the relationships among perceptions of the school, bureaucratic orientation levels and satisfaction-dissatisfaction measures of secondary school students. Unpublished doctoral dissertation, University of Maryland.

HALL, C. S., and LINDZEY, G. (1970). *Theories of Personality* (2d ed.). New York: Wiley.

HALL, D. W. (1962). Vocational development in adolescence: The measurement of vocational maturity. Unpublished master's thesis, University of Iowa.

HALL, L. G. (1976). *Occupational Orientation Inventory* (3rd ed.). Bensenville, IL: Scholastic Testing Service.

HALSTEAD, W. C. (1961). Biological intelligence. In J. J. Jenkins and D. G. Paterson (Eds.), *Studies in individual differences.* New York: Appleton-Century-Crofts.

HAMBLETON, R. K., SWAMINATHAN, H., ALGINA, J., and COULSON, D. (1978). Criterion-referenced testing and measurement: A review of technical issues and developments. *Review of Educational Research, 41,* 1–47.

HANSEN, G. R. (Ed.). (1982). *Measuring student development.* San Francisco: Jossey-Bass.

HANSEN, J. C. (1984a). The measurement of vocational interests: Issues and future directions. In R. B. Lent and S. D. Brown (Eds.), *Handbook of counseling psychology* (pp. 99–136). New York: Wiley.

HANSEN, J. C. (1984b). *User's guide for the SVIB-SCII*. Stanford, CA: Stanford University Press.

HANSEN, J. C. (1986). Strong Vocational Interest Blank/Strong-Campbell Interest Inventory. In W. B. Walsh and S. H. Osipow (Eds.), *Advances in vocational psychology: The assessment of interests, Volume I*. Hillsdale, NJ: Lawrence Erlbaum Associates.

HANSEN, J. C., and CAMPBELL, D. P. (1985). *Manual for the SVIB-SCII* (4th ed.). Palo Alto, CA: Consulting Psychologists Press.

HARGADON, F. (1981). Tests and college admissions. *American Psychologist, 36* (10), 1112–1119.

HARMAN, H. H. (1967). *Modern factor analysis* (rev. ed.). Chicago: University of Chicago Press.

HARRIS, D. B (1963). *Children's drawings as measures of intellectual maturity: A revision and extension of the Goodenough Draw-A-Man Test*. New York: Harcourt, Brace and World.

HARRIS, D. B. (1972). [A review of the Draw-A-Person Test.] In O. K. Buros (Ed.). *The seventh mental measurements yearbook* (Vol. I 401–404). Highland Park, NJ: Gryphon Press.

HARTMAN, D. P., and WOOD, D. D. (1982). Observational methods. In A. S. Bellack, M. Hersen, and A. E. Kazdin (Eds.), *International handbook of behavior modification and therapy*. New York: Plenum Press.

HARTNETT, R. T., and FELDNESSER, R. A. (1980). College admissions testing and the myth of selectivity: Unresolved questions and needed research. *AAHE Bulletin, 32*, 3–6.

HATHAWAY, S. R., and McKINLEY, J. C. (1943). *Manual for the Minnesota Multiphasic Personality Inventory*. New York: Psychological Corporation.

HATHAWAY, S. R., and McKINLEY, J. C. (1967). *Manual for the Minnesota Multiphasic Personality Inventory* (rev. ed.). New York: Psychological Corporation.

HAYNES, S. N. (1978). *Principles of behavioral assessment*. New York: Halstead Press.

HAYNES, S. N. (1983). Behavioral assessment. In M. Hersen, A. E. Kazdin, and A. S. Bellack (Eds.), *The clinical psychology handbook*. New York: Pergamon Press.

HAYNES, S. N., and WILSON, C. C. (1979). *Behavioral assessment*. San Francisco: Jossey-Bass.

HAYS, W. L. (1981). *Statistics* (3rd ed.). New York: Holt, Rinehart and Winston.

HEBB, D. O. (1972). *Textbook of psychology* (3rd ed.). Philadelphia: W. B. Saunders.

HEIST, P., and YONGE, G. (1986). *Manual for the Omnibus Personality Inventory, Form F*. New York: Psychological Corporation.

HELMSTADTER, G. C. (1964). *Principles of psychological measurement*. New York: Appleton-Century-Crofts.

HELSON, H. (1959). Adaptation level theory. In S. Koch (Ed.), *Psychology: A study of science* (Vol. I, pp. 57–85). New York: McGraw-Hill.

HELSON, R., and MITCHELL, V. (1978). Personality. In M. R. Rosenzweig and L. W. Porter (Eds.), *Annual Review of Psychology* (pp. 555–585). Palo Alto, CA: Annual Reviews.

HERR, E. L., and MOORE, G. D. (1968). A pilot study of college expectation and reality perception. *College Student Personnel Abstracts, 3*, 202–203.

HODGSON, R., and RACHMAN, S. (1977). Obsessional-compulsive complaints. *Behavior Research and Therapy, 15*, 389–395.

HOLLAND, J. L. (1959). A theory of vocational choice. *Journal of Counseling Psychology, 6*, 35–45.

HOLLAND, J. L. (1971). *The counselor's guide to the Self-Directed Search*. Palo Alto, CA: Consulting Psychologists Press.

HOLLAND, J. L. (1973). *Making vocational choices: A theory of careers*. Englewood Cliffs, NJ: Prentice Hall.

HOLLAND, J. L. (1977). *The occupations finder*. Palo Alto, CA: Consulting Psychologists Press.

HOLLAND, J. L. (1979). *The Self-Directed Search: Professional manual*. Palo Alto, CA: Consulting Psychologists Press.

HOLLAND, J. L. (1985a). *Making vocational choices: A theory of vocational personalities and work environments*. Englewood Cliffs, NJ: Prentice Hall.

HOLLAND, J. L. (1985b). *Professional manual for the Self-Directed Search*. Odessa, FL: Psychological Assessment Resources.

HOLLAND, J. L., DAIGER, D. C., and POWER, P. G. (1980). *My vocational situation: Description of an experimental diagnostic form for the selection of vocational assistance*. Palo Alto, CA: Consulting Psychologists Press.

HOLLAND, J. L., and GOTTFREDSON, G. D. (1976). Using a typology of persons and environments to explain careers: Some extensions and clarifications. *Counseling Psychologist, 6*, 20–28.

HOLLAND, J. L., and RAYMAN, J. R. (1986). The Self-Directed Search. In W. B. Walsh and S. H. Osipow (Eds.), *Advances in vocational psychology: The assessment of interests, Volume I*. Hillsdale, NJ: Lawrence Erlbaum Associates.

HOLLENDER, J. W. (1964). Interrelationships of vocational maturity, consistency and realism of vocational choice, school grade, and age in adolescence. Unpublished master's thesis, University of Iowa.

HOLTZMAN, W. H. (1975). New developments in Holtzman Inkblot Technique. In P. McReynolds (Ed.), *Advances in psychological assessment* (Vol. III, pp. 124–162). San Francisco: Jossey-Bass.

HOLTZMAN, W. H. (1981). Holtzman Inkblot Technique (HIT). In A. I. Rabin (Ed.), *Assessment with projective techniques: A concise introduction* (pp. 47–83). New York: Springer.

HOLZBERG, J. D., and ALESSI, S. (1949). Reliability of the shortened MMPI. *Journal of Consulting Psychology, 13*, 288–292.

HOLZMAN, T. G., GLASER, R., and PELLEGRINO, J. W. (1976). Process training derived from a computer simulation theory. *Memory and Cognition, 1*, 349–356.

HOOD, A. B. (1986). The Erwin Identity Scale. In A. B. Hood (Ed.), *The Iowa student development inventories*. Iowa City, IA: Hitech Press.

HOOD, A. B., and JACKSON, L. M. (1986a). Assessing the development of competence. In A. B. Hood (Ed.), *The Iowa student development inventories*. Iowa City, IA: Hitech Press.

HOOD, A. B., and JACKSON, L. M. (1986b). The Iowa Developing Autonomy Inventory. In A. B. Hood (Ed.), *The Iowa student development inventories.* Iowa City, IA: Hitech Press.

HOOD, A. B., and JACKSON, L. M. (1986c). The Iowa Managing Emotions Inventory. In A. B. Hood (Ed.), *The Iowa student development inventories.* Iowa City, IA: Hitech Press.

HOOD, A. B., and MINERS, R. A. (1986). Freeing of interpersonal relationships. In A. B. Hood (Ed.), *The Iowa student development inventories.* Iowa City, IA: Hitech Press.

HOWARD, J. A. (1979). Person-situation interaction models. *Personality and social Psychology Bulletin, 5,* 191–195.

HOWARTH, E. (1978). [A review of the Comrey Personality Scales.] In O. K. Buros (Ed.), *The eighth mental measurements yearbook* (Vol. I, pp. 753–755). Highland Park, NJ: Gryphon Press.

HUMPHREYS, L. G. (1962). The organization of human abilities, *American Psychologist, 17,* 475–483.

HUMPHREYS, L. G., and TABER, T. (1973). Ability factors as a function of advantaged and disadvantaged groups. *Journal of Educational Measurement, 10,* 107–115.

HUNT, E. B. (1978). Mechanics of verbal ability. *Psychological Review, 85,* 109–130.

HUNT, E. B., LUNNEBORG, C., and LEWIS, J. (1975). What does it mean to be high verbal? *Cognitive Psychology, 7,* 194–227.

HUNT, J. M. (1961). *Intelligence and Experience.* New York: The Ronald Press.

HUNTER, J. E., and SCHMIDT, F. L. (1981). Fitting people to jobs: The impact of personnel selection for national productivity. In M. D. Dunnette and E. A. Fleishman (Eds.), *Human performance and productivity* (Vol. I, pp. 233–284). Hillsdale, NJ: Lawrence Erlbaum Associates.

HUNTER, J. E., SCHMIDT, F. L., and HUNTER, R. (1979). Differential validity of employment tests by race: A comprehensive review and analysis. *Psychological Bulletin, 86,* 721–735.

HUTT, M. L. (1951). The Bender Gestalt drawings. In E. S. Shneidman, W. Joel, and K. B. Little (Eds.), *Thematic test analysis* (pp. 114–153). New York: Grune and Stratton.

HUTT, M. L. (1977). *The Hutt adaptation of the Bender Gestalt Test.* New York: Grune and Stratton.

HUTT, M. L., and BRISKIN, G. J. (1960). *The clinical use of the Revised Bender Gestalt Test.* New York: Grune and Stratton.

JACKSON, D. N. (1976a). *Jackson Personality Inventory.* Goshen, NY: Research Psychologists Press.

JACKSON, D. N. (1976b). *Manual for the Jackson Personality Inventory.* Goshen, NY: Research Psychologists Press.

JACKSON, D. N. (1977a). Reliability of the Jackson Personality Inventory. *Psychological Report, 40,* 613–614.

JACKSON, D. N. (1977b). *Manual for the Jackson Vocational Interest Survey.* Port Huron, MI: Research Psychologists Press.

JACKSON, D. N. (1978). Interpreter's guide to the Jackson Personality Inventory. In P. McReynolds (Ed.), *Advances in psychological assessment, Volume 4.* San Francisco: Jossey-Bass.

JACKSON, D. N. (1984). *Multidimensional Aptitude Battery manual.* Port Huron, MI: Research Psychologists Press.

JACKSON, D. N., and SKINNER, H. A. (1975). Univocal Varimax: An orthogonal factor rotation program for optimal simple structure. *Educational and Psychological Measurement, 35,* 663–665.

JACKSON, G. (1975). On the report of the ad hoc committee on educational uses of tests with disadvantaged students. *American Psychologist, 30,* 88–92.

JAEGER, R. M. (1985). Review of the GRE. In J. V. Mitchell, Jr. (Ed.), *The ninth mental measurements yearbook.* Lincoln, NE: University of Nebraska Press.

JENSEN, A. R. (1969). How much can we boost IQ and scholastic achievement? *Harvard Educational Review, 39,* 1–123.

JENSEN, A. R. (1979). g: Outmoded theory or unconquered territory? *Creative Science and Technology, 2,* 16–29.

JENSEN, A. R. (1980). *Bias in mental testing.* New York: Free Press.

JENSEN, A. R. (1985) Review of the Armed Services Vocational Aptitude Battery. In J. V. Mitchell, Jr. (Ed.), *Ninth Mental Measurements Yearbook.* Lincoln, NE: University of Nebraska Press.

JOHANSSON, C. B. (1982). *Manual for the Career Assessment Inventory* (2nd ed.). Minneapolis: National Computer Systems Interpretive Scoring System.

JOHANSSON, C. B. (1986). *Career Assessment Inventory: The Enhanced Version.* Minneapolis: National Computer Systems Interpretive Scoring System.

JOHNSON, R. W. (1976). Test review: Strong-Campbell Interest Inventory (Form T325). *Measurement and Evaluation in Guidance, 9,* 40–45.

JOHNSON, R. W. (1978). [Review of the DAT Career Planning Program.] In O. K. Buros (Ed.), *The eighth mental measurements yearbook,* (Vol. II, pp. 1576–1577). Highland Park, NJ: Gryphon Press.

JOLLES, I. (1964). *A catalogue for the qualitative interpretation of the H-T-P* (revised). Beverly Hills, CA: Western Psychological Services.

JONES, L. K. (1979). Occu-Sort: Development and evaluation of an occupational card sort system. *Vocational Guidance Quarterly, 28,* 56–62.

JONES, R. F., and ADAMS, L. N. (1982). *An annotated bibliography of research on the Medical College Admission Test* (Report 82-1, MCAT Interpretive Studies Series). Washington, DC: Association of American Medical Colleges.

JONES, R. G. (1968). *A factored measure of Ellis' irrational belief system with personality and maladjustment correlates.* Unpublished doctoral dissertation. Texas Technological College, Lubbock.

"Judge reiterates IQ Test Ban." (1986, December). *APA Monitor,* p. 18.

JUNG, C. G. (1923). *Psychological types.* London: Routledge and Kegan Paul.

KAHILL, S. (1984). Human figure drawing in adults: An update of the empirical evidence, 1967–1982. *Canadian Psychology, 25*(4) 269–292.

KANFER, F. H., and SASLOW, G. (1969). Behavioral diagnosis. In C. Franks (Ed.), *Assessment and status of the behavior therapies and associated developments* (pp. 417–444). New York: McGraw-Hill.

KANTOR, J. R. (1924). *Principles of psychology* (Vol. I). Bloomington, IN: Principia Press.

KAPLAN, R. M. (1982). Nader's raid on the testing industry: Is it in the best interests of the consumer? *American Psychologist, 37*, 15–23.

KASMAR, J. V. (1970). The development of a usable lexicon of environmental descriptors. *Environment and Behavior, 2*, 153–169.

KATZ, M. R. (1975). *SIGI: A computer-based system of interactive guidance and information.* Princeton, NJ: Educational Testing Service.

KAUFMAN, A. S. (1985). Review of the WAIS-R. In J. V. Mitchell, Jr. (Ed.), *Ninth edition of the mental measurements yearbook.* Lincoln, NE: University of Nebraska Press.

KAUFMAN, A. S., and KAUFMAN, N. L. (1983a). *Kaufman Assessment Battery for Children: Administration and scoring manual.* Circle Pines, MN: American Guidance Service.

KAUFMAN, A. S., and KAUFMAN, N. L. (1983b). *Kaufman Assessment Battery for Children: Interpretive Manual.* Circle Pines, MN: American Guidance Service.

KEATING, D. P., and BOBBITT, B. L. (1978). Individual and developmental differences in cognitive-processing components of mental ability. *Child Development, 49*, 155–167.

KEENE, J. M., JR. (1985). Review of the Tests of Achievement and Proficiency. In J. V. Mitchell, Jr. (Ed.), *Ninth Mental Measurements yearbook.* Lincoln, NE: University of Nebraska Press.

KELLY, G. A. (1955). *The psychology of personal constructs* (Vols. I to II). New York: W. W. Norton.

KEYSER, D. J. and SWEETLAND, R. C. (Eds.) (1985). *Test critiques* (Vol. IV). Kansas City, Missouri: Test Corporation of America.

KIFER, E. (1985). Review of the Iowa Tests of Educational Development. In J. V. Mitchell, Jr. (Ed.), *Ninth Mental Measurements yearbook.* Lincoln, NE: University of Nebraska Press.

KING, P. (1977). *The development of reflective judgment and formal operational thinking in adolescents and young adults.* Unpublished doctoral dissertation, University of Minnesota, Minneapolis.

KING, P. M. (1978). William Perry's theory of intellectual and ethical development. In L. Knefelhamp, C. Widich, and C. Parker (Eds.), *New direction for student services: Applying new developmental findings,* No. 4. San Francisco: Jossey Bass.

KING, P. M., KITCHENER, K. S., DAVISON, M. L., PARKER, C., and WOOD, P. K. (1982). The justification of beliefs in young adults: A longitudinal study. Unpublished manuscript, School of Education, University of Denver.

KITAY, P. M. (1972). [A review of the Bender Gestalt Test.] In O. K. Buros (Ed.), *The seventh mental measurements yearbook* (Vol. I, pp. 394–395). Highland Park, NJ: Gryphon Press.

KITCHENER, K. S. (1977). *Intellectual development in late adolescents and young adults: Reflective judgment and verbal reasoning.* Unpublished doctoral dissertation, University of Minnesota, Minneapolis.

KITCHENER, K. S. (1982). Human development and the college campus: Sequences and tasks. In G. R. Hanson (Ed.), *Measuring Student Development* (pp. 17–45). San Francisco: Jossey Bass.

KITCHENER, K. S., and KING, P. M. (1981). Reflective judgment: Concepts of justification and their relationship to age and education. *Journal of Applied Developmental Psychology, 2*, 89–116.

KLOPFER, B., and KELLEY, D. M. (1942). *The Rorschach technique.* Yonkers, NY: World Book Company.

KLUCKHOHN, C., MURRAY, H. A., and SCHNEIDER, D. M. (Eds.). (1953). *Personality in nature, society, and culture.* New York: Knopf.

KNAPP, L., and KNAPP, R. R. (1980a). *California Occupational Preference System Interest Inventory: Form R.* San Diego: Educational and Industrial Testing Service.

KNAPP, L., and KNAPP, R. R. (1980b). *Manual for the California Occupational Preference System: Form R.* San Diego: Educational and Industrial Testing Service.

KNECHT, S. D., CUNDICK, B. P., EDWARDS, D., and GUNDERSON, E. K. (1972). The prediction of marijuana use from personality scales. *Educational and Psychological Measurement, 32*, 1111–1117.

KNEFELKAMP, L. L. (1974). *Developmental instruction: Fostering intellectual and personal growth.* Unpublished doctoral dissertation, University of Minnesota, Minneapolis.

KNOX, D. (1971). *Marriage happiness: A behavioral approach to counseling.* Champaign, IL: Research Press.

KOFFKA, K. (1935). *Principles of gestalt psychology.* New York: Harcourt Brace.

KOHLBERG, L. (1969). *Stage and sequence: The cognitive developmental approach to socialization theory and research.* New York: Rand McNally.

KOHLBERG, L. (1971). From is to ought: How to commit the naturalistic fallacy and get away with it in the study of moral development. In T. Mischel (Ed.), *Cognitive development and epistemology* (pp. 74–103). New York: Academic Press.

KOHLBERG, L., COLBY, A., GIBBS, J., SPEICHER-DUBIN, B., and POWER, C. (1978). *Assessing moral stages: A manual.* Cambridge, MA: Harvard University, Center for Moral Education.

KOHLBERG, L., and WASSERMAN, E. R. (1980). The cognitive-development approach and the practicing counselor: An opportunity for counselors to rethink their roles. *Personnel and Guidance Journal, 58*, 559–569.

KOHN, M. (1977). The Kohn Social Competence Scale and Kohn Symptom Checklist for the Preschool Child: A follow-up report. *Journal of Abnormal Child Psychology, 5*, 249–264.

KOPPITZ, E. M. (1975). *The Bender Gestalt Test for Young*

Children: Research and application, 1963–1973. New York: Grune and Stratton.

KOVACS, M., and BECK, A. T. (1977). The wish to die and the wish to live in attempted suicides. *Journal of Clinical Psychology, 33*(2), 361–365.

KRAEPELIN, E. (1907). *Clinical psychiatry.* Jena, Germany: Fischer.

KRUG, S. E. (1981). *Interpreting 16 PF profile patterns.* Champaign, IL: Institute of Personality and Ability Testing.

KUDER, G. F. (1934). Kuder General Interest Survey. Chicago: Science Research Associates.

KUDER, G. F. (1946). *Manual, Kuder Preference Record: Vocational.* Chicago: Science Research Associates.

KUDER, G. F. (1966). The Occupational Interest Survey. *Personnel and Guidance Journal, 45,* 72–77.

KUDER, G. F., and DIAMOND, E. E. (1979). *Occupational Interest Survey, general manual* (2d ed.). Chicago: Science Research Associates.

KUDER, G., and RICHARDSON, M. (1937). The theory of estimation of test reliability. *Psychometrika, 2,* 151.

LACHAR, DAVID. (1974). *The MMPI: Clinical assessment and automated interpretation.* Los Angeles: Western Psychological Services.

LACKS, P. (1984). *Bender Gestalt: Screening for brain Dysfunction.* New York: Wiley.

LAMB, R. R., and PREDIGER, D. J. (1981). *Technical report for the unisex edition of the ACT Interest Inventory UNIACT).* Iowa City, IA: American College Testing Program.

LAMKE, T. A., NELSON, M. J., and FRENCH, J. L. (1973a). *The Henman-Nelson Tests of Mental Ability.* Boston: Houghton Mifflin.

LAMKE, T. A., NELSON, M. J., and FRENCH, J. L. (1973b). *Manual for the Henman-Nelson Tests of Mental Ability, 1973 Revision.* Boston: Houghton Mifflin.

LANGE, P. J., and LAZOVIK, A. D. (1963). Experimental desensitization of a phobia. *Journal of Abnormal and Social Psychology, 66,* 519–525.

LANGE, P. J., MELAMED, B. G., and HART, J. (1970). A psycho-physiological analysis of fear modification using an automated desensitization procedure. *Journal of Abnormal Psychology, 76,* 220–234.

LANYON, R. I. (1967). Measurement of social competence in college males. *Journal of Consulting Psychology, 31,* 493–498.

LARRY, P. v. RILES (495 F. Supp. 926) California (No. 80-427) (1980).

LAUMANN, E. O., and HOUSE, J. S. (1970). Living room styles and social attributes: The patterning of material artifacts in a modern urban Community. *Sociological Social Research, 54,* 321–342.

LAUTERBACH, C. G., and VIELHABER, D. P. (1966). Need-press and expectation-press indices are predictors of college achievement. *Educational and Psychological Measurement, 26,* 965–972.

LAYTON, W. L. (1972). [Review of the Stern Environment Indexes.] In O. K. Buros (Ed.), *The seventh mental measurements yearbook* (Vol. I, pp. 343–344). Highland Park, NJ: Gryphon Press.

LEMKE, S., and MOOS, R. (1987). The Sheltered Care Environment Scale: Measuring the social climate of congregate residential settings. *Psychology and Aging, 2,* 20–29.

LEMKE, S., MOOS, R. H., GAUVAIN, M., and MEHREN, B. (1979). *Multiphasic Environmental Assessment Procedure (MEAP) hand scoring booklet.* Palo Alto, CA: Sheltered Care Project of the Social Ecology Laboratory.

LEMKE, S., MOOS, R. H., MEHREN, B., and GAUVAIN, M. (1979). *Multiphasic Environmental Assessment Procedure (MEAP) handbook for users.* Palo Alto, CA: Sheltered Care Project of the Social Ecology Laboratory.

LERNER, B. (1981). The minimum competency testing movement: Social, scientific, and legal implications. *American Psychologist, 36,* 1057–1066.

LERNER, H., and LERNER, P. M. (1985). [Review of the Rorschach Inkblot Test.] In D. J. Keyser and R. C. Sweetland (Eds.), *Test critiques* (Vol. IV, pp. 523–552). Kansas City, MO: Test Corporation of America.

"Less labeling, more help," NRC panel tells educators. (1982, November). *APA Monitor,* p. 4.

LEVINSON, D., DARROW, C., KLEIN, E., LEVINSON, M., McKEE, B. (1978). *The seasons of a man's life.* New York: Knopf.

LEWIN, K. (1935). *A dynamic theory of personality: Selected papers.* New York: McGraw-Hill.

LEWIN, K. (1936). *Principles of topological psychology.* New York: McGraw-Hill.

LINDEN, K. W., and LINDEN, J. P. (1968). *Modern mental measurement: A historical perspective.* Boston: Houghton Mifflin.

LINDQUIST, E. F. (1970). The Iowa Testing Programs: A retrospective view. *Education, 81,* 4–23.

LINDZEY, G. (1959). On the classification of projective techniques. *Psychological Bulletin, 56,* 158–168.

LINDZEY, G. (1961). *Projective techniques and cross cultural research.* New York: Appleton-Century-Crofts.

LINN, R. L. (1982). Admissions testing on trial. *American Psychologist, 37,* 279–291.

LITTLE, B. R. (1973). *Person-thing orientation: A provisional manual for the T-P Scale.* Windsor, Canada: National Foundation for Educational Research.

LITTLEMEYER, M. H., and MAUNEY, A. C. (1977). *New MCAT student manual.* Washington, DC: American Association of Medical Colleges.

LITWIN, G. H., and STRINGER, R. A. (1968). *Motivation and organizational climate.* Cambridge, MA: Harvard University Press.

LOEVINGER, J. (1966). The meaning and measurement of ego development. *American Psychologist, 21,* 195–206.

LOEVINGER, J. (1976). *Ego development: Conceptions and theories.* San Francisco: Jossey-Bass.

LOEVINGER, J., and WESSLER, R. (1970). *Measuring ego development.* San Francisco: Jossey-Bass.

LOFQUIST, L. H., and DAWIS, R. V. (1975). *Counseling use of the Minnesota Importance Questionnaire.* Minneapolis: University of Minnesota, Department of Psychology, Work Adjustment Project.

LOFQUIST, L. H., and DAWIS, R. V. (1984). *Adjustment to work.* New York: Appleton-Century-Crofts.

LONG, J. (1983). Covariance structure models: An introduction to Lisrel. Beverly Hills, CA: Sage.

LORGE, I., THORNDIKE, R. L., and HAGEN, E. P. (1964). *Lorge-Thorndike intelligence tests: Multilevel edition.* Lombard, IL: Riverside Publishing Company.

LUNNEBORG, C. E. (1972). [Review of the Institutional Functioning Inventory.] In O. K. Buros (Ed.), *The seventh mental measurements yearbook* (Vol. I, pp. 190–192). Highland Park, NJ: Gryphon Press.

LUNNEBORG P. W. (1978). [Review of the Strong-Campbell Interest Inventory.] In O. K. Buros (Ed.), *The eighth mental measurements yearbook* (Vol. II, pp. 1627–1628). Highland Park, NJ: Gryphon Press.

LUNNEBORG, P. W. (1979a). Service vs. technical interest: Biggest sex difference of all? *Vocational Guidance Quarterly, 28,* 146–153.

LUNNEBORG, P. W. (1979b). The Vocational Interest Inventory: Development and validation. *Educational and Psychological Measurement, 39,* 445–451.

LUNNEBORG, P. W. (1980). Reducing sex bias in interest measurement at the item level. *Journal of Vocational Behavior, 16,* 226–234.

LUNNEBORG, P. W. (1981). *The Vocational Interest Inventory manual.* Los Angeles: Western Psychological Services.

LUNNEBORG, P. W. (1985). *Review of My Vocational Situation.* In J. V. Mitchell, Jr. (Ed.), *Ninth Mental Measurements Yearbook.* Lincoln, NE: University of Nebraska Press.

LUNNEBORG, P. W., and LUNNEBORG, C. E. (1986). Everyday Spatial Activities Test for studying differential experience and vocational behavior. *Journal of Vocational Behavior, 28,* 135–141.

LYMAN, H. B. (1978). *Test scores and what they mean* (3rd ed.). Englewood Cliffs, NJ: Prentice-Hall.

MACHOVER, K. (1949). *Personality projection in the drawing of the human figure.* Springfield, IL: Charles C. Thomas.

MAGNUSSON, D. (1981a). Problems in environmental analyses: An introduction. In D. Magnusson (Ed.), *Toward a psychology of situations: An interactional perspective* (p. 3–7). Hillsdale, NJ: Lawrence Erlbaum Associates.

MAGNUSSON, D. (Ed.). (1981b). *Toward a psychology of situations: An interactional perspective.* Hillsdale, NJ: Lawrence Erlbaum Associates.

MAGNUSSON, D. (1988). *Individual development from an interactional perspective: A longitudinal study.* Hillsdale, NJ: Lawrence Erlbaum Associates.

MAGNUSSON, D., and ENDLER, N. S. (1977a). Interactional psychology: Present status and future prospects. In D. Magnusson & N. S. Endler (Eds.), *Personality at the crossroads: Current issues in interactional psychology* (pp. 3–31). Hillsdale, NJ: Lawrence Erlbaum Associates.

MAGNUSSON, D., and ENDLER, N. S. (Eds.). (1977b). *Personality at the crossroads: Current issues in interactional psychology.* Hillsdale, NJ: Lawrence Erlbaum Associates.

MALONEY, M. P., and WARD, M. P. (1976). *Psychological assessment: A conceptual approach.* New York: Oxford University Press.

MANN, M. J. (1959). Relationships among certain variables associated with post-college success. *Educational and Psychological Measurement, 19,* 351–362.

MARANELL, G. (Ed.). (1974). *Scaling a sourcebook for behavioral scientists.* Chicago: Aldine.

MARCIA, J. (1966). Development and validation of ego identity status. *Journal of Personality and Social Psychology, 3,* 551–558.

MATARAZZO, J. D. (1972). *Wechsler's measurement and appraisal of adult intelligence* (5th ed.). Baltimore: Williams and Wilkins.

MATARAZZO, J. D. (1978). The interview: Its reliability and validity in psychiatric diagnosis. In B. B. Wolman (Ed.), *Clinical diagnosis of mental disorders* (pp. 47–96). New York: Plenum Press.

MATARAZZO, J. D. (1985). Review of the WAIS-R. In J. Mitchell, Jr. (Ed.), *Ninth edition of the mental measurements yearbook.* Lincoln, NE: University of Nebraska Press.

MCALLISTER, L. W. (1986). *A practical guide to CPI interpretation.* Palo Alto, CA: Consulting Psychologists Press.

MCARTHUR, C. C. (1972). [A review of the Rorschach.] In O. K. Buros (Ed.), *The seventh mental measurements yearbook* (Vol. I, pp. 440–443). Highland Park, NJ: Gryphon Press.

MCCRAE, R. R. (1985). [Review of the Defining Issues Test.] In J. V. Mitchell, Jr. (Ed.), *The ninth mental measurements yearbook* (Vol. I, pp. 439–440). Lincoln, NE: The Buros Institute of Mental Measurements.

MCGRATH, E., and DOLAN, B. B. (1983, January 10). A victory for Christian Schools. *Time,* p. 46.

MCKECHNIE, G. E. (1974). *Manual for the Environmental Response Inventory.* Palo Alto, CA: Consulting Psychologists Press.

MCKECHNIE, G. E. (1978). Environmental dispositions: Concepts and measures. In P. McReynolds (Ed.), *Advances in psychological assessment* (Vol. IV, pp. 141–177). San Francisco: Jossey-Bass.

MCNEMAR, Q. (1969). *Psychological statistics* (4th ed.). New York: Wiley.

MCREYNOLDS, P. (1975). Historical antecedents of personality assessment. In P. McReynolds (Ed.), *Advances in psychological assessment* (Vol. III, pp. 477–532). San Francisco: Jossey-Bass.

MEDVENE, A. M., and SHUEMAN, S. S. (1978). Perceived parental attitudes and choice of vocational specialty area among male engineering students. *Journal of Vocational Behavior, 12,* 208–217.

MEEHL, P. E. (1965). Seer over sign: The first good example. *Journal of Experimental Research in Personality, 1,* 27–32.

MEEHL, P. E., and ROSEN, A. (1955). Antecedent probability and the efficiency of psychometric signs, patterns, or cutting scores. *Psychological Bulletin, 52,* 194–216.

MEGARGEE, E. (1972). *The California Psychological In-*

ventory handbook. Palo Alto, CA: Consulting Psychologists Press.

MEHRABIAN, A., and RUSSELL, J. A. (1973). A measure of arousal-seeking tendency. *Environment and Behavior, 5,* 315–334.

MEIR, E. I., and BARAK, A. (1974). A simple instrument for measuring vocational interests based on Roe's classification of occupations. *Journal of Vocational Behavior, 4,* 33–42.

MELTON, G. B. (1985). Review of the LSAT. In J. Mitchell, Jr. (Ed.), *Ninth mental measurements yearbook.* Lincoln, NE: University of Nebraska Press.

MELTZER, L. (1961). The need for a dual orientation in social psychology. *Journal of Social Psychology, 55,* 43–48.

MERCER, J. R. (1978). *System of multicultural pluralistic assessment.* New York: Psychological Corporation.

MESSICK, S. (1975). The standard problem: Meaning and values in measurement and evaluation. *American Psychologist, 30,* 955–966.

MESSICK, S. (1980). Test validity and the ethics of assessment. *American Psychologist, 35,* 1012–1037.

MEYER, P. (1977). Intellectual development: An analysis of religious content. *Counseling Psychologist, 6*(4), 45–50.

MILHOLLAND, J. (1978). [Review of the Otis Lennon School Ability Test.] In O. K. Buros (Ed.), *The eighth mental measurements yearbook* (Vol. I, pp. 30–32). Highland Park, NJ: Gryphon Press.

MILLER, J. K. (1985). [Review of the College Student Experiences Questionnaire.] In J. V. Mitchell, Jr. (Ed.), *The ninth mental measurements yearbook* (Vol. I, pp. 366–368). Lincoln, NE: The Buros Institute of Mental Measurements.

MILLON, T. (1983). *Millon Clinical Multiaxial Inventory manual* (3rd ed.). Minneapolis: Interpretive Scoring Systems.

MINES, R. A. (1978). *Change in college students along Chickering's vector of freeing interpersonal relationships* (Technical Report on Studies Nos. 12, 15, 26). Iowa City, IA: Iowa Student Development Project.

MINES, R. A. (1982). Student development assessment techniques. In G. R. Hanson (Ed.), *Measuring student development* (pp. 65–91). San Francisco: Jossey-Bass.

MISCHEL, W. (1968). *Personality and assessment.* New York: Wiley.

MISCHEL, W. (1973). Toward a cognitive social learning reconceptualization of personality. *Psychological Review, 80,* 252–283.

MISCHEL, W. (1977a). On the future of personality measurement. *American Psychologist, 32,* 246–255.

MISCHEL, W. (1977b). The interaction of person and situation. In D. Magnusson and N. S. Endler (Eds.), *Personality at the crossroads: Current issues in interactional psychology* (pp. 333–352). Hillsdale, NJ: Lawrence Erlbaum Associates.

MITCHELL, J. V., JR. (1978). [Review of the National Teacher Examinations.] In O. K. Buros (Ed.), *The eighth mental measurements yearbook* (Vol. I, pp. 516–518). Highland Park, NJ: Gryphon Press.

MITCHELL, J. V., JR. (Ed.). (1985). *The ninth mental measurements yearbook* (Vol. I, pp. xiii–xxi). Lincoln, NE: The Buros Institute of Mental Measurements.

MOONEY, R. L., and GORDON, L. V. (1950). *Manual for the Mooney Problem Checklists (Adult Form).* New York: Psychological Corporation.

MOORE, W. S. (1982). The Measure of Intellectual Development: A brief review. Unpublished paper, Center for Application of Developmental Instruction, University of Maryland, College Park.

MOOS, R. H. (1973). Conceptualizations of human environments. *American Psychologist, 28,* 652–665.

MOOS, R. H. (1974). *The Social Climate Scales: An overview.* Palo Alto, CA: Consulting Psychologists Press.

MOOS, R. H. (1975). Assessment and impact of social climate. In P. McReynolds (Ed.), *Advances in psychological assessment* (Vol. III, pp. 8–41), San Francisco: Jossey-Bass.

MOOS, R. H. (1976a). *The human context.* New York: Wiley.

MOOS, R. H. (1979). *Evaluating educational environments.* San Francisco: Jossey-Bass.

MOOS, R. H. (1984). Context and coping: Toward a unifying conceptual framework. *American Journal of Community Psychology, 12,* 1–36.

MOOS, R. (1986a). *Group Environment Scale manual* (2nd ed.). Palo Alto, CA: Consulting Psychologists Press.

MOOS, R. (1986b). *Military Environment Inventory manual* (2nd ed.). Palo Alto, CA: Consulting Psychologists Press.

MOOS, R. (1986c). *Work Environment Scale manual* (2nd ed.). Palo Alto, CA: Consulting Psychologists Press.

MOOS, R. H. (1987a). *Correctional Institutions Environment Scale manual* (2nd ed.). Palo Alto, CA: Consulting Psychologists Press.

MOOS, R. H. (1987b). *The social climate scales: A user's guide.* Palo Alto, CA: Consulting Psychologists Press.

MOOS, R. H. (1987c). *Ward Atmosphere Scale manual* (2nd ed.). Palo Alto, CA: Consulting Psychologists Press.

MOOS, R. H. (1987d). Person-environment congruence in work, school, and health care settings. *Journal of Vocational Behavior, 31,* 222–230.

MOOS, R. (1988a). *Community-Oriented Programs Environment Scale manual* (2nd ed.). Palo Alto, CA: Consulting Psychologists Press.

MOOS, R. (1988b). *University Residence Environment Scale manual* (2nd ed.). Palo Algo, CA: Consulting Psychologists Press.

MOOS, R. H., and LEMKE, S. (1979). *Multiphasic Environmental Assessment Procedure (MEAP) preliminary manual.* Palo Alto, CA: Sheltered Care Project of the Social Ecology Laboratory.

MOOS, R. H., and LEMKE, S. (1984). *Multiphasic Environmental Assessment Procedure (MEAP) manual.* Palo Alto, CA: Sheltered Care Project of the Social Ecology Laboratory.

MOOS, R., and LEMKE, S. (1987). *Sheltered Care Environment Scale manual.* Palo Alto, CA: Social Ecology Laboratory, Stanford University and Veterans Administration Medical Center.

Moos, R., and Moos, B. (1986). *Family Environment Scale manual* (2nd ed.). Palo Alto, CA: Consulting Psychologists Press.

Moos, R., and Trickett, E. (1987). *Classroom Environment Scale manual* (2nd ed.). Palo Alto, CA: Consulting Psychologists Press.

Moreland, K. L. (1985). [Review of the Defining Issues Test.] In J. V. Mitchell, Jr. (Ed.), *The ninth mental measurements yearbook* (Vol. I, pp. 440–442). Lincoln, NE: The Buros Institute of Mental Measurements.

Moreno, K. E., Wetzel, C. D. McBride, J. R., and Weiss, D. J. (1984). Relationship between corresponding ASVAB and computerized adaptive testing (CAT) subtests, *Applied Psychological Measurement, 8,* 155–163.

Mulholland, T. W., Pellegrino, T. W., and Glaser, R. (1980). Components of geometric analogy solution. *Cognitive Psychology, 12,* 252–284.

Munroe, R. (1942). An experiment in large-scale testing by a modification of the Rorschach method. *Journal of Psychology, 13,* 229–263.

Murphy, G. (1947). *Personality: A biosocial approach to origins and structure.* New York: Harper.

Murray, H. A. (1938). *Explorations in personality.* New York: Oxford University Press.

Murray, H. A. (1943). *Thematic Apperception Test manual.* Cambridge, MA: Harvard University Press.

Meyers, I. B. (1962). *Manual for the Myers-Briggs Type Indicator.* Princeton, NJ: Educational Testing Service.

Myers, I. B. (1977). *The Myers-Briggs Type Indicator: Supplementary manual.* Palo Alto, CA: Consulting Psychologists Press.

Myers, I. (1987). *Introduction to type.* Palo Alto, CA: Consulting Psychologists Press.

Myers, I., and McCaulley, M. (1985). *Manual: A guide to the development and use of the Myers-Briggs Type Indicator.* Palo Alto, CA: Consulting Psychologists Press.

Nairn, A. (1980). *The reign of ETS: The corporation that makes up minds.* Washington, DC: Nader.

National Assessment of Educational Progress. (1976). *Functional literacy: Basic reading performance.* Denver: Author.

Nelson, R. O., and Hayes, S. C. (Eds.). (1982). *Conceptual foundations of behavioral assessment.* New York: Guilford Press.

Nevill, D. D., and Super, D. E. (1986). *Values Scale Manual: Theory, application, and research.* Palo Alto, CA: Consulting Psychologists Press.

Novaco, R. W. (1977). Stress inoculation: A cognitive therapy for anger and its application to a case of depression. *Journal of Consulting and Clinical Psychology, 45,* 600–608.

Novick, M. R. (1981). Federal guidelines and professional standards. *American Psychologist, 36,* 1035–1046.

Nunnally, J. C. (1978). *Psychometric theory* (3rd ed.). New York: McGraw-Hill.

Ogdon, D. P. (1978). *Psychodiagnostic and personality assessment: A handbook* (2nd ed.). Los Angeles: Western Psychological Services.

Oliver, L. W. (1978). Outcome measurement in career counseling research. *Journal of Counseling Psychology, 26,* 217–226.

Osipow, S. H. (1980). *Manual for the Career Decision Scale.* Columbus, OH: Marathon Consulting Press.

Osipow, S. H. (1983). *Theories of career development* (3rd ed.). Englewood Cliffs, NJ: Prentice Hall.

Osipow, S. H. (Ed.). (1987). *Manual for the Career Decision Scale.* Odessa, FLA: Psychological Assessment Resources.

Osipow, S. H., Carney, C. G., and Barak, A. (1976). A scale of educational and vocational undecidedness: A typological approach. *Journal of Vocational Behavior, 9,* 233–243.

Osipow, S. H., Carney, C. G., Winer, J. L., Yanico, B., and Koschier, M. (1976). *The Career Decision Scale* (3rd rev.). Columbus, OH: Marathon Consulting Press.

Osipow, S. H., and Walsh, W. B. (1970). *Strategies in counseling for behavior change.* Englewood Cliffs, NJ: Prentice Hall.

Otis, A. S., and Lennon, R. T. (1980). *Manual for the Otis-Lennon School Ability Test.* New York: Psychological Corporation.

Pace, C. R. (1984). *Measuring the quality of college student experiences.* University of California, Los Angeles: Higher Education Research Institute.

Pace, C. R. (1987). *CSEQ: Test manual and norms.* University of California, Los Angeles: Center for the Study of Evaluations.

Pace, C. R., and Stern, G. G. (1958). An approach to the measurement of psychological characteristics of college environments. *Journal of Educational Psychology, 49,* 269–277.

Page, E. B. (1985). Review of the Kaufman Assessment Battery for Children. In J. V. Mitchell, Jr. (Ed.), *Ninth Mental Measurements yearbook.* Lincoln, NE: University of Nebraska Press.

Page, R., and Bode, J. (1980). Comparison of measures of moral reasoning and development of a new objective measure. *Educational and Psychological Measurement, 40,* 317–329.

Parker, C. A. (Ed.). (1978). *Encouraging development in college students.* Minneapolis: University of Minnesota Press.

Parker, J. C., and Hood, A. B. (1986). The Parker Cognitive Development Inventory. In A. B. Hood (Ed.), *The Iowa student development inventories.* Iowa City, IA: Hitech Press.

Parsons, F. (1909). *Choosing a vocation.* Boston: Houghton Mifflin.

Pascal, G. R., and Suttell, B. (1951). *The Bender Gestalt Test.* New York: Grune & Stratton.

PASE v. Hannon (506 F. Supp. 831) Illinois (N.D. Ill. 1980).

Passow, H. (1985). Review of SCAT-III. In J. Mitchell, Jr. (Ed.), *Ninth Edition of the mental measurements yearbook.* Lincoln, NE: University of Nebraska Press.

Paul, G. L. (1966). *Insight versus desensitization in psychotherapy.* Stanford, CA: Stanford University Press.

Payne, R. L., and Pugh, D. S. (1976). Organizational structure and climate. In M. D. Dunette (Ed.), *Hand-*

book of industrial and organizational psychology (pp. 1125–1174). Chicago: Rand McNally.

PERRY, W., JR. (1970). Forms of intellectual and ethical development in the college years. New York: Holt, Rinehart & Winston.

PERVIN, L. A. (1968). Performance and satisfaction as a function of individual-environment fit. Psychological Bulletin, 69, 56–68.

PERVIN, L. A. (1976). A free response description approach to the analysis of person-situation interaction. Journal of Personality and social Psychology, 34, 465–474.

PERVIN, L. A. (1977). The representative design in person-situation research. In D. Magnusson and N. S. Endler (Eds.), Personality at the crossroads: Current issues in interactional psychology (pp. 371–384). Hillsdale, NJ: Lawrence Erlbaum Associates.

PERVIN, L. A., and LEWIS, M. (Eds.). (1978). Perspectives in interactional psychology. New York: Plenum Press.

PERVIN, L. A., and RUBIN, D. B. (1967). Student dissatisfaction with college and the college dropout. Journal of Social Psychology, 72, 285–295.

PETERSON, R. E., CENTRA, J. A., HARTNETT, R. J., and LINN, R. L. (1983). Institutional Functioning Inventory: Preliminary technical manual. Princeton, NJ: Educational Testing Service.

PHEYSEY, D. C., and PAYNE, R. L. (1970). The Hemphill group dimensions description questionnaire: A British industrial application. Human Relations, 23, 473–497.

PIAGET, J. (1950). The psychology of intelligence. New York: Harcourt, Brace and World.

PIAGET, J. (1952). The origins of intelligence in children. New York: International University Press. (Originally published in 1936.)

PIAGET, J. (1965). The moral judgment of the child. New York: Free Press. (Originally published in 1932.)

PIAGET, J. (1972). Intellectual evolution from adolescence to adulthood. Human Development, 15, 1–12.

POPHAM, W. J. (1978). Criterion-referenced measurement. Englewood Cliffs, NJ: Prentice Hall.

POWERS, D. E. (1982). Long term predictive and construct validity of two traditional predictors of law school performance. Journal of Educational Psychology, 74, 568–576.

PRASSE, D. (1978). Federal legislation and school psychology: Impact and implication. Professional Psychology, 9, 592–601.

PREDIGER, D. J. (1980). The determination of Holland types of characterizing occupational groups. Journal of Vocational Behavior, 16, 33–42.

PRICE, G. E. (1984). [Review of the School Environment Preference Survey.] In D. J. Keyser and R. C. Sweetland (Eds.), Test critiques (Volume I, pp. 555–558). Kansas City, MO: Test Corporation of America.

PRINCE, J., MILLER, J., and WINSTON, R. (1974). Student Development Task Inventory guidelines. Athens, GA: Student Development Associates.

PROCIDANO, M. E. (1985). [Review of the Home Observation for Measurement of the Environment.] In D. J. Keyser and R. C. Sweetland (Eds.), Test critiques (Volume II, pp. 337–346). Kansas City, MO: Test Corporation of America.

The Psychological Corporation. (1972). The Differential Aptitude Tests and Career Planning Program. New York: Author.

The Psychological Corporation. (1977). Counseling from profiles: A casebook for the Differential Aptitude Tests (2nd ed.). New York: Author.

The Psychological Corporation. (1982). Resources for decision-making: 1982 catalog. New York: Author.

RABEN, C. S., SNYDER, R. A., HOFFMAN, R. G., and FARR, J. L. (1978). An examination of the construct validity and reliability of the Ghiselli Self-Description Inventory as a measure of self-esteem. Applied Psychological Measure, 2, 73–81.

RAPAPORT, D. G., GILL, M. M., and SCHAFER, R. (1968). Diagnostic psychological testing (rev. ed. by R. R. Holt). New York: International Universities Press.

RAUSH, H. L., DITTMANN, A. T., and TAYLOR, T. J. (1959). Person, setting and change in social interaction. Human Relations, 12, 361–378.

RAVEN, J. C. (1938). Progressive matrices: A perceptual test of intelligence. London: H. K. Lewis.

RESCHLY, D. J. (1981). Psychological testing in educational classification and placement. American Psychologist, 36, 1094–1102.

REST, J. R. (1979a). Development in judging moral issues. Minneapolis: University of Minnesota Press.

REST, J. R. (1979b). Revised manual for the Defining Issues Test. Minneapolis: Moral Research Projects, University of Minnesota.

REST, J. R. (1981, April). The impact of higher education on moral judgment development. Paper presented at the American Education Research Association National Convention, Los Angeles.

REYNOLDS, C. R., KAMPHAUS, R. W., and ROSENTHAL, B. L. (1988). Factor analysis of the Stanford-Binet Fourth Edition for Ages 2 years through 23 years. Measurement and Evaluation in Counseling and Development, 21, 52–63.

RICHARDS, J. M., JR. (1972). [Review of the Medical College Admission Test.] In O. K. Buros (Ed.), The seventh mental measurements yearbook (Vol. II, pp. 1512–1514). Highland Park, NJ: Gryphon Press.

RICHARDS, J. M., JR. (1978). [Review of the Environmental Response Inventory.] In O. K. Buros (Ed.), The eighth mental measurements yearbook (Vol. I, pp. 788–789). Highland Park, NJ: Gryphon Press.

RICHARDSON, F. C., and SUINN, R. M. (1973). The Mathematics Anxiety Rating Scale: Normative data. Journal of Counseling Psychology, 80, 252–283.

RICKS, J. H., JR. (1978). [Review of SRA Career Development Inventory.] In O. K. Buros (Ed.), The eighth mental measurements yearbook. Highland Park, NJ: Gryphon Press.

RODGERS, R. F. (1980). Theories underlying student development. In D. G. Creamer (Ed.), Student development in higher education (pp. 10–95). Washington, D.C.: American College Personnel Association.

ROE, A. (1956). *The psychology of occupations.* New York: Wiley.

ROE, A. (1957). Early determinants of vocational choice. *Journal of Counseling Psychology, 4,* 212–217.

ROE, A., and KLOS, D. (1969). Occupational classification. *The Counseling Psychologist, 1,* 84–92.

ROE, A., and SIEGELMAN, M. (1964). *The origin of interests* (The APGA Inquiry Series, No. 1), Washington, DC: American Personnel and Guidance Association.

ROGERS, C. R. (1951). *Client-centered therapy.* Boston: Houghton Mifflin.

ROGERS, C. R. (1961). *On becoming a person.* Boston: Houghton Mifflin.

ROGERS, W. B. (1977). Review of the Work Environment Preference Schedule. *Journal of Measurement and Evaluation in Guidance, 9,* 216–217.

RORSCHACH, H. (1942). *Psychodiagnostics: A diagnostic test based on perception* (4th ed.). New York: Grune & Stratton. (Originally published in 1921.)

ROSENTHAL, A. C. (1985). [Review of Assessment in Infancy: Ordinal Scales of Psychological Development.] In J. V. Mitchell, Jr. (Ed.), *The ninth mental measurements yearbook* (Vol. I, pp. 85–86). Lincoln, NE: The Buros Institute of Mental Measurements.

ROTTER, J. B. (1946). Thematic Apperception Test: Suggestions for administration and interpretation. *Journal of Personality, 15,* 70–92.

ROTTER, J. B. (1954). *Social learning and clinical psychology.* Englewood Cliffs, NJ: Prentice Hall.

ROTTER, J. B. (1966). Generalized expectancies for internal versus external control of reinforcement. *Psychological Monograph, 80* (Whole No. 609).

ROTTER, J. B., and RAFFERTY, J. E. (1950). *Manual for the Rotter Incomplete Sentences Blank College Form.* New York: Psychological Corporation.

ROUNDS, J. B., JR., HENLY, G. A., DAWIS, R. V., LOFQUIST, L. H., and WEISS, D. J. (1981). *Manual for the Minnesota Importance Questionnaire.* Minneapolis: Vocational Psychology Research, Dept. of Psychology, University of Minnesota.

RUCH, F. L., and RUCH, W. W. (1980). *Employee Aptitude Survey: Technical report.* Los Angeles: Psychological Services.

RUMMELL, R. J. (1970). *Applied factor analysis.* Evanston, IL: Northwestern University Press.

RUSSELL, J. A., and WARD, L. M. (1982). Environmental psychology. In M. R. Rosenzweig and L. W. Portor (Eds.), *Annual review of psychology* (pp. 651–688). Palo Alto, CA: Annual Reviews.

Russell Sage Foundation. (1970). *Guidelines for the collection, maintenance, and dissemination of pupil records.* New York: Author.

RYAN, R. M. (1985). [Review of the Thematic Apperception Test.] In D. J. Keyser and R. C. Sweetland (Eds.), *Test critiques* (Vol. II, pp. 799–814). Kansas City, MO: Test Corporation of America.

SANFORD, N. (1962). Developmental status of the entering freshman. In N. Sanford (Ed.), *The American college* (pp. 253–282). New York: Wiley.

SANFORD, N. (1963). Factors related to the effectiveness of student interaction with the college social system. In B. Barger & E. E. Hall (Eds.), *Higher education and mental health* (pp. 8–26). Conference conducted at the University of Florida, Gainesville.

SAUNDERS, D. R. (1969). A factor analytic study of the AI and the CCI. *Multivariate Behavioral Research, 4,* 329–346.

SCHMIDT, F. L., and HUNTER, J. E. (1977). Development of a general solution to the problem of validity generalization. *Journal of Applied Psychology, 62,* 529–540.

SCHMIDT, F. L., and HUNTER, J. E. (1981). Employment testing: Old theories and new research findings. *American Psychologist, 36,* 1128–1137.

SCHMIDT, F. L., HUNTER, J. E., PEARLMAN, K., and SHANE, G. S. (1979). Further tests of the Schmidt-Hunter Bayesian validity generalization procedures. *Personnel Psychology, 32,* 257–281.

SCHNEIDER, B., and BARTLETT, C. J. (1970). Individual differences and organizational climate: II. Measurement of organizational climate by the multi-trait multi-rater matrix. *Personnel Psychology, 23,* 493–512.

SCHRADER, W. B. (1977). Summary of law school validity studies 1948–1975 (Rep. LSAC-76-8). In Law School Admission Council (Ed.), *Reports of LSAC sponsored research: 1975–1977* (Vol. III). Princeton, NJ: Law School Admission Council.

SCHUSTER, C. S. (1980). Study of the human life cycle. In C. S. Schuster and S. S. Ashburn (Eds.), *The process of human development* (pp. 3–20). Boston: Little, Brown.

SEASHORE, H. G., WESMAN, A. G., and DOPPELT, J. E. (1950). The standardization of the Wechsler Intelligence Scale for Children. *Journal of Consulting Psychology, 14,* 99–110.

SECHREST, L. (1963). Incremental validity. *Educational and Psychological Measurement, 23,* 153–158.

SELKOW, P. (1984). *Assessing sex bias in testing.* Westport, CT: Greenwood Press.

SELLS, S. B. (1963). An interactionist looks at the environment. *American Psychologist, 18,* 696–702.

SHAFER, E. L., JR., and THOMPSON, R. C. (1968). Models that describe use of Adirondack campgrounds. *Forest Science, 14,* 383–391.

SHARP, S. E. (1898/1899). Individual psychology: A study in psychological methods. *American Journal of Psychology, 10,* 329–391.

SILVERMAN, L. H. (1976). Psychoanalytic theory: The reports of my death are greatly exaggerated. *American Psychologist, 31,* 621–638.

SKAGER, R. W. (1972). [Review of the Stern Environmental Indexes.] In O. K. Buros (Ed.), *The seventh mental measurements yearbook* (Vol. I, pp. 344–348). Highland Park, NJ: Gryphon Press.

SLACK, W. V., and PORTER, D. (1980a). The Scholastic Aptitude Test: A critical appraisal. *Harvard Educational Review, 50,* 154–175.

SLACK, W. V., and PORTER, D. (1980b). Training validity, and the issue of aptitude: A reply to Jackson. *Harvard Educational Review, 50,* 392–401.

SLANEY, R. B., PALKO-NONEMAKER, D., and ALEXANDER, R. (1981). An investigation of two measures of career indecision. *Journal of Vocational Behavior, 18*, 92–103.

SPANIER, G. B. (1976). Measuring dyadic adjustment: New scales for assessing the quality of marriage and similar dyads. *Journal of Marriage and the Family, 38*, 15–28.

SPEARMAN, C. (1904). "General intelligence": Objectively determined and measured. *American Journal of Psychology, 15*, 201–292.

SPEARMAN, C. (1923). *The nature of "intelligence" and the principles of cognition.* London: Macmillan.

SPIELBERGER, C. D. (1978). [Review of the Fear Survey Schedule.] In O. K. Buros (Ed.), *The eighth mental measurements yearbook* (Vol. I, pp. 823–825). Highland Park, NJ: Gryphon Press.

SPOKANE, A. R. (1979). Occupational preference and the validity of the Strong-Campbell Interest Inventory for college women and men. *Journal of Counseling Psychology, 26*, 312–318.

SPOKANE, A. R. (1985). A review of research on person-environment congruence in Holland's theory of careers. *Journal of Vocational Behavior, 26*, 306–343.

SPOKANE, A. R. (Ed.). (1987). Conceptual and methodological issues in person-environment fit research: A special issue of the *Journal of Vocational Behavior, 31*, 217–361.

STERN, G. G. (1970). *People in context.* New York: Wiley.

STERN, G. G., STEIN, M. I., and BLOOM, B. S. (1956). *Methods in personality assessment.* Glencoe, IL: Free Press.

STERNBERG, R. J. (1977a). Cognitive processes in analogical reasoning. *Psychological Review, 84*, 353–378.

STERNBERG, R. J. (1977b). *Intelligence, information processing, and analogical reasoning: The componential analysis of human abilities.* Hillsdale, NJ: Lawrence Erlbaum Associates.

STERNBERG, R. J. (1978). Componential investigations of human intelligence. In A. Lesgold, J. Pellegrino, S. Fokkema, and R. Glaser (Eds.), *Cognitive psychology and instruction* (pp. 421–457). New York: Plenum Press.

STERNBERG, R. J. (1979). The nature of mental abilities. *American Psychologist, 34*, 214–230.

STERNBERG, R. J. (1980). Sketch of a componential subtheory of human intelligence. *Behavioral and Brain Sciences, 3*, 573–584.

STERNBERG, R. J. (1981). Testing and cognitive psychology. *American Psychologist, 36*, 1181–1189.

STEVENS, S. S. (1951). *Handbook of experimental psychology.* New York: Wiley.

STRICKER, L. J. (1978). [Review of the Environmental Response Inventory.] In O. K. Buros (Eds.), *The eighth mental measurements yearbook* (Vol. I, pp. 789–791). Highland Park, NJ: Gryphon Press.

STRONG, E. K. (1927). Vocational Interest Test. *Educational Record, 8*, 107–121.

STRONG, E. K., JR. (1933). Strong Vocational Interest Blank for Women. Stanford, CA: Stanford University Press.

SUE, S. Ethnic minority issues in psychology: A reexamination. (1983). *American Psychologist, 38*, 583–592.

SUINN, R. M. (1969a). Changes in non-treated subjects over time: Data on a Fear Survey Schedule and the Test Anxiety Scale. *Behavior Research and Therapy, 7*, 205–206.

SUINN, R. M. (1969b). The STABS, a measure of test anxiety for behavior therapy: Normative data. *Behavior Research and Therapy, 7*, 335–339.

SUNDBERG, N. D. (1990). *Assessment of persons* (2nd ed.). Englewood Cliffs, NJ: Prentice Hall.

SUPER, D. E. (1940). *Avocational interest patterns.* Stanford, CA: Stanford University Press.

SUPER, D. E. (1949). *Appraising vocational fitness.* New York: Harper.

SUPER, D. E. (1957). *The psychology of careers.* New York: Harper.

SUPER, D. E. (1963). Vocational development in adolescence and early adulthood: Tasks and behaviors. In D. E. Super, *Career Development: Self-concept theory.* New York: CEEB Research Monograph No. 4.

SUPER, D. E. (1968–1980). *Work Values Inventory.* Lombard, IL: Riverside.

SUPER, D. E. (1973a). *DAT Career Planning Program: Counselor's manual.* New York: Psychological Corporation.

SUPER, D. E. (1973b). The Working Values Inventory. In D. G. Zytowski (Ed.), *Contemporary approaches to interest measurement* (pp. 189–205). Minneapolis: University of Minnesota Press.

SUPER, D. E. (1982). *DAT Career Planning Program: Counselor's manual* (2nd ed.). New York: Psychological Corporation.

SUPER, D. E., CRITES, J. O., HUMMEL, R. C., MOSER, H. P., OVERSTREET, P. L., and WARNARTH, C. F. (1957). *Vocational development: A framework for research.* New York: Teachers College Press.

SUPER, D. E. and NEVILL, D. (1986). *The Values Scale.* Palo Alto, CA: Consulting Psychologists Press.

SUPER, D. E., THOMPSON, A. S., LINDEMAN, R. H., JORDAN, J. P., and MEYERS, R. A. (1981). *Career Development Inventory.* Palo Alto, CA: Consulting Psychologists Press.

SWENSEN, C. H. (1968). Empirical evaluations of human figure drawings: 1957–1966. *Psychological Bulletin, 70*, 20–44.

TAGIURI, R. (1968). Executive climate. In R. Tagiuri and G. H. Litwin (Eds.), *Organization climate: Exploration of a concept* (pp. 395–449). Cambridge, MA: Harvard University Press.

TASTO, D. L., and SUINN, R. M. (1972). Fear Survey Schedule changes on total and factor scores due to non-treatment effects. *Behavior Therapy, 3*, 275–278.

TAYLOR, K. M. (1988). Advances in career planning systems. In W. B. Walsh and S. H. Osipow (Eds.), *Career decision-making* (pp. 137–211). Hillsdale, NJ: Lawrence Erlbaum Associates.

TERMAN, L. M., and MERRILL, M. A. (1960). *Stanford-Binet Intelligence Scale: Manual for the third revision, Form L-M.* Boston: Houghton Mifflin.

TERMAN, L. M., and MERRILL, M. A. (1973). *Stanford-Binet Intelligence Scale 1972 norms edition.* Boston: Houghton Mifflin.

THORNDIKE, E. L. (1906). *The principles of teaching: Based on psychology.* New York: A. G. Seiler.

THORNDIKE, R. L. (1951). Reliability. In E. F. Lindquist (Ed.), *Educational measurement* (pp. 560–620). Washington, DC: American Council on Education.

THORNDIKE, R. L., and HAGEN, E. (1978). *The Cognitive Abilities Test.* Lombard, IL: Riverside.

THORNDIKE, R. L., and HAGEN, E. (1979). *Examiner's manual for the Cognitive Abilities Test.* Boston: Houghton Mifflin.

THORNDIKE, R. L., HAGEN, E. P., and SATTLER, J. M. (1986a). *Guide for administering and scoring the Fourth Edition Stanford-Binet Intelligence Scale.* Chicago: Riverside.

THORNDIKE, R. L., HAGEN, E. P., and SATTLER, J. M. (1986b). *Technical manual for the Stanford-Binet: Fourth Edition.* Chicago: Riverside.

THURSTONE, L. L. (1938). Primary mental abilities. *Psychometric Monographs* (Whole No. 1).

THURSTONE, L. L., and THURSTONE, T. G. (1941). Factorial studies of intelligence. *Psychometric Monographs* (Whole No. 2).

TIEDEMAN, D. V., and O'HARA, R. P. (1963). *Career development: Choice and Adjustment.* New York: College Entrance Examination Board.

TILTON, J. W. (1937). The measurement of overlapping. *Journal of Educational Psychology, 23,* 656–662.

TITTLE, C. K. (1981). *Careers and family: Sex roles and adolescent life plans.* Beverly Hills, CA: Sage.

TITTLE, C. K., and ZYTOWSKI, D. G. (Eds.). (1978). *Sex fair interest measurement: Research and implications.* Washington, DC: National Institute of Education.

TOBIAS, L. L., and MacDONALD, M. L. (1977). Internal locus of control and weight loss: An insufficient condition. *Journal of Consulting and Clinical Psychology, 45,* 647–653.

TOLMAN, E. C. (1935). Psychology versus immediate experience. *Philosophy of Science, 2,* 356–380.

TOLMAN, E. C. (1951). Psychology versus immediate experience. In E. C. Tolman (Ed.), *Collected papers in psychology* (pp. 356–380). Berkeley: University of California Press.

TOLOR, A., and SCHULBERG, H. (1963). *An evaluation of the Bender Gestalt Test.* Springfield, IL: Charles C. Thomas.

TOMKINS, S. S. (1947). *The Thematic Apperception Test.* New York: Grune and Stratton.

TRAUB, R. E., and ROWLEY, G. L. (1980). Reliability of test scores and decisions. *Applied Psychological Measurement, 4,* 517–546.

TWENTYMAN, C. T., and McFALL, R. M. (1975). Behavioral training of social skills in shy males. *Journal of Consulting and Clinical Psychology, 43,* 384–395.

TYLER, L. E. (1965). *The psychology of human differences* (3rd ed.). New York: Appleton-Century-Crofts.

TYLER, L. E. (1969). Research explorations in the realm of choice. *Journal of Counseling Psychology, 8,* 195–202.

U.S. Department of Defense. (1984). *Counselor's Manual for the ASVAB.* North Chicago, IL: U.S. Military Entrance Processing Command.

U.S. Department of Defense. (1984). *Technical supplement to the counselor's manual for the ASVAB-14.* North Chicago, IL: U.S. Military Entrance Processing Command.

U.S. Department of Education. *Losing the war of letters.* (1986). Washington, D.C.: Goverment Printing Office.

U.S. Department of Labor, Bureau of Statistics. (1983). *Occupational outlook handbook.* Washington, DC: Government Printing Office.

U.S. Department of Labor, Employment and Training Administration. (1970). *Manual for the USES General Aptitude Tests Battery, section III: Development.* Washington, DC: Government Printing Office.

U.S. Department of Labor, Employment and Training Administration. (1977). *Dictionary of occupational titles* (4th ed.). Washington, DC: Government Printing Office.

U.S. Department of Labor, Employment and Training Administration. (1979). *Manual for the USES General Aptitude Tests Battery, section IV: Specific aptitude test batteries.* Washington, DC: Government Printing Office.

U.S. Department of Labor, Employment and Training Administration. (1980a). *Manual for the USES General Aptitude Tests Battery, section II: Occupational aptitude pattern structure.* Washington, DC: Government Printing Office.

U.S. Department of Labor, Employment and Training Administration. (1980b). *Manual for the USES General Aptitude Tests Battery, section IIa: Development of the occupational aptitude pattern structure.* Washington, DC: Government Printing Office.

U.S. Department of Labor, Employment and Training Administration. (1981a). *Guide for occupational exploration.* Washington, DC: Government Printing Office.

U.S. Department of Labor, Employment and Training Administration. (1981b). *A new counselee assessment/occupational exploration system and its interest and aptitude dimensions* (USES Test Research Report No. 35). Washington, DC: Government Printing Office.

U.S. Equal Employment Opportunity Commission, Civil Service Commission, Department of Labor, and Department of Justice. (1978). Uniform guidelines on employee selection procedures. *Federal Register, 43,* 38296–38309.

UZGIRIS, I. C., and HUNT, J. M. (1975). *Assessment of infancy: Ordinal series of psychological development.* Urbana: University of Illinois Press.

VERNON, P. A. (1985). Multidimensional Aptitude Battery. In D. J. Keyser and R. C. Sweetland (Eds.), *Test Critiques* (Vol. II). Kansas City, MO: Test Corporation of America.

VERNON, P. E. (1960). *The structure of human abilities* (rev. ed.). London: Methuen.

VIGLIONE, D., and EXNER, J. (1983). Current research in the comprehensive Rorschach systems. In J. Butcher and C. Spielberger (Eds.), *Advances in personality assessment* (Vol. I). Hillsdale, NJ: Lawrence Erlbaum Associates.

WACHTEL, P. L. (1973). Psychodynamics, behavior therapy, and the implacable experimenter: An inquiry into the consistency of personality. *Journal of Abnormal Psychology, 82*, 324–334.

WATKINS, C. E., JR., CAMPBELL, V. L., and McGREGOR, P. (1988). Counseling psychologists' uses of the opinions about psychological tests: A contemporary perspective. *The Counseling Psychologist, 16*, 476–486.

WALSH, W. B. (1973). *Theories of person-environment interaction.* Iowa City, IA: American College Testing Program.

WALSH, W. B. (1989). *Tests and measurements* (4th ed.). Englewood Cliffs, NJ: Prentice Hall.

WALSH, W. B., CRAIK, K., and PRICE, R. H. (Eds.) (1991). *Person-environment psychology: Models and perspectives.* Hillsdale, NJ: Lawrence Erlbaum Associates.

WALSH, W. B., and OSIPOW, S. H. (1973). Career preferences, self-concept, and vocational maturity. *Research in Higher Education, 1*, 287–295.

WARDROP, J. L. (1985). Review of the Tests of Achievement and Proficiency. In J. V. Mitchell, Jr. (Ed.), *Ninth Mental Measurements yearbook.* Lincoln, NE: University of Nebraska Press.

WATSON, J. B. (1913). Psychology as a behaviorist sees it. *Psychological Review, 20*, 158–177.

WEATHERSBY, R. P. (1981). Ego development. In A. W. Chickering (Ed.), *The modern American college* (pp. 51–75). San Francisco: Jossey-Bass.

WECHSLER, D. (1939). *The measurement of adult intelligence.* Baltimore: Williams and Wilkins.

WECHSLER, D. (1981). *Manual for the Wechsler Adult Intelligence Scale—Revised.* New York: Psychological Corporation.

WEINGARTEN, K. P. (1958). The Picture Interest Inventory. Monterey, CA: California Test Bureau/McGraw Hill, Del Monte Research Park.

WEISS, D. J. (1972). [Review of the General Aptitude Test Battery.] In O. K. Buros (Ed.), *The seventh mental measurements yearbook* (Vol. 2, pp. 1058–1061). Highland Park, NJ: Gryphon Press.

WEISS, D. J. (1974). *Strategies of adaptive ability measurement.* (Res. Rep. 74-5). Minnespolis: University of Minnesota.

WEISS, D. J. (1982). Improving measurement quality and efficiency with adaptive testing. *Applied Psychological Measurement, 6*, 473–492.

WEISS, D. J. (Ed.). (1983). *Latent trait test theory and computerized adaptive testing.* NY: Academic Press.

WEISS, D. J., and BETZ, N. E. (1973). *Ability measurement: Conventional or adaptive?* (Res. Rep. 73-1). Minneapolis: University of Minnesota, Department of Psychology, Psychometric Methods Program.

WEISS, D. J., DAWIS, R. V., LOFQUIST, L. V., GAY, E., and HENDEL, D. D. (1975). *The Minnesota Importance Questionnaire.* Minneapolis, University of Minnesota, Department of Psychology, Work Adjustment Project.

WEISS, R. L., and MARGOLIN, G. (1977). Marital conflict and accord. In A. R. Ciminero, K. S. Calhoun, and H. E. Adams (Eds.), *Handbook for behavioral assessment* (pp. 767–809). New York: Wiley.

WERTHEIMER, L. C. (1980). Relation among developmental dimensions in Jane Loevinger's model of ego development. Unpublished doctoral dissertation, University of Maryland.

WESTBROOK, B. W. (1974). Content analysis of six career development tests. *Measurement and Evaluation in Guidance, 7*, 172–180.

WESTBROOK, B. W. (1985). Review of My Vocational Situation. In J. V. Mitchell, Jr. (Ed.), *Ninth Mental Measurements yearbook.* Lincoln, NE: University of Nebraska Press.

WESTBROOK, B. W., and MASTIE, M. M. (1974). The Cognitive Vocational Maturity Test. In D. E. Super (Ed.), *Measuring vocational maturity for counseling and evaluation* (pp. 41–50). Washington, DC: American Personnel and Guidance Association.

WESTBROOK, B. W., and PARRY-HILL, J. W., JR. (1973). The measurement of cognitive vocational maturity. *Journal of Vocational Behavior, 3*, 239–252.

WHITE, D. B. (1986). An assessment and validation of Chickering's seven vectors of student development. Doctoral Dissertation. The University of Iowa, Iowa City, Iowa.

WHITWORTH, R. H. (1984). [Review of the Bender Visual Motor Gestalt Test.] In D. J. Keyser and R. C. Sweetland (Eds.), *Test critiques* (Vol. I, pp. 90–98). Kansas City, MO: Test Corporation of America.

WICKER, A. W. (1979). Ecological psychology: Some recent and prospective developments. *American Psychologist, 34*, 755–766.

WIDICK, C. (1975). *An evaluation of developmental instruction in a university setting.* Unpublished doctoral dissertation, University of Minnesota, Minneapolis.

WIDICK, C., KNEFELKAMP, L. L., and PARKER, C. A. (1975). The counselor as a developmental instructor. *Counselor Education and Supervision, 14*, 286–296.

WIENER-LEVY, D., and EXNER, J. E. (1981). The Rorschach comprehensive system: An overview. In P. McReynolds (Ed.), *Advances in Psychological Assessment* (Vol. V, pp. 236–293). San Francisco: Jossey-Bass.

WIGGINS, J. S. (1973). *Personality and prediction: Principles of personality assessment.* Reading, MA: Addison-Wesley.

WILLIAMS, R. E., and VINCENT, K. R. (1985). [Review of the Loevinger Sentence Completion Test.] In D. J. Keyser and R. C. Sweetland (Eds.), *Test critiques* (Vol. III, pp. 395–401). Kansas City, MO: Test Corporation of America.

WINER, B. J. (1971). *Statistical principles in experimental design* (2nd ed.). New York: McGraw-Hill.

WINSTON, R. B., JR., and MILLER, T. K. (1987). *Student Developmental Task and Lifestyle Inventory manual.* Athens, GA: Student Development Associates.

WINSTON, R. B., JR., MILLER, T. K., and PRINCE, J. S. (1979). *Assessing student development.* Athens, GA: Student Development Associates.

WINSTON, R. B., JR., MILLER, T. K., and PRINCE, J. S. (1987). *Student Developmental Task and Lifestyle Inventory (Form W87).* Athens, GA: Student Development Associates.

WISSLER, C. (1901). The correlation of mental and physical traits. *Psychological Monographs, 3* (6) (Whole No. 16).

WOLLERSHEIM, J. P. (1970). Effectiveness of group therapy based upon learning principles in the treatment of overweight women. *Journal of Abnormal Psychology, 76,* 462–474.

WOLMAN, B. B. (1978). Classification and diagnosis of mental disorders. In B. B. Wolman (Ed.), *Clinical diagnosis of mental disorders* (pp. 15–45). New York: Plenum Press.

WOLPE, J., and LANGE, P. J. (1964). A Fear Survey Schedule for use in behavior therapy. *Behavior Research and Therapy, 2,* 27.

WOLPE, J., and LANGE, P. J. (1969). *Fear Survey Schedule.* San Diego: Educational and Industrial Testing Service.

WOLPE, J., and LANGE, P. J. (1977). *Manual for the Fear Survey Schedule.* San Diego: Educational and Industrial Testing Service.

WOODWORTH, R. S. (1920). Personal Data Sheet. Chicago: Stoelting.

YERKES, R. M. (Ed.). (1921). Psychological examining in the United States Army. *Memoirs of the National Academy of Sciences, 15* (Whole). Washington, DC: Government Printing Office.

ZIMMERMAN, I. L., and WOO-SAM, J. M. (1973). *Clinical interpretation of the Wechsler Intelligence Scale.* New York: Grune and Stratton.

ZUCKERMAN, M. (1977). Development of a situation-specific trait-state test for the prediction and measurement of affective responses. *Journal of Consulting and Clinical Psychology, 45,* 513–523.

ZUNKER, V. G. (1981). *Career counseling: Applied concepts of life planning.* Monterey, CA: Brooks/Cole.

ZYTOWSKI, D. G. (1976). Predictive validity of the Kuder Occupational Interest Survey: A 12- to 19-year follow-up. *Journal of Counseling Psychology, 23,* 221–233.

ZYTOWSKI, D. G. (1977). The effects of being interest inventoried. *Journal of Vocational Behavior, 11,* 153–158.

ZYTOWSKI, D. G. (1981). *Counseling with the Kuder Occupational Interest Survey.* Chicago: Science Research Associates.

ZYTOWSKI, D. G. (1985). *Kuder DP manual supplement.* Chicago, IL: Science Research Associates.

ZYTOWSKI, D. G., and KUDER, G. F. (1986). Advances in the Kuder Occupational Interest Survey. In W. B. Walsh and S. H. Osipow (Eds.), *Advances in vocational psychology: The assessment of interests, volume I.* Hillsdale, NJ: Lawrence Erlbaum Associates.

ZYTOWSKI, D. G., and LAING, J. (1978). Validity of other-gender-normed scales on the Kuder Occupational Interest Survey. *Journal of Counseling Psychology, 3,* 205–209.

Author Index

Lunneborg, C. E., 158, 341, 431
Lunneborg, P. W., 254, 282, 428, 429, 431
Lyman, H. B., 50

M

MacCulloch, M. J., 141
MacDonald, M. L., 141
Magnusson, D., 15, 88, 89, 317–19, 360–62
Maloney, M. P., 12, 16, 168, 410
Mann, M. J., 354
Maranell, G., 84
Marcia, J., 395
Margolin, G., 141
Maslow, A., 356
Mastie, M., 304, 305
Matarazzo, J. D., 19, 168
Mauney, A. C., 201
McAllister, L. W., 95
McArthur, C. C., 130
McBride, J. R., 81
McCaulley, M., 115, 116
McCrae, R. R., 389
McFall, R. M., 140
McGrath, E. J., 227
McGregor, P., 9, 128, 132, 134, 135, 137
McGuire, J. M., 249
McKechnie, G. E., 335, 336–38, 340, 356
McKee, B., 399
McKinley, F., 6, 91, 117, 120
McNemar, Q., 66
McReynolds, P. 3, 11, 340
Medvene, A. M., 373, 375
Meehl, P., 14, 71
Megargee, E., 94, 95
Mehrabian, A., 356
Mehren, B., 331, 333
Mehrens, W. A., 290
Meir, E. I., 373
Melamed, B. G., 142
Melton, G., 202
Meltzer, L., 360
Mercer, J., 4
Merrill, M. A., 161
Merwin, J. C., 233
Messick, S. M., 416, 419, 425
Meyer, P., 392
Milholland, J., 181
Miller, R., 245
Miller, T. K., 396–98
Mines, R., 387, 389, 392, 397, 399
Mischel, W., 8, 9, 15, 317, 360
Mitchell, J. V., Jr., 7, 91, 117, 128, 132, 135, 137, 252, 362

Mooney, R. L., 141
Moore, G. D., 366
Moore, W. S., 191, 392
Mooreland, K. L., 389
Moos, B., 327–29
Moos, R., 6, 7, 319, 326–31, 333–35, 360, 361, 369, 371, 375–77
Moser, H. P., 291
Morgan, C., 132
Mulholland, T. W., 158
Munday, A., 181
Munroe, R., 130
Murphy, G., 359
Murray, H. A., 7, 8, 15, 128, 132–34, 317, 320, 359, 360, 365–68, 375, 376
Myers, I. B., 115, 116, 118, 356
Myers, R. A., 291, 299–301

N

Nader, R., 423–25
Nairn, A., 423–25
National Academy of Sciences, 418
National Assessment of Educational Progress, 421
National Council on Measurement in Education, 49, 402, 403
Nelson, M. J., 181, 183
Nelson, R. O., 140–42
Nevill, D., 289, 290
Nichols, R. C., 178
Novaco, R. W., 142
Novick, M., 403
Nunnally, J. C., 40, 56, 58, 75, 78

O

Ogdon, D. P., 136, 138
O'Hara, R. P., 289
Osipow, S. H., 139, 297, 306–8, 372, 373
Otis, A. S., 2, 180, 181
Overstreet, P. L., 291
Overton, T. D., 364

P

Pace, C. R., 7, 8, 321, 324–26, 351, 375
Page, R., 390
Palko-Nonemaker, D., 307
Parker, C. A., 382, 391
Parsquarelli, B. A., 133
Parsons, F., 7
Pascal, G. R., 137
PASE v. Hannon, 420

Stern, G. G., 320–23, 351, 361, 365–67, 375, 376

Stern, W., 132

Sternberg, R. J., 158

Stevens, S. S., 18

Stricker, L. J., 337, 338

Stringer, R. A., 356

Strong, E. J., Jr., 6, 21, 249, 250, 253

Suinn, R. M., 142, 347

Sullivan, B. J., 142

Sundberg, N. D., 11, 19, 127, 130, 139, 251

Super, D., 211, 250, 252, 286, 289–91, 299–301, 306, 310

Suttell, B., 137

Swaminathan, H., 225

Sweetland, R., 7

Swensen, C. H., 136

T

Taber, R., 413

Tagiuri, R., 356

Tasto, D. L., 347

Tatsuoka, M. M., 83, 122

Taylor, K. M., 310, 311

Taylor, T. J., 360

Terman, L., 161

Terman, M., 2

Terrell, M. D., 426

Thompson, A. S., 291, 299–301

Thompson, R., 319

Thorndike, E., 6, 12

Thorndike, R. L., 54, 161, 172, 173, 176, 178

Thurstone, E. L., 4, 5, 7, 14, 151, 186

Thurstone, T. G., 151

Tiedeman, D. V., 289

Tilton, J. W., 66

Tittle, C. K., 255, 429

Tobias, L. L., 141

Tolman, E. C., 317, 359

Tolor, A., 138

Tomkins, S. S., 133

Trickett, E., 327, 328

Trishmen, D., 245

Twentyman, C. T., 140

Tyler, L. E., 221, 281, 306

U

United States Department of Defense, 216–19

United States Department of Labor, 83, 215

United States Employment Service, 213

Uzgiris, I., 385

V

Vernon, P. E., 153–56

Vielhaber, D. P., 366

Viglione, D., 130

Vincent, K. R., 387

Voss, J. F., 159

W

Wachtel, P. L., 360

Wallace, W. L., 170

Walsh, W. B., 19, 89, 139, 251, 297, 306, 360, 367, 369

Ward, M. P., 12, 16, 168, 410

Wardrop, J., 239

Warnath, C. F., 291

Wasserman, E. R., 388

Watkins, C. E., Jr., 9, 128, 132, 134, 135, 137

Watson, J., 8

Weathersby, R. P., 385–87

Wechsler, D., 4, 166–68

Weinberg, R. A., 364

Weingarten, K. P., 281

Weiss, D. J., 66, 78, 81, 214, 215, 284–86

Weiss, R. L., 141

Weiss, S. D., 135

Welsh, G. S., 73

Wertheimer, L. C., 392

Wesman, A. G., 169, 209, 419

Wessler, R., 385, 386

Westbrook, B. W., 304, 350

Wetzel, 81

White, D. B., 399

Whitworth, R. H., 138

Wicker, A. W., 379

Widaman, K. F., 389

Widick, C., 391, 392

Wiener-Levy, D., 130

Wiggins, J. S., 20, 40

Williams, B. E., 387

Wilson, C. C., 140–44

Wilson, H. K., 347

Winer, B. J., 66

Winer, J. L., 306

Winston, R. B., 396–98

Wissler, C., 148

Wollersheim, J. P., 141

Wolman, B. B., 16

Wolpe, J., 347–49

Wood, D. D., 143, 144

Wood, P. K., 392

Woodsworth, R. S., 6, 21, 91

Woo-Sam, J. M., 168
Wundt, W., 2

Y

Yanico, B., 306
Yerkes, R. M., 171
Yonge, G., 95, 99

Z

Zimmerman, I. L., 168
Zimmerman, W. S., 83, 110, 112–14
Zuckerman, M., 142
Zunker, V. G., 315
Zytowski, D. G., 263–65, 267, 268, 429

Subject Index

Intelligence, Theories of (*cont.*)
  Spearman's two-factor, 149, 150
  Sternberg, 158
  Thurstones, 151
  Vernon, 153–56
Interactional perspective, 362–71
Interest inventories, 252–82
Interval scale, 18–19
Inventoried interest, 252
Inventory of Psychosocial Development, 395
Iowa Tests of Basic Skills, 229, 230
Iowa Tests of Educational Development,
  235–37
IQ score, 149, 165, 167, 168
Item analysis, 75–81
Item Response Theory, 78–81

J

Jackson Personality Inventory, 104–10
Jackson Vocational Interest Survey, 281, 282
Judgmental approach, 14–15

K

Kohlberg's theory, 387–90
Kuder Occupational Interest Inventory,
  263–68

L

Landscape Adjective Checklist, 355
Latent Trait theory, 78–81
Law School Admission Test, 197, 201, 202
Levinson's theory, 399, 400
Living Room Checklist, 355
Loevinger's theory, 385–87

M

Manifest interest, 252
Measure of Intellectual Development, 391,
  392
Measurement, 17–19
Medical College Admission Test, 197–201
Mental Age, 148, 149
Mental Measurements Yearbook Series, 85
Metropolitan Achievement Tests, 230, 231
Military Company Environment Inventory,
  327, 328, 376
Miller Analogies Test, 197
Millon Clinical Multiaxial Inventory, 123

Miner-Jensen Interpersonal Relationship
  Inventory, 399
Minimum competency testing, 421, 422
  Debra P. v. Turlington, 422
  National Assessment of Educational
    Progress, 421
  Social issues in, 421, 422
Minnesota Importance Questionnaire,
  284–88
Minnesota Multiphasic Personality Inventory,
  117–22
Moos social climate scales, 326–31
Moos social ecological approach, 375–78
Moral Judgment Interview, 388, 389
Multidimensional Aptitude Battery, 221
Multiphasic Environmental Assessment
  Procedure, 330–35
Myers-Briggs Type Indicator, 115–17
My Vocational Situation, 308

N

National Merit Scholarship Qualifying Test,
  193
National Teachers Examination Programs,
  246, 247
Nominal scale, 18
Normal distribution, 29–31
  characteristics of, 29–31
  percentage of cases falling under, 29–31
  and standard scores, 46
Norms, 40–46
  normalized standard scores, 39
  percentiles, 41–43
  standard scores, 43–45
  stanines, 45
  uses of, 40, 41, 47

O

Objective approach, 14–15
Objective personality tests, 90–24
Objectivity in testing, 20–22
Observation in natural environments, 143,
  144
Omnibus Personality Inventory, 95–100
Ordering techniques, 127
Original scale, 18
Organizational Climate Description Scales,
  356
Organizational Climate Index, 320–24, 366
Otis-Lennon School Ability Test, 180, 181